Jon E. Lewis is a writer and historian. He is author of the best-selling *The Mammoth Book of Eyewitness History* and *The Mammoth Book of Eyewitness Britain*.

A

DOCUMENTARY HISTORY OF

HUMAN RIGHTS

A RECORD OF THE EVENTS, DOCUMENTS AND SPEECHES THAT SHAPED OUR WORLD

Edited by Jon E. Lewis

CARROLL & GRAF PUBLISHERS
New York

Carroll & Graf Publishers
An imprint of Avalon Publishing Group, Inc.
161 William Street
16th Floor
NY 10038-2607
www.carrollandgraf.com

First published in the UK by Robinson,
an imprint of Constable & Robinson Ltd 2003

First Carroll & Graf edition 2003

ISBN 0-7867-1268-6

Printed and bound in the EU

For Penny, Tristram and Freda

A scene in heaven after the battle of Thermopylae, 480 BC:

The GREEK: But thou art dead, Leonidas. Why dost thou even among the dead feel so great a hatred of the Persians?

LEONIDAS: The love of liberty dies not.

CONTENTS

INTRODUCTION

The premise of this book is simple, the purpose more simple still.

It premises that Western civilization is the highest form of society yet achieved by humankind, for only the democracies of the West have achieved the historical double bull's-eye of personal freedom and material wellbeing.

Of course, this is an outrageous claim. For all that, if you care to think about it, it is impossible to gainsay. It is a telling point that no country outside the West, or the West's colonial influence, has found an independent path to universal suffrage. And those nations of the East which have achieved the industrialization essential to high living standards have done so under autocracy. The seeming exception that is Japan is no such thing. Japan's present democracy was installed by America following Japan's defeat in World War II.

I don't wish to suggest that there was something inevitable about the West's winning of democracy and economic wealth, or that it is due to some racial superiority. Because it ain't so. The modern West is the result of historical process, one which began around the Mediterranean some 5,000 years ago and realized its first major form in the civilizations of Ancient Greece. One of the states of Ancient Greece, Athens, begat democracy (a Greek word), though on a restricted basis; there was no democracy for the hundreds of thousands of slaves which kept Athens ticking along. Much of Greek culture was swallowed by the Romans, whose major independent contribution to the world was the rule of law; like Greece, however, the glory that was Rome was built on a slave economy. When Rome fell to the barbarians in the 5th century, it was the Christian Church which picked up the baton of Graeco-Roman culture, whilst adding a new strand: a monotheistic religion, the oldest in the world, dating back to Judea in the second millennium BC.

Greece. Rome. Judaeo-Christianity. These were the pillars on which the modern West was built. Unfortunately, history is not a flawless progression of ever greater edifices on the same site. The great "Age of Faith" which followed Rome's collapse was a blessing and a hindrance. More individualistic than most creeds, Judaeo-Christianity fitted well the tradition of personal freedom begun by Greece and Rome, while its spirituality fulfilled a human need hardly glimpsed by the prosaic polytheisms of Greece and Rome. The ethics of Christianity, as codified in Jesus' "Sermon on the Mount" were also wondrously workable. Yet the "Age of Faith" proved inimical to Graeco-Roman rationality. For a thousand years, the Christian Church in the West preserved, but did not progress, philosophy, science, mathematics – indeed any rational discipline at all. The last astronomical observation made in Ancient society was by the Athenian Proclus in AD 475; only after Copernicus published *De Revolutionibus* in 1543 did such studies begin again in the West. Such a resumption of science was predicated on the weakening of the influence of the Catholic Church which attended "humanism" and "the Renaissance". The binds of authoritarian blind faith were cut for ever when Martin Luther nailed his ninety-five theses to the door of Wittenberg church in 1517. Central to the ensuing Protestant "Reformation" was the assertion of the Bible and not the Church as the supreme authority in religious matters. This was a deeply democratic notion; henceforth any man who could read was the master of his religion and his salvation. And his life. The more Protestant the country, as a general rule of thumb, the more democratic it proved. Think of England, Holland and the new world of America. (Germany was an exception, but Germany always was; it was never conquered by the Romans.)

Further, Protestantism had an intimate relationship with the rise of capitalism. Protestantism didn't father capitalism, which was an economic bastard born to the money-bags mercantilism of the Renaissance Italian ports; but Protestantism gave capitalism its ideological head, for it approved worldly pursuits (including science, the midwife of capitalist technologies), thrift, and entrepreneurial endeavour. That the Puritan English Revolution issued a raft of pro-capitalist legislation – most magnificently, the 1651 Navigation Act – was no accident. The English Revolution, the historians' squabbling and blarney about its "myriad causes" aside, made England safe for Protestantism, safe for Capitalism and safe for Democracy. When Oliver Cromwell departed this life for Puritan heaven, the people of England invited the Stuart monarchy back – but only as constitutional throne-sitters. Effectively England was a parliamentary democracy. Meanwhile, courtesy of Cromwell's political legacy, capitalism in England proceeded quick-march to the Industrial Revolution.

The Industrial Revolution is best appreciated in retrospect. The human and environmental misery it caused was incalculable. At the same time it manufactured the wealth and machines which eventually allowed freedom from poverty and domestic drudgery for millions of people in Britain and elsewhere. The benefits of economic wealth are more than material; they tend to include political stability, even the maintenance of democracy. (The Russian revolutionist Trotsky once noted that scarcity causes queues, and these need to be policed. And then a policeman is detailed to look after the first policeman, a third to look after the second . . . and, presto, the result is the tyranny of Stalinism.)

The modern West, then, is the result of history, but the present was not built into the beginning. Despite the certainties and vast impersonal forces beloved of Hegel, Marx, Fukuyama and all, there's no teleology in human society, only in Nature. Ideas and economies have their time and their place; whether they are taken up depends on man and woman. The French *philosophe* Rousseau declared memorably that "Man is born free, but is everywhere in chains". Humans certainly strive for political freedom, whether this is a congentital condition or no. If one casts one's eyes over the course of Western history the sheer bloody struggle of Everyman for Liberty is plain enough to see.

There is, of course, much that is wrong about the modern West. We have become negligent about the environment, family life has corroded, a lumpen under-class persists in most places, we worship too much in the Temple of Shopping and we half close our eyes to the plight of the "Third World". Yet no people are freer to express their political and religious views, no people have greater sex, class and race equality, no people have greater control over their lives. These are heady freedoms and powers.

And they are to be cherished.

Which leads to the purpose of this book. This is a "primer" for citizens of the West and for those elsewhere who wish to emulate its finer points (and let's face it, outside of Taleban mullahs, Maoists, oil sheiks, Asian military gangsters, and puffed-up African dictators, who doesn't want universal suffrage?). A primer which in collecting together the milestones of Western human endeavour – be it in religion, science, ethics, law, politics, culture – seeks to show how we got here and why. It is a "history in documents" of the evolution of democracy, human rights and Western civilization.

History demands our attention. Because we can only guard the future when we value and understand our past.

Part One

The Age of Classical Civilization

The Ancient World 1800 BC – AD 427

INTRODUCTION

If the Bible is put aside, modern anthropology suggests that the higher primates appeared 25 million years ago. Recognizable hominoids began walking the earth four million years ago. Modern variant humankind, *homo sapiens sapiens*, stepped into the proverbial primordial mists 250,000 years ago.

Of these 250,000 years, humankind has spent just five thousand *annae* in a state of civilization.

Civilization was a long time a-coming, but it was worth the wait. Primitive *homo sapiens sapiens* might have been a happy savage as the French *philosophe* Rousseau believed, or a short-lived brutish one as the Englishman Hobbes had it, but he was still savage: burdened by superstition, incapable of controlling Nature, and with a subsistence existence that limited life expectancy to the twenties.

It was in the fertile land between the Tigris and Euphrates that *homo sapiens sapiens* first developed (through an irrigation system supervised by warrior kings) an agriculture that could support large-scale population levels. Whereas a hunter-gatherer needed 100 acres of land to support a family unit, the Sumerian farmer needed only 25. More food meant that more mouths could be fed. Farming also led to a sedentary lifestyle, based around homestead, temple and storehouse. By 3000 BC the Sumerians had built thirteen cities, some of them boasting populations of over 50,000.

This was truly civilization – from the Latin *civitas*, "living in a city". For the first time human beings lived in an environment shaped entirely by their own hands, and produced enough material resources to be spared the constant hunt for food. City life demanded new and complex forms of organization, and by thronging together a mass of people made cultural and technological innovation more likely. So it was that the Sumerians devised the first calendar, invented bronze and, with their hieroglyphic script, developed the first writing.

The importance of writing to human history can scarcely be exaggerated. (Indeed "history" means that part of the past for which there is written record; all before it is "pre-history".) Without writing, government, law and education are impossible on anything other than a parochial basis. The biggest turning point in history was literally "history" itself. The invention of the written word.

From Sumer civilization filtered through to Egypt (in around 3100 BC), and thence to the Eastern Mediterranean and India and China. As civilization spread outwards from its birthplace, it encountered a mass movement of people heading westwards, the Indo-Europeans. Over time, it was the Indo-Europeans who would systematically adopt and adapt the components of civilization – cities, literacy, technology, written codes of law – into something unique: the Western tradition.

The first truly Western civilization – the Minoans of Crete are to be discounted because of the Eastern Mediterranean racial origins and feminized, Egyptianized culture – lay with the Mycenaeans, the Greek-speaking warrior Aryans who colonized the Greek mainland in c. 1900 BC. It was the Zeus-worshipping Mycenaeans who Homer venerated in *The Iliad*. Mycenaean culture burned bright, faded, was trampled by the Dorians (another set of Aryan Greeks), but enough of it survived to stimulate in 800 BC or thereabouts the rise of the city-states of Hellas. And with them came all the glory that was Greece.

Unlike nearly all other previous civilized Ancient peoples, the Greeks set high store by the dignity and rights of the individual human being. From this it followed that their politics (from the Greek "polis", for city) were participatory, hereditary rule was the exception not the norm, and in Chios and Athens there were the world's first experiments in political democracy (another Greek word, from *demos* "the people" and *krateo* "to rule"). Meanwhile, Greek advances in philosophy (courtesy of Socrates, Plato, Aristotle *et al*) and science (which included Leucippus and Democritus' 5th century BC proposal that all matter was composed of atoms) became the building blocks of Western intellectual life. Even modern sport is indebted to the Ancient Greeks (marathon, Olympics, discus). The measure of Greece's impact on the Western world is shown by a single fact: one word out of every eight spoken in the West today is of Greek derivation.

Perhaps this is not surpising when one remembers that, over the course of nigh on 800 years, Hellenistic culture spread around the Mediterranean from France to Libya, as well as into Asia. Sometimes it was carried by traders, but usually it was carried on the end of a hoplite's 21-foot pike. Alexander the Great, after all, was a Greek.

In chronology, at least, the next great civilization in Western antiquity was Rome. Much of Rome's culture was drawn from its Greek neighbour, as was its early politics; republican democracy was quite probably introduced into Rome by Greek residents in the city.

That said, there was a fundamental difference between the Roman and the Grecian way. The Greeks were metaphysicians, the Romans pragmatists. Even in their philosophy, such as it was, the Romans were almost exclusively concerned with the useful end of matters: ethics and politics.

Of course, the professional pragmatism of the Romans meant that *Pax Romana* brought peace, just laws, fine roads, high personal codes of conduct and government to most of Europe for 400 years.

The shadow of Rome still falls on the West. This is particularly evident in jurisprudence, where Emperor Justinian's *Codex* informs the law of nearly all modern European countries. The legal standing of the Roman citizen is indeed the root of the present day notion of political *rights* as opposed to expectations.

Rome's shadow touches us in many other ways, too. Nearly a third of the English language is Latin-based. Our customs too, are remarkably Roman – even to the carrying of brides over thresholds.

Then there is the matter of Christianity. Although official Rome was hostile to Christianity, it was, ironically enough, the very orderliness and straights roads of *Pax Romana* that enabled the "good news" to be spread throughout the Empire. Eventually, under Constantine in 324, Christianity became the state religion of Rome.

Christianity added an entirely new dimension to the Graeco-Roman tradition. The religion of the Greeks was a poor thing, and the Romans added nothing to it; both peoples advocated a life governed by reason. When they did inter-relate with the gods, it was as a business transaction: they offered x in the hopes of y. Christianity, meanwhile, was a reform of a some 2000-year-old deeply spiritual Hebrew religion which was, uniquely, monotheistic with the partial exception of pharaoh Akhenaten's short-lived, foreshadowing Aten cult. As such, Christianity offered faith, without being opposed to reason, a merciful God who was Father to all men and women and the promise for the repentant of eternal life, thanks to Christ's Redemption.

Alongside spirituality, Christianity concerned itself with the compassionate improvement of man's lot in the here and now. It was an active, not a contemplative religion. "Feed my sheep," Jesus said to Peter. It was also a religion which offered particular succour to the masses: "Blessed are the meek: for they shall inherit the earth". Christ's recognition of the importance of Everyman gave a religious sanction to the importance of the individual; in many years to come, this sanction would be used to press for democratic rights in the West.

Since Christianity was all encompassing, it had little difficulty in incorporating Roman law and civics, Greek philosophy and politics.

When the Roman Empire in the West fell to the barbarians in 410, the

Christian Church survived, and within it was preserved not only the Christian religion but all the gains of classical thought and culture.

Greece. Rome. Judaeo-Christianity. These are the foundations of the modern West.

THE CODE OF HAMMURABI, c. 1800 BC

Hammurabi

The Amorite Hammurabi ascended the throne of Babylon in c. 1800 BC and immediately initiated a campaign of territorial conquest which made Babylon the pre-eminent power in the Ancient Near East. But his greater fame in posterity lies in the promise he made to the god Marduk to establish a legal system: the ensuing "Code of Hammurabi" is the earliest complete legislation known to humanity. The Code's 282 clauses cover nearly every aspect of Babylonian life and were, by the standards of the time, humane. Primitive tribalism, such as blood feuding, was avoided, and the Code was transparent – in that it was inscribed on eight-feet stone stele placed around the kingdom in public view – with fixed penalties for transgression. In most Ancient societies – even early Rome – the law was arcane and arbitrary, interpreted and implemented solely by the priesthood or nobility.

The guiding principle of the Code, some several hundred years before Biblical law, was *lex talonis* – "an eye for an eye, a tooth for a tooth". That said, many crimes carried the death penalty whatever, burglary among them. Nor did the Code adhere to *lex talonis* if the victim and perpetrator were of different classes. The nobility and professions (Amelu) were entitled to higher compensations than the middle classes (Muskinu) and the slaves (Ardu). Conversely, the Amelu had to pay higher fines than their lessers if determined to be guilty. Although most of the Code was rational and relied on human deliberation, it was not entirely so: in the trying of some crimes the pantheistic spirit of waster was invoked and the accused thrown into the river. The guilty drowned.

An original stele inscribed with the Code of Hammurabi, in 3,600 lines of cuneiform, is displayed in Paris' Louvre museum. Below are its most significant Clauses. It should be noted that there was no Clause 13 in the original, for 13 was an unlucky number in the world's first civilization.

Extracts:

1. If a citizen has accused a citizen and has indicted him for a murder and has not substantiated the charge, his accuser shall be put to death.

2. If a citizen has indicted a citizen for sorcery and does not substantiate the charge, the one who is indicted for sorcery shall go to the river and shall throw himself in. If the river overwhelms him, (then) his indicter shall take away his house. If the river exculpates that citizen and he is preserved, the one who indicted him for sorcery shall die, (and) the one who threw himself into the river shall take away his house.

3. If a citizen in a case has borne false witness, and does not substantiate the statement which he has made, (and) if that case is one warranting the death-penalty, that citizen shall be put to death.

4. If he comes forward to witness concerning wheat or money, he shall bear the penalty appropriate to that case.

5. If a judge has given a judgment and has passed a sentence and has drawn up a sealed document, and afterwards revises his findings, they shall convict that judge of revising his findings; he shall give the prescribed indemnity which follows from that case twelve-fold, and they shall eject him from the council, from the seat of his judicature; he shall not return and he shall not sit with the judges in judgment.

6. If a citizen has stolen property of the temple or of the crown, that man shall die, and whosoever receives the stolen goods from his hand shall die.

7. If a citizen has purchased or has accepted for safe custody silver, or gold, or serf, or bondmaid, or ox, or sheep, or ass, or whatsoever it may be, from the hand of the son of a citizen, or from the serf of a citizen, without witnesses or contracts, that man is a thief, (and) he shall die.

8. If a citizen has stolen an ox, or a sheep, or an ass, or a pig, or a boat, if it is the property of the temple or of the crown, he shall give thirty-fold, but, if it is the property of a vassal, he shall restore ten-fold, whereas if the thief has nothing to give, he shall die.

14. If a citizen steals the child of a citizen, he shall die.

22. If a citizen has committed a robbery and is caught, that man shall die.

117. If a debt renders a citizen distrainable, and he has sold for money his wife, or son, or daughter, or if anyone is sold for service in lieu of debt, they shall work for three years in the house of their purchaser or their distrainer. In the fourth year they shall attain their freedom.

118. If a serf or bondmaid has been sold, and should the merchant proceed to (re-sell) and either is sold for money, they cannot be reclaimed.

119. If a debt renders a citizen distrainable, and he sells for money his bondmaid who has borne him children, the master of the bondmaid may repay the sum and redeem his bondmaid.

122. If a citizen gives to a citizen for custody silver, or gold, or anything whatsoever, he shall show to witnesses all that is deposited. He shall furnish the contracts, and (then) he shall hand the goods over for safe custody.

123. If he has given into custody without witnesses and contracts, and those to whom he gave it deny the transaction, no claim can lie in such a case.

124. If a citizen has given another citizen silver, or gold, or anything whatsoever for safe custody in the presence of witnesses and he denies it, they shall convict that citizen, and in spite of his denial, he shall restore it twofold.

125. If a citizen has handed over anything of his whatsoever for safe custody, and if the place where it is deposited (is entered) either by breaking in or by (climbing a) ladder, and his property and that of the owner of the house is lost, the householder, who has been negligent, shall make restitution of what was given him for safe custody and was lost, and shall compensate the owner; the householder shall further search for what was lost and recover it from the thief.

127. If a citizen has pointed a finger at a priestess, or the wife of a citizen, and does not substantiate his imputation, they shall charge that citizen before the judge and they shall shave his front hair.

128. If a citizen has taken a wife but has not deposited her contracts, that woman is not a (legal) wife.

129. If the wife of a citizen is taken cohabiting with another male, they shall both be bound and cast into the water; if the husband of the wife reprieves his wife, then the king may reprieve his servant.

130. If a citizen has forced a citizen's wife, who has not known a man, and has lain in her bosom, and they seize him, that man shall be put to death, that wife shall go free.

131. If the wife of a citizen is accused by her husband, but she has not been caught lying with another male, she shall take an oath of the god and return to her house.

132. If the finger is pointed at the wife of a citizen on account of another man, but she has not been caught lying with another man, for her husband's sake she shall throw herself into the river.

133a. If a citizen has been carried away captive, and there is sustenance in his house, his wife . . . shall guard her property and shall not enter the household of another.

133b. If that wife does not guard her property but enters into the household of another, they shall convict this wife and cast her into the water.

134. If a citizen has been carried away captive, and there is no sustenance in his house, his wife may enter into another household, and no crime may be imputed to this woman.

135. If a citizen is carried away captive, and there is no sustenance in his house, (and) before his re-appearance his wife has entered the household of another, and borne children, (and if) subsequently her husband returns and comes to his city, that woman shall return to this her former husband, but the children shall follow their (natural) father.

144. If a citizen has taken a priestess-wife, and that priestess has given a bondmaid to her husband and she has borne children, if that man plan to take a votaress (as concubine), they shall not give that citizen permission, a votaress he may not take.

145. If a citizen has taken a priestess-wife, and she has not presented him with children, and if he plans to take a votaress (as concubine), that citizen may take a votaress, and bring her into his house; but this votaress shall not make herself equal with the priestess-wife.

146. If a citizen has taken a priestess-wife, and she has given a bondmaid to her husband, and she has borne children, and if afterwards that bondmaid has made herself equal with her mistress, her mistress may not sell her for money, since she has borne children; she may, however, impose on her the badge of serfdom and reckon her among the bondmaids.

147. If she has not borne children she may sell her for money.

148. If a citizen has taken a wife, and intermittent fever attacks her, and if he plans to take another wife, he may do so. He may not forsake his wife who is attacked by the intermittent fever, but she shall dwell in a house which he has prepared, and he shall support her for life.

153. If the wife of a citizen through association with another male has caused the death of her husband, they shall impale that woman.

154. If a citizen has known his daughter, they shall cause that citizen to leave the city.

155. If a citizen has chosen a bride for his son, and his son has known her, and he himself (the father) lies in her bosom, they shall seize that citizen and bind him and cast him into the water.

156. If a citizen has chosen a bride for his son, and his son has not known her, and he himself lies in her bosom, he shall pay her a half-mina of silver, and he shall refund to her whatsoever she brought from her father's house. She may take a husband according to her heart.

157. If a citizen after (the death of) his father lies in the bosom of his mother, they shall burn them both.

158. If a citizen after (the death of) his father is seized in the bosom of his foster-mother who has borne children, that man shall be turned out of his father's house.

170. If a citizen, whose wife has borne him children and (also) his bond-maid has borne him children, (and) the father during his lifetime has said to the bondmaid's children, which she has borne him, "My children"; he has added them to the children of the wife. After the father goes to his fate, the children of the wife shall divide the property of the father's house equally with the sons of the bondmaid; the son and heir, the son of the wife, shall choose a share (first) and take it.

195. If a son has struck his father, they shall cut off his hand.

196. If a citizen has destroyed the eye of one of citizen status, they shall destroy his eye.

197. If he has broken the bone of a citizen, his bone shall they break.

198. If he has destroyed the eye, or has broken the bone, of a vassal, he shall pay one mina of silver.

199. If he has destroyed the eye of a slave of a citizen, or has broken the bone of a serf, he shall pay half of his market-value.

200. If a citizen has knocked out the tooth of one of equal status, they shall knock out his tooth.

201. If he has knocked out the tooth of a vassal, he shall pay a third of a mina of silver.

202. If a citizen has struck the cheek of his superior, he shall receive in the council sixty strokes with a thong.

203. If one of citizen status has struck the cheek of his equal, he shall pay one mina of silver.

204. If a vassal has struck the cheek of a fellow vassal, he shall pay ten shekels of silver.

205. If the serf of a citizen has struck the cheek of one of citizen status, they shall cut off his ear.

206. If a citizen has struck a citizen in a quarrel, and has inflicted on him a wound, that citizen shall swear "I struck him unwittingly", and he shall pay the doctor.

207. If he has died as a consequence of his attack, he shall swear, and, if he was of citizen stock, he shall pay a half-mina of silver.

208. If he belonged to the vassal class, he shall pay a third of a mina of silver.

209. If a citizen has struck the daughter of a citizen, and she miscarries, he shall pay ten shekels of silver for her miscarriage.

210. If that woman dies as a result, they shall put his daughter to death.

211. If the blow has caused the daughter of a vassal to miscarry, he shall pay five shekels of silver.

212. If that woman dies as a result, he shall pay a half-mina of silver.

213. If he has struck the bondmaid of a citizen and has caused her to miscarry, he shall pay two shekels of silver.

214. If that bondmaid dies as a result, he shall pay a third of a mina of silver.

250. If an ox has gored a citizen, while going along the road, and has occasioned his death, there shall be no penalty attached to this case.

251. If the offending ox belonged to a citizen who has been notified by the authorities of its propensity to gore, and he has not removed its horns, or has not tethered the ox, and that ox gored a man of citizen status occasioning his death, he shall pay a half-mina of silver.

252. If he was the serf of a citizen, he shall pay a third of a mina of silver.

280. If a citizen has bought in a foreign country a serf or a bondmaid of a man, and when he came home, a (former) owner of the serf or bondmaid recognises either his serf or his bondmaid, if the serf and bondmaid are natives of the land, their emancipation shall be asserted without money.

281. If they are natives of another land, the buyer shall declare before the god the sum he paid, and the owner of the serf or bondmaid shall reimburse the merchant for the (whatever) money he expended, and shall redeem his serf or bondmaid.

282. If a serf has declared to his master – "Thou art not my master," his master shall confirm him (to be) his serf and shall cut off his ear.

THE TEACHING OF AMENHOPE, c. 1400 BC

Anonymous

"The Teaching of Amenhope" is an Egyptian manual of good behaviour from the pharaonic era. Such instructions were phenomenally popular, not because of any fad but because the Ancient Egyptians were earnest in their desire for civilized behaviour. "The Teaching of Amenhope" has clear parallels with the Bible's book of Proverbs, especially *Proverbs* 22:17 and 24:22, suggesting that Hebrew was informed by the Egyptian.

Preface

The beginning of instruction on how to live,
Guidance for well-being;
Every direction for consorting with elders,
Rules for a courtier;
5 Ability to refute him who uttereth an accusation,
And to bring back a report to one who hath sent him.
To direct him to the path of life,
To make him prosper upon the earth;
To let his heart go into its shrine,
10 Steering him clear of evil;
To save him from the mouth of strangers,
Praised in the mouth of men.

He Says: First Chapter

Give thine ears, hear what is said,
Give thy mind to interpret them.
To put them in thy heart is beneficial;
It is detrimental for him who neglecteth them.
5 Let them rest in the casket of thy belly,

That they may be a *pnat* in thy heart.
Even when there is a whirlwind of words,
They shall be a mooring-stake for thy tongue.
If thou spendest thy lifetime while this is in thy heart,
10 Thou wilt find it a success,
Thou wilt find my words a treasury of life;
Thy body will prosper upon earth.

Second Chapter

Guard thyself against robbing the wretched
And against being puissant over the man of broken arm.
Stretch not forth thy hand to repel an old man,
Nor anticipate the aged.
5 Let not thyself be sent on a wicked mission,
Nor love him who hath performed it.
Cry not out against him whom thou hast injured,
Nor answer him back to justify thyself.
He who hath done evil, the river-bank abandons him,
10 And his flooded land carries him away.
The north wind cometh down that it may end his hour;
It is united to the tempest;
The thunder is loud, and the crocodiles are evil.
O hot-head, what is thy condition?
15 He is crying out, his voice to heaven.
O Moon, arraign his crime!
Steer that we may ferry the wicked man across,
For we shall not act like him –
Lift him up, give him thy hand;
20 Leave him (in) the hands of the god;
Fill his belly with bread that thou hast,
So that he may be sated and may cast down his eye.

Fourth Chapter

As for the hot-headed man in a temple,
He is like a tree growing in an enclosed space.
A moment completeth its loss of foliage.
Its end is reached in the *makherma*.
5 It is sunk far from its place;
The flame is its burial shroud.
The truly silent man, he withdraweth himself apart.
He is like a tree growing in a plot.
It groweth green and doubleth its yield;

10 It is before its lord.
Its fruit is sweet; its shade is pleasant.
Its end is reached in the grove.

Sixth Chapter

Remove not the landmark at the boundaries of the arable land,
Nor disturb the position of the measuring-cord;
Covet not a cubit of land,
Nor throw down the boundaries of a widow . . .
5 Beware of throwing down the boundaries of the fields,
Lest a terror carry thee off . . .
Better is poverty in the hand of the god
Than riches in a storehouse;
Better is bread, when the heart is happy,
10 Than riches with vexation.

Seventh Chapter

Cast not thy heart after riches;
There is no ignoring Shay and Renent.
Place not thy heart upon externals;
Every man belongeth to his hour.
5 Labour not to seek for increase;
Thy needs are safe for thee.
If riches are brought to thee by robbery,
They will not spend the night with thee;
At daybreak they are not in thy house:
10 Their places may be seen, but they are not.
The ground has opened its mouth – "Let him enter that it may swallow",
They sink into the underworld.
They have made for themselves a great breach suitable to their size
And are sunken down in the storehouse.
15 They have made themselves wings like geese
And are flown away to heaven.
Rejoice not thyself (over) riches (gained) by robbery,
Nor groan because of poverty

Ninth Chapter

Associate not with the hot-head,
Nor become intimate with him in conversation . . .
Leap not to cleave to such a one,
Lest a terror carry thee off.

Tenth Chapter

Salute not thy hot-headed (opponent) perforce,
And hurt thine own heart (thereby).
Say not to him: "Hail to thee!" falsely,
While there is dread in thy belly.

Eleventh Chapter

Covet not the property of an inferior person,
Nor hunger for his bread.
As for the property of an inferior person, it is an obstruction to the throat,
It maketh a vomiting in the gullet.
5 By false oaths he hath produced it,
His heart being perverted in his body . . .

Thirteenth Chapter

Injure not a man, [with] pen upon papyrus –
O abomination of the god!
Bear not witness with lying words,
Nor seek another's reverse with thy tongue.
5 Make not a reckoning with him who hath nothing,
Nor falsify thy pen.
If thou hast found a large debt against a poor man,
Make it into three parts,
Forgive two, and let one remain,
10 In order that thou shalt find thereby the ways of life.
Thou wilt lie down – the night hasteneth away – (lo!) thou art in
the morning;
Thou hast found it like good news.
Better is praise for one who loves men
Than riches in a storehouse;
15 Better is bread, when the heart is happy,
Than riches with contention.

Sixteenth Chapter

Tamper not with the scales nor falsify the weights,
Nor damage the fractions of the measure.
Desire not the agricultural measure,
And neglect those of the Treasury . . .

Eighteenth Chapter

Lie not down at night being fearful of the morrow.
When the day breaks, what is the morrow like?
Man knoweth not what the morrow is like.
God is (ever) in his success,
5 Whereas man is in his failure;
One thing are the words which men have said,
Another is that which the god doeth . . .

Twenty-first Chapter

Empty not thine inmost self to everybody,
And so damage thine influence.
Spread not thine utterances to the common people,
Nor associate with thyself the over-communicative.
5 Better is a man who concealeth his report in his inmost self
Than he who speaketh it out injuriously.

Twenty-third Chapter

Eat not bread in the presence of a noble,
Nor apply thy mouth at the beginning.
If thou art satisfied – false chewings
Be a diversion for thy saliva!
5 Look at the cup which is in thy presence
And let it serve thy needs.

Twenty-fifth Chapter

Laugh not at a blind man nor tease a dwarf,
Nor injure the plans of the lame.
Tease not a man who is in the hand of the god,
Nor be furious against him when he hath erred.
5 As for man, clay and straw,
The god is his builder.
He teareth down and buildeth up every day.
He maketh a thousand poor men at his will,
(Or) he maketh a thousand men as overseers,
10 When he is in his hour of life.
How joyful is he who hath reached the West,
Being safe in the hand of the god.

Thirtieth Chapter

See for thyself these thirty chapters:
They give pleasure; they instruct;
They are the foremost of all books;
They instruct the ignorant.
5 If they are read out in the presence of the ignorant,
Then he will be cleansed by reason of them.
Fill thyself with them; put them in thy heart,
And be a man who can explain them,
Interpreting them as a teacher.
10 As for the scribe who is experienced in his office,
He shall find himself worthy to be a courtier.

Colophon

It has come to its end
In the writing of Senu, son of the God's Father Pa-miu.

THE HYMN TO ATEN, c. 1345 BC

Akhenaten

Under the 18th Dynasty Pharaoh Amenhotep IV, Egypt ushered in a religious revolution whereby the old ways were banned in favour of the worship of the Sun (specifically the Sun's physical orb – the Aten). To mark the change of religion, Amenhotep himself changed his name to Akhenaten ("Servant of the Aten"). The new cult barely survived Akhenaten's reign; its claim on attention is that it was the first known instance of monotheism. "The Hymn to Aten", ostensibly written by Akenhaten, was the liturgy of the Aten faith.

Thou dost appear beautiful on the horizon of heaven,
   O living Aten, thou who wast the first to live.
When thou hast risen on the eastern horizon,
   Thou hast filled every land with thy beauty.
5 Thou art fair, great, dazzling, high above every land;
   Thy rays encompass the lands to the very limit of all thou hast
      made.
Being Re, thou dost reach to their limit
   And curb them [for] thy beloved son;
Though thou art distant, thy rays are upon the earth;
10   Thou art in their faces, yet thy movements are unknown(?).

When thou dost set on the western horizon,
   The earth is in darkness, resembling death.
Men sleep in the bed-chamber with their heads covered,
   Nor does one eye behold the other.
15 Were all their goods stolen which are beneath their heads,
   They would not be aware of it.
Every lion has come forth from his den,
   All the snakes bite.
Darkness prevails, and the earth is in silence,

20   Since he who made them is resting in his horizon.

At daybreak, when thou dost rise on the horizon,
    Dost shine as Aten by day,
Thou dost dispel the darkness
    And shed thy rays.
25 The Two Lands are in festive mood,
    Awake, and standing on (their) feet,
For thou hast raised them up;
    They cleanse their bodies and take (their) garments;
Their arms are (lifted) in adoration at thine appearing;
30   The whole land performs its labour.

All beasts are satisfied with their pasture;
    Trees and plants are verdant.
The birds which fly from their nests, their wings are (spread)
        in adoration to thy soul;
    All flocks skip with (their) feet;
35 All that fly up and alight
    Live when thou hast risen [for] them.
Ships sail upstream and downstream alike,
    For every route is open at thine appearing.
The fish in the river leap before thee,
40   For thy rays are in the midst of the sea.

Thou creator of issue in woman, who makest semen into mankind,
    And dost sustain the son in his mother's womb,
Who dost soothe him with that which stills his tears,
    Thou nurse in the very womb, giving breath to sustain all thou
        dost make!
45 When he issues from the womb to breathe on the day of his birth,
    Thou dost open his mouth completely and supply his needs.
When the chick in the egg cheeps inside the shell,
    Thou givest it breath within it to sustain it.
Thou hast set it its appointed time in the egg to break it,
50   That it may emerge from the egg to cheep at its appointed time;
    That it may walk with its feet when it emerges from it.

How manifold is that which thou hast made, hidden from view!
    Thou sole god, there is no other like thee!
Thou didst create the earth according to thy will, being alone:
55   Mankind, cattle, all flocks,
Everything on earth which walks with (its) feet,
    And what are on high, flying with their wings.

The foreign lands of Hurru and Nubia, the land of Egypt –
  Thou dost set each man in his place and supply his needs;
60 Each one has his food, and his lifetime is reckoned.
  Their tongues are diverse in speech and their natures likewise;
    Their skins are varied, for thou dost vary the foreigners.
  Thou dost make the Nile in the underworld,
    And bringest it forth as thou desirest to sustain the people,
65 As thou dost make them for thyself,
    Lord of them all, who dost weary thyself with them,
  Lord of every land, who dost rise for them,
    Thou Aten of the day, great in majesty.

As for all distant foreign lands, thou makest their life,
70 For thou hast set a Nile in the sky,
  That it may descend for them,
    That it may make waves on the mountains like the sea,
    To water their fields amongst their towns.
  How excellent are thy plans, thou lord of eternity!
75 The Nile in the sky is for the foreign peoples,
  For the flocks of every foreign land that walk with (their) feet,
    While the (true) Nile comes forth from the underworld for Egypt.

Thy rays suckle every field;
    When thou dost rise, they live and thrive for thee.
80 Thou makest the seasons to nourish all that thou hast made:
    The winter to cool them; the heat that they(?) may taste thee.
  Thou didst make the distant sky to rise in it,
    To see all that thou hast made.
  Being alone, and risen in thy form as the living Aten,
85 Whether appearing, shining, distant, or near,
  Thou makest millions of forms from thyself alone:
    Cities, towns, fields, road, and river.

Every eye perceives thee level with them,
    When thou art the Aten of the day above the earth (?)
90 When thou didst go away because all men existed,
    Thou didst create their faces that thou mightest not see [thy]self [alone],
  . . . one . . . which thou didst make.
  Thou art in my heart;
    There is no other that knows thee,
95 Save thy son Akhenaten,
    For thou hast made him skilled in thy plans and thy might.
  The earth came into being by thy hand,
    Just as thou didst make them (i.e. mankind).

When thou hast risen, they live;
100   When thou dost set, they die.
For thou art lifetime thyself; one lives through thee;
Eyes are upon (thy) beauty until thou dost set.
All labour is put aside when thou dost set in the west;
When [thou] risest [thou] makest . . . flourish for the king.
105 As for all who hasten on foot,
Ever since thou didst fashion the earth,
Thou dost raise them up for thy son who came forth from thyself,
The King of Upper and Lower Egypt, Akhenaten.

THE TEN COMMANDMENTS, c. 1260 BC

In the Christian Old Testament (the Hebrew Torah), it is written that the Ten Commandments were revealed to Moses on Mount Sinai, inscribed by God's finger on two tablets of stone.

There are, confusingly, two versions of the Ten Commandments in the Bible, in *Exodus* 20:1–19 and *Deuteronomy* 5:6–21, though they are substantially the same. Neither is actually composed of ten injunctions, but rather more tradition groups them as a "decalogue". For those who believe in the inerrancy of the Bible, the revelation to Moses is literally true; Old Testament scholars suggest that the Commandments were instead written by four distinct authors ("J", "E", "D", "P") between 922–622 BC, but basing their writings on a much older, possibly Hittite, document.

What is certain is that the Ten Commandments have become central to Judaeo-Christian ethics and law. They were reaffirmed by Jesus in the Sermon on the Mount and throughout the Christian era, particularly from early medieval times, have been the pre-eminent moral code. The version of the Ten Commandments below, together with the manner of their revelation to Moses, is from *Exodus* in the King James Version of the Bible. The common reduction of the Commandments to ten precepts is given afterwards.

In the development of Western thought the first commandment, "I am the Lord thy God. Thou shalt have no other gods before me", is of particular import. The God of the Hebrews was already a "mono-deist" exclusivist by the time He revealed himself to Moses.

Chapter 19

In the third month, when the children of Israel were gone forth out of the land of Egypt, the same day came they *into* the wilderness of Sinai.

2 For they were departed from Rephidim, and were come *to* the desert

of Sinai, and had pitched in the wilderness; and there Israel camped before the mount.

3 And Moses went up unto God, and the LORD called unto him out of the mountain, saying. Thus shalt thou say to the house of Jacob, and tell the children of Israel;

4 Ye have seen what I did unto the Egyptians, and *how* I bare you on eagles' wings, and brought you unto myself.

5 Now therefore, if ye will obey my voice indeed, and keep my covenant, then ye shall be a peculiar treasure unto me above all people: for all the earth *is* mine:

6 And ye shall be unto me a kingdom of priests, and an holy nation. These *are* the words which thou shalt speak unto the children of Israel.

7 ¶ And Moses came and called for the elders of the people, and laid before their faces all these words which the LORD commanded him.

8 And all the people answered together, and said, All that the LORD hath spoken we will do. And Moses returned the words of the people unto the LORD.

9 And the LORD said unto Moses, Lo, I come unto thee in a thick cloud, that the people may hear when I speak with thee, and believe thee for ever. And Moses told the words of the people unto the LORD.

10 ¶ And the LORD said unto Moses, Go unto the people, and sanctify them to day and to morrow, and let them wash their clothes.

11 And be ready against the third day: for the third day the LORD will come down in the sight of all the people upon mount Sinai.

12 And thou shalt set bounds unto the people round about, saying, Take heed to yourselves, *that ye* go *not* up into the mount, or touch the border of it; whosoever toucheth the mount shall be surely put to death:

13 There shall not an hand touch it, but he shall surely be stoned, or shot through; whether *it be* beast or man, it shall not live: when the trumpet soundeth long, they shall come up to the mount.

14 ¶ And Moses went down from the mount unto the people, and sanctified the people: and they washed their clothes.

15 And he said unto the people. Be ready against the third day: come not at *your* wives.

16 ¶ And it came to pass on the third day in the morning, that there were thunders and lightnings, and a thick cloud upon the mount, and the voice of the trumpet exceeding loud; so that all the people that *was* in the camp trembled.

17 And Moses brought forth the people out of the camp to meet with God; and they stood at the nether part of the mount.

18 And mount Sinai was altogether on a smoke, because the LORD descended upon it in fire: and the smoke thereof ascended as the smoke of a furnace, and the whole mount quaked greatly.

19 And when the voice of the trumpet sounded long, and waxed louder and louder, Moses spake, and God answered him by a voice.

20 And the LORD came down upon mount Sinai, on the top of the mount: and the LORD called Moses *up* to the top of the mount; and Moses went up.

21 And the LORD said unto Moses, Go down, charge the people, lest they break through unto the LORD to gaze, and many of them perish.

22 And let the priests also, which come near to the LORD, sanctify themselves, lest the LORD break forth upon them.

23 And Moses said unto the LORD, The people cannot come up to mount Sinai: for thou chargedst us, saying. Set bounds about the mount, and sanctify it.

24 And the LORD said unto him, Away, get thee down, and thou shalt come up, thou, and Aaron with thee: but let not the priests and the people break through to come up unto the LORD, lest he break forth upon them.

25 So Moses went down unto the people, and spake unto them.

Chapter 20

And God spake all these words, saying,

2 I *am* the LORD thy God, which have brought thee out of the land of Egypt, out of the house of bondage.

3 Thou shalt have no other gods before me.

4 Thou shalt not make unto thee any graven image, or any likeness *of any thing* that *is* in heaven above, or that *is* in the earth beneath, or that *is* in the water under the earth:

5 Thou shalt not bow down thyself to them, nor serve them: for I the LORD thy God *am* a jealous God, visiting the iniquity of the fathers upon the children unto the third and fourth *generation* of them that hate me;

6 And shewing mercy unto thousands of them that love me, and keep my commandments.

7 Thou shalt not take the name of the LORD thy God in vain; for the LORD will not hold him guiltless that taketh his name in vain.

8 Remember the sabbath day, to keep it holy.

9 Six days shalt thou labour, and do all thy work:

10 But the seventh day *is* the sabbath of the LORD thy God: *in it* thou shalt not do any work, thou, nor thy son, nor thy daughter, thy manservant, nor thy maidservant, nor thy cattle, nor thy stranger that *is* within thy gates:

11 For *in* six days the LORD made heaven and earth, the sea, and all that in them *is*, and rested the seventh day: wherefore the LORD blessed the sabbath day, and hallowed it.

12 ¶ Honour thy father and thy mother: that thy days may be long upon the land which the LORD thy God giveth thee.

13 Thou shalt not kill.

14 Thou shalt not commit adultery.

15 Thou shalt not steal.

16 Thou shalt not bear false witness against thy neighbour.

17 Thou shalt not covet thy neighbour's house, thou shalt not covet thy neighbour's wife, nor his manservant, nor his maidservant, nor his ox, nor his ass, nor any thing that *is* thy neighbour's.

18 ¶ And all the people saw the thunderings, and the lightnings, and the noise of the trumpet, and the mountain smoking: and when the people saw *it*, they removed, and stood afar off.

19 And they said unto Moses, Speak thou with us, and we will hear: but let not God speak with us, lest we die.

20 And Moses said unto the people, Fear not: for God is come to prove you, and that his fear may be before your faces, that ye sin not.

21 And the people stood afar off, and Moses drew near unto the thick darkness where God *was*.

22 ¶ And the LORD said unto Moses, Thus thou shalt say unto the children of Israel, Ye have seen that I have talked with you from heaven.

23 Ye shall not make with me gods of silver, neither shall ye make unto you gods of gold.

24 ¶ An altar of earth thou shalt make unto me, and shalt sacrifice thereon thy burnt offerings, and thy peace offerings, thy sheep, and thine oxen: in all places where I record my name I will come unto thee, and I will bless thee.

25 And if thou wilt make me an altar of stone, thou shalt not build it of hewn stone: for if thou lift up thy tool upon it, thou hast polluted it.

26 Neither shalt thou go up by steps unto mine altar, that thy nakedness be not discovered thereon.

The traditional abridgement of "The Ten Commandments"

1. I am the Lord thy God. Thou shalt have no other gods before me.
2. Thou shalt not make unto thee any graven image.
3. Thou shalt not take the name of the Lord thy God in vain.
4. Remember the sabbath day, to keep it holy.
5. Honour thy father and thy mother.
6. Thou shalt not kill.
7. Thou shalt not commit adultery.
8. Thou shalt not steal.
9. Thou shalt not bear false witness against thy neighbour.
10. Thou shalt not covet.

THE TWELVE TABLES, c. 450 BC

Displayed in the Forum, "The Twelve Tables" stated the rights and duties of the Roman citizen. Their formulation was the result of considerable agitation by the plebian class, who had hitherto been excluded from the higher benefits of the Republic. (Indeed the law had previously been unwritten and exclusively interpreted by upper-class priests, the *pontifices*). Something of the regard with which later Romans came to view the Twelve Tables is captured in the remark of Cicero (106–43 BC) that the "Twelve Tables . . . seems to me, assuredly to surpass the libraries of all the philosophers, both in weight of authority, and in plenitude of utility". Cicero scarcely exaggerated; the Twelve Tables formed the basis of Roman law for a thousand years. Herewith are excerpts from the main clauses:

Table I

1. If anyone summons a man before the magistrate, he must go. If the man summoned does not go, let the one summoning him call the bystanders to witness and then take him by force.
2. If he shirks or runs away, let the summoner lay hands on him.
3. If illness or old age is the hindrance, let the summoner provide a team. He need not provide a covered carriage with a pallet unless he chooses.
4. Let the protector of a landholder be a landholder; for one of the proletariat, let anyone that cares, be protector.
6–9. When the litigants settle their case by compromise, let the magistrate announce it. If they do not compromise, let them state each his own side of the case, in the *comitium* of the forum before noon. Afterwards let them talk it out together, while both are present. After noon, in case either party has failed to appear, let the magistrate pronounce judgment in favour of the one who is present. If both are present the trial may last until sunset but no later.

Table II

2. He whose witness has failed to appear may summon him by loud calls before his house every third day.

Table III

1. One who has confessed a debt, or against whom judgment has been pronounced, shall have thirty days to pay it in. After that forcible seizure of his person is allowed. The creditor shall bring him before the magistrate. Unless he pays the amount of the judgment or some one in the presence of the magistrate interferes in his behalf as protector the creditor so shall take him home and fasten him in stocks or fetters. He shall fasten him with not less than fifteen pounds of weight or, if he choose, with more. If the prisoner choose, he may furnish his own food. If he does not, the creditor must give him a pound of meal daily; if he choose he may give him more.
2. On the third market day let them divide his body among them. If they cut more or less than each one's share it shall be no crime.
3. Against a foreigner the right in property shall be valid forever.

Table IV

1. A dreadfully deformed child shall be quickly killed.
2. If a father sell his son three times, the son shall be free from his father.
3. As a man has provided in his will in regard to his money and the care of his property, so let it be binding. If he has no heir and dies intestate, let the nearest agnate have the inheritance. If there is no agnate, let the members of his *gens* have the inheritance.
4. If one is mad but has no guardian, the power over him and his money shall belong to his agnates and the members of his *gens*.
5. A child born after ten months since the father's death will not be admitted into a legal inheritance.

Table V

1. Females should remain in guardianship even when they have attained their majority.

Table VI

1. When one makes a bond and a conveyance of property, as he has made formal declaration so let it be binding.
3. A beam that is built into a house or a vineyard trellis one may not take from its place.

5. *Usucapio* of movable things requires one year's possession for its completion; but *usucapio* of an estate and buildings two years.

6. Any woman who does not wish to be subjected in this manner to the hand of her husband should be absent three nights in succession every year, and so interrupt the *usucapio* of each year.

Table VII

1. Let them keep the road in order. If they have not paved it, a man may drive his team where he likes.

9. Should a tree on a neighbour's farm be bend crooked by the wind and lean over your farm, you may take legal action for removal of that tree.

10. A man might gather up fruit that was falling down onto another man's farm.

Table VIII

2. If one has maimed a limb and does not compromise with the injured person, let there be retaliation. If one has broken a bone of a freeman with his hand or with a cudgel, let him pay a penalty of three hundred coins. If he has broken the bone of a slave, let him have one hundred and fifty coins. If one is guilty of insult, the penalty shall be twenty-five coins.

3. If one is slain while committing theft by night, he is rightly slain.

4. If a patron shall have devised any deceit against his client, let him be accursed.

5. If one shall permit himself to be summoned as a witness, or has been a weigher, if he does not give his testimony, let him be noted as dishonest and incapable of acting again as witness.

10. Any person who destroys by burning any building or heap of corn deposited alongside a house shall be bound, scourged, and put to death by burning at the stake provided that he has committed the said misdeed with malice aforethought; but if he shall have committed it by accident, that is, by negligence, it is ordained that he repair the damage or, if he be too poor to be competent for such punishment, he shall receive a lighter punishment.

12. If the theft has been done by night, if the owner kills the thief, the thief shall be held to be lawfully killed.

13. It is unlawful for a thief to be killed by day . . . unless he defends himself with a weapon; even though he has come with a weapon, unless he shall use the weapon and fight back, you shall not kill him. And even if he resists, first call out so that someone may hear and come up.

23. A person who had been found guilty of giving false witness shall be hurled down from the Tarpeian Rock.

26. No person shall hold meetings by night in the city.

Table IX

4. The penalty shall be capital for a judge or arbiter legally appointed who has been found guilty of receiving a bribe for giving a decision.
5. Treason: he who shall have roused up a public enemy or handed over a citizen to a public enemy must suffer capital punishment.
6. Putting to death of any man, whosoever he might be if unconvicted is forbidden.

Table X

1. None is to bury or burn a corpse in the city.
3. The women shall not tear their faces nor wail on account of the funeral.
5. If one obtains a crown himself, or if his chattel does so because of his honour and valour, if it is placed on his head, or the head of his parents, it shall be no crime.

Table XI

1. Marriages should not take place between plebeians and patricians.

Table XII

2. If a slave shall have committed theft or done damage with his master's knowledge, the action for damages is in the slave's name.
5. Whatever the people had last ordained should be held as binding by law.

THE FUNERAL ORATION OF PERICLES, 431 BC

Thucydides

It is to the Ancient Greeks that we owe both the word and concept of "democracy". And this democracy saw its finest flowering in the city-state of Athens, where Solon, Pisistratus, Theomistocles and Pericles successively redistributed the economic and political power of the "oligarchy" to the people, so that by mid 5th-century BC Athens was a participatory democracy in which all citizens (freeborn Athenian males) could attend, speak and vote in the ruling assembly, or Ekklesia. The day-to-day business of the Ekklesia was organized by the Boule of 500 citizens, chosen by lot from those who indicated their willingess to serve. Most public offices – even generalships – were elected annually.

In his celebrated "funeral speech", given over the bodies of Athenians killed in battle against Sparta, Pericles set out "the general principles by virtue of which we came to empire, and of the civic institutions and manners of life in consequence of which our empire became great".

Most of my predecessors in this place have commended him who made this speech part of the law, telling us that it is well that it should be delivered at the burial of those who fall in battle. For myself, I should have thought the worth which had displayed itself in deeds would be sufficiently rewarded by honours also shown by deeds, such as in this funeral prepared at the people's cost; and I could have wished that the reputations of many brave men were not to be imperilled in the mouth of a single individual, to stand or fall accordingly as he spoke well or ill. However, since our ancestors have stamped this custom with their approval, it becomes my duty to obey the law.

I shall begin with our ancestors. They dwelt in the country without break in the succession from generation to generation, and handed it down free to the present time by their valour. And, if our more remote ancestors deserve praise, much more do our own fathers, who added to their inheritance the empire we now possess. Lastly, there are few parts of our dominions that have not been augmented by those of us here, still more or less in the vigour of life; while the Mother Country has been furnished by us with everything that can enable her to depend on her own resources.

Our constitution does not copy the laws of neighbouring States; we are rather a pattern to others than imitators ourselves. Its administration favours the many instead of the few; this is why it is called a democracy. If we look to the laws, they afford equal justice to all in their private differences; if to social standing, advancement in public life falls to reputation for capacity, class considerations not being allowed to interfere with merit; nor again does poverty bar the way; if a man is able to serve the State, he is not hindered by the obscurity of his condition.

Further, we provide plenty of means for the mind to refresh itself from business. We celebrate games and sacrifices all the year round, and the elegance of our private establishments forms a daily source of pleasure and helps to banish the spleen; while the magnitude of our city draws the produce of the world into our harbour, so that to the Athenian the fruits of other countries are as familiar a luxury as those of his own.

If we turn to our military policy, there also we differ from our antagonists. We throw open our city to the world, and never by alien acts exclude foreigners from any opportunity of learning or observing (although the eyes of an enemy may occasionally profit by our liberality), trusting less in system and policy than to the native spirit of our citizens; while in education, where our rivals from their very cradles by a painful discipline seek after manliness, at Athens we live as we please, and yet are ready to encounter every danger.

We cultivate refinement without extravagance and knowledge without effeminacy; wealth we employ more for use than for show, and place the real disgrace of poverty not in owning to the fact but in declining the struggle against it. Our public men have, besides politics, their private affairs to attend to, and our ordinary citizens, though occupied with the pursuits of industry, are still fair judges of public matters. In our enterprises we present the singular spectacle of daring and deliberation, each carried to its highest point, and both united in the same persons, although usually decision is the fruit of ignorance, hesitation of reflection. But the palm of courage will surely be adjudged most justly to those who best know the difference between hardship and pleasure yet are never tempted to shrink from danger. In generosity we are equally singular, acquiring our friends by conferring, not by receiving, favours. Yet, of course, the doer of the favour is the firmer friend of the two, in order by continued kindness to keep the recipient in his debt; while the debtor feels less keenly from the very consciousness that the return he makes will be a payment, not a free gift. And it is only the Athenians who, fearless of consequences, confer their benefits not from calculations of expediency, but in the confidence of liberality.

In short, I say that as a city we are the school of Hellas; while I doubt if the world can produce a man who, where he has only himself to depend upon, is equal to so many emergencies, and graced by so happy a versatility as the Athenian. And that this is no mere boast thrown out for the occasion, but plain matter of fact, the power of the State acquired by these habits proves. For Athens alone of her contemporaries is found when tested to be greater than her reputation, and gives no occasion to her assailants to blush at the antagonist by whom they have been worsted, or to her subjects to question her title by merit to rule. Rather the admiration of the present and succeeding ages will be ours, since we have not left our power without witness, but have shown it by mighty proofs; and, far from needing a Homer for our panegyrist, we have forced every sea and land to be the highway of our daring, and everywhere, whether for evil or for good, have left imperishable monuments behind us.

Such is the Athens for which these men, in the assertion of their resolve not to lose her, nobly fought and died; and well may every one of their survivors be ready to suffer in her cause. The Athens that I have celebrated is only what the heroism of these and their like have made her, men whose fame, unlike that of most Hellenes, will be found to be only commensurate with their deserts. If a test of worth be wanted it is to be found in their closing scene. None of these allowed either wealth, with its prospect of future enjoyment, to unnerve his spirit, or poverty, with its hope of a day of freedom and riches, to tempt him to shrink from danger. Thus choosing to die resisting rather than to live submitting, they fled only from dishonour, but met danger face to face, and after one brief moment, while at the summit of their fortune, escaped, not from their fear, but from their glory.

So died these men as became Athenians. You, their survivors, must determine to have as unfaltering a resolution in the field. Not contented with ideas derived only from words of the advantages which are bound up with the defence of your country, realize the power of Athens, and feed your eyes upon her from day to day, till love of her fills your hearts; and then, when all her greatness shall break upon you, reflect that it was by courage, sense of duty, and a keen feeling of honour in action, that men were enabled to win all this, and that no personal failure in an enterprise could make them consent to deprive their country of their valour; but they laid it at her feet as the most glorious contribution that they could offer.

For this offering of their lives, made in common by them all, they each individually received that renown which never grows old, and for a sepulchre, not so much that in which their bones have been deposited, but that noblest of shrines wherein their glory is laid up to be eternally remembered. For heroes have the whole Earth for their tomb; and in lands far from their own there is enshrined in every breast a record unwritten with no tablet to preserve it except that of the heart. These take as your model, and, judging happiness to be the fruit of freedom and freedom of valour, never decline the dangers of war. For it is not the miserable that would most justly be unsparing of their lives; these have nothing to hope for: it is rather they to whom continued life may bring reverses as yet unknown, and to whom a fall, if it came, would be most tremendous in its consequences. And surely, to a man of spirit, the degradation of cowardice must be immeasurably more grievous than the unfelt death which strikes him in the midst of his strength and patriotism!

Comfort, therefore, not condolence, is what I have to offer to the parents of the dead who may be here. Numberless are the chances to which the life of man is subject; but fortunate indeed are they who draw for their lot a death so glorious as that which has caused your mourning, and to whom life has been so exactly measured as to terminate in the happiness in which it has been passed. Those of you who have passed your prime must congratulate yourselves with the thought that the best part of your life was fortunate, and that the brief span that remains will be cheered by the fame of the departed. For it is only the love of honour that never grows old; and honour it is, not gain, that rejoices the heart of age and help-lessness.

Turning to the sons or brothers of the dead, I see an arduous struggle before you. When a man is gone all are wont to praise him, and should your merit be ever so transcendent you will still find it difficult, not merely to overtake, but even to approach their renown. The living have envy to contend with, while those who are no longer in our path are honoured with a goodwill into which rivalry does not enter. If I must say anything on feminine excellence to those of you who will now be in widowhood, it will be all comprised in this brief exhortation. Great will be your glory in not falling short of your natural character; and greatest will be hers who is least talked of among the men, whether for good or for bad.

My task is now finished. I have performed it to the best of my ability. If deeds be in question, those who are here interred have received part of their honours already, and, for the rest, their children will be brought up till manhood at the public expense. The State thus offers a valuable prize, as the garland of victory in this race of valour, for both those who have fallen and their survivors. Where the rewards for merit are greatest, there are found the best citizens.

And now that you have brought to a close your lamentations for your relatives, you may depart.

SOCRATES ON HIS CONDEMNATION TO DEATH, 399 BC

Plato

Socrates was instrumental in moving the focus of Western philosophy from Nature to the world of man, particularly man's ethics and politics. An Athenian born, he participated like a good citizen in the military campaigns at Potidaea, Delium and Ampholis. Yet his relentless probing of the morals of his fellow Athenians by the "Socratic method" (of analytical discussion about everyday concepts such as justice and duty) was always faintly unnerving to the larger citizenry. In 399 BC Socrates, aged 70, was charged with "not believing in the gods in which the state believes . . . and corrupting the youth". A court of 501 citizens found him guilty, at which he rejected the option of merely paying a fine, instead suggesting that the state provide free meals for him in perpetuity. This antagonized the jury, which ordered him to die by the drinking of hemlock (*Conium maculatum*). For all Socrates' arrogance, his personal integrity was unimpeachable. He believed he had committed no wrong and could not therefore admit any acknowledgment of guilt. Thus Socrates is one of history's first martyrs to conscience.

Socrates' speech on receiving his condemnation to death is recorded by his student Plato in *The Apology*.

Not much time will be gained, O Athenians, in return for the evil name which you will get from the detractors of the city, who will say that you killed Socrates, a wise man; for they will call me wise even although I am not wise when they want to reproach you. If you had waited a little while, your desire would have been fulfilled in the course of nature. For I am far advanced in years, as you may perceive, and not far from death. I am speaking now only to those of you who have condemned me to death. And I have another thing to say to them: You think that I was convicted through deficiency of words – I mean, that if I had thought fit to leave nothing undone, nothing unsaid, I might have gained an acquittal. Not so;

the deficiency which led to my conviction was not of words – certainly not. But I had not the boldness or impudence or inclination to address you as you would have liked me to address you, weeping and wailing and lamenting, and saying and doing many things which you have been accustomed to hear from others, and which, as I say, are unworthy of me. But I thought that I ought not to do anything common or mean in the hour of danger: nor do I now repent of the manner of my defence, and I would rather die having spoken after my manner, than speak in your manner and live. For neither in war nor yet at law ought any man to use every way of escaping death. For often in battle there is no doubt that if a man will throw away his arms, and fall on his knees before his pursuers, he may escape death; and in other dangers there are other ways of escaping death, if a man is willing to say and do anything. The difficulty, my friends, is not in avoiding death, but in avoiding unrighteousness; for that runs faster than death. I am old and move slowly, and the slower runner has overtaken me, and my accusers are keen and quick, and the faster runner, who is unrighteousness, has overtaken them. And now I depart hence condemned by you to suffer the penalty of death, and they, too, go their ways condemned by the truth to suffer the penalty of villainy and wrong; and I must abide by my award – let them abide by theirs. I suppose that these things may be regarded as fated – and I think that they are well.

And now, O men who have condemned me, I would fain prophesy to you; for I am about to die, and that is the hour in which men are gifted with prophetic power. And I prophesy to you who are my murderers, that immediately after my death punishment far heavier than you have inflicted on me will surely await you. Me you have killed because you wanted to escape the accuser, and not to give an account of your lives. But that will not be as you suppose: far otherwise. For I say that there will be more accusers of you than there are now; accusers whom hitherto I have restrained: and as they are younger they will be more severe with you, and you will be more offended at them. For if you think that by killing men you can avoid the accuser censuring your lives, you are mistaken; that is not a way of escape which is either possible or honourable; the easiest and noblest way is not to be crushing others, but to be improving yourselves. This is the prophecy which I utter before my departure, to the judges who have condemned me.

Friends, who would have acquitted me, I would like also to talk with you about this thing which has happened, while the magistrates are busy, and before I go to the place at which I must die. Stay then awhile, for we may as well talk with one another while there is time. You are my friends, and I should like to show you the meaning of this event which has happened to me. O my judges – for you I may truly call judges – I should like to tell you of a wonderful circumstance. Hitherto the familiar oracle within me has constantly been in the habit of opposing me even about trifles, if I was going to make a slip or error about anything; and now as you see there has come upon me that which may be thought, and is generally believed to be, the last and worst evil. But the oracle made no sign of opposition, either as I was leaving my house and going out in the morning, or when I was going up into this court, or while I was speaking, at anything which I was going to say; and yet I have often been stopped in the middle of a speech; but now in nothing I either said or did touching this matter has the oracle opposed me. What do I take to be the explanation of this? I will tell you. I regard this as a proof that what has happened to me is a good, and that those of us who think that death is an evil are in error. This is a great proof to me of what I am saying, for the customary sign would surely have opposed me had I been going to evil and not to good.

Let us reflect in another way, and we shall see that there is great reason to hope that death is a good, for one of two things: – either death is a state of nothingness and utter unconsciousness, or, as men say, there is a change and migration of the soul from this world to another. Now if you suppose that there is no consciousness, but a sleep like the sleep of him who is undisturbed even by the sight of dreams, death will be an unspeakable gain. For if a person were to select the night in which his sleep was undisturbed even by dreams, and were to compare with this the other days and nights of his life, and then were to tell us how many days and nights he had passed in the course of his life better and more pleasantly than this one, I think that any man, I will not say a private man, but even the great king, will not find many such days or nights, when compared with the others. Now if death is like this, I say that to die is gain; for eternity is then only a single night. But if death is the journey to another place, and there, as men say, all the dead are, what good, O my friends and judges, can be greater than this? If indeed when the pilgrim arrives in the world below, he is delivered from the professors of justice in this world, and finds the true judges who are said to give judgment there, Minos and Rhadamanthus and Aeacus and Triptolemus, and other sons of God who were righteous in their own life, that pilgrimage will be worth making. What would not a man give if he might converse with Orpheus and Musaeus and Hesiod and Homer? Nay, if this be true, let me die again and again. I, too, shall have a wonderful interest in a place where I can converse with Palamedes, and Ajax the son of Telamon, and other heroes of old, who have suffered death through an unjust judgment; and there will be no small pleasure, as I think, in comparing my own sufferings with theirs. Above all, I shall be able to continue my search into true and false knowledge; as in this world, so also in that; I shall find out who is wise, and who pretends to be wise, and is not. What would not a man give, O judges, to be able to examine the leader of the great Trojan expedition; or Odysseus or Sisyphus, or numberless others, men and women too! What infinite delight would there be in conversing with them and asking them questions! For in that world they do not put a man to death for this; certainly not. For besides being happier in that world than in this, they will be immortal, if what is said is true.

Wherefore, O judges, be of good cheer about death, and know this of a truth – that no evil can happen to a good man, either in life or after death. He and his are not neglected by the gods; nor has my own approaching end happened by mere chance. But I see clearly that to die and be released was better for me; and therefore the oracle gave no sign. For which reason also, I am not angry with my accusers, or my condemners; they have done me no harm, although neither of them meant to do me any good; and for this I may gently blame them.

Still I have a favour to ask of them. When my sons are grown up, I would ask you, O my friends, to punish them; and I would have you trouble them, as I have troubled you, if they seem to care about riches, or anything, more than about virtue; or if they pretend to be something when they are really nothing – then reprove them, as I have reproved you, for not caring about that for which they ought to care, and thinking that they are something when they are really nothing. And if you do this, I and my sons will have received justice at your hands.

The hour of departure has arrived, and we go our ways – I to die, and you to live. Which is better God only knows.

From THE REPUBLIC, 375 BC

Plato

Aristocles, nicknamed Plato ("broad-shoulders"), was born in Athens in c. 429 BC. Disenchanted by the execution of Socrates (see pp 35–8) and the degeneration of Athenian democracy, Plato sought solace and solution in philosophy. Notable among his subsequent conclusions were the "Theory of Forms" – which distinguished between the temporary nature of the everyday world in which we live and the realm of the eternal – and Platonic love, which elevated spiritual devotion above sexual desire. There were also his political and ethical ideas.

These were most fully expressed in *The Republic* of c. 375 BC, which proposed that philosophers should be rulers (or rulers philosophers) of a rigidly caste-based state in which the family and much else was held in common.

As numerous commentators have pointed out, Stalin's Soviet Union was Plato's *Republic* in motion and have accordingly tended to throw out the philosophical baby with the Platonic political bathwater. *For The Republic* is also a book of ethics, epistemology and education.

Ethics: Justice in the Individual (Book Four)
The Republic starts with the question: what is justice? Something of Plato's answer is given below, which follows an imaginary dialogue between Socrates and Glaucon.

[Socrates] Will the just man or citizen ever be guilty of sacrilege or theft, or treachery either to his friends or to his country?

[Glaucon] Never.
Neither will he ever break faith where there have been oaths or agreements?

Impossible.
No one will be less likely to commit adultery, or to dishonour his father and mother, or to fall in his religious duties?

No one.
And the reason is that each part of him is doing its own business, whether in ruling or being ruled?

Exactly so.
Are you satisfied then that the quality which makes such men and such states is justice, or do you hope to discover some other?

Not I, indeed.
Then our dream has been realized; and the suspicion which we entertained at the beginning of our work of construction, that some divine power must have conducted us to a primary form of justice, has now been verified?

Yes, certainly.
And the division of labour which required the carpenter and the shoemaker and the rest of the citizens to be doing each his own business, and not another's, was a shadow of justice, and for that reason it was of use?

Clearly.
But in reality justice was such as we were describing, being concerned however, not with the outward man, but with the inward, which is the true self and concernment of man: for the just man does not permit the several elements within him to interfere with one another, or any of them to do the work of others – he sets in order his own inner life, and is his own master and his own law, and at peace with himself; and when he has bound together the three principles within him, which may be compared to the higher, lower, and middle notes of the scale, and the intermediate intervals – when he has bound all these together, and is no longer many, but has become one entirely temperate and perfectly adjusted nature, then he proceeds to act, if he has to act, whether in a matter of property, or in the treatment of the body, or in some affair of politics or private business; always thinking and calling that which preserves and co-operates with this harmonious condition, just and good action, and the knowledge which presides over it, wisdom, and that which at any time impairs this condition, he will call unjust action, and the opinion which presides over it ignorance.

You have said the exact truth, Socrates.
Very good; and if we were to affirm that we had discovered the just man

and the just State, and the nature of justice in each of them, we should not be telling a falsehood?

Most certainly not.
May we say so, then?
Let us say so.
And now, I said, injustice has to be considered.
Clearly.
Must not injustice be a strife which arises among the three principles – a meddlesomeness, and interference, and rising up of a part of the soul against the whole, an assertion of unlawful authority, which is made by a rebellious subject against a true prince, of whom he is the natural vassal – what is all this confusion and delusion but injustice, and intemperance and cowardice and ignorance, and every form of vice?

Exactly so.
And if the nature of justice and injustice be known, then the meaning of acting unjustly and being unjust, or, again, of acting justly, will also be perfectly clear?

What do you mean? he said.
Why, I said, they are like disease and health; being in the soul just what disease and health are in the body.

How so? he said.
Why, I said, that which is healthy causes health, and that which is unhealthy causes disease.

Yes.
And just actions cause justice, and unjust actions cause injustice?
That is certain.
And the creation of health is the institution of a natural order and government of one by another in the parts of the body; and the creation of disease is the production of a state of things at variance with this natural order?

True.
And is not the creation of justice the institution of a natural order and government of one by another in the parts of the soul, and the creation of injustice the production of a state of things at variance with the natural order?

Exactly so, he said.
Then virtue is the health and beauty and well-being of the soul, and vice the disease and weakness and deformity of the same?

True.

And do not good practices lead to virtue, and evil practices to vice?

Assuredly.

Still our old question of the comparative advantage of justice and injustice has not been answered: Which is the more profitable, to be just and act justly and practise virtue, whether seen or unseen of gods and men, or to be unjust and act unjustly, if only unpunished and unreformed?

In my judgment, Socrates, the question has now become ridiculous. We know that, when the bodily constitution is gone, life is no longer endurable, though pampered with all kinds of meats and drinks, and having all wealth and all power; and shall we be told that when the very essence of the vital principle is undermined and corrupted, life is still worth having to a man, if only he be allowed to do whatever he likes with the single exception that he is not to acquire justice and virtue, or to escape from injustice and vice; assuming them both to be such as we have described?

Yes, I said, the question is, as you say, ridiculous.

The Cave (Book Six)

This famous simile is a summation of Plato's epistemology: the world which appears to our senses and absolute reality differ. "The Theory of Forms" remained influential in Western philosophy until modern times.

And now, I said, let me show in a figure how far our nature is enlightened or unenlightened; – Behold! human beings living in an underground den, which has a mouth open towards the light and reaching all along the den; here they have been from their childhood, and have their legs and necks chained so that they cannot move and can only see before them, being prevented by the chains from turning round their heads. Above and behind a fire is blazing at a distance, and between the fire and the prisoners there is a raised way, like the screen which marionette players have in front of them, over which they show the puppets.

I see.

And do you see, I said, men passing along the wall carrying all sorts of vessels, and statues and figures of animals made of wood and stone and various materials, which appear over the wall? Some of them are talking, others silent.

You have shown me a strange image, and they are strange prisoners.

Like ourselves, I replied; and they see only their own shadows, or the shadows of one another, which the fire throws on the opposite wall of the cave?

True, he said; how could they see anything but the shadows if they were never allowed to move their heads?

And of the objects which are being carried in like manner they would only see the shadows?

Yes, he said.

And if they were able to converse with one another, would they not suppose that they were naming what was actually before them?

Very true.

And suppose further that the prison had an echo which came from the other side, would they not be sure to fancy when one of the passers-by spoke that the voice which they heard came from the passing shadow?

No question, he replied.

To them, I said, the truth would be literally nothing but the shadows of the images.

That is certain.

And now look again, and see what will naturally follow if the prisoners are released and disabused of their error. At first, when any of them is liberated and compelled suddenly to stand up and turn his neck round and walk and look towards the light, he will suffer sharp pains: the glare will distress him, and he will be unable to see the realities of which in his former state he had seen the shadows; and then conceive someone saying to him, that what he saw before was an illusion, but that now, when he is approaching nearer to being and his eye is turned towards more real existence, he has a clearer vision – what will be his reply? And you may further imagine that his instructor is pointing to the objects as they pass and requiring him to name them – will he not be perplexed? Will he not fancy that the shadows which he formerly saw are truer than the objects which are now shown to him?

Far truer.

And if he is compelled to look straight at the light, will he not have a pain in his eyes which will make him turn away to take refuge in the objects of vision which he can see, and which he will conceive to be in reality clearer than the things which are now being shown to him?

True, he said.

And suppose once more, that he is reluctantly dragged up a steep and rugged ascent, and held fast until he is forced into the presence of the sun himself, is he not likely to be pained and irritated? When he approaches the light his eyes will be dazzled, and he will not be able to see anything at all of what are now called realities.

Not all in a moment, he said.

He will require to grow accustomed to the sight of the upper world. And first he will see the shadows best, next the reflections of men and other objects in the water, and then the objects themselves; then he will gaze upon the light of the moon and the stars and the spangled heaven; and he will see the sky and the stars by night better than the sun or the light of the sun by day?

Certainly.

Last of all he will be able to see the sun, and not mere reflections of it in the water, but he will see it in its own proper place, and not in another; and he will contemplate it as it is.

Certainly.

He will then proceed to argue that this is it which gives the season and the years, and is the guardian of all that is in the visible world, and in a certain way the cause of all things which he and his fellows have been accustomed to behold?

Clearly, he said, he would first see the sun and then reason about it.

And when he remembered his old habitation, and the wisdom of the den and his fellow-prisoners, do you not suppose that he would congratulate himself on the change and pity them?

Certainly, he would.

And if they were in the habit of conferring honours among themselves on those who were quickest to observe the passing shadows and to remark which of them went before, and which followed after, and which were together; and who were therefore best able to draw conclusions as to the future, do you think that he would care for such honours and glories, or envy the possessors of them? Would he not say with Homer,

"Better to be the poor servant of a poor master," and to endure anything, rather than think as they do and live after their manner?

Yes, he said, I think that he would rather suffer anything than entertain these false notions and live in this miserable manner.

Imagine once more, I said, such a one coming suddenly out of the sun to be replaced in his old situation; would he not be certain to have his eyes full of darkness?

To be sure, he said.

And if there were a contest, and he had to compete in measuring the shadows with the prisoners who had never moved out of the den, while his sight was still weak, and before his eyes had become steady (and the time which would be needed to acquire this new habit of sight might be very considerable), would he not be ridiculous? Men would say of him that up he went and came back without his eyes; and that it was better not even to think of ascending; and if any one tried to loose another and lead him up to the light, let them only catch the offender, and they would put him to death.

No question, he said.

This entire allegory, I said, you may now append, dear Glaucon, to the previous argument; the prison-house is the world of sight, the light of the fire is the sun, and you will not misapprehend me if you interpret the journey upwards to be the ascent of the soul into the intellectual world according to my poor belief, which, at your desire, I have expressed – whether rightly or wrongly God knows. But whether true or false, my opinion is that in the world of knowledge the idea of good appears last of all, and is seen only with an effort; and when seen, is also inferred to be the universal author of all things beautiful and right, parent of light and of the lord of light in this visible world, and the immediate source of reason and truth in the intellectual; and that this is the power upon which he who would act rationally either in public or private life must have his eye fixed.

I agree, he said, as far as I am able to understand you.

Moreover, I said, you must not wonder that those who attain to this beatific vision are unwilling to descend to human affairs; for their souls are ever hastening into the upper world where they desire to dwell; which desire of theirs is very natural, if our allegory may be trusted.

Yes, very natural.

And is there anything surprising in one who passes from divine contemplations to the evil state of man, misbehaving himself in a ridiculous manner; if, while his eyes are blinking and before he has become accustomed to the surrounding darkness, he is compelled to fight in courts of law. or in other places, about the images or the shadows of images of justice, and is endeavoring to meet the conceptions of those who have never yet seen absolute justice?

Anything but surprising, he replied.

Anyone who has common sense will remember that the bewilderments of the eyes are of two kinds, and arise from two causes, either from coming out of the light or from going into the light, which is true of the mind's eye, quite as much as of the bodily eye; and he who remembers this when he sees anyone whose vision is perplexed and weak, will not be too ready to laugh; he will first ask whether that soul of man has come out of the brighter life, and is unable to see because unaccustomed to the dark, or having turned from darkness to the day is dazzled by excess of light.

The business of us who are the founders of the State will be to compel the best minds to attain that knowledge which we have already shown to be the greatest of all – they must continue to ascend until they arrive at the good; but when they have ascended and seen enough we must not allow them to do as they do now.

What do you mean?

I mean that they remain in the upper world; but this must not be allowed; they must be made to descend again among the prisoners in the den, and partake of their labours and honours, whether they are worth having or not.

Education for Leadership (Book Seven)

Plato's notions on education for the philosopher-kings of *The Republic* command attention because he was the first person in the world to found a university – the Academy in Athens in c. 387. He did so because he pioneeringly proposed that education had the potential to transform society. Here Plato outlines the higher course of education for "philosopher-rulers", it complements an earlier stage, lasting until the age of 18, described in *The Republic*'s Book Three.

Solon was under a delusion when he said that a man when he grows old may learn many things – for he can no more learn much than he can run much; youth is the time for any extraordinary toil.

Of course.

And, therefore, calculation and geometry and all the other elements of instruction, which are a preparation for dialectic, should be presented to the mind in childhood; not, however, under any notion of forcing our system of education.

Why not?

Because a freeman ought not to be a slave in the acquisition of knowledge of any kind. Bodily exercise, when compulsory, does no harm to the body; but knowledge which is acquired under compulsion obtains no hold on the mind.

Very true.

Then, my good friend, I said, do not use compulsion, but let early education be a sort of amusement; you will then be better able to find out the natural bent.

That is a very rational notion, he said.

Do you remember that the children, too, were to be taken to see the battle on horseback; and that if there were no danger they were to be brought close up and, like young hounds, have a taste of blood given them?

Yes, I remember.

The same practice may be followed, I said, in all these things – labours, lessons, dangers – and he who is most at home in all of them ought to be enrolled in a select number.

At what age?

At the age when the necessary gymnastics are over: the period whether of two or three years which passes in this sort of training is useless for any other purpose; for sleep and exercise are unpropitious to learning; and the trial of who is first in gymnastic exercises is one of the most important tests to which our youth are subjected.

Certainly, he replied.

After that time those who are selected from the class of twenty years old will be promoted to higher honours, and the sciences which they learned without any order in their early education will now be brought together, and they will be able to see the natural relationship of them to one another and to true being.

Yes, he said, that is the only kind of knowledge which takes lasting root.

Yes, I said; and the capacity for such knowledge is the great criterion of dialectical talent: the comprehensive mind is always the dialectical.

I agree with you, he said.

These, I said, are the points which you must consider; and those who have most of this comprehension, and who are most steadfast in their learning and in their military and other appointed duties, when they have arrived at the age of thirty will have to be chosen by you out of the select class, and elevated to higher honour; and you will have to prove them by the help of dialectic, in order to learn which of them is able to give up the use of sight and the other senses, and in company with truth to attain absolute being. And here, my friend, great caution is required.

Why great caution? . . .

There is a danger lest they should taste the dear delight too early; for youngsters, as you may have observed, when they first get the taste in their mouths, argue for amusement, and are always contradicting and refuting others in imitation of those who refute them; like puppy-dogs, they rejoice in pulling and tearing at all who come near them.

Yes, he said, there is nothing which they like better.

And when they have made many conquests and received defeats at the hands of many, they violently and speedily get into a way of not believing anything which they believed before, and hence, not only they, but philosophy and all that relates to it is apt to have a bad name with the rest of the world.

Too true, he said.

But when a man begins to get older, he will no longer be guilty of such insanity; he will imitate the dialectician who is seeking for truth, and not the eristic, who is contradicting for the sake of amusement; and the greater moderation of his character will increase instead of diminishing the honour of the pursuit.

Very true, he said.

And did we not make special provision for this, when we said that the disciples of philosophy were to be orderly and steadfast, not, as now, any chance aspirant or intruder?

Very true.

Suppose, I said, the study of philosophy to take the place of gymnastics and to be continued diligently and earnestly and exclusively for twice the number of years which were passed in bodily exercise – will that be enough?

Would you say six or four years? he asked.

Say five years, I replied; at the end of the time they must be sent down again into the den and compelled to hold any military or other office which young men are qualified to hold: in this way they will get their experience of life, and there will be an opportunity of trying whether, when they are drawn all manner of ways by temptation, they will stand firm or flinch.

And how long is this state of their lives to last?

Fifteen years, I answered; and when they have reached fifty years of age, then let those who still survive and have distinguished themselves in every action of their lives and in every branch of knowledge come at last to their consummation: the time has now arrived at which they must raise the eye of the soul to the universal light which lightens all things, and behold the absolute good; for that is the pattern according to which they are to order the State and the lives of individuals, and the remainder of their own lives also; making philosophy their chief pursuit, but, when their turn comes, toiling also at politics and ruling for the public good, not as though they were performing some heroic action, but simply as a matter of duty; and when they have brought up in each generation others like themselves and left them in their place to be governors of the State, then they will depart to the Islands of the Blest and dwell there; and the city will give them public memorials and sacrifices and honour them, if the Pythian oracle consent, as demigods, but if not, as in any case blessed and divine.

You are a sculptor, Socrates, and have made statues of our governors faultless in beauty.

Yes, I said, Glaucon, and of our governesses too; for you must not suppose that what I have been saying applies to men only and not to women as far as their natures can go.

There you are right, he said, since we have made them to share in all things like the men.

Well, I said, and you would agree (would you not?) that what has been said about the State and the government is not a mere dream, and although difficult not impossible, but only possible in the way which has been supposed; that is to say, when the true philosopher kings are born in a State, one or more of them, despising the honours of this present world which they deem mean and worthless, esteeming above all things right and the honour that springs from right, and regarding justice as the greatest and most necessary of all things, whose ministers they are, and whose principles will be exalted by them when they set in order their own city?

How will they proceed?

They will begin by sending out into the country all the inhabitants of the city who are more than ten years old, and will take possession of their children, who will be unaffected by the habits of their parents; these they will train in their own habits and laws, I mean in the laws which we have given them: and in this way the State and constitution of which we were speaking will soonest and most easily attain happiness, and the nation which has such a constitution will gain most.

Yes, that will be the best way. And I think, Socrates, that you have very well described how, if ever, such a constitution might come into being.

Enough then of the perfect State, and of the man who bears its image – there is no difficulty in seeing how we shall describe him.

There is no difficulty, he replied; and I agree with you in thinking that nothing more need be said.

From THE POLITICS, c. 330 BC

Aristotle

Aristotle (384–322 BC) was born in Macedon, but was educated in Athens, where he studied under Plato (see pp 35–49) for 20 years. Around 335 BC Aristotle opened his own school in the Lyceum grove, and those works of his which survive are believed to be his lecture notes; these encompass ethics, logic, poetics, zoology, political theory and much else. Aristotle and his followers – called "peripatetics", after his habit of walking up and down whilst teaching – indelibly shaped the later intellectual thought of the Christian medieval world, largely through the offices of St Aquinas. Unfortunately, on almost every conceivable scientific subject Aristotle was mistaken, due to the shortcoming of his deductive method of reasoning, later corrected by Francis Bacon (see pp 224–7) in the 17th century. However, Aristotle's "empirical" approach made for a valuable record and analysis of Greek politics. In this extract from *The Politics* Aristotle examines the nature of the State.

The Purpose of the State

Seeing that every state is a sort of association and every association is formed for the attainment of some Good – for some presumed Good is the end of all action – it is evident that, as some Good is the object of all associations, so in the highest degree is the supreme Good the object of that association which is supreme and embraces all the rest, in other words, of the State or political association.

Now it is wrong to confound, as some do, the functions of the constitutional statesman, king, householder and slavemaster. They hold that the difference between them is not one of kind, but depends simply upon the number of persons ruled, i.e. that a man is a slavemaster if he has but few subjects; if he has more, a householder; if still more, a constitutional statesman or king, there being no distinction between a large household and a small State; also that a man is either a king or a constitutional statesman according as he governs absolutely or in conformity to the laws of political science, being alternately ruler and subject. Such an opinion is erroneous. Our meaning will be clear, however, if we follow our usual method of investigation. For as in other cases we have to analyse a compound whole into the uncompounded elements which are its least parts, so in examining the constituents of a State we shall incidentally best ascertain the points of difference between the above mentioned forms of government and the possibility of arriving at a scientific conclusion in regard to each of them.

Here, as elsewhere, the best system of examination will be to begin at the beginning and observe things in their growth.

There are certain primary essential combinations of those who cannot exist independently one of another. Thus male and female must combine in order to procreate children, nor is there anything deliberate or arbitrary in their so doing; on the contrary, the desire of leaving an offspring like oneself is natural to man as to the whole animal and vegetable world. Again, natural rulers and subjects combine for safety, and when I say "natural" I mean that there are some persons qualified intellectually to form projects, and these are natural rulers or natural masters: while there are others qualified physically to carry them out, and these are subjects or natural slaves, so that the interests of master and slave are coincident.

Now Nature has differentiated females from slaves. None of Nature's products wears a poverty-stricken look like the Delphian knife, as it is called, that cutlers make [a many-purpose knife, not very good for any]; each has a single definite object on the principle that any instrument admits of the highest finish, only if it subserves a single purpose rather than several. Among non-Greek peoples on the other hand females and slaves stand on one and the same footing. The reason is that natural rulers do not exist among them, and the association they form consists of none but slaves male and female; hence the poet says: "Tis meet Greeks rule barbarians," implying the natural identity of barbarians or non-Greeks and slaves.

But to resume: the associations of male and female, master and slave, constitute the primary form of household, and Hesiod was right when he wrote: "Get thee first house and wife and ox to plough withal," for an ox is to the poor what a servant is to the rich.

Thus the association naturally formed for the supply of everyday wants is a household; its members, according to Charondas, are "those who eat of the same store," or, according to the Cretan Epimenides, "those who sit around the same hearth."

Again, the simplest association of several households for something more than ephemeral purposes is a village. It seems that the village in its most natural form is derived from the household, including all the children of certain parents, and the children's children or, as the phrase sometimes is, "all who are suckled upon the same milk."

This is the reason why States were originally governed by kings, as is still the case with uncivilized peoples; they were composed of units accustomed to this form of government. For as each household is under the kingly government of its eldest member, so were also the offshoot-households as comprising none but blood relations. It is this condition of things that Homer means when he describes the Cyclops as "lawgivers each of his own wives and children," in allusion to their want of corporate life. This patriarchal government was universal in primitive times; in fact, the reason why all nations represent the polity of the Gods as monarchical is that such originally was, if it is not still, their own polity, and men assimilate the lives no less than the bodily form of the Gods to their own.

Lastly, the association composed of several villages in its complete form is the State, in which the goal of full independence may be said to be first attained. For as the State was formed to make life possible, so it exists to make life good. Consequently if it be allowed that the simple associations, i.e. the household and the village, have a natural existence, so has the State in all cases; for in the State they attain complete development, and Nature implies complete development, as the Nature of anything, e.g. of a man, a house, or a horse, may be defined to be conditioned when the process of production is complete. Or the naturalness of the State may be proved in another way: the object proposed or the complete development of a thing is its highest Good; but independence which is first attained in the State is a complete development or the highest Good and is therefore natural.

Thus we see that the State is a natural institution, that Man is naturally a political animal and that one who is not a citizen of any State, if the cause of his isolation be natural and not accidental, is either a superhuman being or low in the scale of civilization, as he stands alone like a blot "on the backgammon board." The "clanless, lawless, heartless" man so bitterly described by Homer is a case in point; for he is naturally a citizen of no State and a lover of war. Also that Man is a political animal in a higher sense than a bee or any other gregarious creature is evident from the fact that Nature, as we are fond of asserting, creates nothing without a purpose and man is the only animal endowed with speech. Now mere sounds serve to indicate sensations of pain and pleasure and are therefore a sign to other animals as to Man; for their nature does not advance beyond the point of perceiving pain and pleasure and signifying these perceptions to one another. The object of speech on the other hand is to indicate advantage and disadvantage and therefore also justice and injustice. For it is a special characteristic which distinguishes Man from all other animals that he alone enjoys perception of good and evil, justice and injustice, and the like. But these are the principles of that association which constitutes a household or a State.

Again, in the order of Nature the State is prior to the household or the individual. For the whole must needs be prior to its parts. For instance, if you take away the body which is the whole, there will not remain any such thing as a foot or a hand, unless we use the same word in a different sense as when we speak of a stone hand as a hand. For a hand separated from the body will be a disabled hand; whereas it is the function or faculty of a thing which makes it what it is, and therefore when things lose their function or faculty it is not correct to call them the same things but rather homonymous, i.e. different things having the same name.

We see then that the State is a natural institution, and also that it is prior to the individual. For if the individual as a separate unit is not independent, he must be a part and must bear the same relation to the State as other parts to their wholes; and one who is incapable of associations with others, or is independent and has no need of such association, is no member of a State, in other words he is either a brute or a God. Now the impulse to political association is innate in all men. Nevertheless the author of the first combination, whoever he was, was a great benefactor of humankind. For Man, as in his condition of complete development, i.e. in the State, he is the noblest of all animals, so apart from law and justice he is the vilest of all. For justice is always most formidable when it is armed; and Nature has endowed Man with arms which are intended to subserve the purpose of prudence and virtue but are capable of being wholly turned to contrary ends. Hence if Man be devoid of virtue, no animal is so unscrupulous or savage, none so sensual, none so gluttonous. Just action, on the other hand, is bound up with the existence of a State; for the administration of justice is an ordinance of the political association and the administration of justice is nothing else than the decision of what is just.

The Nature Of The State

In any inquiry into the nature and character of particular polities we may say that the first point to be considered is the nature of the State. At present there is often a difference of opinion, as one party asserts that it is the State which has done a certain action, and another that it is not the State but the Oligarchy, or the Tyrant, by whom it was governed. Also it is necessary to settle this point, as a State is the sphere in which all the activity of a statesman or legislator is displayed, and the polity itself is nothing more than a certain order of the inhabitants of the State. But as the State belongs to the category of compound things, like anything else which is a whole but composed of many parts, it is clear that we must first investigate the conception of the citizen; for the State is composed of a number of citizens. We have to inquire then to whom the title "citizen" belongs, or, in other words, what is the nature of a citizen. For the conception of the citizen as of the State is often disputed, nor is the world agreed in recognizing the same person as a citizen. Thus it often happens that one who is a citizen in a Democracy is not a citizen in an Oligarchy.

Now putting out of sight persons who acquire the title of citizen in some exceptional way, e.g. honorary citizens, we may lay it down that it is not residence which constitutes a citizen, as the qualification of residence belongs equally to aliens settled in the country and to slaves. Nor again does citizenship consist simply in the participation in legal rights to the extent of being party to an action as defendant or plaintiff, for this is a qualification possessed equally by the members of different States who associate on the basis of commercial treaties. (It may be observed that in many places resident aliens are not admitted to the full enjoyment even of these legal rights, but are obliged to put themselves under the protection of a patron. It is only in a certain imperfect sense then that they are members of an association so constituted.) Such persons on the contrary are much in the same position as children who are too young to be entered upon the register of the deme or old men who are exempted from civil duties; for although these classes are to be called citizens in a certain sense, it is not in a sense quite absolute and unlimited, but with some such qualifying word as "immature" or "superannuated" or the like, it does not matter what. Our meaning at least is plain; we want a definition of the citizen in the absolute sense, one to whom no such exception can be taken as makes it necessary to correct our definition. For difficulties of a similar kind may be discussed and settled respecting persons who have been disfranchised or exiled. There is nothing whereby a citizen in the absolute sense is so well defined as by participation in judicial power and public office. But the offices of State are of two kinds. Some are determinate in point of time; thus there are certain offices which may never in any circumstances or may only after certain definite intervals be held a second time by the same person. Other officers again are perpetual, e.g. jurors and members of the Public Assembly. It will be objected perhaps that jurors and members of the Public Assembly are not officers of State at all and that their functions do not invest them with an official status; although it is ridiculous to deny the title of "officers" to the supreme authorities in the State. But this matter we may regard as unimportant; it is a mere question of name. The fact is that there is no word to express rightly the common function of a juror and a member of the Public Assembly. Let us call it for distinction's sake a perpetual office. Citizens, then, we may define as those who participate in judicial and deliberative office.

This is perhaps the definition of a citizen which is most appropriate to all who are so called. It is to be observed however that, where things included under a general head are specifically different and one is conceived of as first, another as second, and another as third, there is either no characteristic whatever in common to them all as such, or the common characteristic exists only in a slight degree. But polities, as we see, differ specifically from each other, some are later and others earlier; for the corrupt or perverted forms are necessarily later than the uncorrupted. What we mean by perverted forms will appear hereafter. It follows then that the citizen in each polity must also be different. Accordingly it is principally to the citizen in a Democracy that our definition applies; it is possibly true in the other polities, but not necessarily. For in some there is no democratical element, nor are there any regular public assemblies but only extraordinary ones, and the administration of justice is divided among various boards as, e.g. at Lacedaemon, where different civil cases are decided by different Ephors, cases of homicide by the Senate, and no doubt other cases by some other magistracy. It is the same at Carthage, where all suits are tried by certain magistrates. However, we need not give up our definition of citizen as it admits of correction. For in all polities except Democracy the right of voting in the Assembly and of acting as jurors belongs not to perpetual officers but to persons whose term of office is strictly defined; as it is either to such officers collectively or to some of them that judicial and deliberative functions, whether upon all or upon certain matters only, are assigned.

Thus we see clearly the nature of the citizen. One who enjoys the privilege of participation in deliberative or judicial office, he only is, according to our definition, a citizen of the State in question, and a State is in general terms such a number of persons thus qualified as is sufficient for an independent life.

Different Polities

We have next to consider whether it is right to assume a single polity or several and, if several, what is the nature of each, and how many there are, and what are the points of distinction between them. A polity may be defined as an order of the State in respect of its offices generally, and especially of the supreme office. For the governing class is everywhere supreme in the State, and the nature of the polity is determined by the governing class. I mean, e.g. that it is the commons who are supreme in a Democracy, and the Few on the other hand in an Oligarchy, and accordingly we call their polities distinct. The same remark may be extended to all the rest; if the governing class is different, so is the polity.

We must begin by laying down (1) the object for which a State is framed and (2) the various kinds of rule which may be exercised over Man in his social existence.

It has been stated at the very outset of our treatise . . . that Man is naturally a political animal, and consequently even where there is no need of mutual service, men are nonetheless anxious to live together. Still, it cannot be denied that the common advantage of all is also a motive of union, more or less operative according to the degree in which each individual is capable of the higher life. Although to the citizens, both collectively and individually, this higher life is emphatically the end proposed, yet life itself is also an object for which they unite and maintain the corporate political association; for it is probable that some degree of the higher life is necessarily implied in merely living, unless there is a great preponderance of hardship in the life. Certain it is that the majority of men endure much suffering without ceasing to cling to life, a proof that a certain happiness or natural sweetness resides in it.

It is because the object of political rule is the benefit of the subjects that in any State framed on the principle of equality and similarity among the citizens a claim is put forward for an alteration of rule. It was originally claimed, as is natural enough, that all should serve the State in turn, and that, as each citizen during his period of rule or office had already paid regard to the interest of another, so that other should in turn pay regard to his. But nowadays the profits derivable from the public service and an official status create a desire for perpetuity of office; it is as though the officers of State, being invalids, were to enjoy good health during all their term of power, in which case it is probable that they would be equally eager for office.

It is evident then that all such polities as regard the good of the community are really normal according to the principle of abstract justice, while such as regard the private good of the rulers are all corruptions or perversions of the normal polities; for the relations of rulers to the subjects in them are like the relations of a master to his slaves, whereas the State is properly a society of free persons.

Having now settled these points, we have next to consider the number of different polities and their nature. We will begin with the normal polities; for when they are determined the perverted forms will be evident at once.

As in any State the polity and the governing class are virtually the same, i.e. the polity is determined by the governing class, as the governing class is the supreme authority in a State, and as supreme power must be vested either in an individual or in a Few, or in the Many, it follows that when the rule of the individual, or the Few, or the Many, is exercised for the benefit of the community at large, the polities are normal, whereas the polities which subserve the private interest either of the individual or the Few or the masses are perversions; for either the members of the State do not deserve the name of citizens, or they ought to have a share in its advantages. The form of Monarchy in which regard is paid to the interest of the community is commonly known as Kingship, and the government of the Few, although of a number exceeding one, for the good of all, as Aristocracy, whether because the rule is in the hands of the best citizens or because they exercise it for the best interests of the State and all its members; while when it is the masses who direct public affairs for the interest of the community, the government is called by the name which is common to all the polities, viz. a Polity. The result in this case is such as might have been expected. For although it is possible to find an individual or a few persons of eminent virtue, it can hardly be the case that a large number are perfectly accomplished in every form of virtue; at the best they will only be accomplished only in military virtue, as it is the only one of which the masses are capable. The consequence is that in this polity, viz. the Polity proper, the military class is supreme, and all who bear arms enjoy full political privileges.

As perverted forms of the polities just mentioned we have Tyranny by the side of Kingship, Oligarchy of Aristocracy, and Democracy of Polity. For Tyranny is monarchical rule for the good of the Monarch; Oligarchy the rule of a Few for the good of the wealthy; and Democracy the rule of the Many for the good of the poor; none of them subserve the interest of the community at large . . .

The really distinctive characteristics of Democracy and Oligarchy are poverty and wealth; and it is a necessary law that wherever wealth constitutes the title to rule, whether the rulers are a minority or a majority, the polity is an Oligarchy, whereas if the poor are rulers, it is a Democracy. But as a matter of fact, it happens, as we said, that in the one case the rulers are few, and in the other many; for there are only few people who are wealthy, whereas liberty is enjoyed by all alike, and wealth and liberty are the grounds upon which the two parties respectively base their claim to be masters of the polity.

In endeavouring to estimate the claims of the two parties, we must first ascertain what are the definitions they give of Oligarchy and Democracy, and what is the principle of justice characteristic of the one or the other. For Oligarchs and Democrats agree in this, that they both adhere to a certain principle of justice; but they do not advance beyond a certain point or put forward a full statement of justice in the proper sense of the word. Thus the one party, i.e. the Democrats, hold that justice is equality; and so it is, but not for all the world, but only for equals. The others, i.e. the Oligarchs, hold that inequality is just, as indeed it is, but not for all the world, but only for unequals. Both put out of sight one side of the relation, viz. the persons who are to enjoy the equality or inequality, and consequently form a wrong judgment. The reason is that they are judging of matters which affect themselves, and we are all sorry judges when our personal interests are at stake. And thus whereas justice is a relative term and . . . implies that the ratio of distribution is constant in respect of the things distributed and the persons who receive them, the two parties, while they are of one mind about the equality of the thing, differ as to what constitutes equality in the recipients, principally for the reason just alleged, viz. that they are bad judges where their own interests are concerned, but secondly also because the fact that each maintains a certain principle of justice up to a certain point is one which itself leads them to suppose that they are maintaining a principle of justice in the absolute sense. For the Oligarchs, if they are superior in a particular point, viz. in money, assume themselves to be superior altogether; while the Democrats, if they are equal in a particular point, viz. in personal liberty, assume themselves to be equal altogether. But they omit the point of capital importance. If a multitude of possessions was the sole object of their association or union, then their share in the State is proportionate to their share in the property, and in this case there would seem to be no resisting the argument of the Oligarchical party that, where there is, e.g. a capital of one hundred *minae* the contributor of a single *mina* ought not, in justice, to enjoy the same share either of the principal or of the profits accruing as a person who has given the remaining ninety-nine. But the truth is that the object of their association is to live well, not merely to live; otherwise slaves and the lower animals might form a State, whereas this is in fact impossible, as they are incapable of happiness or of a life regulated by a definite moral purpose, i.e. of the conditions necessary to a State. Nor is the object military alliance and security against injury from any quarter. Nor again is the end proposed barter and intercommunion; for, if it were, the Tyrrhenians and Carthaginians and such nations as are connected by commercial treaties might be regarded as citizens of a single State. Among them there certainly exist contracts in regard to Customs, covenants against mutual injury, and formal articles of alliance. But there are no magistracies common to all the contracting parties instituted to secure these objects, but different magistracies exist in each of the States; nor do the members of the one feel concerned about the right character of members of the other or about the means of preserving all who come under the treaties from being unjust and harbouring any kind of wickedness or indeed about any point whatever, except the prevention of mutually injurious actions. Virtue and vice on the other hand are matters of earnest consideration to all whose hearts are set upon good and orderly government. And from this fact it is evident that a State which is not merely nominally but in the true sense of the word a State should devote its attention to virtue. To neglect virtue is to convert the political association into an alliance differing in nothing except in the local contiguity of its members from the alliances formed between distant States, to convert the law into a mere covenant or, as the sophist Lycophron said, a mere surety for the mutual respect of rights, without any qualification for producing goodness or justice in the citizens. But it is clear that this is the true view of the State, i.e. that it promotes the virtue of its citizens. For if we were to combine different localities in one so that, e.g. the walls of Megara and Corinth were contiguous, yet the result would not be a single State. Nor again does the practice of intermarriage necessarily imply a single State, although intermarriage is one of the forms of association which are especially characteristic of States. So too if we suppose the case of certain persons living separately, although not so far apart as to prevent association, but under laws prohibitive of mutual injury in the exchange of goods, if we suppose, e.g. A to be a carpenter, B a husbandman, C a cobbler, D something else, and the total to amount to 10,000, but their association to be absolutely confined to such things as barter and military alliance, here again there would certainly not be a State. What then is the reason? It is assuredly not the absence of local contiguity in the association. For suppose the members were actually to form a union upon such terms of association as we have described, suppose at the same time that each individual were to use his own household as a separate State, and their intercourse were limited as under the condition of a defensive alliance to rendering mutual assistance against aggression, still the conception of a State in the strict view would not even then be realized, if their manner of social dealings after the union were to be precisely the same as when they lived apart.

It is clear then that the State is not merely a local association or an association existing to prevent mutual injury and to promote commercial exchange. So far is this from being the case that, although these are indispensable conditions, if a State is to exist, yet all these conditions do not necessarily imply a State. A State on the contrary is first realized when there is an association of households and families in living well, with a view to a complete and independent existence . . . It is for this reason that there were established in different States matrimonial connections, clanships, common sacrifices and such amusements as promote a common life. But all this is the work of friendship, for the choice of a common life implies no more than friendship. And thus while the end of a State is living well, these are only means to the end. A State, on the contrary, is the association of families and villages in a complete and independent existence or in other words, according to our definition, in a life of felicity and nobleness. We must assume then that the object of the political association is not merely a common life but noble action. And from this it follows that they who contribute most to the association, as so conceived, possess a larger interest in the State than they who are equal or superior in personal liberty, or birth, but inferior in political virtue, or than they who have the superiority in wealth but the inferiority in virtue.

From NICOMACHEAN ETHICS, c. 330 BC

Aristotle

If Aristotelian science is fallen stock, his ethics have held their value. His appeal to individual responsibility, his belief that human good needs to be achieved within community, resonates as well in the modern world as it did in Ancient Athens.

. . . To say however that the Supreme Good is happiness will probably appear a truism; we still require a more explicit account of what constitutes happiness. Perhaps then we may arrive at this by ascertaining what is man's function. For the goodness or efficiency of a flute-player or sculptor or craftsman of any sort, and in general of anybody who has some function or business to perform, is thought to reside in that function; and similarly it may be held that the good of man resides in the function of man, if he has a function.

Are we then to suppose that, while the carpenter and the shoemaker have definite functions or businesses belonging to them, man as such has none, and is not designed by nature to fulfil any function? Must we not rather assume that, just as the eye, the hand, the foot and each of the various members of the body manifestly has a certain function of its own, so a human being also has a certain function over and above all the functions of his particular members. What then precisely can this function be? The mere act of living appears to be shared even by plants, whereas we are looking for the function peculiar to man; we must therefore set aside the vital activity of nutrition and growth. Next in the scale will come some form of sentient life; but this too appears to be shared by horses, oxen, and animals generally. There remains therefore what may be called the practical life of the rational part of man. (This part has two divisions, one rational as obedient to principle, the other as possessing principle and exercising intelligence.) Rational life again has two meanings; let us assume that we are here concerned with the active exercise of the rational faculty, since this seems to be the more proper sense of the term. If then the function of man is the active exercise of the soul's faculties in conformity with rational principle, or at all events not in dissociation from rational principle, and if we acknowledge the function of an individual and of a good individual of the same class (for instance, a harper and a good harper, and so generally with all classes) to be generically the same, the qualification of the latter's superiority in excellence being added to the function in his case (I mean that if the function of a harper is to play the harp, that of a good harper is to play the harp well): if this is so, and if we declare that the function of man is a certain form of life, and define that form of life as the exercise of the soul's faculties and activities in association with rational principle, and say that the function of a good man is to perform these activities well and rightly, and if a function is well performed when it is performed in accordance with its own proper excellence – if then all this be so, the Good of man proves to be the active exercise of his soul's faculties in conformity with excellence or virtue, or if there be several human excellencies or virtues, in conformity with the best and most perfect among them.

Moreover, to be happy takes a complete lifetime. For one swallow does not make summer, nor does one fine day; and similarly one day or a brief period of happiness does not make a man supremely blessed and happy . . .

Moreover, the faculties given us by nature are bestowed on us first in a potential form; we develop their exercise afterwards. This is clearly so with our senses: we did not acquire the faculty of sight or hearing by repeatedly seeing or repeatedly listening, but the other way about – because we had the senses we began to use them, we did not get them by using them. The virtues on the other hand we acquire by first having actually practised them, just as we do the arts. We learn an art or craft by doing the things that we shall have to do when we have learnt it: for instance, men become builders by building houses, harpers by playing on the harp. Similarly we become just by doing just acts, temperate by doing temperate acts, brave by doing brave acts. This truth is attested by the experience of states: lawgivers make the citizens good by training them in habits of right action – this is the aim of all legislation, and if it fails to do this it is a failure; this is what distinguishes a good form of constitution from a bad one. Again, the actions from or through which any virtue is produced are the same as those through which it also is destroyed – just as is the case with skill in the arts, for both the good harpers and the bad ones are produced by harping, and similarly with builders and all the other craftsmen: as you will become a good builder from building well, so you will become a bad one from building badly. Were this not so, there would be no need for teachers of the arts, but everybody would be born a good or bad craftsman as the case might be. The same then is true of the virtues. It is by taking part in transactions with our fellow-men that some of us become just and others unjust; by acting in dangerous situations and forming a habit of fear or of confidence we become courageous or cowardly. And the same holds good of our dispositions with regard to the appetites, and anger; some men become temperate and gentle, others profligate and irascible, by actually comporting themselves in one way or the other in relation to those passions. In a word, our moral dispositions are formed as a result of the corresponding activities. Hence it is incumbent on us to control the character of our activities, since on the quality of these depends the quality of our dispositions. It is therefore not of small moment whether we are trained from childhood in one set of habits or another; on the contrary it is of very great, or rather of supreme, importance . . .

But if happiness consists in activity in accordance with virtue, it is reasonable that it should be activity in accordance with the highest virtue; and this will be the virtue of the best part of us. Whether then this be the intellect, or whatever else it be that is thought to rule and lead us by nature, and to have cognizance of what is noble and divine, either as being itself also actually divine, or as being relatively the divinest part of us, it is the activity of this part of us in accordance with the virtue proper to it that will constitute perfect happiness; and it has been stated already that this activity is the activity of contemplation.

And that happiness consists in contemplation may be accepted as agreeing both with the results already reached and with the truth. For contemplation is at once the highest form of activity, since the intellect is the highest thing in us, and the objects with which the intellect deals are the highest things that can be known; and also it is the most continuous, for we can reflect more continuously than we can carry on any form of action. And again, we suppose that happiness must contain an element of pleasure; now activity in accordance with wisdom is admittedly the most pleasant of the activities in accordance with virtue; at all events it is held that philosophy or the pursuit of wisdom contains pleasures of marvellous purity and permanence, and it is reasonable to suppose that the enjoyment of knowledge is a still pleasanter occupation than the pursuit of it. Also the activity of contemplation will be found to possess in the highest degree the quality that is termed self-sufficiency; for while it is true that the wise man equally with the just man and the rest requires the necessaries of life, yet, these being adequately supplied, whereas the just man needs other persons towards whom or with whose aid he may act justly, and so likewise do the temperate man and the brave man and the others, the wise man on the contrary can also contemplate by himself, and the more so the wiser he is; no doubt he will study better with the aid of fellow-workers, but still he is the most self-sufficient of men. Also the activity of contemplation may be held to be the only activity that is loved for its own sake: it produces no results beyond the actual act of contemplation, whereas from practical pursuits we look to secure some advantage greater or smaller, beyond the action itself. Also happiness is thought to involve leisure, for we do business in order that we may have leisure, and carry on war in order that we may have peace . . .

THE WISDOM OF SOLOMON, c. 100 BC

The authorship of this book of the biblical *Apocrypha* is unknown; its ascription to Solomon is pure licence. Most modern critics consider that it was written by a Greek-speaking Jew in Alexandria (the Egypt port had a large Jewish quarter). Its words of intrinsic wisdom aside, the book has importance as an historical artefact: it is one of the earliest examples of fusion between two of the main currents which made Western culture: Greek philosophy and Hebrew thought. The following translations are from the Revised Version of the Bible.

Wisdom of Solomon (I:12–II: 15; II: 21–III:15)

Court not death in the error of your life;
Neither draw upon yourselves destruction by the works of your hands:
Because God made not death;
Neither delighteth he when the living perish:
For he created all things that they might have being:
And the generative powers of the world are healthsome,
And there is no poison of destruction in them:
Nor hath Hades royal dominion upon earth,
For righteousness is immortal:
But ungodly men by their hands and their words called death unto them:
Deeming him a friend they consumed away,
And they made a covenant with him,
Because they are worthy to be of his portion.

For they said within themselves, reasoning not aright,
Short and sorrowful is our life;
And there is no healing when a man cometh to his end,
And none was ever known that gave release from Hades.

Because by mere chance were we born,
And hereafter we shall be as though we had never been:
Because the breath in our nostrils is smoke,
And while our heart beateth reason is a spark,
Which being extinguished, the body shall be turned into ashes,
And the spirit shall be dispersed as thin air;
And our name shall be forgotten in time,
And no man shall remember our works;
And our life shall pass away as the traces of a cloud,
And shall be scattered as is a mist,
When it is chased by the beams of the sun,
And overcome by the heat thereof.
For our allotted time is the passing of a shadow,
And our end retreateth not;
Because it is fast sealed, and none turneth it back.
Come therefore and let us enjoy the good things that now are;
And let us use the creation with all our soul as youth's possession.
Let us fill ourselves with costly wine and perfumes;
And let no flower of spring pass us by:
Let us crown ourselves with rosebuds, before they be withered:
Let none of us go without his share in our proud revelry:
Everywhere let us leave tokens of our mirth:
Because this is our portion, and our lot is this.
Let us oppress the righteous poor;
Let us not spare the widow,
Nor reverence the hairs of the old man gray for length of years.
But let our strength be to us a law of righteousness;
For that which is weak is found to be of no service.
But let us lie in wait for the righteous man,
Because he is of disservice to us,
And is contrary to our works,
And upbraideth us with sins against the law,
And layeth to our charge sins against our discipline.
He professeth to have knowledge of God,
And nameth himself servant of the Lord.
He became to us a reproof of our thoughts.
He is grievous unto us even to behold,
Because his life is unlike other men's,
And his paths are of strange fashion . . .

Thus reasoned they, and they were led astray;
For their wickedness blinded them,
And they knew not the mysteries of God,
Neither hoped they for wages of holiness,

Nor did they judge that there is a prize for blameless souls.
Because God created man for incorruption,
And made him an image of his own proper being;
But by the envy of the devil death entered into the world,
And they that are of his portion make trial thereof.
But the souls of the righteous are in the hand of God,
And no torment shall touch them.
In the eyes of the foolish they seemed to have died;
And their departure was accounted to be their hurt,
And their journeying away from us to be their ruin:
But they are in peace.
For even if in the sight of men they be punished,
Their hope is full of immortality;
And having borne a little chastening, they shall receive great good;
Because God made trial of them, and found them worthy of himself.

Wisdom of Solomon (V:6–14)

Verily we went astray from the way of truth,
And the light of righteousness shined not for us,
And the sun rose not for us.
We took our fill of the paths of lawlessness and destruction,
And we journeyed through trackless deserts,
But the way of the Lord we knew not.
What did our arrogancy profit us?
And what good have riches and vaunting brought us?
Those things all passed away as a shadow,
And as a message that runneth by:
As a ship passing through the billowy water,
Whereof, when it is gone by, there is no trace to be found,
Neither pathway of its keel in the billows:
Or as when a bird flieth through the air,
No token of her passage is found,
But the light wind, lashed with the stroke of her pinions,
And rent asunder with the violent rush of the moving wings, is
    passed through,
And afterwards no sign of her coming is found therein:
Or as when an arrow is shot at a mark,
The air disparted closeth up again immediately,
So that men know not where it passed through:
So we also, as soon as we were born, ceased to be;
And of virtue we had no sign to shew,
But in our wickedness we were utterly consumed.
Because the hope of the ungodly man is as chaff carried by the wind,

And as foam vanishing before a tempest;
And is scattered as smoke is scattered by the wind,
And passeth by as the remembrance of a guest that tarrieth but a day.

Wisdom of Solomon (XI, 21–6)

For to be greatly strong is thine at all times;
And the might of thine arm who shall withstand?
Because the whole world before thee is as a grain in a balance,
And as a drop of dew that at morning cometh down upon the earth.
But thou hast mercy on all men, because thou hast power to do all things,
And thou overlookest the sins of men to the end they may repent.
For thou lovest all things that are,
And abhorrest none of the things which thou didst make;
For never wouldest thou have formed anything if thou didst hate it.
And how would anything have endured, except thou hadst willed it?
Or that which was not called by thee, how would it have been preserved?
But thou sparest all things, because they are thine,
O Sovereign Lord, thou lover of men's lives.

From *DE RERUM NATURA,* c. 65 BC

Lucretius

Titus Lucretius Carus (c. 99–55 BC) was a Roman poet and philosopher. Under the ideological sway of Democritus and Epicurus, Lucretius propounded a thoroughgoing materialism in which events were not the doings of whimsical gods but natural, explicable processes. There was no room for religion in Lucretius' great hexameter poem *De Rerum Natura* ("On the Nature of Things"), but there was unbridled belief in mankind's ability to free himself from primitive fear and superstition. The translation below is in iambic pentameter.

Huge the first race of men, their limbs well strung,
Hardy as hardy earth from which they sprung;
On strong and massy bones their structure rose,
Firm as the firmest oak that towering grows:
Nor heat nor cold they felt, nor weakness knew,
Nor from voluptuous feasts diseases drew;
Through long revolving years on nature thrived,
And, wildly bold, in savage freedom lived.
No sturdy husbandmen the land prepare,
Plant the young stocks, or guide the shining share:
For future crops the seed no sower throws,
Nor dresser clips the wild luxuriant boughs.
What earth spontaneous gave, and sun and showers,
Careless they took, and propt their nervid powers;
Their giant energies with acorns fed,
Wild summer apples, indurate and red:
Such in our wintry orchards sparing hang;
But larger theirs, and more abundant, sprang.
Earth in her primal strength these things bestowed,
With rich fecundity her bosom glowed;

O'er her broad surface various plenty reigned;
Her voluntary gifts man's race sustained.
Thus by her fruits the human race was nursed;
And springs and rivers slaked their parching thirst;
Called them, as now the fall from pouring heights
The thirst afflicted savage tribes invites.
For nightly roofs to hollow caves they hied,
Or with their gods in sylvan fanes reside;
Whence a sweet spring in silvery drops distills,
And rolls o'er polished stones, its bubbling rills;
O'er polished stones, and mossy greens they flow,
Meandering through the fertile vales below.

As yet, no fire their simple food prepared;
Nor spoils of beasts their hardened bodies shared:
Naked among the rocks and woods they ran,
And hollow mountains formed the abodes of man.
Shelter from winds and rains in groves they sought,
And nature's wants supplied as nature taught.

No common good they felt, no laws ordained,
Nor public justice private wrong restrained;
What power or fortune offered, no one spared;
Each his own welfare sought, nor further cared.

Then Venus' fire was all the lover's law,
And groves and woods the consummation saw;
Or mutual flames inspired the burning pair;
Or manhood's force compelled the unwilling fair;
Or softening presents taught her heart to yield;
Berries or acorns, fresh from bower or field.

Bold in their native vigour, men pursued
With flying feet the fierce and savage brood;
With missile weapons urged the hardy chase;
And stones and clubs subdued the brutal race.
Some they hunt down, some their swift staves o'ertake,
Others they fled, and sought the sheltering brake,
When night o'ertook them with her sable shades,
Like bristly boars they pressed the grassy glades,
In leaves enwrapt; nor mourned the absent light,
Nor wandered through the darkness of the night;
But, in soft sleep dissolved, contented lay
Till rosy dawn proclaimed expected day:
For observation from their childhood taught
That day the night, and night the morning, brought.
Hence, they ne'er dreaded an eternal night,
But woke to hail the sure return of light:

Yet feared, lest prowling beasts that shun the day,
Should fall destructive on their human prey:
Roused from their sleep, and filled with timely dread
Of boars and lions, from their haunts they fled;
Trembling, resigned the leafy couch to those
Whom nature framed for their relentless foes.
  Yet, fewer, then, the call of death obeyed,
Left the sweet light of day for endless shade,
Than now; though, hapless, some were seized, o'erpowered,
Then by their fierce and savage foes devoured:
These, as the brutes their reeking bowels rend,
See to a living grave their flesh descend;
Wake, with their piercing screams, the affrighted skies
And fill the woods and mountains with their cries:
And those who fly, the cloud of fate surrounds;
Pressing with trembling hands their throbbing wounds,
Death they implore, till gnawing worms consume
Their putrid flesh, and consummate their doom:
For then no healing science blessed mankind
No skilful hand the gushing wound could bind,
But then, fell war no thousands swept away
Hurled to destruction in a single day:
In vain the raging ocean rolls and roars;
No ships were dashed upon the rocky shores:
Though calm again the sinking billows grew,
And all their awful violence withdrew,
Yet no smooth surface, no deceitful smile,
Could the fond, thoughtless mariner beguile:
No dangerous art, then, traced the briny path,
No floating castles braved the ocean's wrath.
Grim Want o'er many urged his fatal power;
But now to ruin Plenty hurries more.
From noxious herbs some, thoughtless, drew their death;
Now studied poisons urge the fleeting breath.
  At length they bade the bough-built hut aspire,
And learned the luxury of skins and fire:
Then One to One in silken bondage held,
Raised man above the savage of the field;
Connubial love a purer bliss bestowed,
And with a chaste delight the bosom glowed;
While, pressing to the heart his smiling boy,
The ennobled father felt a father's joy.
Then, by indulgence softened, men no more
Braved the sharp cold, rude winds uninjured bore;

Hymen their fierceness tamed, and fondling arts
Of darling children humanized their hearts.
Then neighbourhoods grew and social compacts rose;
To reason waked, no more they lived as foes;
To women, children, kind protection yield;
The softer, weaker, from the stronger shield.
Though not yet all by order's voice were swayed,
The greater part the laws of faith obeyed:
Man the approach of peace and union hailed,
And universal war no more prevailed:
Or gradual ravage, with its wide embrace,
Had, long ere this, suppressed the human race.
Dumb motion now no longer things proclaimed;
By nature taught, the tongue each object named;
As infants, ere they speak, by signs express
Their simple thoughts, and all their wants confess.
. . . And is it wonderful that men, supplied
With vocal organs, and in whom reside
The powers of intellect, should names devise
For objects constantly before their eyes?
Would they of things the various nature know,
Nor appellations on those things bestow;
Since e'en the mute creation signals find,
To speak the thoughts and feelings of their mind;
Their love, their joy, their sorrow and their ire,
And all the passions which their breasts inspire?
    When grim Molossian mastiffs are enraged,
And by no soothing art their wrath assuaged,
When fierce they snarl, they grin, their fangs display,
From their deep throats gruff murmurs break their way,
Unlike the sounds that rend our startled ears
When their loud clamorous voice the welkin tears.
But view them when, with soft caressing tongue,
Gently they lick their sprawling, playful young;
Now feign to bite, now roll them o'er and o'er,
Now, fondly gaping, threaten to devour;
But cautiously their harmless teeth employ,
And in soft whinings tell their tender joy:
Not as when left at home, they howl and cry,
Or when with trembling fear they, crouching, eye
The uplifted whip, and whimper as they lie . . .
    Since, then, these creatures' dull perceptions cause
Their different notes, how clear that nature's laws
Stronger must act on intellectual man!

That sounds have varied since the world began;
And human speech was part of nature's plan.
   Let thirst of knowledge still thy mind inspire:
Now sings the Muse the origin of fire.
Thunder this element to earth conveyed,
When loud it rattled, and its lightnings played:
On their red wings the ardent vapours came,
And wrapped whole groves and forests in their flame.
For now we see the same effect arise
When dart the flashing terrors of the skies:
Or, pressed by winds the labouring branches meet,
Strike, chafe and kindle to devouring heat;
From tree to tree it flies, from grove to grove
Climb the broad flames, and fire the realms above.
From friction, hence, or lightning's rage, might spring
The igniting cause, and fierce combustion bring.
   From the sun's heat men first acquired the art
Their viands to prepare; his rays that dart,
Ripening the yellow corn; that flowers unfold,
Play on the fruits and change their green to gold,
The use of fire revealed: the wiser few
The lesson caught, and by example drew
Their fellow men; new habits were assumed
And savoury meats the cloudy air perfumed.
   Then kings arose, fair cities then appeared,
Armies were formed, and citadels were reared;
Lands were divided, separate beeves assigned,
As merit claimed, of body and of mind.
But chief the powers of body held the sway,
And strength and beauty bore the palm away.
Then gold was found, and men for riches burn,
And strength and beauty yielded in their turn;
The shining ore prevailed o'er old and young,
And gold was stronger than the brave and strong.
But once did reason rectify the mind
And chase the vain delusions of mankind;
The bliss of little with content and health,
This were their noblest boon, their truest wealth.
And, say, this little who should fear to want?
To whom this little would not fortune grant?
But for renown and power we every day
See mortals fling the sweets of life away:
These to their wealth a lasting base will give,
Then in soft ease and pleasure they will live.

But vain their labours, and absurd as vain,
Since those who anxiously aspire to gain
Nay, who secure, high honours and estate
(The greatest mid the wealthy and the great),
But journey haplessly; for Envy arms
Her hand with thunder, and their soul alarms;
Aims at their glory her destroying blow,
Their fame extinguishes and lays them low.
How happier they who peacefully obey,
Than those who struggle for imperial sway!
Who prostitute their anxious, wasted life
In sordid efforts and ambitious strife;
Climb the steep, thorny path, where perils wait,
And Envy urges with her deadly hate;
Arms with her bolts the candidates for power
And most delights to see her flames devour
The highest. These let pomp and pride excite
And drive them struggling up the dangerous height;
Let Flattery's voice their eager ear beguile,
And stimulate their never ceasing toil.
This folly still behold, this ancient rage,
It maddens ours and will the latest age.
    Those monarchs slain, the glory of their throne
And sparkling diadem no longer shone.
The sceptre, emblem of their regal trust,
Stained with their blood and trodden in the dust,
Mourns its lost honours; while the rabble raise
Loud clamours, where they lately shouted praise;
Base in their power insult the mighty dead,
And triumph o'er whom living they would dread.
    Now to the mob the varying sway returned,
And vulgar breasts with wild ambition burned:
Fired by the thirst for power, for power they strain:
Empire's the dazzling prize, and all would reign.
Wearied with jarring interests, fierce disputes,
Where each man reasons, and where each refutes;
Tired of a state where all men all assailed,
Where equity nor polity prevailed;
Where the mad Many hold the Wise in awe
And violence usurps the throne of law;
All the fell power of anarchy deplore
And government and order would restore;
At length the sager few a code ordain;
And, future feuds and contests to restrain,

Rulers elect and check Contention's reign.
. . . Wretched the man who lives in lawless strife;
Who bursts the sacred bonds of social life:
Though Gods and men his cunning arts deceive,
In his own bosom fear and conscience live.
Hence, oft in slumber men their guilt betray;
Oft, when their fevered minds deliriums sway,
The plots discover long concealed by time
And tell in broken speech the secret crime.

　　To Memmius now, inspiring Muse, disclose
Whence of the Gods our first conceptions rose:
Whence altars towns adorned; whence solemn rites
And sacred festivals, divine delights,
And smoking hecatombs whose fumes arise
And roll in curling volumes to the skies:
Whence the sad terror that all earth pervades,
Temples erects and plants the sacred shades.
Nor sure too high my ardent zeal aspires;
Obvious the course, nor keen research requires.
At first creation, forms divinely bright,
Radiant in beauty, burst upon the sight:
Men, e'en awake, the shadows wondering saw
Glowed as they gazed and felt a secret awe:
But to their dreams still grander visions came;
Visions of brighter, more gigantic, frame;
Whose active limbs astonishment excite,
Clothed in the glories of supernal night.
On these bright forms their fancy sense bestowed,
Language superb and worthy of a God.
Eternal, too, the shining phantoms seem,
Since on the sight descends a constant stream
Of images: and then what power can harm
Such mighty beings? What their fears alarm?
And those whom mortal terrors ne'er annoy
Peaceful must live, and perfect bliss enjoy.
Then, too, their shadowy wonders they display
With wondrous ease their limbs their will obey,
Nor ever dull fatigue or lassitude betray.

　　In order, too, the rolling heavens appear,
And varied seasons of the circling year:
But still the source of motion was concealed;
The Primum Mobile was unrevealed.
Hence, men to Gods creation's frame assigned:
Themselves and all things to their will resigned.

Where glide the shining orbs for ever bright,
For ever rolling in refulgent light,
There they established the celestial bowers,
There fixed the mansions of the heavenly powers;
There, where the sun and moon their fires display,
The beam nocturnal and the flame of day;
The stars serene that shed their mingled rays,
The flying lightnings and the meteor's blaze;
The hail, the rain, the dews that float on high,
The thunder's awful bolts that threatening fly,
And all the dread commotions of the sky.
　Oh, hapless mortals! blindly pious race!
Why with such troublous rage the Gods disgrace?
To your own age what idle fears ye taught!
On us what needless woes those fears have brought!
And still what griefs, what evils, shall supply
What floods of tears, to our posterity!
　Strange piety the crouching head to veil!
Fondly to sticks and stones to make appeal!
To every fane with spreading arms to fly,
Fall on the earth, and in dependence lie
Before the sacred shrines! with blood to stain
The sprinkled altars, and with praises vain
And vows on vows the heedless Gods obtest!
Calmly all things to view, be this confest
True piety. For, when the soul surveys
The grandeur heaven's illumined dome displays;
The blue expanse, with sparkling stars o'er spread,
And sun and moon that constant courses lead,
Then doubts that other evils had suppressed
Cloud the sad mind, and agitate the breast;
Doubts whether Gods the potent sinews claim
Yon orbs to wield, and heaven's stupendous frame.
To ignorance these evils mortals owe;
From doubts what terrors spring! what ceaseless woe!
From ignorance we doubt Creation's birth;
The wandering stars and stationary earth;
How long the heavens great Nature will defend;
Whether their motion and their being end;
Or if, unfading, by the Gods they're framed
By everlasting energies inflamed;
In endless orbits formed to roll sublime
And triumph o'er the ravages of Time.
　Who calmly contemplates the blest abodes?

What heart but faints with terror of the Gods?
Whose limbs so nervid not to quake, when roll
The pealing thunders, and from pole to pole
Thick lightnings flash? What nations, free from fear,
Eye the blue fires, the loud explosions hear?
Proud tyrants tremble, fears their members thrill,
Forms of avenging gods their fancy fill;
Lest their foul crimes have armed the powers on high
And the dread day of retribution's nigh.
And o'er the seas when winds and tempests roar
And heave the rolling mountains to the shore,
The gallant Admiral with legions armed,
And mighty elephants, with soul alarmed,
Falls he not prostrate to the powers above
To soothe their anger and their pity move?
Praying the blest Immortals to be kind
And make his peace with the reluctant wind;
Grant to his squadron soft, propitious gales,
And gently swell the bosom of his sails?
In vain! No prayers his tossing legions save;
Cold death awaits them and the Stygian wave.
Such the contempt some hidden power awards
To human greatness! Such its high regards
For rods and axes (glories of a day)
And all the ensigns of imperial sway!
With scornful sport it treats the gaudy things,
And on the proudly great its reckless vengeance flings!
And then, when tremors seize this earthly ball,
And death and ruin threat to swallow all,
Should we, whilst all are trembling, feel surprise
If men their weakness see, themselves despise,
Give to the Gods omnipotence, and place
With them the government of being and of space?
  Now learn that Earth disclosed her various ores
Lead, iron, silver, brass and golden stores
When to her hills fierce fires devouring came
And blazing forests fed the raging flame;
Whether from heaven the wasting fury spring,
Borne on the lightning's coruscating wing,
Or from fierce war the devastations flow
And woods were fired to scare the distant foe;
Or men, resolved to enlarge the fruitful soil,
Of their green pride the encumbered wilds despoil;
Or dauntlessly their savage tenants prest,

And with their shaggy hides themselves invest;
(For ere with nets and dogs they snared their prey,
With fire they drove them to the light of day . . .)
Whether from lurid heaven's ethereal flame
Or from mankind the wide destruction came;
Sprang the fierce fires from art or nature's power
That to their roots the crackling trees devour,
Spread unrestrained through wide extended woods,
Melt the burnt earth and boil the hissing floods;
Then from the earth's smoking veins red metals flow
Through delving channels, gliding as they glow:
When they to hardness cool, and men behold
The argent silver and the ruddy gold,
View the rich beauty of the shining ores
Thrown to the day from nature's latent stores;
See them the figures of their beds assume;
By fire if molten, aptly they presume
That various forms the fluid ores would take
And pointed instruments, or edged, might make;
To hew the woods, rough timbers smooth or cleave,
And the rude block a shapely figure give . . .
. . . And now my Memmius will perceive the source
Whence the Rude Ages learned hard iron's force.
The earliest weapons hostile mortals tried,
Hands, teeth and nails and broken boughs supplied:
With chasing fire the foe they next assailed;
Then the tough brass, then iron's strength prevailed.
But brass, less stubborn and more plenteous found,
Claimed the first use: with brazen shares the ground
At first was ploughed, with brazen arms the field
Of battle blazed, brass taught the foe to yield;
Brass bade the suffering weak the strong obey,
Seized on their lands and bore their herds away.
Then hardier iron gradual use obtained
And brass, contemned, no more triumphant reigned:
The fertile glebe endured the iron share,
And iron gleamed in instruments of war.
   To mount the war horse heroes first aspired,
With the left hand to guide, the art acquired;
Full on the foe, with rushing force they sprung
And with the dexter hand the javelin they flung.
Ere with the flying car and mettled pair
They swept the field and crushed the ranks of war.
First with a Pair, then Double Pair, they strove;

Fixed the keen, cleaving scythe, and slaughtering drove . . .
These are of war the earliest arts; but who
Can think the inventors ne'er the effects foreknew
So sure to follow; all the ills that rise?
Dread catalogue of human miseries!
Safer, perchance, to say these things had birth
In various worlds, and not alone on earth:
Obtained throughout the Universal State,
Nor here, nor there, could claim their earliest date.
But not alone for victory brutes were brought
Against the foe; but leaders chiefly sought
Vexatious combat – though, their numbers small
And slightly skilled in arms, they saw their certain fall.
Their vests the shaggy spoils of beasts supplied,
And thorns inserted held the folding hide:
For Reason tells no weaving arts had birth
Till iron left the bosom of the earth:
Iron the chief, the grand material proved,
Iron the treadles, shuttles, spindles moved.
Had iron still been locked from human sight,
Nor these, nor rattling beams, had sprung to light.
But the first wheels and distaffs Men employed
Since more inventive powers their minds enjoyed
Than those of women; more they claim of arts,
And all that borrows mind, or mind imparts.
But the rough peasant mocked the slender toil,
Called the male spinsters to the needy soil:
In softer hands the nimble shutters played
And the smooth treadles shapelier feet obeyed.
Men to superior tasks their efforts turned;
For nobler arts and hardier labours burned.
   Creative Nature (whence all things began)
To sow, to plant, engraft, instructed man.
Berries and acorns as they fell to earth,
Giving, in season, kindred shoots to birth,
Taught him to plant; and bid the cultured field
With fruitage teem, and fair abundance yield;
Taught him to graft the tender slips, and raise
In ordered rows, the suckling's blooming sprays.
   Then rising art to rising plenty led;
Improving earth enriching labour fed:
Wild fruits to ripeness swelled and, sweet as fair,
With mellow juice repaid the peasant's care.
The mountain woods a narrower bound assumed,

And valleys waved with corn, with golden produce bloomed.
Then cultivated Earth, no longer wild,
Her meadows, rivers, lakes and mountains smiled!
Cornfields and vineyards waked to new delight
The peasant's heart, and charmed his gladdened sight! . . .
. . . While the glad mind no higher good conceives,
The present good delight and pleasure gives:
But doth a more exalted bliss arise?
The joy that lived till then, that moment dies.
Hence acorns that could once the taste invite,
In time the pampered palate learned to slight.
The downy couch supplants the leafy bed
And glossy robes to shaggy skins succeed.
Yet the first man these savage spoils that wore
Such envy raised, his earth-born fellows tore
Quick from his back the vest his courage gained
And with his blood his shaggy honours stained;
Their murderous hands upon the victim laid;
And death the price of his invention paid.

Then hides, now Gold and Purple, men delight;
No more for those, but fierce for these they fight;
And, sure, more folly we betray than those
Whose naked limbs the shivering winter froze;
While without gold and purple we, as well
Might all the rigours of the winds repel:
Since simplest habits will protection yield
And richest vestments but the body shield.

How vain, then, all the troubles, cares and strife
That cheat weak mortals of the sweets of life!
No limits they assign to flattering wealth,
Nor know felicity is peace and health.
Ignorant of where the bounds of pleasure lie,
Into a sea of woes they anxious fly;
Evils unceasing court, and round the world
With maddening rage the flames of war are hurled.

At length the Sun and Moon, that wakeful roll
Their radiant orbs around the steady pole;
That to the circling skies their light display
To cheer the silent night or give the day;
Taught watchful man that Order governs all,
And wheels the seasons round this central ball.

Now for defence arose embattled towers,
To castles chiefs withdrew their marshalled powers;
Lands were divided, spacious seas explored,

And civic union swayed the guardian sword;
Extending concord state with state combined
And held in welcome bondage humankind.
Then various arts appeared, then letters sprung,
Poets exploits divine in strains diviner sung:
But deeds of ages past were all unknown,
Or but by Reason's light obscurely shone.
Custom and slow Experience knowledge brought;
(Knowledge, with all the nobler blessings fraught;)
What life improves, or fosters Virtue's cause;
Fair Agriculture, Navigation, Laws,
Cities and Public Ways, rich Vestments, Arms,
Aspiring Temples, and the immortal charms
Of Painting, Sculpture, all that man refine;
Philosophy and Poesy divine.
   Thus Time with gradual light the mind illumes;
Thus new born energies the soul assumes;
From art to art the brightening radiance flies,
And to their full perfection all things rise.

FIRST ORATION AGAINST CATILINE, 63 BC

Cicero

Orator, advocate and statesman, Cicero (106–43 BC) was the leading defender of the Roman Republic in its twilight. Here is Cicero's famous speech against Catiline, an aristocratic malcontent who was plotting a coup d'état. Eventually, Catiline was foiled – not least because of Cicero's oration against him – and was killed in a battle with Republican forces in January 62.

The Romans considered oration one of the highest art forms; and Cicero was master of it.

When, O Catiline, do you mean to cease abusing our patience? How long is that madness of yours still to mock us? When is there to be an end of that unbridled audacity of yours, swaggering about as it does now? Do not the mighty guards placed on the Palatine Hill – do not the watches posted throughout the city – does not the alarm of the people, and the union of all good men – does not the precaution taken of assembling the senate in this most defensible place – do not the looks and countenances of this venerable body here present, have any effect upon you? Do you not feel that your plans are detected? Do you not see that your conspiracy is already arrested and rendered powerless by the knowledge which everyone here possesses of it? What is there that you did last night, what the night before – where is it that you were – who was there that you summoned to meet you – what design was there which was adopted by you, with which you think that any one of us is unacquainted?

Shame on the age and on its principles! The senate is aware of these things; the consul sees them; and yet this man lives. Lives! aye, he comes even into the senate. He takes a part in the public deliberations; he is watching and marking down and checking off for slaughter every individual among us. And we, gallant men that we are, think that we are doing our duty to the republic if we keep out of the way of his frenzied attacks.

You ought, O Catiline, long ago to have been led to execution by command of the counsel: That destruction which you have been long plotting against us ought to have already fallen on your own head.

What? Did not that most illustrious man, Publius Scipio, the Pontifex Maximus, in his capacity of a private citizen, put to death Tiberius Gracchus, though but slightly undermining the constitution? And shall we, who are the consuls, tolerate Catiline, openly desirous to destroy the whole world with fire and slaughter? For I pass over older instances, such as how Caius Servilius Ahala with his own hand slew Spurius Mælius when plotting a revolution in the state. There was – there was once such virtue in this republic that brave men would repress mischievous citizens with severer chastisement than the most bitter enemy. For we have a resolution of the senate, a formidable and authoritative decree against you, O Catiline; the wisdom of the republic is not at fault, nor the dignity of this senatorial body. We, we alone – I say it openly – we, the consuls, are wanting in our duty.

The senate once passed a decree that Lucius Opimius, the consul, should take care that the republic suffered no injury. Not one night elapsed. There was put to death, on some mere suspicion of disaffection, Caius Gracchus, a man whose family had borne the most unblemished reputation for many generations. There was slain Marcus Fulvius, a man of consular rank, and all of his children. By a like decree of the senate the safety of the republic was intrusted to Caius Marius and Lucius Valerius, the consuls. Did not the vengeance of the republic, did not execution overtake Lucius Saturninus, a tribune of the people, and Caius Servilius, the prætor, without the delay of one single day? But we, for these twenty days, have been allowing the edge of the senate's authority to grow blunt, as it were. For we are in possession of a similar decree of the senate, but we keep it locked up in its parchment – buried, I may say, in the sheath; and according to this decree you ought. O Catiline, to be put to death this instant. You live – and you live, not to lay aside, but to persist in your audacity.

I wish, O conscript fathers, to be merciful; I wish not to appear negligent amid such danger to the state; but I do now accuse myself of remissness and culpable inactivity. A camp is pitched in Italy, at the entrance of Etruria, in hostility to the republic; the number of the enemy increases every day; and yet the general of that camp, the leader of those enemies, we see within the walls – aye, and even in the senate – planning every day some internal injury to the republic. If, O Catiline, I should now order you to be arrested, to be put to death, I should I suppose, have to fear lest all good men should say that I had acted tardily, rather than that any one should affirm that I acted cruelly. But yet this, which ought to have been done long since, I have good reason for not doing as yet; I will put you to death, then, when there shall be not one person possible to be found so wicked, so abandoned, so like yourself, as not to allow that it has been rightly done. As long as one person exists who can dare to defend you, you shall live; but you shall live as you do now, surrounded by my many and trusted guards, so that you shall not be able to stir one finger against the republic; many eyes and ears shall still observe and watch you as they have hitherto done, though you shall not perceive them.

For what is there, O Catiline, that you can still expect, if night is not able to veil your nefarious meetings in darkness, and if private houses cannot conceal the voice of your conspiracy within their walls – if everything is seen and displayed? Change your mind: trust me: forget the slaughter and conflagration you are meditating. You are hemmed in on all sides; all your plans are clearer than the day to us; let me remind you of them. Do you recollect that on the 21st of October I said in the senate, that on a certain day, which was to be the 27th of October, C. Manlius, the satellite and servant of your audacity, would be in arms? Was I mistaken, Catiline, not only in so important, so atrocious, so incredible a fact, but, what is much more remarkable, in the very day? I said also in the senate that you had fixed the massacre of the nobles for the 28th of October, when many chief men of the senate had left Rome, not so much for the sake of saving themselves as of checking your designs. Can you deny that on that very day you were so hemmed in by my guards and my vigilance, that you were unable to stir one finger against the republic; when you said that you would be content with the flight of the rest, and the slaughter of us who remained? What? when you made sure that you would be able to seize Præneste on the 1st of November by a nocturnal attack, did you not find that that colony was fortified by my order, by my garrison, by my watchfulness and care? You do nothing, you plan nothing, think of nothing which I not only do not hear but which I do not see and know every particular of.

Listen while I speak of the night before. You shall now see that I watch far more actively for the safety than you do for the destruction of the republic. I say that you came the night before (I will say nothing obscurely) into the Scythe-dealers' street, to the house of Marcus Lecca; that many of your accomplices in the same insanity and wickedness came there, too. Do you dare to deny it? Why are you silent? I will prove it if you do deny it; for I see here in the senate some men who were there with you.

O ye immortal gods, where on earth are we? in what city are we living? what constitution is ours? There are here – here in our body, O conscript fathers, in this the most holy and dignified assembly of the whole world, men who meditate my death, and the death of all of us, and the destruction of this city, and of the whole world. I, the consul, see them; I ask them their opinion about the republic, and I do not yet attack, even by words, those who ought to be put to death by the sword. You were, then, O Catiline, at Lecca's that night; you divided Italy into sections; you settled where every one was to go; you fixed whom you were to leave at Rome, whom you were to take with you; you portioned out the divisions of the city for conflagration; you undertook that you yourself would at once leave the city, and said that there was then only this to delay you, that I was still alive. Two Roman knights were found to deliver you from this anxiety, and to promise that very night, before daybreak, to slay me in my bed. All this I knew almost before your meeting had broken up. I strengthened and fortified my house with a stronger guard; I refused admittance, when they came, to those whom you sent in the morning to salute me, and of whom I had foretold to many eminent men that they would come to me at that time.

As, then, this is the case, O Catiline, continue as you have begun. Leave the city at last: the gates are open; depart. That Manlian camp of yours has been waiting too long for you as its general. And lead forth with you all your friends, or at least as many as you can; purge the city of your presence; you will deliver me from a great fear, when there is a wall between me and you. Among us you can dwell no longer – I will not bear it, I will not permit it, I will not tolerate it. Great thanks are due to the immortal gods, and to this very Jupiter Stator, in whose temple we are, the most ancient protector of this city, that we have already so often escaped so foul, so horrible, and so deadly an enemy to the republic. But the safety of the commonwealth must not be too often allowed to be risked on one man. As long as you, O Catiline, plotted against me while I was the consul-elect, I defended myself not with a public guard, but by my own private diligence. When, in the next consular comitia, you wished to slay me when I was actually consul, and your competitors also, in the Campus Martius, I checked your nefarious attempt by the assistance and resources of my own friends, without exciting any disturbance publicly. In short, as often as you attacked me, I by myself opposed you, and that, too, though I saw that my ruin was connected with great disaster to the republic. But now you are openly attacking the entire republic.

You are summoning to destruction and devastation the temples of the immortal gods, the houses of the city, the lives of all the citizens; in short, all Italy. Wherefore, since I do not yet venture to do that which is the best thing, and which belongs to my office and to the discipline of our ancestors, I will do that which is more merciful if we regard its rigour, and more expedient for the state. For if I order you to be put to death, the rest of the conspirators will still remain in the republic; if, as I have long been exhorting you, you depart, your companions, these worthless dregs of the republic, will be drawn off from the city too. What is the matter, Catiline? Do you hesitate to do that when I order you which you were already doing of your own accord? The consul orders an enemy to depart from the city. Do you ask me, Are you to go into banishment? I do not order it; but if you consult me, I advise it.

For what is there, O Catiline, that can now afford you any pleasure in this city? for there is no one in it, except that band of profligate conspirators of yours, who does not fear you – no one who does not hate you. What brand of domestic baseness is not stamped upon your life? What disgraceful circumstance is wanting to your infamy in your private affairs? From what licentiousness have your eyes, from what atrocity have your hands, from what iniquity has your whole body ever abstained? Is there one youth, when you have once entangled him in the temptations of your corruption, to whom you have not held out a sword for audacious crime, or a torch for licentious wickedness?

What? when lately by the death of your former wife you had made your house empty and ready for a new bridal, did you not even add another incredible wickedness to this wickedness? But I pass that over, and willingly allow it to be buried in silence, that so horrible a crime may not be seen to have existed in this city, and not to have been chastised. I pass over the ruin of your fortune, which you know is hanging over you against the Ides of the very next month; I come to those things which relate not to the infamy of your private vices, not to your domestic difficulties and baseness, but to the welfare of the republic and to the lives and safety of us all.

Can the light of this life, O Catiline, can the breath of this atmosphere be pleasant to you, when you know that there is not one man of those here present who is ignorant that you, on the last day of the year, when Lepidus and Tullus were consuls, stood in the assembly armed; that you had prepared your hand for the slaughter of the consuls and chief men of the state, and that no reason or fear of yours hindered your crime and madness, but the fortune of the republic? And I say no more of these things, for they are not unknown to every one. How often have you endeavoured to slay me, both as consul-elect and as actual consul? how many shots of yours, so aimed that they seemed impossible to be escaped, have I avoided by some slight stooping aside, and some dodging, as it were, of my body? You attempt nothing, you execute nothing, you devise nothing that can be kept hid from me at the proper time; and yet you do not cease to attempt and to contrive. How often already has that dagger of yours been wrested from your hands? How often has it slipped through them by some chance, and dropped down? and yet you cannot any longer do without it; and to what sacred mysteries it is consecrated and devoted by you I know not, that you think it necessary to plunge it in the body of the consul.

But now, what is that life of yours that you are leading? For I will speak to you not so as to seem influenced by the hatred I ought to feel, but by pity, nothing of which is due to you. You came a little while ago into the senate: in so numerous an assembly, who of so many friends and connections of yours saluted you? If this in the memory of man never happened to any one else, are you waiting for insults by word of mouth, when you are overwhelmed by the most irresistible condemnation of silence? Is it nothing that at your arrival all those seats were vacated? that all the men of consular rank, who had often been marked out by you for slaughter, the very moment you sat down, left that part of the benches bare and vacant? With what feelings do you think you ought to bear this? On my honour, if my slaves feared me as all your fellow-citizens fear you, I should think I must leave my house. Do not you think you should leave the city? If I saw that I was even undeservedly so suspected and hated by my fellow-citizens, I would rather flee from their sight than be gazed at by the hostile eyes of every one. And do you, who, from the consciousness of your wickedness, know that the hatred of all men is just and has been long due to you, hesitate to avoid the sight and presence of those men whose minds and senses you offend? If your parents feared and hated you, and if you could by no means pacify them, you would, I think, depart somewhere out of their sight. Now your country, which is the common parent of all of us, hates and fears you, and has no other opinion of you than that you are meditating parricide in her case; and will you neither feel awe of her authority, nor deference for her judgment, nor fear of her power?

And she, O Catiline, thus pleads with you, and after a manner silently speaks to you: there has now for many years been no crime committed but by you; no atrocity has taken place without you; you alone unpunished and unquestioned have murdered the citizens, have harassed and plundered the allies; you alone have had power not only to neglect all laws and investigations, but to overthrow and break through them. Your former actions, though they ought not to have been borne, yet I did bear as well as I could; but now that I should be wholly occupied with fear of you alone, that at every sound I should dread Catiline, that no design should seem possible to be entertained against me which does not proceed from your wickedness, this is no longer endurable. Depart, then, and deliver me from this fear; that, if it be a just one, I may not be destroyed; if an imaginary one, that at least I may at last cease to fear.

If, as I have said, your country were thus to address you, ought she not to obtain her request, even if she were not able to enforce it? What shall I say of your having given yourself into custody? what of your having said, for the sake of avoiding suspicion, that you were willing to dwell in the house of Marcus Lepidus? And when you were not received by him, you dared even to come to me, and begged me to keep you in my house; and when you had received answer from me that I could not possibly be safe in the same house with you, when I considered myself in great danger as long as we were in the same city, you came to Quintus Metellus, the prætor, and being rejected by him, you passed on to your associate, that most excellent man, Marcus Marcellus, who would be, I suppose you thought, most diligent in guarding you, most sagacious in suspecting you, and most bold in punishing you; but how far can we think that man ought to be from bonds and imprisonment who has already judged himself deserving of being given into custody?

Since, then, this is the case, do you hesitate, O Catiline, if you cannot remain here with tranquillity, to depart to some distant land, and to trust your life, saved from just and deserved punishment, to flight and solitude? Make a motion, say you, to the senate (for that is what you demand), and if this body votes that you ought to go into banishment, you say that you will obey. I will not make such a motion, it is contrary to my principles, and yet I will let you see what these men think of you. Begone from the city, O Catiline, deliver the republic from fear; depart into banishment, if that is the word you are waiting for. What now, O Catiline? Do you not perceive, do you not see the silence of these men? They permit it, they say nothing; why wait you for the authority of their words, when you see their wishes in their silence?

But had I said the same to this worthy young man, Publius Sextius, or to that brave man, Marcus Marcellus, before this time the senate would deservedly have laid violent hands on me, consul though I be, in this very temple. But as to you, Catiline, while they are quiet they approve, while they permit me to speak they vote, while they are silent they are loud and eloquent. And not they alone, whose authority forsooth is dear to you, though their lives are unimportant, but the Roman knights, too, those most honourable and excellent men, and the other virtuous citizens who are now surrounding the senate, whose numbers you could see, whose desires you could know, and whose voices you a few minutes ago could hear – aye, whose very hands and weapons I have for some time been scarcely able to keep off from you; but those, too, I will easily bring to attend you to the gates if you leave these places you have been long desiring to lay waste.

And yet, why am I speaking? that anything may change your purpose? that you may ever amend your life? that you may meditate flight or think of voluntary banishment? I wish the gods may give you such a mind; though I see, if alarmed at my words you bring your mind to go into banishment, what a storm of unpopularity hangs over me, if not at present, while the memory of your wickedness is fresh, at all events hereafter. But it is worth while to incur that, as long as that is but a private misfortune of my own, and is unconnected with the dangers of the republic. But we cannot expect that you should be concerned at your own vices, that you should fear the penalties of the laws, or that you should yield to the necessities of the republic, for you are not, O Catiline, one whom either shame can recall from infamy, or fear from danger, or reason from madness.

Wherefore, as I have said before, go forth, and if you wish to make me, your enemy as you call me, unpopular, go straight into banishment. I shall scarcely be able to endure all that will be said if you do so; I shall scarcely be able to support my load of unpopularity if you do go into banishment at the command of the consul; but if you wish to serve my credit and reputation, go forth with your ill-omened band of profligates; betake yourself to Manlius, rouse up the abandoned citizens, separate yourselves from the good ones, wage war against your country, exult in your impious banditti, so that you may not seem to have been driven out by me and gone to strangers, but to have gone invited to your friends.

Though why should I invite you, by whom I know men have been already sent on to wait in arms for you at the Forum Aurelium; who I know has fixed and agreed with Manlius upon a settled day; by whom I know that that silver eagle, which I trust will be ruinous and fatal to you and to all your friends, and to which there was set up in your house a shrine, as it were, of your crimes, has been already sent forward. Need I fear that you can long do without that which you used to worship when going out to murder, and from whose altars you have often transferred your impious hand to the slaughter of citizens?

You will go at last where your unbridled and mad desire has been long hurrying you. And this causes you no grief, but an incredible pleasure. Nature has formed you, desire has trained you, fortune has preserved you for this insanity. Not only did you never desire quiet, but you never even desired any war but a criminal one; you have collected a band of profligates and worthless men, abandoned not only by all fortune but even by hope.

Then what happiness will you enjoy! with what delight will you exult! in what pleasure will you revel! when in so numerous a body of friends you neither hear nor see one good man. All the toils you have gone through have always pointed to this sort of life; your lying on the ground not merely to lie in wait to gratify your unclean desires, but even to accomplish crimes; your vigilance, not only when plotting against the sleep of husbands, but also against the goods of your murdered victims, have all been preparations for this. Now you have an opportunity of displaying your splendid endurance of hunger, of cold, of want of everything; by which in a short time you will find yourself worn out. All this I effected when I procured your rejection from the consulship, that you should be reduced to make attempts on your country as an exile, instead of being able to distress it as consul, and that that which had been wickedly undertaken by you should be called piracy rather than war.

Now that I may remove and avert, O conscript fathers, any in the least reasonable complaint from myself, listen, I beseech you, carefully to what I say, and lay it up in your inmost hearts and minds. In truth, if my country, which is far dearer to me than my life – if all Italy – if the whole republic were to address me, Marcus Tullius, what are you doing? will you permit that man to depart whom you have ascertained to be an enemy? whom you see ready to become the general of the war? whom you know to be expected in the camp of the enemy as their chief, the author of all this wickedness, the head of the conspiracy, the instigator of the slaves and abandoned citizens, so that he shall seem not driven out of the city by you, but let loose by you against the city? will you not order him to be thrown into prison, to be hurried off to execution, to be put to death with the most prompt severity? What hinders you? is it the customs of our ancestors? But even private men have often in this republic slain mischievous citizens. Is it the laws which have been passed about the punishment of Roman citizens? But in this city those who have rebelled against the republic have never had the rights of citizens. Do you fear odium with posterity? You are showing fine gratitude to the Roman people which has raised you, a man known only by your own actions, of no ancestral renown, through all the degrees of honour at so early an age to the very highest office, if from fear of unpopularity or of any danger you neglect the safety of your fellow-citizens. But if you have a fear of unpopularity, is that arising from the imputation of vigour and boldness, or that arising from that of inactivity and indecision most to be feared? When Italy is laid waste by war, when cities are attacked and houses in flames, do you not think that you will be then consumed by a perfect conflagration of hatred?

To this holy address of the republic, and to the feelings of those men who entertain the same opinion, I will make this short answer: if, O conscript fathers, I thought it best that Catiline should be punished with death, I would not have given the space of one hour to this gladiator to live in. If, forsooth, those excellent men and most illustrious cities not only did not pollute themselves, but even glorified themselves by the blood of Saturninus, and the Gracchi, and Flaccus, and many others of old time, surely I had no cause to fear lest for slaying this parricidal murderer of the citizens any unpopularity should accrue to me with posterity. And if it did threaten me to ever so great a degree, yet I have always been of the disposition to think unpopularity earned by virtue and glory not unpopularity.

Though there are some men in this body who either do not see what threatens, or dissemble what they do see; who have fed the hope of Catiline by mild sentiments, and have strengthened the rising conspiracy by not believing it; influenced by whose authority many, and they not wicked, but only ignorant, if I punished him would say that I had acted cruelly and tyrannically. But I know that if he arrives at the camp of Manlius to which he is going, there will be no one so stupid as not to see that there has been a conspiracy, no one so hardened as not to confess it. But if this man alone were put to death, I know that this disease of the republic would be only checked for a while, not eradicated forever. But if he banishes himself, and takes with him all his friends, and collects at one point all the ruined men from every quarter, then not only will this full grown plague of the republic be extinguished and eradicated, but also the root and seed of all future evils.

We have now for a long time, O conscript fathers, lived among these dangers and machinations of conspiracy; but somehow or other, the ripeness of all wickedness, and of this long-standing madness and audacity, has come to a head at the time of my consulship. But if this man alone is removed from this piratical crew, we may appear, perhaps, for a short time relieved from fear and anxiety, but the danger will settle down and lie hid in the veins and bowels of the republic. As it often happens that men afflicted with a severe disease, when they are tortured with heat and fever, if they drink cold water seem at first to be relieved, but afterwards suffer more and more severely; so this disease which is in the republic, if relieved by the punishment of this man, will only get worse and worse, as the rest will be still alive.

Wherefore, O conscript fathers, let the worthless begone – let them separate themselves from the good – let them collect in one place – let them, as I have often said before, be separated from us by a wall; let them cease to plot against the consul in his own house – to surround the tribunal of the city prætor – to besiege the senate house with swords – to prepare brands and torches to burn the city; let it, in short, be written on the brow of every citizen what are his sentiments about the republic. I promise you this, O conscript fathers, that there shall be so much diligence in us the consuls, so much authority in you, so much virtue in the Roman knights, so much unanimity in all good men, that you shall see everything made plain and manifest by the departure of Catiline – everything checked and punished.

With these omens, O Catiline, begone to your impious and nefarious war, to the great safety of the republic, to your own misfortune and injury, and to the destruction of those who have joined themselves to you in every wickedness and atrocity. Then do you, O Jupiter, who were consecrated by Romulus with the same auspices as this city, whom we rightly call the stay of this city and empire, repel this man and his companions from your altars and from the other temples – from the houses and walls of the city – from the lives and fortunes of all the citizens; and overwhelm all the enemies of good men, the foes of the republic, the robbers of Italy, men bound together by a treaty and infamous alliance of crimes, dead and alive, with eternal punishments.

From *ON THE STATE*, c. 53 BC

Cicero

Cicero's famous treatise on the constitution, *De Republica* ("On the State"), takes the form of an imaginary dialogue between prominent Roman men of a previous generation. The voice of Scipio Aemilianus is the voice of Cicero himself.

XXXI. SCIPIO: . . . and every State is such as its ruler's character and will make it. Hence liberty has no dwelling-place in any State except that in which the people's power is the greatest, and surely nothing can be sweeter than liberty; but if it is not the same for all, it does not deserve the name of liberty. And how can it be the same for all, I will not say in a kingdom, where there is no obscurity or doubt about the slavery of the subject, but even in States where everyone is ostensibly free? I mean States in which the people vote, elect commanders and officials, are canvassed for their votes, and have bills proposed to them, but really grant only what they would have to grant even if they were unwilling to do so, and are asked to give to others what they do not possess themselves. For they have no share in the governing power, in the deliberative function, or in the courts, over which selected judges preside, for those privileges are granted on the basis of birth or wealth. But in a free nation, such as the Rhodians or the Athenians, there is not one of the citizens who [may not hold the offices of State and take an active part in the government.] . . .

XXXII. [Our authorities] say [that] when one person or a few stand out from the crowd as richer and more prosperous, then, as a result of the haughty and arrogant behaviour of these, there arises [a government of one or a few], the cowardly and weak giving way and bowing down to the pride of wealth. But if the people would maintain their rights, they say that no form of government would be superior, either in liberty or happiness, for they themselves would be masters of the laws and the courts, of war and peace, of international agreements, and of every citizen's life and property; this government alone, they believe, can rightly be called a commonwealth, that is, "the property of the people". And it is for that reason, they say, that "the property of the people" is often liberated from the domination of kings or senators, while free peoples do not seek kings or the power and wealth of aristocracies. And indeed they claim that this free popular government ought not to be entirely rejected on account of the excesses of an unbridled mob, for, according to them, when a sovereign people is pervaded by a spirit of harmony and tests every measure by the standard of their own safety and liberty, no form of government is less subject to change or more stable. And they insist that harmony is very easily obtainable in a State where the interests of all are the same, for discord arises from conflicting interests, where different measures are advantageous to different citizens. Therefore they maintain that when a senate has been supreme, the State has never had a stable government, and that such stability is less attainable by far in kingdoms, in which, as Ennius says,

> No sacred partnership or honour is.

Therefore, since law is the bond which unites the civic association, and the justice enforced by law is the same for all, by what justice can an association of citizens be held together when there is no equality among the citizens? For if we cannot agree to equalize men's wealth, and equality of innate ability is impossible, the legal rights at least of those who are citizens of the same commonwealth ought to be equal. For what is a State except an association or partnership in justice? . . .

XXXIII. . . . Indeed they think that States of the other kinds have no right at all to the names which they arrogate to themselves. For why should I give the name of king, the title of Jupiter the Best, to a man who is greedy for personal power and absolute authority, a man who lords it over an oppressed people? Should I not rather call him tyrant? For tyrants may be merciful as well as oppressive: so that the only difference between the nations governed by these rulers is that between the slaves of a kind and those of a cruel master; for in any case the subjects must be slaves. And how could Sparta, at the time when the mode of life inculcated by her constitution was considered so excellent, be assured of always having good and just kings, when a person of any sort, if he was born of the royal family, had to be accepted as king? As to aristocrats, who could tolerate men that have claimed the title without the people's acquiescence, but merely by their own will? For how is a man adjudged to be "the best"? On the basis of knowledge, skill, learning, [and similar qualities surely, not because of his own desire to possess the title!] . . .

XXXIV. . . . If [the State] leaves [the selection of its rulers] to chance, it will be as quickly overturned as a ship whose pilot should be chosen by lot from among the passengers. But if a free people chooses the men to whom it is to entrust its fortunes, and, since it desires its own safety, chooses the best men, then certainly the safety of the State depends upon the wisdom of its best men, especially since Nature has provided not only that those men who are superior in virtue and in spirit should rule the weaker, but also that the weaker should be willing to obey the stronger.

But they claim that this ideal form of State has been rejected on account of the false notions of men, who, through their ignorance of virtue – for just as virtue is possessed by only a few, so it can be distinguished and perceived by only a few – think that the best men are those who are rich, prosperous, or born of famous families. For when, on account of this mistaken notion of the common people, the State begins to be ruled by the riches, instead of the virtue, of a few men, these rulers tenaciously retain the title, though they do not possess the character, of the "best". For riches, names, and power, when they lack wisdom and the knowledge of how to live and to rule over others, are full of dishonour and insolent pride, nor is there any more depraved type of State than that in which the richest are accounted the best. But what can be nobler than the government of the State by virtue? For then the man who rules others is not himself a slave to any passion, but has already acquired for himself all those qualities to which he is training and summoning his fellows. Such a man imposes no laws upon the people that he does not obey himself, but puts his own life before his fellow-citizens as their law. If a single individual of this character could order all things properly in a State, there would be no need of more than one ruler; or if the citizens as a body could see what was best and agree upon it, no one would desire a selected group of rulers. It has been the difficulty of formulating policies that has transferred the power from a king to a larger number; and the perversity and rashness of popular assemblies that have transferred it from the many to the few. Thus, between the weakness of a single ruler and the rashness of the many, aristocracies have occupied that intermediate position which represents the utmost moderation; and in a State ruled by its best men, the citizens must necessarily enjoy the greatest happiness, being freed from all cares and worries, when once they have entrusted the preservation of their tranquillity to others, whose duty it is to guard it vigilantly and never to allow the people to think that their interests are being neglected by their rulers. For that equality of legal rights of which free peoples are so found cannot be maintained (for the people themselves, though free and unrestrained, give very many special powers to many individuals, and create great distinctions among men and the honours granted to them), and what is called equality is really most inequitable. For when equal honour is given to the highest and the lowest – for men of both types must exist in every nation – then this very "fairness" is most unfair; but this cannot happen in States ruled by their best citizens. These arguments and others like them,

Laelius, are approximately those which are advanced by men who consider this form of government the best.

XXXV. LAELIUS: But what about yourself, Scipio? Which of these three forms do you consider the best?

SCIPIO: You are right to ask which I consider the best of the three, for I do not approve of any of them when employed by itself, and consider the form which is a combination of all of them superior to any single one of them. But if I were compelled to approve one single unmixed form, [I might choose] the kingship . . . the name of king seems like that of father to us, since the king provides for the citizens as if they were his own children, and is more eager to protect them than . . . to be sustained by the care of one man who is the most virtuous and most eminent. But here are the aristocrats, with the claim that they can do this more effectively, and that there will be more wisdom in the counsels of several than in those of one man, and an equal amount of fairness and scrupulousness. And here also are the people, shouting with a loud voice that they are willing to obey neither one nor a few, that nothing is sweeter than liberty even to wild beasts, and that all who are slaves, whether to a king or to an aristocracy, are deprived of liberty. Thus kings attract us by our affection for them, aristocracies by their wisdom, and popular governments by their freedom, so that in comparing them it is difficult to say which one prefers.

XLII. When I have set forth my ideas in regard to the form of State which I consider the best, I shall have to take up in greater detail those changes to which States are liable, though I think it will not be at all easy for any such changes to take place in the State which I have in mind. But the first and most certain of these changes is the one that takes place in kingships: when the king begins to be unjust, that form of government is immediately at an end, and the king has become a tyrant. This is the worst sort of government, though closely related to the best. If the best men overthrow it, as usually happens, then the State is in the second of its three stages; for this form is similar to a kingship, being one in which a paternal council of leading men makes good provision for the people's welfare. But if the people themselves have killed or driven out the tyrant, they govern rather moderately, as long as they are wise and prudent, and, delighting in their exploit, they endeavour to maintain the government they have themselves set up. But if the people ever rebel against a just king and deprive him of his kingdom, or, as happens more frequently, taste the blood of the aristocracy and subject the whole State to their own caprices (and do not dream, Laelius, that any sea or any conflagration is so powerful that it cannot be more easily subdued than an unbridled multitude enjoying unwonted power), then we have a condition which is splendidly described by Plato, if only I can reproduce his description in Latin; it is difficult, but I will attempt it. XLIII. He says: "When the insatiable throats of the people have become dry with the thirst for liberty, and, served by evil ministers, they have drained in their thirst a draught of liberty which, instead of being moderately tempered, is too strong for them, then, unless the magistrates and men of high rank are very mild and indulgent, serving them with liberty in generous quantities, the people persecute them, charge them with crime and impeach them, calling them despots, kings, and tyrants." I think you are acquainted with this passage.

LAELIUS: It is very familiar to me.

SCIPIO: He continues thus: "Those who follow the lead of prominent citizens are persecuted by such a people and called willing slaves; but those who, though in office, try to act like private citizens, and those private citizens who try to destroy all distinction between a private citizen and a magistrate are praised to the skies and loaded with honours. It necessarily follows in such a State that liberty prevails everywhere, to such an extent that not only are homes one and all without a master, but the vice of anarchy extends even to the domestic animals, until finally the father fears his son, the son flouts his father, all sense of shame disappears, and all is so absolutely free that there is no distinction between citizen and alien; the schoolmaster fears and flatters his pupils, and pupils despise their masters; youths take on the gravity of age, and old men stoop to the games of youth, for fear they may be disliked by their juniors and seem to them too serious. Under such conditions even the slaves come to behave with unseemly freedom, wives have the same rights as their husbands, and in the abundance of liberty even the dogs, the horses, and the asses are so free in their running about that men must make way for them in the streets. Therefore," he concludes, "the final result of this boundless licence is that the minds of the citizens become so squeamish and sensitive that, if the authority of government is exercised in the smallest degree, they become angry and cannot bear it. On this account they begin to neglect the laws as well, and so finally are utterly without a master of any kind."

XLIV. LAELIUS: You have given us his description with great exactness.

SCIPIO: Well, to return now to my own style of discourse, he also says that from this exaggerated licence, which is the only thing such people call liberty, tyrants spring up as from a root, and are, as it were, engendered. For just as an excess of power in the hands of the aristocrats results in the overthrow of an aristocracy, so liberty itself reduces a people who possess it in too great degree to servitude. Thus everything which is in excess – when, for instance, either in the weather, or in the fields, or in men's bodies, conditions have been too favourable – is usually changed into its opposite: and this is especially true in States, where such excess of liberty either in nations or in individuals turns into an excess of servitude. This extreme liberty gives birth to a tyrant and the utterly unjust and cruel servitude of the tyranny. For out of such an ungoverned, or rather, untamed, populace someone is usually chosen as leader against those leading citizens who have already been subjected to persecution and cast down from their leadership – some bold and depraved man, who shamelessly harasses oftentimes even those who have deserved well of the State, and curries favour with the people by bestowing upon them the property of others as well as his own. To such a man, because he has much reason to be afraid if he remains a private citizen, official power is given and continually renewed: he is also surrounded by armed guards, as was Pisistratus at Athens; and finally he emerges as a tyrant over the very people who have raised him to power. If the better citizens overthrow such a tyrant, as often happens, then the State is re-established; but if it is the bolder sort who do so, then we have that oligarchy which is only a tyranny of another kind. This same form of government also arises from the excellent rule of an aristocracy, when some bad influence turns the leading citizens themselves from the right path. Thus the ruling power of the State, like a ball, is snatched from kings by tyrants, from tyrants by aristocrats or the people, and from them again by an oligarchical faction or a tyrant, so that no single form of government ever maintains itself very long.

XLV. Since this is true, the kingship, in my opinion, is by far the best of the three primary forms, but a moderate and balanced form of government which is a combination of the three good simple forms is preferable even to the kingship. For there should be a supreme and royal element in the State, some power also ought to be granted to the leading citizens, and certain matters should be left to the judgment and desires of the masses. Such a constitution, in the first place, offers in a high degree a sort of equality, which is a thing free men can hardly do without for any considerable length of time, and, secondly, it has stability. For the primary forms already mentioned degenerate easily into the corresponding perverted forms, the king being replaced by a despot, the aristocracy by an oligarchical faction, and the people by a mob and anarchy; but whereas these forms are frequently changed into new ones, this does not usually happen in the case of the mixed and evenly balanced constitution, except through great faults in the governing class. For there is no reason for a change when every citizen is firmly established in his own station, and there underlies it no perverted form into which it can plunge and sink.

XLVI. But I am afraid that you Laelius, and you, my very dear and learned friends, may think, if I spend more time upon this aspect of the subject, that my discourse is rather that of a master or teacher than of one who is merely considering these matters in company with yourselves. Therefore I will pass to a topic which is familiar to everyone, and which we ourselves discussed some time ago. For I am convinced, I believe, and I declare that no other form of government is comparable, either in its general character, in its distribution of powers, or in the training it gives, with that which our ancestors received from their own forefathers, and have handed down to us. Therefore, if you have no objection – since you have desired to hear me discourse upon matters with which you are already familiar – I will explain the character of this constitution and show why it is the best; and, using our own government as my pattern, I will fit to it, if I can, all I have to say about the ideal State. If I can keep to this intention and carry it through, the task that Laelius has imposed upon me will, in my opinion, have been abundantly accomplished.

XLVII. LAELIUS: The task is yours indeed, Scipio, and yours alone; for who is better qualified than yourself to speak of the institutions of our ancestors, since you yourself are descended from most famous fore-fathers? Or who is better able to speak of the ideal State? For if we are to have such a constitution (surely at present that is not the case), who would be more prominent in its administration than yourself? Or who is better qualified to speak of provisions for the future, when you have provided for all future time by freeing our city from the two dangers that threatened it?

Cicero's endeavours on behalf of the Republic ultimately came to nought. Dictatorship was established under Julius Caesar in 49 BC. Six years later Cicero was murdered by the military triumvirate of Mark Antony – whom he'd attacked in his Philippics – Lepidus and Octavian. (The latter was soon to rule solo as Rome's first Emperor, Augustus). Cicero met his end calmly by putting his head outside the litter in which he was being carried and telling the murderers to strike.

THE BIRTH OF CHRIST, c. 6 BC

St Luke

An old mistake in calculation gives the birth of the founder of Christianity as AD 1; he was almost certainly born in 6 or 4 BC. The only remotely contemporaneous accounts of the Nativity are the gospels of Matthew and Luke. Luke omits the wise men, but has shepherds; Mark vice versa.

The Gospel According to St. Luke
(Authorized version; II:1–21)

Chapter 2

And it came to pass in those days, that there went out a decree from Cæsar Augustus, that all the world should be taxed.

2 (*And* this taxing was first made when Cyrenius was governor of Syria.)

3 And all went to be taxed, every one into his own city.

4 And Joseph also went up from Galilee, out of the city of Nazareth, into Judæa, unto the city of David, which is called Bethlehem; (because he was of the house and lineage of David:)

5 To be taxed with Mary his espoused wife, being great with child.

6 And so it was, that, while they were there, the days were accomplished that she should be delivered.

7 And she brought forth her firstborn son, and wrapped him in swaddling clothes, and laid him in a manger; because there was no room for them in the inn.

8 And there were in the same country shepherds abiding in the field, keeping watch over their flock by night.

9 And, lo, the angel of the Lord came upon them, and the glory of the Lord shone round about them: and they were sore afraid.

10 And the angel said unto them. Fear not: for, behold, I bring you good tidings of great joy, which shall be to all people.

11 For unto you is born this day in the city of David a Saviour, which is Christ the Lord.

12 And this *shall be* a sign unto you; Ye shall find the babe wrapped in swaddling clothes, lying in a manger.

13 And suddenly there was with the angel a multitude of the heavenly host praising God, and saying.

14 Glory to God in the highest, and on earth peace, good will toward men.

15 And it came to pass, as the angels were gone away from them into heaven, the shepherds said one to another, Let us now go even unto Bethlehem, and see this thing which is come to pass, which the Lord hath made known unto us.

16 And they came with haste, and found Mary, and Joseph, and the babe lying in a manger.

17 And when they had seen *it*, they made known abroad the saying which was told them concerning this child.

18 And all they that heard *it* wondered at those things which were told them by the shepherds.

19 But Mary kept all these things, and pondered *them* in her heart.

20 And the shepherds returned, glorifying and praising God for all the things that they had heard and seen, as it was told unto them.

21 And when eight days were accomplished for the circumcising of the child, his name was called JESUS, which was so named of the angel before he was conceived in the womb.

THE SERMON ON THE MOUNT, c. AD 30

This was the main pedagogic event in the ministry of Jesus Christ (from the Greek "khristos," the anointed one). As a young man Jesus had followed his earthly father's occupation, carpentry, but around AD 27 John the Baptist began to preach that the Kingdom of God (the day of judgment) was nigh and urged baptism and repentance as preparation. Those baptized included his relative Jesus, who then began his public ministry, mostly in the area of Galilee. Unlike the temple Pharisees, Jesus did not rely on exposition of the sacred texts but on parables and aphorisms. His demotic style antagonized the Hebrew religious establishment, but not as much as his message, which is summarized in the Sermon on the Mount as the imminence of the Kingdom of God, the need for repentance and for virtue (faith, hope, charity and all) over strict observance of Mosaic Law. Above all, in the Sermon on the Mount Jesus established universal spiritual and ethical standards. These are mostly clearly expressed in Sermon's the Beatitudes (the eight blessings, Matthew 5:3–12) and the Lord's Prayer (Matthew 6:9–13).

The Sermon on the Mount is recounted twice in the New Testament, in the Gospels of Matthew and Luke. Both Gospels, which were written sometimes after Christ's Crucifixion in c. AD 30, seem to have drawn on a contemporary source ("Q"), long lost. The Mount on which Jesus delivered the Sermon was probably the Horns of Hattin, near Capernaum.

Chapter 5

And seeing the multitudes, he went up into a mountain; and when he was set, his disciples[1] came unto him:

2 And he opened his mouth, and taught them, saying,

---

[1] Not just the 12 disciples, but all Jesus' followers

3 Blessed *are* the poor in spirit: for theirs is the kingdom of heaven.

4 Blessed *are* they that mourn: for they shall be comforted.

5 Blessed *are* the meek: for they shall inherit the earth.

6 Blessed *are* they which do hunger and thirst after righteousness: for they shall be filled.

7 Blessed *are* the merciful: for they shall obtain mercy.

8 Blessed *are* the pure in heart: for they shall see God.

9 Blessed *are* the peacemakers: for they shall be called the children of God.

10 Blessed *are* they which are persecuted for righteousness' sake: for theirs is the kingdom of heaven.

11 Blessed are ye, when *men* shall revile you, and persecute *you*, and shall say all manner of evil against you falsely, for my sake.

12 Rejoice, and be exceeding glad: for great *is* your reward in heaven: for so persecuted they the prophets which were before you.

13 ¶ Ye are the salt of the earth: but if the salt have lost his savour, wherewith shall it be salted? it is thenceforth good for nothing, but to be cast out, and to be trodden under foot of men.

14 Ye are the light of the world. A city that is set on an hill cannot be hid.

15 Neither do men light a candle, and put it under a bushel, but on a candlestick; and it giveth light unto all that are in the house.

16 Let your light so shine before men, that they may see your good works, and glorify your Father which is in heaven.

17 ¶ Think not that I am come to destroy the law, or the prophets: I am not come to destroy, but to fulfil.

18 For verily I say unto you. Till heaven and earth pass, one jot or one tittle shall in no wise pass from the law, till all be fulfilled.

19 Whosoever therefore shall break one of these least commandments, and shall teach men so, he shall be called the least in the kingdom of heaven: but whosoever shall do and teach *them*, the same shall be called great in the kingdom of heaven.

20 For I say unto you, That except your righteousness shall exceed *the righteousness* of the scribes and Pharisees, ye shall in no case enter into the kingdom of heaven.

21 ¶ Ye have heard that it was said by them of old time, Thou shalt not kill; and whosoever shall kill shall be in danger of the judgment:

22 But I say unto you, That whosoever is angry with his brother without a cause shall be in danger of the judgment: and whosoever shall say to his brother, Raca, shall be in danger of the council: but whosoever shall say, Thou fool, shall be in danger of hell fire.

23 Therefore if thou bring thy gift to the altar, and there rememberest that thy brother hath aught against thee:

24 Leave there thy gift before the altar, and go thy way; first be reconciled to thy brother, and then come and offer thy gift.

25 Agree with thine adversary quickly, whiles thou art in the way with him; lest at any time the adversary deliver thee to the judge, and the judge deliver thee to the officer, and thou be cast into prison.

26 Verily I say unto thee, Thou shalt by no means come out thence, till thou hast paid the uttermost farthing.

27 ¶ Ye have heard that it was said by them of old time, Thou shalt not commit adultery:

28 But I say unto you, That whosoever looketh on a woman to lust after her hath committed adultery with her already in his heart.

29 And if thy right eye offend thee, pluck it out, and cast *it* from thee: for it is profitable for thee that one of thy members should perish, and not *that* thy whole body should be cast into hell.

30 And if thy right hand offend thee, cut it off, and cast *it* from thee: for it is profitable for thee that one of thy members should perish, and not *that* thy whole body should be cast into hell.

31 It hath been said, Whosoever shall put away his wife, let him give her a writing of divorcement:

32 But I say unto you, That whosoever shall put away his wife, saving for the cause of fornication, causeth her to commit adultery: and whosoever shall marry her that is divorced committeth adultery.

33 ¶ Again, ye have heard that it hath been said by them of old time, Thou shalt not forswear thyself, but shalt perform unto the Lord thine oaths:

34 But I say unto you, Swear not at all; neither by heaven; for it is God's throne:

35 Nor by the earth; for it is his footstool: neither by Jerusalem; for it is the city of the great King.

36 Neither shalt thou swear by thy head, because thou canst not make one hair white or black.

37 But let your communication be, Yea, yea; Nay, nay: for whatsoever is more than these cometh of evil.

38 ¶ Ye have heard that it hath been said, An eye for an eye, and a tooth for a tooth:

39 But I say unto you, That ye resist not evil: but whosoever shall smite thee on thy right cheek, turn to him the other also.

40 And if any man will sue thee at the law, and take away thy coat, let him have *thy* cloak also.

41 And whosoever shall compel thee to go a mile, go with him twain.

42 Give to him that asketh thee, and from him that would borrow of thee turn not thou away.

43 ¶ Ye have heard that it hath been said, Thou shalt love thy neighbour, and hate thine enemy.

44 But I say unto you, Love your enemies, bless them that curse you, do good to them that hate you, and pray for them which despitefully use you, and persecute you:

45 That ye may be the children of your Father which is in heaven: for he maketh his sun to rise on the evil and on the good, and sendeth rain on the just and on the unjust.

46 For if ye love them which love you, what reward have ye? do not even the publicans the same?

47 And if ye salute your brethren only, what do ye more *than others?* do not even the publicans so?

48 Be ye therefore perfect, even as your Father which is in heaven is perfect.

Chapter 6

Take heed that ye do not your alms before men, to be seen of them: otherwise ye have no reward of your Father which is in heaven.

2 Therefore when thou doest *thine* alms, do not sound a trumpet before thee, as the hypocrites do in the synagogues and in the streets, that they may have glory of men. Verily I say unto you, They have their reward.

3 But when thou doest alms, let not thy left hand know what thy right hand doeth:

4 That thine alms may be in secret: and thy Father which seeth in secret himself shall reward thee openly.

5 ¶ And when thou prayest, thou shalt not be as the hypocrites *are*: for they love to pray standing in the synagogues and in the corners of the streets, that they may be seen of men. Verily I say unto you, They have their reward.

6 But thou, when thou prayest, enter into thy closet, and when thou hast shut thy door, pray to thy Father which is in secret; and thy Father which seeth in secret shall reward thee openly.

7 But when ye pray, use not vain repetitions, as the heathen *do*: for they think that they shall be heard for their much speaking.

8 Be not ye therefore like unto them: for your Father knoweth what things ye have need of, before ye ask him.

9 After this manner therefore pray ye: Our Father which art in heaven, Hallowed be thy name.

10 Thy kingdom come. Thy will be done in earth, as *it is* in heaven.

11 Give us this day our daily bread.

12 And forgive us our debts, as we forgive our debtors.

13 And lead us not into temptation, but deliver us from evil: For thine is the kingdom, and the power, and the glory, for ever, Amen.

14 For if ye forgive men their trespasses, your heavenly Father will also forgive you:

15 But if ye forgive not men their trespasses, neither will your Father forgive your trespasses.

16 ¶ Moreover when ye fast, be not, as the hypocrites, of a sad

countenance: for they disfigure their faces, that they may appear unto men to fast. Verily I say unto you, They have their reward.

17 But thou, when thou fastest, anoint thine head, and wash thy face;

18 That thou appear not unto men to fast, but unto thy Father which is in secret: and thy Father, which seeth in secret, shall reward thee openly.

19 ¶ Lay not up for yourselves treasures upon earth, where moth and rust doth corrupt, and where thieves break through and steal:

20 But lay up for yourselves treasures in heaven, where neither moth nor rust doth corrupt, and where thieves do not break through nor steal:

21 For where your treasure is, there will your heart be also.

22 The light of the body is the eye: if therefore thine eye be single, thy whole body shall be full of light.

23 But if thine eye be evil, thy whole body shall be full of darkness. If therefore the light that is in thee be darkness, how great *is* that darkness!

24 ¶ No man can serve two masters: for either he will hate the one, and love the other; or else he will hold to the one, and despise the other. Ye cannot serve God and mammon.

25 Therefore I say unto you, Take no thought for your life, what ye shall eat, or what ye shall drink: nor yet for your body, what ye shall put on. Is not the life more than meat, and the body than raiment?

26 Behold the fowls of the air: for they sow not, neither do they reap, nor gather into barns; yet your heavenly Father feedeth them. Are ye not much better than they?

27 Which of you by taking thought can add one cubit unto his stature?

28 And why take ye thought for raiment? Consider the lilies of the field, how they grow; they toil not, neither do they spin:

29 And yet I say unto you, That even Solomon in all his glory was not arrayed like one of these.

30 Wherefore, if God so clothe the grass of the field, which to day is, and to morrow is cast into the oven, *shall he* not much more *clothe* you, O ye of little faith?

31 Therefore take no thought, saying, What shall we eat? or, What shall we drink? or, Wherewithal shall we be clothed?

32 (For after all these things do the Gentiles seek:) for your heavenly Father knoweth that ye have need of all these things.

33 But seek ye first the kingdom of God, and his righteousness; and all these things shall be added unto you.

34 Take therefore no thought for the morrow: for the morrow shall take thought for the things of itself. Sufficient unto the day *is* the evil thereof.

Chapter 7

Judge not, that ye be not judged.

2 For with what judgment ye judge, ye shall be judged: and with what measure ye mete, it shall be measured to you again.

3 And why beholdest thou the mote that is in thy brother's eye, but considerest not the beam that is in thine own eye?

4 Or how wilt thou say to thy brother, Let me pull out the mote out of thine eye; and, behold, a beam *is* in thine own eye?

5 Thou hypocrite, first cast out the beam out of thine own eye; and then shalt thou see clearly to cast out the mote out of thy brother's eye.

6 ¶ Give not that which is holy unto the dogs, neither cast ye your pearls before swine, lest they trample them under their feet, and turn again and rend you.

7 ¶ Ask, and it shall be given you; seek, and ye shall find; knock, and it shall be opened unto you:

8 For every one that asketh receiveth; and he that seeketh findeth; and to him that knocketh it shall be opened.

9 Or what man is there of you, whom if his son ask bread, will he give him a stone?

10 Or if he ask a fish, will he give him a serpent?

11 If ye then, being evil, know how to give good gifts unto your children, how much more shall your Father which is in heaven give good things to them that ask him?

12 Therefore all things whatsoever ye would that men should do to you, do ye even so to them: for this is the law and the prophets.

13 ¶ Enter ye in at the strait gate: for wide *is* the gate, and broad *is* the way, that leadeth to destruction, and many there be which go in thereat:

14 Because strait *is* the gate, and narrow *is* the way, which leadeth unto life, and few there be that find it.

15 ¶ Beware of false prophets, which come to you in sheep's clothing, but inwardly they are ravening wolves.

16 Ye shall know them by their fruits. Do men gather grapes of thorns, or figs of thistles?

17 Even so every good tree bringeth forth good fruit; but a corrupt tree bringeth forth evil fruit.

18 A good tree cannot bring forth evil fruit, neither *can* a corrupt tree bring forth good fruit.

19 Every tree that bringeth not forth good fruit is hewn down, and cast into the fire.

20 Wherefore by their fruits ye shall know them.

21 ¶ Not every one that saith unto me, Lord, Lord, shall enter into the kingdom of heaven; but he that doeth the will of my Father which is in heaven.

22 Many will say to me in that day, Lord, Lord, have we not prophesied in thy name? and in thy name have cast out devils? and in thy name done many wonderful works?

23 And then will I profess unto them, I never knew you: depart from me, ye that work iniquity.

24 ¶ Therefore whosoever heareth these sayings of mine, and doeth them, I will liken him unto a wise man, which built his house upon a rock:

25 And the rain descended, and the floods came, and the winds blew, and beat upon that house: and it fell not: for it was founded upon a rock.

26 And every one that heareth these sayings of mine, and doeth them not, shall be likened unto a foolish man, which built his house upon the sand:

27 And the rain descended, and the floods came, and the winds blew, and beat upon that house; and it fell: and great was the fall of it.

28 And it came to pass, when Jesus had ended these sayings, the people were astonished at his doctrine:

29 For he taught them as *one* having authority, and not as the scribes.

From MEDITATIONS, c. AD 177

Marcus Aurelius

Matthew Arnold once called Aurelius "perhaps the most beautiful figure in history"; certainly he was amongst the most dutiful of Roman Emperors. A Stoic by inclination and education, his *Meditations*, composed whilst defending the Danube, outline the high ideals by which he lived his life. He died in AD 180, aged 59.

1. Injustice is a sin. Nature has constituted rational beings for their own mutual benefit, each to help his fellows according to their worth, and in no wise to do them hurt; and to contravene her will is plainly to sin against this eldest of all the deities. Untruthfulness, too, is a sin, and against the same goddess. For Nature is the nature of Existence itself; and existence connotes the kinship of all created beings. Truth is but another name for this Nature, the original creator of all true things. So, where a wilful lie is a sin because the deception is an act of injustice, an involuntary lie is also a sin because it is a discordant note in Nature's harmony, and creates mutinous disorder in an orderly universe. For mutinous indeed it is, when a man lets himself be carried, even involuntarily, into a position contrary to truth; seeing that he has so neglected the faculties Nature gave him that he is no longer able to distinguish the false from the true.

Again, it is a sin to pursue pleasure as a good and to avoid pain as an evil. It is bound to result in complaints that Nature is unfair in her rewarding of vice and virtue; since it is the bad who are so often in enjoyment of pleasures and the means to obtain them, while pains and events that occasion pains descend upon the heads of the good. Besides, if a man is afraid of pain, he is afraid of something happening which will be part of the appointed order of things, and this is itself a sin; if he is bent on the pursuit of pleasure, he will not stop at acts of injustice, which again is manifestly sinful. No; when Nature herself makes no distinction and if she did, she would not have brought pains and pleasures into existence side by side – it behoves those who would follow in her footsteps to be like-minded and exhibit the same indifference. He therefore who does not view with equal unconcern pain or pleasure, death or life, fame or dishonour – all of them employed by Nature without any partiality – clearly commits a sin. And in saying that Nature employs them without partiality, I mean that every successive generation of created things equally passes through the same experiences in turn; for this is the outcome of the original impulse which in the beginning moved Providence – by taking certain germs of future existences, and endowing them with productive powers of self-realization, of mutation, and of succession – to progress from the inception of the universe to its present orderly system.

2. A man of finer feelings would have taken leave of the world before ever sampling its falsehood, double-dealing, luxury, and pride; but now that all these have been tasted to satiety, the next best course would be to end your life forthwith. Or are you really resolved to go on dwelling in the midst of iniquity and has experience not yet persuaded you to flee from the pestilence? For infection of the mind is a far more dangerous pestilence than any unwholesomeness or disorder in the atmosphere around us. Insofar as we are animals, the one attacks our lives; but as men, the other attacks our manhood.

3. Despise not death; smile, rather, at its coming; it is among the things that Nature wills. Like youth and age, like growth and maturity, like the advent of teeth, beard, and grey hairs, like begetting, pregnancy, and childbirth, like every other natural process that life's seasons bring us, so is our dissolution. Never, then, will a thinking man view death lightly, impatiently, or scornfully; he will wait for it as but one more of Nature's processes. Even as you await the baby's emergence from the womb of your wife, so await the hour when the little soul shall glide forth from its sheath.

But if your heart would have comfort of a simpler sort, then there is no better solace in the face of death than to think on the nature of the surroundings you are leaving, and the characters you will no longer have to mix with. Not that you must find these offensive; rather, your duty is to care for them and bear with them mildly; yet never forget that you are parting from men of far other principles than your own. One thing, if any, might have held you back and bound you to life; the chance of fellowship with kindred minds. But when you contemplate the weariness of an existence in company so discordant, you cry, "Come quickly, Death, lest I too become forgetful of myself."

4. The sinner sins against himself; the wrongdoer wrongs himself, becoming the worse by his own action.

5. A man does not sin by commission only, but often by omission.

6. Enough if your present opinion be grounded in conviction, your present action grounded in unselfishness, and your present disposition contented with whatever befalls you from without.

7. Erase fancy; curb impulse; quench desire; let sovereign reason have the mastery.

8. A single life-principle is divided amongst all irrational creatures, and a single mind-principle distributed among the rational; just as this one earth gives form to all things earthy, and just as all of us who have sight and breath see by the self-same light and breathe of the self-same air.

9. All things that share the same element tend to seek their own kind. Things earthy gravitate towards earth, things aqueous flow towards one another, things aerial likewise – whence the need for the barriers which keep them forcibly apart. The tendency of flames is to mount skyward, because of the elemental fire; even here below, they are so eager for the company of their own kind that any sort of material, if it be reasonably dry, will ignite with ease, since there is only a minority of its ingredients which is resistant to fire. In the same way, therefore, all portions of the universal Mind are drawn towards one another. More strongly, indeed; since, being higher in the scale of creation, their eagerness to blend and combine with their affinities is proportionately keener. This instinct for reunion shows itself in its first stage among the creatures without reason, when we see bees swarming, cattle herding, birds nesting in colonies, and couples mating; because in them soul has already emerged, and in such relatively higher forms of life as theirs the desire for union is found at a level of intensity which is not present in stones or sticks. When we come to beings with reason, there are political associations, comradeships, family life, public meetings, and in times of war treaties and armistices; and among the still higher orders, a measure of unity even exists between bodies far separated from one another – as for example with the stars. Thus ascent in the ranks of creation can induce fellow-feeling even where there is no proximity.

Yet now see what happens. It is we – we, intelligent beings – who alone have forgotten this mutual zeal for unity; among us alone the currents are not seen to converge. Nevertheless, though man may flee as he will, he is still caught and held fast; Nature is too strong for him. Observe with care, and you will see: you will sooner find a fragment of earth unrelated to the rest of earth than a man who is utterly without some link with his fellows.

10. Everything bears fruit; man, God, the whole universe, each in its proper season. No matter that the phrase is restricted in common use to vines and such like. Reason, too, yields fruit, both for itself and for the world; since from it comes a harvest of other good things, themselves all bearing the stamp of reason.

11. Teach them better, if you can; if not, remember that kindliness has been given you for moments like these. The gods themselves show kindness to such men; and at times, so indulgent are they, will even aid them in their endeavours to secure health, wealth, or reputation. This you too could do; who is there to hinder you?

12. Work yourself hard, but not as if you were being made a victim, and not with any desire for sympathy or admiration. Desire one thing alone: that your actions or inactions alike should be worthy of a reasoning citizen.

13. Today I have got myself out of all my perplexities; or rather, I have got the perplexities out of myself – for they were not without, but within; they lay in my own outlook.

14. Everything is banal in experience, fleeting in duration, sordid in content; in all respects the same today as generations now dead and buried have found it to be.

15. Facts stand wholly outside our gates; they are what they are, and no more; they know nothing about themselves, and they pass no judgment upon themselves. What is it, then, that pronounces the judgment? Our own guide and ruler, Reason.

16. A rational and social being is not affected in himself for either better or worse by his feelings, but by his will; just as his outward behaviour, good or bad, is the product of will, not of feelings.

17. For the thrown stone there is no more evil in falling than there is good in rising.

18. Penetrate into their inmost minds, and you will see what manner of critics you are afraid of, and how capable they are of criticizing themselves.

19. All things are in process of change. You yourself are ceaselessly undergoing transformation, and the decay of some of your parts, and so is the whole universe.

20. Leave another's wrongdoing where it lies.

21. In the interruption of an activity, or the discontinuance and, as it were, death of an impulse, or an opinion, there is no evil. Look back at the phases of your own growth: childhood, boyhood, youth, age: each change itself a kind of death. Was this so frightening? Or take the lives you lived under your grandfather and then under your mother and then your father; trace the numerous differences and changes and discontinuances there were in those days, and ask yourself, "Were they so frightening?" No more so, then, is the cessation, the interruption, the change from life itself.

22. Your own mind, the Mind of the universe, your neighbour's mind – be prompt to explore them all. Your own, so that you may shape it to justice; the universe's, that you may recollect what it is you are a part of; your neighbour's, that you may understand whether it is informed by ignorance or knowledge, and also may recognize that it is kin to your own.

23. As a unit yourself, you help to complete the social whole; and similarly, therefore, your every action should help to complete the social life. Any action which is not related either directly or remotely to this social end disjoints that life, and destroys its unity. It is as much the act of a schismatic as when some citizen in a community does his utmost to dissociate himself from the general accord.

24. Childish squabbles, childish games, "petty breaths supporting corpses" – why, the ghosts in Homer have more evident reality!

25. First get at the nature and quality of the original cause, separate it from the material to which it has given shape, and study it; then determine the possible duration of its effects.

26. The woes you have had to bear are numberless because you were not content to let Reason, your guide and master, do its natural work. Come now, no more of this!

27. When those about you are venting their censure or malice upon you, or raising any other sort of injurious clamour, approach and penetrate into their souls, and see what manner of men they are. You will find little enough reason for all your painstaking efforts to win their good opinion. All the same, it still remains your duty to think kindly of them; for Nature has made them to be your friends, and even the gods themselves lend them every sort of help, by dreams and by oracles, to gain the ends on which their hearts are set.

28. Upwards and downwards, from age to age, the cycles of the universe follow their unchanging round. It may be that the World-Mind wills each separate happening in succession; and if so, then accept the consequences. Or, it may be, there was but one primal act of will, of which all else is the sequel; every event being thus the germ of another. To put it another way, things are either isolated units, or they form one inseparable whole. If that whole be God, then all is well; but if aimless chance, at least you need not be aimless also.

Soon earth will cover us all. Then in time earth, too, will change; later, what issues from this change will itself in turn incessantly change, and so again will all that then takes its place, even unto the world's end. To let the mind dwell on these swiftly rolling billows of change and transformation is to know a contempt for all things mortal.

29. The primal Cause is like a river in flood; it bears everything along. How ignoble are the little men who play at politics and persuade themselves that they are acting in the true spirit of philosophy. Babes, incapable even of wiping their noses! What then, you who are a man? Why, do what nature is asking of you at this moment. Set about it as the opportunity offers, and no glancing around to see if you are observed. But do not expect Plato's ideal commonwealth; be satisfied if even a trifling endeavour comes off well, and count the result no mean success. For who can hope to alter men's convictions; and without change of conviction what can there be but grudging subjection and feigned assent? Oh yes; now go on and talk to me of Alexander, and Philip, and Demetrius of Phaleron. If those men did in truth understand the will of Nature and school themselves to follow it, that is their own affair. But if it was nothing more than a stage-role they were playing, no court has condemned me to imitate their example. Philosophy is a modest profession, all simplicity and plain dealing. Never try to seduce me into solemn pretentiousness.

30. Look down from above on the numberless herds of mankind, with their mysterious ceremonies, their divers voyagings in storm and calm, and all the chequered pattern of their comings and gatherings and goings. Go on to consider the life of bygone generations; and then the life of all those who are yet to come; and even at the present day, the life of the hordes of far-off savages. In short, reflect what multitudes there are who are ignorant of your very name; how many more will have speedily forgotten it; how many, perhaps praising you now, who will soon enough be abusing you; and that therefore remembrance, glory, and all else together are things of no worth.

31. When beset from without by circumstance, be unperturbed; when prompted from within to action, be just and fair: in fine, let both will and deed issue in behaviour that is social and fulfils the law of your being.

32. Many of the anxieties that harass you are superfluous: being but creatures of your own fancy, you can rid yourself of them and expand into an ampler region, letting your thought sweep over the entire universe, contemplating the illimitable tracts of eternity, marking the swiftness of change in each created thing, and contrasting the brief span between birth and dissolution with the endless aeons that precede the one and the infinity that follows the other.

33. A little while, and all that is before your eyes now will have perished. Those who witness its passing will go the same road themselves before long; and then what will there be to choose between the oldest grandfather and the baby that died in its cradle?

34. Observe the instincts that guide these men; the ends they struggle for; the grounds on which they like and value things. In short, picture their souls laid bare. Yet they imagine their praises or censures have weight to help or hurt. What presumption!

35. Loss is nothing else but change, and change is Nature's delight. Ever since the world began, things have been ordered by her decree in the selfsame fashion as they are at this day, and as other similar things will be ordered to the end of time. How, then, can you say that it is all amiss, and ever will be so; that no power among all the gods in heaven can avail to mend it; and that the world lies condemned to a thraldom of ills without end?

36. The substance of us all is doomed to decay; the moisture and the clay, the bones, and the fetor. Our precious marble is but a callosity of the earth, our gold and silver her sediment; our raiment shreds of hair, our purple a fish's gore; and thus with all things else. So too is the very breath of our lives – ever passing as it does from this one to that.

37. Enough of this miserable way of life, these everlasting grumbles, these monkey antics. Why must you agitate yourself so? Nothing unprecedented is happening; so what is it that disturbs you? The form of it? Take a good look at it. The matter of it? Look well at that, too. Beyond

form and matter, there is nothing more. Even at this late hour, set yourself to become a simpler and better man in the sight of the gods. For the mastering of that lesson, three years are as good as a hundred.

38. If he sinned, the harm is his own. Yet perhaps, after all, he did not.

39. Either things must have their origin in one single intelligent source, and all fall into place to compose, as it were, one single body – in which case no part ought to complain of what happens for the good of the whole – or else the world is nothing but atoms and their confused minglings and dispersions. So why be so harassed? Say to the Reason at your helm, "Come, are you dead and in decay? Is this some part you are playing? Have you sunk to the level of a beast of the field, grazing and herding with the rest?"

40. The gods either have power or they have not. If they have not, why pray to them? If they have, then instead of praying to be granted or spared such-and-such a thing, why not rather pray to be delivered from dreading it, or lusting for it, or grieving over it? Clearly, if they can help a man at all, they can help him in this way. You will say, perhaps, "But all that is something they have put in my own power." Then surely it were better to use your power and be a free man, than to hanker like a slave and a beggar for something that is not in your power. Besides, who told you the gods never lend their aid even towards things that do lie in our own power? Begin praying in this way, and you will see. Where another man prays "Grant that I may possess this woman," let your own prayer be, "Grant that I may not lust to possess her." Where he prays, "Grant me to be rid of such-and-such a one," you pray, "Take from me my desire to be rid of him." Where he begs, "Spare me the loss of my precious child," beg rather to be delivered from the terror of losing him. In short, give your petitions a turn in this direction, and see what comes.

41. "When I was sick," says Epicurus, "I never used to talk about my bodily ailments. I did not," he says, "discuss any topics of that kind with my visitors. I went on dealing with the principles of natural philosophy; and the point I particularly dwelt on was how the mind, while having its part in all these commotions of the flesh, can still remain unruffled and pursue its own proper good. Nor," he adds, "did I give the doctors a chance to brag of their own triumphs; my life merely went on its normal way, smoothly and happily." In sickness, then, if you are sick, or in trouble of any other kind, be like Epicurus. Never let go your hold on philosophy for anything that may befall, and never take part in the nonsense that is talked by the ignorant and uninstructed (this is a maxim on which all schools agree). Concentrate wholly on the task before you, and on the instrument you possess for its accomplishment.

42. When you are outraged by somebody's impudence, ask yourself at once, "Can the world exist without impudent people?" It cannot; so do not ask for impossibilities. That man is simply one of the impudent whose

existence is necessary to the world. Keep the same thought present, whenever you come across roguery, double-dealing or any other form of obliquity. You have only to remind yourself that the type is indispensable, and at once you will feel kindlier towards the individual. It is also helpful if you promptly recall what special quality Nature has given us to counter such particular faults. For there are antidotes with which she has provided us: gentleness to meet brutality, for example, and other correctives for other ills. Generally speaking, too, you have the opportunity of showing the culprit his blunder – for everyone who does wrong is failing of his proper objective, and is thereby a blunderer. Besides, what harm have you suffered? Nothing has been done by any of these victims of your irritation that could hurtfully affect your own mind; and it is in the mind alone that anything evil or damaging to the self can have reality. What is there wrong or surprising, after all, in a boor behaving boorishly? See then if it is not rather yourself you ought to blame, for not foreseeing that he would offend in this way. You, in virtue of your reason, had every means for thinking it probable that he would do so; you forgot this, and now his offence takes you by surprise. When you are indignant with anyone for his perfidy or ingratitude, turn your thoughts first and foremost upon yourself. For the error is clearly your own, if you have put any faith in the good faith of a man of that stamp, or, when you have done him a kindness, if it was not done unreservedly and in the belief that the action would be its own full reward. Once you have done a man a service, what more would you have? Is it not enough to have obeyed the laws of your own nature, without expecting to be paid for it? That is like the eye demanding a reward for seeing, or the feet for walking. It is for that very purpose that they exist; and they have their due in doing what they were created to do. Similarly, man is born for deeds of kindness; and when he has done a kindly action, or otherwise served the common welfare, he has done what he was made for, and has received his quittance.

THE EDICT OF MILAN, AD 313

Emperors Constantine and Licinius

The legislation by which Christians were given toleration and civil rights throughout the Roman Empire. Constantine himself was converted to Christianity after beholding a vision of a flaming cross inscribed "In this conquer" before his successful battle against the rivalrous Maxentius at Milvian Bridge in 312. Christianity became the state religion of Rome in 324.

When I, Constantine Augustus, as well as I, Licinius Augustus, had fortunately met near Mediolanum [Milan] and were considering everything that pertained to the public welfare and security, we thought that, among other things which we saw would be for the good of many, those regulations pertaining to the reverence of the Divinity ought certainly to be made first, so that we might grant to the Christians and to all others full authority to observe that religion which each preferred; whence any Divinity whatsoever in the seat of the heavens may be propitious and kindly disposed to us and all who are placed under our rule. And thus by this wholesome counsel and most upright provision we thought to arrange that no one whatsoever should be denied the opportunity to give his heart to the observance of the Christian religion, or of that religion which he should think best for himself, so that the supreme Deity, to whose worship we freely yield our hearts, may show in all things His usual favour and benevolence. Therefore, your Worship should know that it has pleased us to remove all conditions whatsoever, which were in the rescripts formerly given to you officially, concerning the Christians, and now any one of these who wishes to observe the Christian religion may do so freely and openly, without any disturbance or molestation. We thought it fit to commend these things most fully to your care that you may know that we have given to those Christians free and unrestricted opportunity of religious worship. When you see that this has been granted to them by us, your Worship will know that we have also conceded to other religions the right of open and free observance of their worship for the sake of the peace of our times, that each one may have the free opportunity to worship as he pleases; this regulation is made that we may not seem to detract aught from any dignity or any religion. Moreover, in the case of the Christians especially, we esteemed it best to order that if it happens that anyone heretofore has bought from our treasury or from anyone whatsoever those places where they were previously accustomed to assemble, concerning which a certain decree had been made and a letter sent to you officially, the same shall be restored to the Christians without payment or any claim of recompense and without any kind of fraud or deception. Those, moreover, who have obtained the same by gift, are likewise to return them at once to the Christians. Besides, both those who have purchased and those who have secured them by gift, are to appeal to the vicar if they seek any recompense from our bounty, that they may be cared for through our clemency. All this property ought to be delivered at once to the community of the Christians through your intercession, and without delay. And since these Christians are known to have possessed not only those places in which they were accustomed to assemble, but also other property, namely the churches, belonging to them as a corporation and not as individuals, all these things which we have included under the above law, you will order to be restored, without any hesitation or controversy at all, to these Christians, that is to say to the corporations and their conventicles: – providing, of course, that the above arrangements be followed so that those who return the same without payment, as we have said, may hope for an indemnity from our bounty. In all these circumstances you ought to tender your most efficacious intervention to the community of the Christians, that our command may be carried into effect as quickly as possible, whereby, moreover, through our clemency, public order may be secured. Let this be done so that, as we have said above, Divine favour towards us, which, under the most important circumstances we have already experienced, may, for all time, preserve and prosper our successes together with the good of the state. Moreover, in order that the statement of this decree of our good will come to the notice of all, this rescript, published by your decree, shall be announced everywhere and brought to the knowledge of all, so that the decree of this, our benevolence, cannot be concealed.

From THE CONFESSIONS/
THE CITY OF GOD, AD 397/412–27

St Augustine

Augustine (354–430) was a ne'er-do-well in his youth, and his conversion
to Christianity – like many in his age – came only after an intense
personal struggle. He later related the experience in his spiritual auto-
biography, *The Confessions* (397). Once converted, however, Augustine
became one of the early church's most productive and deepest thinkers.
The City of God was begun as a riposte to the claims that the fall of Rome
in 410 was due to the enervating effect of Christianity on the Empire, but
in the writing became something altogether grander, a philosophy of
history, which presented human endeavour as a conflict between the
sacred (The City of Jerusalem: ie God) and the temporal (the City of
Babylon) which destined to end in the triumph of the City of God. This
was the first Christian philosophy of history, and its assurance of victory
would help maintain the morale of the Christian Church – which
embodied within it all the gains of Western civilization – through the
ensuing 1,000 years that were the Dark Ages.

From The Confessions

I desire to record all my past vileness and the carnal corruption of my soul:
not that I love the retrospect, but that I may love Thee, O my God. For
love of Thy love do I travel over again in the bitterness of my self-
examination my most wicked ways; that Thou mayest be my joy, my
never-failing joy, my blessed and fearless joy; that Thou mayest gather me
again from the scattering wherein I was torn limb from limb; for, when I
turned from the One, I melted away into the Many.

For in the time of youth I took my fill passionately among the wild
beasts, and I dared to roam the woods and pursue my vagrant loves

beneath the shade; and my beauty consumed away, and I was loathsome in Thy sight, pleasing myself and desiring to please the eyes of men.

God Is That True and Perfect Goodness, Whereof Temptation Is the Semblance

Alas, what was it then that I loved in thee, O my theft, thou midnight crime of my sixteenth year? How couldest thou be beautiful, seeing that thou wert a theft? Nay, art thou anything that I should thus apostrophise thee? Those pears that we stole were fair to look upon, because they were Thy creatures, O Thou Fairest of all and Creator of all, Thou good God, Thou Chief Good, my true Good. They were fair; but it was not for them that my wretched soul lusted. I had plenty of better pears; I gathered them only to steal. For I flung them away when gathered, and tasted no enjoyment but the wickedness, which gave me all my delight. For, if I did eat one of those pears, its flavour came from the sin . . .

Thus doth the soul play the harlot, when she turns away, and seeks outside Thee those joys which she can only find in their purity by returning to Thee. He does but imitate Thee badly who flies from Thee, and lifts up his horn against Thee. Yet by that bad imitation he proves that Thou art the Creator of all nature, and that therefore it is not possible to fly from Thee. What was it then that I loved in that theft of mine? How was I imitating my Lord in my bad and vicious way? Was there a pleasure in defying the law, by fraud if not by force, in playing at freedom in the prison-house, in showing that I could do wrong with impunity, which might seem a phantom of omnipotence? Lo, such is the servant who runs away from his Lord and attains a shadow. O what corruption! What a horrible life, what a deep gulf of death! To think that one should love what is forbidden, just because it is forbidden!

Pontitianus Describes the Life of Antony, the Egyptian Monk

And now will I tell and confess unto Thy Name, O Lord my Helper and my Redeemer, how Thou didst deliver me from the bond of the sexual desire by which I was so tightly held, and from the slavery of worldly affairs. I was pursuing my usual life, with ever-growing dissatisfaction, and daily was I sighing unto Thee. I attended Thy church, whenever there was a pause in that business under the burden whereof I groaned. With me was Alypius, now released from his legal duties after a third term of office as assessor, waiting to sell his experience to a new purchaser, as I was selling such faculty of speech as could be imparted by a teacher. Nebridius had proved his affection for us by accepting the post of lecturer under Verecundus, a citizen of Milan, professor of grammar, and one of our closest allies, who was in great need of a loyal colleague, and called, with the right of friendship, for the services of one of our company.

It was no desire of advancement, therefore, that had attracted Nebridius, for he might have obtained higher remuneration if he had chosen to keep to the teaching of literature, but he was too sweet and gentle a friend to refuse a request which appealed to his love. Yet he bore himself most discreetly, shunning the acquaintance of the great ones of this world, lest it should unsettle his mind; he wished to keep his freedom and reserve as many hours as possible of leisure for thought, or reading, or hearing lectures on philosophy.

On a certain day, then, when Nebridius for some reason was not present, it happened that Pontitianus paid a visit to Alypius and myself at our house. He was an African, and so a fellow-countryman, and held high rank in the household. He had some request to make, and we sat down and conversed. He noticed a volume lying on the draught table before us, picked it up, opened it, and to his great surprise found that it was the Apostle Paul, for what he expected to see was one of my wearisome rhetorical manuals. He looked at me with a smile, and told me how delighted he was to find so unexpectedly that book, and that alone on my table. For he was a faithful Christian, and often prostrated himself before Thee, our God, in church in long and frequent prayer. I replied that I spent much time over the scriptures, and this led him on to speak of Antony, the Egyptian monk, whose name was held in high honour by Thy servants, though I had never heard it till that hour. When he discovered my ignorance he enlarged his discourse, marvelling at our ignorance of so great a man, and gently showing us how great he was.

We listened with amazement to the tale of Thy wonders, so freshly wrought, almost in our own lifetime, so well attested, springing from the true faith and the bosom of the Catholic Church. We were all alike surprised, Alypius and I because the history was so extraordinary; he because we had never heard it. Thence he passed to speak of the crowded monasteries, and the ways of Thy sweetness, and the teeming solitudes of the desert, all strange news to us. There was a monastery at Milan, outside the city walls, full of good brothers, of whom Ambrose was foster-father; yet we had never heard of it. He went on talking, and we listened in silence. So he was led to tell us how once he and three of his comrades at Treves – the Emperor being detained at the afternoon games in the circus – went out for a stroll in the gardens beneath the city walls; how they parted company, two going off by themselves; how these two entered aimlessly into a house wherein dwelt certain of Thy servants, men poor in spirit, of whom is the kingdom of heaven, and found there a volume containing the life of Antony.

One of them began to read, and as he read his soul caught fire, so that then and there he began to think of plunging into the monastic life, and exchanging his worldly service for Thine. He was one of the officials of the Ministry of the Interior. Suddenly he was filled with holy love and sober shame, and, as if angered with himself, fixed his eyes upon his friend, saying. "Tell me, prithee, what goal are we seeking in all these toils of ours? What is it that we desire? What do we look to gain in the service? Can we hope in the palace to attain anything better than the friendship of the Emperor? How frail, how beset with perils is that prize! Through what dangers must we climb to a greater danger! And when shall we succeed? But, if I choose, I can be the friend of God from this moment."

He spoke, and, torn by the pangs of the new birth, returned to the book. As he read he was changed in the inner man, which Thou canst see, and his mind was alienated from the world, as soon appeared. For he read, with heart like a stormy sea; more than once he groaned, but he saw the better course, and made up his resolve. And so at last he said quite calmly to his friend, "I have broken with ambition, and determined to serve God. I am going to begin this moment, and here. If you do not care to follow my example, do not oppose me." "The service," replied the other, "is noble, and the wage is great; I will be your brother in arms." So both became Thine, and "built a tower at their own cost," having determined to give up all and follow Thee. Shortly afterwards Pontitianus and his companions, who had been walking in a different part of the garden and looking for the lost couple, arrived at the house, where they found them, and pressed them to return, as the sun had already set. But the two friends told them of the resolve which had so wonderfully sprung up and taken shape in their minds, and begged them not to take it ill if they refused to go with them. "So we," said Pontitianus, "who could not change our course, shed tears, not for them but for ourselves; we congratulated them on their godly decision, commended ourselves to their prayers, and went back to the palace, dragging our hearts along the ground, while they remained in the house, with hearts uplifted to heaven." Both these men were betrothed, but their wives that should have been, followed the example of their lovers, and consecrated their virginity to Thee.

How the Narrative of Pontitianus Pricked Augustine to the Heart
Such was the story that Pontitianus told. But, whilst he was speaking. Thou, O Lord, didst turn me round into my own sight. I had set myself, as it were, upon my own back, because I was unwilling to see myself, and now Thou didst place me before my own eyes so that I beheld how ugly I was, how deformed, and filthy, and spotted, and ulcerous. I beheld and shuddered, yet whither could I flee from myself? And, if I strove not to look upon myself, the tale of Pontitianus caught me again, and again didst Thou hold up to me my own portrait, and forced my eyes to gaze upon my very features, so that I might discover and loathe my own iniquity. I knew it; but feigned ignorance, and winked at it, and forgot it. But at that moment the warmer my love for that pair of friends, whose wholesome resolve to give themselves up altogether into Thy healing hands was still ringing in my ears, the deeper was my hatred of myself. How many of my

years – perhaps twelve whole years – had run to waste since the day when, as a youth of nineteen, I had read the Hortensius of Cicero, and heard the call to the study of wisdom. My plain duty was to scorn earthly delights and devote myself to the search after that happiness whereof the mere pursuit – not to speak of its attainment – is better than the possession of all the treasures and kingdoms of the world, better than all bodily pleasures, though they were to be had for a word. And yet I was wasting time.

Yea, wretched, O wretched youth that I had been, on the very threshold of my youth, I had even begged of Thee the gift of chastity; but I had said, "Give me chastity and self-control, but not just yet." For I was afraid lest Thou shouldest hear me in a moment, and in a moment heal that disease of lust, which I wanted to be sated, not eradicated. And I had wandered along the evil ways of godless superstition, not that I thought them right, only because I preferred them to others, which I angrily denounced without any serious reflection. And I flattered myself that the reason why, from day to day, I hesitated to cast off the world and its hopes and follow Thee alone, was that I could find no certain goal. And now the day had come when I was laid bare in my own sight, and the stern voice of conscience demanded, "Where is thy tongue? Wast thou not wont to say that thou wouldest not cast off the pack of thy vanity for an uncertain truth? Lo, the truth is certain, and thou art still bending under thy pack, while others, who have not wearied themselves in research, nor spent a long ten years in study, are putting forth wings from free shoulders."

Thus did a horrible shame gnaw and confound my soul while Pontitianus was speaking. He ended his tale, despatched the business which had brought him to our house, and departed. But how did I reproach myself! With what sharp reasons did I flog my soul to make it follow me in my effort to follow Thee! And it would not; it refused and would not even make an excuse. All its arguments had been tried and found wanting, yet it resisted in sullen disquiet, fearing, as if it were death, the closing of that running sore of evil habit by which it was being wasted to death.

He Goes into the Garden. What Befell Him There

Disordered in look and mind by this desperate wrestle with my own soul in the secret chambers of my own heart, I fell upon Alypius, crying out, "What has come to us? What means this tale that thou hast heard? Simple men arise and take heaven by violence, and we with all our heartless learning – see how we are wallowing in flesh and blood. Shall we stand still because they have taken the lead? Shall we not follow if we could not lead?" I scarcely knew what I said, and flung away, leaving him staring in silent astonishment. For my voice was changed; my face, eyes, colour, tone expressed my meaning more clearly than my words.

There was a garden to our lodging, of which we were free, as indeed we were of the whole house. For our host, the master of the house, did not live there. Thither the tumult of my breast drove me, where no one could interrupt the duel into which I had entered with myself, until it should reach the issue which Thou alone couldest foresee. I was mad, unto salvation; I was dying, unto life; I knew what evil thing I was; what good thing I was soon to be I knew not. I fled then into the garden, and Alypius followed me step for step. For I had no secret wherein he did not share, and how could he leave me in such distress? We sat down, as far from the house as possible. I was groaning in spirit, shaken with a gust of indignation, because I could not enter into Thy Will and Covenant, O my God; yet all my bones were crying out that this was the way, the best of all ways, and no ship is needed for that way, nor chart, no, nor feet, for it is not so far as from the house to the spot where we were seated.

For to go along that road, aye, and to reach the goal, is all one with the will to go; but it must be a strong and single will, not a broken-winged wish fluttering hither and thither, rising with one pinion, struggling and falling with the other. In fine, in the midst of that passionate indecision, I was doing many things which men sometimes will, yet cannot perform, because they have lost a limb, because their limbs are bound with fetters, or enfeebled by disease, or incapacitated in some other way. If I tore my hair, or beat my brow, or clasped my hands about my knees, it was because I willed to do so. Yet I might have willed in vain, if the nerves had not obeyed my bidding. Many things then I did, in which will and power to do were not the same, yet did not that one thing which seemed to me infinitely more desirable, which, before long, I should have power to will, because, before long, I should certainly will to will it. For in this the power of willing is the power of doing, and yet I could not do it. And so my body lent a ready obedience to the slightest desire of the soul, moving its limbs in instant compliance, while my soul could not aid itself in carrying out its great resolve, which needed but resolve to accomplish it.

Why the Mind Is Not Obeyed When It Commands Itself

Now whence and why is this strange anomaly? Let Thy mercy shine as the light; and suffer me to ask, if perchance I may find an answer amid the dark places of human chastisement, and the midnight of the contrition of the sons of Adam. Whence is this anomaly and why? Mind commands body, and there is instant obedience; mind commands mind, and there is rebellion. Mind commands the hand to move, and so facile is the process that you can hardly distinguish the order from its fulfilment; now the mind is mind and the hand is body. Mind commands mind to will, and, though it is one, it will not hear. Whence and why is this anomaly? I say it commands to will; and it would not command unless it did will, and yet its command is inoperative.

But it does not will wholly, and therefore it does not command wholly. For it commands, in so far as it wills, and its command is not executed, in so far as it does not will. For the will commands that there should be a will, and not another will but itself. Certainly it is not the full will that commands, hence it is not the very thing that it commands. For if it were the full will, it would not even command itself to be, because it would be already. And so this "will and will not" is no anomaly, but a sickness of the mind, which is weighed down by evil habit, and cannot rise wholly when uplifted by truth. And so there are two wills, because one of them is not whole, and one of them possesses what the other lacks.

Against the Manicheans Who Because There Are Two Contrary Wills Affirm the Existence of Two Contrary Natures

Let them perish from Thy presence, O God, yea, and they do perish, those vain talkers and seducers of the soul, who, because they have observed that in the act of deliberation there are two wills, maintain that there are two minds of differing natures, the one good and the other bad. They themselves are bad, while they hold these bad ideas, yet will they become good, if they see the truth and assent unto the truth, that Thy Apostle may say to them, "Ye were sometimes darkness, but now are ye light in the Lord." For these Manichees, wishing to be light not in the Lord but in themselves, imagining the essence of the soul to be the essence of God, have become thicker darkness than they were, for in their dread arrogance they have gone farther away from Thee, from Thee, the true Light which lighteth every man that cometh into the world. Mark what you say, and blush for shame. Draw near unto Him and be lightened, and your faces shall not be ashamed. Who was it that willed, who was it that could not will, when I was deliberating whether I should not at once serve the Lord my God, as I had long purposed to do? Was it not I, I myself? I could not fully will, I could not fully will not. And so I was at war with myself, and dragged asunder by myself. And the strife was against my will, yet it showed not the presence of a second mind, but the punishment of the one I had. Therefore it was no more I that wrought it, but sin that dwelt in me, the punishment of a sin that was more voluntary, because I was a son of Adam. For, if there are as many opposing natures as opposing wills, there will be not two but many more.

If a man deliberates whether he shall go to their conventicle or to the theatre they cry, "See, he has two natures; the good one draws him to us, the evil drags him back. For how else shall we account for this halting between conflicting wills?" But I say that both wills are bad, that which draws him to them, not less than that which drags him back to the theatre. They naturally think it a good will which pulls in their direction. But suppose one of our people is tossed about between two wills, to go to the theatre or to go to our church – will they not be puzzled what to say? Either they must reluctantly confess that the will which carries a man to our church is as good as that which carries their own professors and adherents to theirs, or they must allow that two evil natures and two evil minds are fighting in one man, and in this case their favourite doctrine that one is good and the other evil falls to the ground, or they must be converted to the truth, and cease to deny that, when a man deliberates, one soul is agitated by opposing wills. Let them then no longer maintain that, when two wills are contending in one man, two antagonistic minds, one good and one evil, are struggling over two antagonistic substances, created by two antagonistic principles.

For Thou, O God of truth, dost reprove and confute and convict them, for both wills may be bad, as when a man deliberates whether he shall murder by poison or by knife; whether he shall seize upon this field or the other, supposing that he cannot get both; whether he shall purchase pleasure by wantonness, or keep his money through covetousness; whether he shall go to the theatre or the circus, if there are shows at both on the same day; and there may be a third course open to him, for there may be a chance of robbing a house, and even a fourth, for there may be an opportunity of committing adultery as well.

Suppose that all these objects present themselves at the same time, and are all equally desired, yet cannot all be secured together, in this case they rend the mind with four conflicting wills, or even more, if there are more objects of desire. Yet they would not say that all these are different substances. The case is the same with good wills. For I ask them whether it is good to find sober delight in reading the Apostle, or in a psalm, or in discoursing upon the Gospel. They will say that each is good. What then if all are equally delightful, and all at the same time? Are not different wills distracting the heart, when we consider which we shall prefer? All are good, but they are in conflict, till one is chosen, and the will is no longer divided between many objects but poured in its full strength upon that one. So also, when eternity attracts us from above and the pleasure of earthly goods pulls us down from below, the soul does not will either the one or the other with all its force, but it is the same soul; and the reason why it is so vexed and torn is that truth forces it to love the better, while custom will not suffer it to cast away the worse.

The Flesh Wrestles with the Spirit in Augustine

Thus was I sick and tormented, reproaching myself more bitterly than ever, rolling and writhing in my chain till it should be wholly broken, for at present, though all but snapped, it still held me fast. And Thou, O Lord, wast urgent in my inmost heart, plying with austere mercy the scourges of fear and shame, lest I should fail once more, and the remnant of my worn and slender fetter, instead of breaking, should grow strong again, and bind me harder than ever. For I kept saying within myself, "O let it be now, let it be now"; and as I spoke the word I was on the verge of resolution. I was on the point of action, yet acted not; still I did not slip back into my former indifference, but stood close and took fresh breath. I tried again, and came a little nearer and a little nearer, I could all but touch and reach the goal, yet I did not quite reach or touch it, because I still shrank from dying unto death and living unto life, and the worse, which was ingrained, was stronger in me than the better, which was unstrained. And the moment, which was to make me different, affrighted me more the nearer it drew, but it no longer repelled or daunted, it only chilled me.

Trifles of trifles and vanities of vanities, my old mistresses, held me back; they caught hold of the garment of my flesh and whispered in my ear, "Can you let us go? and from that instant we shall see you no more for ever; and from that instant this and that will be forbidden you for ever." What did they mean, O my God, what did they mean by "this and that?" O let Thy mercy guard the soul of Thy servant from the vileness, the shame that they meant! As I heard them, they seemed to have shrunk to half their former size. No longer did they meet me face to face with open contradiction, but muttered behind my back, and, when I moved away, plucked stealthily at my coat to make me look back. Yet, such was my indecision, that they prevented me from breaking loose, and shaking myself free, and running after the voice that called me away; for strong habit supported them, asking me, "Do you think you can live without them?"

But the voice of Habit had lost its persuasion. For in that quarter to which I had set my face and was fain to fly, there dawned upon me the chaste dignity of Continence, calm and cheerful but not wanton, modestly alluring me to come and doubt not, holding out to welcome and embrace me her pious hands full of good examples. There might I see boys and girls, a goodly array of youth and of every age, grave widows and aged virgins, and in every one of them all was Continence herself, not barren but a fruitful mother of children, of joys born of Thee, her husband, O Lord. And she smiled upon me with a challenging smile, as if she would say, "Canst not thou do what these have done? Was it their power, was it not that of the Lord their God, that gave them strength? The Lord their God gave me unto them. Thou standest on thyself, and therefore standest not. Cast thyself on Him; fear not; He will not flinch, and thou wilt not fall. Cast thyself boldly upon Him; He will sustain thee, and heal thee." And I blushed, for still I heard the whispers of the daughters of vanity, and still I hung in the wind. And again she seemed to say, "Stop thine ears against thy unclean members upon earth, that they may be mortified. They tell thee of delights, but not according to the law of the Lord thy God." Such was the debate that raged in my heart, myself battling against myself. Alypius kept close to my side and waited in silence to see the issue of my strange agitation.

How by a Voice and by the Words of the Apostle He Was Wholly Converted

Now, when deep reflection brought forth from its secret stores the whole cloud of my misery, and piled it up in the sight of my heart, there rose a whirlwind, carrying with it a violent burst of tears. And hereupon I rose and left Alypius, till my weeping and crying should be spent. For solitude seemed fitter for tears. So I went farther off, till I could feel that even his presence was no restraint upon me. Thus it was with me, and he guessed my feelings. I suppose I had said something before I started up; and he noticed that my voice was fraught with tears. So he remained upon the bench lost in wonder. I flung myself down under a fig tree, and gave my tears free course, and the floods of mine eyes broke forth, an acceptable sacrifice in Thy sight. And I cried unto Thee incessantly, not in these words, but to this purpose, "And Thou, O Lord, how long? How long, O Lord; wilt Thou be angry for ever? O remember not our iniquities of old times." For I felt that I was held fast by them, and I went on wailing, "How long, how long? tomorrow and tomorrow? Why not now? why not this hour make an end of my vileness?"

Thus I spoke, weeping in bitter contrition of heart, when, lo, I heard a voice from the neighbouring house. It seemed as if some boy or girl, I knew not which, was repeating in a kind of chant the words, "Take and read, take and read." Immediately, with changed countenance, I began to think intently whether there was any kind of game in which children sang those words; but I could not recollect that I had ever heard them. I stemmed the rush of tears, and rose to my feet; for I could not think but that it was a divine command to open the Bible, and read the first passage I lighted upon. For I had heard that Antony had happened to enter a church at the moment when this verse of the Gospel was being read, "Go, sell all that thou hast and give to the poor, and thou shalt have treasure in heaven; and come and follow Me," that he had taken these words home to himself, and by this oracle been converted to Thee on the spot.

I ran back then to the place where Alypius was sitting; for, when I quitted him, I had left the volume of the Apostle lying there. I caught it up, opened it, and read in silence the passage on which my eyes first fell, "Not in rioting and drunkenness, not in chambering and wantonness, not in strife and envying: but put ye on the Lord Jesus Christ, and make not provision for the flesh to fulfil the lusts thereof." No further would I read, nor was it necessary. As I reached the end of the sentence, the light of peace seemed to be shed upon my heart, and every shadow of doubt melted away. I put my finger, or some other mark, between the leaves, closed the volume, and with calm countenance told Alypius. And then he revealed to me his own feelings, which were unknown to me. He asked to see what I had read. I showed him the text, and he read a little further than I had done, for I knew not what followed.

What followed was this: "Him that is weak in the faith receive." This he explained to me as applying to himself. These words of warning gave him strength, and with good purpose and resolve, following the bent of his moral character, which had always been much better than mine, without any painful hesitation, he cast in his lot with me. Immediately we went in to my mother, and to her great joy told her what had happened. But, when we explained to her how it had come to pass, she was filled with exultation and triumph, and blessed Thee, who art able to do above that we ask or think. For she saw that Thou hadst granted her far more than she had ever asked for me in all her tearful lamentations. For so completely didst Thou convert me to Thyself that I desired neither wife nor any hope of this world, but set my feet on the rule of faith, as she had seen me in her vision so many years ago. So Thou didst turn her mourning into joy, joy fuller by far than she had ventured to pray for, dearer and purer by far than that which she had hoped to find in the children of my flesh.

From *The City of God*: "The State of the Two Cities, the Heavenly and the Earthly"

Two loves therefore, have given original to these two cities: self-love in contempt of God unto the earthly, love of God in contempt of one's self to the heavenly; the first seeks the glory of men, and the latter desires God only as the testimony of the conscience, the greatest glory. That glories in itself, and this in God. That exalts itself in self-glory: this says to God: "My glory and the lifter up of my head." That boasts of the ambitious conquerors, led by the lust of sovereignty: in this every one serves other in charity, both the rulers in counselling and the subjects in obeying. That loves worldly virtue in the potentates: this says unto God, "I will love Thee, O Lord, my strength." And the wise men of that, follow either the good things of the body, or mind, or both: living according to the flesh: and such as might know God, honoured Him not as God, nor were thankful but became vain in their own imaginations, and their foolish heart was darkened: for professing themselves to be wise, that is, extolling themselves proudly in their wisdom, they became fools: changing the glory of the incorruptible God to the likeness of the image of a corruptible man, and of birds and four-footed beasts and serpents: for they were the people's guides or followers unto all those idolatries, and served the creature more than the Creator who is blessed for ever. But in this other, this heavenly city, there is no wisdom of man, but only the piety that serves the true God and expects a reward in the society of the holy angels, and men, that God may be all in all.

Part Two

The Age of Faith

The Medieval World, 515–1516

INTRODUCTION

With the fall of Rome to Alaric the Visigoth, the West entered the Dark Ages. For four centuries, Europe was in almost constant flux as barbarian tribes uprooted and migrated under pressure of advancing nomads from the east. One former province alone, England, endured invasions by Angles, Saxons and Jutes from north Germany and Denmark. Then, in the 780s, the Vikings of Scandinavia bore down on the country in their longships. At first there was stout resistance, but by 1016 England had become part of the Danish empire of Canute. With war came, always, its attendants of famine and pestilence. Population stagnated.

England was not particularly unfortunate – most other western realms endured changes of tenure. In the midst of this anarchy, vestiges of civilization continued. Barbarians they might have been, but most Germanic tribesmen were quick to see the advantages of Roman law, while a distinct corner of the Mediterranean remained forever (until 1452, anyway) Roman with the city-state of Byzantium. But much the most important citadel of civilization in wider Europe was the Christian Church which endured, even triumphed; for the story of the Middle Ages in the West is the story of the growth of faith. After establishing the supremacy of the Church in Rome, successive popes, beginning with Gregory the Great (AD 540–604) sent out missions to heathen lands, their efforts consolidated by the vigorous monastic movement inaugurated by Benedict of Nursia. Everywhere they were founded, monasteries acted as centres of worship, of scholarship, and even welfare centres for the local poor. By 700 most of Western Europe had been converted. In 732, a tribe of former heathens, the Franks, saved Christian Europe from an invasion by followers of another dynamic monotheistic religion – Islam, founded by the prophet Muhammad (AD 570–632). The Arab

Muslim onrush into Europe was stopped at Tours[1] by a Frankish force under Charles Martel.

Culturally, it might be said, the Frankish triumph at Tours was not much of a victory. Islam, following the injunction of Muhammad to "seek knowledge", was far advanced in astronomy, medicine and much else. Arab cities even had pavements and lights. Some cultural seepage from Islam came into Christian Europe, notably through the south of Spain (held by the Muslims until 1492), but in general Christendom was intellectually defensive. (This seepage included the arithmetical concept of "zero".) The great walls of medieval Europe, around cities and forts, were but the physical manifestation of the fortifications around the medieval mind.

Of course, these walls could be breached. The German and Scandinavian "heathen" tribes had already done so, introducing their heroic-warrior culture into the urbane Graeco-Romano-Judaeo tradition of Christian culture. Depressing as the epic *Beowulf* might be – for Beowulf dies fighting the dragon – it communicated important ideas of heroism, of physical courage and dynamic energy. By the 10th century at the latest, the northern warrior-ideal had become synthesized into the Western tradition, just as the northerns themselves had become assimilated and Christianized.

The end of that selfsame century witnessed a millennial angst, especially among the peasantry shackled to land and lord by the economic and social system known as feudalism. The doom which gripped the peasantry was that the world would end of the last day of 999. It didn't, of course, and the medieval world collectively sighed its relief.

Perhaps the sense of reprieve stirred the medieval spirit. For over the next 100 years there was a distinct awakening of Europe. Economically, improved agriculture and trade stimulated the growth of cities, which themselves were quick to dissolve old bonds. Serfs who escaped to cities became freemen: "City air is free air," cried medieval peasants. Many of these freemen set up as artisans, formed themselves into guilds – the first trades unions – and guildsmen came to play a part in the government of their city. (Modern local political democracy dates directly from this development.) Into the city also escaped new ideas, particularly from the men (and women) who participated in the Crusades to the Holy Land, which began with Pope Urban II's call to the warriors of Christendom in 1095. Reflecting – or even underpinning – the whole process of awakening was a philosophic ferment in the Christian Church: "the Battle of Universals".

[1] Feudalism, incidentally, was born at the battle of Tours; Martel, impressed by the Muslim cavalryman's use of stirrups – which enabled him to fight with lance or sword – emulated him in the creation of a cadre of horsemen who received a grant of land – *feudum*- in return for an oath of service).

The main doctrine of the Christian Church since St Augustine (354–430) was quite simply "faith". As Augustine put it: "I believe in order that I might know." Faith in the scriptures gave knowledge; if reason ever seemed at variance with this knowledge then it – reason – was wrong. Upon such belief was built the Medieval Cathedral – one of the finest expressions of man's artistry – but so too were the edifices of Scholasticism and Realism. The first was dry-as-dust study of the Bible (the Pharisees would have approved) and the second was Augustine's adaptation of Plato, whereby ultimate reality existed in the Mind of God only. The ins and outs of neo-platonism confused even medieval theologians, but suffice it to say, the practical result was that the human being and the earthly world was not deemed worthy of study. As Augustine put it: "go not out of doors . . . in the Inner Man dwells truth."

"The Battle of Universals" began when Roscellinus put forward his doctrine of Nominalism which held that physical things were the only reality (which is the "common sense" position of most people today). The Parisian scholar Peter Abelard, perhaps best known for his tragic love affair with Heloïse, maintained a middle-road position of Conceptualism.

There was another contributor to "the Battle of Universals", Aristotle. Although Aristotle's logic was familiar to most medieval Christian scholars his other works were unknown. This changed in about 1200 when Arabic editions of almost his entire *oeuvre* were discovered and translated into Latin. That Aristotelian scientific method eventually proved flawed (see pp 224–7) hardly mattered; it was Aristotle's objects of study which mesmerized medieval man. Nothing human or natural was alien to Aristotle.

Initially, the Church reacted by banning, then "abridging" Aristotle's books, but the intellectual cat was out of the bag. It took the magnificent mind of St Thomas Aquinas to develop a reconciliation of faith and reason (one which remains the official position of the Catholic Church today), whereby man's soul and body were of equal veneration.

Thus justified, medieval man could look beyond the walls. The doors to science and art were open.

Alas for the Church, Aquinas' endeavour ran contrary to one current of the times. In *Summa contra Gentiles*, 1259–64, and *Summa Theologiae*, 1266–73, Aquinas provides elaborate justification for the pyramid structure of feudal society, with king and pope at top, the peasants at the bottom. This conservatism, which would eventually relegate Catholicism to the backburner of democratic Western history, met neither the political nor social-mobility aspirations of the artisan class, and had no chance at all of success with the king. The nation state, headed by the monarch, was already on the rise and, far from sharing power with the pope at the top of the pyramid, the king would seek to chuck him off. It was precisely this dispute between State and Church which caused Henry II of England to call for Archbishop Thomas à Becket's murder in 1170. The Church's political woes were only increased by its corruption. "God has given us the papacy." said the Borgia Pope Alexander VI, "let us enjoy it." Such manifest sin alienated many.

The king had his problems too. This was most evident in England where the tree of political liberty had already been planted. Under the Saxon kings, the nobles of the land had been accustomed to being consulted by the king at the Witan, or council. The Normans might have invaded in 1066 but the remembrance of customs past lived on; besides the Norman barons themselves soon wanted a voice in the place where things were discussed (in Norman French, a place of *parlement*). Through successive legislation, the 1101 Coronation Charter of Henry I, the 1135 Charter of King Stephen, the 1166 Assize of Clarendon, and the famous 1215 *Magna Carta*, the royal prerogative was curtailed, a parliamentary tradition established (only for the nobles as yet, but the rest would come) and a legal system begun that allowed individual rights and trial by jury.

England was unique in these things, but by the middle of the 14th century it was clear that monarchical grip was slipping in other European countries. This was especially evident in Italy where merchant families – led by the Medicis of Florence – were the harbingers of capitalism, their liquid money destroying the lod systems of feudal oaths and tied land. These monied merchants also helped pay, with their patronage, for the revival of Italian interest in the classical civilizations of antiquity which proceed through the Aquinas-influenced humanism of Petrarca's "Letter to Posterity" to the full-blown "Renaissance". Against the otherwordly concerns of the medieval craftsman, the artist of the Renaissance took pride in worldly affairs and Man himself. In Michelangelo Buonarroti's painting *Creation of Man*, the man is the focus, dominating even God.

Michelangelo was the archetypal "Renaissance Man", magnificent as painter, poet and sculptor alike. There were other such cultural prodigies – Leonardo da Vinci, Raphael, Benvenuto Cellini among them. Underpinning their achievements was patronage by a wealthy merchant class. One of the by-products of the Crusades had been to stimulate trade in such north Italian cities as Genoa, Florence, Milan and Venice. The rich merchant families – led by the Medicis in Florence – largely paid for the Renaissance. The self same merchants were the harbingers of capitalism; it was the money of the towns which sounded the death knell for feudalism.

The humanistic, enquiring spirit of the Renaissance, however, was not confined to artistic endeavour. Above all it caused men to explore the world around them.

Exploration was not merely a matter of the mind's desire. It was predicated on technological developments. Apart from the Atlantic voyages of the Vikings in the tenth century and Marco Polo's overland journey to China, medieval Europeans had made few long-distance explorations. A chief reason was the poor manoeuvrability of the medieval "cog" ship, with its single square sail and lack of navigational aids. Medieval ships rarely sailed out of sight of land. But by the end of the fifteenth century, the cog had been replaced by the three-master with variable sails and a stern rudder. The magnetic compass had also arrived (probably from China, via the Arabs, who had sent an embassy to China as early as 651). Thus equipped, European sailors could sail far over the Ocean Blue.

One who did so, in 1492, was Christopher Columbus. A Genoese in the employ of the Spanish throne, Columbus was possessed by the revolutionary idea that by sailing westwards across the Atlantic he would reach Asia – this is at a time when almost everyone thought the world was flat. After 69 days afloat Columbus landed in the Bahamas. Inadvertently, he had discovered a New World. The importance of Christopher Columbus's journey is difficult to overestimate. Because of him, other Europeans sailed to America and colonized it; because of him Ferdinand Magellan would lead an expedition that circumnavigated the globe for the first time; because of him Europe would come to dominate the modern world.

If the precise moment when the medieval became the modern world is impossible to pin down, 1517 is as good a year as any. The New World had been discovered and the Renaissance was at its apogee. Capitalism was seeded in the merchant towns of Europe, and in Germany a little-known theologian by the name of Martin Luther would in this year pin a set of proclamations on a church door in Wittenberg.
So was Protestantism established.

And it was the creed of Protestantism which would dominate and direct the advances of Western civilization throughout the modern era.

THE MONASTIC RULE OF ST BENEDICT, c. 515

The *Regula Monachorum* of Benedict of Nursia (c. 480–547) was the model
of organization for all Western monasteries.

Prologue. We are about to found *a school for the Lord's service*; in the
organization of which we trust that we shall ordain nothing severe and
nothing burdensome. But even if, the demands of justice dictating it,
something a little irksome shall be the result . . . thou shalt not therefore,
struck by fear, flee the way of salvation. But as one's way of life and one's
faith progresses, the heart becomes broadened, and with unutterable
sweetness of love, the way of the mandates of the Lord is traversed.

What the Abbot should be like. An abbot who is worthy to preside over a
monastery ought always to remember what he is called, and carry out with
his deeds the *name* of a "Superior"; for he is believed to be Christ's
representative. And so the abbot should not teach or decree or order
anything apart from the precept of the Lord; but his order or teaching
should be sprinkled with the ferment of divine justice in the minds of his
disciples. . . . [Only where he has exercised his uttermost care and ability
can he be absolved of responsibility to God if his monks go astray.]

Concerning obedience. [The monks are to practise humility by implicitly
obeying their superiors.] And in the same moment let command of the
master and the perfected work of the disciple – both together in the
swiftness of the fear of God – be called into being by those who are
possessed with a desire of advancing to eternal salvation. Thus living not
according to their own judgment, nor obeying their own desires and
commands, let them desire an abbot to rule over them.

Whether the monks should have anything of their own? More than any
other thing is this special vice to be cut off root and branch from the
monastery, that one should presume to give or receive *anything* without
the order of the abbot, or should have anything of his own. He should have

absolutely nothing – neither a book, nor tablets, nor a pen – nothing at all – for indeed it is not allowable to the monks to have their own bodies or wills in their own power; but all things necessary they must expect of the Father of the monastery.

Concerning the food allowance. We believe that for the daily refection of the sixth as well as of the ninth hour two cooked dishes, on account of the infirmities of the different ones, are enough for all tables; so that, per-chance, whoever cannot eat of one dish may partake of the other. Therefore let two cooked dishes suffice for all the brothers; if it is possible to obtain apples or growing vegetables, a third may be added. One full pound of bread shall suffice for a day; and [. . . half a hemina of wine,[1] but care must be taken to prevent overindulgence].

Concerning the daily manual labour. Idleness is the enemy of the soul. And therefore, at fixed times, the brothers ought to be occupied in manual labour; and again at fixed times in sacred reading. Therefore we believe that both seasons ought to be arranged [so that the time for sleeping, praying, working, eating, and reading be carefully apportioned].

Whether a monk should be allowed to receive letters or anything? By no means shall it be allowed to a monk – either from his relatives, or from any man, or from one of his fellows – to receive or give, without order of the abbot, letters, presents, or any gift however small. But even if by his relatives anything has been sent to him, he shall not presume to receive it, unless it has been first shown to the abbot. But if he order it to be received, it shall be in the power of the abbot to give it to whomever he will; and the brother to whom it happened to be sent shall not be chagrined.

[*The Independence of the monastery from the world.*] A monastery ought – if it can be done – to be so arranged that everything necessary – water, a mill, a garden, a bakery – may be made use of, and different arts be carried on within the monastery, so that there shall be no need for the monks to wander about outside; for this is not at all good for their souls.

How the monks shall sleep. They shall sleep separately in separate beds. If it can be done, they shall all sleep in one place; [if too numerous] by tens and twenties. A candle shall always be burning in that same cell until early in the morning. They shall sleep clothed, and girt with belts or with ropes, and they shall not have their knives at their sides while they sleep, lest perchance in a dream they should wound the sleepers. And let the monks be always on the alert [to rise with great promptness, without grumbling, upon the signal].

---

[1] About half a pint.

THE RULES OF COURTLY LOVE, c. 1150

Andreas Capellanus

The "Courts of Love" of medieval France (predominantly) produced *faux* legal codes governing aristocratic etiquette. Manifestly superficial and elitist they nonethless played a part in the civilizing of feudal Europe. The Courts were overseen by women whose husbands were away at the wars and crusades, thus allowing a rare chance for the feminization of public behaviour, then based on a feudal martial code. The whole chivalric ideal of Sir Lancelot is heavily perfumed by feminine mystique.

Love is a certain inborn suffering derived from the sight of and excessive meditation upon the beauty of the opposite sex, which causes each one to wish above all things the embraces of the other and by common desire to carry out all of love's precepts in the other's embrace.

The Rules

1. Marriage is no real excuse for not loving.
2. He who is not jealous cannot love.
3. No one can be bound by a double love.
4. It is well known that love is always increasing or decreasing.
5. That which a lover takes against the will of his beloved has no relish.
6. Boys do not love until they arrive at the age of maturity.
7. When one lover dies, a widowhood of two years is required of the survivor.
8. No one should be deprived of love without the very best of reasons.
9. No one can love unless he is impelled by the persuasion of love.
10. Love is always a stranger in the home of avarice.
11. It is not proper to love any woman whom one would be ashamed to seek to marry.

12. A true lover does not desire to embrace in love anyone except his beloved.
13. When made public love rarely endures.
14. The easy attainment of love makes it of little value: difficulty of attainment makes it prized.
15. Every lover regularly turns pale in the presence of his beloved.
16. When a lover suddenly catches sight of his beloved his heart palpitates.
17. A new love puts to flight an old one.
18. Good character alone makes any man worthy of love.
19. If love diminishes, it quickly fails and rarely revives.
20. A man in love is always apprehensive.
21. Real jealousy always increases the feeling of love.
22. Jealousy, and therefore love, are increased when one suspects his beloved.
23. He whom the thought of love vexes eats and sleeps very little.
24. Every act of a lover ends in the thought of his beloved.
25. A true lover considers nothing good except what he thinks will please his beloved.
26. Love can deny nothing to love.
27. A lover can never have enough of the solaces of his beloved.
28. A slight presumption causes a lover to suspect his beloved.
29. A man who is vexed by too much passion usually does not love.
30. A true lover is constantly and without intermission possessed by the thought of his beloved.
31. Nothing forbids one woman being loved by two men or one man by two women.

MAGNA CARTA, 1215

The most famous document in English history, the "Great Charter" was negotiated over five days in 1215 in a meadow at Runnymede, beside the Thames. A dog's dinner of demands and compromises between the dissident barons and King John, it failed miserably to achieve the aim to which it was set: a political ceasefire. No sooner had the barons and monarch signed the charter on June 15 than they regretted it and embarked upon civil war.

That said, *Magna Carta* was destined to become the "Palladium of Liberty" for good reason. Although the baronial class sought mostly in *Magna Carta* to protect itself from feudal financial abuse by their overlord, the king (see, *inter alia*, Clauses 2, 8, 12, 20), they also formulated and codified notions of government from which the English have never departed. In Clause 39, no freeman is to be punished except by lawful judgment of his equals and the law of the land – thus guaranteeing trial by jury. The selfsame principle of trial by jury also prevented government from misusing the courts to silence its critics or to disguise tyranny in the cloak of justice. Additionally, Clause 40 opened up the courts to all freemen without payment and regardless of the king's favour.

The definite beginnings of Parliament are to be seen in Clause 14 which provided for a meeting of those which held land of the crown to consent (or not) to levies of "aid" requested by the monarch. Those "summoned" were the great and the powerful; it was representation of the rich, of course, but representation nontheless.

Other freedoms are enshrined in Magna Carta. A subject is free to leave and re-enter the country (save in times of war) in Clause 42. A subject is protected from arbitrary confiscations of property by the state in Clauses 28, 30 and 31.

Yet the importance of *Magna Carta* in the history of liberty lay less in its individual provisions than for the principle which overarched it – that the power of the king (read: government) is subject to the law of the land and the voice of his subjects. This principle quickly entered common law and the popular psyche.

Indeed *Magna Carta* became a state of mind: succeeding generations joyfully proclaimed all sorts of liberties in the name of *Magna Carta* which were not actually intended by the constitutional document itself. "Freeman", for instance, which had a particular and narrow meaning in 1215, was soon held to mean "Everyman", and trial by jury was transmogrified from a specific right to a universal one. In the name of *Magna Carta* the English revolted against Stuart tyranny in 1642. Even as late as the 20th century, *Magna Carta* served to rally the libertarian sensibilities of the English (and by extension under the Act of Union, the remainder of the peoples of the British isles), who fought Nazidom as the people of *Magna Carta*.

John, by the grace of God King of England, Lord of Ireland, Duke of Normandy and Aquitaine, and Count of Anjou, to his archbishops, bishops, abbots, earls, barons, justices, foresters, sheriffs, stewards, servants, and to all his officials and loyal subjects, Greeting.

Know that before God, for the health of our soul and those of our ancestors and heirs, to the honour of God, the exaltation of the holy Church, and the better ordering of our kingdom, at the advice of our reverend fathers Stephen, archbishop of Canterbury, primate of all England, and cardinal of the holy Roman Church, Henry archbishop of Dublin, William bishop of London, Peter bishop of Winchester, Jocelin bishop of Bath and Glastonbury, Hugh bishop of Lincoln, Walter bishop of Coventry, Benedict bishop of Rochester, Master Pandulf subdeacon and member of the papal household, Brother Aymeric master of the knighthood of the Temple in England, William Marshal earl of Pembroke, William earl of Salisbury, William earl of Warren, William earl of Arundel, Alan de Galloway constable of Scotland, Warin Fitz Gerald, Peter Fitz Herbert, Hubert de Burgh seneschal of Poitou, Hugh de Neville, Matthew Fitz Herbert, Thomas Basset, Alan Basset, Philip Daubeny, Robert de Roppeley, John Marshal, John Fitz Hugh and other loyal subjects:

(1) First, that we have granted to God, and by this present charter have confirmed for us and our heirs in perpetuity, that the English Church shall be free, and shall have its rights undiminished, and its liberties unimpaired. That we wish this so to be observed, appears from the fact that of our own free will, before the outbreak of the present dispute between us and our barons, we granted and confirmed by charter the freedom of the Church's elections – a right reckoned to be of the greatest necessity and importance to it – and caused this to be confirmed by Pope Innocent III. This freedom we shall observe ourselves, and desire to be observed in good faith by our heirs in perpetuity.

To all free men of our kingdom we have also granted, for us and our heirs for ever, all the liberties written out below, to have and to keep for them and their heirs, of us and our heirs:

(2) If any earl, baron, or other person that holds lands directly of the Crown, for military service, shall die, and at his death his heir shall be of full age and owe a "relief", the heir shall have his inheritance on payment of the ancient scale of "relief". That is to say, the heir or heirs of an earl shall pay £100 for the entire earl's barony, the heir or heirs of a knight 100s. at most for the entire knight's "fee", and any man that owes less shall pay less, in accordance with the ancient usage of "fees".

(3) But if the heir of such a person is under age and a ward, when he comes of age he shall have his inheritance without "relief" or fine.

(4) The guardian of the land of an heir who is under age shall take from it only reasonable revenues, customary dues, and feudal services. He shall do this without destruction or damage to men or property. If we have given the guardianship of the land to a sheriff, or to any person answerable to us for the revenues, and he commits destruction or damage, we will exact compensation from him, and the land shall be entrusted to two worthy and prudent men of the same "fee", who shall be answerable to us for the revenues, or to the person to whom we have assigned them. If we have given or sold to anyone the guardianship of such land, and he causes destruction or damage, he shall lose the guardianship of it, and it shall be handed over to two worthy and prudent men of the same "fee", who shall be similarly answerable to us.

(5) For so long as a guardian has guardianship of such land, he shall maintain the houses, parks, fish preserves, ponds, mills, and everything else pertaining to it, from the revenue of the land itself. When the heir comes of age, he shall restore the whole land to him, stocked with plough-teams and such implements of husbandry as the season demands and the revenues from the land can reasonably bear.

(6) Heirs may be given in marriage, but not to someone of lower social standing. Before a marriage takes place, it shall be made known to the heir's next-of-kin.

(7) At her husband's death, a widow may have her marriage portion and inheritance at once and without trouble. She shall pay nothing for her dower, marriage portion, or any inheritance that she and her husband held jointly on the day of his death. She may remain in her husband's house for forty days after his death, and within this period her dower shall be assigned to her.

(8) No widow shall be compelled to marry, so long as she wishes to remain without a husband. But she must give security that she will not marry without royal consent, if she holds her lands of the Crown, or without the consent of whatever other lord she may hold them of.

(9) Neither we nor our officials will seize any land or rent in payment of a debt, so long as the debtor has movable goods sufficient to discharge the

debt. A debtor's sureties shall not be distrained upon so long as the debtor himself can discharge his debt. If, for lack of means, the debtor is unable to discharge his debt, his sureties shall be answerable for it. If they so desire, they may have the debtor's lands and rents until they have received satisfaction for the debt that they paid for him, unless the debtor can show that he has settled his obligations to them.

(10) If anyone who has borrowed a sum of money from Jews dies before the debt has been repaid, his heir shall pay no interest on the debt for so long as he remains under age, irrespective of whom he holds his lands. If such a debt falls into the hands of the Crown, it will take nothing except the principal sum specified in the bond.

(11) If a man dies owing money to Jews, his wife may have her dower and pay nothing towards the debt from it. If he leaves children that are under age, their needs may also be provided for on a scale appropriate to the size of his holding of lands. The debt is to be paid out of the residue, reserving the service due to his feudal lords. Debts owed to persons others than Jews are to be dealt with similarly.

(12) No "scutage"[1] or "aid" may be levied in our kingdom without its general consent, unless it is for the ransom of our person, to make our eldest son a knight, and (once) to marry our eldest daughter. For these purposes only a reasonable "aid" may be levied. "Aids" from the city of London are to be treated similarly.

(13) The city of London shall enjoy all its ancient liberties and free customs, both by land and by water. We also will and grant that all other cities, boroughs, towns, and ports shall enjoy all their liberties and free customs.

(14) To obtain the general consent of the realm for the assessment of an "aid" – except in the three cases specified above – or a "scutage", we will cause the archbishops, bishops, abbots, earls, and greater barons to be summoned individually by letter. To those who hold lands directly of us we will cause a general summons to be issued, through the sheriffs and other officials, to come together on a fixed day (of which at least forty days notice shall be given) and at a fixed place. In all letters of summons, the cause of the summons will be stated. When a summons has been issued, the business appointed for the day shall go forward in accordance with the resolution of those present, even if not all those who were summoned have appeared.

(15) In future we will allow no one to levy an "aid" from his free men, except to ransom his person, to make his eldest son a knight, and (once) to marry his eldest daughter. For these purposes only a reasonable "aid" may be levied.

(16) No man shall be forced to perform more service for a knight's "fee", or other free holding of land, than is due from it.

[1] "Scutage" or "shield-money" was paid in lieu of physical participation in the king's wars.

(17) Ordinary lawsuits shall not follow the royal court around, but shall be held in a fixed place.

(18) Inquests of *novel disseisin*, *mort d'ancestor*, and *darrein presentment* shall be taken only in their proper county court. We ourselves, or in our absence abroad our chief justice, will send two justices to each county four times a year, and these justices, with four knights of the county elected by the county itself, shall hold the assizes in the county court, on the day and in the place where the court meets.

(19) If any assizes cannot be taken on the day of the county court, as many knights and freeholders shall afterwards remain behind, of those who have attended the court, as will suffice for the administration of justice, having regard to the volume of business to be done.

(20) For a trivial offence, a free man shall be fined only in proportion to the degree of his offence, and for a serious offence correspondingly, but not so heavily as to deprive him of his livelihood. In the same way, a merchant shall be spared his merchandise, and a husbandman the implements of his husbandry, if they fall upon the mercy of a royal court. None of these fines shall be imposed except by the assessment on oath of reputable men of the neighbourhood.

(21) Earls and barons shall be fined only by their equals, and in proportion to the gravity of their offence.

(22) A fine imposed upon the lay property of a clerk in holy orders shall be assessed upon the same principles, without reference to the value of his ecclesiastical benefice.

(23) No town or person shall be forced to build bridges over rivers except those with an ancient obligation to do so.

(24) No sheriff, constable, coroners, or other royal officials are to hold lawsuits that should be held by the royal justices.

(25) Every county, hundred, wapentake, and tithing shall remain at its ancient rent, without increase, except the royal demesne manors.

(26) If at the death of a man who holds a lay "fee" of the Crown, a sheriff or royal official produces royal letters patent of summons for a debt due to the Crown, it shall be lawful for them to seize and list movable goods found in the lay "fee" of the dead man to the value of the debt, as assessed by worthy men. Nothing shall be removed until the whole debt is paid, when the residue shall be given over to the executors to carry out the dead man's will. If no debt is due to the Crown, all the movable goods shall be regarded as the property of the dead man, except the reasonable shares of his wife and children.

(27) If a free man dies intestate, his movable goods are to be distributed by his next-of-kin and friends under the supervision of the Church. The rights of his debtors are to be preserved.

(28) No constable or other royal official shall take corn or other

movable goods from any man without immediate payment, unless the seller voluntarily offers postponement of this.

(29) No constable may compel a knight to pay money for castle-guard if the knight is willing to undertake the guard in person, or with reasonable excuse to supply some other fit man to do it. A knight taken or sent on military service shall be excused from castle-guard for the period of this service.

(30) No sheriff, royal official, or other person shall take horses or carts for transport from any free man, without his consent.

(31) Neither we nor any royal official will take wood for our castle, or for any other purpose, without the consent of the owner.

(32) We will not keep the lands of people convicted of felony in our hand for longer than a year and a day, after which they shall be returned to the lords of the "fees" concerned.

(33) All fish-weirs shall be removed from the Thames, the Medway, and throughout the whole of England, except on the sea coast.

(34) The writ called *precipe* shall not in future be issued to anyone in respect of any holding of land, if a free man could thereby be deprived of the right of trial in his own lord's court.

(35) There shall be standard measures of wine, ale, and corn (the London quarter), throughout the kingdom. There shall also be a standard width of dyed cloth, russett, and haberject, namely two ells within the selvedges. Weights are to be standardised similarly.

(36) In future nothing shall be paid or accepted for the issue of a writ of inquisition of life or limbs. It shall be given gratis, and not refused.

(37) If a man holds land of the Crown by "fee-farm", "socage", or "burgage", and also holds land of someone else for knight's service, we will not have guardianship of his heir, nor of the land that belongs to the other person's "fee", by virtue of the "fee-farm", "socage", or "burgage", unless the "fee-farm" owes knight's service. We will not have the guardianship of a man's heir, or of land that he holds of someone else, by reason of any small property that he may hold of the Crown for a service of knives, arrows, or the like.

(38) In future no official shall place a man on trial upon his own unsupported statement, without producing credible witnesses to the truth of it.

(39) No free man shall be seized or imprisoned, or stripped of his rights or possessions, or outlawed or exiled, or deprived of his standing in any other way, nor will we proceed with force against him, or send others to do so, except by the lawful judgement of his equals or by the law of the land.

(40) To no one will we sell, to no one deny or delay right or justice.

(41) All merchants may enter or leave England unharmed and without fear, and may stay or travel within it, by land or water, for purposes of

trade, free from all illegal exactions, in accordance with ancient and lawful customs. This, however, does not apply in time of war to merchants from a country that is at war with us. Any such merchants found in our country at the outbreak of war shall be detained without injury to their persons or property, until we or our chief justice have discovered how our own merchants are being treated in the country at war with us. If our own merchants are safe they shall be safe too.

(42) In future it shall be lawful for any man to leave and return to our kingdom unharmed and without fear, by land or water, preserving his allegiance to us, except in time of war, for some short period for the common benefit of the realm. People that have been imprisoned or outlawed in accordance with the law of the land, people from a country that is at war with us, and merchants – who shall be dealt with as stated above – are excepted from this provision.

(43) If a man holds lands of any "escheat" such as the "honour" of Wallingford, Nottingham, Boulogne, Lancaster, or of other "escheats" in our hand that are baronies, at his death his heir shall give us only the "relief" and service that he would have made to the baron, had the barony been in the baron's hand. We will hold the "escheat" in the same manner as the baron held it.

(44) People who live outside the forest need not in future appear before the royal justices of the forest in answer to general summonses, unless they are actually involved in proceedings or are sureties for someone who has been seized for a forest offence.

(45) We will appoint as justices, constables, sheriffs, or other officials, only men that know the law of the realm and are minded to keep it well.

(46) All barons who have founded abbeys, and have charters of English kings or ancient tenure as evidence of this, may have guardianship of them when there is no abbot, as is their due.

(47) All forests that have been created in our reign shall at once be disafforested. River-banks that have been enclosed in our reign shall be treated similarly.

(48) All evil customs relating to forests and warrens, foresters, warreners, sheriffs and their servants, or river-banks and their wardens, are at once to be investigated in every county by twelve sworn knights of the county, and within forty days of their enquiry the evil customs are to be abolished completely and irrevocably. But we, or our chief justice if we are not in England, are first to be informed.

(49) We will at once return all hostages and charters delivered up to us by Englishmen as security for peace or for loyal service.

(50) We will remove completely from their offices the kinsmen of Gerard de Athée, and in future they shall hold no offices in England. The people in question are Engelard de Cigogné, Peter, Guy, and Andrew de Chanceaux, Guy de Cigogné, Geoffrey de Martigny and his brothers,

Philip Marc and his brothers, with Geoffrey his nephew, and all their followers.

(51) As soon as peace is restored, we will remove from the kingdom all the foreign knights, bowmen, their attendants, and their mercenaries that have come to it, to its harm, with horses and arms.

(52) To any man whom we have deprived or dispossessed of lands, castles, liberties, or rights, without the lawful judgement of his equals, we will at once restore these. In cases of dispute the matter shall be resolved by the judgement of the twenty-five barons referred to below in the clause for securing the peace (§61). In cases, however, where a man was deprived or dispossessed of something without the lawful judgement of his equals by our father King Henry or our brother King Richard, and it remains in our hands or is held by others under our warranty, we shall have respite for the period commonly allowed to Crusaders, unless a lawsuit had been begun, or an enquiry had been made at our order, before we took the Cross as a Crusader. On our return from the Crusade, or if we abandon it, we will at once render justice in full.

(53) We shall have similar respite in rendering justice in connexion with forests that are to be disafforested, or to remain forests, when these were first afforested by our father Henry or our brother Richard; with the guardianship of lands in another person's "fee", when we have hitherto had this by virtue of a "fee" held of us for knight's service by a third party; and with abbeys founded in another person's "fee", in which the lord of the "fee" claims to own a right. On our return from the Crusade, or if we abandon it, we will at once do full justice to complaints about these matters.

(54) No one shall be arrested or imprisoned on the appeal of a woman for the death of any person except her husband.

(55) All fines that have been given to us unjustly and against the law of the land, and all fines that we have exacted unjustly, shall be entirely remitted or the matter decided by a majority judgement of the twenty-five barons referred to below in the clause for securing the peace together with Stephen, archbishop of Canterbury, if he can be present, and such others as he wishes to bring with him. If the archbishop cannot be present, proceedings shall continue without him, provided that if any of the twenty-five barons has been involved in a similar suit himself, his judgement shall be set aside, and someone else chosen and sworn in his place, as a substitute for the single occasion, by the rest of the twenty-five.

(56) If we have deprived or dispossessed any Welshmen of lands, liberties, or anything else in England or in Wales, without the lawful judgement of their equals, these are at once to be returned to them. A dispute on this point shall be determined in the Marches by the judgement of equals. English law shall apply to holdings of land in England, Welsh

law to those in Wales, and the law of the Marches to those in the Marches. The Welsh shall treat us and ours in the same way.

(57) In cases where a Welshman was deprived or dispossessed of anything, without the lawful judgement of his equals, by our father King Henry or our brother King Richard, and it remains in our hands or is held by others under our warranty, we shall have respite for the period commonly allowed to Crusaders, unless a lawsuit has been begun, or an enquiry had been made at our order, before we took the Cross as a Crusader. But on our return from the Crusade, or if we abandon it, we will at once do full justice to the laws of Wales and the said regions.

(58) We will at once return the son of Llywelyn, all Welsh hostages, and the charters delivered to us as security for the peace.

(59) With regard to the return of the sisters and hostages of Alexander, king of Scotland, his liberties and his rights, we will treat him in the same way as our other barons of England, unless it appears from the charters that we hold from his father William, formerly king of Scotland, that he should be treated otherwise. This matter shall be resolved by the judgement of his equals in our court.

(60) All these customs and liberties that we have granted shall be observed in our kingdom in so far as concerns our own relations with our subjects. Let all men of our kingdom, whether clergy or laymen, observe them similarly in their relations with their own men.

(61) Since we have granted all these things for God, for the better ordering of our kingdom, and to allay the discord that has arisen between us and our barons, and since we desire that they shall be enjoyed in their entirety, with lasting strength, for ever, we give and grant to the barons the following security:

> The barons shall elect twenty-five of their number to keep, and cause to be observed with all their might, the peace and liberties granted and confirmed to them by this charter.
>
> If we, our chief justice, our officials, or any of our servants offend in any respect against any man, or transgress any of the articles of the peace or of this security, and the offence is made known to four of the said twenty-five barons, they shall come to us – or in our absence from the kingdom to the chief justice – to declare it and claim immediate redress. If we, or in our absence abroad the chief justice, make no redress within forty days, reckoning from the day on which the offence was declared to us or to him, the four barons shall refer the matter to the rest of the twenty-five barons, who may distrain upon and assail us in every way possible, with the support of the whole community of the land, by seizing our castles, lands, possessions, or anything else saving only our own person and those of the

queen and our children, until they have secured such redress as they have determined upon. Having secured the redress, they may then resume their normal obedience to us.

Any man who so desires may take an oath to obey the commands of the twenty-five barons for the achievement of these ends, and to join with them in assailing us to the utmost of his power. We give public and free permission to take this oath to any man who so desires, and at no time will we prohibit any man from taking it. Indeed, we will compel any of our subjects who are unwilling to take it to swear it at our command.

If one of the twenty-five barons dies or leave the country, or is prevented in any other way from discharging his duties, the rest of them shall choose another baron in his place, at their discretion, who shall be duly sworn in as they were.

In the event of disagreement among the twenty-five barons on any matter referred to them for decision, the verdict of the majority present shall have the same validity as a unanimous verdict of the whole twenty-five, whether these were all present or some of those summoned were unwilling or unable to appear.

The twenty-five barons shall swear to obey all the above articles faithfully, and shall cause them to be obeyed by others to the best of their power.

We will not seek to procure from anyone, either by our own efforts or those of a third party, anything by which any part of these concessions or liberties might be revoked or diminished. Should such a thing be procured, it shall be null and void and we will at no time make use of it, either ourselves or through a third party.

(62) We have remitted and pardoned fully to all men any ill-will, hurt, or grudges that have arisen between us and our subjects, whether clergy or laymen, since the beginning of the dispute. We have in addition remitted fully, and for our own part have also pardoned, to all clergy and laymen any offences committed as a result of the said dispute between Easter in the sixteenth year of our reign and the restoration of peace.

In addition we have caused letters patent to be made for the barons, bearing witness to this security and to the concessions set out above, over the seals of Stephen, archbishop of Canterbury, Henry archbishop of Dublin, the other bishops named above, and Master Pandulf.

(63) It is accordingly our wish and command that the English Church shall be free, and that men in our kingdom shall have and keep all these liberties, rights, and concessions, well and peaceably in their fulness and entirety for them and their heirs, of us and our heirs, in all things and all places for ever.

Both we and the barons have sworn that all this shall be observed in good faith and without deceit. Witness the above-mentioned people and many others.

Given by our hand in the meadow that is called Runnymede, between Windsor and Staines, on the fifteenth day of June in the seventeenth year of our reign.

From THE LIFE OF ST FRANCIS, 1228–9

Thomas of Celano

Renouncing, in c. 1205, the wealth of his merchant father following a dream, the Italian Giovanni Bernadone dedicated his life to the care of the poor. His ascetic and altrustic example was infectious and thousands flocked to join him; in 1210 Bernadone founded the Franciscan monastic order (Bernadone's nickname was "Il Francesco", the little Frenchman, after his former love of French song) and in 1212 the Poor Clares. Bernadone believed in the union of man and nature, and preached the gospel to all of God's creatures. He was canonized as Saint Francis of Assisi by Pope Gregory IX in 1228. In 1980 he was made the patron saint of ecology.

Celano was one of St Francis' friars.

Francis, therefore, Christ's valiant knight, went round the cities and fortresses proclaiming the Kingdom of God, preaching peace, teaching salvation and repentance for the remission of sins, not with plausible words of human wisdom, but with the learning and power of the Spirit. The Apostolic authority which had been granted him enabled him to act in all things with greater confidence, without using flattery or seducing blandishments. Incapable of showing favour to the lives of sinners, he could smite them with sharp reproof because he had first persuaded himself by practice of that which he endeavoured to commend to others by his words; and without fear of any reprover he uttered the truth most confidently, so that even the most learned men, mighty in renown and dignity, wondered at his discourses and were smitten by his presence with wholesome fear. Men ran, women too ran, clerks hastened, and Religious made speed to see and hear the Saint of God who seemed to all to be a man of another world. People of every age and either sex hastened to behold the wonders which the Lord was newly working in the world by His servant. Surely at that time, whether by holy Francis' presence or by the fame [of him], it seemed that, as it were, a new light had been sent from heaven on earth, scattering the universal blackness of darkness which had so seized on well-nigh the whole of that region, that scarce any one knew whither he must go. For such depth of forgetfulness of God and such slumber of neglect of His commandments had oppressed almost all that they could scarce endure to be roused, even slightly, from their old and inveterate sins . . .

But the chief matter of our discourse is the Order which as well from charity as by profession he took upon him and maintained. What then shall we say of it? He himself first planted the Order of Friars Minor (Lesser Brethren) and on that very occasion gave it that name; since (as is well known) it was written in the Rule: "And be they lesser": and in that hour, when those words were uttered, he said: "I will that this brotherhood be called the Order of Lesser Brethren" (Friars Minor). And truly they were "lesser", for, being subject to all, they ever sought for lowly dwellings, and for occupations in the discharge of which they might appear in some sort to suffer wrong, that they might deserve to be so founded on the solid basis of true humility that in happy disposition the spiritual building of all the virtues might arise in them. Verily on the foundation of stedfastness a noble structure of charity arose, wherein living stones heaped together from all parts of the world were built up into an habitation of the Holy Spirit. Oh, with what ardour of charity did Christ's new disciples burn! What love of their pious fellowship flourished among them! For whenever they came together in any place or met one another in the way (as is usual), there sprang up a shoot of spiritual love scattering over all love the seeds of true affection. What can I say more? Their embraces were chaste, their feelings gentle, their kisses holy, their intercourse sweet, their laughter modest, their look cheerful, their eye single, their spirit submissive, their tongue peaceable, their answer soft, their purpose identical, their obedience ready, their hand untiring.

And for that they despised all earthly things, and never loved one another with private love, but poured forth their whole affection in common, the business of all alike was to give up themselves as the price of supplying their brethren's need. They came together with longing, they dwelt together with delight; but the parting of companions was grievous on both sides, a bitter divorce, a cruel separation. But these obedient knights durst put nothing before the orders of holy Obedience, and before the word of command was finished they were preparing to fulfil the order; not knowing how to distinguish between precept and precept, they ran, as it were, headlong to perform whatever was enjoined, all contradiction being put aside.

The followers of most holy Poverty, having nothing, loved nothing, and therefore had no fear of losing anything. They were content with a tunic only, patched sometimes within and without; no elegance was seen in it, but great abjectness and vileness, to the end they might wholly appear therein as crucified to the world. They were girt with a cord, and wore drawers of common stuff; and they were piously purposed to remain in that state, and to have nothing more. Everywhere, therefore, they were secure, nor kept in suspense by any fear; distracted by no care, they awaited the morrow without solicitude, nor, though oftentimes in great straits in their journeyings, were they ever in anxiety about a night's lodging. For when, as often happened, they lacked a lodging in the coldest weather, an oven sheltered them, or, at least, they lay hid by night humbly in underground places or in caves. And by day those who knew how to, worked with their hands, and they stayed in lepers' houses, or in other decent places, serving all with humility and devotion.

They would exercise no calling whence scandal might arise, but, by always doing holy, just, virtuous, and useful deeds, they provoked all with whom they lived to copy their humility and patience. The virtue of patience had so compassed them about that they rather sought to be where they might suffer persecution of their bodies than where they might be uplifted by the world's favour, if their holiness was acknowledged or praised. For many times when they were reviled, insulted, stripped naked, scourged, bound or imprisoned, they would not avail themselves of any one's protection, but bore all so bravely that the voice of praise and thanksgiving alone sounded in their mouth. Scarcely, or not at all, did they cease from praising God and from prayer; but, recalling by constant examination what they had done, they rendered thanks to God for what they had done well, and groans and tears for what they had neglected or unadvisedly committed. They deemed themselves forsaken by God unless they knew themselves to be constantly visited in their devotions by their wonted piety. And so when they would apply themselves to prayer they sought the support of certain appliances lest their prayer should be disturbed by sleep stealing over them. Some were held up by hanging ropes, some surrounded themselves with instruments of iron, while others shut themselves up in wooden cages. If ever their sobriety were disturbed (as commonly happens) by abundance of food or drink, or if, tired by a journey, they overpassed, though but a little, the bounds of necessity, they tortured themselves most severely by many days' abstinence. In short they made it their business to keep down the promptings of the flesh with such maceration that they shrank not from often stripping themselves naked in the sharpest frost, and piercing their whole body with thorns so as to draw blood.

And so vigorously did they set at naught all earthly things that they scarce submitted to take the barest necessities of life, and shrank not from any hardships, having been parted from bodily comfort by such long usage. Amid all this they followed peace and gentleness with all men, and, ever behaving themselves modestly and peaceably, were most zealous in avoiding all occasions of scandal. For they scarcely spoke even in time of need, nor did any jesting or idle words proceed out of their mouth, in order that nothing immodest or unseemly might by any means be found in all their behaviour and conversation. Their every act was disciplined, their every movement modest, all the senses had been so mortified in them that they scarce submitted to hear or see anything but what their purpose demanded; their eyes were fixed on the ground, their mind clave to Heaven. No envy, malice, rancour, evil-speaking, suspicion or bitterness had place in them, but great concord, continual quietness, thanksgiving, and the voice of praise were in them. Such were the teachings wherewith the tender father, not by word and tongue only, but above all in deed and truth, was fashioning his new sons . . .

Of his Preaching to the Birds and of the Obedience of the Creatures.

During the time when (as has been said) many joined themselves to the brethren, the most blessed father Francis was journeying through the valley of Spoleto, and came to a spot near Bevagna where a very great number of birds of different sorts were gathered together, viz., doves, rooks, and those other birds that are called in the vulgar tongue *monade*. When he saw them, being a man of the most fervent temper and also very tender and affectionate toward all the lower and irrational creatures, Francis the most blessed servant of God left his companions in the way and ran eagerly toward the birds. When he was come close to them and saw that they were awaiting him, he gave them his accustomed greeting. But, not a little surprised that the birds did not fly away (as they are wont to do) he was filled with exceeding joy and humbly begged them to hear the word of God: and, after saying many things to them he added: "My brother birds, much ought ye to praise your Creator, and ever to love Him who has given you feathers for clothing, wings for flight, and all that ye had need of. God has made you noble among His creatures, for He has given you a habitation in the purity of the air, and, whereas ye neither sow nor reap, He Himself doth still protect and govern you without any care of your own." On this (as he himself and the brethren who had been with him used to say) those little birds rejoicing in wondrous fashion, after their nature, began to stretch out their necks, to spread their wings, to open their beaks and to gaze on him. And then he went to and fro amidst them, touching their heads and bodies with his tunic. At length he blessed them, and, having made the sign of the cross, gave them leave to fly away to another place. But the blessed father went on his way with his companions, rejoicing and giving thanks to God Whom all creatures humbly acknowledge and revere. Being now, by grace become simple (though he was not so by nature) he began to charge himself with negligence for not having preached to the birds before, since they listened so reverently to God's word. And so it came to pass that from that day he diligently exhorted all winged creatures, all beasts, all reptiles and even creatures insensible, to praise and love the Creator, since daily, on his calling on the Saviour's name, he had knowledge of their obedience by his own experience.

One day (for instance) when he was come to the fortress called Alviano to set forth the word of God, he went up on an eminence where all could see him, and asked for silence. But though all the company held their peace and stood reverently by, a great number of swallows who were building their nests in that same place were chirping and chattering loudly. And, as Francis could not be heard by the men for their chirping, he spoke to the birds and said: "My sisters, the swallows, it is now time for me to speak too, because you have been saying enough all this time. Listen to the word of God and be in silence, and quiet, until the sermon is finished!" And those little birds (to the amazement and wonder of all the bystanders) kept silence forthwith, and did not move from that place till the preaching was ended. So those men, when they had seen the sign, were filled with the greatest admiration, and said: "Truly this man is a Saint, and a friend of the Most High." And with the utmost devotion they hastened at least to touch his clothes, praising and blessing God.

And it is certainly wonderful how even the irrational creatures recognized his tender affection towards them and perceived beforehand the sweetness of his love.

For once when he was staying at the fortress of Greccio, one of the brethren brought him a live leveret that had been caught in a snare; and when the blessed man saw it he was moved with compassion and said: "Brother leveret, come to me. Why didst thou let thyself be so deceived?" And forthwith the leveret, on being released by the brother who was holding him fled to the holy man, and, without being driven thither by any one, lay down in his bosom as being the safest place. When he had rested there a little while the holy father, caressing him with maternal affection, let him go, so that he might freely return to the woodland. At last, after the leveret had been put down on the ground many times, and had every time returned to the holy man's bosom, he bade the brethren carry it into a wood which was hard by. Something of the same kind happened with a rabbit (which is a very wild creature) when he was on the island in the lake of Perugia. He was also moved by the same feeling of pity towards fish, for if they had been caught, and he had the opportunity, he would throw them back alive into the water, bidding them beware of being caught a second time.

Once accordingly when he was sitting in a boat near a port on the lake of Rieti a fisherman caught a big fish called a tench, and respectfully offered it to him. He took it up joyfully and kindly, began to call it by the name of

brother, and then putting it back out of the boat into the water he began
devoutly to bless the name of the Lord. And while he continued thus for
some time in prayer, the said fish played about in the water close to the
boat, and did not leave the place where Francis had put him, until, having
finished his prayer, the holy man of God gave him leave to depart. Even so
did the glorious father Francis, walking in the way of obedience, and
taking upon him perfectly the yoke of Divine submission, acquire great
dignity before God in that the creatures obeyed him. For water was even
turned to wine for him when he was once in grievous sickness at the
hermitage of Sant' Urbano; and when he had tasted it he got well so easily
that all believed it to be a Divine miracle, as indeed it was. And truly he is a
Saint whom the creatures thus obey and at whose nod the very elements
are transmuted for other uses.

Of his Preaching at Ascoli; and How the Sick Were Healed in His Absence by Things that his Hand had Touched

At the time when (as has been said) the venerable father Francis preached
to the birds, as he went round about the cities and fortresses scattering
seeds of blessing everywhere, he came to the city of Ascoli. Here, when
according to his wont he was most fervently uttering the word of God,
almost all the people, changed by the right hand of the Highest, were filled
with such grace and devotion that in their eagerness to see and hear him
they trod on one another. And at that time thirty men, clerks and lay
people, received from him the habit of holy Religion. Such was the faith of
men and women, such their devotion of mind toward God's Saint that he
who could but touch his garment called himself happy. If he entered any
city the clergy were joyful, the bells were rung, the men exulted, the
women rejoiced together, the children clapped their hands and often took
boughs of trees and went in procession to meet him singing Psalms.
Heretical wickedness was confounded, the Church's faith was magnified;
and while the faithful shouted for joy, the heretics slunk away. For the
tokens of holiness that appeared in him were such that no one durst speak
against him; seeing that the crowds hung on him alone. Amidst and above
all else he pronounced that the faith of the Holy Roman Church, wherein
alone consists the salvation of all that are to be saved, must be kept,
revered, and imitated. He revered the priests and embraced the whole
hierarchy with exceeding affection.

The people would offer him loaves to bless, and would keep them for
long after, and by tasting them they were healed of divers sicknesses.
Many times also in their great faith in him they cut up his tunic so that he
was left almost naked; and, what is more wonder, some even recovered
their health by means of objects which the holy father had touched with his
hand, as happened in the case of a woman who lived in a little village near

Arezzo. She was with child, and when the time of her delivery came was in labour for several days and hung between life and death in incredible suffering. Her neighbours and kinsfolk had heard that the blessed Francis was going to a certain hermitage and would pass by that way. But while they were waiting for him it chanced that he went to the place by a different way, for he was riding because he was weak and ill. When he reached the place he sent back the horse to the man who had lent it him out of charity, by a certain brother named Peter. Brother Peter, in bringing the horse back passed through the place where the suffering woman was. The inhabitants on seeing him ran to him in haste, thinking he was the blessed Francis, but were exceedingly disappointed when they found he was not. At length they began to inquire together if anything might be found which the blessed Francis had touched with his hand; and after spending a long time over this they at last hit upon the reins which he had held in his hand when riding: so they took the bit out of the mouth of the horse on which the holy father had sat, and laid the reins which he had touched with his own hands upon the woman: and forthwith her peril was removed and she brought forth her child with joy and in safety.

Gualfreduccio, who lived at Castel della Pieve, a religious man fearing and worshipping God with all his house, had by him a cord wherewith the blessed Francis had once been girded. Now it came to pass that in that place many men and not a few women were suffering from various sicknesses and fevers; and this man went through the houses of the sick, and, after dipping the cord in water or mixing with water some of the strands, made the sufferers drink of it, and so, in Christ's name, they all recovered. Now these things were done in blessed Francis' absence, besides many others which we could in nowise unfold in the longest discourse. But a few of those things which the Lord our God deigned to work by means of his presence we will briefly insert in this work . . .

Of the Love Which he Bore to All Creatures for the Creator's Sake. Description of his Inner and Outer Man

It were exceeding long, and indeed impossible, to enumerate and collect all the things which the glorious father Francis did and taught while he lived in the flesh. For who could ever express the height of the affection by which he was carried away as concerning all the things that are God's? Who could tell the sweetness which he enjoyed in contemplating in His creatures the wisdom, power and goodness of the Creator? Truly such thoughts often filled him with wondrous and unspeakable joy as he beheld the sun, or raised his eyes to the moon, or gazed on the stars, and the firmament. O simple piety! O pious simplicity! Even towards little worms he glowed with exceeding love, because he had read that word concerning the Saviour: "I am a worm, and no man." Wherefore he used to pick them up in the way and put them in a safe place, that they might not be crushed by the feet of passers-by. What shall I say of other lower creatures, when in winter he would cause honey or the best wine to be provided for bees, that they might not perish from cold? And he used to extol, to the glory of the Lord, the efficacy of their works and the excellence of their skill with such abundant utterance that many times he would pass a day in praise of them and of the other creatures. For as of old the three children placed in the burning fiery furnace invited all the elements to praise and glorify the Creator of the universe, so this man also, full of the spirit of God, ceased not to glorify, praise, and bless in all the elements and creatures the Creator and Governor of them all.

What gladness thinkest thou the beauty of flowers afforded to his mind as he observed the grace of their form and perceived the sweetness of their perfume? For he turned forthwith the eye of consideration to the beauty of that Flower which, brightly coming forth in spring-time from the root of Jesse, has by its perfume raised up countless thousands of the dead. And when he came upon a great quantity of flowers he would preach to them and invite them to praise the Lord, just as if they had been gifted with reason. So also cornfields and vineyards, stones, woods, and all the beauties of the field, fountains of waters, all the verdure of gardens, earth and fire, air and wind would he with sincerest purity exhort to the love and willing service of God. In short he called all creatures by the name of brother, and in a surpassing manner, of which other men had no experience, he discerned the hidden things of creation with the eye of the heart, as one who had already escaped into the glorious liberty of the children of God.

Now, O good Jesus, in the heavens with the angels he is praising Thee as admirable who when on earth did surely preach Thee to all creatures as lovable.

THE END OF MAN, 1259–64

St Thomas Aquinas

Aquinas (1225–74) sought to reconcile the Christian doctine of faith with Aristotle's rationalism. So successful was this project, which bore its finest fruit in *Summa contra Gentiles* and *Summa Theologiae*, that Aquinas was able to show "five ways" (proofs) for God's existence; his conclusions remain the standard teachings of the Catholic Church.

From Summa contra Gentiles

Now of all the parts of man, the intellect is the highest mover: for it moves the appetite, by proposing its object to it; and the intellective appetite, or will, moves the sensitive appetites, namely the irascible and concupiscible, so that we do not obey the concupiscence, unless the will command; and the sensitive appetite, the will consenting, moves the body. Therefore the end of the intellect is the end of all human actions. *Now the intellect's end and good are the true*; and its last end is the first truth. Therefore the last end of all man and of all his deeds and desires, is to know the first truth, namely God.

Moreover. Man has a natural desire to know the causes of whatever he sees: wherefore through wondering at what they saw, and ignoring its cause, men first began to philosophize, and when they had discovered the cause they were at rest. Nor do they cease inquiring until they come to the first cause; and *then do we deem ourselves to know perfectly when we know the first cause*. Therefore man naturally desires, as his last end, to know the first cause. But God is the first cause of all. Therefore man's last end is to know God . . .

Now the last end of man and of any intelligent substance is called happiness or beatitude; for it is this that every intelligent substance desires as its last end, and for its own sake alone. Therefore the last beatitude or happiness of any intelligent substance is to know God.

Hence it is said (Matthew V, 8): "Blessed are the clean of heart, for they shall see God": and (John XVII, 3): "This is eternal life: that they may know Thee, the only true God." Aristotle agrees with this statement (10 *Ethic*, VII) when he says that man's ultimate happiness is "contemplative, in regard to his contemplating the highest object of contemplation." . . .

It remains for us to inquire in what kind of knowledge of God the ultimate happiness of the intellectual substance consists. For there is a certain general and confused knowledge of God, which is in almost all men, whether from the fact that, as some think, the existence of God, like other principles of demonstration, is self-evident, as we have stated in the First Book: or, as seems nearer to the truth, because by his natural reason, man is able at once to arrive at some knowledge of God. For seeing that natural things are arranged in a certain order – since there cannot be order without a cause of order – men, for the most part, perceive that there is one who arranges in order the things that we see. But who or of what kind this cause of order may be, or whether there be but one, cannot be gathered from this general consideration: even, so, when we see a man in motion, and performing other works, we perceive that in him there is a cause of these operations, which is not in other things, and we give this cause the name of "soul," but without knowing yet what the soul is, whether it be a body, or how it brings about operations in question.

Now, this knowledge of God cannot possibly suffice for happiness . . .

There is yet another knowledge of God, in one respect superior to the knowledge we have been discussing, namely that whereby God is known to men through faith. In this respect it surpasses the knowledge of God through demonstration, because by faith we know certain things about God, which are so sublime that reason cannot reach them by means of demonstration, as we have stated at the beginning of this work. But not even in this knowledge of God can man's ultimate happiness consist.

For happiness is the intellect's perfect operation, as already declared. But in knowledge by faith the operation of the intellect is found to be most imperfect as regards that which is on the part of the intellect: although it is the most perfect on the part of the object: for the intellect in believing does not grasp the object of its assent. Therefore neither does man's happiness consist in this knowledge of God.

Again. It has been shown that ultimate happiness does not consist chiefly in an act of will. Now in knowledge by faith the will has the leading place: for the intellect assents by faith to things proposed to it, because it wills, and not through being constrained by the evidence of their truth. Therefore man's final happiness does not consist in this knowledge . . .

Seeing that man's ultimate happiness does not consist in that knowledge of God whereby He is known by all or many in a vague kind of opinion, nor again in that knowledge of God whereby He is known in science through demonstration; nor in that knowledge whereby He is known through faith, as we have proved above: and seeing that it is not possible in this life to arrive at a higher knowledge of God in His essence, or at least so that we understand other separate substances, and thus know God through that which is nearest to Him, so to say, as we have proved; and since we must place our ultimate happiness in some kind of knowledge of God, as we have shown; it is impossible for man's happiness to be in this life.

Again. Man's last end is the term of his natural appetite, so that when he has obtained it, he desires nothing more: because if he still has a movement towards something, he has not yet reached an end wherein to be at rest. Now, this cannot happen in this life: since the more man understands, the more is the desire to understand increased in him – this being natural to man – unless perhaps someone there be who understands all things: and in this life this never did nor can happen to anyone that was a mere man; seeing that in this life we are unable to know separate substances which in themselves are most intelligible, as we have proved. Therefore man's ultimate happiness cannot possibly be in this life.

Besides. Whatever is in motion towards an end has a natural desire to be established and at rest therein: hence a body does not move away from the place towards which it has a natural movement, except by a violent movement which is contrary to that appetite. Now happiness is the last end which man desires naturally. Therefore it is his natural desire to be established in happiness. Consequently unless together with happiness he acquires a state of immobility, he is not yet happy, since his natural desire is not yet at rest. When therefore a man acquires happiness, he also acquires stability and rest; so that all agree in conceiving stability as a necessary condition of happiness: hence the philosopher says (1 *Ethic*, x): "We do not look upon the happy man as a kind of chameleon." Now, in this life there is no sure stability; since, however happy a man may be, sickness and misfortune may come upon him, so that he is hindered in the operation, whatever it be, in which his happiness consists. Therefore man's ultimate happiness cannot be in this life . . .

Further. All admit that happiness is a perfect good: else it would not bring rest to the appetite. Now perfect good is that which is wholly free from any admixture of evil: just as that which is perfectly white is that which is entirely free from any admixture of black. But man cannot be wholly free from evils in this state of life; not only from evils of the body, such as hunger, thirst, heat, cold, and the like, but also from evils of the soul. For no one is there who at times is not disturbed by inordinate passion; who sometimes does not go beyond the mean, wherein virtue consists, either in excess or in deficiency; who is not deceived in some thing or another; or at least ignores what he would wish to know, or feels doubtful about an opinion of which he would like to be certain. Therefore no man is happy in this life.

Again. Man naturally shuns death, and is sad about it: not only shunning it now when he feels its presence, but also when he thinks about it. But man, in this life, cannot obtain not to die. Therefore it is not possible for man to be happy in this life . . .

Again. The natural desire cannot be void; since *nature does nothing in vain*. But nature's desire would be void if it could never be fulfilled. Therefore man's natural desire can be fulfilled. But not in this life, as we have shown. Therefore it must be fulfilled after this life. Therefore man's ultimate happiness is after this life.

Besides. As long as a thing is in motion towards perfection it has not reached its last end. Now in the knowledge of truth all men are ever in motion and tending towards perfection: because those who follow, make discoveries in addition to those made by their predecessors, as stated in 2 *Metaph.* Therefore in the knowledge of truth man is not situated as though he had arrived at his last end. Since then as Aristotle himself shows (10 *Ethic,* VII) man's ultimate happiness in this life consists apparently in speculation, whereby he seeks the knowledge of truth, we cannot possibly allow that man obtains his last end in this life . . .

For these and like reasons Alexander and Averroes held that man's ultimate happiness does not consist in human knowledge obtained through speculative sciences, but in that which results from conjunction with a separate substance, which conjunction they deemed possible to man in this life. But as Aristotle realized that man has no knowledge in this life other than that which he obtains through speculative sciences, he maintained that man attains to happiness, not perfect, but proportionate to his capacity.

Hence it becomes sufficiently clear how these great minds suffered from being so straitened on every side. We, however, will avoid these straits if we suppose, in accordance with the foregoing arguments, that man is able to reach perfect happiness after this life, since man has an immortal soul; and that in that state his soul will understand in the same way as separate substances understand, as we proved in the Second Book.

Therefore man's ultimate happiness will consist in that knowledge of God which he possesses after this life; a knowledge similar to that by which separate substances know him. Hence our Lord promises us a "reward . . . in heaven" (Matthew v, 12) and (Matthew xxii, 30) states that the saints "shall be as the angels": who always see God in heaven (Matthew xviii, 10).

WRIT OF SUMMONS TO PARLIAMENT, 1295

Edward I

During the 13th century almost all of the fundamentals of the English parliament – the "Mother of Parliaments' – were established. Following *Magna Carta* (see pp 140–50) more baronial struggle – led by Simon de Montfort – resulted in the 1258 "Provisions of Oxford" which allowed an elected council to meet at least three times a year as a "parliament" When Henry II tried to rescind the measure, civil war saw de Montfort become the effective ruler of England; to buttress his rule de Montfort called a parliament of two knights from every shire and two citizens from every borough. That is, de Montfort gave – revolutionary measure – the "commonalty" a role in government

De Montfort was killed at Evesham in 1265 by Prince Edward, but his reforms were not. Indeed, Edward on his accession to the throne was obliged to confirm and even extend them. By the First Statutes of Westminster, 1275, Edward I agreed not only a place for the "commonalty" in parliament, but in Article 5 that: ". . . because elections ought to be free, the King commandeth upon great forfeiture, that no man by force of arms, nor by malice or menacing, shall disturb any to make free election."

Hence the historic importance of this seemingly innocuous "summons to parliament" from Edward. For, not only is it addressed to bishops and magnates, but to sheriffs, with these latter enjoined with organizing the election of representatives for the local commonalty. The king still wore the crown, but his subjects were ineluctably taking their political liberty.

The King to the venerable father in Christ, Robert, by the same grace Archbishop of Canterbury, primate of all England, greeting. As a most just law, established by the careful providence of sacred princes, exhorts and decrees that what affects all, should be approved by all, so also, very evidently should common danger be met by means provided in common. You know sufficiently well, and it is now, as we believe, known through all regions of the world, how the King of France fraudulently and craftily deprived us of our land of Gascony, by withholding it unjustly from us. Now, however, not satisfied with the aforesaid fraud and injustice, having gathered together for the conquest of our kingdom a very great fleet, and a very large force of warriors, with which he has made a hostile attack on our kingdom and the inhabitants of the kingdom, he now proposes to stamp out the English language altogether from the earth if his power should be equal to the detestable task of the proposed iniquity, which God forbid. Because, therefore, darts seen beforehand do less injury, and your interest especially, as that of other fellow citizens of the same realm, is concerned in this affair, we command you, strictly enjoining you in the fidelity and love in which you are bound to us, that on the Lord's day next after the feast of St Martin, in the approaching winter, you be present in person at Westminster; citing beforehand the dean and chapter of your church, the archdeacons and all the clergy of your diocese, causing the same dean and archdeacons in their own persons, and the said chapter by one suitable proctor, and the said clergy by two, to be present along with you, having full and sufficient power of themselves from the chapter and clergy, for considering, ordaining and providing along with us and with the rest of the prelates and principal men and other inhabitants of our kingdom how the dangers and threatened evils of this kind are to be met. Witness, the King at Wengham, the thirtieth day of September.

[Like summons were sent to the Archbishop of York, to 18 bishops and with the omission of the last paragraph to 70 abbots and other leading churchmen]

The King to his beloved and faithful kinsman, Edmund, Earl of Cornwall, greeting. Because we wish to have a conference and meeting with you and with the rest of the principal men of our kingdom, to provide remedies for the dangers which in these days threaten our whole kingdom; we command you, strictly enjoining you by the fidelity and love in which you are bound to us, that on the Lord's day next after the feast of St Martin, in the approaching winter, you be present in person at Westminster, for considering, ordaining and doing with us, and with the prelates, and the rest of the magnates and other inhabitants of our kingdom, as may be necessary to meet dangers of this kind. Witness, the King at Canterbury, on the first day of October.

[Like summons were sent to 7 earls and 41 barons]

The King to the sheriff of Northamptonshire. Since we purpose to have a conference and meeting, with the earls, barons, and other principal men of our kingdom to provide remedies for the dangers which in these days threaten the same kingdom; and on that account, have commanded them to be with us, on the Lord's day next after the feast of St Martin, in the approaching winter, at Westminster, to consider, ordain, and do, as may be necessary for the avoidance of these dangers; we strictly require you to cause two knights from the aforesaid county, two citizens from each city in the same county, and two burgesses from each borough, of the more discreet and capable, to be elected without delay, and to cause them to come to us, at the aforesaid time and place.

Moreover, the said knights are to have full and sufficient power, for themselves and for the commonalty of the aforesaid county, and the said citizens and burgesses for themselves and for the commonalty of the aforesaid cities and boroughs separately, then and there to do what shall be ordained by the common advice in the premises; so that the aforesaid business shall not remain unfinished in any way for defect of this power. And you shall have there the names of the knights, citizens and burgesses, and this writ.

Witness, the King at Canterbury, on the third day of October.

[Like summons were sent to the sheriffs of all English counties]

From THE DIVINE COMEDY, c. 1307

Dante Alighieri

The Florentine poet Alighieri (1265–1321) was for much of his life a wandering political exile; this experience is "literarily" reflected in the *Divina Commedia*, which narrates Dante's journey through Hell and Purgatory until he finally reaches Heaven. The most profound aspect of the poem – and there are many – is that it achieves in art the reason-faith synthesis which Aquinas achieved in philosophy. By the lights of the time *Commedia* was scientific; simultaneously it showed the way to God. Dante also allows a very modern sense of personal freedom. God is a matter of individual free choice, not a decision made by an external force. It might have been sinful not to choose God – "Abandon hope all ye that enter here" is the inscription Dante puts over the mouth of Hell – but it was still a *choice*.

In the extact below Dante is in Hell, guided by the poet Vergil. There they see Dis (Satan) devouring Judas, Brutus and Cassius (ie Traitors), and escape by crawling along Dis' body until they reach the centre of the Earth. From there they follow the stream of Lethe upwards until it brings them out onto Mount Purgatory. And Dante is a step closer to Heaven:

Canto XXXIV

"*Vexilla regis prodeunt inferni*
   Encountering us: canst thou distinguish him,
   Look forward," said the master, "as we journey."
As, when a thick mist breathes, or when the rim
   Of night creeps up across our hemisphere,
   A turning windmill looms in the distance dim,
I thought I saw a shadowy mass appear;
   Then shrank behind my leader from the blast,
   Because there was no other cabin here.

I stood (with fear I write it) where at last
  The shades, quite covered by the frozen sheet,
  Gleamed through the ice like straws in crystal glassed;
Some lie at length and others stand in it,
  This one upon his head, and that upright,
  Another like a bow bent face to feet.
And when we had come so far that it seemed right
  To my dear master, he should let me see
  That creature fairest once of the sons of light,
He moved him from before me and halted me,
  And said: "Behold now Dis! behold the place
  Where thou must steel thy soul with constancy."
How cold I grew, how faint with fearfulness,
  Ask me not, Reader; I shall not waste breath
  Telling what words are powerless to express;
This was not life, and yet it was not death;
  If thou hast wit to think how I might fare
  Bereft of both, let fancy aid thy faith.
The Emperor of the sorrowful realm was there,
  Out of the girding ice he stood breast-high,
  And to his arm alone the giants were
Less comparable than to a giant I;
  Judge then how huge the stature of the whole
  That to so huge a part bears symmetry.
If he was once as fair as now he's foul,
  And dared outface his Maker in rebellion,
  Well may he be the fount of all our dole.
And marvel 'twas, out-marvelling a million,
  When I beheld three faces in his head;
  The one in front was scarlet like vermilion;
And two, mid-centred on the shoulders, made
  Union with this, and each with either fellow
  Knit at the crest, in triune junction wed.
The right was of a hue 'twixt white and yellow;
  The left was coloured like the men who dwell
  Where Nile runs down from source to sandy shallow.
From under each sprang two great wings that well
  Befitted such a monstrous bird as that;
  I ne'er saw ship with such a spread of sail.
Plumeless and like the pinions of a bat
  Their fashion was: and as they flapped and whipped
  Three winds went rushing over the icy flat
And froze up all Cocytus; and he wept
  From his six eyes, and down his triple chin

Runnels of tears and bloody slaver dripped.
Each mouth devoured a sinner clenched within,
　　Frayed by the fangs like flax beneath a brake;
　　Three at a time he tortured them for sin.
But all the bites the one in front might take
　　Were nothing to the claws that flayed his hide
　　And sometimes stripped his back to the last flake.
"That wretch up there whom keenest pangs divide
　　Is Judas called Iscariot," said my lord,
　　"His head within, his jerking legs outside;
As for the pair whose heads hang hitherward:
　　From the black mouth the limbs of Brutus sprawl –
　　See how he writhes and utters never a word;
And strong-thewed Cassius is his fellow-thrall.
　　But come; for night is rising on the world
　　Once more: we must depart; we have seen all."
Then, as he bade, about his neck I curled
　　My arms and clasped him. And he spied the time
　　And place; and when the wings were wide unfurled
Set him upon the shaggy flanks to climb.
　　And thus from shag to shag descended down
　　'Twixt matted hair and crusts of frozen rime.
And when we had come to where the huge thigh-bone
　　Rides in its socket at the haunch's swell.
　　My guide, with labour and great exertion,
Turned head to where his feet had been, and fell
　　To hoisting himself up upon the hair.
　　So that I thought us mounting back to Hell.
"Hold fast to me, for by so steep a stair."
　　My master said, panting like one forspent.
　　"Needs must we quit this realm of all despair."
At length, emerging through a rocky vent.
　　He perched me sitting on the rim of the cup
　　And crawled out after, heedful how he went.
I raised my eyes, thinking to see the top
　　Of Lucifer, as I had left him last;
　　But only saw his great legs sticking up.
And if I stood dumbfounded and aghast,
　　Let those thick-witted gentry judge and say.
　　Who do not see what point it was I'd passed.
"Up on thy legs!" the master said; "the way
　　Is long, the road rough going for the feet,
　　And at mid-terce already stands the day."
The place we stood in was by no means fit

For a king's palace, but a natural prison,
  With a vile floor, and very badly lit.
"One moment, sir," said I, when I had risen;
  "Before I pluck myself from the Abyss,
  Lighten my darkness with a word in season.
Kindly explain; what's happened to the ice?
  What's turned him upside-down? or in an hour
  Thus whirled the sun from dusk to dawning skies?"
"Thou think'st," he said, "thou standest as before
  Yon side the centre, where I grasped the hair
  Of the ill Worm that pierces the world's core.
So long as I descended, thou wast there;
  But when I turned, then was the point passed by
  Toward which all weight bears down from everywhere.
The other hemisphere doth o'er thee lie –
  Antipodal to that which land roofs in.
  And under whose meridian came to die
The Man born sinless and who did no sin;
  Thou hast thy feet upon a little sphere
  Of whose far side Judecca forms the skin.
When it is evening there, it's morning here;
  And he whose pelt our ladder was, stands still
  Fixt in the self-same place, and does not stir.
This side the world from out high Heaven he fell;
  The land which here stood forth fled back dismayed.
  Pulling the sea upon her like a veil,
And sought our hemisphere; with equal dread.
  Belike, that peak of earth which still is found
  This side, rushed up, and so this void was made."
There is a place low down there underground.
  As far from Belzebub as his tomb's deep.
  Not known to sight, but only by the sound
Of a small stream which trickles down the steep,
  Hollowing its channel, where with gentle fall
  And devious course its wandering waters creep.
By that hid way my guide and I withal,
  Back to the lit world from the darkened dens
  Toiled upward, caring for no rest at all.
He first, I following; till my straining sense
  Glimpsed the bright burden of the heavenly cars
  Through a round hole; by this we climbed, and thence
Came forth, to look once more upon the stars.

PIERS PLOWMAN'S PROTEST. c. 1362

William Langland

Langland's long poem *The Vision of William concerning Piers Plowman* has
been called "the first authentic cry of the poor in British history". That cry,
which came in the wake of the Black Death and attempts by aristocracy to
fix down wages, took a more violent expression in 1381 with the Peasants'
Revolt. Little is known of the life of Langland (c. 1330–1386), although it is
supposed that he took minor orders and guessed that he was the illegitimate
son of the rector of Shipton-under-Wychwood in Oxfordshire.

Therefore I warn you rich, who are able in this world
On trust of your treasure to have triennials and pardons,
Be never the bolder to break the ten commandments;
And most of all you masters, mayors and judges,
Who have the wealth of this world, and are held wise by your neighbours,
You who purchase your pardons and papal charters:
At the dread doom, when the dead shall rise
And all come before Christ, and give full accounting,
When the doom will decide what day by day you practised,
How you led your life and were lawful before him,
Though you have pocketfuls of pardons there or provincial letters,
Though you be found in the fraternity of all the four orders,
Though you have double indulgences – unless Do Well help you
I set your patents and your pardons at the worth of a peascod!
Therefore I counsel all Christians to cry God mercy,
And Mary His Mother be our mean between Him,
That God may give us grace, ere we go hence,
To work with such a will, while we are here,
That after our death day, and at the Day of Doom,
Do Well may declare that we did as He commanded.

The poor may plead and pray in the doorway;
They may quake for cold and thirst and hunger;
None receives them rightfully and relieves their suffering.
They are hooted at like hounds and ordered off.
Little does he love the Lord, who lent him all these favours,
And who so parts his portion with the poor who are in trouble.
If there were no more mercy among poor than among rich men,
Mendicants might go meatless to slumber.
God is often in the gorge of these great masters,
But among lowly men are his mercy and his works;
And so says the psalter, as I have seen it often:
Ecce audivimus eam in Effrata, invenimus eam in campis silvae.
Clerics and other conditions converse of God readily,
And have him much in the mouth, but mean men in their hearts.

Friars and false men have found such questions
To please proud men since the pestilence season,
And have so preached at Saint Paul's from pure envy of clerics,
That men are not firm in faith nor free in bounty
Nor sorry for their sins. Pride has so multiplied
In religious orders and in the realm, among rich and poor folk,
That prayers have no power to prevent the pestilence,
Yet the wretches of this world are not warned by each other.
The dread of death cannot draw pride from them;
Nor are they plentiful to the poor as plain charity wishes;
But glut themselves with their goods in gaiety and gluttony,
And break no bread with the beggar as the Book teaches.

Lo, lords, lo, and ladies! witness
That the sweet liquor lasts but a little season,
Like peapods, and early pears, plums and cherries.
What lances up lightly lasts but a moment,
And what is readiest to ripen rots soonest.
A fat land full of dung breeds foul weeds rankly,
And so are surely all such bishops,
Earls and archdeacons and other rich clerics
Who traffic with tradesmen and turn on them if they are beaten,
And have the world at their will to live otherwise.
As weeds run wild on ooze or on the dunghill,
So riches spread upon riches give rise to all vices.
The best wheat is bent before ripening
On land that is overlaid with marle or the dungheap.
And so are surely all such people:
Overplenty feeds the pride which poverty conquers.

The wealth of this world is evil to its keeper,
Howsoever it may be won, unless it be well expended.
If he is far from it, he fears often
That false men or felons will fetch away his treasure.
Moreover wealth makes men on many occasions
To sin, and to seek out subtlety and treason,
Or from coveting of goods to kill the keepers.
Thus many have been murdered for their money or riches,
And those who did the deed damned forever,
And he himself, perhaps, in hell for his hard holding;
And greed for goods was the encumbrance of all together.
Pence have often purchased both palaces and terror;
Riches are the root of robbery and of murder;
He who so gathers his goods prizes God at little.

Ah! well may it be with poverty, for he may pass untroubled,
And in peace among the pillagers if patience follow him!
Our Prince Jesus and His Apostles chose poverty together,
And the longer they lived the less wealth they mastered.

"When the kindness of Constantine gave Holy Church endowments
In lands and leases, lordships and servants,
The Romans heard an angel cry on high above them:
'This day *dos ecclesiae* has drunk venom
And all who have Peter's power are poisoned forever.'
But a medicine may be given to amend prelates
Who should pray for the peace and whose possessions prevent
    them.
Take your lands, you lords, and let them live by tithing!
If possession is poison and makes imperfect orders,
It were good to dislodge them for the Church's profit,
And purge them of that poison before the peril is greater.

"If priesthood were perfect all the people would be converted
Who are contrary to Christ's law and who hold Christendom in
    dishonour.
All pagans pray and believe rightly
In the great and holy God, and ask His grace to aid them.
Their mediator is Mohammed to move their petition.
Thus the folk live in a faith but with a false advocate,
Which is rueful for righteous men in the realms of Christendom,
And a peril to the pope and to the prelates of his creation
Who bear the names of the bishops of Bethlehem and Babylon."

"And would that you, Conscience, were in the court of the king always,
That Grace, whom you commend so, were the guide of all clergy,
And that Piers with his plows, the newer and the older,
Were emperor of all the world, and all men Christian!
He is but a poor pope who should be the peoples' helper
And who sends men to slay the souls that they should rescue.
But well be it with Piers the Plowman who pursues his duty!
Qui pluit super justos et injustos equally,
Sends forth the sun to shine on the villein's tillage
As brightly as on the best man's and on the best woman's.
So Piers the Plowman is at pains to harrow
As well for a waster and for wenches in the brothels
As for himself and his servants, though he is served sooner.
He toils and tills for a traitor as earnestly
As for an honest husbandman, and at all times equally.
May he be worshipped who wrought all, both the good and the wicked,
And suffers the sinful till the season of their repentance!
God amend the pope, who pillages Holy Church,
Who claims that before the king he is the keeper of Christians,
Who accounts it nothing that Christians are killed and beaten,
Who leads the people to battle and spills the blood of Christians,
Against the Old Law and the New Law, as Luke witnesses . . .
Surely it seems that if himself has his wishes
He recks nothing of the right nor of the rest of the people.
But may Christ in His Kindness save the cardinals and prelates
And turn their wits into wisdom and to welfare of the spirit!"

"Charity is God's champion, like a child that is gentle,
And the merriest of mouth at meat and at table.
For the love that lies in his heart makes him lightsome in language,
And he is companionable and cheerful as Christ bids him.
Nolite fieri sicut hypocritae tristes, etc.
I have seen him in silk and sometimes in russet,
In grey and in furred gowns and in gilt armour;
And he gave them as gladly to any creature who needed them.
Edmund and Edward were each kings
And considered saints when Charity followed them.
I have seen Charity also singing and reading,
Riding, and running in ragged clothing;
But among bidders and beggars I beheld him never.
In rich robes he is most rarely witnessed,
With a cap or a crown glistening and shaven,
Or in cleanly clothes of gauze or Tartary.
In a friar's frock he was found once,

But that was afar back in Saint Francis' lifetime;
In that sect since he has been too seldom witnessed.
He receives the robes of the rich, and praises
All who lead their lives without deception.
Beatus est dives qui, etc.
He comes often in the king's court where the council is honest,
But if Covetousness is of the council he will not come into it.
He comes but seldom in court with jesters,
Because of brawling and backbiting and bearing false witness.
He comes but rarely in the consistory where the commissary is seated,
For their lawsuits are overlong unless they are lifted by silver,
And they make and unmake matrimony for money.
Whom Conscience and Christ have combined firmly
They undo unworthily, these Doctors of Justice.
His ways were once among the clergy,
With archbishops and bishops and prelates of Holy Church,
To apportion Christ's patrimony to the poor and needy.
But now Avarice keeps the keys and gives to his kinsmen,
To his executors and his servants and sometimes to his children.

"I blame no man living; but Lord amend us
And give us all grace, good God, to follow Charity!
Though he mistrusts such manners in all men who meet him,
He neither blames nor bans nor boasts nor praises,
Nor lowers nor lauds nor looks sternly
Nor craves nor covets nor cries after more.
In pace in idipsum dormiam, etc.
The chief livelihood that he lives by is love in God's passion.
He neither bids nor begs nor borrows to render.
He misuses no man and his mouth hurts no one."

LETTER TO POSTERITY, c. 1370

Francesco Petrarca

If there is such a thing as the founding text of humanism, Petrarca's "Letter to Posterity" has a claim to it.

Whereas Aquinas and Dante sought a balanced synthesis between Man and God, humanist went a distinct step beyond this to preoccupation with Man himself. Thus, whereas the architects of the great medieval cathedrals are anonymous, the humanist artists took pride in their Earthly achievements. The most startling aspect of "Letter to Posterity" by the Florentine poet Petrarca (1304–74) is simply its existence. Its humility is all pretence. Petrarca hoped – expected – to have his name remembered down the centuries. No Gothic builder would have dared or dreamed of such human self-importance.

c. 1370

Greeting. It is possible that some word of me may have come to you, though even this is doubtful, since an insignificant and obscure name will scarcely penetrate far in either time or space. If, however, you should have heard of me, you may desire to know what manner of man I was, or what was the outcome of my labours, especially those of which some description or, at any rate, the bare titles may have reached you.

To begin with myself, then, the utterances of men concerning me will differ widely, since in passing judgment almost everyone is influenced not so much by truth as by preference, and good and evil report alike know no bounds. I was, in truth, a poor mortal like yourself, neither very exalted in my origin, nor, on the other hand, of the most humble birth, but belonging, as Augustus Caesar says of himself, to an ancient family. As to my disposition, I was not naturally perverse or wanting in modesty, however the contagion of evil associations may have corrupted me. My youth was gone before I realized it; I was carried away by the strength of manhood; but a riper age brought me to my senses and taught me by experience the truth I had long before read in books, that youth and pleasure are vanity – nay, that the Author of all ages and times permits us miserable mortals, puffed up with emptiness, thus to wander about, until finally, coming to a tardy consciousness of our sins, we shall learn to know ourselves. In my prime I was blessed with a quick and active body, although not exceptionally strong; and while I do not lay claim to remarkable personal beauty, I was comely enough in my best days. I was possessed of a clear complexion, between light and dark, lively eyes, and for long years a keen vision, which however deserted me, contrary to my hopes, after I reached my sixtieth birthday, and forced me, to my great annoyance, to resort to glasses. Although I had previously enjoyed perfect health, old age brought with it the usual array of discomforts.

My parents were honourable folk, Florentine in their origin, of medium fortune, or, I may as well admit it, in a condition verging upon poverty. They had been expelled from their native city, and consequently I was born in exile, at Arezzo, in the year 1304 of this latter age which begins with Christ's birth, July the twentieth, on a Monday, at dawn. I have always possessed an extreme contempt for wealth; not that riches are not desirable in themselves, but because I hate the anxiety and care which are invariably associated with them. I certainly do not long to be able to give gorgeous banquets. I have, on the contrary, led a happier existence with plain living and ordinary fare than all the followers of Apicius, with their elaborate dainties. So-called *convivia*, which are but vulgar bouts, sinning against sobriety and good manners, have always been repugnant to me. I have ever felt that it was irksome and profitless to invite others to such affairs, and not less so to be bidden to them myself. On the other hand, the pleasure of dining with one's friends is so great that nothing has ever given me more delight than their unexpected arrival, nor have I ever willingly sat down to table without a companion. Nothing displeases me more than display, for not only is it bad in itself, and opposed to humility, but it is troublesome and distracting.

I struggled in my younger days with a keen but constant and pure attachment, and would have struggled with it longer had not the sinking flame been extinguished by death – premature and bitter, but salutary. I should be glad to be able to say that I had always been entirely free from irregular desires, but I should lie if I did so. I can, however, conscientiously claim that, although I may have been carried away by the fire of youth or by my ardent temperament, I have always abhorred such sins from the depths of my soul. As I approached the age of forty, while my powers were unimpaired and my passions were still strong, I not only abruptly threw off my bad habits, but even the very recollection of them, as if I had never looked upon a woman. This I mention as among the greatest of my blessings, and I render thanks to God, who freed me, while still sound and vigorous, from a disgusting slavery which had always been hateful to me. But let us turn to other matters.

I have taken pride in others, never in myself, and however insignificant I may have been, I have always been still less important in my own judgment. My anger has very often injured myself, but never others. I have always been most desirous of honourable friendships, and have faithfully cherished them. I make this boast without fear, since I am confident that I speak truly. While I am very prone to take offence, I am equally quick to forget injuries, and have a memory tenacious of benefits. In my familiar associations with kings and princes, and in my friendship with noble personages, my good fortune has been such as to excite envy. But it is the cruel fate of those who are growing old that they can commonly only weep for friends who have passed away. The greatest kings of this age have loved and courted me. They may know why; I certainly do not. With some of them I was on such terms that they seemed in a certain sense my guests rather than I theirs; their lofty position in no way embarrassing me, but, on the contrary, bringing with it many advantages. I fled, however, from many of those to whom I was greatly attached; and such was my innate longing for liberty, that I studiously avoided those whose very name seemed incompatible with the freedom that I loved.

I possessed a well-balanced rather than a keen intellect, one prone to all kinds of good and wholesome study, but especially inclined to moral philosophy and the art of poetry. The latter, indeed, I neglected as time went on, and took delight in sacred literature. Finding in that a hidden sweetness which I had once esteemed but lightly, I came to regard the works of the poets as only amenities. Among the many subjects which interested me, I dwelt especially upon antiquity, for our own age has always repelled me, so that, had it not been for the love of those dear to me. I should have preferred to have been born in any other period than our own. In order to forget my own time, I have constantly striven to place myself in spirit in other ages, and consequently I delighted in history; not that the conflicting statements did not offend me, but when in doubt I accepted what appeared to me most probable, or yielded to the authority of the writer.

My style, as many claimed, was clear and forcible; but to me it seemed weak and obscure. In ordinary conversation with friends, or with those about me, I never gave any thought to my language, and I have always wondered that Augustus Caesar should have taken such pains in this respect. When, however, the subject itself, or the place or listener, seemed to demand it, I gave some attention to style, with what success I cannot pretend to say; let them judge in whose presence I spoke. If only I have lived well, it matters little to me how I talked. Mere elegance of language can produce at best but an empty renown.

My life up to the present has, either through fate or my own choice, fallen into the following divisions. A part only of my first year was spent at

Arezzo, where I first saw the light. The six following years were, owing to the recall of my mother from exile, spent upon my father's estate in Ancisa, about fourteen miles above Florence. I passed my eighth year at Pisa, the ninth and following years in Farther Gaul, at Avignon, on the left bank of the Rhone, where the Roman pontiff holds and has long held the Church of Christ in shameful exile . . .

On the windy banks of the river Rhone I spent my boyhood, guided by my parents, and then, guided by my own fancies, the whole of my youth. Yet there were long intervals spent elsewhere, for I first passed four years at the little town of Carpentras, somewhat to the east of Avignon: in these two places I learned as much of grammar, logic, and rhetoric as my age permitted, or rather, as much as it is customary to teach in school: how little that is, dear reader, thou knowest. I then set out for Montpellier to study law, and spent four years there, then three at Bologna. I heard the whole body of the civil law, and would, as many thought, have distinguished myself later, had I but continued my studies. I gave up the subject altogether, however, so soon as it was no longer necessary to consult the wishes of my parents. My reason was that, although the dignity of the law, which is doubtless very great, and especially the numerous references it contains to Roman antiquity, did not fail to delight me, I felt it to be habitually degraded by those who practise it. It went against me painfully to acquire an art which I would not practise dishonestly, and could hardly hope to exercise otherwise. Had I made the latter attempt, my scrupulousness would doubtless have been ascribed to simplicity.

So at the age of two and twenty I returned home. I call my place of exile home, Avignon, where I had been since childhood; for habit has almost the potency of nature itself. I had already begun to be known there, and my friendship was sought by prominent men; wherefore I cannot say. I confess this is now a source of surprise to me, although it seemed natural enough at an age when we are used to regard ourselves as worthy of the highest respect. I was courted first and foremost by that very distinguished and noble family, the Colonnesi, who, at that period, adorned the Roman Curia with their presence. However it might be now, I was at that time certainly quite unworthy of the esteem in which I was held by them . . .

About this time, a youthful desire impelled me to visit France and Germany. While I invented certain reasons to satisfy my elders of the propriety of the journey, the real explanation was a great inclination and longing to see new sights. I first visited Paris, as I was anxious to discover what was true and what fabulous in the accounts I had heard of that city. On my return from this journey I went to Rome, which I had since my infancy ardently desired to visit. There I soon came to venerate Stephano, the noble head of the family of the Colonnesi, like some ancient hero, and was in turn treated by him in every respect like a son . . .

On my return, since I experienced a deep-seated and innate repugnance to town life, especially in that disgusting city of Avignon which I heartily abhorred, I sought some means of escape. I fortunately discovered, about fifteen miles from Avignon, a delightful valley, narrow and secluded, called Vaucluse, where the Sorgue, the prince of streams, takes its rise. Captivated by the charms of the place, I transferred thither myself and my books. Were I to describe what I did there during many years, it would prove a long story. Indeed, almost every bit of writing which I have put forth was either accomplished or begun, or at least conceived, there, and my undertakings have been so numerous that they still continue to vex and weary me. My mind, like my body, is characterized by a certain versatility and readiness, rather than by strength, so that many tasks that were easy of conception have been given up by reason of the difficulty of their execution . . .

While I was wandering in those mountains upon a Friday in Holy Week, the strong desire seized me to write an epic in an heroic strain, taking as my theme Scipio Africanus the Great, who had, strange to say, been dear to me from my childhood. But although I began the execution of this project with enthusiasm, I straightway abandoned it, owing to a variety of distractions. The poem was, however, christened *Africa*, from the name of its hero, and, whether from his fortunes or mine, it did not fail to arouse the interest of many before they had seen it.

While leading a leisurely existence in this region, I received, remarkable as it may seem, upon one and the same day, letters both from the Senate at Rome and the chancellor of the University of Paris, pressing me to appear in Rome and Paris, respectively, to receive the poet's crown of laurel. In my youthful elation I convinced myself that I was quite worthy of this honour; the recognition came from eminent judges, and I accepted their verdict rather than that of my own better judgment. I hesitated for a time which I should give ear to, and sent a letter to Cardinal Giovanni Colonna, of whom I have already spoken, asking his opinion. He was so near that, although I wrote late in the day, I received his reply before the third hour on the morrow. I followed his advice, and recognized the claims of Rome as superior to all others . . .

So I decided, first to visit Naples, and that celebrated king and philosopher, Robert, who was not more distinguished as a ruler than as a man of culture. He was, indeed, the only monarch of our age who was the friend at once of learning and of virtue, and I trusted that he might correct such things as he found to criticize in my work. The way in which he received and welcomed me is a source of astonishment to me now, and, I doubt not, to the reader also, if he happens to know anything of the matter. Having learned the reason of my coming, the king seemed mightily pleased. He was gratified, doubtless, by my youthful faith in him, and felt, perhaps, that he shared in a way the glory of my coronation, since I had chosen him from all others as the only suitable critic. After talking over a great many things, I showed him my *Africa*, which so delighted him that he asked that it might be dedicated to him in consideration of a handsome reward. This was a request that I could not well refuse, nor, indeed, would I have wished to refuse it, had it been in my power. He then fixed a day upon which we could consider the object of my visit. This occupied us from noon until evening, and the time proving too short, on account of the many matters which arose for discussion, we passed the two following days in the same manner. Having thus tested my poor attainments for three days, the king at last pronounced me worthy of the laurel. He offered to bestow that honour upon me at Naples, and urged me to consent to receive it there, but my veneration for Rome prevailed over the insistence of even so great a monarch as Robert. At length, seeing that I was inflexible in my purpose, he sent me on my way accompanied by royal messengers and letters to the Roman Senate, in which he gave enthusiastic expression to his flattering opinion of me. This royal estimate was, indeed, quite in accord with that of many others, and especially with my own, but today I cannot approve either his or my own verdict. In his case, affection and the natural partiality to youth were stronger than his devotion to truth.

On arriving at Rome, I continued, in spite of my unworthiness, to rely upon the judgment of so eminent a critic, and, to the great delight of the Romans who were present, I who had been hitherto a simple student received the laurel crown . . .

On leaving Rome, I went to Parma, and spent some time with the members of the house of Correggio, who, while they were most kind and generous towards me, agreed but ill among themselves. They governed Parma, however, in a way unknown to that city within the memory of man, and the like of which it will hardly again enjoy in this present age . . .

I had already passed my thirty-fourth year when I returned thence to the Fountain of the Sorgue, and to my transalpine solitude. I had made a long stay both in Parma and Verona, and everywhere I had, I am thankful to say, been treated with much greater esteem than I merited.

Some time after this, my growing reputation procured for me the goodwill of a most excellent man, Giacomo the Younger, of Carrara, whose equal I do not know among the rulers of his time. For years he wearied me with messengers and letters when I was beyond the Alps, and with his petitions whenever I happened to be in Italy, urging me to accept his friendship . . . I appeared, though tardily, at Padua, where I was received by him of illustrious memory, not as a mortal, but as the blessed are greeted in heaven – with such delight and such unspeakable affection and esteem, that I cannot adequately describe my welcome in words, and must, therefore, be silent. Among other things, learning that I had led a clerical life from boyhood, he had me made a canon of Padua, in order to bind me the closer to himself and his city. In fine, had his life been spared, I should have found there an end to all my wanderings. But alas! nothing mortal is enduring, and there is nothing sweet which does not presently end in bitterness. Scarcely two years was he spared to me, to his country, and to the world . . .

I returned to Gaul, not so much from a desire to see again what I had already beheld a thousand times, as from the hope, common to the afflicted, of coming to terms with my misfortunes by a change of scene.

From *WYCLIF'S DOCTRINES, 1382*

John Wyclif

The English theologian and scholar John Wyclif (c. 1329–1384) has been termed the "prophet of the Reformation" for his anticipation of its prime ideas. Not only did he roundly attack Church corruption, but he placed the scriptures as a higher authority than the papacy and asserted that Everyman had the right to read the Bible himself. The first English translation of the Bible duly ensued. After the Great Schism in the Church of 1378, Wyclif's radicalism increased and he entered dangerous waters in 1380 when he questioned the sacraments of the eucharist and penance. In 1382 Archbishop Courtenay convoked a council at Blackfriars Hall, London, which condemned 24 of Wyclif's doctrines, some as heretical and some as erroneous. Despite this condemnation, Lollardy (as Wyclif's theology was called, after the Dutch for "mumbling") endured at low-level in English society until the Reformation.

Some of the doctrines condemned at Blackfriars are reprinted here.

1. That the substance of material bread and wine doth remain in the sacrament of the altar after consecration.

2. That the "accidents" do not remain without the "subject" in the same sacrament after consecration.

3. That Christ is not in the sacrament of the altar identically, truly, and really in His proper corporeal person.

4. That if a bishop or a priest be in mortal sin, he doth not ordain [validly], consecrate the elements . . , nor baptize.

5. That if a man be duly contrite, all outer confession is for him superfluous and invalid . . .

8. That if the pope . . . be an evil man . . ., he hath no power over the faithful of Christ given to him by any, unless, peradventure, by the emperor.

9. That after Urban VI none other is to be received for pope . . .

10. The assertion that it is contrary to Holy Scripture that ecclesiastical persons should have temporal possessions.

11. That no prelate ought to excommunicate any man except he first know him to be excommunicated by God . . .

13. That a bishop excommunicating a cleric who hath appealed to the king or . . . to the council of the realm . . . is a traitor to God, the king, and the realm . . .

15. The assertion that it is lawful for any deacon or presbyter to preach the word of God without the authority of the Apostolic See, or of a Catholic bishop, or of other recognized authority . . .

17. That temporal lords may at will withdraw their temporal goods from ecclesiastics habitually delinquent . . .

18. That tithes are pure alms, and that parishioners may, on account of the sins of their curates, detain them and bestow them on others at pleasure . . .

20. Moreover, in that any man doth enter into any private religion whatsoever, he is thereby made more unapt and unable to observe the commandments of God . . .

23. That friars are bound to obtain their living by the labour of their hands, and not by begging . . .

ON REACHING THE NEW WORLD, 1492

Christopher Columbus

Columbus (1451–1506) was manifestly not the discoverer of the New World; it was, after all, already inhabited by "Indians", and the Viking Bjarni Herjolsson explored the coast of Labrador in c. AD 985 Nevertheless, Columbus' voyage of 1492, undertaken in the minuscule *Santa Maria*, *Pinta* and *Nina* ships from Spain with a bare 120 men, unveiled the continent's existence to medieval Europe. The voyage proved, in contra-distinction to common sense and religious dogma, that the Earth was spherical, not flat. A revolution in exploration followed and when in 1519–22 Ferdinand Magellan's expedition sailed the world round, the whole globe came within the reach of mankind.

More, Columbus' redisovery of the New World stimulated a revolution in the medieval mind. All the old religious shibboleths became questionable. The traveller's tales of new lands suggested to the oppressed a place of hope and freedom, beginning America's career as Utopia.

A native of Genoa (Italy), Columbus undertook his 1492 journey on behalf of Isabella and Ferdinand of Spain. The purpose of the voyage was the discovery of a trade route to China and India by sailing westwards. Columbus rediscovery of the Americas was hence an utter accident.

Below, in a letter to Isabella and Ferdinand, Columbus recounts this his first sighting of the Americas – probably Watling's Island in the Bahamas – on 12 October 1492.

I was on the poop deck at ten o'clock in the evening when I saw a light. It was so indistinct that I could not be sure it was land, but I called Gutiérrez, the Butler of the King's Table and told him to look at what I thought was a light.

He looked and saw it. I also told Rodrigo Sánchez de Segovia, Your Majesties' observer on board, but he saw nothing because he was standing in the wrong place. After I had told them, the light appeared once or twice more, like a wax candle rising and falling. Only a few people thought it was a sign of land, but I was sure we were close to a landfall.

Then the *Pinta*, being faster and in the lead, sighted land and made the signal as I had ordered. The first man to sight land was called Rodrigo de Triana. The land appeared two hours after midnight, about two leagues away. We furled all sail except the *treo*, the mainsail with no bonnets, and we jogged off and on until Friday morning, when we came to an island. We saw naked people, and I went ashore in a boat with armed men, taking Martín Alonso Pinzón and his brother Vicente Yáñez, captain of the *Nina*. I took the royal standard, and the captains each took a banner with the Green Cross, which each of my ships carries as a device, with the letters F and Y, surmounted by a crown, at each end of the cross.

When we stepped ashore we saw fine green trees, streams everywhere and different kinds of fruit. I called to the two captains to jump ashore with the rest, who included Rodrigo de Escobedo, secretary of the fleet, and Rodrigo Sánchez de Segovia, asking them to bear solemn witness that in the presence of them all I was taking possession of this island for their Lord and Lady the King and Queen, and I made the necessary declaration which are set down at greater length in the written testimonies.

Soon many of the islanders gathered round us. I could see that they were people who would be more easily converted to our Holy Faith by love than by coercion, and wishing them to look on us with friendship I gave some of them red bonnets and glass beads which they hung round their necks, and many other things of small value, at which they were so delighted and so eager to please us that we could not believe it. Later they swam out to the boats to bring us parrots and balls of cotton thread and darts, and many other things, exchanging them for such objects as glass beads and hawk bells. They took anything, and gave willingly whatever they had.

However, they appeared to me to be a very poor people in all respects. They go about as naked as the day they were born, even the women, though I saw only one, who was quite young. All the men I saw were quite young, none older than thirty, all well built, finely bodied and handsome in the face. Their hair is coarse, almost like a horse's tail, and short; they wear it short, cut over the brow, except a few strands of hair hanging down uncut at the back.

Some paint themselves with black, some with the colour of the Canary islanders, neither black nor white, others with white, others with red, others with whatever they can find. Some have only their face painted, others their whole body, others just their eyes or nose. They carry no weapons, and are ignorant of them; when I showed them some swords they took them by the blade and cut themselves. They have no iron; their darts are just sticks without an iron head, though some of them have a fish tooth or something else at the tip.

They are all the same size, of good stature, dignified and well formed. I saw some with scars on their bodies, and made signs to ask about them, and they indicated to me that people from other islands nearby came to capture them and they defended themselves. I thought, and still think, that people from the mainland come here to take them prisoner. They must be good servants, and intelligent, for I can see that they quickly repeat everything said to them. I believe they would readily become Christians; it appeared to me that they have no religion. With God's will, I will take six of them with me for Your Majesties when I leave this place, so that they may learn Spanish.

I saw no animals on the island, only parrots.

From UTOPIA, 1516

Sir Thomas More

Thomas More (1478–1535) introduced the word "Utopia" into the English language, though the contents of the book which bear that name are unfamiliar to most outside the 16th century.

Utopia was one of the most significant expressions of Renaissance humanism in England. For someone who, as Lord Chancellor, might have been expected to produce an authoritarian-monarchical-clerical "ideal state", More's Utopia is an idyll where – in an anticipation of Rousseau – property is regarded as the root of all social evil. In Utopia, land is held in common, hours of work are regulated, there is free education for men and women, and there is religious tolerance.

More himself was a deeply contradictory figure, an almost personal embodiment of the tension between passing feudalism and the growing Renaissance. There might have been religious freedom in Utopia, but More himself was a ruthless persecutor of heretics. He was eventually beheaded by Henry VIII for refusing to recognise him (and not the Pope) as head of the English Church.

The Description of Utopia

The Island of Utopia containeth in breadth in the middle part of it (for there it is broadest) two hundred miles. Which breadth continueth through the most part of the land, saving that by little and little it cometh in and waxeth narrower towards both the ends. Which fetching about a circuit or compass of five hundred miles, do fashion the whole island like to the new moon. Between these two corners the sea runneth in, dividing them asunder by the distance of eleven miles or thereabouts, and there sumounteth into a large and wide sea, which by reason that the land on every side compasseth it about, and sheltereth it from the winds, is not rough, nor mounteth not with great waves, but almost floweth quietly, not much unlike a great standing pool; and maketh well-nigh all the space within the belly of the land in manner of a haven; and to the great commodity of the inhabitants receiveth in ships towards every part of the land. The forefronts or frontiers of the two corners, what with fords and shelves, and what with rocks, be very jeopardous and dangerous. In the middle distance between them both standeth up above the water a great rock, which therefore is nothing perilous because it is in sight. Upon the top of this rock is a fair and a strong tower built, which they hold with a garrison of men. Other rocks there be lying hid under the water, which therefore be dangerous. The channels be known only to themselves. And therefore it seldom chanceth that any stranger, unless he be guided by an Utopian, can come into this haven. Insomuch that they themselves could scarcely enter without jeopardy, but that their way is directed and ruled by certain landmarks standing on the shore. By turning, translating, and removing these marks into other places they may destroy their enemies' navies, be they ever so many. The outside or utter circuit of the land is also full of havens, but the landing is so surely fenced, what by nature, and what by workmanship of man's hand, that a few defenders may drive back many armies.

Howbeit as they say, and as the fashion of the place itself doth partly show, it was not ever compassed about with the sea. But King Utopus, whose name, as conqueror, the island beareth (for before his time it was called Abraxa), which also brought the rude and wild people to that excellent perfection in all good fashions, humanity, and civil gentleness, wherein they now go beyond all the people of the world; even at his first arriving and entering upon the land, forthwith obtaining the victory, caused fifteen miles' space of uplandish ground, where the sea had no passage, to be cut and digged up, and so brought the sea round about the land. He set to this work not only the inhabitants of the island (because they should not think it done in contumely and despite), but also all his own soldiers. Thus the work being divided into so great a number of workmen, was with exceeding marvellous speed dispatched. Insomuch that the borderers, which at the first began to mock and to jest at this vain enterprise, then turned their derision to marvel at the success, and to fear.

There be in the island fifty-four large and fair cities, or shire towns, agreeing altogether in one tongue, in like manners, institutions, and laws. They be all set and situated alike, and in all points fashioned alike, as far north as the place or plot suffereth. Of these cities they that be nighest together be twenty-four miles asunder. Again there is none of them distant from the next above one day's journey on foot.

There come yearly to Amaurote out of every city three old men, wise and well experienced, there to entreat and debate of the common matters of the land. For this city (because it standeth just in the middle of the island, and is therefore most meet for the ambassadors of all parts of the realm) is taken for the chief and head city. The precincts and bounds of the shires be so commodiously appointed out, and set forth for the cities, that none of them all hath of any side less than twenty miles of ground, and of some side also much more, as of that part where the cities be of farther distance asunder. None of the cities desire to enlarge the bounds and limits of their shires. For they count themselves rather the good husbands, than the owners of their lands.

They have in the country in all parts of the shire houses or farms built, well appointed and furnished with all sorts of instruments and tools belonging to husbandry. These houses be inhabited of the citizens, which come thither to dwell by course. No household or farm in the country hath fewer than forty persons, men and women, besides two bondmen, which be all under the rule and order of the good-man and the good-wife of the house, being both very sage, discreet, and ancient persons. And every thirty farms or families have one head ruler, which is called a Philarch, being as it were, a head bailiff. Out of every one of these families or farms cometh every year into the city twenty persons which have continued two years before in the country. In their place so many fresh be sent thither out of the city, who, of them that have been there a year already, and be therefore expert and cunning in husbandry, shall be instructed and taught. And they the next year shall teach other. This order is used for fear that either scarceness of victuals, or some other like incommodity should chance, through lack of knowledge, if they should be altogether new, and fresh, and unexpert in husbandry. This manner and fashion of yearly changing and renewing the occupiers of husbandry, though it be solemn and customably used, to the intent that no man shall be constrained against his will to continue long in that hard and sharp kind of life, yet many of them have such a pleasure and delight in husbandry, that they obtain a longer space of years. These husbandmen plough and till the ground, and breed up cattle, and provide and make ready wood, which they carry to the city either by land, or by water, as they may most conveniently.

They bring up a great multitude of pulleyn, and that by a marvellous policy. For the hens do not sit upon the eggs, but by keeping them in a certain equal heat they bring life into them, and hatch them. The chickens, as soon as they become out of the shell, follow men and women instead of the hens.

They bring up very few horses, nor none but very fierce ones; and that for none other use or purpose, but only to exercise their youth in riding and feats of arms. For oxen be put to all the labour of ploughing and drawing. Which they grant to be not so good as horses at a sudden brunt, and (as we say) at a dead lift, but yet they hold opinion, that oxen will abide and suffer much more labour, pain, and hardness, than horses will. And they think that oxen be not in danger and subject unto so many diseases, and that they be kept and maintained with much less cost and charge; and, finally, that they be good for meat when they be past labour.

They sow corn only for bread. For their drink is either wine made of grapes, or else of apples, or pears, or else it is clear water. And many times mead made of honey or liquorice sodden in water, for thereof they have great store. And though they know certainly (for they know it perfectly indeed) how much victuals the city with the whole country or shire round about it doth spend, yet they sow much more corn, and breed up much more cattle, than serveth for their own use, parting the overplus among their borderers. Whatsoever necessary things be lacking in the country, all such stuff they fetch out of the city; where without any exchange they easily obtain it of the magistrates of the city. For every month many of them go into the city on the holy day. When their harvest day draweth near, and is at hand, then the Philarchs, which be the head officers and bailiffs of husbandry, send word to the magistrates of the city what number of harvestmen is needful to be sent to them out of the city. The which company of harvestmen being ready at the day appointed, almost in one fair day dispatcheth all the harvest work.

Of the Magistrates

Every thirty families or farms choose them yearly an officer, which in their old language is called the Syphogrant, and by a newer name the Philarch. Every ten Syphogrants, with all their thirty families, be under an officer which was once called the Tranibor, now the chief Philarch. Moreover, as concerning the election of the prince, all the Syphogrants, which be in number two hundred, first be sworn to choose him whom they think most meet and expedient. Then by a secret election, they name prince one of those four whom the people before named unto them. For out of the four quarters of the city there be four chosen, out of every quarter one, to stand for the election; which be put up to the council. The prince's office continueth all his lifetime, unless he be deposed or put down for suspicion of tyranny. They choose the Tranibors yearly, but lightly they change them not. All the other officers be but for one year. The Tranibors every third day, and sometimes, if need be, oftener, come into the council-house with the prince. Their counsel is concerning the commonwealth. If there be any controversies among the commoners, which be very few, they dispatch and end them by and by. They take ever two Syphogrants to them in counsel, and every day a new couple. And it is provided that nothing touching the commonwealth shall be confirmed and ratified, unless it have been reasoned of and debated three days in the council before it be decreed.

It is death to have any consultation for the commonwealth out of the council, or the place of the common election. This statute, they say, was made to the intent, that the prince and Tranibors might not easily conspire together to oppress the people by tyranny, and to change the state of the weal public. Therefore matters of great weight and importance be brought to the election-house of the Syphogrants, which open the matter to their families. And afterwards, when they have consulted among themselves, they show their device to the council. Sometimes the matter is brought before the council of the whole island.

Furthermore, this custom also the council useth, to dispute or reason of no matter the same day that it is first proposed or put forth, but to defer it to the next sitting of the council. Because that no man when he hath rashly there spoken that cometh to his tongue's end, shall then afterward rather study for reasons wherewith to defend and maintain his first foolish sentence, than for the commodity of the commonwealth; as one rather willing the harm or hindrance of the weal public than any loss or diminution of his own existimation. And as one that would be ashamed (which is a very foolish shame) to be counted anything at the first overseen in the matter; who at the first ought to have spoken rather wisely, than hastily or rashly.

Of Sciences, Crafts and Occupations

Husbandry is a science common to them all in general, both men and women, wherein they be all expert and cunning. In this they be all instructed even from their youth; partly in their schools with traditions and precepts, and partly in the country nigh the city, brought up as it were in playing, not only beholding the use of it, but by occasion of exercising their bodies practising it also.

Besides husbandry, which (as I said) is common to them all, every one of them learneth one or other several and particular science, as his own proper craft. That is most commonly either clothworking in wool or flax, or masonry, of the smith's craft, or the carpenter's science. For there is none other occupation that any number to speak of doth use there. For their garments, which throughout all the island be of one fashion (saving that there is a difference between the man's garment and the woman's, between the married and the unmarried), and this one continueth for evermore unchanged, seemly and comely to the eye, no let to the moving and welding of the body, also fit both for winter and summer: as for these garments (I say) every family maketh their own. But of the other foresaid crafts every man learneth one. And not only the men, but also the women. But the women, as the weaker sort, be put to the easier crafts; as to work wool and flax. The more laboursome sciences be committed to the men. For the most part every man is brought up in his father's craft. For most commonly they be naturally thereto bent and inclined. But if a man's mind stand to any other, he is by adoption put into a family of that occupation,

which he doth most fantasy. Whom not only his father, but also the
magistrates do diligently look to, that he be put to a discreet and an honest
householder. Yea, and if any person, when he hath learned one craft, be
desirous to learn also another, he is likewise suffered and permitted.

When he hath learned both, he occupieth whether he will; unless the city
have more need of the one than of the other. The chief and almost the only
office of the Syphogrants is, to see and take heed that no man sit idle, but
that every one apply his own craft with earnest diligence; and yet for all
that, not to be wearied, from early in the morning to late in the evening,
with continual work, like labouring and toiling beasts. For this is worse
than the miserable and wretched condition of bondmen, which nevertheless is almost everywhere the life of workmen and artificers, saving in
Utopia.

For they, dividing the day and the night into twenty-four just hours,
appoint and assign only six of those hours to work; three before noon,
upon the which they go straight to dinner; and after dinner, when they
have rested two hours, then they work three hours, and upon that they go
to supper. About eight of the clock in the evening (counting one of the
clock at the first hour after noon) they go to bed; eight hours they give to
sleep. All the void time, that is between the hours of work, sleep, and meat,
that they be suffered to bestow, every man as he liketh best himself. Not to
the intent that they should misspend this time in riot or slothfulness; but
being then licensed from the labour of their own occupations, to bestow
the time well and thriftily upon some other science, as shall please them.
For it is a solemn custom there to have lectures daily early in the morning;
where to be present they only be constrained that be namely chosen and
appointed to learning. Howbeit a great multitude of every sort of people,
both men and women, go to hear lectures, some one and some another, as
every man's nature is inclined. Yet, this notwithstanding, if any man had
rather bestow this time upon his own occupation (as it chanceth in many,
whose minds rise not in the contemplation of any science liberal) he is not
letted nor prohibited, but is also praised and commended, as profitable to
the commonwealth.

After supper they bestow one hour in play; in summer in their gardens,
in winter in their common halls where they dine and sup. There they
exercise themselves in music, or else in honest and wholesome communication. Dice-play, and such other foolish and pernicious games they
know not. But they use two games not much unlike the chess. The one is
the battle of numbers, wherein one number stealeth away another. The
other is wherein vices fight with virtues, as it were in battle array, or a set
field. In the which game is very properly showed both the strife and
discord that vices have among themselves, and again their unity and
concord against virtues; and also what vices be repugnant to what virtues:
with what power and strength they assail them openly; by what wiles and

subtlety they assault them secretly: with what help and aid the virtues resist, and overcome the puissance of the vices; by what craft they frustrate their purposes: and finally by what sleight or means the one getteth the victory . . .

Of their Living and Mutual Conversation Together

But now will I declare how the citizens use themselves one towards another; what familiar occupying and entertainment there is among the people, and what fashion they use in the distribution of everything. First the city consisteth of families, the families most commonly be made of kindreds. For the women, when they be married at a lawful age, they go into their husbands' houses. But the male children, with all the whole male offspring, continue still in their own family and be governed of the eldest and ancientest father, unless he dote for age; for then the next to him in age is placed in his room.

But to the intent the prescript number of the citizens should neither decrease nor above measure increase, it is ordained that no family, which in every city be six thousand in the whole, besides them of the country, shall at once have fewer children of the age of fourteen years or thereabout than ten or more than sixteen, for of children under this age no number can be prescribed or appointed. This measure or number is easily observed and kept, by putting them that in fuller families be above the number into families of smaller increase. But if chance be that in the whole city the store increase above the just number, therewith they fill up the lack of other cities.

But if so be that the multitude throughout the whole island pass and exceed the due number, then they choose out of every city certain citizens, and build up a town under their own laws in the next land where the inhabitants have much waste and unoccupied ground, receiving also of the same country people to them, if they will join and dwell with them. They thus joining and dwelling together do easily agree in one fashion of living, and that to the great wealth of both the peoples. For they so bring the matter about by their laws, that the ground which before was neither good nor profitable for the one nor for the other, is now sufficient and fruitful enough for them both. But if the inhabitants of that land will not dwell with them to be ordered by their laws, then they drive them out of those bounds which they have limited and appointed out for themselves. And if they resist and rebel, then they make war against them. For they count this the most just cause of war, when any people holdeth a piece of ground void and vacant to no good nor profitable use, keeping others from the use and possession of it, which notwithstanding by the law of nature ought thereof to be nourished and relieved. If any chance do so much diminish the number of any of their cities that it cannot be filled up again, without the diminishing of the just number of the other cities (which they say chanced but twice since the beginning of the land through a great pestilent plague), then they fulfil and make up the number with citizens fetched out of their own foreign towns, for they had rather suffer their foreign towns to decay and perish, than any city of their own island to be diminished.

But now again to the conversation of the citizens among themselves. The eldest (as I said) ruleth the family. The wives be ministers to their husbands, the children to their parents, and, to be short, the younger to their elders. Every city is divided into four equal parts or quarters. In the midst of every quarter there is a market-place of all manner of things. Thither the works of every family be brought into certain houses. And every kind of thing is laid up several in barns or storehouses. From thence the father of every family, or every householder, fetcheth whatsoever he and his hath need of, and carrieth it away with him without money, without exchange, without any gage, pawn, or pledge. For why should anything be denied unto him? Seeing there is abundance of all things, and that it is not to be feared lest any man will ask more than he needeth. For why should it be thought that that man would ask more than enough which is sure never to lack? Certainly in all kinds of living creatures either fear of lack doth cause covetousness and raven, or in man only pride, which counteth it a glorious thing to pass and excel others in the superfluous and vain ostentation of things. The which kind of vice among the Utopians can have no place.

Next to the market-places that I spake of, stand meat markets; whither be brought not only all sorts of herbs, and the fruits of trees, with bread, but also fish, and all manner of four-footed beasts and wild-fowl that be man's meat. But first the filthiness and odour thereof is clean washed away in the running river without the city, in places appointed meet for the same purpose. From thence the beasts be brought in killed, and clean washed by the hands of their bondmen. For they permit not their free citizens to accustom themselves to the killing of beasts, through the use whereof they think clemency, the gentlest affection of our nature, by little and little to decay and perish. Neither they suffer anything that is filthy, loathsome, or uncleanly, to be brought into the city, lest the air by the stench thereof, infected and corrupt, should cause pestilent diseases.

Moreover, every street hath certain great large halls set in equal distance one from another, every one known by a several name. In these halls dwell the Syphogrants. And to every one of the same halls be appointed thirty families, on either side fifteen. The stewards of every hall at a certain hour come in to the meat markets, where they receive meat according to the number of their halls.

But first, and chiefly of all, respect is had to the sick, that be cured in the hospitals. For in the circuit of the city, a little without the walls, they have four hospitals, so big, so wide, so ample, and so large, that they may seem four little towns, which were devised of that bigness partly to the intent the sick, be they never so many in number, should not lie too throng or strait, and, therefore, uneasily and incommodiously; and partly that they which were taken and holden with contagious diseases, such as be wont by infection to creep from one to another, might be laid apart far from the company of the residue. These hospitals be so well appointed, and with all things necessary to health so furnished, and, moreover, so diligent attendance through the continual presence of cunning physicians is given, that though no man be sent thither against his will, yet, notwithstanding, there is no sick person in all the city that had not rather lie there than at home in his own house . . .

Of Bondmen, Sick Persons, Wedlock, and divers other Matters

They neither make bondmen of prisoners taken in battle, unless it be in battle that they fought themselves, nor of bondmen's children, nor, to be short, of any such as they can get out of foreign countries, though he were there a bondman. But either such as among themselves for heinous offences be punished with bondage, or else such as in the cities of other lands for great trespasses be condemned to death. And of this sort of bondmen they have most store. For many of them they bring home, sometimes paying very little for them, yea, most commonly getting them for gramercy. These sorts of bondmen they keep not only in continual work and labour, but also in bands. But their own men they handle hardest, whom they judge more desperate, and to have deserved greater punishment, because they being so godly brought up to virtue in so excellent a commonwealth, could not for all that be refrained from misdoing.

Another kind of bondman they have, when a vile drudge being a poor labourer in another country doth choose of his own free will to be a bondman among them. These they entreat and order honestly, and entertain almost as gently as their own free citizens, saving that they put them to a little more labour, as thereto accustomed. If any such be disposed to depart thence (which seldom is seen), they neither hold him against his will, neither send him away with empty hands.

The sick (as I said) they see to with great affection, and let nothing at all pass concerning either physic or good diet, whereby they may be restored again to their health. Such as be sick of incurable diseases they comfort with sitting by them, with talking with them, and, to be short, with all manner of helps that may be. But if the disease be not only incurable, but also full of continual pain and anguish, then the priests and the magistrates exhort the man, seeing he is not able to do any duty of life, and by overliving his own death is noisome and irksome to others, and grievous to himself, that he will determine with himself no longer to cherish that pestilent and painful disease. And seeing his life is to him but a torment, that he will not be unwilling to die, but rather take a good hope to him, and either despatch himself out of that painful life, as out of a prison, or a rack of torment, or else suffer himself willingly to be rid out of it by others. And in so doing they tell him he shall do wisely, seeing by his death he shall lose no commodity, but end his pain. And because in that act he shall follow the counsel of the priests, that is to say, of the interpreters of God's will and pleasure, they show him that he shall do like a godly and a virtuous man.

They that be thus persuaded, finish their lives willingly, either with hunger, or else die in their sleep without any feeling of death. But they cause none such to die against his will, nor they use no less diligence and attendance about him, believing this to be an honourable death. Else he that killeth himself before that the priests and the counsel have allowed the cause of his death, him as unworthy either to be buried, or with fire to be consumed, they cast unburied into some stinking marsh.

The woman is not married before she be eighteen years old. The man is four years older before he marry. If either the man or the woman be proved to have actually offended before their marriage, with another, the party that so hath trespassed is sharply punished. And both the offenders be forbidden ever after in all their life to marry, unless the fault be forgiven by the prince's pardon. But both the goodman and the goodwife of the house where that offence was committed, as being slack and negligent in looking to their charge, be in danger of great reproach and infamy. That offence is so sharply punished, because they perceive, that unless they be diligently kept from the liberty of this vice, few will join together in the love of marriage, wherein all the life must be led with one, and also all the griefs and displeasures coming therewith patiently be taken and borne.

Furthermore in choosing wives and husbands they observe earnestly and straightly a custom which seemed to us very fond and foolish. For a sad and honest matron showeth the woman, be she maid or widow, naked to the wooer. And likewise a sage and discreet man exhibiteth the wooer naked to the woman.[1] At this custom we laughed, and disallowed it as foolish.

[1] In this respect, More practised what he preached. According to John Aubrey's *Brief Lives*, c. 1690:

> Memorandum that in his *Utopia*, his lawe is that the young people are to see each other stark-naked before marriage. Sir [William] Roper, of . . . ('tis by Eltham in Kent), came one morning pretty early to my Lord, with a proposall to marry one of [his] daughters. My Lord's daughters were then both together a bed in a truckle-bed in their father's chamber asleep. He carries Sir [William] into the chamber, and takes the sheet by the corner and suddenly whippes it off. They lay on their backs, and their smocks up as high as their arme pitts; this awakened them, and immediately they turned on their bellies. Quoth Sir William Roper, "I have seen both sides", and so gave a patt on her buttock, he made choice of, sayeing, "Thou art mine."
>
> Here was all the trouble of the wooeing.

But they on the other part do greatly wonder at the folly of all other nations, which in buying a colt, whereas a little money is in hazard, be so chary and circumspect, that though he be almost all bare, yet they will not buy him, unless the saddle and all the harness be taken off, lest under those coverings be hid some gall or sore. And yet in choosing a wife, which shall be either pleasure or displeasure to them all their life after, they be so reckless, that all the residue of the woman's body being covered with clothes, they esteem her scarcely by one handbreath (for they can see no more but her face), and so to join her to them not without great jeopardy of evil agreeing together, if anything in her body afterward should chance to offend and mislike them. For all men be not so wise as to have respect to the virtuous conditions of the party. And the endowments of the body cause the virtues of the mind more to be esteemed and regarded, yea, even in the marriages of wise men. Verily so foul deformity may be hid under those coverings, that it may quite alienate and take away the man's mind from his wife, when it shall not be lawful for their bodies to be separate again. If such deformity happen by any chance after the marriage is consummate and finished, well, there is no remedy but patience. Every man must take his fortune well a worth. But it were well done that a law were made whereby all such deceits might be eschewed and avoided beforehand.

And this were they constrained more earnestly to look upon, because they only of the nations in that part of the world be content every man with one wife apiece. And matrimony is there never broken, but by death; except adultery break the bond, or else the intolerable wayward manners of either party. For if either of them find themselves for any such cause grieved, they may by the licence of the council change and take another. But the other party liveth ever after in infamy and out of wedlock. Howbeit the husband to put away his wife for no other fault, but for that some mishap is fallen to her body, this by no means they will suffer. For they judge it a great point of cruelty, that anybody in their most need of help and comfort should be cast off and forsaken, and that old age, which both bringeth sickness with it, and is a sickness itself, should unkindly and unfaithfully be dealt withal.

But now and then it chanceth, whereas the man and the woman cannot well agree between themselves, both of them finding other with whom they hope to live more quietly and merrily, that they by the full consent of them both be divorced asunder and married again to other. But that not without the authority of the council. Which agreeth to no divorces before they and their wives have diligently tried and examined the matter. Yea, and then also they be loth to consent to it, because they know this to be the next way to break love between man and wife, to be in easy hope of a new marriage.

Breakers of wedlock be punished with most grievous bondage. And if both the offenders were married, then the parties which in that behalf have suffered wrong, being divorced from the advoutrers, be married together, if they will, or else to whom they lust. But if either of them both do still continue in love toward so unkind a bedfellow, the use of wedlock is not to them forbidden, if the party faultless be disposed to follow in toiling and drudgery the person which for that offence is condemned to bondage. And very oft it chanceth that the repentance of the one, and the earnest diligence of the other, doth so move the prince with pity and compassion, that he restoreth the bond person from servitude to liberty and freedom again. But if the same party be taken eftsoons in that fault, there is no other way but death.

To other trespasses no prescript punishment is appointed by any law. But according to the heinousness of the offence, or contrary, so the punishment is moderated by the discretion of the council. The husbands chastise their wives, and the parents their children, unless they have done any so horrible an offence that the open punishment thereof maketh much for the advancement of honest manners. But most commonly the most heinous faults be punished with the incommodity of bondage. For that they suppose to be to the offenders no less grief, and to the commonwealth more profit, than if they should hastily put them to death, and so make them quite out of the way. For there cometh more profit of their labour than of their death, and by their example they fear other the longer from like offences. But if they being thus used, do rebel and kick again, then forsooth they be slain as desperate and wild beasts, whom neither prison nor chain could restrain and keep under. But they which take their bondage patiently be not left all hopeless. For after they have been broken and tamed with long miseries, if then they show such repentance, as thereby it may be perceived that they be sorrier for their offence than for their punishment, sometimes by the prince's prerogative, and sometimes by the voice and consent of the people, their bondage either is mitigated, or else clean released and forgiven. He that moveth to advoutry is in no less danger and jeopardy than if he had committed advoutry in deed. For in all offences they count the intent and pretensed purpose as evil as the act or deed itself, thinking that no let ought to excuse him that did his best to have no let.

They have singular delight and pleasure in fools. And as it is a great reproach to do any of them hurt or injury, so they prohibit not to take pleasure of foolishness. For that, they think, doth much good to the fools. And if any man be so sad and stern, that he cannot laugh neither at their words, nor at their deeds, none of them be committed to his tuition, for fear lest he would not entreat them gently and favourably enough; to whom they should bring no delectation (for other goodness in them is none), much less any profit should they yield him.

To mock a man for his deformity, or for that he lacketh any part or limb of his body, is counted great dishonesty and reproach, not to him that is mocked, but to him that mocketh. Which unwisely doth upbraid any man of that as a vice, that was not in his power to eschew. Also as they count and reckon very little wit to be in him that regardeth not natural beauty and comeliness, so to help the same with paintings is taken for a vain and a wanton pride, not without great infamy. For they know even by very experience that no comeliness of beauty doth so highly commend and advance the wives in the conceit of their husbands, as honest conditions and lowliness. For as love is oftentimes won with beauty, so it is not kept, preserved, and continued but by virtue and obedience.

They do not only fear their people from doing evil by punishments, but also allure them to virtue with rewards of honour. Therefore they set up in the market-place the images of notable men, and of such as have been great and bountiful benefactors to the commonwealth, for the perpetual memory of their good acts: and also that the glory and renown of the ancestors may stir and provoke their posterity to virtue. He that inordinately and ambitiously desireth promotions is left all hopeless for ever attaining any promotion as long as he liveth.

They live together lovingly. For no magistrate is either haughty or fearful. Fathers they be called, and like fathers they use themselves. The citizens (as it is their duty) willingly exhibit unto them due honour without any compulsion. Nor the prince himself is not known from the other by princely apparel, or a robe of state, not by a crown or diadem royal, or cap of maintenance, but by a little sheaf of corn carried before him. And so a taper of wax is borne before the bishop, whereby only he is known . . .

Part Three

The Age of Freedom

The Modern World, 1517–

INTRODUCTION

When Martin Luther nailed his Theses to the door of Wittenberg church in 1517, he had set in train a revolution. This was not his intention (Luther, in most respects, was deeply conservative), but there were forces abroad in Europe outside his purview.

These forces would find Luther's Protestantism a justification, a fillip, even a necessity. There were the kings, such as Henry VIII of England, who used Protestantism to weaken, then break, their ties to the Roman Catholic Church for reason of pure, selfish realpolitik – a divorce from Anne Boleyn, in Henry's case. More uncomprehending, but even more needy, were those burgeoning capitalists who grasped Protestantism's stress on the individual and on industriousness ("the Protestant work ethic") to validate their lives. The "individualism" of Protestanism stemmed largely from Luther's belief in the Bible, not the established Church, as the supreme religious arbiter, and anyone who was literate could read the Bible. The liberating potentialities of Protestantism were enormous.

Henceforth the rise of Protestantism, capitalism and political freedom tended to go hand in hand. The proof was in Protestant Holland and England, the most advanced economic countries in the world in the 16th and 17th centuries. The north of Holland declared itself a republic in its war of liberation from Spain in 1581; England achieved the world's first democratic revolution in 1642. And this at a time when most of the West was ruled by preening monarchs who claimed the "divine right" to do so. (Of course, the English put a monarch back on the throne, but one with trimmed feathers; Parliament remained the real power in the land.) Holland and England were also the world's leading scientific and intellectual powers. In Catholic countries, meanwhile, the Inquisition of the Catholic "Counter-Reformation" was paranoically banning anything not in accordance with the precepts of Aquinas.

Not that the Inquisition was entirely successful. The French philosopher René Descartes, perhaps mindful of the house arrest of the Italian scientist Galileo, was careful in the expression of his ideas, but they would prove deeply damaging to Catholicism nonetheless. And indeed, to Protestanism too, in due course.

In his 1637 *Discourse de la Méthode* Descartes decided to reject all received wisdom and authority, and begin at the beginning. The one unassailable truth was that his own mind was thinking, and that he himself must therefore exist: *Cogito, ergo sum* ("I think, therefore I am"). Descartes accepted God, but a God proven by Rationalism, not faith. Fifty years on, Sir Isaac Newton furnished powerful support for Descartes' contention that the great truth of life and the universe might be discovered by reason alone. In *Philosophiae Naturalis Principia Mathematica*, 1687, Newton declared that one force – gravity – held the universe together. The Western world was now entering the "Age of Enlightenment", the "Age of Reason". Phenomena previously attributable to God were now explained by science. Descartes and Newton were religious men. But the logical step was to use science to explain away God. Atheism was at hand.

Meanwhile, it was perhaps just a matter of time before someone would suggest that society, as well as the universe, was subject to an all embracing natural law. And that this law held that all men were free and equal. The philosopher who did so was the Englishman John Locke in *Two Treatises on Government*, 1690, which for good measure also rejected the Divine Right of kings to rule. Much of Locke's book was influenced by recent historical practice, namely the English Revolutions of 1642 and 1688. Yet, just as Locke drew on history, so he made it. His contention that any ruling body which offended against natural law should be removed had a direct influence on the American Revolution of 1775, which threw off British colonial rule. Thomas Jefferson's draft of the Declaration of Independence, based on his reading of Locke (and other democrats such as Montesquieu, Rousseau and Paine), declared: "We hold these truths to be self-evident. That all men are created equal, that they are endowed by their Creator with certain inalienable rights, that among these are Life, Liberty and the Pursuit of Happiness."

Revolution for democratic rights was infectious. In 1789 it reached France, the exemplar of the absolutist state, where Louis XIV, the "Sun King" had opined "*L'état c'est moi*" (I am the state). On 14 July 1789 the Parisians stormed the Bastille fortress. Within a year the monarchy had been swept away, and a republic declared in its place. Eventually, under attack by foreign states, the French Republic fell into terror, but its purest and best ideals lived on to cross the boundaries of most of the Western world. The liberal nationalism of the early 19th century – the most fervent and potent ideology in the West since the Reformation – was directly descended from the French Revolution. So too, in the arts, the Romantic poetry of Shelley and Wordsworth, the Transcendentalist essays of Emerson and Thoreau.

Upheaval in this Age of Revolution was not only political. The most fundamental change was economic: the coming of the Industrial Revolution, which began in Britain as early as 1750. The factory system – Blake's "Dark Satanic Mills" – desecrated the landscape and squeezed teeming millions into overcrowded conurbations.

This selfsame Industrial Revolution brought *Home sapiens sapiens* fantastic economic and political freedom.

It would be cold comfort to the first generations of industrial workers but their labours massively raised the productive basis of society and their machines, as Oscar Wilde prophesied in *The Soul of Socialism Under Man*, would eventually set men and women free from much drudgery. Industrial capitalism has replaced the washtub with the washing machine, the candle with the electric light, the brush with the vacuum cleaner.

It would be cold comfort to the first generations of industrial workers but their sheer crowded togetherness enabled them to organize for political change. Notions of individual liberty and participatory democracy had in Britain, for example, a long history but the franchise was restricted to men of property. The final pushes to universal suffrage, in the Acts of 1832 and 1918, came because the people protested for them. But nothing in history worth the winning came without a struggle.

Material quality and political liberalism. These have been the hallmarks of the new civilization of the West. Over the last century, this new civilization has largely maintained representative democracy throughout nearly all of the Western world, liberated its own women and black minorities (or at least allowed their liberation), and set free colonial possessions. Over the same timespan, the new West has – largely – enjoyed universal education, health provision, improved mental well-being, paid holidays, longer holidays and a life expectancy which has, because of better food and wonder drugs such as penicillin, almost doubled to 80 years or so.

It can be correctly complained that there are things wrong with the modern West. A glance around London, Chicago or Paris will show disquieting inequalities of wealth, environmental vandalism and spiritual impoverishment.

Yet the modern West is unique because it alone in the history of the world has the means – economic, political and moral – to set set right wrongs.

These means, which are collected together in the pages of this book, are our inheritance. We only have to cherish and share them.

THE NINETY-FIVE THESES, 1517

Martin Luther

A priest at the University of Wittenberg, Martin Luther (1483–1546) attacked the corrupt sale of "indulgences" (remissions of sin) in 95 theses which he nailed to the door of the local church on Halloween, 1517. This small defiance of papal practice set in train the Protestant Reformation.

Luther was not the first to bemoan the scandals of the Catholic Church; Wyclif and Huss had done so in the preceding centuries, with the latter burned at the stake for his impudence. Luther, however, had the benefit of timing: the Renaissance had created a continental climate of intellectual questioning; many burgeoning European princes wanted a stick to beat the papacy for their own fiscal and nationalistic ends; and mercantile capitalism was on the rise. The new economy needed a new ideology, and found it in Martin Luther's "Protestantism". This soon moved beyond mere criticism of "indulgences" to the doctrine of salvation through faith not good works, and the assertion that the Bible, not the Church, was final authority for conduct and belief. If this was the case then any individual who could read the Bible was an independent in religion. Luther's promotion of individuality accorded strongly with capitalistic entrepreneurial spirit.

Luther himself was excommunicated from the Church of Rome in 1521, the same year in which he was called by Charles V, the Holy Roman Emperor, to defend himself at the Diet of Worms (see pp 214–6). For his own protection thereafter, Luther was lodged by the elector of Saxony in the Wartburg, where he translated the Bible into German. In many respects, Luther himself was a religious and political moderate (his primary, if not his only, interest was the salvation of souls) but the logic of Protestantism was unstoppable. By the time of Luther's death in 1546, numerous "Protestant" nations in Europe had already broken away from Catholicism, and the inherent radicalism of the new religion was being zealously articulated by French theologian John Calvin (1509–64), whose *Institutes of the Christian Religion* from 1536 was strongly democratic and egalitarian. The "elect", sermonized the *Institutes*, had no need of a priest and managed their churches by election. It is no accident that Calvinism, reworked as Puritanism, helped make the English Revolution.

In the desire and with the purpose of elucidating the truth, a disputation will be held on the underwritten propositions at Wittenberg, under the presidency of the Reverend Father Martin Luther, Monk of the Order of St Augustine, Master of Arts and of Sacred Theology, and ordinary Reader of the same in that place. He therefore asks those who cannot be present and discuss the subject with us orally, to do so by letter in their absence. In the name of our Lord Jesus Christ. Amen.

1. Our Lord and Master Jesus Christ in saying "Repent ye" (*poenitentiam agite*), etc., intended that the whole life of believers should be penitence (*poenitentia*).
2. This word cannot be understood as sacramental penance (*poenitentia*), that is, of the confession and satisfaction which are performed under the ministry of priests.
3. It does not, however, refer solely to inward penitence (*poenitentia*); nay, such inward penitence is naught, unless it outwardly produces various mortifications of the flesh.
4. The penalty (*poena*) thus continues as long as the hatred of self (that is, true inward penitence); namely, till our entrance into the Kingdom of Heaven.
5. The Pope has neither the will nor the power to remit any penalties except those which he has imposed by his own authority, or by that of the canons.
6. The Pope has no power to remit any guilt, except by declaring and warranting it to have been remitted by God; or at most by remitting cases reserved for himself; in which cases, if his power were despised, guilt would certainly remain.
7. Certainly God remits no man's guilt without at the same time subjecting him, humbled in all things, to the authority of his representative the priest.
8. The penitential canons are imposed only on the living, and no burden ought to be imposed on the dying, according to them.
9. Hence, the Holy Spirit acting in the Pope does well for us in that, in his decrees, he always makes exception of the article of death and of necessity.
10. Those priests act unlearnedly and wrongly who, in the case of the dying, reserve the canonical penances for Purgatory.
11. Those tares about changing the canonical penalty into the penalty of Purgatory seem surely to have been sown while the bishops were asleep.

12. Formerly the canonical penalties were imposed not after but before absolution, as tests of true contrition.
13. The dying pay all penalties by death, and are already dead to the canon laws, and are by right relieved from them.
14. The imperfect vigour or love of a dying person necessarily brings with it great fear, and the less it is, the greater the fear it brings.
15. This fear and horror is sufficient by itself, to say nothing of other things, to constitute the pains of Purgatory, since it is very near to the horror of despair.
16. Hell, Purgatory, and Heaven appear to differ as despair, almost despair, and peace of mind differ.
17. With souls in Purgatory it seems that it must needs be that as horror diminishes so love increases.
18. Nor does it seem to be proved by any reasoning or any Scriptures, that they are outside of the state of merit or of the increase of love.
19. Nor does this appear to be proved, that they are sure and confident of their own blessedness, at least all of them, though we may be very sure of it.
20. Therefore the Pope, when he speaks of the plenary remission of all penalties, does not mean really of all, but only of those imposed by himself.
21. Thus those preachers of indulgences are in error who say that by the indulgences of the Pope a man is freed and saved from all punishment.
22. For in fact he remits to souls in Purgatory no penalty which they would have had to pay in this life according to the canons.
23. If any entire remission of all penalties can be granted to any one it is certain that it is granted to none but the most perfect, that is to very few.
24. Hence, the greater part of the people must needs be deceived by this indiscriminate and high-sounding promise of release from penalties.
25. Such power over Purgatory as the Pope has in general, such has every bishop in his own diocese, and every parish priest in his own parish, in particular.
26. The Pope acts most rightly in granting remission to souls not by the power of the keys (which is of no avail in this case), but by the way of intercession.
27. They preach man who say that the soul flies out of Purgatory as soon as the money thrown into the chest rattles.
28. It is certain that, when the money rattles in the chest, avarice and gain may be increased, but the effect of the intercession of the Church depends on the will of God alone.
29. Who knows whether all the souls in Purgatory desire to be redeemed from it – witness the story told of Saints Severinus and Paschal?

30. No man is sure of the reality of his own contrition, much less of the attainment of plenary remission.

31. Rare as is a true penitent, so rare is one who truly buys indulgences – that is to say, most rare.

32. Those who believe that, through letters of pardon, they are made sure of their own salvation will be eternally damned along with their teachers.

33. We must especially beware of those who say that these pardons from the Pope are that inestimable gift of God by which man is reconciled to God.

34. For the grace conveyed by these pardons has respect only to the penalties of sacramental satisfaction, which are of human appointment.

35. They preach no Christian doctrine who teach that contrition is not necessary for those who buy souls (out of Purgatory) or buy confessional licences.

36. Every Christian who feels true compunction has of right plenary remission of punishment and guilt even without letters of pardon.

37. Every true Christian, whether living or dead, has a share in all the benefits of Christ and of the Church, given by God, even without letters of pardon.

38. The remission, however, imparted by the Pope is by no means to be despised, since it is, as I have said, a declaration of the divine remission.

39. It is a most difficult thing, even for the most learned theologians, to exalt at the same time in the eyes of the people the ample effect of pardons and the necessity of true contrition.

40. True contrition seeks and loves punishment; while the ampleness of pardons relaxes it, and causes men to hate it, or at least gives occasion for them to do so.

41. Apostolic pardons ought to be proclaimed with caution, lest the people should falsely suppose that they are placed before other good works of charity.

42. Christians should be taught that it is not the wish of the Pope that the buying of pardons should be in any way compared to works of mercy.

43. Christians should be taught that he who gives to a poor man, or lends to a needy man, does better than if he bought pardons.

44. Because by works of charity, charity increases, and the man becomes better; while by means of pardons, he does not become better, but only freer from punishment.

45. Christians should be taught that he who sees any one in need, and, passing him by, gives money for pardons, is not purchasing for himself the indulgences of the Pope but the anger of God.

46. Christians should be taught that, unless they have superfluous wealth,

they are bound to keep what is necessary for the use of their own households, and by no means to lavish it on pardons.

47. Christians should be taught that while they are free to buy pardons they are not commanded to do so.

48. Christians should be taught that the Pope, in granting pardons, has both more need and more desire that devout prayer should be made for him than that the money should be readily paid.

49. Christians should be taught that the Pope's pardons are useful if they do not put their trust in them, but most hurtful if through them they lose the fear of God.

50. Christians should be taught that, if the Pope were acquainted with the exactions of the Preachers of pardons, he would prefer that the Basilica of St Peter should be burnt to ashes rather than that it should be built up with the skin, flesh, and bones of his sheep.

51. Christians should be taught that as it would be the duty so would it be the wish of the Pope even to sell, if necessary, the Basilica of St Peter, and to give of his own money to very many of those from whom the Preachers of pardons extract money.

52. Vain is the hope of salvation through letters of pardon, even if a commissary – nay, the Pope himself – were to pledge his own soul for them.

53. They were enemies of Christ and of the Pope who, in order that the pardons may be preached, condemn the Word of God to utter silence in other churches.

54. Wrong is done to the Word of God when, in the same sermon, an equal or longer time is spent on pardons than on it.

55. The mind of the Pope necessarily is that, if pardons, which are a very small matter, are celebrated with single bells, single processions, and single ceremonies, the Gospel, which is a very great matter, should be preached with a hundred bells, a hundred processions, and a hundred ceremonies.

56. The treasures of the Church, whence the Pope grants indulgences, are neither sufficiently named nor known among the people of Christ.

57. It is clear that they are at least not temporal treasures, for these are not so readily lavished, but only accumulated, by means of the preachers.

58. Nor are they the merits of Christ and of the saints, for these, independently of the Pope, are always working grace to the inner man, and the cross, death, and hell to the outer man.

59. St Lawrence said that the treasures of the Church are the poor of the Church, but he spoke according to the use of the term in his time.

60. We are not speaking rashly when we say that the keys of the Church, bestowed through the merits of Christ, are that treasure.

61. For it is clear that the power of the Pope is sufficient of itself for the remission of [canonical] penalties and of [reserved] cases.

62. The true treasure of the Church is the Holy Gospel of the glory and grace of God.

63. This treasure, however, is deservedly most hateful, because it makes the first to be last.

64. While the treasure of indulgences is deservedly most acceptable, because it makes the last to be first.

65. Hence the treasures of the Gospel are nets, wherewith of old they fished for the men of riches.

66. The treasures of indulgences are nets, wherewith they now fish for the riches of men.

67. Those indulgences, which the preachers loudly proclaim to be the greatest graces, are seen to be truly such as regards the promotion of gain.

68. Yet they are in reality most insignificant when compared to the grace of God and the piety of the cross.

69. Bishops and parish priests are bound to receive the commissaries of apostolical pardons with all reverence.

70. But they are still more bound to see to it with all their eyes, and take heed with all their ears, that these men do not preach their own dreams in place of the Pope's commission.

71. He who speaks against the truth of apostolical pardons, let him be anathema and accursed.

72. But he, on the other hand, who exerts himself against the wantonness and licence of speech of the Preachers of pardons, let him be blessed.

73. As the Pope justly thunders against those who use any kind of contrivance to the injury of the traffic in pardons.

74. Much more is it his intention to thunder against those who, under the pretext of pardons, use contrivances to the injury of holy charity and of truth.

75. To think that the Papal pardons have such power that they could absolve a man even if – by an impossibility – he had violated the Mother of God, is madness.

76. We affirm on the contrary that Papal pardons cannot take away even the least of venial sins, as regards its guilt.

77. The saying that, even if St Peter were now Pope, he could grant no greater graces, is blasphemy against St Peter and the Pope.

78. We affirm on the contrary that both he and any other Pope has greater graces to grant, namely, the Gospel, powers, gifts of healing, etc. (I Cor. XII).

79. To say that the cross set up among the insignia of the Papal arms is of equal power with the cross of Christ, is blasphemy.

80. Those bishops, priests and theologians who allow such discourses to have currency among the people will have to render an account.

81. This licence in the preaching of pardons makes it no easy thing, even

for learned men, to protect the reverence due to the Pope against the calumnies, or at all events, the keen questioning of the laity.

82. As for instance: why does not the Pope empty Purgatory for the sake of most holy charity and of the supreme necessity of souls – this being the most just of all reasons – if he redeems an infinite number of souls for the sake of that most fatal thing, money, to be spent on building a basilica – this being a very slight reason?

83. Again; why do funeral masses and anniversary masses for the deceased continue, and why does not the Pope return, or permit the withdrawal of, the funds bequeathed for this purpose, since it is a wrong to pray for those who are already redeemed?

84. Again; what is this new kindness of God and the Pope, in that, for money's sake, they permit an impious man and an enemy of God to redeem a pious soul which loves God, and yet do not redeem that same pious and beloved soul out of free charity on account of its own need?

85. Again; why is it that the penitential canons, long since abrogated and dead in themselves, in very fact and not only by usage, are yet still redeemed with money, through the granting of indulgences, as if they were full of life?

86. Again; why does not the Pope, whose riches are at this day more ample than those of the wealthiest of the wealthy, build the single Basilica of St Peter with his own money rather than with that of poor believers?

87. Again; what does the Pope remit or impart to those who through perfect contrition have a right to plenary remission and participation?

88. Again; what greater good could the Church receive than if the Pope, instead of once, as he does now, were to bestow these remissions and participations a hundred times a day on any one of the faithful?

89. Since it is the salvation of souls, rather than money, that the Pope seeks by his pardons, why does he suspend the letters and pardons granted long ago, since they are equally efficacious?

90. To repress these scruples and arguments of the laity by force alone, and not to resolve them by giving reasons, is to expose the Church and the Pope to the ridicule of their enemies, and to make Christian men unhappy.

91. If then pardons were preached according to the spirit and mind of the Pope, all these questions would be resolved with ease; nay, would not exist.

92. Away then with all those prophets who say to the people of Christ: "Peace, peace," and there is no peace.

93. Blessed be all those prophets who say to the people of Christ: "The cross, the cross," and there is no cross.

94. Christians should be exhorted to strive to follow Christ their head through pains, deaths, and hells.
95. And thus trust to enter Heaven through many tribulations, rather than in the security of peace.

SPEECH BEFORE THE DIET OF WORMS, 1521

Martin Luther

Tried before the Holy Roman Emperor, Charles V, at the Diet of Worms, the founder of Protestantism (see pp 206–13) made a celebrated address, reproduced below.

Most serene Emperor, and You Illustrious Princes and Gracious Lords:– I this day appear before you in all humility, according to your command, and I implore your majesty and your august highnesses, by the mercies of God, to listen with favour to the defence of a cause which I am well assured is just and right. I ask pardon, if by reason of my ignorance, I am wanting in the manners that befit a court; for I have not been brought up in kings' palaces, but in the seclusion of a cloister.

Two questions were yesterday put to me by his imperial majesty; the first, whether I was the author of the books whose titles were read; the second, whether I wished to revoke or defend the doctrine I have taught. I answered the first, and I adhere to that answer.

As to the second, I have composed writings on very different subjects. In some I have discussed Faith and Good Works, in a spirit at once so pure, clear, and Christian, that even my adversaries themselves, far from finding anything to censure, confess that these writings are profitable, and deserve to be perused by devout persons. The pope's bull, violent as it is, acknowledges this. What, then, should I be doing if I were now to retract these writings? Wretched man! I alone, of all men living, should be abandoning truths approved by the unanimous voice of friends and enemies, and opposing doctrines that the whole world glories in confessing!

I have composed, secondly, certain works against popery, wherein I have attacked such as by false doctrines, irregular lives, and scandalous examples, afflict the Christian world, and ruin the bodies and souls of men. And is not this confirmed by the grief of all who fear God? Is it not manifest that the laws and human doctrines of the popes entangle, vex, and distress the consciences of the faithful, while the crying and endless extortions of Rome engulf the property and wealth of Christendom, and more particularly of this illustrious nation?

If I were to revoke what I have written on that subject, what should I do . . . but strengthen this tyranny, and open a wider door to so many and flagrant impieties? Bearing down all resistance with fresh fury, we should behold these proud men swell, foam, and rage more than ever! And not merely would the yoke which now weighs down Christians be made more grinding by my retraction – it would thereby become, so to speak, lawful – for, by my retraction, it would receive confirmation from your most serene majesty, and all the States of the Empire. Great God! I should thus be like to an infamous cloak, used to hide and cover over every kind of malice and tyranny.

In the third and last place, I have written some books against private individuals, who had undertaken to defend the tyranny of Rome by destroying faith. I freely confess that I may have attacked such persons with more violence than was consistent with my profession as an ecclesiastic: I do not think of myself as a saint; but neither can I retract these books, because I should, by so doing, sanction the impieties of my opponents, and they would thence take occasion to crush God's people with still more cruelty.

Yet, as I am a mere man, and not God, I will defend myself after the example of Jesus Christ, who said: "If I have spoken evil, bear witness against me" (John xviii, 23). How much more should I, who am but dust and ashes, and so prone to error, desire that every one should bring forward what he can against my doctrine.

Therefore, most serene emperor, and you illustrious princes, and all, whether high or low, who hear me, I implore you by the mercies of God to prove to me by the writings of the prophets and apostles that I am in error. As soon as I shall be convinced, I will instantly retract all my errors, and will myself be the first to seize my writings, and commit them to the flames.

What I have just said I think will clearly show that I have well considered and weighed the dangers to which I am exposing myself; but far from being dismayed by them, I rejoice exceedingly to see the Gospel this day, as of old, a cause of disturbance and disagreement. It is the character and destiny of God's word. "I came not to send peace unto the earth, but a sword," said Jesus Christ. God is wonderful and awful in His counsels. Let us have a care, lest in our endeavours to arrest discords, we be bound to fight against the holy word of God and bring down upon our heads a frightful deluge of inextricable dangers, present disaster, and everlasting desolations . . . Let us have a care lest the reign of the young and noble prince, the Emperor Charles, on whom, next to God, we build so many hopes, should not only commence, but continue and terminate its course under the most fatal auspices. I might cite examples drawn from the oracles of God. I might speak of Pharaohs, of kings of Babylon, or of Israel, who were never more contributing to their own ruin that when, by measures in appearances most prudent, they thought to establish their authority! "God removeth the mountains and they know not" (Job ix, 5).

In speaking thus, I do not suppose that such noble princes have need of my poor judgment; but I wish to acquit myself of a duty that Germany has a right to expect from her children. And so commending myself to your august majesty, and your most serene highnesses, I beseech you in all humility, not to permit the hatred of my enemies to rain upon me an indignation I have not deserved.

Since your most serene majesty and your high mightinesses require of me a simple, clear and direct answer, I will give one, and it is this: I cannot submit my faith either to the pope or to the council, because it is as clear as noonday that they have fallen into error and even into glaring inconsistency with themselves. If, then, I am not convinced by proof from Holy Scripture, or by cogent reasons, if I am not satisfied by the very text I have cited, and if my judgment is not in this way brought into subjection to God's word, I neither can nor will retract anything; for it cannot be right for a Christian to speak against his conscience. I stand here and can say no more. God help me. Amen.

THE CANDLE THAT SHALL NEVER BE PUT OUT: THE MARTYRDOM OF RIDLEY AND LATIMER, 1555

John Foxe

When Mary Tudor aceeded to the throne, a period of Catholic reaction was ushered into the land of England. Among those found guilty of the heresy of Protestantism by the committee of Convocation at Oxford were the bishops Nicholas Ridley and Hugh Latimer. They were duly burnt outside Balliol College. This account of their death, with its ringing last utterance from Hugh Latimer, is from Foxe's *History of the Acts and Monuments of the Church*, more popularly known as *Foxe's Book of Martyrs*.

Dr Ridley had a black gown such as he used to wear when he was a bishop; a tippet of velvet furred likewise about his neck, a velvet nightcap upon his head, and slippers on his feet. He walked to the stake between the mayor and an alderman.

After him came Mr Latimer in a poor Bristol frieze frock much worn, with his buttoned cap and kerchief on his head, all ready to the fire, a new long shroud hanging down to the feet; which at the first sight excited sorrow in the spectators, beholding on the one side the honour they some time had, and on the other the calamity into which they had fallen.

Dr Ridley, then looking back, saw Mr Latimer coming after, unto whom he said, "Oh, are you there?" "Yea," said Mr Latimer, "have after, as fast as I can." So he followed a pretty way off, and at length they came to the stake. Dr Ridley, first entering the place, earnestly held up both his hands, looking towards Heaven, then, shortly after seeing Mr Latimer with a cheerful look, he ran up to him and embraced him, saying, *Be of good heart, brother, for God will assuage the fury of the flames, or else strengthen us to abide it.*

He went then to the stake, and, kneeling down, prayed with great fervour, while Mr Latimer kneeled also, and prayed as earnestly as he.

After this they arose and conversed together, and while they were thus employed Dr Smith began his sermon to them upon the text, "If I yield my body to the fire to be burnt, and have not charity, I shall gain nothing thereby."

They were commanded to prepare immediately for the stake. They accordingly with all meekness obeyed. Dr Ridley made presents of small things to gentlemen standing by, divers of them pitifully weeping; happy was he who could get the least trifle for a remembrance of this good man. Mr Latimer quietly suffered his keeper to pull off his hose and his other apparel, which was very simple, and being stripped to his shroud he seemed as comely a person as one could well see.

Then Dr Ridley unlaced himself, and held up his hand and said, "O heavenly Father, I give unto thee most hearty thanks that thou hast called me to be a professor of thee, even unto death; I beseech thee, Lord God, have mercy upon this realm of England, and deliver it from all her enemies."

Then the smith took a chain of iron, and brought it about both their middles; and as he was knocking in the staple Dr Ridley took the chain in his hand, and, looking aside to the smith; said, "Good fellow, knock it in hard, for the flesh will have its course." Then his brother brought him a bag of gunpowder, and tied it about his neck. Dr Ridley asked him what it was, and he answered, Gunpowder. "Then (said he), I will take it to be sent of God; therefore I will receive it. And have you any for my brother?" "Yes, sir, that I have," said he. "Then give it unto him in time (said he), lest you come too late." So his brother went and carried it to Mr Latimer.

Dr Ridley said to my lord Williams, "My lord, I must be a suitor unto your lordship in the behalf of divers poor men, and especially in the cause of my poor sister. I beseech your lordship, for Christ's sake, to be a means of grace for them. There is nothing in all the world that troubles my conscience, this only excepted. While I was in the See of London divers poor men took leases of me; now I hear that the bishop, who occupieth the same room, will not allow my grants made to them, but, contrary to all law and conscience, hath taken from them their livings. I beseech you, my lord, be a means for them; you shall do a good deed and God will reward you."

They then brought a lighted faggot and laid it at Dr Ridley's feet, upon which Mr Latimer said,

Be of good comfort, Master Ridley, and play the man; we shall this day light such a candle by God's grace in England as I trust shall never be put out.

When Dr Ridley saw the flame leaping up towards him he cried with an amazing loud voice, "Into thy hands, O Lord, I commend my spirit; Lord receive my spirit," and continued oft to repeat, "Lord, Lord receive my spirit." Mr Latimer, on the other side, cried as vehemently, "O Father of Heaven, receive my soul." After which he soon died, seemingly with little pain.

But Dr Ridley, from the ill-making of the fire (the faggots being green, and piled too high, so that the flames being kept down by the green wood, burned fiercely beneath, was put to such exquisite pain that he desired them, for God's sake, to let the fire come unto him. His brother-in-law hearing, but not very well understanding, to rid him out of his pain and not well knowing what he did, heaped faggots upon him, so that he quite covered him, which made the fire so vehement beneath that it burned all his nether parts before it touched the upper, and made him struggle under the faggots, and often desire them to let the fire come unto him, saying, "I cannot burn." Yet in all his torments he forgot not to call upon God, still having in his mouth, "Lord have mercy upon me," mingling with his cry, "Let the fire come unto me; I cannot burn."

In these pains he laboured till one of the standers-by pulled the faggots from above, and when he saw the fire flame up he wrested himself to that side, and when the fire touched the gunpowder, he was seen to stir no more, but fell down at Mr Latimer's feet.

The dreadful sight filled almost every eye with tears. Some took it grievously to see their deaths whose lives they had held so dear. Some pitied their persons, who thought their souls had no need thereof. But the sorrow of his brother, whose extreme anxiety had led him to attempt to put a speedy end to his sufferings, but who, from error and confusion, had so unhappily prolonged them, surpassed them all; and so violent was his grief that the spectators pitied him almost as much as they did the martyr.

THE POOR LAW ACT, 1598

There was, of course, a great deal of self-interest in this measure passed by the Elizabethan state. Economic change in the countryside, particularly the sharper gentry's switch to sheep farming on previously common land, had created a vast crowd of the jobless. Consecutive bad harvests promised famine in the land. With the whiff of riot in the air, Parliament passed the Poor Law Act. The Act's merit was to understand that the state, as well as private conscience, had a role in succouring the poor and that unemployment was subject to rational controls. The main provisions of the Act remained the basis of poor relief in Britain until 1834.

An Act for the Relief of the Poor

Be it enacted by the authority of this present Parliament, that the Churchwardens of every parish, and four substantial householders there . . . who shall be nominated yearly in Easter week, under the hand and seal of two or more Justices of the Peace in the same county, whereof one to be of the Quorum, dwelling in or near the same parish, shall be called Overseers of the Poor of the same parish; and they or the greater part of them shall take order from time to time by and with the consent of two or more such Justices of Peace for setting to work of the children of all such whose parents shall not by the said persons be thought able to keep and maintain their children, And also all such persons married or unmarried as having no means to maintain them use no ordinary and daily trade of life to get their living by; and also to raise weekly or otherwise (by taxation of every inhabitant and every occupier of lands in the said parish in such competent sum and sums of money as they shall think fit) a convenient stock of flax, hemp, wool, thread, iron, and other necessary ware and stuff to set the poor on work, and also competent sums of money for and towards the necessary relief of the lame, impotent, old, blind, and such other among them being poor and not able to work, and also for the putting out of such children to be apprentices, to be gathered out of the same parish according to the ability of the said parish; and to do and execute all other things, as well for disposing of the said stock as otherwise concerning the premises, as to them shall seem convenient: which said Churchwardens, and Overseers so to be nominated, or such of them as shall not be let by sickness or other just excuse to be allowed by such two Justices of Peace or more, shall meet together at the least once every month in the church of the said parish, upon the Sunday in the afternoon after divine service, there to consider of some good course to be taken and of some meet orders to be set down in the premises; . . . upon pain that every one of them absenting themselves without lawful cause as aforesaid from such monthly meeting for the purpose aforesaid, or being negligent in their office or in the execution of the orders aforesaid being made by and with the assent of the said Justices of Peace, to forfeit for every such default twenty shillings.

II. And be it also enacted, that if the said Justices of Peace do perceive that the inhabitants of any parish are not able to levy among themselves sufficient sums of money for the purposes aforesaid, that then the said Justices shall and may tax, rate, and assess as aforesaid any other of other parishes, or out of any parish within the hundred where the said parish is, to pay such sum and sums of money to the Churchwardens and Overseers of the said poor parish for the said purpose as the said Justices shall think fit, according to the intent of this law; and if the said hundred shall not be thought to the said Justices able and fit to relieve the said several parishes not able to provide for themselves as aforesaid, then the Justices of Peace at their general Quarter Sessions, or the greater number of them, shall rate and assess as aforesaid, . . . other parishes . . . as in their discretion shall seem fit . . .

IV. And be it further enacted, that it shall be lawful for the said Churchwardens and Overseers or the greater part of them, by the assent of any two Justices of the Peace, to bind any such children as aforesaid to be apprentices where they shall see convenient, till such man-child shall come to the age of four and twenty years, and such woman-child to the age of one and twenty years; the same to be as effectual to all purposes as if such child were of full age and by indenture of covenant bound him or herself.

V. And to the intent that necessary places of habitation may more conveniently be provided for such poor impotent people, Be it enacted by the authority aforesaid, That it shall and may be lawful for the said Churchwardens and Overseers or the greater part of them, by the leave of the lord or lords of the manor whereof any waste or common within their parish is or shall be parcel . . . to erect, build, and set up in fit and convenient places of habitation in such waste or common, at the general charges of the parish or otherwise of the hundred or county as aforesaid, to be taxed, rated, and gathered in manner before expressed, convenient Houses of Dwelling for the said impotent poor; And also to place inmates or more families than one in one cottage or house . . .

XII. And forasmuch as all begging is forbidden by this present Act; be it further enacted by the authority aforesaid, that the Justices of Peace for every county or place corporate, or the more part of them, in their general Sessions to be holden next after the end of this session of Parliament, or in default thereof at the Quarter Sessions to be holden about the Feast of Easter next, shall rate every parish to such a weekly sum of money as they shall think convenient, so as no parish be rated above the sum of 6d. nor under the sum of an half-penny weekly to be paid, and so as the total sum of such taxation of the parishes in every county amount not above the rate of twopence for every parish in the said county; which sums so taxed shall be yearly assessed by the agreement of the parishioners within themselves, or in default thereof by the Churchwardens and Constables of the same parish or the more part of them, or in default of their agreement by the order of such Justice or Justices of Peace as shall dwell in the same parish or (if none be there dwelling) in the parts next adjoining; and if any person shall refuse or neglect to pay any such portion of money so taxed, it shall be lawful for the said Churchwardens and Constables or in their default for the Justices of the Peace, to levy the same by distress and sale of the goods of the party so refusing or neglecting, rendering to the party the overplus, and in default of such distress it shall be lawful to any Justice of that limit to commit such persons to prison, there to abide without bail or mainprize till he have paid the same.

XIII. And be it also enacted, that the said Justices of the Peace at their general Quarter Sessions to be holden at the time of such taxation, shall set down what competent sum of money shall be sent quarterly out of every county or place corporate for the relief of the poor prisoners of the King's Bench and Marshalsea, and also of such hospitals and almshouses as shall be in the said county, and what sums of money shall be sent to every one of the said hospitals and almshouses, so as there be sent out of every county yearly twenty shillings at the least to the prisoners of the King's Bench and Marshalsea; which sums, rateably to be assessed upon every parish, the Churchwardens of every parish shall truly collect and pay over to the High Constable in whose division such parish shall be situate . . .

XVI. Provided always nevertheless, that every soldier being discharged of his service or otherwise lawfully licensed to pass into his country, and not having wherewith to relieve himself in his travel homewards, and every seafaring man landing from sea not having wherewith to relieve himself in his travel homewards, having a testimonial under the hand of some one Justice of Peace of or near the place where he was landed or was discharged, setting down therein the place and time where and when he landed or was discharged, and the place of the party's dwelling-place or birth unto which he is to pass, and a convenient time to be limited therein for his passage, shall and may, without incurring the danger or penalty of this Act, in the usual ways directly to the place unto which he is directed to pass and within the time in such his testimonial limited for his passage, ask and receive such relief as shall be necessary in and for his passage; This Act or anything therein contained to the contrary notwithstanding.

XVII. Provided always, that this Act shall endure no longer than to the end of the next Session of Parliament.[1]

(39 Eliz. I, c. 3.)

---

[1] It was afterwards prolonged by numerous Acts, being made permanent in 1640.

From *NOVUM ORGANUM, 1620*

Francis Bacon

The sometime Lord Chancellor of England, Francis Bacon (1561–1626) has a claim to be the pioneer of the modern scientific inductive method. In his principal works, *The Advancement of Learning*, 1605, and *Novum Organum*, 1620, Bacon – a lawyer by training – abandoned the pervasive deductive method of Aristotle for a procedure in which the scientist formed an hypothesis which was tested by experiment. If the experiment confirmed the facts, the original hypothesis was deemed to be true.

There was little in Bacon's personal life to admire. He was an obsequious, vainglorious spendthrift of little loyalty to anyone. His commitment to science was absolute, however, he died from a cold caught whilst stuffing a chicken with snow in order to observe the latter substance's preserving effects.

Preface

. . . They who have presumed to dogmatize on Nature, as on some well-investigated subject, either from self-conceit or arrogance, and in the professorial style, have inflicted the greatest injury on philosophy and learning. For they have tended to stifle and interrupt inquiry exactly in proportion as they have prevailed in bringing others to their opinion: and their own activity has not counterbalanced the mischief they have occasioned by corrupting and destroying that of others. They again who have entered upon a contrary course, and asserted that nothing whatever can be known, whether they have fallen into this opinion from their hatred of the ancient sophists, or from the hesitation of their minds, or from an exuberance of learning, have certainly adduced reasons for it which are by no means contemptible. They have not, however, derived their opinion from true sources, and, hurried on by their zeal, and some affectation, have certainly exceeded due moderation. But the more ancient Greeks (whose writings have perished) held a more prudent mean, between the arrogance of dogmatism, and the despair of scepticism; and though too frequently intermingling complaints and indignation at the difficulty of inquiry, and the obscurity of things, and champing, as it were, at the bit, have still persisted in pressing their point, and pursuing their intercourse with nature: thinking, as it seems, that the better method was not to dispute upon the very point of the possibility of any thing being known, but to put it to the test of experience. Yet they themselves, by only employing the power of the understanding, have not adopted a fixed rule, but have laid their whole stress upon intense meditation, and a continual exercise and perpetual agitation of the mind.

Our method, though difficult in its operation, is easily explained. It consists in determining the degrees of certainty, whilst we, as it were, restore the senses to their former rank, but generally reject that operation of the mind which follows close upon the senses, and open and establish a new and certain course for the mind from the first actual perceptions of the senses themselves. This no doubt was the view taken by those who have assigned so much to logic; showing clearly thereby that they sought some support for the mind, and suspected its natural and spontaneous mode of action. But this is now employed too late as a remedy, when all is clearly lost, and after the mind, by the daily habit and intercourse of life, has become prepossessed with corrupted doctrines, and filled with the vainest idols. The art of logic therefore being (as we have mentioned) too late a precaution, and in no way remedying the matter, has tended more to confirm errors, than to disclose truth. Our only remaining hope and salvation is to begin the whole labour of the mind again; not leaving it to itself, but directing it perpetually from the very first, and attaining our end as it were by mechanical aid. If men, for instance, had attempted mechanical labours with their hands alone, and without the power and aid of intruments, as they have not hesitated to carry on the labours of their understanding with the unaided efforts of their mind, they would have been able to move and overcome but little, though they had exerted their utmost and united powers. And, just to pause a while on this comparison, and look into it as a mirror; let us ask, if any obelisk of a remarkable size were perchance required to be moved, for the purpose of gracing a triumph or any similar pageant, and men were to attempt it with their bare hands, would not any sober spectator avow it to be an act of the greatest madness? And if they should increase the number of workmen, and imagine that they could thus succeed, would he not think so still more? But if they chose to make a selection, and to remove the weak, and only employ the strong and vigorous, thinking by this means, at any rate, to achieve their object, would he not say that they were more fondly deranged? Nay, if, not content with this, they were to determine on consulting the athletic art, and were to give orders for all to appear with their hands, arms, and muscles regularly oiled and prepared, would he not exclaim that they were taking pains to rave by method and design? Yet men are hurried on with the same senseless energy and useless combination in intellectual matters, so long as they expect great results either from the number and agreement, or the excellence and acuteness of their wits; or even strengthen their minds with logic, which may be considered as an athletic preparation, but yet do not desist (if we rightly consider the matter) from applying their own understandings merely with all this zeal and effort. Whilst nothing is more clear, than that in every great work executed by the hand of man without machines or implements, it is impossible for the strength of individuals to be increased, or for that of the multitude to combine.

Having premised so much, we lay down two points on which we would admonish mankind, lest they should fail to see or to observe them. The first of these is: that it is our good fortune (as we consider it), for the sake of extinguishing and removing contradiction and irritation of mind, to leave the honour and reverence due to the ancients untouched and undiminished, so that we can perform our intended work, and yet enjoy the benefit of our respectful moderation. For if we should profess to offer something better than the ancients, and yet should pursue the same course as they have done, we could never, by any artifice, contrive to avoid the imputation of having engaged in a contest or rivalry as to our respective wits, excellences, or talents; which, though neither inadmissible or new (for why should we not blame and point out any thing that is imperfectly discovered or laid down by them, of our own right, a right common to all) yet, however just and allowable, would perhaps be scarcely an equal match, on account of the disproportion of our strength. But, since our present plan leads us to open an entirely different course to the understanding, and one unattempted and unknown to them, the case is altered. There is an end to party zeal, and we only take upon ourselves the character of a guide, which requires a moderate share of authority and good fortune, rather than talents and excellence. This first admonition relates to persons, the next to things.

We make no attempt to disturb the system of philosophy that now prevails, or any other which may or will exist, either more correct or more complete. For we deny not that the received system of philosophy, and others of a similar nature, encourage discussion, embellish harangues, are employed and are of service in the duties of the professor, and the affairs of civil life. Nay, we openly express and declare that the philosophy we offer will not be very useful in such respects. It is not obvious, nor to be understood in a cursory view, nor does it flatter the mind in its preconceived notions, nor will it descend to the level of the generality of mankind, unless by its advantages and effects.

Let there exist then (and may it be of advantage to both) two sources, and two distributions of learning, and in like manner two tribes, and as it were kindred families of contemplators or philosophers, without any hostility or alienation between them; but rather allied and united by mutual assistance. Let there be, in short, one method of cultivating the sciences, and another of discovering them. And as for those who prefer and more readily receive the former, on account of their haste, or from motives arising from their ordinary life, or because they are unable from weakness of mind to comprehend and embrace the other (which must necessarily be the case with by far the greater number), let us wish that they may prosper as they desire in their undertaking, and attain what they pursue. But if any individual desire and is anxious not merely to adhere to and make use of present discoveries, but to penetrate still further, and not to overcome his adversaries in disputes, but nature by labour, not, in short, to give elegant and specious opinions, but to know to a certainty and demonstration, let him, as a true son of science (if such be his wish), join with us; that when he has left the antechambers of nature trodden by the multitude, an entrance at last may be discovered to her inner apartments. And, in order to be better understood, and to render our meaning more familiar by assigning determinate names, we have accustomed ourselves to call the one method the anticipation of the mind, and the other the interpretation of nature.

We have still one request left. We have at least reflected and taken pains in order to render our propositions not only trtce, but of easy and familiar access to men's minds, however wonderfully prepossessed and limited. Yet it is but just that we should obtain this favour from mankind, (especially in so great a restoration of learning and the sciences), that whosoever may be desirous of forming any determination upon an opinion of this our work, either from his own perceptions, or the crowd of authorities, or the forms of demonstrations, he will not expect to be able to do so in a cursory manner, and whilst attending to other matters; but in order to have a thorough knowledge of the subject, will himself by degrees attempt the course which we describe and maintain; will become accustomed to the subtlety of things which is manifested by experience; and will correct the depraved and deeply rooted habits of his mind by a seasonable and as it were just hesitation: and then finally (if he will) use his judgment when he has begun to be master of himself.

THE MAYFLOWER COMPACT, 1620

William Bradford

Bradford was one of the leaders of the Pilgrim Fathers, a group of religious non-conformists who sailed to America to escape the religious intolerance of James I of England. In the cabin of the *Mayflower*, the Pilgrims made a compact with their non-Pilgrim passengers by which they agreed a form of self-government for the colony they were about to found. The notion of government by consent was thus sown early in the English colonies of the New World.

In the name of God, Amen.

We whose names are underwritten, the loyal subjects of our dread sovereign Lord, King James, by the grace of God, of Great Britain, France and Ireland king, defender of the faith, etc., having undertaken, for the glory of God, and advancement of the Christian faith, and honour of our king and country, a voyage to plant the first colony in the Northern parts of Virginia, do by these presents solemnly and mutually in the presence of God, and one of another, covenant and combine ourselves together into a civil body politic, for our better ordering and preservation and furtherance of the ends aforesaid; and by virtue hereof to enact, constitute, and frame such just and equal laws, ordinances, acts, constitutions, and offices, from time to time, as shall be thought most meet and convenient for the general good of the colony, unto which we promise all due submission and obedience.

In witness whereof we have hereunder subscribed our names at Cape-Cod the 11 of November, in the year of the reign of our sovereign lord, King James, of England, France, and Ireland the eighteenth, and of Scotland the fifty-fourth. Anno Domini 1620.

THE PETITION OF RIGHT, 1628

During the reign of Charles I, the centuries-old tension between the British monarchy and Parliament reached its climax. Suspicious of Charles' use of the royal prerogative, his resistance to the Puritanization of the Anglican Church, his imprisoning – even execution – of subjects without trial, his forced loans, Parliament presented Charles with "The Petition of Right" in 1628. This "humbly" sought to show Charles the error of his ways. Clause I reminded Charles that, since the reign of Edward III, no man could be compelled to loan money to the king; Clause II recalled the Great Charter – as vivid in the mind of the 17th century Englishman as it was his 13th century forbear – whereby no freeman (and since by statute of Elizabeth I this meant *no* Englishman) could be imprisoned without due legal process. There were other clauses but these were the most important.

To the King's Most Excellent Majesty

Humbly show unto our Sovereign Lord the King, the Lords Spiritual and Temporal, and Commons in Parliament assembled, that whereas it is declared and enacted by a statute made in the time of the reign of King Edward the First, commonly called *Statutum de tallagio non concedendo*, that no tallage or aid shall be laid or levied by the King or his heirs in this realm, without the good will and assent of the Archbishops, Bishops, Earls, Barons, Knights, Burgesses, and other the freemen of the commonalty of this realm: and by authority of Parliament holden in the five and twentieth year of the reign of King Edward the Third, it is declared and enacted, that from thenceforth no person shall be compelled to make any loans to the King against his will, because such loans were against reason and the franchise of the land; and by other laws of this realm it is provided, that none should be charged by any charge or imposition, called a Benevolence, nor by such like charge: by which, the statutes before-mentioned, and other the good laws and statutes of this realm, your subjects have inherited this freedom, that they should not be compelled to contribute to any tax, tallage, aid, or other like charge, not set by common consent in Parliament:

II. Yet nevertheless, of late divers commissions directed to sundry Commissioners in several counties, with instructions, have issued, by means whereof your people have been in divers places assembled, and required to lend certain sums of money unto your Majesty, and many of them upon their refusal so to do, have had an oath administered unto them, not warrantable by the laws or statutes of this realm, and have been constrained to become bound to make appearance and give attendance before your Privy Council, and in other places, and others of them have been therefore imprisoned, confined, and sundry other ways molested and disquieted: and divers other charges have been laid and levied upon your people in several counties, by Lords Lieutenants, Deputy Lieutenants, Commissioners for Musters, Justices of Peace and others, by command or direction from your Majesty or your Privy Council, against the laws and free customs of this realm.

III. And where also by the statute called, "The Great Charter of the Liberties of England", it is declared and enacted that no freeman may be taken or imprisoned or be disseised of his freehold or liberties, or his free customs, or be outlawed or exiled, or in any manner destroyed, but by the lawful judgment of his peers, or by the law of the land:

IV. And in the eight and twentieth year of the reign of King Edward the Third, it was declared and enacted by authority of Parliament, that no man of what estate or condition that he be, should be put out of his lands or tenements, nor taken, nor imprisoned, nor disinherited, nor put to death, without being brought to answer by due process of law:

V. Nevertheless, against the tenor of the said statutes, and other the good laws and statutes of your realm, to that end provided, divers of your subjects have of late been imprisoned without any cause showed, and when for their deliverance they were brought before your Justices, by your Majesty's writs of Habeas Corpus, there to undergo and receive as the Court should order, and their keepers commanded to certify the causes of their detainer; no cause was certified, but that they were detained by your Majesty's special command, signified by the Lords of your Privy Council, and yet were returned back to several prisons, without being charged with anything to which they might make answer according to the law.

VI. And whereas of late great companies of soldiers and mariners have been dispersed into divers counties of the realm, and the inhabitants against their wills have been compelled to receive them into their houses, and there to suffer them to sojourn, against the laws and customs of this realm, and to the great grievance and vexation of the people.

VII. And whereas also by authority of Parliament, in the 25th year of the reign of King Edward the Third, it is declared and enacted, that no man shall be forejudged of life or limb against the form of the Great Charter, and the law of the land; and by the said Great Charter and other the laws and statutes of this your realm, no man ought to be adjudged to death, but by the laws established in this your realm, either by the customs of the same realm or by Acts of Parliament: and whereas no offender of what kind soever is exempted from the proceedings to be used, and punishments to be inflicted by the laws and statutes of this your realm; nevertheless of late divers commissions under your Majesty's Great Seal have issued forth, by which certain persons have been assigned and appointed Commissioners with power and authority to proceed within the land, according to the justice of martial law against such soldiers and mariners, or other dissolute persons joining with them, as should commit any murder, robbery, felony, mutiny, or other outrage or misdemeanour whatsoever, and by such summary course and order, as is agreeable to martial law, and is used in armies in time of war, to proceed to the trial and condemnation of such offenders, and them to cause to be executed and put to death, according to the law martial:

VIII. By pretext whereof, some of your Majesty's subjects have been by some of the said Commissioners put to death when and where, if by the laws and statutes of the land they had deserved death, by the same laws and statutes also they might, and by no other ought to have been, adjudged and executed:

IX. And also sundry grievous offenders by colour thereof, claiming an exemption, have escaped the punishments due to them by the laws and statutes of this your realm, by reason that divers of your officers and ministers of justice have unjustly refused, or forborne to proceed against such offenders according to the same laws and statutes, upon pretence that the said offenders were punishable only by martial law, and by authority of such commissions as aforesaid; which commissions, and all other of like nature, are wholly and directly contrary to the said laws and statutes of this your realm.

X. They do therefore humbly pray your Most Excellent Majesty, that no man hereafter be compelled to make or yield any gift, loan, benevolence, tax, or such like charge, without common consent by Act of Parliament; and that none be called to make answer, or take such oath, or to give attendance, or be confined, or otherwise molested or disquieted concerning the same, or for refusal thereof; and that no freeman, in any such manner as is before-mentioned, be imprisoned or detained; and that your Majesty will be pleased to remove the said soldiers and mariners, and that your people may not be so burdened in time to come; and that the aforesaid commissions for proceeding by martial law, may be revoked and annulled; and that hereafter no commissions of like nature may issue forth to any person or persons whatsoever, to be executed as aforesaid, lest by colour of them any of your Majesty's subjects be destroyed or put to death, contrary to the laws and franchise of the land.

XI. All of which they most humbly pray of your Most Excellent Majesty, as their rights and liberties according to the laws and statutes of this realm: and that your Majesty would also vouchsafe to declare that the awards, doings, and proceedings to the prejudice of your people, in any of the premises, shall not be drawn hereafter into consequence or example: and that your Majesty would be also graciously pleased, for the further comfort and safety of your people, to declare your royal will and pleasure, that in the things aforesaid all your officers and ministers shall serve you, according to the laws and statutes of this realm, as they tender the honour of your Majesty, and the prosperity of this kingdom.

Which Petition being read the 2nd of June 1628, the King's answer was thus delivered unto it:

The King willeth that right be done according to the laws and customs of the realm; and that the statutes be put in due execution, that his subjects may have no cause to complain of any wrong or oppressions, contrary to their just rights and liberties, to the preservation whereof he holds himself as well obliged as of his prerogative.

On June 7 the answer was given in the accustomed form, *Soit droit fait comme il est désiré.*

From *DIALOGUE CONCERNING TWO CHIEF WORLD SYSTEMS, 1632*

Galileo Galilei

As early as 1530, in his *De Revolutionibus*, the Polish astronomer Nicolas Copernicus (1473–1543) had proved that the sun was the centre of the universe. The book was placed on the Index of books prohibited by the Catholic Church. A century later, the Pisan astronomer and physicist Galileo Galilei (1564–1642), using his new refractor telescope, once again showed that the Earth revolved around the Sun. He published his proofs several times, including in his *Dialogo sopra i due massimi sistemi del Mondo* of 1632. The treatise was banned and Galileo forced into a recantation by the Inquisition. As he left his trial, he is said to have muttered "Eppur si muove" ("But it moves, just the same"). He spent the remainder of his life under house arrest, adding to his treasure of other scientifc disoveries. These included the law that all bodies have weight, and the law of uniformly accelerated motion towards Earth, both of which anticipated the findings of Isaac Newton.

Simplicio

How do you deduce that it is not the earth, but the sun, which is at the centre of the universe?

Salvato

That is deduced from most obvious and therefore most powerfully convincing observations. The most palpable of these, which excludes the earth from the centre and places the sun there, is that we find all the planets closer to the earth at one time and farther from it at another. The differences are so great that Venus, for example, is six times as distant from us at its furthest or at its closest, and Mars soars nearly eight times as high in one state as in the other. You may then see whether Aristotle was not some trifle deceived in believing that they were always equally distant from us.

Simplicio

But what are the signs that they move around the sun?

Salvato

This is reasoned out from finding the three other planets – Mars, Jupiter and Saturn – always quite close to the earth when they are in opposition to the sun and very distant when they are in conjunction with it. This approach and recession is of such moment that Mars when close looks sixty times as large as when it is most distant. Next, it is certain that Venus and Mercury must revolve around the sun, because of their never moving far away from it, and because of their being seen now beyond it and now by the side of it, as Venus's changes of shape conclusively prove.

From THE DISCOURSE UPON METHOD, 1637

René Descartes

The concept of doubt was nothing new in philosophy before Descartes. The Frenchman, however, insisted that the first duty of the philosopher was to rid himself of all prejudice and doubt *everything*; the result, Descartes found, was to arrive at a single certainty: doubt itself cannot be doubted. Hence Descartes' famous formulation, *Cogito, ergo sum* ("I think, therefore I am"). Descartes' "Rationalist" method, which essentially sought to extend reason to all fields of human knowledge, laid the basis for modern philosophy. During his lifetime (1596–1650) Descartes also made important contributions to astronomy and mathematics (analytical geometry's "Cartesian coordinates").

Unlike many philosophers, Descartes had the gift of readability and compression. *The Discourse Upon Method* presents in remarkably small span a summary of Descartes' philosopical doctrines.

Part Second

I was then in Germany[1], whither the wars, which were not yet ended there, had summoned me; and when I was returning to the army, from the coronation of the emperor, the coming on of the winter detained me in a quarter where, finding no one I wished to talk with, and fortunately having no cares nor passions to trouble me, I spent the whole day shut up in a room heated by a stove, where I had all the leisure I desired to hold converse with my own thoughts. One of the first thoughts to occur to me was that there is often less completeness in works made up of many parts and by the hands of different masters than in those upon which only one has laboured. Thus we see that buildings which a single architect has

---

[1] Descartes enlisted at his own expense in the Thirty Years War, mainly for the pleasure of travelling.

undertaken and erected are usually much more beautiful and symmetrical than those which many have tried to reconstruct, using old walls which were built for other purposes.

. . . And so I thought that the sciences contained in books, at least those in which the proofs were merely probable and not demonstrations, being the gradual accumulation of opinions of many different persons, by no means come so near the truth as the plain reasoning of a man of good sense in regard to the matters which present themselves to him.

And I thought still further that, because we all have been children before we were men, and for a long time of necessity were under the control of our inclinations and our tutors, who were often of different minds, and none of whom perhaps gave us the best of counsels, it is almost impossible that our judgments should be as free from error and as solid as they would have been if we had had the entire use of our reason from the moment of our birth, and had always been guided by that alone . . .

As for all the opinions which I had accepted up to that time, I was persuaded that I could do no better than get rid of them at once, in order to replace them afterward with better ones, or perhaps with the same, if I should succeed in making them square with reason. And I firmly believed that in this way I should have much greater success in the conduct of my life than if I should build only on the old foundations, and should rely only on the principles which I had allowed myself to be persuaded of in my youth, without ever having examined whether they were true. . . .

My design has never reached further than the attempt to reform my own opinions, and to build upon a foundation altogether my own. But although I am well enough pleased with my work to present you here a sketch of it, I would not on that account advise anyone to imitate me . . . The simple resolution to strip one's self of all that he has hitherto believed is not an example for everyone to follow . . .

But having discovered while at college that there is nothing whatever so strange or incredible that has not been said by some philosopher; and afterward, in my travels, having observed that not all those who cherish opinions quite contrary to our own are therefore barbarians or savages, but that many of these peoples use their reason as well or better than we do; and having considered how differently the same man, with the same mind, would turn out, if he were brought up from infancy among the French or the Germans, from what he would if he always lived among the Chinese or with cannibals; and observing how, even in fashions of dress, the same thing which pleased us ten years ago, and, it may be, will please us again ten years hence, appears to us now extravagant and ridiculous; so that it is rather custom and example than certain knowledge which persuades us; and yet a plurality of votes is no proof that a thing is true, especially where truths are difficult of discovery, in which case it is much more likely that a man left to himself will find them out sooner than people in general – taking all these things into consideration, and not being able to select anyone whose opinions seemed to me to be preferable to those of others, I found myself, as it were, compelled to take myself as my guide. But like a man who walks alone and in the dark, I resolved to go so slowly and to use so much caution in everything, that, even if I did not get on very far, I should at least keep from falling. Likewise I was unwilling at the start to reject summarily any opinion which might have insinuated itself into my belief without having been introduced there by reason, but I would first spend time enough to draw up a plan of the work I was undertaking and to discover the true method for arriving at the knowledge of whatever my mind was capable of.

I had studied, in earlier years, of the branches of philosophy, logic, and in mathematics, geometrical analysis and algebra, three arts or sciences which seemed likely to afford some assistance to my design. But on examination of them I observed, in respect to logic, that its syllogisms and the greater part of its processes are of service principally in explaining to another what one already knows himself, or, like the art of Lully, they enable him to talk without judgment on matters in which he is ignorant, rather than help him to acquire knowledge of them; and while it contains in reality many very true and very excellent precepts, there are nevertheless mixed with these many others which are either harmful or superfluous, and which are almost as difficult to separate from the rest as to draw forth a Diana or a Minerva from a block of marble which is not yet rough-hewn . . . For this reason I thought that some other method should be sought out which, comprising the advantages of these three, should be exempt from their defects. And as a multiplicity of laws often furnishes excuses for vices, so that a state is best governed which has but few and those strictly obeyed; in like manner, in place of the multitude of precepts of which logic is composed, I believed I should find the four following rules quite sufficient, provided I should firmly and steadfastly resolve not to fail of observing them in a single instance.

The first rule was never to receive anything as a truth which I did not clearly know to be such; that is, to avoid haste and prejudice, and not to comprehend anything more in my judgments than that which should present itself so clearly and so distinctly to my mind that I should have no occasion to entertain a doubt of it.

The second rule was to divide every difficulty which I should examine into as many parts as possible, or as might be required for resolving it.

The third rule was to conduct my thoughts in an orderly manner, beginning with objects the most simple and the easiest to understand, in order to ascend as it were by steps to the knowledge of the most composite, assuming some order to exist even in things which did not appear to be naturally connected.

The last rule was to make enumerations so complete, and reviews so comprehensive, that I should be certain of omitting nothing.

Those long chains of reasoning, quite simple and easy, which geometers are wont to employ in the accomplishment of their most difficult demonstrations, led me to think that everything which might fall under the cognizance of the human mind might be connected together in a similar manner, and that, provided only one should take care not to receive anything as true which was not so, and if one were always careful to preserve the order necessary for deducing one truth from another, there would be none so remote at which he might not at last arrive, nor so concealed which he might not discover . . .

And I am free to say that the exact observance of these few rules which I had laid down gave me such facility in solving all the questions to which these two sciences apply, that in the two or three months which I spent in examining them, having begun with the simplest and most general, and each truth that I discovered being a rule which was of service to me afterward in the discovery of others, not only did I arrive at many which formerly I had considered very difficult, but it seemed to me, toward the end, that I was able to determine even in those matters where I was ignorant by what means and how far it would be possible to resolve them. In this I shall not appear to you to be very vain, perhaps, if you will only consider that there is, in respect to each case, but one truth, and that he who finds it knows as much about it as anyone can know; as, for example, a child, who has learned arithmetic, when he has made an addition according to the rules, can be assured that he has found out, in respect to the sum that he has computed, all that it is possible for the human mind to discover. Because, in a word, the method which shows one how to follow the true order, and to take account exactly of all the circumstances of the subject under investigation, contains all that which gives certitude to the rules of arithmetic. But that which pleased me most in this method was the fact that by means of it I was using my reason in everything, if not perfectly, yet in a manner the very best in my power . . .

Part Fourth

I am in doubt as to the propriety of making my first meditations in the place above mentioned a matter of discourse; for these are so metaphysical, and so uncommon, as not, perhaps, to be acceptable to every one. And yet, that it may be determined whether the foundations that I have laid are sufficiently secure, I find myself in a measure constrained to advert to them. I had long before remarked that, in relation to practice, it is sometimes necessary to adopt, as if above doubt, opinions which we discern to be highly uncertain, as had been already said; but as I then desired to give my attention solely to the search after truth, I thought that a procedure exactly the opposite was called for, and that I ought to reject as absolutely false all opinions in regard to which I could suppose the least ground for doubt, in order to ascertain whether after that there remained aught in my belief that was wholly indubitable. Accordingly, seeing that our senses sometimes deceive us, I was willing to suppose that there existed nothing really such as they presented to us; and because some men err in reasoning, and fall into paralogisms, even on the simplest matters of Geometry, I, convinced that I was as open to error as any other, rejected as false all the reasonings I had hitherto taken for demonstrations; and finally, when I considered that the very same thoughts [presentations] which we experience when awake may also be experienced when we are asleep, while there is at that time not one of them true, I supposed that all the objects [presentations] that had ever entered into my mind when awake, had in them no more truth than the illusions of my dreams. But immediately upon this I observed that, whilst I thus wished to think that all was false, it was absolutely necessary that I, who thus thought, should be somewhat; and as I observed that this truth, *I think, hence I am,* was so certain and of such evidence, that no ground of doubt, however extravagant, could be alleged by the Sceptics capable of shaking it, I concluded that I might, without scruple, accept it as the first principle of the Philosophy of which I was in search.

In the next place, I attentively examined what I was, and as I observed that I could suppose that I had no body, and that there was no world nor any place in which I might be; but that I could not therefore suppose that I was not; and that, on the contrary, from the very circumstance that I thought no doubt of the truth of other things, it most clearly and certainly followed that I was; while, on the other hand, if I had only ceased to think, although all the other objects which I had ever imagined had been in reality existent, I would have had no reason to believe that I existed; I thence concluded that I was a substance whose whole essence or nature consists only in thinking, and which, that it may exist, has need of no place, nor is dependent on any material thing; so that "I", that is to say, the mind by which I am what I am, is wholly distinct from the body, and is even more easily known than the latter, and is such, that although the latter were not, it would still continue to be all that it is.

After this I inquired in general into what is essential to the truth and certainty of a proposition; for since I had discovered one which I knew to be true, I thought that I must likewise be able to discover the ground of this certitude. And as I observed that in the words *I think, hence I am,* there is nothing at all which gives me assurance of their truth beyond this, that I see very clearly that in order to think it is necessary to exist, I concluded that I might take, as a general rule, the principle, that all the things which we very clearly and distinctly conceive are true, only observing, however, that there is some difficulty in rightly determining the objects which we distinctly conceive.

In the next place, from reflecting on the circumstance that I doubted, and that consequently my being was not wholly perfect (for I clearly saw that it was a greater perfection to know than to doubt), I was led to inquire whence I had learned to think of something more perfect than myself; and I clearly recognized that I must hold this notion from some Nature which in reality was more perfect. As for the thoughts of many other objects external to me, as of the sky, the earth, light, heat, and a thousand more, I was less at a loss to know whence these came; for since I remarked in them nothing which seemed to render them superior to myself, I could believe that, if these were true, they were dependencies on my own nature, in so far as it possessed a certain perfection, and, if they were false, that I held them from nothing, that is to say, that they were in me because of a certain imperfection of my nature. But this could not be the case with the idea of a Nature more perfect than myself; for to receive it from nothing was a thing manifestly impossible; and, because it is not less repugnant that the more perfect should be an effect of, and dependence on the less perfect, than that something should proceed from nothing, it was equally impossible that I could hold it from myself: accordingly, it but remained that it had been placed in me by a Nature which was in reality more perfect than mine, and which even possessed within itself all the perfections of which I could form any idea; that is to say, in a single word, which was God. And to this I added that, since I knew some perfections which I did not possess, I was not the only being in existence (I will here, with your permission, freely use the terms of the schools), but, on the contrary, that there was of necessity some other more perfect Being upon whom I was dependent, and from whom I had received all that I possessed; for if I had existed alone, and independently of every other being, so as to have had from myself all the perfection, however little, which I actually possessed, I should have been able, for the same reason, to have had from myself the whole remainder of perfection, of the want of which I was conscious, and thus could of myself have become infinite, eternal, immutable, omniscient, all-powerful, and, in fine, have possessed all the perfections which I could recognize in God. For in order to know the nature of God (whose existence has been established by the preceding reasonings), as far as my own nature permitted, I had only to consider in reference to all the properties of which I found in my mind some idea, whether their possession was a mark of perfection; and I was assured that no one which indicated any imperfection was in him, and that none of the rest was wanting. Thus I perceived that doubt, inconstancy, sadness, and such like, could not be found in God, since I myself would have been happy to be free from them. Besides, I had ideas of many sensible and corporeal things; for although I might suppose that I was dreaming, and that all which I saw or imagined was false, I could not, nevertheless, deny that the ideas were in reality in my thoughts. But, because I had already very clearly recognized in myself that the intelligent nature is distinct from the corporeal, and as I observed that all composition is an evidence of dependency, and that a state of dependency is manifestly a state of imperfection, I therefore determined that it could not be a perfection in God to be compounded of these two natures, and that consequently he was not so compounded; but that if there were any bodies in the world, or even any intelligences, or other natures that were not wholly perfect, their existence depended on his power in such a way that they could not subsist without him for a single moment.

I was disposed straightway to search for other truths; and when I had represented to myself the object of the geometers, which I conceived to be a continuous body, or a space indefinitely extended in length, breadth, and height or depth, divisible into divers parts which admit of different figures and sizes, and of being moved or transposed in all manner of ways (for all this the geometers suppose to be in the object they contemplate), I went over some of their simplest demonstrations. And, in the first place, I observed, that the great certitude which by common consent is accorded to these demonstrations, is founded solely upon this, that they are clearly conceived in accordance with the rules I have already laid down. In the next place, I perceived that there was nothing at all in these demonstrations which could assure me of the existence of their object: thus, for example, supposing a triangle to be given, I distinctly perceived that its three angles were necessarily equal to two right angles, but I did not on that account perceive anything which could assure me that any triangle existed: while, on the contrary, recurring to the examination of the idea of a Perfect Being, I found that the existence of the Being was comprised in the idea in the same way that the equality of its three angles to two right angles is comprised in the idea of a triangle, or as in the idea of a sphere, the equidistance of all points on its surface from the centre, or even still more clearly; and that consequently it is at least as certain that God, who is this Perfect Being, is, or exists, as any demonstration of Geometry can be.

But the reason which leads many to persuade themselves that there is a difficulty in knowing this truth, and even also in knowing what their mind really is, is that they never raise their thoughts above sensible objects, and are so accustomed to consider nothing except by way of imagination, which is a mode of thinking limited to material objects, that all that is not imaginable seems to them not intelligible. The truth of this is sufficiently manifest from the single circumstance, that the philosophers of the Schools accept as a maxim that there is nothing in the Understanding which was not previously in the Senses, in which however it is certain that the ideas of God and of the soul have never been; and it appears to me that they who make use of their imagination to comprehend these ideas do exactly the same thing as if, in order to hear sounds or smell odours, they strove to avail themselves of their eyes; unless indeed that there is this difference, that the sense of sight does not afford us an inferior assurance to those of smell or hearing; in place of which, neither our imagination nor our senses can give us assurance of anything unless our Understanding intervene.

Finally, if there be still persons who are not sufficiently persuaded of the existence of God and of the soul, by the reasons I have adduced, I am desirous that they should know that all the other propositions, of the truth of which they deem themselves perhaps more assured, as that we have a body, and that there exist stars and an earth, and such like, are less certain; for, although we have a moral assurance of these things, which is so strong that there is an appearance of extravagance in doubting of their existence, yet at the same time no one, unless his intellect is impaired, can deny, when the question relates to a metaphysical certitude, that there is sufficient reason to exclude entire assurance, in the observation that when asleep we can in the same way imagine ourselves possessed of another body and that we see other stars and another earth, when there is nothing of the kind. For how do we know that the thoughts which occur in dreaming are false rather than those other which we experience when awake, since the former are often not less vivid and distinct than the latter? And though men of the highest genius study this question as long as they please, I do not believe that they will be able to give any reason which can be sufficient to remove this doubt, unless they presuppose the existence of God. For, in the first place, even the principle which I have already taken as a rule, viz., that all the things which we clearly and distinctly conceive are true, is certain only because God is or exists, and because he is a Perfect Being, and because all that we possess is derived from him: whence it follows that our ideas or notions, which to the extent of their clearness and distinctness are real, and proceed from God, must to that extent be true. Accordingly, whereas we not unfrequently have ideas or notions in which some falsity is contained, this can only be the case with such as are to some extent confused and obscure, and in this proceed from nothing, [participate of negation,] that is, exist in us thus confused because we are not wholly perfect. And it is evident that it is not less repugnant that falsity or imperfection, in so far as it is imperfection, should proceed from God, than that truth or perfection should proceed from nothing. But if we did not know that all which we possess of real and true proceeds from a Perfect and Infinite Being, however clear and distinct our ideas might be, we should have no ground on that account for the assurance that they possessed the perfection of being true.

But after the knowledge of God and of the soul has rendered us certain of this rule, we can easily understand that the truth of the thoughts we experience when awake, ought not in the slightest degree to be called in question on account of the illusions of our dreams. For if it happened that an individual, even when asleep, had some very distinct idea, as, for example, if a geometers should discover some new demonstration, the circumstance of his being asleep would not militate against its truth; and as for the most ordinary error of our dreams, which consists in their representing various objects in the same way as our external senses, this is not prejudicial, since it leads us very properly to suspect the truth of the ideas of sense; for we are not unfrequently deceived in the same manner when awake; as when persons in the jaundice see all objects yellow, or when the stars or bodies at a great distance appear to us much smaller than they are. For, in fine, whether awake or asleep, we ought never to allow ourselves to be persuaded of the truth of anything unless on the evidence of our Reason. And it must be noted that I say of our *Reason*, and not of our imagination or of our senses: thus, for example, although we very clearly see the sun, we ought not therefore to determine that it is only of the size which our sense of sight presents; and we may very distinctly imagine the head of a lion joined to the body of a goat, without being therefore shut up to the conclusion that a chimaera exists; for it is not a dictate of Reason that what we thus see or imagine is in reality existent; but it plainly tells us that all our ideas or notions contain in them some truth; for otherwise it could not be that God, who is wholly perfect and veracious, should have placed them in us. And because our reasonings are never so clear or so complete during sleep as when we are awake, although sometimes the acts of our imagination are then as lively and distinct, if not more so than in our waking moments, Reason further dictates that, since all our thoughts cannot be true because of our partial imperfection, those possessing truth must infallibly be found in the experience of our waking moments rather than in that of our dreams.

THE ATTEMPTED ARREST OF THE
FIVE MEMBERS, 1642

John Rushworth

Although Charles I granted the Petition of Right (see pp 229–32) royal assent, he had no intention of being bound by Parliament, which he dissolved shortly afterwards. For eleven years, Charles ruled without Parliament until desperate finances obliged him to summon one in 1640, in the hope that it would vote aid.

Once called, Parliament wasted little time in establishing its ascendancy. The cruelly anti-Puritan Archbishop Laud was imprisoned (later executed). MPs imprisoned by Royal Courts – which did not possess the jury system – were released and the courts themselves abolished. In 1641 Parliament passed the "Grand Remonstrance" by 159 votes to 148. The Grand Remonstrance was uncompromising – despite the usual formal obsequies – and demanded that the king deprive the bishops of their votes in Parliament and remove all councillors to which Parliament objected.

On 4 January 1642 the King went personally, in a bid to reassert his power, to the House of Commons to arrest five members – Pym, Hampden, Hesilrige, Holles and Strode – for treason. The Commons bravely defied him. (To this day no sovereign is allowed to enter the House.) Foiled in this design, Charles shillied and shallied, until he raised his standard at Nottingham on 2 August 1642. Parliament determined to oppose him.

The English Revolution was the first democratic revolt of an entire nation in the history of the world.

. . . The said five accused Members this day *after dinner* came into the House, and did appear according to the special Order and Injunction of the House laid upon them yesterday, to give their attendance upon the House, *de die in dim* and their appearance was entered in the Journal.

They were no sooner sate in their places, but the House was informed by one Captain *Langrish*, lately an Officer in Arms in *France*, that he came from among the Officers, and souldiers at *White Hall*, and understanding by them, that his Majesty was coming with a Guard of Military Men, Commanders and Souldiers, to the House of Commons, he passed by them with some difficulty to get to the House before them, and sent in word how near the said Officers and Souldiers were come; Whereupon a certain Member of the House having also private Intimation from the Countess of *Carlile*, Sister to the Earl of *Northumberland*, that endeavours would be used this day to apprehend the five Members, the House required the five Members to depart the House forthwith, to the end to avoid Combustion in the House, if the said Souldiers should use Violence to pull any of them out. To which Command of the House, four of the said Members yielded ready Obedience, but Mr *Stroud* was obstinate, till Sir *Walter Earle* (his ancient acquaintance) pulled him out by force, the King being at that time entring into the *New Pallace-yard*, in *Westminster*. And as his Majesty came through *Westminster Hall*, the Commanders, Reformadoes, &c. that attended him, made a Lane on both sides the Hall (through which his Majesty passed and came up the Stairs to the House of Commons) and stood before the Guard of Pentioners, and Halberteers (who also attended the King Person), and the door of the House of Commons being thrown open, his Majesty entred the House, and as he passed up towards *the Chair* he cast his eye on the Right-hand near the Bar of the House, where Mr *Pym* used to sit, but his Majesty not seeing him there (knowing him well) went up to the Chair, and said, "By your leave (Mr Speaker), I must borrow your Chair a little," whereupon the Speaker came out of the Chair, and his Majesty stept up into it, after he had stood in the Chair a while, casting his Eye upon the Members as they stood up *uncovered*; but could not discern any of the five Members to be there, nor indeed were they easie to be discerned (had they been there) among so many bare Faces all standing up together.

Then his Majesty made this Speech,

"Gentlemen,

I Am sorry for this occasion of coming unto you: Yesterday I sent a Serjeant at Arms upon a very Important occasion to apprehend some that by my command were accused of High Treason, whereunto I did expect Obedience and not a Message. And I must declare unto you here, that albeit, no King that ever was in *England*, shall be more careful of your Priviledges, to maintain them to the uttermost of his power then I shall be; yet you must know that in Cases of Treason, no person hath a priviledge. And therefore I am come to know if any of these persons that were accused are here: For I must tell you Gentlemen, that so long as these persons that I have accused (for no slight Crime but for Treason) are here, I cannot expect that this House will be in the Right way that I do heartily wish it: Therefore I am come to tell you that I must have them wheresoever I find them. Well since I see all the Birds are Flown, I do expect from you, that you shall send them unto me, as soon as they return hither. But I assure you, in the word of a King, I never did intend any Force, but shall proceed against them in a legal and fair way, for I never meant any other.

And now since I see I cannot do what I came for, I think this no unfit occasion to repeat what I have said formerly, That whatsoever I have done in favour, and to the good of my Subjects, I do mean to maintain it.

I will trouble you no more, but tell you I do expect as soon as they come to the House, you will send them to me: otherwise I must take my own Course to find them."

When the King was looking about the House, the Speaker standing below by the Chair, his Majesty ask'd him, whether any of these persons were in the House? Whether he saw any of them? and where they were? To which the Speaker falling on his Knee, thus Answered.

"*May it please your Majesty*, I Have neither Eyes to see, nor Tongue to speak in this place, but as the House is pleased to direct me, whose Servant I am here, and humbly beg your Majesties Pardon, that I cannot give any other Answer than this, to what your Majesty is pleased to demand of me."

The King having Concluded his Speech, went out of the House again which was in great disorder, and many Members cried out, aloud so as he might hear them, "Priviledge! Priviledge!" and forthwith Adjourned till the next Day at One of the Clock . . .

A DECLARATION FROM THE POOR OPPRESSED PEOPLE OF ENGLAND, 1649

Gerrard Winstanley et al

Winstanley was a member of the Diggers or True Levellers, a radical movement of the English Revolution which demanded that all crown lands and commons should be cultivated by the poor in communal ownership.

We whose names are subscribed, do in the name of all the poor oppressed people in England, declare unto you, that call your selves Lords of Manors, and Lords of the Land, that in regard the King of Righteousness, our Maker, hath inlightened our hearts so far, as to see, that the earth was not made purposely for you, to be Lords of it, and we to be your Slaves, Servants, and Beggers; but it was made to be a common Livelihood to all, without respect of persons: And that your buying and selling of Land, and the Fruits of it, one to another, is the cursed thing, and was brought in by War, which hath, and still does establish murder, and theft, in the hands of some branches of Mankinde over others, which is the greatest outward burden, and unrighteous power, that the Creation groans under: For the power of inclosing Land, and owning Propriety, was brought into the Creation by your Ancestors by the Sword; which first did murther their fellow Creatures, Men, and after plunder or steal away their Land, and left this Land successively to you, their Children. And therefore, though you did not kill or theeve, yet you hold that cursed thing in your hand, by the power of the Sword; and so you justifie the wicked deeds of your Fathers; and that sin of your Fathers, shall be visited upon the Head of you, and your Children, to the third and fourth Generation, and longer too, till your bloody and theeving power be rooted out of the Land.

And further, in regard the King of Righteousness hath made us sensible of our burthens, and the cryes and groanings of our hearts are come before him: We take it as a testimony of love from him, that our hearts begin to be freed from slavish fear of men, such as you are; and that we find Resolutions in us, grounded upon the inward law of Love, one towards another, to Dig and Plough up the Commons, and waste Lands through England; and that our conversation shall be so unblameable, That your Laws shall not reach to oppress us any longer, unless you by your Laws will shed the innocent blood that runs in our veins.

For though you and your Ancestors got your Propriety by murther and theft, and you keep it by the same power from us, that have an equal right to the Land with you, by the righteous Law of Creation, yet we shall have no occasion of quarrelling (as you do) about that disturbing devil, called Particular Propriety: For the Earth, with all her Fruits of Corn, Cattle, and such like, was made to be a common Store-house of Livelihood to all Mankinde, friend, and foe, without exception.

And to prevent your scrupulous Objections, know this, that we must neither buy nor sell; Money must not any longer (after our work of the Earths community is advanced) be the great god, that hedges in some, and hedges out others; for Money is but part of the Earth: And surely, the Righteous Creator, who is King, did never ordain, That unless some of Mankinde, do bring that Mineral (Silver and Gold) in their hands, to others of their own kinde, that they should neither be fed, nor be clothed; no surely, For this was the project of Tyrant-flesh (which Land-lords are branches of) to set his Image upon Money. And they make this unrighteous Law, That none should buy or sell, eat, or be clothed, or have any comfortable Livelihood among men, unless they did bring his Image stamped upon Gold or Silver in their hands.

And whereas the Scriptures speak, That the mark of the Beast is 666, the number of a man; and that those that do not bring that mark in their hands, or in their foreheads, they should neither buy nor sell, Revel. 13.16. And seeing the numbering Letters round about the English money make 666, which is the number of that Kingly Power and Glory (called a Man), And seeing the age of the Creation is now come to the Image of the Beast, or Half day. And seeing 666 is his mark, we expect this to be the last Tyrannical power that shall raign; and that people shall live freely in the enjoyment of the Earth, without bringing the mark of the Beast in their hands, or in their promise; and that they shall buy Wine and Milk, without Money, or without price, as Isiah speaks.

For after our work of the Earthly community is advanced, we must make use of Gold and Silver, as we do of other metals, but not to buy and sell withal; for buying and selling is the great cheat, that robs and steals the Earth one from another: it is that which makes some Lords, others Beggers, some Rulers, others to be ruled; and makes great Murderers and Theeves to be imprisoners, and hangers of little ones, or of sincere-hearted men.

And while we are made to labour the Earth together, with one consent and willing minde; and while we are made free, that every one, friend and foe, shall enjoy the benefit of their Creation, that is, to have food and rayment from the Earth, their Mother; and every one subject to give accompt of his thoughts, words, and actions to none, but to the one onely righteous Judge, and Prince of Peace; the Spirit of Righteousness that dwells, and that is now rising up to rule in every Creature, and in the whole Globe. We say, while we are made to hinder no man of his Priviledges given him in his Creation, equal to one, as to another, what Law then can you make, to take hold upon us, but Laws of Oppression and Tyranny, that shall enslave or spill the blood of the Innocent? And so your Selves, your judges, Lawyers, and Justices, shall be found to be the greatest Transgressors, in, and over Mankinde.

But to draw neerer to declare our meaning, what we would have, and what we shall endevour to the uttermost to obtain, as moderate and righteous Reason directs us; seeing we are made to see our Priviledges, given us in our Creation, which have hitherto been denied to us, and our Fathers, since the power of the Sword began to rule. And the secrets of the Creation have been locked up under the traditional, Parrat-like speaking, from the Universities, and Colledges for Scholars, And since the power of the murdering, and theeving Sword, formerly, as well as now of late yeers, hath set up a Government, and maintains that Government; for what are prisons, and putting others to death, but the power of the Sword to enforce people to that Government which was got by Conquest and Sword, and cannot stand of it self, but by the same murdering power? That Government that is got over people by the Sword and kept by the Sword, is not set up by the King of Righteousness to be his Law, but by Covetousness, the great god of the world; who hath been permitted to raign for a time, times, and dividing of time, and his government draws to the period of the last term of his allotted time; and then the Nations shall see the glory of that Government that shall rule in Righteousness, without either Sword or Spear,

And seeing further, the power of Righteousness in our hearts, seeking the Livelihood of others as well as our selves, hath drawn forth our bodies to begin to dig, and plough, in the Commons and waste Land, for the Reasons already declared,

And seeing and finding ourselves poor, wanting Food to feed upon, while we labour the Earth to cast in Seed, and to wait till the first Crop comes up; and wanting Ploughs, Carts, Corn, and such materials to plant the Commons withal we are willing to declare our condition to you, and to all, that have the Treasury of the Earth, locked up in your Bags, Chests, and Barns, and will offer up nothing to this publike Treasury; but will rather see your fellow Creatures starve for want of Bread, that have an equal right to it with your selves, by the Law of Creation: But this by the way we onely declare to you, and to all that follow the subtle art of buying and selling the Earth, with her Fruits, meerly to get the Treasury thereof into their hands, to lock it up from them, to whom it belongs; that so, such covetous, proud, unrighteous, selfish flesh, may be left without excuse in the day of Judgment.

And therefore, the main thing we aym at, and for which we declare our Resolutions to go forth, and act, is this. To lay hold upon, and as we stand in need, to cut and fell, and make the best advantage we can of the Woods and Trees, that grow upon the Commons, to be a stock for our selves, and our poor Brethren, through the land of *England*, to plant the Commons withal; and to provide us bread to eat, till the Fruit of our labours in the Earth bring forth increase; and we shall meddle with none of your Proprieties (but what is called Commonage) till the Spirit in you, make you cast up your Lands and Goods, which were got, and still is kept in your hands by murder, and theft; and then we shall take it from the Spirit, that hath conquered you, and not from our Swords, which is an abominable, and unrighteous power, and a destroyer of the Creation: But the Son of man comes not to destroy, but to save.

And we are moved to send forth this Declaration abroad, to give notice to every one whom it concerns, in regard we hear and see, that some of you, that have been Lords of Manors, do cause the Trees and Woods that grow upon the Commons, which you pretend a Royalty unto, to be cut down and sold, for your own private use, whereby the Common Land, which your own mouths doe say belongs to the poor, is impoverished, and the poor oppressed people robbed of their Rights, while you give them creating words, by telling some of our poor oppressed Brethren, That those of us that have begun to Dig and Plough up the Commons, will hinder the poor and so blinde their eyes, that they see not their Priviledge, while you, and the rich Free-holders make the most profit of the Commons, by your over-stocking of them with Sheep and Cattle; and the poor that have the name to own the Commons, have the least share therein; nay, they are checked by you, if they cut Wood, Heath, Turf, or Furseys, in places about the Common, where you disallow.

Therefore we are resolved to be cheated no longer, nor be held under the slavish fear of you no longer, seing the Earth was made for us, as well as for you: And if the Common Land belongs to us who are the poor oppressed, surely the woods that grow upon the Commons belong to us likewise: therefore we are resolved to try the uttermost in the light of reason, to know whether we shall be free men, or slaves. If we lie still, and let you steale away our birthrights, we perish; and if we Petition we perish also, though we have paid taxes, given free quarter, and ventured our lives to preserve the Nations freedom as much as you, and therefore by the law of contract with you, freedom in the land is our portion as well as yours, equal with you: And if we strive for freedom, and your murdering, governing Laws destroy us, we can but perish.

Therefore we require, and we resolve to take both Common Land, and Common woods to be a livelihood for us, and look upon you as equal with us, not above us, knowing very well, that *England* the land of our Nativity, is to be a common Treasury of livelihood to all, without respect of persons.

So then, we declare unto you, that do intend to cut our Common Woods and Trees, that you shall not do it; unlesse it be for a stock for us, as aforesaid, and we to know of it, by a publick declaration abroad, that the poor oppressed, that live thereabouts, may take it, and employ it, for their publike use, therefore take notice we have demanded it in the name of the Commons of *England*, and of all the Nations of the world, it being the righteous freedom of the Creation.

Likewise we declare to you that have begun to cut down our Common Woods and Trees, and to fell and carry away the same for your private use, that you shall forbear, and go no farther, hoping, that none that are friends to the Commonwealth of England, will endeavour to buy any of those Common Trees and Woods of any of those Lords to Mannors, so called, who have, by the murdering and cheating law of the sword, stoln the Land from younger brothers, who have by the law of Creation, a standing portion in the Land, as well, and equall with others. Therefore we hope all Wood-mongers will disown all such private merchandize, as being a robbing of the poor oppressed, and take notice, that they have been told our resolution: But if any of you that are Wood-mongers, will buy it of the poor, and for their use, to stock the Commons, from such as may be appointed by us to sell it, you shall have it quietly, without diminution; but if you will slight us in this thing, blame us not, if we make stop of the Carts you send and convert the Woods to our own use, as need requires, it being our own, equal with him that calls himself the Lord of the Mannor, and not his peculiar right, shutting us out, but he shall share with us as a fellow-creature.

For we say our purpose is, to take those Common Woods to sell them, now at first, to be a stock for our selves, and our children after us, to plant and manure the Common land withall; for we shall endeavour by our righteous acting not to leave the earth any longer intangled unto our children, by self-seeking proprietors; But to leave it a free store-house, and common treasury to all, without respect of persons; And this we count is our dutie, to endeavour to the uttermost, every man in his place (according to the national Covenant which the Parliament set forth) a Reformation to preserve the peoples liberties, one as well as another. As well those as have paid taxes, and given free quarter, as those that have either born the sword, or taken our moneys to dispose of them for publike use: for if the Reformation must be according to the word of God, then every one is to have the benefit and freedom of his creation, without respect of persons; we count this our duty, we say, to endeavour to the uttermost, and so shall leave those that rise up to oppose us without excuse, in their day of

Judgment; and our precious blood, we hope, shall not be dear to us, to be willingly laid down at the door of a prison, or foot of a gallows, to justifie this righteous cause; if those that have taken our money from us, and promised to give us freedom for it, should turn Tyrants against us: for we must not fight, but suffer.

And further we intend, that not one, two, or a few men of us shall sell or exchange the said woods, but it shall be known publikly in Print or writing to all, how much every such, and such parcell of wood is sold for, and how it is laid out, either in victualls, corn, ploughs, or other materials necessary.

And we hope we may not doubt (at least we expect) that they that are called the great Councel and powers of *England*, who so often have declared themselves, by promises and Covenants, and confirmed them by multitude of fasting daies, and devout Protestations, to make *England* a free people, upon condition they would pay moneys, and adventure their lives against the successor of the *Norman* Conqueror; under whose oppressing power *England* was enslaved; And we look upon that freedom promised to be the inheritance of all, without respect of persons; And this cannot be, unless the Land of *England* be freely set at liberty from proprietors, and become a common Treasury to all her children, as every portion of the Land of *Canaan* was the Common livelihood of such and such a Tribe, and of every member in that Tribe, without exception, neither hedging in any, nor hedging out.

We say we hope we need not doubt of their sincerity to us herein, and that they will not gainsay our determinate course; howsoever, their actions will prove to the view of all, either their sinceritie, or hypocrisie: We know what we speak is our priviledge, and our cause is righteous, and if they doubt of it, let them but send a childe for us to come before them, and we shall make it manifest four wayes.

First, by the National Covenant, which yet stands in force to bind Parliament and people to be faithful and sincere, before the Lord God Almighty, wherein every one in his several place hath covenanted to preserve and seek the liberty each of other, without respect of persons.

Secondly, by the late Victory over King *Charls*, we do claime this our priviledge, to be quietly given us, out of the hands of Tyrant-Government, as our bargain and contract with them; for the Parliament promised, if we would pay taxes, and give free quarter, and adventure our lives against *Charls* and his party, whom they called the Common enemy, they would make us a free people; These three being all done by us, as well as by themselves, we claim this our bargain, by the law of contract from them, to be a free people with them, and to have an equall priviledge of Common livelihood with them, they being chosen by us, but for a peculiar worke, and for an appointed time, from among us, not to be our oppressing Lords, but servants to succour us. But these two are our weakest proofs. And yet by them (in the light of reason and equity that dwells in mens hearts) we shall with ease cast down, all those former enslaving *Norman* reiterated laws, in every Kings raigne since the Conquest, which are as thornes in our eyes, and pricks in our sides, and which are called the Ancient Government of *England*.

Thirdly, we shall prove, that we have a free right to the land of *England*, being born, therein as well as elder brothers, and that it is our right equal with them, and they with us, to have a comfortable livelihood in the earth, without owning any of our own kinde, to be either Lords, or Land-Lords over us: And this we shall prove by plain Text of Scripture, without exposition upon them, which the Scholars and great ones generally say, is their rule to walk by.

Fourthly, we shall prove it by the Righteous Law of our Creation, That mankinde in all his branches, is the Lord of the Earth and ought not to be in subjection to any of his own kinde without him, but to live in the light of the law of righteousness, and peace established in his heart.

And thus in love we have declared the purpose of our hearts plainly, without flatterie, expecting love, and the same sincerity from you, without grumbling or quarreling, being Creatures of your own Image and mould, intending no other matter herein, but to observe the Law of righteous action, endeavouring to shut out of the Creation, the cursed thing, called *Particular Propriety*, which is the cause of all wars, bloud-shed, theft, and enslaving Laws, that hold the people under miserie.

Signed for and in behalf of all the poor oppressed people of *England*, and the whole world.

Gerrard Winstanley
John Coulton
John Palmer
Thomas Star
Samuel Webb
John Hayman
Thomas Edcer
William Hogrill
Daniel Weeden
Richard Wheeler
Nathaniel Yates
et al

From *AREOPAGITICA, 1644*

John Milton

The greater fame of Milton (1608–74) rests on his epic poems, *Paradise Lost* and *Paradise Regained*. In his own times, he was equally esteemed – and feared – as a pamphleteer. *Areopagitica, A Speech for the Liberty of Unlicensed Printing* was issued in 1644 in response to a Puritan act of parliament from the previous year which stated that "no book . . . be printed unless approved of and licensed" by government. Milton's protest took the literary form of ancient Greek speeches, addressed by Isocartes to the Areopagus or High Court of Athens. *Areopagitica* is still referred to in vindication of the freedom of the press.

I deny not, but that it is of greatest concernment in the Church and Commonwealth, to have a vigilant eye how books demean themselves as well as men; and thereafter to confine, imprison, and do sharpest justice on them as malefactors. For books are not absolutely dead things, but do contain a potency of life in them to be as active as that soul was whose progeny they are; nay, they do preserve as in a vial the purest efficacy and extraction of that living intellect that bred them. I know they are as lively, and as vigorously productive, as those fabulous dragon's teeth; and being sown up and down, may chance to spring up armed men. And yet, on the other hand, unless wariness be used, as good almost kill a man as kill a good book. Who kills a man kills a reasonable creature, God's image; but he who destroys a good book, kills reason itself, kills the image of God, as it were in the eye. Many a man lives a burden to the earth; but a good book is the precious life-blood of a master spirit, embalmed and treasured up on purpose to a life beyond life. 'Tis true, no age can restore a life, whereof perhaps there is no great loss; and revolutions of ages do not oft recover the loss of a rejected truth, for the want of which whole nations fare the worse.

We should be wary therefore what persecutions we raise against the living labours of public men, how we spill that seasoned life of man, preserved and stored up in books; since we see a kind of homicide may be thus committed, sometimes a martyrdom, and if it extend to the whole impression, a kind of massacre; whereof the execution ends not in the slaying of an elemental life, but strikes at that ethereal and fifth essence, the breath of reason itself, slays an immortality rather than a life. But lest I should be condemned of introducing licence, while I oppose licensing, I refuse not the pains to be so much historical, as will serve to show what hath been done by ancient and famous commonwealths against this disorder, till the very time that this project of licensing crept out of the inquisition, was catched up by our prelates, and hath caught some of our presbyters . . .

If we think to regulate printing, thereby to rectify manners, we must regulate all recreations and pastimes, all that is delightful to man. No music must be heard, no song be set or sung, but what is grave and Doric. There must be licensing dancers, that no gesture, motion, or deportment be taught our youth but what by their allowance shall be thought honest; for such Plato was provided of; it will ask more than the work of twenty licensers to examine all the lutes, the violins, and the guitars in every house; they must not be suffered to prattle as they do, but must be licensed what they may say. And who shall silence all the airs and madrigals that whisper softness in chambers? The windows also, and the balconies must be thought on; there are shrewd books, with dangerous frontispieces, set to sale; who shall prohibit them, shall twenty licensers? The villages also must have their visitors to inquire what lectures the bagpipe and the rebeck reads, even to the ballatry and the gamut of every municipal fiddler, for these are the countryman's Arcadias, and his Monte Mayors.

Next, what more national corruption, for which England hears ill abroad, than household gluttony: who shall be the rectors of our daily rioting? And what shall be done to inhibit the multitudes that frequent those houses where drunkenness is sold and harboured? Our garments also should be referred to the licensing of some more sober workmasters to see them cut into a less wanton garb. Who shall regulate all the mixed conversation of our youth, male and female together, as is the fashion of this country? Who shall still appoint what shall be discoursed, what presumed, and no further? Lastly, who shall forbid and separate all idle resort, all evil company? These things will be, and must be; but how they shall be least hurtful, how least enticing, herein consists the grave and governing wisdom of a state . . .

They are not skilful considers of human things, who imagine to remove sin by removing the matter of sin; for, besides that it is a huge heap increasing under the very act of diminishing, though some part of it may for a time be withdrawn from some persons, it cannot from all, in such a universal thing as books are; and when this is done, yet the sin remains entire. Though ye take from a covetous man all his treasure, he has yet one jewel left, ye cannot bereave him of his covetousness. Banish all objects of lust, shut up all youth into the severest discipline that can be exercised in any hermitage, ye cannot make them chaste, that came not thither so: such great care and wisdom is required to the right managing of this point. Suppose we could expel sin by this means; look how much we thus expel of sin, so much we expel of virtue: for the matter of them both is the same; remove that, and ye remove them both alike . . .

I cannot set so light by all the invention, the art, the wit, the grave and solid judgment which is in England, as that it can be comprehended in any twenty capacities how good soever, much less that it should not pass except their superintendence be over it, except it be sifted and strained with their strainers, that it should be uncurrent without their manual stamp. Truth and understanding are not such wares as to be monopolized and traded in by tickets and statutes and standards. We must not think to make a staple commodity of all the knowledge in the land, to mark and license it like our broadcloth and our woolpacks. What is it but a servitude like that imposed by the Philistines, not to be allowed the sharpening of our own axes and coulters, but we must repair from all quarters to twenty licensing forges? . . .

Nor is it to the common people less than a reproach; for if we be so jealous over them, as that we dare not trust them with an English pamphlet, what do we but censure them for a giddy, vicious, and ungrounded people; in such a sick and weak state of faith and discretion, as to be able to take nothing down but through the pipe of a licenser? . . .

Where there is much desire to learn, there of necessity will be much arguing, much writing, many opinions; for opinion in good men is but knowledge in the making . . .

Methinks I see in my mind a noble and puissant nation rousing herself like a strong man after sleep, and shaking her invincible locks. Methinks I see her as an eagle mewing her mighty youth, and kindling her undazzled eyes at the full midday beam; purging and unscaling her long-abused sight at the fountain itself of heavenly radiance; while the whole noise of timorous and flocking birds, with those also that love the twilight, flutter about, amazed at what she means, and in their envious gabble would prognosticate a year of sects and schisms.

What would ye do then? should ye suppress all this flowery crop of knowledge and new light sprung up and yet springing daily in this city? should ye set an obligarchy of twenty engrossers over it, to bring a famine upon our minds again, when we shall know nothing but what is measured to us by their bushel? Believe it, Lords and Commons, they who counsel ye to such a suppressing do as good as bid ye suppress yourselves; and I will soon show how. If it be desired to know the immediate cause of all this free writing and free speaking, there cannot be assigned a truer than your own mild and free and humane government. It is the liberty, Lords and Commons, which your own valorous and happy counsels have purchased us, liberty which is the nurse of all great wits; this is that which hath rarefied and enlightened our spirits like the influence of heaven; this is that which hath enfranchised, enlarged and lifted up our apprehensions degrees above themselves.

Ye cannot make us now less capable, less knowing, less eagerly pursuing of the truth, unless ye first make yourselves, that made us so, less the lovers, less the founders of our true liberty. We can grow ignorant again, brutish, formal and slavish, as ye found us; but you then must first become that which ye cannot be, oppressive, arbitrary and tyrannous, as they were from whom ye have freed us. That our hearts are now more capacious, our thoughts more erected to the search and expectation of greatest and exactest things, is the issue of your own virtue propagated in us; ye cannot suppress that, unless ye reinforce an abrogated and merciless law, that fathers may dispatch at will their own children. And who shall then stick closest to ye, and excite others? not he who takes up arms for coat and conduct, and his four nobles of Danegelt. Although I dispraise not the defence of just immunities, yet love my peace better, if that were all. Give me the liberty to know, to utter, and to argue freely according to conscience, above all liberties.

From THE PILGRIM'S PROGRESS, 1678–84

John Bunyan

Subtitled *from This World to that Which is to Come*, Bunyan's masterpiece is a prose allegory in which the author dreams, in Part I, that he sees Christian flee the City of Destruction and progress on a pilgrimage – through the Slough of Despond, the Valley of the Shadow of Death, Doubting Castle and all – until he reaches the Celestial City (the "New Jerusalem" of Revelations 21:2); in Part II, Christian's wife, Christiana, and her children set out on the same pilgrimage, accompanied by neighbour Mrs Mercy, against the objections of Mrs Timorous. Much of the book was written while Bunyan (1628–88) himself was in Bedford Jail, England, for preaching without a licence; this "crime" was a convenient excuse, for in truth the Restoration authorities simply disliked Bunyan's Puritan Non-conformist's politics. A former soldier in the Parliamentary army, Bunyan remained faithfully married to political radicalism, religious dissent, and compassion for "Christ's poor" – the very ideas in which *Pilgrim's Progress* is soaked. Its influence over the struggle of the 18th-century British "Everyman" for political representation was only rivalled by Tom Paine's *Rights of Man* (see pp 355–99). Meanwhile, the moral message of Pilgrim's Progress, together with its vivid and humorous prose, its exciting narrative, gave it another existence as a children's classic. It has been translated into more than 100 languages.

The Fight with Apollyon[1] (Part I)

Then Apollyon straddled quite over the whole breadth of the way, and said, "I am void of fear in this matter, prepare thyself to die, for I swear by my infernal den that thou shalt go no further, here will I spill thy soul"; and with that, he threw a flaming dart at his breast, but Christian had a shield

---

[1] Apollyon: the angel of the bottomless pit, from Revelations 9:2.

in his hand, with which he caught it, and so prevented the danger of that. Then did Christian draw, for he saw 'twas time to bestir him; and Apollyon as fast made at him, throwing darts as thick as hail; by the which, notwithstanding all that Christian could do to avoid it, Apollyon wounded him in his head, his hand and foot; this made Christian give a little back: Apollyon therefore followed his work amain, and Christian again took courage, and resisted as manfully as he could. This sore combat lasted for above half a day, even till Christian was almost quite spent. For you must know that Christian by reason of his wounds, must needs grow weaker and weaker.

Then Apollyon espying his opportunity, began to gather up close to Christian, and wrestling with him, gave him a dreadful fall; and with that Christian's sword flew out of his hand. Then said Apollyon, "I am sure of thee now"; and with that, he had almost pressed him to death, so that Christian began to despair of life. But as God would have it, while Apollyon was fetching of his last blow, thereby to make a full end of this good man, Christian nimbly reached out his hand for his sword, and caught it, saying, "Rejoice not against me, O mine enemy! when I fall, I shall arise"; and with that, gave him a deadly thrust, which made him give back, as one that had received his mortal wound: Christian perceiving that, made at him again, saying, "Nay, in all these things we are more than conquerors, through Him that loved us." And with that, Apollyon spread forth his dragon's wings, and sped him away, that Christian saw him no more.

In this combat no man can imagine, unless he had seen and heard as I did, what yelling, and hideous roaring Apollyon made all the time of the fight, he spake like a dragon: and on the other side, what sighs and groans brast from Christian's heart. I never saw him all the while give so much as one pleasant look, till he perceived he had wounded Apollyon with his two edged sword, then indeed he did smile, and look upward: but 'twas the dreadfullest sight that ever I saw.

So when the battle was over, Christian said, "I will here give thanks to Him that hath delivered me out of the mouth of the lion; to him that did help me against Apollyon": and so he did, saying,

> "Great Beelzebub, the captain of this fiend,
> Designed my ruin; therefore to this end
> He sent him harnessed out, and he with rage
> That hellish was, did fiercely me engage:
> But blessèd Michael helpèd me, and I,
> By dint of sword, did quickly make him fly:
> Therefore to him let me give lasting praise,
> And thank and bless his holy name always."

Then there came to him an hand, with some of the leaves of the tree of life, the which Christian took, and applied to the wounds that he had received in the battle, and was healed immediately. He also sat down in that place to eat bread, and to drink of the bottle that was given him a little before; so being refreshed, he addressed himself to his journey, with his sword drawn in his hand, for he said, "I know not but some other enemy may be at hand." But he met with no other affront from Apollyon quite through this valley.

The Trial of Christian and Faithful (Part I)

Then proclamation was made, that they that had aught to say for their lord the king against the prisoner at the bar, should forthwith appear and give in their evidence. So there came in three witnesses, to wit, *Envy, Superstition,* and *Pick-thank.* They were then asked if they knew the prisoner at the bar; and what they had to say for their lord the king against him.

Then stood forth *Envy,* and said to this effect: My Lord, I have known this man a long time, and will attest upon my oath before this honourable bench that he is –

Judge. Hold! Give him his oath. (So they sware him.) Then he said –

Envy. My Lord, this man, notwithstanding his plausible name, is one of the vilest men in our country. He neither regardeth prince nor people, law nor custom; but doth all that he can to possess all men with certain of his disloyal notions, which he in the general calls principles of faith and holiness. And, in particular, I heard him once myself affirm that Christianity and the customs of our town of *Vanity* were diametrically opposite, and could not be reconciled. By which saying, my Lord, he doth at once not only condemn all our laudable doings, but us in the doing of them.

Judge. Then did the Judge say to him, Hast thou any more to say?

Envy. My Lord, I could say much more, only I would not be tedious to the court. Yet, if need be, when the other gentlemen have given in their evidence, rather than anything shall be wanting that will despatch him, I will enlarge my testimony against him. So he was bid to stand by.

Then they called *Superstition,* and bid him look upon the prisoner. They also asked, what he could say for their lord the king against him. Then they sware him; so he began.

Super. My Lord, I have no great acquaintance with this man, nor do I desire to have further knowledge of him; however, this I know, that he is a very pestilent fellow, from some discourse that, the other day, I had with him in this town; for then, talking with him, I heard him say, that our religion was nought, and such by which a man could by no means please God. Which sayings of his, my Lord, your Lordship very well knows, what necessarily thence will follow, to wit, that we do still worship in vain, are yet in our sins, and finally shall be damned; and this is that which I have to say.

Then was *Pickthank* sworn, and bid say what he knew in behalf of their lord the king, against the prisoner at the bar.

Pick. My Lord, and you gentlemen all – This fellow I have known of a long time, and have heard him speak things that ought not to be spoke; for he hath railed on our noble prince *Beelzebub*, and hath spoken contemptibly of his honourable friends, whose names are the Lord *Old Man*, the Lord *Carnal Delight*, the Lord *Luxurious*, the Lord *Desire of Vain Glory*, my old Lord *Lechery*, Sir *Having Greedy*, with all the rest of our nobility; and he hath said, moreover, That if all men were of his mind, if possible, there is not one of these noblemen should have any longer a being in this town. Besides, he hath not been afraid to rail on you, my Lord, who are now appointed to be his judge, calling you an ungodly villain, with many other such like vilifying terms, with which he hath bespattered most of the gentry of our town.

When this *Pickthank* had told his tale, the Judge directed his speech to the prisoner at the bar, saying, Thou runagate, heretic, and traitor, hast thou heard what these honest gentlemen have witnessed against thee?

Faith. May I speak a few words in my own defence?

Judge. Sirrah! sirrah! thou deservest to live no longer, but to be slain immediately upon the place; yet, that all men may see our gentleness towards thee, let us hear what thou, vile runagate, hast to say.

Faith. 1. I say, then, in answer to what Mr *Envy* hath spoken, I never said aught but this, That what rule, or laws, or customs, or people, were flat against the Word of God, are diametrically opposite to Christianity. If I have said amiss in this, convince me of my error, and I am ready here before you to make my recantation.

2. As to the second, to wit, Mr *Superstition*, and his charge against me, I said only this, That in the worship of God there is required a Divine faith; but there can be no Divine faith without a Divine revelation of the will of God. Therefore, whatever is thrust into the worship of God that is not agreeable to Divine revelation, cannot be done but by a human faith, which faith will not be profitable to eternal life.

3. As to what Mr *Pickthank* hath said, I say (avoiding terms, as that I am said to rail, and the like) that the prince of this town, with all the rabblement, his attendants, by this gentleman named, are more fit for a being in hell, than in this town and country: and so, the Lord have mercy upon me!

Then the Judge called to the jury (who all this while stood by, to hear and observe): Gentlemen of the jury, you see this man about whom so great an uproar hath been made in this town. You have also heard what these worthy gentlemen have witnessed against him. Also you have heard his reply and confession. It lieth now in your breasts to hang him or save his life; but yet I think meet to instruct you into our law.

There was an Act made in the days of Pharaoh the Great, servant to our prince, that lest those of a contrary religion should multiply and grow too strong for him, their males should be thrown into the river. There was also an Act made in the days of Nebuchadnezzar the Great, another of his servants, that whosoever would not fall down and worship his golden image, should be thrown into a fiery furnace. There was also an Act made in the days of Darius, that whoso, for some time, called upon any god but him, should be cast into the lions' den. Now the substance of these laws this rebel has broken, not only in thought (which is not to be borne), but also in word and deed, which must therefore needs be intolerable.

For that of Pharaoh, his law was made upon a supposition, to prevent mischief, no crime being yet apparent; but here is a crime apparent. For the second and third, you see he disputeth against our religion; and for the treason he hath confessed, he deserveth to die the death.

Then went the jury out, whose names were, Mr *Blind-man*, Mr *No-good*, Mr *Malice*, Mr *Love-lust*, Mr *Live-loose*, Mr *Heady*, Mr *High-mind*, Mr *Enmity*, Mr *Liar*, Mr *Cruelty*, Mr *Hate-light*, and Mr *Implacable*; who every one gave in his private verdict against him among themselves, and afterwards unanimously concluded to bring him in guilty before the Judge. And first, among themselves, Mr *Blind-man*, the foreman, said, I see clearly that this man is a heretic. Then said Mr *No-good*, Away with such a fellow from the earth. Ay, said Mr *Malice*, for I hate the very looks of him. Then said Mr *Love-lust*, I could never endure him. Nor I, said Mr *Live-loose*, for he would always be condemning my way. Hang him, hang him, said Mr *Heady*. A sorry scrub, said Mr *High-mind*. My heart riseth against him, said Mr *Enmity*. He is a rogue, said Mr *Liar*. Hanging is too good for him, said Mr *Cruelty*. Let us despatch him out of the way, said Mr *Hate-light*. Then said Mr *Implacable*, Might I have all the world given me, I could not be reconciled to him; therefore, let us forthwith bring him in guilty of death. And so they did; therefore he was presently condemned to be had from the place where he was to the place from whence he came, and there to be put to the most cruel death that could be invented.

They, therefore, brought him out, to do with him according to their law; and, first, they scourged him, then they buffeted him, then they lanced his flesh with knives; after that, they stoned him with stones, then pricked him with their swords; and, last of all, they burned him to ashes at the stake. Thus came *Faithful* to his end.

Now I saw that there stood behind the multitude a chariot and a couple of horses, waiting for *Faithful*, who (so soon as his adversaries had despatched him) was taken up into it, and straightway was carried up through the clouds, with sound of trumpet, the nearest way to the *Celestial Gate*.

"Brave *Faithful*, bravely done in word and deed;
Judge, witnesses, and jury have, instead
Of overcoming thee, but shewn their rage:
When they are dead, thou'lt live from age to age."

But as for *Christian*, he had some respite, and was remanded back to prison. So he there remained for a space; but He that overrules all things, having the power of their rage in his own hand, so wrought it about, that *Christian* for that time escaped them, and went his way.

The Crossing of the River (Part II)

Now the day drew on that Christiana must be gone. So the road was full of people to see her take her journey. But, behold, all the banks beyond the river were full of horses and chariots, which were come down from above to accompany her to the city gate. So she came forth, and entered the river, with a beckon of farewell to those that followed her to the river side. The last words that she was heard to say here were, I come, Lord, to be with thee, and bless thee.

So her children and friends returned to their place, for that those that waited for Christiana had carried her out of their sight. So she went and called, and entered in at the gate with all the ceremonies of joy that her husband Christian had done before her.

At her departure her children wept; but Mr Great-heart and Mr Valiant played upon the well-tuned cymbal and harp for joy. So all departed to their respective places.

In process of time there came a post to the town again, and his business was with Mr Ready-to-halt. So he inquired him out, and said to him, I am come to thee in the name of him whom thou hast loved and followed, though upon crutches; and my message is to tell thee, that he expects thee at his table to sup with him, in his kingdom, the next day after Easter; wherefore prepare thyself for this journey.

Then he also gave him a token that he was a true messenger, saying, I have broken thy golden bowl, and loosed thy silver cord. (Eccles. xii. 6.)

After this, Mr Ready-to-halt called for his fellow-pilgrims, and told them, saying, I am sent for, and God shall surely visit you also. So he desired Mr Valiant to make his will; and because he had nothing to bequeath to them that should survive him but his crutches and his good wishes, therefore thus he said, These crutches I bequeath to my son that shall tread in my steps, with a hundred warm wishes that he may prove better than I have done.

Then he thanked Mr Great-heart for his conduct and kindness, and so addressed himself to his journey. When he came at the brink of the river, he said, Now I shall have no more need of these crutches, since yonder are chariots and horses for me to ride on. The last words he was heard to say was, Welcome life! So he went his way.

After this, Mr Feeble-mind had tidings brought him, that the post sounded his horn at his chamber-door. Then he came in, and told him, saying, I am come to tell thee that thy Master hath need of thee; and that, in very little time, thou must behold his face in brightness. And take this as a token of the truth of my message, "Those that look out of the windows shall be darkened." (Eccles. xii. 3.)

Then Mr Feeble-mind called for his friends, and told them what errand had been brought unto him, and what token he had received of the truth of the message. Then he said, Since I have nothing to bequeath to any, to what purpose should I make a will? As for my feeble mind, that I will leave behind me, for that, I have no need of that in the place whither I go. Nor is it worth bestowing upon the poorest pilgrim; wherefore, when I am gone, I desire that you, Mr Valiant, would bury it in a dunghill. This done, and the day being come in which he was to depart, he entered the river as the rest. His last words were, Hold out, faith and patience. So he went over to the other side.

When days had many of them passed away, Mr Despondency was sent for; for a post was come, and brought this message to him: Trembling man, these are to summon thee to be ready with thy King by the next Lord's day, to shout for joy for thy deliverance from all thy doubtings.

And, said the messenger, that my message is true, take this for a proof; so he gave him the grasshopper to be a burden unto him. (Eccles. xii. 5.) Now, Mr Despondency's daughter, whose name was Much-afraid, said, when she heard what was done, that she would go with her father. Then Mr Despondency said to his friends, Myself and my daughter, you know what we have been, and how troublesome we have behaved ourselves in every company. My will and my daughter's is, that our desponds and slavish fears be by no man ever received, from the day of our departure, for ever; for I know that after my death they will offer themselves to others. For, to be plain with you, they are ghosts the which we entertained when we first began to be pilgrims, and could never shake them off after; and they will walk about and seek entertainment of the pilgrims; but, for our sakes, shut ye the doors upon them.

When the time was come for them to depart, they went to the brink of the river. The last words of Mr Despondency were, Farewell night, welcome day. His daughter went through the river singing, but none could understand what she said.

Then it came to pass, a while after, that there was a post in the town that inquired for Mr Honest. So he came to his house where he was, and delivered to his hand these lines: Thou art commanded to be ready against this day seven-night, to present thyself before the Lord, at his Father's house. And for a token that my message is true, "All the daughters of music shall be brought low." (Eccles. xii. 4.) Then Mr Honest called for his friends, and said unto them, I die, but shall make no will. As for my honesty, it shall go with me; let him that comes after be told of this. When the day that he was to be gone was come, he addressed himself to go over the river. Now the river at that time overflowed the banks in some places; but Mr Honest in his lifetime had spoken to one Good-conscience to meet him there, the which he also did, and lent him his hand, and so helped him over. The last words of Mr Honest were, Grace reigns. So he left the world.

After this it was noised abroad, that Mr Valiant-for-truth was taken with a summons by the same post as the other; and had this for a token that the summons was true, "That his pitcher was broken at the fountain." (Eccles. xii. 6.) When he understood it, he called for his friends, and told them of it. Then, said he, I am going to my Father's; and though with great difficulty I am got hither, yet now I do not repent me of all the trouble I have been at to arrive where I am. My sword I give to him that shall succeed me in my pilgrimage, and my courage and skill to him that can get it. My marks and scars I carry with me, to be a witness for me, that I have fought his battle who now will be my rewarder. When the day that must go hence was come, many accompanied him to the river side, into which as he went he said, "Death, where is thy sting?" And as he went down deeper, he said, "Grave, where is thy victory?" So he passed over, and all the trumpets sounded for him on the other side.

Then there came forth a summons for Mr Stand-fast – this Mr Stand-fast was he that the rest of the pilgrims found upon his knees in the Enchanted Ground – for the post brought it him open in his hands. The contents whereof were, that he must prepare for a change of life, for his Master was not willing that he should be so far from him any longer. At this Mr Stand-fast was put into a muse. Nay, said the messenger, you need not doubt the truth of my message, for here is a token of the truth thereof: "Thy wheel is broken at the cistern." (Eccles. xii. 6.) Then he called unto him Mr Great-heart, who was their guide, and said unto him, Sir, although it was not my hap to be much in your good company in the days of my pilgrimage; yet, since the time I knew you, you have been profitable to me. When I came from home, I left behind me a wife and five small children; let me entreat you, at your return (for I know that you will go and return to your Master's house, in hopes that you may yet be a conductor to more of the holy pilgrims), that you send to my family, and let them be acquainted with all that hath or shall happen unto me. Tell them, moreover, of my happy arrival to this place, and of the present [and] late blessed condition that I am in. Tell them also of Christian, and Christiana his wife, and how she and her children came after her husband. Tell them also of what a happy end she made, and whither she has gone. I have little or nothing to send to my family, except it be prayers and tears for them; of which it will suffice if thou acquaint them, if peradventure they may prevail.

When Mr Stand-fast had thus set things in order, and the time being come for him to haste him away, he also went down to the river. Now there was a great calm at that time in the river; wherefore Mr Stand-fast, when he was about half-way in, stood awhile, and talked to his companions that had waited upon him thither; and he said, This river has been a terror to many; yea, the thoughts of it also have often frightened me. Now, methinks, I stand easy, my foot is fixed upon that upon which the feet of the priests that bare the ark of the covenant stood, while Israel went over this Jordan. (Jos. iii. 17.) The waters, indeed, are to the palate bitter, and to the stomach cold; yet the thoughts of what I am going to, and of the conduct that waits for me on the other side, doth lie as a glowing coal at my heart.

I see myself now at the end of my journey, my toilsome days are ended. I am going now to see that head that was crowned with thorns, and that face that was spit upon for me.

I have formerly lived by hearsay and faith; but now I go where I shall live by sight, and shall be with him in whose company I delight myself.

I have loved to hear my Lord spoken of; and wherever I have seen the print of his shoe in the earth, there I have coveted to set my foot too.

His name has been to me as a civet-box; yea, sweeter than all perfumes. His voice to me has been most sweet; and his countenance I have more desired than they that have most desired the light of the sun. His word I did use to gather for my food, and for antidotes against my faintings. "He has held me, and hath kept me from mine iniquities; yea, my steps hath he strengthened in his way."

Now, while he was thus in discourse, his countenance changed, his strong man bowed under him; and after he had said, Take me, for I come unto thee, he ceased to be seen of them.

But glorious it was to see how the open region was filled with horses and chariots, with trumpeters and pipers, with singers and players on stringed instruments, to welcome the pilgrims as they went up, and followed one another in at the beautiful gate of the city.

HABEAS CORPUS ACT, 1679

In 1660 the Stuarts re-ascended the throne of England. Old tendencies towards Catholicism and absolutism proved little diminished, however, and a prudently watchful parliament determined to pass an Act enshrining *Habeas Corpus*.

This was an ancient English right that, if a man was imprisoned by a local lord, his friends could request the king to issue a writ commanding the man who "have the body" (*Habeas Corpus*) of the prisoner to bring the prisoner before a magistrate for a proper trial. Under a tyrannous king, such as Charles I, the process could be wilfully ignored. In 1679 Parliament passed the Habeas Corpus Act against future abuse. The following are the main provisions:

Whereas great delays have been used by sheriffs, gaolers and other officers, to whose custody any of the king's subjects have been committed for criminal or supposed criminal matters, in making returns of writs of Habeas Corpus to them directed by standing out an Alias and Pluries Habeas Corpus and sometimes more, and by other shifts to avoid their yielding obedience to such writs, contrary to their duty and the known laws of the land, whereby many of the king's subjects have been and hereafter may be long detained in prison in such cases where by law they are bailable, to their great charge and vexation.

II. For the prevention whereof and the more speedy relief of all persons imprisoned for any such criminal or supposed criminal matters; be it enacted by the king's most excellent Majesty, by and with the advice and consent of the lords spiritual and temporal and commons in this present parliament assembled, and by the authority thereof, that whensoever any person or persons shall bring any habeas corpus directed unto any sheriff or sheriffs, gaoler, minister or other person whatsoever for any person in his or their custody, and the said writ shall be served upon the said officer or left at the gaol or prison with any of the under officers, under keepers or deputy of the said officers or keepers, that the said officer or officers, his or their under officers, under keepers or deputies shall within three days after service thereof as aforesaid (unless the commitment aforesaid were for treason or felony, plainly and specially expressed in the warrant of commitment) upon payment or tender of the charges of bringing the said prisoner, to be ascertained by the judge or court that awarded the same and endorsed upon the said writ, not exceeding twelve pence per mile, and upon security given by his own bond to pay the charges of carrying back the prisoner, if he shall be remanded by the court or judge to which he shall be brought according to the true intent of this present act, and that he will not make any escape by the way, make return of such writ; and bring or cause to be brought the body of the party so committed or restrained unto or before the lord chancellor, or lord keeper of the great seal of England, for the time being, or the judges or barons of the said court from whence the said writ shall issue, or unto and before such other person or persons before whom the said writ is made returnable, according to the command thereof; and shall then likewise certify the true causes of his detainer or imprisonment; unless the commitment of the said party be in any place beyond the distance of twenty miles from the place or places where such court or person is or shall be residing, and if beyond the distance of twenty miles and not above one hundred miles then within the space of ten days after such delivery aforesaid, and not longer.

III. And to the intent that no sheriff, gaoler or other officer may pretend ignorance of the import of any such writ; be it enacted by the authority aforesaid, that all such writs shall be marked in this manner, *Per statutum tricesimo primo Caroli Secundi regis*, and shall be signed by the person that awards the same; and if any person or persons shall be or stand committed or detained as aforesaid, for any crime, unless for treason or felony plainly expressed in the warrant of commitment, in the vacation time, and out of term, it shall and may be lawful to and for the person or persons so committed or detained (other than persons convict or in execution by legal process) or any one on his or their behalf to appeal or complain to the lord chancellor or lord keeper or any one of His Majesty's justices, either of the one bench or of the other, or the barons of the exchequer of the degree of the coif; and the said lord chancellor, lord keeper, justices or barons or any of them, upon view of the copy or copies of the warrant or warrants of commitment and detainer, or otherwise upon oath made that such copy or copies were denied to be given by such person or persons in whose custody the prisoner or prisoners is or are detained, are hereby authorised and required, upon request made in writing by such person or persons or any on his, her or their behalf, attested and subscribed by two witnesses who were present at the delivery of the same, to award and grant an habeas corpus, under the seal of such court whereof he shall then be one of the judges, to be directed to the officer or officers in whose custody the party so committed or detained shall be, returnable immediate before the said lord chancellor or lord keeper, or such justice, baron or any other justice or baron of the degree of the coif of any of the said courts; and upon service thereof as aforesaid, the officer or officers, his or their under officer or under officers, under keeper or under keepers, or deputy, in whose custody the party is so committed or detained, shall within the times respectively before limited bring such prisoner or prisoners before the said lord chancellor or lord keeper or such justices, barons or one of them, before whom the said writ is made returnable, and in case of his absence before any other of them, with the return of such writ and the true causes of the commitment and detainer; and thereupon within two days after the party shall be brought before them, the said lord chancellor or lord keeper, or such justice or baron before whom the prisoner shall be brought as aforesaid, shall discharge the said prisoner from his imprisonment, taking his or their recognisance with one or more surety or sureties in any sum according to their discretions, having regard to the quality of the prisoner and nature of the offence, for his or their appearance in the court of king's bench the term following or at the next assizes, sessions or general gaol-delivery of and for such county, city or place where the commitment was, or where the offence was committed, or in such other court where the said offence is properly cognizable, as the case shall require, and then shall certify the said writ with the return thereof and the said recognizance or recognizances into the said court where such appearance is to be made; unless it shall appear unto the said lord chancellor or lord keeper, or justice or justices, or baron or barons, that the party so committed is detained upon a legal process, order or warrant out of some court that hath jurisdiction of criminal matters, or by some warrant signed and sealed with the hand and seal of any of the said justices or barons, or some justice or justices of the peace, for such matters or offences for the which by the law the prisoner is not bailable.

IV. Provided always, and be it enacted, that if any person shall have wilfully neglected by the space of two whole terms after his imprisonment to pray a habeas corpus for his enlargement, such person so wilfully neglecting shall not have any habeas corpus to be granted in vacation time in pursuance of this act.

V. And be it further enacted by the authority aforesaid, that if any officer or officers, his or their under-officer or under-officers, under-keeper or under-keepers, or deputy, shall neglect or refuse to make the returns aforesaid, or to bring the body or bodies of the prisoner or prisoners according to the command of the said writ, within the respective times aforesaid, or upon demand made by the prisoner or person in his behalf shall refuse to deliver, or within the space of six hours after demand shall not deliver, to the person so demanding, a true copy of the warrant or warrants of commitment and detainer of such prisoner, which he and they are hereby required to deliver accordingly; all and every the head gaolers and keepers of such prisons, and such other person in whose custody the prisoner shall be detained, shall for the first offence forfeit to the prisoner or party grieved the sum of one hundred pounds; and for the second offence the sum of two hundred pounds and shall and is hereby made incapable to hold or execute his said office; the said penalties to be recovered by the prisoner or party grieved, his executors or administrators, against such offender, his executors or administrators, by any action of debt, suit, bill, plaint or information, in any of the king's courts at Westminster, wherein no essoin, protection, privilege, injunction wager of laws or stay of prosecution by *Non vult ulterious prosequi* or otherwise shall be admitted or allowed, or any more than one imparlance; and any recovery or judgment at the suit of any party grieved shall be a sufficient conviction for the first offence; and any after recovery or judgment at the suit of a party grieved for any offence after the first judgment shall be a sufficient conviction to bring the officers or person within the said penalty for the second offence.

VI. And for the prevention of unjust vexation by reiterated commitments for the same offence; be it enacted by the authority aforesaid, that no person or persons, which shall be delivered or set at large upon any habeas corpus, shall at any time hereafter be again imprisoned or committed for the same offence by any person or persons whatsoever, other than by the legal order and process of such court wherein he or they shall be bound by recognizance to appear or other court having jurisdiction of the cause; and if any other person or persons shall knowingly contrary to this act recommit or imprison or knowingly procure or cause to be recommitted or imprisoned for the same offence or pretended offence any person or persons delivered or set at large as aforesaid, or be knowingly aiding or assisting therein, then he or they shall forfeit to the prisoner or party grieved the sum of five hundred pounds, any colourable pretence or variation in the warrant or warrants or commitment notwithstanding, to be recovered as aforesaid.

VII. Provided always, and be it further enacted, that if any person or persons shall be committed for high treason or felony, plainly and specially expressed in the warrant of commitment, upon his prayer or petition in open court the first week of the term or first day of the sessions of oyer and terminer or general gaol delivery to be brought to his trial, shall not be indicted sometime in the next term, sessions of oyer and terminer or general gaol delivery after such commitment; it shall and may be lawful to and for the judges of the court of king's bench and justices of oyer and terminer or general gaol delivery and they are hereby required, upon motion to them made in open court the last day of the term, sessions or gaol delivery, either by the prisoner or any one in his behalf, to set at liberty the prisoner upon bail, unless it appear to the judges and justices upon oath made, that the witnesses for the king could not be produced the same term, sessions or general goal delivery; and if any person or persons, committed as aforesaid, upon his prayer or petition in open court the first week of the term or first day of the sessions of oyer and terminer or general gaol delivery to be brought to his trial, shall not be indicted and tried the second term, sessions of oyer and terminer or general gaol delivery after his commitment, or upon his trial shall be acquitted, he shall be discharged from his imprisonment.

VIII. Provided always, that nothing in this act shall extend to discharge out of prison any person charged in debt or other action or with process in any civil cause, but that after he shall be discharged of his imprisonment for such his criminal offence, he shall be kept in custody according to law for such other suit.

IX. Provided always, and be it enacted by the authority aforesaid, that if any person or persons, subjects of this realm, shall be committed to any prison or in custody of any officer or officers whatsoever for any criminal or supposed criminal matter, that the said person shall not be removed from the said prison and custody into the custody of any other officer or officers; unless it be by habeas corpus or some other legal writ, or where the prisoner is delivered to the constable or other inferior officer to carry such prisoner to some common gaol, or where any person is sent by order of any judge of assize or justice of the peace to any common work-house or house of correction, or where the prisoner is removed from one prison or place to another within the same county, in order to his or her trial or discharge in due course of law, or in case of sudden fire or infection or other necessity; and if any person or persons shall after such commitment aforesaid make out and sign or countersign any warrant or warrants for such removal aforesaid, contrary to this act, as well he that makes or signs or countersigns such warrant or warrants as the officer or officers that obey or execute the same shall suffer and incur the pains and forfeitures in this act beforementioned, both for the first and second offence respectively, to be recovered in manner aforesaid by the party grieved.

X. Provided also, and be it further enacted by the authority aforesaid, that it shall and may be lawful to and for any prisoner and prisoners as aforesaid to move and obtain his or their habeas corpus as well out of the high court of chancery or court of exchequer as out of the court of king's bench or common pleas or either of them; and if the said lord chancellor or lord keeper, or any judge or judges, baron or barons for the time being of the degree of the coif, of any of the courts aforesaid, in the vacation time upon view of the copy or copies of the warrant or warrants of commitment or detainer, or upon oath made that such copy or copies were denied as aforesaid, shall deny any writ of habeas corpus by this act required to be granted being moved for as aforesaid, they shall severally forfeit to the prisoner or party grieved the sum of five hundred pounds, to be recovered in manner aforesaid.

XI. And be it enacted and declared by the authority aforesaid, that an habeas corpus according to the true intent and meaning of this act may be directed and run into any county palatine, the Cinque ports, or other privileged places within the kingdom of England, dominion of Wales or town of Berwick upon Tweed, and the islands of Jersey or Guernsey, any law or usage to the contrary notwithstanding.

XII. And for preventing illegal imprisonments in prisons beyond the seas; be it further enacted by the authority aforesaid, that no subject of this realm that now is or hereafter shall be an inhabitant or resident of this kingdom of England, dominion of Wales or town of Berwick upon Tweed shall or may be sent prisoner into Scotland, Ireland, Jersey, Guernsey, Tangier or into any parts, garrisons, islands or places beyond the seas, which are or at any time hereafter shall be within or without the dominions of his majesty, his heirs or successors; and that every such imprisonment is hereby enacted and adjudged to be illegal; and that if any of the said subjects now is or hereafter shall be so imprisoned every such person and persons so imprisoned shall and may for every such imprisonment maintain by virtue of this act an action or actions of false imprisonment in any of his majesty's courts of record against the person or persons by whom he or she shall be so committed, detained, imprisoned, sent prisoner or transported, contrary to the true meaning of this act, and against all or any person or persons that shall frame, contrive, write, seal or countersign any warrant or writing for such commitment, detainer, imprisonment or transportation, or shall be advising, aiding or assisting in the same or any of them; and the plaintiff in every such action shall have judgment to recover his treble costs, besides damages, which damages so to be given shall not be less than five hundred pounds; in which action no delay, stay or stop of proceeding by rule, order or command, nor no injunction, protection or privilege whatsoever, nor any more than one imparlance, shall be allowed, excepting such rule of the court wherein the action shall depend, made in open court, as shall be thought in justice necessary, for special cause to be expressed in the said rule; and the person or persons who shall knowingly frame, contrive, write, seal or countersign any warrant for such commitment, detainer or transportation, or shall so commit, detain, imprison or transport any person or persons, contrary to this act, or be any ways advising, aiding or assisting therein, being lawfully convicted thereof, shall be disabled from thenceforth to bear any office of trust or profit within the said realm of England, dominion of Wales or town of Berwick upon Tweed, or any of the islands, territories or dominions thereunto belonging; and shall incur and sustain the pains, penalties and forfeitures limited, ordained and provided in and by the statute of provision and præmunire, made in the sixteenth year of King

Richard the Second; and be incapable of any pardon from the king, his heirs or successors, of the said forfeitures, losses or disabilities, or any of them.

XIII. Provided always, that nothing in this act shall extend to give benefit to any person who shall by contract in writing agree with any merchant or owner of any plantation, or other person whatsoever, to be transported to any parts beyond seas, and receive earnest upon such agreement, although that afterwards such person shall renounce such contract.

XIV. Provided always, and be it enacted, that if any person or persons lawfully convicted of any felony shall in open court pray to be transported beyond the seas, and the court shall think fit to leave him or them in prison for that purpose, such person or persons may be transported into any parts beyond the seas, this act or anything therein contained to the contrary notwithstanding.

XV. Provided also, and be it enacted, that nothing herein contained shall be deemed, construed or taken to extend to the imprisonment of any person before the first day of June one thousand six hundred seventy and nine, or to anything advised, procured or otherwise done relating to such imprisonment, anything herein contained to the contrary notwithstanding.

XVI. Provided also, that if any person or persons at any time resident in this realm shall have committed any capital offence in Scotland or Ireland or any of the islands or foreign plantations of the king, his heirs or successors, where he or she ought to be tried for such offence, such person or persons may be sent to such place there to receive such trial in such manner as the same might have been used before the making of this act, anything herein contained to the contrary notwithstanding.

XVII. Provided also, and be it enacted, that no person or persons shall be sued, impleaded, molested or troubled for any offence against this act, unless the party offending be sued or impleaded for the same within two years at the most after such time wherein the offence shall be committed, in case the party grieved shall not be then in prison; and if he shall be in prison, then within the space of two years after the decease of the person imprisoned, or his or her delivery out of prison, which shall first happen.

XVIII. And to the intent no person may avoid his trial at the assizes or general gaol delivery by procuring his removal before the assizes, at such time as he cannot be brought back to receive his trial there; be it enacted, that after the assizes proclaimed for that county where the prisoner is detained, no person shall be removed from the common gaol upon any habeas corpus granted in pursuance of this act, but upon any such habeas corpus shall be brought before the judge of assize in open court, who is thereupon to do what to justice shall appertain.

XIX. Provided nevertheless, that after the assizes are ended any person or persons detained may have his or her habeas corpus according to the direction and intention of this act.

XX. And be it also enacted by the authority aforesaid, that if any information, suit or action shall be brought or exhibited against any person or persons for any offence committed or to be committed against the form of this law, it shall be lawful for such defendants to plead the general issue that they are not guilty, or that they owe nothing, and to give such special matter in evidence to the jury that shall try the same, which matter being pleaded had been good and sufficient matter in law to have discharged the said defendant or defendants against the said information, suit or action, and the said matter shall then be as available to him or them to all intents and purposes, as if he or they had sufficiently pleaded, set forth or alleged the same matter in bar or discharge of such information, suit or action.

XXI. And because many times persons charged with petty treason or felony or as accessories thereunto are committed upon suspicion only, whereupon they are bailable or not according as the circumstances making out that suspicion are more or less weighty, which are best known to the justices of peace that committed the persons, and have the examinations before them, or to other justices of the peace in the county; be it therefore enacted, that where any person shall appear to be committed by any judge or justice of the peace and charged as accessory before the fact to any petty treason or felony or upon suspicion thereof, or with suspicion of petty treason or felony which petty treason or felony shall be plainly and specially expressed in the warrant of commitment, that such person shall not be removed or bailed by virtue of this act, or in any other manner than they might have been before the making of this act.

THE BILL OF RIGHTS (BRITAIN), 1689

By the "Glorious Revolution" of 1688 the people of Britain removed another absolutist, papist-inclined Stuart monarch from the throne. The Revolution was "glorious" because it was bloodless, and James II was merely dispatched to another land on the Earth and not from it. The throne was handed to James Dutch Protestant son-in-law, William of Orange. This was an effective *quid pro quo*: William and his wife Mary got the throne, Parliament got a (Protestant) monarch who acceded to its "Declaration of Rights".

The Declaration in due course became the basis for the "Bill of Rights", which settled the "religion, laws, and liberties of the kingdom, so that for the future might not be in danger of again being subverted". This was achieved, *inter alia*, by parliamentary control of the army, the regular calling of Parliament and an independent judiciary. To ensure a co-operative monarchy, Parliament made William and Mary – and all subsequent monarchs – financially dependent upon it.

The Bill of Rights curtailed the royal prerogative forever. It also ushered in the "party political era", for after 1689 no monarch in Britain could govern without majority support in Parliament.

Whereas the lords spiritual and temporal and commons assembled at Westminster lawfully, fully and freely representing all the estates of the people of this realm, did upon the thirteenth day of February in the year of our Lord one thousand six hundred eighty-eight, present unto Their Majesties, then called and known by the names and style of William and Mary, prince and princess of Orange, being present in their proper persons, a certain declaration in writing made by the said lords and commons in the words following viz:

Whereas the late king James the Second by the assistance of divers evil counsellors, judges and ministers employed by him did endeavour to subvert and extirpate the Protestant religion and the laws and liberties of this kingdom.

By assuming and exercising a power of dispensing with and suspending of laws, and the execution of laws, without consent of parliament.

By committing and prosecuting divers worthy prelates for humbly petitioning to be excused from concurring to the said assumed power.

By issuing and causing to be executed a commission under the great seal for erecting a court, called the court of commissioners for ecclesiastical causes.

By levying money for and to the use of the crown, by pretence of prerogative, for other time and in other manner than the same was granted by parliament.

By raising and keeping a standing army within this kingdom in time of peace, without consent of parliament, and quartering of soldiers contrary to law.

By causing several good subjects being Protestants to be disarmed, at the same time when papists were both armed and employed, contrary to law.

By violating the freedom of election of members to serve in parliament.

By prosecutions in the court of king's bench for matters and causes cognizable only in parliament, and by divers other arbitrary and illegal courses.

And whereas of late years partial, corrupt and unqualified persons have been returned and served on juries in trials, and particularly divers jurors in trials for high treason, which were not freeholders.

And excessive bail hath been required of persons committed in criminal cases, to elude the benefit of the laws made for the liberty of subjects.

And excessive fines have been imposed.

And illegal and cruel punishments have been inflicted.

And several grants and promises made of fines and forfeitures before any conviction or judgment against the persons upon whom the same were to be levied.

All of which are utterly and directly contrary to the known laws and statutes and freedom of this realm.

And whereas the said late king James the Second having abdicated the government and the throne being thereby vacant. His Highness the prince of Orange (whom it hath pleased Almighty God to make the glorious instrument of delivering this kingdom from popery and arbitrary power) did (by the advice of the lords spiritual and temporal and divers principal persons of the commons) cause letters to be written to the lords spiritual and temporal, being Protestants; and other letters to the several counties, cities, universities, boroughs and Cinque ports for the choosing of such persons to represent them, as were of right to be sent to parliament, to meet and sit at Westminster upon the two and twentieth day of January in this year one thousand six hundred eighty and eight, in order to such an establishment as that their religion, laws and liberties might not again be in danger of being subverted; upon which letters elections having been accordingly made.

And thereupon the said lords spiritual and temporal and commons pursuant to their respective letters and elections being now assembled in a full and free representative of this nation, taking into their most serious consideration the best means for attaining the ends aforesaid, do in the first place (as their ancestors in like cases have usually done) for the vindicating and asserting their ancient rights and liberties, declare:

That the pretended power of suspending of laws or the execution of laws by regal authority without consent of parliament is illegal.

That the pretended power of dispensing with laws or the execution of laws by regal authority as it hath been assumed and exercised of late is illegal.

That the commission for erecting the late court of commissioners for ecclesiastical causes and all other commissions and courts of like nature are illegal and pernicious.

That the levying money for or to the use of the crown by pretence of prerogative without grant of parliament for a longer time or in other manner than the same is or shall be granted is illegal.

That it is the right of the subjects to petition the king and all commitments and prosecutions for such petitioning are illegal.

That the raising or keeping a standing army within the kingdom in time of peace unless it be with consent of parliament is against law.

That the subjects which are Protestants may have arms for their defence suitable to their conditions and as allowed by law.

That election of members of parliament ought to be free.

That the freedom of speech and debates or proceedings in parliament ought not to be impeached or questioned in any court or place out of parliament.

That excessive bail ought not to be required nor excessive fines imposed nor cruel and unusual punishments inflicted.

That jurors ought to be duly impanelled and returned and jurors which pass upon men in trials for high treason ought to be freeholders.

That all grants and promises of fines and forfeitures of particular persons before conviction are illegal and void.

And that for redress of all grievances and for the amending, strengthening and preserving of the laws parliaments ought to be held frequently.

And they do claim, demand and insist upon all and singular the premises as their undoubted rights and liberties and that no declarations, judgments, doings or proceedings to the prejudice of the people in any of the said premises ought in any wise to be drawn hereafter into consequence or example. To which demand of their rights they are particularly encouraged by the declaration of His Highness the prince of Orange as being the only means for obtaining a full redress and remedy therein. Having therefore an entire confidence that His said Highness the prince of Orange will perfect the deliverance so far advanced by him, and will still preserve them from the violation of their rights, which they have here asserted, and from all other attempts upon their religion, rights and liberties, the said lords spiritual and temporal and commons assembled at Westminster do resolve, that William and Mary, prince and princess of Orange, be and be declared king and queen of England, France and Ireland and the dominions thereunto belonging, to hold the crown and royal dignity of the said kingdoms and dominions to them the said prince and princess during their lives and the life of the survivor of them; and that the sole and full exercise of the regal power be only in and executed by the said prince of Orange in the names of the said prince and princess during their joint lives; and after their deceases the said crown and royal dignity of the said kingdoms and dominions to be to the heirs of the body of the said princess; and for default of such issue to the princess Anne of Denmark and the heirs of her body; and for default of such issue to the heirs of the body of the said prince of Orange. And the lords spiritual and temporal and commons do pray the said prince and princess to accept the same accordingly. And that the oaths hereafter mentioned to be taken by all persons of whom the oaths of allegiance and supremacy might be required by law instead of them; and that the said oaths of allegiance and supremacy be abrogated.

"I, A.B., do sincerely promise and swear, that I will be faithful and bear true allegiance to Their Majesties King William and Queen Mary."

"I, A.B., do swear, that I do from my heart abhor, detest and abjure as impious and heretical this damnable doctrine and position, that princes excommunicated or deprived by the pope or any authority of the see of Rome may be deposed or murdered by their subjects or any other whatsoever. And I do declare that no foreign prince, person, prelate, state or potentate hath or ought to have any jurisdiction, power, superiority, preeminence or authority, ecclesiastical or spiritual, within this realm. So help me God."

Upon which Their said Majesties did accept the crown and royal dignity of the kingdoms of England, France and Ireland and the dominions thereunto belonging, according to the resolution and desire of the said lords and commons, contained in the said declaration. And thereupon Their Majesties were pleased, that the said lords spiritual and temporal and commons being the two houses of parliament should continue to sit, and with Their Majesties' royal concurrence make effectual provision for the settlement of the religion, laws and liberties of this kingdom, so that the same for the future might not be in danger again of being subverted, to which the lords spiritual and temporal and commons did agree and proceed to act accordingly. Now in pursuance of the premises, the lords spiritual and temporal and commons in parliament assembled for the ratifying, confirming and establishing the said declaration and the articles, clauses, matters and things therein contained, by the force of a law made in due form by authority of parliament, do pray that it may be declared and enacted, that all and singular the rights and liberties asserted and claimed in the said declaration are the true, ancient and indubitable rights and liberties of the people of this kingdom, and so shall be esteemed, allowed, adjudged, deemed and taken to be, and that all and every the particulars aforesaid shall be firmly and strictly holden and observed, as they are expressed in the said declaration; and all officers and ministers whatsoever shall serve Their Majesties and their successors according to the same in all times to come. And the said lords spiritual and temporal and commons, seriously considering how it hath pleased Almighty God in His marvellous providence and merciful goodness to this nation to provide and preserve Their said Majesties' royal persons most happily to reign over us upon the throne of their ancestors, for which they render unto Him from the bottom of their hearts their humblest thanks and praises, do truly, firmly, assuredly and in the sincerity of their hearts think, and do hereby humbly recognise, acknowledge and declare, that King James the Second having abdicated the government and Their Majesties having accepted the crown and royal dignity [as] aforesaid, Their said Majesties did become, were, are and of right ought to be by the laws of this realm our sovereign liege lord and lady, king and queen of England, France and Ireland and the dominions thereunto belonging, in and to whose princely persons the royal state, crown and dignity of the said realms, with all honours, styles, titles, regalities, prerogatives, powers, jurisdictions and authorities to the same belonging and appertaining, are most fully, rightfully and entirely invested and incorporated, united and annexed; and for preventing all questions and divisions in this realm by reason of any pretended titles to the crown and for preserving a certainty in the succession thereof, in and upon which the unity, peace, tranquillity and safety of this nation doth under God wholly consist and depend, the said lords spiritual and temporal and commons do beseech Their Majesties, that it may be enacted, established and declared, that the crown and regal government of the said kingdom and dominions, with all and singular the premises thereunto belonging and appertaining, shall be and continue to Their said Majesties and the survivor of them during their lives and the life of the survivor of them; and that the entire, perfect and full exercise of the regal power and government be only in and executed by His Majesty, in the names of both Their Majesties, during their joint lives; and after their deceases the said crown and premises shall be and remain to the heirs of the body of Her Majesty; and for default of such issue to Her Royal Highness the princess Anne of Denmark and the heirs of her body;

and for default of such issue to the heirs of the body of His said Majesty; and thereunto the said lords spiritual and temporal and commons do in the name of all the people aforesaid most humbly and faithfully submit themselves, their heirs and posterities forever; and do faithfully promise that they will stand to, maintain and defend Their said Majesties, and also the limitation and succession of the crown herein specified and contained, to the utmost of their powers with their lives and estates against all persons whatsoever that shall attempt anything to the contrary. And whereas it hath been found by experience, that it is inconsistent with the safety and welfare of this Protestant kingdom to be governed by a popish prince or by any king or queen marrying a papist, the said lords spiritual and temporal and commons do further pray, that it may be enacted, that all and every person and persons that is, are or shall be reconciled to or shall hold communion with the See or Church of Rome, or shall profess the popish religion, or shall marry a papist, shall be excluded and be forever incapable to inherit, possess or enjoy the crown and government of this realm and Ireland and the dominions thereunto belonging, or any part of the same, or to have, use or exercise any regal power, authority or jurisdiction within the same; and in all and every such case or cases the people of these realms shall be and are hereby absolved of their allegiance; and the said crown and government shall from time to time descend to and be enjoyed by such person or persons, being Protestants, as should have inherited and enjoyed the same, in case the said person or persons so reconciled, holding communion, or professing, or marrying, as aforesaid, were naturally dead; and that every king and queen of this realm, who at any time hereafter shall come to and succeed in the imperial crown of this kingdom, shall on the first day of the meeting of the first parliament, next after his or her coming to the crown, sitting in his or her throne in the house of peers, in the presence of the lords and commons therein assembled, or at his or her coronation, before such person or persons who shall administer the coronation oath to him or her at the time of his or her taking the said oath, (which shall first happen), make, subscribe and audibly repeat the declaration mentioned in the statute made in the thirtieth year of the reign of King Charles the Second, entitled, An Act for the more effectual preserving the King's Person and Government by disabling Papists from sitting in either House of Parliament; but if it shall happen that such king or queen upon his or her succession to the crown of this realm shall be under the age of twelve years, then every such king or queen shall make, subscribe and audibly repeat the said declaration at his or her coronation, or the first day of the meeting of the first parliament as aforesaid, which shall first happen after such king or queen shall have attained the said age of twelve years. All which Their Majesties are contented and pleased shall be declared, enacted and established by authority of this present parliament, and shall stand, remain and be the law of this realm forever; and the same are by Their said Majesties, by and with the advice and consent of the lords spiritual and temporal and commons in parliament assembled, and by the authority of the same, declared, enacted and established accordingly.

II. And be it further declared and enacted by the authority aforesaid, that, from and after this present session of parliament, no dispensation by *non obstante* of or to any statute or any part thereof shall be allowed, but that the same shall be held void and of no effect, except a dispensation be allowed of in such statute, and except in such a case as shall be specially provided for by one or more bill or bills to be passed during this present session of parliament.

III. Provided that no charter or grant or pardon, granted before the three and twentieth day of October in the year of our Lord one thousand six hundred eighty-nine, shall be any ways impeached or invalidated by this act, but that the same shall be and remain of the same force and effect in law and no other than as if this act had never been made.

From *THE SECOND TREATISE ON GOVERNMENT, 1690*

John Locke

John Locke (1632–1704) published his *Two Treatises on Government* anonymously. They are a justification of the 1688 Revolution and a direct attack on the absolutism propounded by Thomas Hobbes in his *Leviathan* of 1651. Locke maintains in the *Two Treatises* that there is "natural law" in the political affairs of men (in much the same way that Isaac Newton believed that there was a single principle which organized the physical universe); according to this natural law, men had certain inalienable rights – life, liberty and property – which were protected by a "social contract" from violators. The purpose, then, of state and society is to enable men to enjoy their natural rights. Any government which fails to uphold the social contract is illegitimate and should be replaced.

This approval of rebellion certainly justified the 1688 Revolution; the dissemination of Locke's *Treatises* also ensured that his imprimatur was given the forthcoming American and French Revolutions. The more general aspects of Locke's political theory reverberated for considerably longer. Indeed, any appeal to "natural rights of man" – of which Locke was the original conceptualist – summons up his ghost.

It should be added that Locke's contribution to culture did not end with liberal democratic politics. His *Essay concerning Human Understanding*, published in 1690 after 20 years in the making, was the founding text of the "empiricist" theory of knowledge.

Of the State of Nature (Chapter II)

Sec. 4. To understand political power right, and derive it from its original, we must consider, what state all men are naturally in, and that is, a state of perfect freedom to order their actions, and dispose of their possessions and persons, as they think fit, within the bounds of the law of nature, without asking leave, or depending upon the will of any other man.

A state also of equality, wherein all the power and jurisdiction is reciprocal, no one having more than another; there being nothing more evident, than that creatures of the same species and rank, promiscuously born to all the same advantages of nature, and the use of the same faculties, should also be equal one amongst another without subordination or subjection, unless the lord and master of them all should, by any manifest declaration of his will, set one above another, and confer on him, by an evident and clear appointment, an undoubted right to dominion and sovereignty.

Sec. 6. But though this be a state of liberty, yet it is not a state of licence: though man in that state have an uncontrollable liberty to dispose of his person or possessions, yet he has not liberty to destroy himself, or so much as any creature in his possession, but where some nobler use than its bare preservation calls for it. The state of nature has a law of nature to govern it, which obliges every one: and reason, which is that law, teaches all mankind, who will but consult it, that being all equal and independent, no one ought to harm another in his life, health, liberty, or possessions: for men being all the workmanship of one omnipotent, and infinitely wise maker; all the servants of one sovereign master, sent into the world by his order, and about his business; they are his property, whose workmanship they are, made to last during his, not one another's pleasure: and being furnished with like faculties, sharing all in one community of nature, there cannot be supposed any such subordination among us, that may authorize us to destroy one another, as if we were made for one another's uses, as the inferior ranks of creatures are for ours. Every one, as he is bound to preserve himself, and not to quit his station wilfully, so by the like reason, when his own preservation comes not in competition, ought he, as much as he can, to preserve the rest of mankind, and may not, unless it be to do justice on an offender, take away, or impair the life, or what tends to the preservation of the life, the liberty, health, limb, or goods of another.

Sec. 7. And that all men may be restrained from invading others' rights, and from doing hurt to one another, and the law of nature be observed, which willeth the peace and preservation of all mankind, the execution of the law of nature is, in that state, put into every man's hands, whereby every one has a right to punish the transgressors of that law to such a degree, as may hinder its violation: for the law of nature would, as all other laws that concern men in this world be in vain, if there were no body that in the state of nature had a power to execute that law, and thereby preserve the innocent and restrain offenders. And if any one in the state of nature may punish another for any evil he has done, every one may do so: for in that state of perfect equality, where naturally there is no superiority or jurisdiction of one over another, what any may do in prosecution of that law, every one must needs have a right to do.

Sec. 8. And thus, in the state of nature, one man comes by a power over another; but yet no absolute or arbitrary power, to use a criminal, when he has got him in his hands, according to the passionate heats, or boundless extravagancy of his own will; but only to retribute to him, so far as calm reason and conscience dictate, what is proportionate to his transgression, which is so much as may serve for reparation and restraint: for these two are the only reasons, why one man may lawfully do harm to another, which is that we call punishment. In transgressing the law of nature, the offender declares himself to live by another rule than that of reason and common equity, which is that measure God has set to the actions of men, for their mutual security; and so he becomes dangerous to mankind, the tye, which is to secure them from injury and violence, being slighted and broken by him. Which being a trespass against the whole species, and the peace and safety of it, provided for by the law of nature, every man upon this score, by the right he hath to preserve mankind in general, may restrain, or where it is necessary, destroy things noxious to them, and so may bring such evil on any one, who hath transgressed that law, as may make him repent the doing of it, and thereby deter him, and by his example others, from doing the like mischief. And in the case, and upon this ground, EVERY MAN HATH A RIGHT TO PUNISH THE OFFENDER, AND BE EXECUTIONER OF THE LAW OF NATURE . . .

Of the Ends of Political Society and Government (Chapter IX)

Sec. 123. If man in the state of nature be so free, as has been said; if he be absolute lord of his own person and possessions, equal to the greatest, and subject to no body, why will he part with his freedom? why will he give up this empire, and subject himself to the dominion and control of any other power? To which it is obvious to answer, that though in the state of nature he hath such a right, yet the enjoyment of it is very uncertain, and constantly exposed to the invasion of others: for all being kings as much as he, every man his equal, and the greater part no strict observers of equity and justice, the enjoyment of the property he has in this state is very unsafe, very unsecure. This makes him willing to quit a condition, which, however free, is full of fears and continual dangers: and it is not without reason, that he seeks out, and is willing to join in society with others, who are already united, or have a mind to unite, for the mutual preservation of their lives, liberties and estates, which I call by the general name, property.

Sec. 124. The great and chief end, therefore, of men's uniting into commonwealths, and putting themselves under government, is the preservation of their property. To which in the state of nature there are many things wanting.

First, there wants an established, settled, known law, received and allowed by common consent to be the standard of right and wrong, and the common measure to decide all controversies between them: for though the law of nature be plain and intelligible to all rational creatures; yet men being biased by their interest, as well as ignorant for want of study of it, are not apt to allow of it as a law binding to them in the application of it to their particular cases.

Sec. 125. Secondly, in the state of nature there wants a known and indifferent judge, with authority to determine all differences according to the established law: for every one in that state being both judge and executioner of the law of nature, men being partial to themselves, passion and revenge is very apt to carry them too far, and with too much heat, in their own cases; as well as negligence, and unconcernedness, to make them too remiss in other men's.

Sec. 126. Thirdly, in the state of nature there often wants power to back and support the sentence when right, and to give it due execution. They who by any injustice offended, will seldom fail, where they are able, by force to make good their injustice; such resistance many times makes the punishment dangerous, and frequently destructive, to those who attempt it.

Sec. 127. Thus mankind, notwithstanding all the privileges of the state of nature, being but in an ill condition, while they remain in it, are quickly driven into society. Hence it comes to pass, that we seldom find any number of men live any time together in this state. The inconveniencies that they are therein exposed to, by the irregular and uncertain exercise of the power every man has of punishing the transgressions of others, make them take sanctuary under the established laws of government, and therein seek the preservation of their property. It is this makes them so willingly give up every one his single power of punishing, to be exercised by such alone, as shall be appointed to it amongst them; and by such rules as the community, or those authorized by them to that purpose, shall agree on. And in this we have the original right and rise of both the legislative and executive power, as well as of the governments and societies themselves.

Sec. 128. For in the state of nature, to omit the liberty he has of innocent delights, a man has two powers.

The first is to do whatsoever he thinks fit for the preservation of himself, and others within the permission of the law of nature: by which law, common to them all, he and all the rest of mankind are one community, make up one society, distinct from all other creatures. And were it not for the corruption and vitiousness of degenerate men, there would be no need of any other, no necessity that men should separate from this great and natural community, and by positive agreements combine into smaller and divided associations.

The other power a man has in the state of nature, is the power to punish the crimes committed against that law. Both these he gives up, when he joins in a private, if I may so call it, or particular politic society, and incorporates into any commonwealth, separate from the rest of mankind.

Sec. 129. The first power, viz. of doing whatsoever he thought for the preservation of himself, and the rest of mankind, he gives up to be regulated by laws made by the society, so far forth as the preservation of himself, and the rest of that society shall require; which laws of the society in many things confine the liberty he had by the law of nature.

Sec. 130. Secondly, the power of punishing he wholly gives up, and engages his natural force (which he might before employ in the execution of the law of nature, by his own single authority, as he thought fit), to assist the executive power of the society, as the law thereof shall require: for being now in a new state, wherein he is to enjoy many conveniencies, from the labour, assistance, and society of others in the same community, as well as protection from its whole strength; he is to part also with as much of his natural liberty, in providing for himself, as the good, prosperity, and safety of the society shall require; which is not only necessary, but just, since the other members of the society do the like.

Sec. 131. But though men, when they enter into society, give up the equality, liberty, and executive power they had in the state of nature, into the hands of the society, to be so far disposed of by the legislative, as the good of the society shall require; yet it being only with an intention in every one the better to preserve himself, his liberty and property; (for no rational creature can be supposed to change his condition with an intention to be worse) the power of the society, or legislative constituted by them, can never be supposed to extend farther, than the common good; but is obliged to secure every one's property, by providing against those three defects above mentioned, that made the state of nature so unsafe and uneasy. And so whoever has the legislative or supreme power of any common-wealth, is bound to govern by established standing laws, pro-mulgated and known to the people, and not by extemporary decrees; by indifferent and upright judges, who are to decide controversies by those laws; and to employ the force of the community at home, only in the execution of such laws, or abroad to prevent or redress foreign injuries, and secure the community from inroads and invasion. And all this to be directed to no other end, but the peace, safety, and public good of the people.

Of the Extent of the Legislative Power (Chapter XI)

Sec. 134. The great end of men's entering into society, being the enjoyment of their properties in peace and safety, and the great instrument and means of that being the laws established in that society; the first and fundamental positive law of all commonwealths is the establishing of the legislative power; as the first and fundamental natural law, which is to govern even the legislative itself, is the preservation of the society, and (as far as will consist with the public good) of every person in it. This legislative is not only the supreme power of the commonwealth, but sacred and unalterable in the hands where the community have once placed it; nor can any edict of any body else, in what form soever conceived, or by what power soever backed, have the force and obligation of a law, which has not its sanction from that legislative which the public has chosen and appointed: for without this the law could not have that, which is absolutely necessary to its being a law, the consent of the society, over whom no body can have a power to make laws, but by their own consent, and by authority received from them; and therefore all the obedience, which by the most solemn ties any one can be obliged to pay, ultimately terminates in this supreme power, and is directed by those laws which it enacts: nor can any oaths to any foreign power whatsoever, or any domestic subordinate power, discharge any member of the society from his obedience to the legislative, acting pursuant to their trust; nor oblige him to any obedience contrary to the laws so enacted, or farther than they do allow; it being ridiculous to imagine one can be tied ultimately to obey any power in the society, which is not the supreme . . .

Sec. 135. Though the legislative, whether placed in one or more, whether it be always in being, or only by intervals, though it be the supreme power in every commonwealth; yet,

First, it is not, nor can possibly be absolutely arbitrary over the lives and fortunes of the people: for it being but the joint power of every member of the society given up to that person, or assembly, which is legislator; it can be no more than those persons had in a state of nature before they entered into society, and gave up to the community: for no body can transfer to another more power than he has in himself; and no body has an absolute arbitrary power over himself, or over any other, to destroy his own life, or take away the life or property of another. A man, as has been proved, cannot subject himself to the arbitrary power of another; and having in the state of nature no arbitrary power over the life, liberty, or possession of another, but only so much as the law of nature gave him for the preservation of himself, and the rest of mankind; this is all he cloth, or can give up to the commonwealth, and by it to the legislative power, so that the legislative can have no more than this. Their power, in the utmost bounds of it, is limited to the public good of the society. It is a power, that hath no other end but preservation, and therefore can never have a right to destroy, enslave, or designedly to impoverish the subjects. The obligations of the law of nature cease not in society, but only in many cases are drawn closer, and have by human laws known penalties annexed to them, to inforce their observation. Thus the law of nature stands as an eternal rule to all men, legislators as well as others. The rules that they make for other men's actions, must, as well as their own and other men's actions, be conformable to the law of nature, i.e. to the will of God, of which that is a declaration, and the fundamental law of nature being the preservation of mankind, no human sanction can be good, or valid against it . . .

Sec. 136. Secondly, the legislative, or supreme authority, cannot assume to its self a power to rule by extemporary arbitrary decrees, but is bound to dispense justice, and decide the rights of the subject by promulgated standing laws, and known authorized judges: for the law of nature being unwritten, and so no where to be found but in the minds of men, they who through passion or interest shall miscite, or misapply it, cannot so easily be convinced of their mistake where there is no established judge: and so it serves not, as it ought, to determine the rights, and fence the properties of those that live under it, especially where every one is judge, interpreter, and executioner of it too, and that in his own case: and he that has right on his side, having ordinarily but his own single strength, hath not force enough to defend himself from injuries, or to punish delinquents. To avoid these inconveniences, which disorder men's properties in the state of nature, men unite into societies, that they may have the united strength of the whole society to secure and defend their properties, and may have standing rules to bound it, by which every one may know what is his. To this end it is that men give up all their natural power to the society which they enter into, and the community put the legislative power into such hands as they think fit, with this trust, that they shall be governed by declared laws, or else their peace, quiet, and property will still be at the same uncertainty, as it was in the state of nature . . .

Sec. 137. Absolute arbitrary power, or governing without settled standing laws, can neither of them consist with the ends of society and government, which men would not quit the freedom of the state of nature for, and tie themselves up under, were it not to preserve their lives, liberties and fortunes, and by stated rules of right and property to secure their peace and quiet. It cannot be supposed that they should intend, had they a power so to do, to give to any one, or more, an absolute arbitrary power over their persons and estates, and put a force into the magistrate's hand to execute his unlimited will arbitrarily upon them. This were to put themselves into a worse condition than the state of nature, wherein they had a liberty to defend their right against the injuries of others, and were upon equal terms of force to maintain it, whether invaded by a single man, or many in combination. Whereas by supposing they have given up themselves to the absolute arbitrary power and will of a legislator, they have disarmed themselves, and armed him, to make a prey of them when he pleases; he being in a much worse condition, who is exposed to the arbitrary power of one man, who has the command of 100,000, than he that is exposed to the arbitrary power of 100,000 single men; no body being secure, that his will, who has such a command, is better than that of other men, though his force be 100,000 times stronger. And therefore, whatever form the common-wealth is under, the ruling power ought to govern by declared and received laws, and not by extemporary dictates and undetermined resolutions: for then mankind will be in a far worse condition than in the state of nature, if they shall have armed one, or a few men with the joint power of a multitude, to force them to obey at pleasure the exorbitant and unlimited decrees of their sudden thoughts, or unrestrained, and till that moment unknown wills, without having any measures set down which may guide and justify their actions: for all the power the government has, being only for the good of the society, as it ought not to be arbitrary and at pleasure, so it ought to be exercised by established and promulgated laws; that both the people may know their duty, and be safe and secure within the limits of the law; and the rulers too kept within their bounds, and not be tempted, by the power they have in their hands, to employ it to such purposes, and by such measures, as they would not have known, and own not willingly.

Sec. 138. Thirdly, the supreme power cannot take from any man any part of his property without his own consent: for the preservation of property being the end of government, and that for which men enter into society, it necessarily supposes and requires, that the people should have property, without which they must be supposed to lose that, by entering into society, which was the end for which they entered into it; too gross an absurdity for any man to own. Men therefore in society having property, they have such a right to the goods, which by the law of the community are their's, that no body hath a right to take their substance or any part of it from them, without their own consent: without this they have no property at all; for I have truly no property in that, which another can by right take from me, when he pleases, against my consent. Hence it is a mistake to think, that the supreme or legislative power of any commonwealth, can do what it will, and dispose of the estates of the subject arbitrarily, or take any part of them at pleasure. This is not much to be feared in governments where the legislative consists, wholly or in part, in assemblies which are variable, whose members, upon the dissolution of the assembly, are subjects under the common laws of their country, equally with the rest. But in governments, where the legislative is in one lasting assembly always in being, or in one man, as in absolute monarchies, there is danger still, that they will think themselves to have a distinct interest from the rest of the community; and so will be apt to increase their own riches and power, by taking what they think fit from the people: for a man's property is not at all secure, tho' there be good and equitable laws to set the bounds of it between him and his fellow subjects, if he who commands those subjects have power to take from any private man, what part he pleases of his property, and use and dispose of it as he thinks good.

Sec. 139. But government, into whatsoever hands it is put, being, as I have before shewed, intrusted with this condition, and for this end, that men might have and secure their properties; the prince, or senate, however it may have power to make laws, for the regulating of property between the subjects one amongst another, yet can never have a power to take to themselves the whole, or any part of the subjects property, without their own consent: for this would be in effect to leave them no property at all. And to let us see, that even absolute power, where it is necessary, is not arbitrary by being absolute, but is still limited by that reason, and confined to those ends, which required it in some cases to be absolute, we need look no farther than the common practice of martial discipline: for the preservation of the army, and in it of the whole common-wealth, requires an absolute obedience to the command of every superior officer, and it is justly death to disobey or dispute the most dangerous or unreasonable of them; but yet we see, that neither the serjeant, that could command a soldier to march up to the mouth of a cannon, or stand in a breach, where he is almost sure to perish, can command that soldier to give him one penny of his money; nor the general, that can condemn him to death for deserting his post, or for not obeying the most desperate orders, can yet, with all his absolute power of life and death, dispose of one farthing of that soldier's estate, or seize one jot of his goods; whom yet he can command any thing, and hang for the least disobedience; because such a blind obedience is necessary to that end, for which the commander has his power, viz. the preservation of the rest; but the disposing of his goods has nothing to do with it.

Sec. 140. It is true, governments cannot be supported without great charge, and it is fit every one who enjoys his share of the protection, should pay out of his estate his proportion for the maintenance of it. But still it must be with his own consent, i.e. the consent of the majority, giving it either by themselves, or their representatives chosen by them: for if any one shall claim a power to lay and levy taxes on the people, by his own authority, and without such consent of the people, he thereby invades the fundamental law of property, and subverts the end of government: for what property have I in that, which another may by right take, when he pleases, to himself?

Sec. 141. Fourthly, the legislative cannot transfer the power of making laws to any other hands: for it being but a delegated power from the people, they who have it cannot pass it over to others. The people alone can appoint the form of the common-wealth, which is by constituting the legislative, and appointing in whose hands that shall be. And when the people have said, We will submit to rules, and be governed by laws made by such men, and in such forms, no body else can say other men shall make laws for them; nor can the people be bound by any laws, but such as are enacted by those whom they have chosen, and authorized to make laws for them. The power of the legislative, being derived from the people by a positive voluntary grant and institution, can be no other than what that positive grant conveyed, which being only to make laws, and not to make legislators, the legislative can have no power to transfer their authority of making laws, and place it in other hands.

Sec. 142. These are the bounds which the trust, that is put in them by the society, and the law of God and nature, have set to the legislative power of every common-wealth, in all forms of government.

First, they are to govern by promulgated established laws, not to be varied in particular cases, but to have one rule for rich and poor, for the favourite at court, and the country man at plough.

Secondly, these laws also ought to be designed for no other end ultimately, but the good of the people.

Thirdly, they must not raise taxes on the property of the people, without the consent of the people, given by themselves, or their deputies. And this properly concerns only such governments where the legislative is always in being, or at least where the people have not reserved any part of the legislative to deputies, to be from time to time chosen by themselves.

Fourthly, the legislative neither must nor can transfer the power of making laws to any body else, or place it any where, but where the people have.

Of Tyranny (Chapter XVIII)

Sec. 199. As usurpation is the exercise of power, which another hath a right to; so tyranny is the exercise of power beyond right, which no body can have a right to. And this is making use of the power any one has in his hands, not for the good of those who are under it, but for his own private separate advantage. When the governor, however intitled, makes not the law, but his will, the rule; and his commands and actions are not directed to the preservation of the properties of his people, but the satisfaction of his own ambition, revenge, covetousness, or any other irregular passion.

Sec. 200. If one can doubt this to be truth, or reason, because it comes from the obscure hand of a subject, I hope the authority of a king will make it pass with him. King James the first, in his speech to the parliament, 1603, tells them thus, I will ever prefer the weal of the public, and of the whole commonwealth, in making of good laws and constitutions, to any particular and private ends of mine; thinking ever the wealth and weal of the commonwealth to be my greatest weal and worldly felicity; a point wherein a lawful king doth directly differ from a tyrant: for I do acknowledge, that the special and greatest point of difference that is between a rightful king and an usurping tyrant, is this, that whereas the proud and ambitious tyrant doth think his kingdom and people are only ordained for satisfaction of his desires and unreasonable appetites, the righteous and just king doth by the contrary acknowledge himself to be ordained for the procuring of the wealth and property of his people, And again, in his speech to the parliament, 1609, he hath these words, The king binds himself by a double oath, to the observation of the fundamental laws of his kingdom; tacitly, as by being a king, and so bound to protect as well the people, as the laws of his kingdom; and expressly, by his oath at his coronation, so as every just king, in a settled kingdom, is bound to observe that paction made to his people, by his laws, in framing his government agreeable thereunto, according to that paction which God made with Noah after the deluge. Hereafter, seed-time and harvest, and cold and heat, and summer and winter, and day and night, shall not cease while the earth remaineth. And therefore a king governing in a settled kingdom, leaves to be a king, and degenerates into a tyrant, as soon as he leaves off to rule according to his laws, And a little after, Therefore all kings that are not tyrants, or perjured, will be glad to bound themselves within the limits of their laws; and they that persuade them the contrary, are vipers, and pests both against them and the commonwealth. Thus that learned king, who well understood the notion of things, makes the difference betwixt a king and a tyrant to consist only in this, that one makes the laws the bounds of his power, and the good of the public, the end of his government; the other makes all give way to his own will and appetite.

Sec. 201. It is a mistake, to think this fault is proper only to monarchies; other forms of government are liable to it, as well as that: for wherever the power, that is put in any hands for the government of the people, and the preservation of their properties, is applied to other ends, and made use of to impoverish, harass, or subdue them to the arbitrary and irregular commands of those that have it; there it presently becomes tyranny, whether those that thus use it are one or many. Thus we read of the thirty tyrants at Athens, as well as one at Syracuse; and the intolerable dominion of the Decemviri at Rome was nothing better.

Sec. 202. Where-ever law ends, tyranny begins, if the law be transgressed to another's harm; and whosoever in authority exceeds the power given him by the law, and makes use of the force he has under his command, to compass that upon the subject, which the law allows not, ceases in that to be a magistrate; and, acting without authority, may be opposed, as any other man, who by force invades the right of another. This is acknowl-edged in subordinate magistrates. He that hath authority to seize my person in the street, may be opposed as a thief and a robber, if he endeavours to break into my house to execute a writ, notwithstanding that I know he has such a warrant, and such a legal authority, as will impower him to arrest me abroad. And why this should not hold in the highest, as well as in the most inferior magistrate, I would gladly be informed. Is it reasonable, that the eldest brother, because he has the greatest part of his father's estate, should thereby have a right to take away any of his younger brothers portions? or that a rich man, who possessed a whole country, should from thence have a right to seize, when he pleased, the cottage and garden of his poor neighbour? The being rightfully possessed of great power and riches, exceedingly beyond the greatest part of the sons of Adam, is so far from being an excuse, much less a reason, for rapine and oppression, which the endamaging another without authority is, that it is a great aggravation of it: for the exceeding the bounds of authority is no more a right in a great, than in a petty officer; no more justifiable in a king than a constable; but is so much the worse in him, in that he has more trust put in him, has already a much greater share than the rest of his brethren, and is supposed, from the advantages of his education, employment, and counsellors, to be more knowing in the measures of right and wrong . . .

Of the Dissolution of Government (Chapter XIX)

Sec. 211. He that will with any clearness speak of the dissolution of government, ought in the first place to distinguish between the dissolution of the society and the dissolution of the government. That which makes the community, and brings men out of the loose state of nature, into one politic society, is the agreement which every one has with the rest to incorporate, and act as one body, and so be one distinct commonwealth. The usual, and almost only way whereby this union is dissolved, is the inroad of foreign force making a conquest upon them: for in that case, (not being able to maintain and support themselves, as one intire and independent body) the union belonging to that body which consisted therein, must necessarily cease, and so every one return to the state he was in before, with a liberty to shift for himself, and provide for his own safety, as he thinks fit, in some other society. Whenever the society is dissolved, it is certain the government of that society cannot remain. Thus conquerors swords often cut up governments by the roots, and mangle societies to pieces, separating the subdued or scattered multitude from the protection of, and dependence on, that society which ought to have preserved them from violence. The world is too well instructed in, and too forward to allow of, this way of dissolving of governments, to need any more to be said of it; and there wants not much argument to prove, that where the society is dissolved, the government cannot remain; that being as impossible, as for the frame of an house to subsist when the materials of it are scattered and dissipated by a whirl-wind, or jumbled into a confused heap by an earthquake.

Sec. 212. Besides this over-turning from without, governments are dissolved from within,

First, when the legislative is altered. Civil society being a state of peace, amongst those who are of it, from whom the state of war is excluded by the umpirage, which they have provided in their legislative, for the ending all differences that may arise amongst any of them, it is in their legislative, that the members of a commonwealth are united, and combined together into one coherent living body. This is the soul that gives form, life, and unity, to the commonwealth: from hence the several members have their mutual influence, sympathy, and connexion: and therefore, when the legislative is broken, or dissolved, dissolution and death follows: for the essence and union of the society consisting in having one will, the legislative, when once established by the majority, has the declaring, and as it were keeping of that will. The constitution of the legislative is the first and fundamental act of society, whereby provision is made for the continuation of their union, under the direction of persons, and bonds of laws, made by persons authorized thereunto, by the consent and appointment of the people, without which no one man, or number of men, amongst them, can have authority of making laws that shall be binding to the rest. When any one, or more, shall take upon them to make laws, whom the people have not appointed so to do, they make laws without authority, which the people are not therefore bound to obey; by which means they come again to be out of subjection, and may constitute to themselves a new legislative, as they think best, being in full liberty to resist the force of those, who without authority would impose any thing upon them. Every one is at the disposure of his own will, when those who had, by the delegation of the society, the declaring of the public will, are excluded from it, and others usurp the place, who have no such authority or delegation.

Sec. 213. This being usually brought about by such in the commonwealth who misuse the power they have; it is hard to consider it aright, and know at whose door to lay it, without knowing the form of government in which it happens. Let us suppose then the legislative placed in the concurrence of three distinct persons.

  1. A single hereditary person, having the constant, supreme, executive power, and with it the power of convoking and dissolving the other two within certain periods of time.

  2. An assembly of hereditary nobility.

  3. An assembly of representatives chosen, *pro tempore*, by the people . . .

Sec. 214. first, that when such a single person, or prince, sets up his own arbitrary will in place of the laws, which are the will of the society, declared by the legislative, then the legislative is changed: for that being in effect the legislative, whose rules and laws are put in execution, and required to be obeyed; when other laws are set up, and other rules pretended, and inforced, than what the legislative, constituted by the society, have enacted, it is plain that the legislative is changed. Whoever introduces new laws, not being thereunto authorized by the fundamental appoint-ment of the society, or subverts the old, disowns and overturns the power by which they were made, and so sets up a new legislative.

Sec. 215. Secondly, when the prince hinders the legislative from assem-bling in its due time, or from acting freely, pursuant to those ends for which it was constituted, the legislative is altered: for it is not a certain number of men, no, nor their meeting, unless they have also freedom of debating, and leisure of perfecting, what is for the good of the society, wherein the legislative consists: when these are taken away or altered, so as to deprive the society of the due exercise of their power, the legislative is truly altered; for it is not names that constitute governments, but the use and exercise of those powers that were intended to accompany them; so that he, who takes away the freedom, or hinders the acting of the legislative in its due seasons, in effect takes away the legislative, and puts an end to the government.

Sec. 216. Thirdly, when, by the arbitrary power of the prince, the electors, or ways of election, are altered, without the consent, and contrary to the common interest of the people, there also the legislative is altered: for, if others than those whom the society hath authorized thereunto, do chuse, or in another way than what the society hath prescribed, those chosen are not the legislative appointed by the people.

Sec. 217. Fourthly, the delivery also of the people into the subjection of a foreign power, either by the prince, or by the legislative, is certainly a change of the legislative, and so a dissolution of the government: for the end why people entered into society being to be preserved one intire, free, independent society, to be governed by its own laws; this is lost, whenever they are given up into the power of another.

Sec. 218. Why, in such a constitution as this, the dissolution of the government in these cases is to be imputed to the prince, is evident; because he, having the force, treasure and offices of the state to employ, and often persuading himself, or being flattered by others, that as supreme magistrate he is uncapable of control; he alone is in a condition to make great advances toward such changes, under pretence of lawful authority, and has it in his hands to terrify or suppress opposers, as factious, seditious, and enemies to the government: whereas no other part of the legislative, or people, is capable by themselves to attempt any alteration of the legislative, without open and visible rebellion, apt enough to be taken notice of, which, when it prevails, produces effects very little different from foreign conquest. Besides, the prince in such a form of government, having the power of dissolving the other parts of the legislative, and thereby rendering them private persons, they can never in opposition to him, or without his concurrence, alter the legislative by a law, his conse power, neglects and abandons that charge, so that the laws already made can no longer be put in execution. This is demonstratively to reduce all to anarchy, and so effectually to dissolve the government: for laws not being made for themselves, but to be, by their execution, the bonds of the society, to keep every part of the body politic in its due place and function; when that totally ceases, the government visibly ceases, and the people become a confused multitude, without order or connexion. Where there is no longer the administration of justice, for the securing of men's rights, nor any remaining power within the community to direct the force, or provide for the necessities of the public, there certainly is no government left. Where the laws cannot be executed, it is all one as if there were no laws; and a government without laws is, I suppose, a mystery in politics, unconceivable to human capacity, and inconsistent with human society.

Sec. 220. In these and the like cases, when the government is dissolved, the people are at liberty to provide for themselves, by erecting a new legislative, differing from the other, by the change of persons, or form, or both, as they shall find it most for their safety and good: for the society can never, by the fault of another, lose the native and original right it has to preserve itself, which can only be done by a settled legislative, and a fair and impartial execution of the laws made by it. But the state of mankind is not so miserable that they are not capable of using this remedy, till it be too late to look for any. To tell people they may provide for themselves, by erecting a new legislative, when by oppression, artifice, or being delivered over to a foreign power, their old one is gone, is only to tell them, they may expect relief when it is too late, and the evil is past cure. This is in effect no more than to bid them first be slaves, and then to take care of their liberty; and when their chains are on, tell them, they may act like freemen. This, if barely so, is rather mockery than relief; and men can never be secure from tyranny, if there be no means to escape it till they are perfectly under it: and therefore it is, that they have not only a right to get out of it, but to prevent it.

Sec. 221. There is therefore, secondly, another way whereby governments are dissolved, and that is, when the legislative, or the prince, either of them, act contrary to their trust. First, the legislative acts against the trust reposed in them, when they endeavour to invade the property of the subject, and to make themselves, or any part of the community, masters, or arbitrary disposers of the lives, liberties, or fortunes of the people.

Sec. 222. The reason why men enter into society, is the preservation of their property; and the end why they chuse and authorize a legislative, is, that there may be laws made, and rules set, as guards and fences to the properties of all the members of the society, to limit the power, and moderate the dominion, of every part and member of the society: for since it can never be supposed to be the will of the society, that the legislative should have a power to destroy that which every one designs to secure, by entering into society, and for which the people submitted themselves to legislators of their own making; whenever the legislators endeavour to take away, and destroy the property of the people, or to reduce them to slavery under arbitrary power, they put themselves into a state of war with the people, who are thereupon absolved from any farther obedience, and are left to the common refuge, which God hath provided for all men, against force and violence. Whensoever therefore the legislative shall transgress this fundamental rule of society; and either by ambition, fear, folly or corruption, endeavour to grasp themselves, or put into the hands of any other, an absolute power over the lives, liberties, and estates of the people; by this breach of trust they forfeit the power the people had put into their hands for quite contrary ends, and it devolves to the people, who have a right to resume their original liberty, and, by the establishment of a new legislative, (such as they shall think fit) provide for their own safety and security, which is the end for which they are in society. What I have said here, concerning the legislative in general, holds true also concerning the supreme executor, who having a double trust put in him, both to have a part in the legislative, and the supreme execution of the law, acts against both, when he goes about to set up his own arbitrary will as the law of the society. He acts also contrary to his trust, when he either employs the force, treasure, and offices of the society, to corrupt the representatives, and gain them to his purposes; or openly preengages the electors, and prescribes to their choice, such, whom he has, by solicitations, threats, promises, or otherwise, won to his designs; and employs them to bring in such, who have promised beforehand what to vote, and what to enact. Thus to regulate candidates and electors, and new-model the ways of election, what is it but to cut up the government by the roots, and poison the very fountain of public security? for the people having reserved to themselves the choice of their representatives, as the fence to their properties, could do it for no other end, but that they might always be freely chosen, and so chosen, freely act, and advise, as the necessity of the commonwealth, and the public good should, upon examination, and mature debate, be judged to require. This, those who give their votes before they hear the debate, and have weighed the reasons on all sides, are not capable of doing. To prepare such an assembly as this, and endeavour to set up the declared abettors of his own will, for the true representatives of the people, and the law-makers of the society, is certainly as great a breach of trust, and as perfect a declaration of a design to subvert the government, as is possible to be met with. To which, if one shall add rewards and punishments visibly employed to the same end, and all the arts of perverted law made use of, to take off and destroy all that stand in the way of such a design, and will not comply and consent to betray the liberties of their country, it will be past doubt what is doing. What power they ought to have in the society, who thus employ it contrary to the trust went along with it in its first institution, is easy to determine; and one cannot but see, that he, who has once attempted any such thing as this, cannot any longer be trusted.

Sec. 223. To this perhaps it will be said, that the people being ignorant, and always discontented, to lay the foundation of government in the unsteady opinion and uncertain humour of the people, is to expose it to certain ruin; and no government will be able long to subsist, if the people may set up a new legislative, whenever they take offence at the old one. To this I answer, Quite the contrary. People are not so easily got out of their old forms, as some are apt to suggest. They are hardly to be prevailed with to amend the acknowledged faults in the frame they have been accustomed to. And if there be any original defects, or adventitious ones introduced by time, or corruption; it is not an easy thing to get them changed, even when all the world sees there is an opportunity for it. This slowness and aversion in the people to quit their old constitutions, has, in the many revolutions which have been seen in this kingdom, in this and former ages, still kept us to, or, after some interval of fruitless attempts, still brought us back again to our old legislative of king, lords and commons: and whatever provocations have made the crown be taken from some of our princes heads, they never carried the people so far as to place it in another line.

Sec. 224. But it will be said, this hypothesis lays a ferment for frequent rebellion. To which I answer,

First, no more than any other hypothesis: for when the people are made miserable, and find themselves exposed to the ill usage of arbitrary power, cry up their governors, as much as you will, for sons of Jupiter; let them be sacred and divine, descended, or authorized from heaven; give them out for whom or what you please, the same will happen. The people generally ill treated, and contrary to right, will be ready upon any occasion to ease themselves of a burden that sits heavy upon them. They will wish, and seek for the opportunity, which in the change, weakness and accidents of human affairs, seldom delays long to offer itself. He must have lived but a little while in the world, who has not seen examples of this in his time; and he must have read very little, who cannot produce examples of it in all sorts of governments in the world.

Sec. 225. Secondly, I answer, such revolutions happen not upon every little mismanagement in public affairs. Great mistakes in the ruling part, many wrong and inconvenient laws, and all the slips of human frailty, will be born by the people without mutiny or murmur. But if a long train of abuses, prevarications and artifices, all tending the same way, make the design visible to the people, and they cannot but feel what they lie under, and see whither they are going; it is not to be wondered, that they should then rouze themselves, and endeavour to put the rule into such hands which may secure to them the ends for which government was at first erected; and without which, ancient names, and specious forms, are so far from being better, that they are much worse, than the state of nature, or pure anarchy; the inconveniencies being all as great and as near, but the remedy farther off and more difficult.

Sec. 226. Thirdly, I answer, that this doctrine of a power in the people of providing for their safety a-new, by a new legislative, when their legislators have acted contrary to their trust, by invading their property, is the best fence against rebellion, and the probablest means to hinder it: for rebellion being an opposition, not to persons, but authority, which is founded only in the constitutions and laws of the government; those, whoever they be, who by force break through, and by force justify their violation of them, are truly and properly rebels: for when men, by entering into society and civil-government, have excluded force, and introduced laws for the preservation of property, peace, and unity amongst themselves, those who set up force again in opposition to the laws, do rebellare, that is, bring back again the state of war, and are properly rebels: which they who are in power, (by the pretence they have to authority, the temptation of force they have in their hands, and the flattery of those about them) being likeliest to do; the properest way to prevent the evil, is to shew them the danger and injustice of it, who are under the greatest temptation to run into it.

Sec. 227. In both the fore-mentioned cases, when either the legislative is changed, or the legislators act contrary to the end for which they were constituted; those who are guilty are guilty of rebellion: for if any one by force takes away the established legislative of any society, and the laws by them made, pursuant to their trust, he thereby takes away the umpirage, which every one had consented to, for a peaceable decision of all their controversies, and a bar to the state of war amongst them. They, who remove, or change the legislative, take away this decisive power, which no body can have, but by the appointment and consent of the people; and so destroying the authority which the people did, and no body else can set up, and introducing a power which the people hath not authorized, they actually introduce a state of war, which is that of force without authority: and thus, by removing the legislative established by the society, (in whose decisions the people acquiesced and united, as to that of their own will) they untie the knot, and expose the people a-new to the state of war, And if those, who by force take away the legislative, are rebels, the legislators themselves, as has been shewn, can be no less esteemed so; when they, who were set up for the protection, and preservation of the people, their liberties and properties, shall by force invade and endeavour to take them away; and so they putting themselves into a state of war with those who made them the protectors and guardians of their peace, are properly, and with the greatest aggravation, rebellantes, rebels.

Sec. 228. But if they, who say it lays a foundation for rebellion, mean that it may occasion civil wars, or intestine broils, to tell the people they are absolved from obedience when illegal attempts are made upon their liberties or properties, and may oppose the unlawful violence of those who were their magistrates, when they invade their properties contrary to the trust put in them; and that therefore this doctrine is not to be allowed, being so destructive to the peace of the world: they may as well say, upon the same ground, that honest men may not oppose robbers or pirates, because this may occasion disorder or bloodshed. If any mischief come in such cases, it is not to be charged upon him who defends his own right, but on him that invades his neighbours. If the innocent honest man must quietly quit all he has, for peace sake, to him who will lay violent hands upon it, I desire it may be considered, what a kind of peace there will be in the world, which consists only in violence and rapine; and which is to be maintained only for the benefit of robbers and oppressors. Who would not think it an admirable peace betwix the mighty and the mean, when the lamb, without resistance, yielded his throat to be torn by the imperious wolf? Polyphemus' den gives us a perfect pattern of such a peace, and such a government, wherein Ulysses and his companions had nothing to do, but quietly to suffer themselves to be devoured. And no doubt Ulysses, who was a prudent man, preached up passive obedience, and exhorted them to a quiet submission, by representing to them of what concernment peace was to mankind; and by shewing the inconveniences might happen, if they should offer to resist Polyphemus, who had now the power over them.

Sec. 229. The end of government is the good of mankind; and which is best for mankind, that the people should be always exposed to the boundless will of tyranny, or that the rulers should be sometimes liable to be opposed, when they grow exorbitant in the use of their power, and employ it for the destruction, and not the preservation of the properties of their people? . . .

From *THE SOCIAL CONTRACT, 1762*

Jean Jacques Rousseau

Du contract social by the Genevan philosopher Rousseau (1712–78) might be said to be the Bible of the French Revolution. It postulated a "social contract" in which the individual voluntarily abdicated his individual liberty to the collective "general will", which was sovereign and always working for the popular good. If aspects of the *Social Contract* were questionable – it suggested that citizens uncooperative about the contract might be "forced to be free" – its advocacy of liberty and democracy was overwhelming. The French Revolution, it was no coincidence, had the same slogan as Rousseau's book: "Liberty, Equality, Fraternity".

The Social Contract acted as literary midwife to more than the French Revolution. Along with Rousseau's other writings, it helped birth the Romantic movement. Against Enlightenment rationality Rousseau praised intuition, spirit, and man's original state – a state which might be described as "noble unsavagery". (Thus Rousseau's opinion of the natural state of man was the diametric opposite of the short and brutish one diagnosed by Thomas Hobbes in the previous century's *Leviathan*.) The corrupter of man was civilization itself. The more a man was civilized, the corrupter he became. A remedy lay in the political reorganization suggested by *The Social Contract*, together with a progressive "natural" education, which Rousseau outlined in *Emile* (see pp 310–19).

Subject of the First Book (Chapter I)

Man is born free; and everywhere he is in chains. One thinks himself the master of others, and still remains a greater slave than they. How did this change come about? I do not know. What can make it legitimate? That question I think I can answer.

If I took into account only force, and the effects derived from it, I should say: "As long as a people is compelled to obey, and obeys, it does well; as soon as it can shake off the yoke, and shakes it off, it does still better; for, regaining its liberty by the same right as took it away, either it is justified in resuming it, or there was no justification for those who took it away." But the social order is a sacred right which is the basis of all other rights. Nevertheless, this right does not come from nature, and must therefore be founded on conventions. Before coming to that, I have to prove what I have just asserted.

The Right of the Strongest (Chapter III)

The strongest is never strong enough to be always the master, unless he transforms strength into right, and obedience into duty. Hence the right of the strongest, which, though to all seeming meant ironically, is really laid down as a fundamental principle. But are we never to have an explanation of this phrase? Force is a physical power, and I fail to see what moral effect it can have. To yield to force is an act of necessity, not of will – at the most, an act of prudence. In what sense can it be a duty?

Suppose for a moment that this so-called "right" exists. I maintain that the sole result is a mass of inexplicable nonsense. For, if force creates right, the effect changes with the cause: every force that is greater than the first succeeds to its right. As soon as it is possible to disobey with impunity, disobedience is legitimate; and, the strongest being always in the right, the only thing that matters is to act so as to become the strongest. But what kind of right is that which perishes when force fails? If we must obey perforce, there is no need to obey because we ought; and if we are not forced to obey, we are under no obligation to do so. Clearly, the word "right" adds nothing to force: in this connection, it means absolutely nothing.

Obey the powers that be. If this means yield to force, it is a good precept, but superfluous: I can answer for its never being violated. All power comes from God, I admit; but so does all sickness: does that mean that we are forbidden to call in the doctor? A brigand surprises me at the edge of a wood: must I not merely surrender my purse on compulsion; but, even if I could withhold it, am I in conscience bound to give it up? For certainly the pistol he holds is also a power.

Let us then admit that force does not create right, and that we are obliged to obey only legitimate powers. In that case, my original question recurs.

Slavery (Chapter IV)

Since no man has a natural authority over his fellow, and force creates no right, we must conclude that conventions form the basis of all legitimate authority among men.

If an individual, says Grotius, can alienate his liberty and make himself the slave of a master, why could not a whole people do the same and make itself subject to a king? There are in this passage plenty of ambiguous words which would need explaining; but let us confine ourselves to the word *alienate*. To alienate is to give or to sell. Now, a man who becomes the slave of another does not give himself; he sells himself, at the least for his subsistence: but for what does a people sell itself? A king is so far from furnishing his subjects with their subsistence that he gets his own only from them; and, according to Rabelais, kings do not live on nothing. Do subjects then give their persons on condition that the king takes their goods also? I fail to see what they have left to preserve.

It will be said that the despot assures his subjects civil tranquillity. Granted; but what do they gain, if the wars his ambition brings down upon them, his insatiable avidity, and the vexatious conduct of his ministers press harder on them than their own dissensions would have done? What do they gain, if the very tranquillity they enjoy is one of their miseries? Tranquillity is found also in dungeons; but is that enough to make them desirable places to live in? The Greeks imprisoned in the cave of the Cyclops lived there very tranquilly, while they were awaiting their turn to be devoured.

To say that a man gives himself gratuitously, is to say what is absurd and inconceivable; such an act is null and illegitimate, from the mere fact that he who does it is out of his mind. To say the same of a whole people is to suppose a people of madmen; and madness creates no right.

Even if each man could alienate himself, he could not alienate his children: they are born men and free; their liberty belongs to them, and no one but they has the right to dispose of it. Before they come to years of discretion, the father can, in their name, lay down conditions for their preservation and well-being, but he cannot give them irrevocably and without conditions: such a gift is contrary to the ends of nature, and exceeds the rights of paternity. It would therefore be necessary, in order to legitimize an arbitrary government, that in every generation the people should be in a position to accept or reject it; but, were this so, the government would be no longer arbitrary.

To renounce liberty is to renounce being a man, to surrender the rights of humanity and even its duties. For him who renounces everything no indemnity is possible. Such a renunciation is incompatible with man's nature; to remove all liberty from his will is to remove all morality from his acts. Finally, it is an empty and contradictory convention that sets up, on the one side, absolute authority, and, on the other, unlimited obedience. Is it not clear that we can be under no obligation to a person from whom we have the right to exact everything? Does not this condition alone, in the absence of equivalence or exchange, in itself involve the nullity of the act? For what right can my slave have against me, when all that he has belongs to me, and, his right being mine, this right of mine against myself is a phrase devoid of meaning?

The Social Compact (Chapter VI)

I suppose men to have reached the point at which the obstacles in the way of their preservation in the state of nature show their power of resistance to be greater than the resources at the disposal of each individual for his maintenance in that state. That primitive condition can then subsist no longer; and the human race would perish unless it changed its manner of existence.

But, as men cannot engender new forces, but only unite and direct existing ones, they have no other means of preserving themselves than the formation, by aggregation, of a sum of forces great enough to overcome the resistance. These they have to bring into play by means of a single motive power, and cause to act in concert.

This sum of forces can arise only where several persons come together: but, as the force and liberty of each man are the chief instruments of his self-preservation, how can be pledge them without harming his own interests, and neglecting the care he owes to himself? This difficulty, in its bearing on my present subject, may be stated in the following terms:

"The problem is to find a form of association which will defend and protect with the whole common force the person and goods of each associate, and in which each, while uniting himself with all, may still obey himself alone, and remain as free as before." This is the fundamental problem of which the social contract provides the solution.

The clauses of this contract are so determined by the nature of the act that the slightest modification would make them vain and ineffective; so that, although they have perhaps never been formally set forth, they are everywhere the same and everywhere tacitly admitted and recognized, until, on the violation of the social compact, each regains his original rights and resumes his natural liberty, while losing the conventional liberty in favour of which he renounced it.

These clauses, properly understood, may be reduced to one – the total alienation of each associate, together with all his rights, to the whole community; for, in the first place, as each gives himself absolutely, the conditions are the same for all; and, this being so, no one has any interest in making them burdensome to others.

Moreover, the alienation being without reserve, the union is as perfect as it can be, and no associate has anything more to demand: for, if the individuals retained certain rights, as there would be no common superior to decide between them and the public, each, being on one point his own judge, would ask to be so on all; the state of nature would thus continue, and the association would necessarily become inoperative or tyrannical.

Finally, each man, in giving himself to all, gives himself to nobody; and as there is no associate over which he does not acquire the same right as he yields others over himself, he gains an equivalent for everything he loses, and an increase of force for the preservation of what he has.

If then we discard from the social compact what is not of its essence, we shall find that it reduces itself to the following terms:

"Each of us puts his person and all his power in common under the supreme direction of the general will, and, in our corporate capacity, we receive each member as an indivisible part of the whole."

At once, in place of the individual personality of each contracting party, this act of association creates a corporate and collective body, composed of as many members as the assembly contains voters, and receiving from this act its unity, its common identity, its life, and its will. This public person, so formed by the union of all other persons, formerly took the name of *city*, and now takes that of *Republic* or *body politic*; it is called by its members *State* when passive, *Sovereign* when active, and *Power* when compared with others like itself. Those who are associated in it take collectively the name of *people*, and severally are called *citizens*, as sharing in the sovereign authority, and *subjects*, as being under the laws of the State. But these terms are often confused and taken one for another: it is enough to know how to distinguish them when they are being used with precision.

The Limits of Sovereign Power (Book II: Chapter IV)

If the State is a moral person whose life is in the union of its members, and if the most important of its cares is the care for its own preservation, it must have a universal and compelling force, in order to move and dispose each part as may be most advantageous to the whole. As nature gives each man absolute power over all his members, the social compact gives the body politic absolute power over all its members also; and it is this power which, under the direction of the general will, bears, as I have said, the name of Sovereignty.

But, besides the public person, we have to consider the private persons composing it, whose life and liberty are naturally independent of it. We are bound then to distinguish clearly between the respective rights of the citizens and the Sovereign, and between the duties the former have to fulfil as subjects, and the natural rights they should enjoy as men.

Each man alienates, I admit, by the social compact, only such part of his powers, goods, and liberty as it is important for the community to control; but it must also be granted that the Sovereign is sole judge of what is important.

Every service a citizen can render the State he ought to render as soon as the Sovereign demands it; but the Sovereign, for its part, cannot impose upon its subjects any fetters that are useless to the community, nor can it even wish to do so; for no more by the law of reason than by the law of nature can anything occur without a cause.

The undertakings which bind us to the social body are obligatory only because they are mutual; and their nature is such that in fulfilling them we cannot work for others without working for ourselves. Why is it that the general will is always upright, and that all continually will the happiness of each one, unless it is because there is not a man who does not think of "each" as meaning him, and consider himself in voting for all? This proves that equality of rights and the idea of justice which such equality creates originate in the preference each man gives to himself, and accordingly in the very nature of man. It proves that the general will, to be really such, must be general in its object as well as its essence; that it must both come from all and apply to all; and that it loses its natural rectitude when it is directed to some particular and determinate object, because in such a case we are judging of something foreign to us, and have no true principle of equity to guide us.

Indeed, as soon as a question of particular fact or right arises on a point not previously regulated by a general convention, the matter becomes contentious. It is a case in which the individuals concerned are one party, and the public the other, but in which I can see neither the law that ought to be followed nor the judge who ought to give the decision. In such a case, it would be absurd to propose to refer the question to an express decision of the general will, which can be only the conclusion reached by one of the parties and in consequence will be, for the other party, merely an external and particular will, inclined on this occasion to injustice and subject to error. Thus, just as a particular will cannot stand for the general will, the general will, in turn, changes its nature, when its object is particular, and, as general, cannot pronounce on a man or a fact. When, for instance, the people of Athens nominated or displaced its rulers, decreed honours to one, and imposed penalties on another, and, by a multitude of particular decrees, exercised all the functions of government indiscriminately, it had in such cases no longer a general will in the strict sense; it was acting no longer as Sovereign, but as magistrate. This will seem contrary to current views; but I must be given time to expound my own.

It should be seen from the foregoing that what makes the will general is less the number of voters than the common interest uniting them; for, under this system, each necessarily submits to the conditions he imposes on others: and this admirable agreement between interest and justice gives to the common deliberations an equitable character which at once vanishes when any particular question is discussed, in the absence of a common interest to unite and identify the ruling of the judge with that of the party.

From whatever side we approach our principle, we reach the same conclusion, that the social compact sets up among the citizens an equality of such a kind, that they all bind themselves to observe the same conditions and should therefore all enjoy the same rights. Thus, from the very nature of the compact, every act of Sovereignty, i.e. every authentic act of the general will, binds or favours all the citizens equally; so that the Sovereign recognizes only the body of the nation, and draws no distinctions between those of whom it is made up. What, then, strictly speaking, is an act of Sovereignty? It is not a convention between a superior and an inferior, but a convention between the body and each of its members. It is legitimate, because based on the social contract, and equitable, because common to all; useful, because it can have no other object than the general good, and stable, because guaranteed by the public force and the supreme power. So long as the subjects have to submit only to conventions of this sort, they obey no one but their own will; and to ask how far the respective rights of the Sovereign and the citizens extend, is to ask up to what point the latter can enter into undertakings with themselves, each with all, and all with each.

We can see from this that the sovereign power, absolute, sacred, and inviolable as it is, does not and cannot exceed the limits of general conventions, and that every man may dispose at will of such goods and liberty as these conventions leave him; so that the Sovereign never has a right to lay more charges on one subject than on another, because, in that case, the question becomes particular, and ceases to be within its competency.

When these distinctions have once been admitted, it is seen to be so untrue that there is, in the social contract, any real renunciation on the part of the individuals, that the position in which they find themselves as a result of the contract is really preferable to that in which they were before. Instead of a renunciation, they have made an advantageous exchange: instead of an uncertain and precarious way of living they have got one that is better and more secure; instead of natural independence they have got liberty, instead of the power to harm others security for themselves, and instead of their strength, which others might overcome, a right which social union makes invincible. Their very life, which they have devoted to the State, is by it constantly protected; and when they risk it in the State's defence, what more are they doing than giving back what they have received from it? What are they doing that they would not do more often and with greater danger in the state of nature, in which they would inevitably have to fight battles at the peril of their lives in defence of that which is the means of their preservation? All have indeed to fight when their country needs them; but then no one has ever to fight for himself. Do we not gain something by running, on behalf of what gives us our security, only some of the risks we should have to run for ourselves, as soon as we lost it?

The Various Systems of Legislation (Book II: Chapter XI)

If we ask in what precisely consists the greatest good of all, which should be the end of every system of legislation, we shall find it reduce itself to two main objects, liberty and equality – liberty, because all particular dependence means so much force taken from the body of the State, and equality, because liberty cannot exist without it.

I have already defined civil liberty; by equality, we should understand, not that the degrees of power and riches are to be absolutely identical for everybody; but that power shall never be great enough for violence, and shall always be exercised by virtue of rank and law; and that, in respect of riches, no citizen shall ever be wealthy enough to buy another, and none poor enough to be forced to sell himself: which implies, on the part of the great, moderation in goods and position, and, on the side of the common sort, moderation in avarice and covetousness.

Such equality, we are told, is an unpractical ideal that cannot actually exist. But if its abuse is inevitable, does it follow that we should not at least make regulations concerning it? It is precisely because the force of circumstances tends continually to destroy equality that the force of legislation should always tend to its maintenance . . .

From EMILE, 1762

Jean Jacques Rousseau

This novel of romance about the eponymous child was, as its subtitle – *ou Traite de l'education* – suggested, a vehicle for Rousseau's principles for a new scheme of education and child-rearing. Prime among these was that children should develop "freely" and independently in a natural environment. Froebel and Steiner and a number of other latterday progressive educationalists have an obvious indebtedness to *Emile*.

Book I

Everything is good as it comes from the hand of the Author of things: everything degenerates in the hand of man. He forces a piece of ground to nourish harvests alien to it, a tree to bear fruit not its own; he mingles and confounds climates, elements, seasons; he mutilates his dog, his horse, his slave; he turns everything upside down, he disfigures everything; he loves deformity and monsters. He does not want anything to be as nature made it, not even man; it must be groomed for him, like a riding-school horse; it must conform to his whim like a tree in his garden . . .

It is you I address, gentle and far-seeing mother, who know that you must withdraw yourself from the established highway and protect the tender sapling from the shock of human opinion! Cultivate, water the young plant before it dies; its fruits will one day be your greatest joy. Build early a protecting wall about the soul of your child: another may mark out the boundary, but you alone must erect the barrier.

Plants are formed by cultivation and men by education. If a man were born tall and strong, his height and strength would be worthless to him until he had learned to make use of them; both could be harmful to him, in keeping others from thinking he needed help; left to himself, he could die of misery before he understood his own needs. We pity the childish state;

we do not see that the human race would have perished if man had not started out as a child.

We are born feeble, we need strength; we are born deprived of everything, we need help; we are born stupid, we need judgment. Everything we lack at our birth, but need when we are grown, is given by our education.

This education comes to us from nature, from men, or from things. The internal development of our faculties and organs is the education of nature; the use we learn to make of this development is the education of men; and the acquisition of our own experience from the objects which affect us is the education of things.

Each one of us, then, is fashioned by three sorts of teachers. The pupil in whom their various teachings clash is badly educated, and will never be at peace with himself; the one in whom they all emphasize the same purpose and tend towards the same ends, goes straight to his goal and lives harmoniously. Such an one is well educated.

Now, of these three different educations, that of nature is the only one that does not depend on us at all; that of things depends on man only in certain respects. That of man is the only one of which we are truly the masters: even here we are in control only theoretically; for who can hope to direct completely the discourse and actions of all those surrounding a child?

Since, then, education is an art, it is almost impossible that it should be successful, for the circumstances necessary to its success are determined by no one person. All that one can do with the greatest care is, more or less, to approach the goal, but one needs good luck to reach it.

What is this goal? It is the very same as nature's; that has just been proved. Since the combination of these educations is necessary for their perfecting, it is toward the one over which we have no control that we must direct the other two. But perhaps this word nature is too vague a term; we must try here to define it.

Nature, we are told, is only habit. What does that mean? Are there not habits which are developed only with effort, and which never stifle nature? Such is, for example, the habit of plants, the vertical direction of which is interfered with. Once the restraints are removed, the plant retains the inclination which it has been forced to take; but even so the sap has not changed its primitive direction, and, if the plant continues to thrive, its growth will return to the vertical. It is the same with the tendencies of man. As long as we stay in one situation, we keep those which are the result of custom and which are the least natural to us; but as soon as the situation changes the learned habit stops and the natural returns. Education is certainly a habit. Now are there not people who forget and lose their education and others who retain it? From whence comes this difference? If we limit the meaning of nature to the habits which conform to the natural, we may spare ourselves this nonsense.

We are born sensitive, and from our birth we are affected in diverse ways by the objects which surround us. As soon as we have, so to speak, the consciousness of our sensations, we are disposed to seek out or to flee from the objects which produce them, first according as to whether they are agreeable or displeasing to us, then according to the harmony or discord which we find between ourselves and these objects, and finally according to the judgments which we form concerning the idea of happiness and perfection which our reason gives us. These judgments are extended and strengthened in accordance with our becoming more sensitive and more enlightened; but limited by our habits, they are changed more or less by our opinions. Before this change, they are what I call nature in us.

It is to these primitive urges, then, that we must relate everything; and this could be done if our three educations were merely different; but what is to be done when they are opposed? – when, instead of educating a man for himself, we wish to educate him for others, then harmony is impossible. Forced to combat nature or social institutions, we must choose between making a man or a citizen: for one cannot do both at the same time.

All small societies, when confined and close-knit, draw away from the world at large. Every patriot is intolerant of foreigners; they are mere men, they have no worth to him. This difficulty is inevitable but it is a slight one. It is essential to be kind to the people with whom one lives. Outside, the Spartan was ambitious, miserly, unrighteous: but disinterestedness, justice, and concord reigned within his walls. Beware of those citizens of the world who study their books for dutiful acts which they disdain to carry out at home. This kind of philosopher loves the barbarian in order to be free from loving his neighbour.

The natural man is all for himself; he is a numerical unity, the absolute entity, in harmony only with himself or his equals. The civil man (the man in society) is but a fractional unit belonging to the denominator whose sole value is in relation to the whole, which is the social body. Good social institutions are those that know best how to strip man of his nature, to take from him his real existence and give him one which is only relative, and to add his personality to the common unity: to the end that each individual will no longer think of himself as one, but as a part of the whole, no longer a thinking being except in the group. A Roman citizen was neither a Caius nor a Lucius: he was a Roman . . .

A woman of Sparta had five sons in the army and awaited news of the battle. A helot arrived and she asked for news, trembling. "Your five sons have been killed." "Ignoble slave, did I ask you that?" "We are victorious!" The mother ran to the temple and gave thank-offerings to the gods. There is your citizen.

One who, in civilized society, hopes to maintain the pre-eminence of the natural does not know what he asks. Always at odds with himself, forever vacillating between his inclinations and his duty, he will never be either man or citizen; he will be no good to himself or others. He will be one of those contemporary men, a Frenchman, an Englishman, a citizen. He will be a nonentity.

To be something, to be himself and always whole, a man must act as he speaks, he must be sure always of the road he must take, take it resolutely and follow it always. I am waiting for someone to show me such a prodigy to know if he is man or citizen, or how he undertakes to be both at the same time.

From these necessarily opposed aims come two forms of contrary institutions: the one held in common and public, the other individual and private.

If you want to get an idea of public education, read Plato's Republic. It is not at all a political work, as those who judge a book only by its title believe it to be: it is the finest treatise on education that anyone ever wrote.

When people want to return to a never-never land, they think of Plato's institution: if Lycurgus[1] had done no more than put his in writing, I should find it much more fanciful. Plato simply purified the heart of man: Lycurgus denaturalized it.

That public system exists no longer, and can exist no longer, because where there is no nation there can be no citizen. These two words *Nation* and *Citizen* should be removed from modern languages. I know quite well the reason for this, but I do not want to discuss it: it has nothing to do with my subject.

Those laughable institutions they call "colleges" I do not think of in connection with public education. Neither do I count the education of the world, because this education leads toward two contrary goals, and misses both of them; it is useful only to produce two-faced men, who seem always to defer to others but who are really interested only in pleasing themselves. Now this behaviour, being common to all, deceives no one in particular. It is so much wasted effort.

From these contradictions arises the one which we feel constantly within ourselves. Pulled by nature and by man in opposite directions; forced to divide ourselves among these different compulsions, we make compromises which lead neither to one goal nor the other. Thus besieged and vacillating during the whole course of our life, we end it without having found peace within ourselves and without having been any good to ourselves or others.

There remains finally private education, or that of nature, but what can a man mean to others if he is educated only for himself? If perhaps the proposed double object could be resolved into one, by removing the

[1] Lycurgus, king of Sparta, established the system of training to which Rousseau refers

contradictions of man we could remove a great obstacle to his happiness. To make a judgment, we must see the finished man; we must have observed his tendencies, seen his progress, followed his advance; in a word, we must know the natural man. I believe you will have taken some steps (made some progress) in our research after having read this discussion.

What must we do to fashion this rare being? – much, without doubt: that is, prevent anything from being done. When it is only a question of sailing against the wind, we tack; but if the sea is high and we want to stay in one place, we must drop anchor. Take care, young pilot, that your cable does not slip or your anchor drag, and that your vessel does not drift without your noticing it.

In the social order where every place is allocated, each one must be educated for his niche. If a man leaves the place for which he was prepared, he no longer fits anywhere. Education is useful to the extent that destiny harmonizes it with the vocation of the parents; in all other instances, it is harmful to the student, if only for the prejudices it gives him. In Egypt, where the son was obliged to step into his father's place, education at least had an assured purpose: but among us where only classes remain, and where men change from one to the other constantly, no one knows whether, in educating his son to take his place, a father may be working against the son's best interests.

In the natural order, since men are equal, their common calling is man's estate, and whoever is well educated for this, cannot fill unworthily any position which relates to it. Whether I destine my pupil for the army, the church, the bar, is of little importance. No matter what the calling of his parents, nature calls him to human life. Living is the trade I should like to teach him. Leaving my hands, he will not be, I admit, magistrate, soldier, or priest; he will be first of all a man: everything that a man should be, he will know how to be, when called on, as well as any man; and in vain will fortune change his place, for he will always be at home . . .

Book II

. . . Far from trying to prevent Emile from hurting himself, I would be worried if he never hurt himself, if he grew up not knowing pain. To suffer is the first thing that he must learn and the one that he will have the greatest need to know. It seems that children are small and weak only in order to learn these important lessons without any danger. The child has such a little way to fall he will not break his leg; if he knocks himself with a stick he will not break his arm; if he grabs a sharp knife he will not grasp it tight enough to make a deep wound. So far as I know, no child left to himself has ever been known to kill or maim himself or even to do himself any serious harm, unless he has been foolishly left on a high place or alone near the fire or within reach of dangerous weapons. What is there to be said for all the paraphernalia which surrounds the child to protect him on every side against pain until, having grown up, he remains at its mercy without courage and without experience, and believes himself dead at the first pinprick and faints at the sight of blood? . . .

Men, be humane; that is your first duty. Be humane toward every condition, every age, toward all that is not foreign to humanity. What wisdom is there for you outside of humanity? Love childhood, promote its pleasures, its lovable instincts. Who among you has not sometimes missed that age when laughter was always on our lips, and when the soul was always at peace? Why take away from these innocent little people the joys of a time that will escape them so quickly and gifts that could never cause any harm? Why fill with bitterness the fleeting days of early childhood, days which will no more return for them than for you? Fathers, can you tell the moment when death awaits your children? Do not prepare yourself for regrets by robbing them of the few moments which nature has given them. As soon as they are aware of the pleasure of existence, let them rejoice in it; make it so that whenever God calls them they will not die without having tasted life . . .

The only man who follows his own will is he who has no need to put another man's arms at the end of his own. From this it follows that the greatest good is not authority but *freedom*. The truly free man wants only what he can do and does what he pleases. This is my fundamental maxim. Apply it to childhood, and all the rules of education spring from it.

Society has weakened man not only by depriving him of the right to his own strength, but above all by making his strength insufficient for his needs. This is why his desires are multiplied with his weakness; and this is why the child is weaker than the man. If a man is strong and a child is weak it is not because the strength of the one is absolutely greater than the strength of the other, but because the one can naturally provide for himself and the other cannot. Thus the man will have more wishes and the child more *whims*, a word which I take to mean desires which are not true needs, desires which can only be satisfied with the help of others . . .

To strengthen the body and make it grow, nature has means that should never be opposed. One must not force a child to stay when he wants to go, nor to go when he wants to stay. When we have not spoiled the wills of children by our own fault they want nothing arbitrarily. They must jump, run, shout when they wish. All their movements are from the needs of their constitution which seeks to strengthen itself. But one should be mistrustful of their wanting to do things that they cannot do themselves and that others are obliged to do for them. Then one must distinguish carefully between the true need, the natural need, and the needs of budding whim or those which come only from the overflowing life just described.

I have *already* told you what you ought to do when a child cries for this thing or that. I will only add that as soon as he has words to ask for what he wants and accompanies his demands with tears, either to get his own way quicker or to override a refusal, he should never have his way. If his words were prompted by a real need you should recognize it and satisfy it at once. But to yield to his tears is to encourage him to cry, to teach him to doubt your kindness, and to think that you are influenced more by his impertinence than your own goodwill. If he does not think you good, soon he will be evil; if he thinks you weak he will soon become obstinate. It is important to grant at his first sign anything that you do not wish to refuse him. Do not overdo your refusals, but, having refused, do not change your mind . . .

Above all, beware of teaching the child empty phrases of politeness that only serve as magic words to subdue those around him to his will and to get him what he wants at once. The artificial education of the rich never fails to make them politely imperious by teaching them the words to use so that no one will dare to resist them. Their children have neither the tone nor the manner of suppliants; they are as haughty or even more haughty in their entreaties than in their commands, as though they were more certain to be obeyed. It is obvious that "If you please" means "It pleases me," and "I beg" means "I command." What admirable politeness, which only succeeds in changing the meaning of words so that every word is a command! For my own part, I would rather Emile were rude than arrogant, that he should say "Do this" as a request, rather than "Please" as a command. What concerns me is not the term that he uses but the meaning that he gives to it.

There is such a thing as excessive severity as well as excessive indulgence, and both should be equally avoided. If you let children suffer you risk their health and life; you make them miserable now. If you take too many pains to spare them every kind of discomfort you are laying up much unhappiness for them in the future; you are making them delicate and over-sensitive; you are taking them out of their place among men, a place to which they must sooner or later return in spite of all your pains. You will say I am falling into the same mistake as those bad fathers whom I blamed for sacrificing the present happiness of their children to a future which may never be theirs.

Not so. For the freedom I give my pupil makes up for the slight hardships to which he is exposed. I see little rascals playing in the snow, stiff and blue with cold, scarcely able to move their fingers. They could go and warm themselves if they chose, but they do not. If you forced them to come in they would feel the harshness of constraint a hundred times more than the sharpness of the cold. So what are you complaining about? Shall I make your child miserable by exposing him to hardships which he is perfectly ready to endure? I do what is good for him in the present moment by letting him be free; I do what is good for him in the future good by arming him against the evils he will have to bear. If he had his choice to be my pupil or yours, would he hesitate even for a moment?

Can one imagine that true happiness is possible for anyone outside of his constitution? And is not trying to spare man all the ills of his species an effort to remove him from his constitution? Indeed I maintain that to enjoy great goodness he must experience slight ills; such is his nature. If the physical is too healthy the moral will be corrupted. A man who knew nothing of suffering would not feel tenderness towards humanity nor the sweetness of *pity*. His heart would be moved by nothing; he would be unsociable, a monster among his fellow men.

Do you know the surest way to make your child miserable? Let him have everything he wants; for as his wants increase in proportion to the ease with which they are satisfied, you will be compelled, sooner or later, to refuse his demands, and this unlooked-for refusal will hurt him more than the lack of what he wants. First he'll want the cane that you are holding, soon he'll want your watch, then the bird that flies, or the star that shines above him. He will want everything that he sees. Unless you were God himself, how could you satisfy him?

It is a disposition natural to man to regard as his own everything that is in his power. In this sense *Hobbes'* principle is true up to a certain point. Multiply both our wishes and the means of satisfying them, and each will make himself the master of all. Thus the child who has only to want something in order to obtain it thinks himself the owner of the universe; he regards all men as his slaves. And finally when one is forced to refuse him something, he, believing anything is possible when he asks for it, takes the refusal as an act of rebellion. All the reasons you give him while he is still too young to reason are so many pretences in his eyes; in all of that he sees only ill will. The sense of a so-called injustice embitters his disposition; he hates every one. Though he has never felt grateful for kindness, he resents all opposition.

How could I conceive that a child thus dominated by anger and devoured by the fiercest passions could ever be happy? Him happy? He is a despot, at once the vilest of slaves and the most miserable of creatures. I have known children raised in this way who expected you to knock the house down, to give them the weather-vane on the steeple, to stop a regiment on the march so that they might listen to the band, and who, without listening to anyone, would pierce the air with their cries as soon as they were not obeyed. Everyone strove vainly to please them. Since their desires were stimulated by the ease with which they got their own way, they set their hearts on impossibilities, and found themselves face to face with opposition and difficulty, pain and grief. Always whining, always rebellious, always in a rage, they spent their days crying and complaining. Were these beings so fortunate? Weakness combined with domination produces nothing but folly and misery. One spoiled child beats the table; another whips the sea. They may beat and whip in vain before they find contentment.

If these ideas of empire and tyranny make them miserable during childhood, what about when they grow up, when their relations with their fellow-men begin to expand and multiply? They are used to finding everything give way to them; what a painful surprise to enter society and meet with opposition on every side, to be crushed beneath the weight of a universe which they expected to move at will.

Their insolent manners, their childish vanity, only draw down upon them mortification, scorn, and mockery; they swallow insults like water. Sharp experience soon teaches them that they have realised neither their position nor their strength. Being unable to do everything, they think they can do nothing. They are daunted by unexpected obstacles, degraded by the scorn of men. They become base, cowardly, and deceitful, and fall as far below their true level as they formerly soared above it.

Let us come back to the first rule. Nature has made children to be loved and helped, but did it make them to be obeyed and feared? Has nature given them an imposing manner, a stern eye, a loud and threatening voice with which to make people wary of them? I understand how the roaring of the lion frightens the other beasts, so that they tremble when they behold his terrible mane, but of all unseemly, hateful, and ridiculous sights, was there ever anything like a group of statesmen, with their leader in front of them in his ceremonial robes, bowing down before a swaddled *babe*, addressing him in pompous phrases, while he cries and drools in reply?

If we consider childhood itself, is there in the world a being weaker and more miserable, more at the mercy of everthing that surrounds it, who has a greater need of pity, care, and affection, than a child? Does it not seem as if his gentle face and touching appearance were intended to interest every one on behalf of his weakness and to make them eager to help him? And what is there more offensive, more contrary to order, than the sight of an unruly or imperious child commanding those about him and impudently taking on the tones of a master towards those without whom he would perish?

On the other hand, is it not clear that the weakness of the first age enchains children in so many ways that it is barbarous to add our own whims to this subjection by depriving them of the limited freedom that they do have – a freedom which they can scarcely abuse and the loss of which will do so little good to them or us? If there is nothing more ridiculous than a haughty child, there is nothing that claims our pity like a timid child. Since civil servitude begins with the age of reason, then why anticipate this by private servitude? Allow one moment of life to be free from this yoke that nature has not imposed upon it. Leave to the child the exercise of his natural freedom, which, for a time at least, keeps him away from the vices contracted in slavery. Let harsh masters and those fathers who are the slaves of their children both come forward with their petty objections; and before they boast of their own methods, let them for once learn the method of nature.

I return to practical matters. I have already said your child must not get what he asks, but what he needs; he must never act from obedience, but from necessity. Thus the very words obey and command will be excluded from his vocabulary, still more those of duty and obligation. But the words strength, necessity, weakness, and constraint must have a large place in it. Before the age of reason it is impossible to form any idea of moral beings or social relations. One must thus avoid as much as possible the use of words which express these ideas lest the child at an early age should attach wrong ideas to them, ideas which you cannot or will not destroy when he is older. The first mistaken idea he gets into his head is the germ of error and vice; it is the first step that needs watching. Act in such a way that while he only notices external objects his ideas are confined to sensations; let him only see the physical world around him. If not, you may be sure that either he will not hear you at all, or that he will form of this moral world you speak about some farfetched notions that you will never erase as long as he lives.

To reason with children was *Locke*'s chief maxim. It is even more in vogue today. Its success however does not seem to me strong enough to give it credit; for me I see nothing more stupid that these children with whom people reasoned so much. Of all man's faculties, reason, which is, so to speak, the one composed of all the others, is the one that develops with the most difficulty and the latest, and yet you want to use it to develop the earlier ones! The culmination of a good education is to make a man reasonable, and you claim to raise a child with reason! You begin at the wrong end; you make the end the means. If children understood reason they would not need education. But by talking to them from their earliest age in a language they do not understand you accustom them to manipulate with words, to control all that is said to them, to think themselves as wise as their teachers, to become argumentative and rebellious. And whatever you think you gain from motives of reason you really gain from the greediness, or fear, or vanity, which you are always forced to add to your reasoning.

From THE PHILOSOPHICAL DICTIONARY, 1764

Voltaire

Voltaire (1694–1778), born Francois Marie Arouet, was the French embodiment of the Enlightenment. A workaholic playwright, author of the
blackly satirical novel *Candide*, a letterist, a pamphleteer, historian and
philosopher, he is said to have dictated to his secretary even whilst dressing
in the morning. Despite the multiplicity of his talents, there was a unity of
rationalist principle behind them: to combat superstition, intolerance and
prejudice in the *ancien régime* and the Catholic Church. This was a
dangerous pursuit which landed him in the Bastille prison and in exile
in England (which he admired for its religious and political tolerance, and
accordingly lauded in his *Letters on the English*). Yet his gallant campaigns
on behalf of those persecuted by the French church, his wit, his self-earned
wealth and the sheer longevity of his life eventually reconciled most of
France to him. After the Revolution of 1734 which, along with Rousseau, he
was a prime philosophical instigator, his body was interred in the Pantheon.

The *Philosophical Dictionary* is the main anti-religious work of Voltaire's
evening.

Religion

I meditated last night; I was absorbed in the contemplation of nature; I
admired the immensity, the course, the harmony of these infinite globes
which the vulgar do not know how to admire.

I admired still more the intelligence which directs these vast forces. I
said to myself: "One must be blind not to be dazzled by this spectacle; one
must be stupid not to recognize the author of it; one must be mad not to
worship Him. What tribute of worship should I render Him? Should not
this tribute be the same in the whole of space, since it is the same supreme
power which reigns equally in all space? Should not a thinking being who
dwells in a star in the Milky Way offer Him the same homage as the

thinking being on this little globe where we are? Light is uniform for the star Sirius and for us; moral philosophy must be uniform. If a sentient, thinking animal in Sirius is born of a tender father and mother who have been occupied with his happiness, he owes them as much love and care as we owe to our parents. If someone in the Milky Way sees a needy cripple, if he can relieve him and if he does not do it, he is guilty toward all globes. Everywhere the heart has the same duties: on the steps of the throne of God, if He has a throne; and in the depth of the abyss, if He is an abyss."

I was plunged in these ideas when one of those genii who fill the intermundane spaces came down to me. I recognized this same aerial creature who had appeared to me on another occasion to teach me how different God's judgments were from our own, and how a good action is preferable to a controversy.

He transported me into a desert all covered with piled up bones; and between these heaps of dead men there were walks of ever-green trees, and at the end of each walk a tall man of august mien, who regarded these sad remains with pity.

"Alas! my archangel," said I, "where have you brought me?"

"To desolation," he answered.

"And who are these fine patriarchs whom I see sad and motionless at the end of these green walks? They seem to be weeping over this countless crowd of dead."

"You shall know, poor human creature," answered the genius from the intermundane spaces; "but first of all you must weep."

He began with the first pile. "These," he said, "are the twenty-three thousand Jews who danced before a calf, with the twenty-four thousand who were killed while lying with Midianitish women. The number of those massacred for such errors and offences amounts to nearly three hundred thousand.

"In the other walks are the bones of the Christians slaughtered by each other for metaphysical disputes. They are divided into several heaps of four centuries each. One heap would have mounted right to the sky; they had to be divided."

"What!" I cried, "brothers have treated their brothers like this, and I have the misfortune to be of this brotherhood!"

"Here," said the spirit, "are the twelve million Americans killed in their fatherland because they had not been baptized."

"My God! why did you not leave these frightful bones to dry in the hemisphere where their bodies were born, and where they were consigned to so many different deaths? Why assemble here all these abominable monuments to barbarism and fanaticism?"

"To instruct you."

"Since you wish to instruct me," I said to the genius, "tell me if there have been peoples other than the Christians and the Jews in whom zeal and religion wretchedly transformed into fanaticism, have inspired so many horrible cruelties."

"Yes," he said. "The Mohammedans were sullied with the same inhumanities, but rarely; and when one asked *amman*, pity, of them, and offered them tribute, they pardoned. As for the other nations there has not been one right from the existence of the world which has ever made a purely religious war. Follow me now." I followed him.

A little beyond these piles of dead men we found other piles; they were composed of sacks of gold and silver, and each had its label: *Substance of the heretics massacred in the 18th century, the 17th and the 16th.* And so on in going back: *Gold and silver of Americans slaughtered,* etc., etc. And all these piles were surmounted with crosses, mitres, croziers, triple crowns studded with precious stones.

"What, my genius! it was then to have these riches that these dead were piled up?"

"Yes, my son."

I wept; and when by my grief I had merited to be led to the end of the green walks, he led me there.

"Contemplate," he said, "the heroes of humanity who were the world's benefactors, and who were all united in banishing from the world, as far as they were able, violence and rapine. Question them."

I ran to the first of the band; he had a crown on his head, and a little censer in his hand; I humbly asked him his name. "I am Numa Pompilius," he said to me. "I succeeded a brigand, and I had brigands to govern: I taught them virtue and the worship of God; after me they forgot both more than once; I forbade that in the temples there should be any image, because the Deity which animates nature cannot be represented. During my reign the Romans had neither wars nor seditions, and my religion did nothing but good. All the neighbouring peoples came to honour me at my funeral: that happened to no one but me."

I kissed his hand, and I went to the second. He was a fine old man about a hundred years old, clad in a white robe. He put his middle-finger on his mouth, and with the other hand he cast some beans behind him. I recognized Pythagoras. He assured me he had never had a golden thigh, and that he had never been a cock; but that he had governed the Crotoniates with as much justice as Numa governed the Romans, almost at the same time; and that this justice was the rarest and most necessary thing in the world. I learned that the Pythagoreans examined their consciences twice a day. The honest people! how far we are from them! But we who have been nothing but assassins for thirteen hundred years, we say that these wise men were arrogant.

In order to please Pythagoras, I did not say a word to him and I passed to Zarathustra, who was occupied in concentrating the celestial fire in the focus of a concave mirror, in the middle of a hall with a hundred doors which all led to wisdom. (Zarathustra's precepts are called doors, and are a hundred in number.) Over the principal door I read these words which are the precis of all moral philosophy, and which cut short all the disputes of the causists: "When in doubt if an action is good or bad, refrain."

"Certainly," I said to my genius, "the barbarians who immolated all these victims had never read these beautiful words."

We then saw the Zaleucus, the Thales, the Aniximanders, and all the sages who had sought truth and practised virtue.

When we came to Socrates, I recognized him very quickly by his flat nose. "Well," I said to him, "here you are then among the number of the Almighty's confidants! All the inhabitants of Europe, except the Turks and the Tartars of the Crimea, who know nothing, pronounce your name with respect. It is revered, loved, this great name, to the point that people have wanted to know those of your persecutors. Melitus and Anitus are known because of you, just as Ravaillac is known because of Henry IV; but I know only this name of Anitus. I do not know precisely who was the scoundrel who calumniated you, and who succeeded in having you condemned to take hemlock."

"Since my adventure," replied Socrates, "I have never thought about that man; but seeing that you make me remember it, I have much pity for him. He was a wicked priest who secretly conducted a business in hides, a trade reputed shameful among us. He sent his two children to my school. The other disciples taunted them with having a father who was a currier; they were obliged to leave. The irritated father had no rest until he had stirred up all the priests and all the sophists against me. They persuaded the counsel of the five hundred that I was an impious fellow who did not believe that the Moon, Mercury and Mars were gods. Indeed, I used to think, as I think now that there is only one God, master of all nature. The judges handed me over to the poisoner of the republic; he cut short my life by a few days: I died peacefully at the age of seventy; and since that time I pass a happy life with all these great men whom you see, and of whom I am the least."

After enjoying some time in conversation with Socrates, I went forward with my guide into a grove situated above the thickets where all the sages of antiquity seemed to be tasting sweet repose.

I saw a man of gentle, simple countenance, who seemed to me to be about thirty-five years old. From afar he cast compassionate glances on these piles of whitened bones, across which I had had to pass to reach the sages' abode. I was astonished to find his feet swollen and bleeding, his hands likewise, his side pierced, and his ribs flayed with whip cuts. "Good heavens!" I said to him, "is it possible for a just man, a sage, to be in this state? I have just seen one who was treated in a very hateful way, but there is no comparison between his torture and yours. Wicked priests and wicked judges poisoned him; is it by priests and judges that you have been so cruelly assassinated?"

He answered with much courtesy – "*Yes.*"

"And who were these monsters?"

"*They were hypocrites.*"

"Ah! that says everything; I understand by this single word that they must have condemned you to death. Had you then proved to them, as Socrates did, that the Moon was not a goddess, and that Mercury was not a god?"

"*No, these planets were not in question. My compatriots did not know at all what a planet is; they were all arrant ignoramuses. Their superstitions were quite different from those of the Greeks.*"

"You wanted to teach them a new religion, then?"

"*Not at all; I said to them simply – 'Love God with all your heart and your fellow-creature as yourself, for that is man's whole duty.' Judge if this precept is not as old as the universe; judge if I brought them a new religion. I did not stop telling them that I had come not to destroy the law but to fulfil it; I had observed all their rites; circumcised as they all were, baptized as were the most zealous among them, like them I paid the Corban; I observed the Passover as they did, eating standing up a lamb cooked with lettuces. I and my friends went to pray in the temple; my friends even frequented this temple after my death; in a word, I fulfilled all their laws without a single exception.*"

"What! these wretches could not even reproach you with swerving from their laws?"

"*No, without a doubt.*"

"Why then did they put you in the condition in which I now see you?"

"*What do you expect me to say? They were very arrogant and selfish. They saw that I knew them; they knew that I was making the citizens acquainted with them; they were the stronger; they took away my life: and people like them will always do as much, if they can, to whoever does them too much justice.*"

"But did you say nothing, do nothing that could serve them as a pretext?"

"*To the wicked everything serves as pretext.*"

"Did you not say once that you were come not to send peace, but a sword?"

"*It is a copyist's error; I told them that I sent peace and not a sword. I have never written anything; what I said can have been changed without evil intention.*"

"You therefore contributed in no way by your speeches, badly reported, badly interpreted, to these frightful piles of bones which I saw on my road in coming to consult you?"

"*It is with horror only that I have seen those who have made themselves guilty of these murders.*"

"And these monuments of power and wealth, of pride and avarice, these treasures, these ornaments, these signs of grandeur, which I have seen piled up on the road while I was seeking wisdom, do they come from you?"

"*That is impossible; I and my people lived in poverty and meanness: my grandeur was in virtue only.*"

I was about to beg him to be so good as to tell me just who he was. My guide warned me to do nothing of the sort. He told me that I was not made to understand these sublime mysteries. Only did I conjure him to tell me in what true religion consisted. "*Have I not already told you? Love God and your fellow-creature as yourself.*"

"What! if one loves God, one can eat meat on Friday?"

"*I always ate what was given me; for I was too poor to give anyone food.*"

"In loving God, in being just, should one not be rather cautious not to confide all the adventures of one's life to an unknown man?"

"*That was always my practice.*"

"Can I not, by doing good, dispense with making a pilgrimage to St James of Compostella?"

"*I have never been in that country.*"

"Is it necessary for me to imprison myself in a retreat with fools?"

"*As for me, I always made little journeys from town to town.*"

"Is it necessary for me to take sides either for the Greek Church or the Latin?"

"*When I was in the world I never made any difference between the Jew and the Samaritan.*"

"Well, if that is so, I take you for my only master." Then he made me a sign with his head which filled me with consolation. The vision disappeared, and a clear conscience stayed with me.

THE ABOLITION OF TORTURE, 1764

Cesare Beccaria

One of the great advances of the Enlightenment was the humanization of the criminal process. Cesare Beccaria (1738–94), an Italian marquis and intellectual, published in 1764 *An Essay on Crimes and Punishments* which argued for the abolition of judicial torture and the death sentence. He also advocated commensurability in the punishment of crimes and the eradication of crime through education. Although he borrowed many of these ideas from Montesquieu's *The Spirit of the Laws*, Beccaria was a persuasive and succinct expositionist. An *Essay on Crimes and Punishments* (*Dei delitti e delle pene*) was an immediate bestseller and influenced legislation in Europe and America.

In every human society, there is an effort continually tending to confer on one part the height of power and happiness, and to reduce the other to the extreme of weakness, and misery. The intent of good laws is to oppose this effort, and to diffuse their influence, universally, and equally. But men generally abandon the care of their most important concerns to the uncertain prudence, and discretion of those, whose interest it is to reject the best, and wisest institutions; and it is not till they have been led into a thousand mistakes in matters, the most essential to their lives and liberties, and are weary of suffering, that they can be induced to apply a remedy to the evils, with which they are oppressed. It is then they begin to conceive, and acknowledge the most palpable truths, which, from their very simplicity, commonly escape vulgar minds, incapable of analysing objects, accustomed to receive impressions without distinction, and to be determined rather by the opinions of others, than by the result of their own examination.

If we look into history we shall find, that laws, which are, or ought to be, conventions between men in a state of freedom, have been, for the most part, the work of the passions of a few, or the consequences of a fortuitous, or temporary necessity; not dictated by a cool examiner of human nature, who knew how to collect in one point, the actions of a multitude, and had this only end in view, *the greatest happiness of the greatest number*. Happy are those few nations, who have not waited, till the slow succession of human vicissitudes, should, from the extremity of evil, produce a transition to good; but, by prudent laws, have facilitated the progress from one to the other! And how great are the obligations due from mankind to that philosopher, who from the obscurity of his closet, had the courage to scatter amongst the multitude, the seeds of useful truths, so long unfruitful!

The art of printing has diffused the knowledge of those philosophical truths, by which the relations between sovereigns and their subjects, and between nations, are discovered. By this knowledge, commerce is animated, and there has sprung up a spirit of emulation, and industry, worthy of rational beings. These are the produce of this enlightened age; but the cruelty of punishments, and the irregularity of proceedings in criminal cases, so principal a part of the legislation, and so much neglected throughout Europe, has hardly ever been called in question. Errors, accumulated through many centuries, have never yet been exposed by ascending to general principles; nor has the force of acknowledged truths been ever opposed to the unbounded licentiousness of ill-directed power, which has continually produced so many authorized examples of the most unfeeling barbarity. Surely, the groans of the weak, sacrificed to the cruel ignorance, and indolence of the powerful; the barbarous torments lavished, and multiplied with useless severity, for crimes either not proved, or in their nature impossible; the filth, and horrors of a prison, increased by the most cruel tormentor of the miserable, uncertainty, ought to have roused the attention of those, whose business is to direct the opinions of mankind.

The immortal *Montesquieu* has but slightly touched on this subject. Truth, which is eternally the same, has obliged me to follow the steps of that great man; but the studious part of mankind, for whom I write, will easily distinguish the superstructure from the foundation. I shall be happy, if, with him, I can obtain the secret thanks of the obscure, and peaceful disciples of reason, and philosophy, and excite that tender emotion, in which sensible minds sympathize with him, who pleads the cause of humanity.

Of the Proportion between Crimes and Punishments

It is not only the common interest of mankind, that crimes should not be committed, but that crimes of every kind should be less frequent, in proportion to the evil they produce to society. Therefore, the means made use of by the legislature to prevent crimes, should be more powerful, in proportion as they are destructive of the public safety and happiness, and as the inducements to commit them are stronger. Therefore there ought to be a fixed proportion between crimes and punishments.

It is impossible to prevent entirely all the disorders which the passions of mankind cause in society. These disorders increase in proportion to the number of people, and the opposition of private interests. If we consult history, we shall find them increasing, in every state, with the extent of dominion. In political arithmetic, it is necessary to substitute a calculation of probabilities, to mathematical exactness. That force, which continually impels us to our own private interest, like gravity, acts incessantly, unless it meets with an obstacle to oppose it. The effects of this force are the confused series of human actions. Punishments, which I would call political obstacles, prevent the fatal effects of private interest, without destroying the impelling cause, which is that sensibility inseparable from man. The legislator acts, in this case, like a skilful architect, who endeavours to counteract the force of gravity by combining the circumstances which may contribute to the strength of his edifice.

The necessity of uniting in society being granted, together with the conventions, which the opposite interests of individuals must necessarily require, a scale of crimes may be formed, of which the first degree should consist of those, which immediately tend to the dissolution of society, and the last, of the smallest possible injustice done to a private member of that society. Between these extremes will be comprehended, all actions contrary to the public good, which are called criminal, and which descend by insensible degrees, decreasing from the highest to the lowest. If mathematical calculation could be applied to the obscure and infinite combinations of human actions, there might be a corresponding scale of punishments, descending from the greatest to the least: but it will be sufficient that the wise legislator mark the principal divisions, without disturbing the order, lest to crimes of the *first* degree, be assigned punishments of the *last*. If there were an exact and universal scale of crimes and punishments, we should there have a common measure of the degree of liberty and slavery, humanity and cruelty of different nations.

Any action, which is not comprehended in the above-mentioned scale, will not be called a crime, or punished as such, except by those who have an interest in the denomination. The uncertainty of the extreme points of this scale, hath produced a system of morality which contradicts the laws; a multitude of laws that contradict each other; and many, which expose the best men to the severest punishments, rendering the ideas of *vice* and *virtue* vague, and fluctuating, and even their existence doubtful. Hence that fatal lethargy of political bodies, which terminates in their destruction.

Whoever reads, with a philosophic eye, the history of nations, and their laws, will generally find, that the ideas of virtue and vice, of a good or a bad citizen, change with the revolution of ages; not in proportion to the

alteration of circumstances, and consequently conformable to the common good; but in proportion to the passions and errors by which the
different law-givers were successively influenced. He will frequently
observe, that the passions and vices of one age are the foundation of
the morality of the following; that violent passion, the offspring of
fanatiscism and enthusiasm, being weakened by time, which reduces
all the phenomena of the natural and moral world to an equality, become,
by degrees, the prudence of the age, and a useful instrument in the hands
of the powerful, or artful politician. Hence the uncertainty of our notions
of honour and virtue; an uncertainty which will ever remain, because they
change with the revolutions of time, and names survive the things they
originally signified; they change with the boundaries of states, which are
often the same both in physical and moral geography.

Pleasure and pain are the only springs of action in beings endowed with
sensibility. Even amongst the motives which incite men to acts of religion,
the invisible legislator has ordained rewards and punishments. From a
partial distribution of these, will arise that contradiction, so little observed,
because so common; I mean, that of punishing by the laws, the crimes
which the laws have occasioned. If an equal punishment be ordained for
two crimes that injure society in different degrees, there is nothing to deter
men from committing the greater, as often as it is attended with greater
advantage.

Of Estimating the Degree of Crimes

The foregoing reflections authorise me to assert, that crimes are only to be
measured by the injury done to society.

They err, therefore, who imagine that a crime is greater, or less,
according to the intention of the person by whom it is committed; for
this will depend on the actual impression of objects on the senses, and on
the previous disposition of the mind; both which will vary in different
persons, and even in the same person at different times, according to the
succession of ideas, passions, and circumstances. Upon that system, it
would be necessary to form, not only a particular code for every individual, but a new penal law for every crime. Men, often with the best
intention, do the greatest injury to society, and with the worst, do it the
most essential services.

Others have estimated crimes rather by the dignity of the person
offended, than by their consequences to society. If this were the true
standard, the smallest irreverence to the divine Being ought to be punished
with infinitely more severity, than the assassination of a monarch.

In short, others have imagined, that the greatness of the sin should
aggravate the crime. But the fallacy of this opinion will appear on the
slightest consideration of the relations between man and man, and

between God and man. The relations between man and man, are relations of equality. Necessity alone hath produced, from the opposition of private passions and interests, the idea of public utility, which is the foundation of human justice. The other are relations of dependence, between an imperfect creature and his creator, the most perfect of beings, who has reserved to himself the sole right of being both lawgiver, and judge; for he alone can, without injustice, be, at the same time, both one and the other. If he hath decreed eternal punishments for those who disobey his will, shall an insect dare to put himself in the place of divine justice, or pretend to punish for the Almighty, who is himself all-sufficient; who cannot receive impressions of pleasure, or pain, and who alone, of all other beings, acts without being acted upon? The degree of sin depends on the malignity of the heart, which is impenetrable to finite beings. How then can the degree of sin serve as a standard to determine the degree of crimes? If that were admitted, men may punish when God pardons, and pardon when God condemns; and thus act in opposition to the supreme Being.

Of the Division of Crimes

We have proved, then, that crimes are to be estimated by *the injury done to society*. This is one of those palpable truths, which, though evident to the meanest capacity, yet, by a combination of circumstances, are only known to a few thinking men in every nation, and in every age. But opinions, worthy only of the despotism of Asia, and passions, armed with power and authority, have, generally by insensible and sometimes by violent impressions on the timid credulity of men, effaced those simple ideas, which perhaps constituted the first philosophy of infant society. Happily the philosophy of the present enlightened age seems again to conduct us to the same principles, and with that degree of certainty, which is obtained by a rational examination, and repeated experience.

Of Torture

The torture of a criminal, during the course of his trial, is a cruelty consecrated by custom in most nations. It is used with an intent either to make him confess his crime, or explain some contradictions, into which he had been led during his examination; or discover his accomplices; or for some kind of metaphysical and incomprehensible purgation of infamy; or, finally, in order to discover other crimes, of which he is not accused, but of which he may be guilty.

No man can be judged a criminal until he be found guilty; nor can society take from him the public protection, until it have been proved that he has violated the conditions on which it was granted. What right, then, but that of power, can authorize the punishment of a citizen, so long as there remains any doubt of his guilt? The dilemma is frequent. Either he is guilty, or not guilty. If guilty, he should only suffer the punishment ordained by the laws, and torture becomes useless, as his confession is unnecessary. If he be not guilty, you torture the innocent; for in the eye of the law, every man is innocent, whose crime has not been proved. Besides, it is confounding all relations, to expect that a man should be both the accuser and accused; and that pain should be the test of truth, as if truth resided in the muscles and fibres of a wretch in torture. By this method, the robust will escape, and the feeble be condemned. These are the inconveniences of this pretended test of truth, worthy only of a cannibal; and which the Romans, in many respects, barbarous, and whose savage virtue has been too much admired, reserved for the slaves alone.

What is the political intention of punishments? To terrify, and be an example to others. Is this intention answered, by thus privately torturing the guilty and the innocent? It is doubtless of importance, that no crime should remain unpunished; but it is useless to make a public example of the author of a crime hid in darkness. A crime already committed, and for which there can be no remedy, can only be punished by a political society, with an intention, that no hopes of impunity should induce others to commit the same. If it be true, that the number of those, who from fear or virtue respect the laws, is greater than of those by whom they are violated, the risk of torturing an innocent person is greater, as there is a greater probability, that, *caeteris paribus*, an individual hath observed, than that he hath infringed the laws.

There is another ridiculous motive for torture, namely, *to purge a man from infamy*. Ought such an abuse to be tolerated in the eighteenth century? Can pain, which is a sensation, have any connexion with a moral sentiment, a matter of opinion? Perhaps the rack may be considered as a refiner's furnace, the unerring light of revelation; and in the times of tractable ignorance, having no other, they naturally had recourse to it on every occasion, making the most remote and absurd applications. Moreover, infamy is a sentiment regulated neither by the laws nor by reason, but entirely by opinion. But torture renders the victim infamous, and therefore cannot take infamy away.

Another intention of torture is, to oblige the supposed criminal to reconcile the contradictions into which he may have fallen, during his examination; as if the dread of punishment, the uncertainty of his fate, the solemnity of the court, the majesty of the judge, and the ignorance of the accused, were not abundantly sufficient to account for contradictions, which are so common to men, even in a state of tranquility; and which must necessarily be multiplied by the perturbation of the mind of a man, entirely engaged in the thoughts of saving himself from imminent danger.

This infamous test of truth is a remaining monument of that antient and savage legislation, in which trials by fire, by boiling water, or the uncertainty of combats, were called *Judgments of God*; as if the links of that eternal chain, whose beginning is in the breast of the first cause of all things, could ever be disunited by the institutions of men. The only difference between torture, and trials by fire and boiling water, is, that the event of the first depends on the will of the accused; and of the second, on a fact entirely physical and external: but this difference is apparent only, not real. A man on the rack, in the convulsions of torture, has it as little in his power to declare the truth, as in former times, to prevent without fraud the effects of fire or of boiling water.

Every act of the will is invariably in proportion to the force of the impression on our senses. The impression of pain, then, may increase to such a degree, that occupying the mind entirely, it will compel the sufferer to use the shortest method of freeing himself from torment. His answer, therefore, will be an effect, as necessary as that of fire or boiling water; and he will accuse himself of crimes of which he is innocent. So that the very means employed to distinguish the innocent from the guilty, will most effectually destroy all difference between them.

It would be superfluous to confirm these reflections by examples of innocent persons, who, from the agony of torture, have confessed themselves guilty: innumerable instances may be found in all nations, and in every age. How amazing, that mankind have always neglected to draw the natural conclusion! Lives there a man who, if he have carried his thoughts ever so little beyond the necessities of life, when he reflects on such cruelty, is not tempted to fly from society, and return to his natural state of independence?

THE DECLARATION OF INDEPENDENCE, 4 JULY 1776

The War of Independence was the first political revolution of the Enlightenment. For all the American colonists' fiscal, purse-watching complaints about taxation by their overlords in London – manifested most famously in the "Boston Tea Party" incident – the true cause of the war was philosophical. It was about the right to representation ("no tax without representation"), the right to democracy and to self-nationhood. The irony that Britain, the freest nation in the world, held another in right-less, colonial status was lost on few in America. (And indeed, on few in Britain outside the court of George III and the cabinet of Lord North.)

A Continental Congress of delegates from all 13 American colonies, except Georgia, first voiced the demand for independence in 1774. A Congress in 1775 called the colonies to arms and appointed George Washington, a Virginia planter (and veteran of the French and Indian Wars) as commander-in-chief. In April of the same year British forces seized military stores at Lexington and Concord. The War of Independence had begun.

Over the next eight years, the British won most of the battles but nonethless lost the war. The canny guerilla tactics of Washington in America's vast landscape played their part, but the major cause of American victory was the colonists' state of mind. Fired up on libertarian fevour, they endured and persevered, even through the desperate winter of 1777 at Valley Forge. Right, it might be said, beat might.

"The Declaration of Independence" was the foundation document of free America. It was proposed on 7 June 1776, by Continental Congress delegate Richard Henry Lee of Virginia, and on 10 June a Congressional committee of five was appointed to prepare a declaration of independence. The committee consisted of John Adams, Benjamin Franklin, Roger Sherman, R.R. Livingston and Thomas Jefferson (1743–1826) as the writer. Basing his ideas on Montesquieu, Locke, Rousseau and Paine, Jefferson's final draft of the Declaration summed up the democratic ideas of the Enlightenment in a sentence which has become immortal: "We hold these truths to be self-evident, that all men are created equal, they they are endowed by their creator with certain unalienable rights, that among these are Life, Liberty and the Pursuit of Happiness." The Declaration was agreed on 4 July 1776 and sent to the legislatures of the States for approval.

In Congress, 4 July 1776, The Unanimous Declaration of the Thirteen United States of America

When in the Course of human events, it becomes necessary for one people to dissolve the political bands which have connected them with another, and to assume among the Powers of the earth, the separate and equal station to which the Laws of Nature and of Nature's God entitle them, a decent respect to the opinions of mankind requires that they should declare the causes which impel them to the separation.

We hold these truths to be self-evident, that all men are created equal, that they are endowed by their Creator with certain unalienable Rights, that among these are Life, Liberty and the pursuit of Happiness. That to secure these rights, Governments are instituted among Men, deriving their just powers from the consent of the governed, That whenever any Form of Government becomes destructive of these ends, it is the Right of the People to alter or to abolish it, and to institute new Government, laying its foundation on such principles and organizing its powers in such form, as to them shall seem most likely to effect their Safety and Happiness. Prudence, indeed, will dictate that Governments long established should not be changed for light and transient causes; and accordingly all experience hath shown, that mankind are more disposed to suffer, while evils are sufferable, than to right themselves by abolishing the forms to which they are accustomed. But when a long train of abuses and usurpations, pursuing invariably the same Object evinces a design to reduce them under absolute Despotism, it is their right, it is their duty, to throw off such Government, and to provide new Guards for their future security. – Such has been the patient sufferance of these Colonies; and such is now the necessity which constrains them to alter their former Systems of Government. The history of the present King of Great Britain is a history of repeated injuries and usurpations, all having in direct object the establishment of an absolute Tyranny over these States. To prove this, let Facts be submitted to a candid world.

He has refused his Assent to Laws, the most wholesome and necessary for the public good.

He has forbidden his Governors to pass Laws of immediate and pressing importance, unless suspended in their operation till his Assent should be obtained; and when so suspended, he has utterly neglected to attend to them.

He has refused to pass other Laws for the accommodation of large districts of people, unless those people would relinquish the right of Representation in the Legislature, a right inestimable to them and formidable to tyrants only.

He has called together legislative bodies at places unusual, uncomfortable, and distant from the depository of their Public Records, for the sole purpose of fatiguing them into compliance with his measures.

He has dissolved Representative Houses repeatedly, for opposing with manly firmness his invasions on the rights of the people.

He has refused for a long time, after such dissolutions, to cause others to be elected; whereby the Legislative Powers, incapable of Annihilation, have returned to the People at large for their exercise; the State remaining in the mean time exposed to all the dangers of invasion from without, and convulsions within.

He has endeavoured to prevent the population of these States; for that purpose obstructing the Laws of Naturalization of Foreigners, refusing to pass others to encourage their migration hither, and raising the conditions of new Appropriations of Lands.

He has obstructed the Administration of Justice, by refusing his Assent to Laws for establishing Judiciary Powers.

He has made Judges dependent on his Will alone, for the tenure of their offices, and the amount and payment of their salaries.

He has erected a multitude of New Offices, and sent hither swarms of Officers to harass our People, and eat out their substance.

He has kept among us, in times of peace, Standing Armies without the Consent of our legislature.

He has affected to render the Military independent of and superior to the Civil Power.

He has combined with others to subject us to a jurisdiction foreign to our constitution, and unacknowledged by our laws; giving his Assent to their acts of pretended legislation:

For quartering large bodies of armed troops among us:

For protecting them, by a mock Trial, from Punishment for any Murders which they should commit on the Inhabitants of these States:

For cutting off our Trade with all parts of the world:

For imposing taxes on us without our Consent:

For depriving us in many cases, of the benefits of Trial by Jury:

For transporting us beyond Seas to be tried for pretended offences:

For abolishing the free System of English Laws in a neighbouring Province, establishing therein an Arbitrary government, and enlarging its Boundaries so as to render it at once an example and fit instrument for introducing the same absolute rule into these Colonies:

For taking away our Charters, abolishing our most valuable Laws, and altering fundamentally the Forms of our Governments:

For suspending our own Legislature, and declaring themselves invested with Power to legislate for us in all cases whatsoever.

He has abdicated Government here, by declaring us out of his Protection and waging War against us.

He has plundered our seas, ravaged our Coasts, burnt our towns, and destroyed the lives of our people.

He is at this time transporting large armies of foreign mercenaries to compleat the works of death, desolation, and tyranny, already begun with circumstances of Cruelty & perfidy scarcely paralleled in the most barbarous ages, and totally unworthy the Head of a civilized nation.

He has constrained our fellow Citizens taken Captive on the high Seas to bear Arms against their Country, to become the executioners of their friends and Brethren, or to fall themselves by their Hands.

He has excited domestic insurrections amongst us, and has endeavoured to bring on the inhabitants of our frontiers, the merciless Indian Savages, whose known rule of warfare, is an undistinguished destruction of all ages, sexes and conditions.

In every stage of these Oppressions We have Petitioned for Redress in the most humble terms: Our repeated Petitions have been answered only by repeated injury. A Prince, whose character is thus marked by every act which may define a Tyrant, is unfit to be the ruler of a free People.

Nor have We been wanting in attention to our British brethren. We have warned them from time to time of attempts by their legislature to extend an unwarrantable jurisdiction over us. We have reminded them of the circumstances of our emigration and settlement here. We have appealed to their native justice and magnanimity, and we have conjured them by the ties of our common kindred to disavow these usurpations, which, would inevitably interrupt our connections and correspondence. They too have been deaf to the voice of justice and of consanguinity. We must, therefore, acquiesce in the necessity, which denounces our Separation, and hold them, as we hold the rest of mankind, Enemies in War, in Peace Friends.

We, therefore, the Representatives of the united States of America, in General Congress, Assembled, appealing to the Supreme Judge of the world for the rectitude of our intentions, do, in the Name, and by Authority of the good People of these Colonies, solemnly publish and declare, That these United Colonies are, and of Right ought to be Free and Independent States; that they are Absolved from all Allegiance to the British Crown, and that all political connection between them and the State of Great Britain, is and ought to be totally dissolved; and that as Free and Independent States, they have full Power to levy War, conclude Peace, contract Alliances, establish Commerce, and to do all other Acts and Things which Independent States may of right do. And for the support of this Declaration, with a firm reliance on the Protection of Divine Providence, we mutually pledge to each other our Lives, our Fortunes and our sacred Honour.

JOHN HANCOCK.

New Hampshire
 JOSIAH BARTLETT,
 WM. WHIPPLE,
 MATTHEW THORNTON.

Massachusetts-Bay
 SAML. ADAMS,
 JOHN ADAMS,
 ROBT. TREAT PAINE,
 ELBRIDGE GERRY.

Rhode Island
 STEP. HOPKINS,
 WILLIAM ELLERY.

Connecticut
 ROGER SHERMAN,
 SAM'EL HUNTINGTON,
 WM. WILLIAMS,
 OLIVER WOLCOTT.

New York
 WM. FLOYD,
 PHIL. LIVINGSTON,
 FRANS. LEWIS,
 LEWIS MORRIS.

Pennsylvania
 ROBT. MORRIS,
 BENJAMIN RUSH,
 BENJA. FRANKLIN,
 JOHN MORTON,
 GEO. CLYMER,
 JAS. SMITH,
 GEO. TAYLOR,
 JAMES WILSON,
 GEO. ROSS.

Delaware
CAESAR RODNEY,
GEO. READ,
THO. M'KEAN.

Georgia
BUTTON GWINNETT,
LYMAN HALL,
GEO. WALTON.

Maryland
SAMUEL CHASE,
WM. PACA,
THOS. STONE,
CHARLES CARROLL of Carrollton.

Virginia
GEORGE WYTHE,
RICHARD HENRY LEE,
TH. JEFFERSON,
BENJA. HARRISON,
THS. NELSON, JR.,
FRANCIS LIGHTFOOT LEE,
CARTER BRAXTON.

North Carolina
WM. HOOPER,
JOSEPH HEWES,
JOHN PENN.

South Carolina
EDWARD RUTLEDGE,
THOS. HEYWARD, JUNR.,
THOMAS LYNCH, JUNR,
ARTHUR MIDDLETON.

New Jersey
RICHD. STOCKTON,
JNO. WITHERSPOON,
FRAS. HOPKINSON,
JOHN HART,
ABRA. CLARK.

From AN INQUIRY INTO THE NATURE AND CAUSES OF THE WEALTH OF NATIONS, 1776

Adam Smith

Published by Smith (1723–90) in the same year as the Declaration of Independence, *The Wealth of Nations* examined the sources of society's increasing riches and exulted free enterprise as the cause. Acquisitive self-interest, non-regulation, the division of labour and competition were the means, according to the Scots economist, to "the progress of opulence".

The Wealth of Nations has never lost its lustre as a work of political economy, although Smith was not quite the hardcore, heartless advocate of "laissez faire" it is usually assumed. He disliked government because he considered it aided the rich against the poor, and intended that economics would implement a sympathetic morality.

On Freedom of Trade

The unproductive class, that of merchants, artificers, and manufacturers, is maintained and employed altogether at the expense of the two other classes – of that of proprietors, and of that of cultivators. They furnish it both with the materials of its work and with the fund of its subsistence, with the corn and cattle which it consumes while it is employed about that work. The proprietors and cultivators finally pay both the wages of all the workmen of the unproductive class, and the profits of all their employers. Those workmen and their employers are properly the servants of the proprietors and cultivators. They are only servants who work without doors, as menial servants work within. Both the one and the other, however, are equally maintained at the expense of the same masters. The labour of both is equally unproductive. It adds nothing to the value of the sum total of the rude produce of the land. Instead of increasing the value of that sum total, it is a charge and expense which must be paid out of it.

The unproductive class, however, is not only useful, but greatly useful to the other two classes. By means of the industry of merchants, artificers, and manufacturers, the proprietors and cultivators can purchase both the foreign goods and the manufactured produce of their own country which they have occasion for, with the produce of a much smaller quantity of their own labour than what they would be obliged to employ if they were to attempt, in an awkward and unskilful manner, either to import the one or to make the other for their own use. By means of the unproductive class, the cultivators are delivered from many cares which would otherwise distract their attention from the cultivation of land. The superiority of produce, which, in consequence of this undivided attention, they are enabled to raise, is fully sufficient to pay the whole expense which the maintenance and employment of the unproductive class costs either the proprietors or themselves. The industry of merchants, artificers, and manufacturers, though in its own nature altogether unproductive, yet contributes in this manner indirectly to increase the produce of the land. It increases the productive powers of productive labour, by leaving it at liberty to confine itself to its proper employment, the cultivation of land; and the plough goes frequently the easier and the better by means of the labour of the man whose business is most remote from the plough.

It can never be the interest of the proprietors and cultivators to restrain or to discourage in any respect the industry of merchants, artificers, and manufacturers. The greater the liberty which this unproductive class enjoys, the greater will be the competition in all the different trades which compose it, and the cheaper will the other two classes be supplied, both with foreign goods and with the manufactured produce of their own country.

It can never be the interest of the unproductive class to oppress the other two classes. It is the surplus produce of the land, or what remains after deducting the maintenance, first, of the cultivators, and afterwards of the proprietors, that maintains and employs the unproductive class. The greater this surplus, the greater must likewise be the maintenance and employment of that class. The establishment of perfect justice, of liberty, and of perfect equality, is the very simple secret which most effectually secures the highest degree of prosperity to all the three classes.

The merchants, artificers, and manufacturers of those mercantile states which, like Holland and Hamburg, consist chiefly of this unproductive class, are in the same manner maintained and employed altogether at the expense of the proprietors and cultivators of land. The only difference is, that those proprietors and cultivators are, the greater part of them, placed at a most inconvenient distance from the merchants, artificers, and manufacturers whom they supply with the materials of their work and the fund of their subsistence, are the inhabitants of other countries, and the subjects of other governments.

Such mercantile states, however, are not only useful, but greatly useful to the inhabitants of those other countries. They fill up, in some measure, a very important void, and supply the place of the merchants, artificers, and manufacturers whom the inhabitants of those countries ought to find at home, but whom, from some defect in their policy, they do not find at home.

It can never be the interest of those landed nations, if I may call them so, to discourage or distress the industry of such mercantile states, by imposing high duties upon their trade, or upon the commodities which they furnish. Such duties, by rendering those commodities dearer, could serve only to sink the real value of the surplus produce of their own land, with which, or, what comes to the same thing, with the price of which those commodities are purchased. Such duties could serve only to discourage the increase of that surplus produce, and consequently the improvement and cultivation of their own land. The most effectual expedient, on the contrary, for raising the value of that surplus produce, for encouraging its increase, and consequently the improvement and cultivation of their own land, would be to allow the most perfect freedom to the trade of all such mercantile nations.

This perfect freedom of trade would even be the most effectual expedient for supplying them, in due time, with all the artificers, man-ufacturers, and merchants whom they wanted at home, and for filling up in the properest and most advantageous manner that very important void which they felt there.

The continual increase of the surplus produce of their land would, in due time, create a greater capital than what could be employed with the ordinary rate of profit in the improvement and cultivation of land; and the surplus part of it would naturally turn itself to the employment of artificers and manufacturers at home. But those artificers and manufacturers, finding at home both the materials of their work and the fund of their subsistence, might immediately, even with much less art and skill, be able to work as cheap as the like artificers and manufacturers of such mer-cantile states, who had both to bring from a great distance. Even though, from want of art and skill, they might not for some time be able to work as cheap, yet, finding a market at home, they might be able to sell their work there as cheap as that of the artificers and manufacturers of such mercantile states, which could not be brought to that market but from so great a distance; and as their art and skill improved, they would soon be able to sell it cheaper. The artificers and manufacturers of such mercantile states, therefore, would immediately be rivalled in the market of those landed nations, and soon after undersold and justled out of it altogether. The cheapness of the manufactures of those landed nations, in conse-quence of the gradual improvements of art and skill, would, in due time, extend their sale beyond the home market, and carry them to many foreign markets, from which they would in the same manner gradually justle out many of the manufactures of such mercantile nations.

This continual increase both of the rude and manufactured produce of those landed nations would in due time create a greater capital than could, with the ordinary rate of profit, be employed either in agriculture or in manufactures. The surplus of this capital would naturally turn itself to foreign trade, and be employed in exporting to foreign countries such parts of the rude and manufactured produce of its own country as exceeded the demand of the home market. In the exportation of the produce of their own country, the merchants of a landed nation would have an advantage of the same kind over those of mercantile nations, which its artificers and manufacturers had over the artificers and manufacturers of such nations: the advantage of finding at home that cargo, and those stores and provisions, which the others were obliged to seek for at a distance. With inferior art and skill in navigation, therefore, they would be able to sell that cargo as cheap in foreign markets as the merchants of such mercantile nations; and with equal art and skill they would be able to sell it cheaper. They would soon, therefore, rival those mercantile nations in this branch of foreign trade, and in due time would justle them out of it altogether.

According to this liberal and generous system, therefore, the most advantageous method in which a landed nation can raise up artificers, manufacturers, and merchants of its own, is to grant the most perfect freedom of trade to the artificers, manufacturers, and merchants of all other nations. It thereby raises the value of the surplus produce of its own land, of which the continual increase gradually establishes a fund which in due time necessarily raises up all the artificers, manufacturers, and merchants whom it has occasion for.

RELIGIOUS TOLERATION, 1779

Gotthold Ephraim Lessing

Lessing was a leading figure in the German Enlightenment, both as dramatist and philosopher. In this extract from his play *Nathan the Wise*, 1779, the Jewish Nathan is answering Saladin's persistent question, "Which is the true religion?"

NATHAN

In days of yore a man lived in the East,
Who owned a ring of marvellous worth,
Given to him by a hand beloved.
The stone was opal, and shed a hundred lovely rays,
But chiefly it possessed the secret power
To make the owner loved of God and man,
If he but wore it in this faith and confidence;
What wonder then that this man in the East
Ne'er from his finger took the ring,
And so arranged it should forever with his house remain,
Namely, thus: He bequeathed it to
The most beloved of his sons,
Firmly prescribing that he in turn
Should leave it to the dearest of his sons;
And always thus the dearest, without respect to birth,
Became the head and chieftain of the house
By virtue of the ring alone.
You understand me, Sultan?

SALADIN

I understand. Proceed.

NATHAN

The ring, descending thus from son to son,
Came to the father of three sons at last,
All three of whom obeyed him equally,
And all of whom he therefore loved alike.
From time to time indeed, now one seemed worthiest of the ring,
And now another, now the third,
Just as it happened one or other with him were alone;
And his o'erflowing heart was not divided with the other two;
And so to each one of the three he gave
The promise – in pious weakness done –
He should possess the wondrous ring.
This then went on long as it could;
But then at last it came to dying,
Which brings the father into sore perplexity.
It pains him much to practise such deceit
Upon two sons who rested so upon his word.
What can be done? In secret
He seeks out a skilful artist,
And from him orders yet two other rings,
Just to the pattern of his own,
And urges him to spare neither pains nor gold,
To make a perfect match.
The artist so succeeded in his task,
That, when he brought the jewels home,
The father even failed to tell which was the pattern ring.
Now, glad and joyous, he calls his sons –
But separately of course – gives each
A special blessing with his ring, and dies.
You hear me, Sultan?

SALADIN
(*Who, somewhat moved, turns from him*)

I hear, I hear;
But pray get ended with your tale.
You soon will be?

NATHAN

I'm at the end,
For what still follows is self-understood.
Scarce was the father dead,
When each one with his ring appears
Claiming each the headship of the house.
Inspections, quarrelling, and complaints ensue;

But all in vain, the veritable ring
Was not distinguishable –

   (*After a pause, during which he expects the Sultan's answer*)

Almost as indistinguishable as to us,
Is now – the true religion.

SALADIN

What? Is that meant as answer to my question?

NATHAN

'Tis meant but to excuse myself, because
I lack the boldness to discriminate between the rings,
Which the father by express intent had made
So that they might not be distinguished.

SALADIN

The rings! Don't play with me.
I thought the faiths which I have named
Were easily distinguishable,
Even to their raiment, even to meat and drink.

NATHAN

But yet not as regards their proofs;
For do not all rest upon history, written or traditional?
And history can also be accepted
Only on faith and trust. Is it not so?
Now, whose faith and confidence do we least misdoubt?
That of our relatives? Of those whose flesh and blood we are,
Of those who from our childhood
Have lavished on us proofs of love,
Who ne'er deceived us, unless 'twere wholesome for us so?
How can I place less faith in my forefathers
Than you in yours? or the reverse?
Can I desire of you to load your ancestors with lies,
So that you contradict not mine? Or the reverse?
And to the Christian the same applies.
Is that not so?

SALADIN

[By the living God, the man is right. I must be dumb.]

NATHAN

Let us return unto our rings.
As said, the sons accused each other,
And each one swore before the judge
He had received his ring directly
From his father's hand – which was quite true –
And that, indeed, after having long his promise held,
To enjoy eventually the ring's prerogative,
Which was no less the truth.
Each one insisted that it was impossible
His father could play false with him,
And ere he could suspect so dear and true a father,
He was compelled, howe'er inclined to think
The best of them, to accuse his brothers
Of this treacherous act, to unmask the traitors,
And avenge himself.

SALADIN

Well, and the judge?
I'm curious to hear what you will give
The judge to say. Go on.

NATHAN

The judge said this: Produce your father here
At once, or I'll dismiss you from this court.
Think you I'm here but to solve riddles?
Or would you wait till the true ring itself will speak?
But stop; I've just been told that the right ring,
Contains the wondrous gift to make its wearer loved,
Agreeable alike to God and man.
That must decide, for the false rings will not have this power.
Now which one do the other two love most?
Come, speak out; you're silent?
Do the rings work only backwards and not outwardly?
Does each one love himself the best?
Then you're all three deceived deceivers;
None of your rings are genuine.
The genuine ring is no doubt lost.
To hide the loss and to supply its place
The father ordered other three.

SALADIN

Splendid, splendid!

NATHAN

The judge went further on to say:
If you will have my judgment, not my advice,
Then go. But my advice is this:
You take the matter as it stands.
If each one had his ring straight from his father,
So let each believe *his* ring the true one.
'Tis possible your father would no longer tolerate
The tyranny of this one ring in his family,
And surely loved you all – and all alike,
And that he would not two oppress
By favouring the third.
Now then, let each one emulate in affection
Untouched by prejudice. Let each one strive
To gain the prize of proving by results
The virtue of his ring, and aid its power
With gentleness and heartiest friendliness,
With benevolence and true devotedness to God;
And if the virtue of the ring will then
Have proved itself among your children's children.
I summon them to appear again
Before this judgment seat,
After a thousand thousand years.
Here then will sit a judge more wise than I,
Who will pronounce. Go you.
So said the modest judge.

SALADIN

God, oh God!

NATHAN

Saladin, if now you feel yourself to be
That promised sage –

SALADIN
(*Who rushes to him and seizes his hand, which to the end he does not let go*)
I dust? I nothing? Oh God!

NATHAN

What ails thee, Sultan?

SALADIN

Nathan, dear Nathan, your judge's thousand
Thousand years have not yet fled,
His judgment seat's not become mine.
Go, go; but be my friend.

THE DECLARATION OF THE RIGHTS OF MAN AND CITIZEN (FRANCE), 1789

Inspired by the lofty teachings of the Enlightenment, by the still warm example of the American Revolution, the people of France seized their opportunity to overthrow royal despotism in 1789. Obliged by bankruptcy to convene an Estates General – the first time a monarch had called one for 150 years – Louis XVI was promptly told by that body politic that "The assembled nation cannot receive orders." That done, the National Assembly proceeded during August to draft the death notice of the French feudal order. The final version of "The Declaration of the Rights of Man and Citizen" was approved by vote on 26 August.

The representatives of the French people, organized in National Assembly, considering that ignorance, forgetfulness, or contempt of the rights of man, are the sole causes of the public miseries and of the corruption of governments, have resolved to set forth in a solemn declaration the natural, inalienable and sacred rights of man, in order that this declaration, being ever present to all the members of the social body, may unceasingly remind them of their rights and duties; in order that the acts of the legislative power and those of the executive power may be each moment compared with the aim of every political institution and thereby may be more respected: and in order that the demands of the citizens, grounded henceforth upon simple and incontestable principles, may always take the direction of maintaining the constitution and the welfare of all.

In consequence, the National Assembly recognizes and declares, in the presence and under the auspices of the Supreme Being, the following rights of man and citizen.

1. Men are born and remain free and equal in rights. Social distinctions can be based only upon public utility.
2. The aim of every political association is the preservation of the natural and imprescriptible rights of man. These rights are liberty, property, security and resistance to oppression.
3. The source of all sovereignty is essentially in the nation; no body, no individual can exercise authority that does not proceed from it in plain terms.
4. Liberty consists in the power to do anything that does not injure others; accordingly, the exercise of the natural rights of each man has no limits except those that secure to the other members of society the enjoyment of these same rights. These limits can be determined only by law.
5. The law has the right to forbid only such actions as are injurious to society. Nothing can be forbidden that is not interdicted by the law, and no one can be constrained to do that which it does not order.
6. Law is the expression of the general will. All citizens have the right to take part personally, or by their representatives, in its formation. It must be the same for all whether it protects or punishes. All citizens, being equal in its eyes, are equally eligible to all public dignities, places, and employments, according to their capacities, and without other distinction than that of their virtues and their talents.
7. No man can be accused, arrested, or detained, except in the cases determined by the law and according to the forms that it has pre-scribed. Those who procure, expedite, execute, or cause to be executed arbitrary orders ought to be punished; but every citizen summoned or seized in virtue of the law ought to render instant obedience; he makes himself guilty by resistance.
8. The law ought to establish only penalties that are strictly and obviously necessary, and no one can be punished except in virtue of a law established and promulgated prior to the offence and legally applied.
9. Every man being presumed innocent until he has been pronounced guilty; if it is thought indispensable to arrest him, all severity that may not be necessary to secure his person ought to be strictly suppressed by law.
10. No one should be disturbed on account of his opinions, even religious, provided their manifestation does not derange the public order established by law.
11. The free communication of ideas and opinions is one of the most precious of the rights of man; every citizen then can freely speak, write and print, subject to responsibility for the abuse of this freedom in the cases determined by law.

12. The guarantee of the rights of man and citizen requires a public force; this force then is instituted for the advantage of all and not for the personal benefit of those to whom it is entrusted.

13. For the maintenance of the public force and for the expenses of administration a general tax is indispensable; it ought to be equally apportioned among all the citizens according to their means.

14. All the citizens have the right to ascertain by themselves or by their representatives, the necessity of the public tax, to consent to it freely, to follow the employment of it, and to determine the quota, the assessment, the collection, and the duration of it.

15. Society has the right to call for an account of his administration from every public agent.

16. Any society in which the guarantee of rights is not secured, or the separation of powers not determined, has no constitution at all.

17. Property being a sacred and inviolable right, no one can be deprived of it, unless a legally established public necessity evidently demands it, under the condition of a just and prior indemnity.

THE BILL OF RIGHTS, 1791

Which comprises the first ten Amendments of the Constitution of the United States of America, ratified by the states in December 1791:

Art. I

Congress shall make no law respecting an establishment of religion, or prohibiting the free exercise thereof; or abridging the freedom of speech, or of the press; or the right of the people peaceably to assemble, and to petition the government for a redress of grievances.

Art. II

A well regulated Militia, being necessary to the security of a free State, the right of the people to keep and bear Arms, shall not be infringed.

Art. III

No Soldier shall, in time of peace be quartered in any house, without the consent of the Owner, nor in time of war, but in a manner to be prescribed by law.

Art. IV

The right of the people to be secure in their persons, houses, papers, and effects, against unreasonable searches and seizures, shall not be violated, and no Warrants shall issue, but upon probable cause, supported by Oath or affirmation, and particularly describing the place to be searched, and the persons or things to be seized.

Art. V

No person shall be held to answer for a capital, or otherwise infamous crime, unless on a presentment or indictment of a Grand Jury, except in cases arising in the land or naval forces, or in the Militia, when in actual service in time of War or public danger; nor shall any person be subject for the same offence to be twice put in jeopardy of life or limb; nor shall be compelled in any criminal case to be a witness against himself, nor be deprived of life, liberty, or property, without due process of law; nor shall private property be taken for public use, without just compensation.

Art. VI

In all criminal prosecutions, the accused shall enjoy the right to a speedy and public trial, by an impartial jury of the State and district wherein the crime shall have been committed, which district shall have been previously ascertained by law, and to be informed of the nature and cause of the accusation; to be confronted with the witnesses against him; to have compulsory process for obtaining witnesses in his favour, and to have the Assistance of Counsel for his defence.

Art. VII

In Suits at common law, where the value in controversy shall exceed twenty dollars, the right of trial by jury shall be preserved, and no fact tried by a jury, shall be otherwise re-examined in any Court of the United States, than according to the rules of the common law.

Art. VIII

Excessive bail shall not be required, nor excessive fines imposed, nor cruel and unusual punishments inflicted.

Art. IX

The enumeration in the Constitution, of certain rights, shall not be construed to deny or disparage others retained by the people.

Art. X

The powers not delegated to the United States by the Constitution, nor prohibited by it to the States, are reserved to the States respectively, or to the people.

Since 1791, there have been sixteen additional amendments to the Constitution. These include:

Art. XIII 18 Dec. 1865

Sec. 1. Neither slavery nor involuntary servitude, except as a punishment for crime whereof the party shall have been duly convicted, shall exist within the United States, or any place subject to their jurisdiction.
Sec. 2. Congress shall have power to enforce this article by appropriate legislation.

Art. XIV 28 July 1868

Sec. 1. All persons born or naturalized in the United States, and subject to the jurisdiction thereof, are citizens of the United States and of the State wherein they reside. No State shall make or enforce any law which shall abridge the privileges or immunities of citizens of the United States; nor shall any State deprive any person of life, liberty, or property, without due process of law; nor deny to any person within its jurisdiction the equal protection of the laws.
Sec. 2. Representatives shall be apportioned among the several States according to their respective numbers, counting the whole number of persons in each State, excluding Indians not taxed. But when the right to vote at any election for the choice of electors for President and Vice President of the United States, Representatives in Congress, the Executive and Judicial officers of a State, or the members of the Legislature thereof, is denied to any of the male inhabitants of such State, being twenty-one years of age, and citizens of the United States, or in any way abridged, except for participation in rebellion, or other crime, the basis of representation therein shall be reduced in the proportion which the number of such male citizens shall bear to the whole number of male citizens twenty-one years of age in such State.
Sec. 3. No person shall be a Senator or Representative in Congress, or elector of President and Vice President, or hold any office, civil or military, under the United States, or under any State, who, having previously taken an oath, as a member of Congress, or as an officer of the United States, or as a member of any State legislature, or as an executive or judicial officer of any State, to support the Constitution of the United States, shall have engaged in insurrection or rebellion against the same, or given aid or comfort to the enemies thereof. But Congress may by a vote of two-thirds of each House, remove such disability.
Sec. 4. The validity of the public debt of the United States, authorized by law, including debts incurred for payment of pensions and bounties for services in suppressing insurrection or rebellion, shall not be questioned.

But neither the United States nor any State shall assume or pay any debt or obligation incurred in aid of insurrection or rebellion against the United States, or any claim for the loss or emancipation of any slave; but all such debts, obligations and claims shall be held illegal and void.

Sec. 5. The Congress shall have power to enforce, by appropriate legislation, the provisions of this article.

Art. XV 30 March 1870

Sec. 1. The right of citizens of the United States to vote shall not be denied or abridged by the United States or by any State on account of race, colour, or previous condition of servitude –

Sec. 2. The Congress shall have power to enforce this article by appropriate legislation –

Art. XIX 26 August 1920

The right of citizens of the United States to vote shall not be denied or abridged by the United States or by any States on account of sex.

The Congress shall have power to enforce this article by appropriate legislation.

From THE RIGHTS OF MAN, 1791–2

Thomas Paine

The Rights of Man was written in reply to Edmund Burke's *Reflections on the Revolution in France*. It was Burke's contention that societies grew organically over time, it was habit which ordered citizenish behaviour; thus no society could be suddenly improved to meet a set of abstract standards. Accordingly, the French Revolution was illegitimate.

Paine's *Rights of Man* defended the French Revolution. More than that, it made a classic statement of the perfectability of humanity, of the possibility of rational government. Against Burke, Paine maintained that legitimate government proceeded not from continuity, but from recognition of natural rights, which were possessed by all men in equal measure. Accordingly any society *not* based on democratic republicanism (such as revolutionary France) was illegitimate. Not that Paine was merely an idealist; part II of *Rights of Man* advocated such practical measures as old age pensions and free education – more than a hundred years before they were introduced in Britain – and contained a fully-costed budget for their financing.

Paine was arguably the most unpopular personage of the late 18th century. A British subject, born in 1737 to a Norfolk Quaker family, his support for the French Revolution (and criticism of the British monarchy) earned him a treason charge in his native land. He escaped to France, where he was feted for *Rights of Man* and elected to the National Convention; alas, his opposition to the execution of Louis XVI caused his imprisonment, and only a technicality saved him from the guillotine. In 1802 he revisited America, where his pamphlet *Common Sense*, 1776, had played an important part in steeling America to declare Independence. Unfortunately Paine's American friends – which included George Washington – cold-shouldered him because of the atheistic attack on religion he had mounted in *The Age of Reason*, 1794–6. He died impoverished and alone in 1809, on the small farm at New Rochelle which the once admiring state of New York had granted him.

Before anything can be reasoned upon to a conclusion, certain facts, principles, or data, to reason from, must be established, admitted, or denied. Mr Burke, with his usual outrage, abuses the *Declaration of the Rights of Man*, published by the National Assembly of France as the basis on which the constitution of France is built. This he calls "paltry and blurred sheets of paper about the rights of man." Does Mr Burke mean to deny that man has any rights? If he does, then he must mean that there are no such things as rights anywhere, and that he has none himself; for who is there in the world but man? But if Mr Burke means to admit that man has rights, the question then will be: What are those rights, and how came man by them originally?

The error of those who reason by precedents drawn from antiquity, respecting the rights of man, is that they do not go far enough into antiquity. They do not go the whole way. They stop in some of the intermediate stages of a hundred or a thousand years, and produce what was then done, as a rule for the present day. This is not authority at all. If we travel still farther into antiquity, we shall find a direct contrary opinion and practice prevailing; and if antiquity is to be authority, a thousand such authorities may be produced, successively contradicting each other; but if we proceed on, we shall at last come out right; we shall come to the time when man came from the hand of his Maker. What was he then? Man. Man was his high and only title, and a higher cannot be given him. But of titles I shall speak hereafter.

We are now got at the origin of man, and at the origin of his rights. As to the manner in which the world has been governed from that day to this, it is no farther any concern of ours than to make a proper use of the errors or the improvements which the history of it presents. Those who lived a hundred or a thousand years ago, were then moderns, as we are now. They had *their* ancients, and those ancients had others, and we also shall be ancients in our turn. If the mere name of antiquity is to govern in the affairs of life, the people who are to live an hundred or a thousand years hence, may as well take us for a precedent, as we make a precedent of those who lived a hundred or a thousand years ago. The fact is, that portions of antiquity, by proving everything, establish nothing. It is authority against authority all the way, till we come to the divine origin of the rights of man at the creation. Here our inquiries find a resting-place, and our reason finds a home. If a dispute about the rights of man had arisen at the distance of an hundred years from the creation, it is to this source of authority they must have referred, and it is to this same source of authority that we must now refer.

Though I mean not to touch upon any sectarian principle of religion, yet it may be worth observing, that the genealogy of Christ is traced to Adam. Why then not trace the rights of man to the creation of man? I will answer the question. Because there have been upstart Governments, thrusting themselves between and presumptuously working to *un-make* man.

If any generation of men ever possessed the right of dictating the mode by which the world should be governed for ever, it was the first generation that existed; and if that generation did it not, no succeeding generation can show any authority for doing it, nor can set any up. The illuminating and divine principle of the equal rights of man (for it has its origin from the Maker of man) relates, not only to the living individuals, but to generations of men succeeding each other. Every generation is equal in rights to the generations which preceded it, by the same rule that every individual is born equal in rights with his contemporary.

Every history of the creation, and every traditionary account, whether from the lettered or unlettered world, however they may vary in their opinion or belief of certain particulars, all agree in establishing one point, *the unity of man*; by which I mean that men are all of *one degree*, and consequently that all men are born equal, and with equal natural rights, in the same manner as if posterity had been continued by *creation* instead of *generation*, the latter being only the mode by which the former is carried forward; and consequently every child born into the world must be considered as deriving its existence from God. The world is as new to him as it was to the first man that existed, and his natural right in it is of the same kind.

The Mosaic account of the creation, whether taken as divine authority or merely historical, is fully up to this point, *the unity or equality of man*. The expressions admit of no controversy. "And God said, Let us make man in our own image. In the image of God created he him; male and female created he them." The distinction of sexes is pointed out, but no other distinction is even implied. If this be not divine authority, it is at least historical authority, and shows that the equality of man, so far from being a modern doctrine, is the oldest upon record.

It is also to be observed that all the religions known in the world are founded, so far as they relate to man, on the *unity of man*, as being all of one degree. Whether in heaven or in hell, or in whatever state man may be supposed to exist hereafter, the good and the bad are the only distinctions. Nay, even the laws of Governments are obliged to slide into this principle, by making degrees to consist in crimes and not in persons.

It is one of the greatest of all truths, and of the highest advantage to cultivate. By considering man in this light, and by instructing him to consider himself in this light, it places him in a close connection with all his duties, whether to his Creator or to the creation, of which he is a part; and it is only when he forgets his origin, or, to use a more fashionable phrase, his *birth and family*, that he becomes dissolute. It is not among the least of the evils of the present existing Governments in all parts of Europe that man, considered as man, is thrown back to a vast distance from his Maker, and the artificial chasm filled up by a succession of barriers, or sort of turnpike gates, through which he has to pass. I will quote Mr Burke's catalogue of barriers that he has set up between Man and his Maker. Putting himself in the character of a herald, he says: *We fear God – we look with* AWE *to kings – with affection to Parliaments – with duty to magistrates – with reverence to priests, and with respect to nobility.* Mr Burke has forgotten to put in "*chivalry*". He has also forgotten to put in Peter.

The duty of man is not a wilderness of turnpike gates, through which he is to pass by tickets from one to the other. It is plain and simple, and consists but of two points. His duty to God, which every man must feel; and with respect to his neighbour, to do as he would be done by. If those to whom power is delegated do well, they will be respected; if not, they will be despised; and with regard to those to whom no power is delegated, but who assume it, the rational world can know nothing of them.

Hitherto we have spoken only (and that but in part) of the natural rights of man. We have now to consider the civil rights of man, and to show how the one originates from the other. Man did not enter into society to become *worse* than he was before, not to have fewer rights than he had before, but to have those rights better secured. His natural rights are the foundation of all his civil rights. But in order to pursue this distinction with more precision, it will be necessary to mark the different qualities of natural and civil rights.

A few words will explain this. Natural rights are those which appertain to man in right of his existence. Of this kind are all the intellectual rights, or rights of the mind, and also all those rights of acting as an individual for his own comfort and happiness, which are not injurious to the natural rights of others. Civil rights are those which appertain to man in right of his being a member of society. Every civil right has for its foundation some natural right pre-existing in the individual, but to the enjoyment of which his individual power is not, in all cases, sufficiently competent. Of this kind are all those which relate to security and protection.

From this short view it will be easy to distinguish between that class of natural rights which man retains after entering into society and those which he throws into the common stock as a member of society.

The natural rights which he retains are all those in which the *power* to execute it is as perfect in the individual as the right itself. Among this class, as is before mentioned, are all the intellectual rights, or rights of the mind; consequently religion is one of those rights. The natural rights which are not retained, are all those in which, though the right is perfect in the individual, the power to execute them is defective. They answer not his purpose. A man, by natural right, has a right to judge in his own cause; and so far as the right of the mind is concerned, he never surrenders it. But what availeth it him to judge, if he has not power to redress? He therefore deposits this right in the common stock of society, and takes the arm of society, of which he is a part, in preference and in addition to his own. Society *grants* him nothing. Every man is a proprietor in society, and draws on the capital as a matter of right.

From *VINDICATION OF THE RIGHTS OF WOMAN,* 1792

Mary Wollstonecraft

Wollstonecraft's *Vindication of the Rights of Woman* has been called the 'feminist declaration of independence".[1] If all the Western world of the late 18th century was consumed by the yeas and nays of the rights of man, it was literally the male human that was meant. Women had little protection under law, no representation in politics, whatever their class, and small opportunity to make a life in public. Nearly all professions were barred them. It was into this patriarchal universe that Wollstonecraft's *Vindication of the Rights of Woman* dropped like a cannon ball in 1792. Wollstonecraft, an Anglo radical writer born in 1759, argued with "energetic emotions" for the equality of the sexes, beginning with the education system. Her arguments were too revolutionary raw for most of her contemporaries, and when John Stuart Mill rehearsed them in his 1869 *On the Subjection of Women* he fared little better. (*Subjection* was the only one of Mill's books to lose money). As time has marched on, however, it has caught up with Wollstonecraft and she indelibly impressed the women's liberation campaigners of the 60s and 70s, among them Germaine Greer (*The Female Eunuch*, 1970) and Kate Millett (*Sexual Politics*, 1971).

Wollstonecraft married the anarchist author William Godwin in 1797, but died in childbirth shortly afterwards. The child, Mary, survived, and later married Percy Shelley. She became famous in her own right as the author of *Frankenstein*, 1818.

I shall not go back to the remote annals of antiquity to trace the history of woman; it is sufficient to allow that she has always been either a slave or a despot, and to remark that each of these situations equally retards the

---

[1] Miriam Brody (ed) *Vindication of the Rights of Woman*, Pelican Books, 1975

progress of reason. The grand source of female folly and vice has ever appeared to me to arise from narrowness of mind; and the very constitution of civil governments has put almost insuperable obstacles in the way to prevent the cultivation of the female understanding; yet virtue can be built on no other foundation. The same obstacles are thrown in the way of the rich, and the same consequences ensue.

Necessity has been proverbially termed the mother of invention; the aphorism may be extended to virtue. It is an acquirement, and an acquirement to which pleasure must be sacrificed; and who sacrifices pleasure when it is within the grasp, whose mind has not been opened and strengthened by adversity, or the pursuit of knowledge goaded on by necessity? Happy is it when people have the cares of life to struggle with, for these struggles prevent their becoming a prey to enervating vices, merely from idleness. But if from their birth men and women be placed in a torrid zone, with the meridian sun of pleasure darting directly upon them, how can they sufficiently brace their minds to discharge the duties of life, or even to relish the affections that carry them out of themselves?

Pleasure is the business of woman's life, according to the present modification of society; and while it continues to be so, little can be expected from such weak beings. Inheriting in a lineal descent from the first fair defect in nature – the sovereignty of beauty – they have, to maintain their power, resigned the natural rights which the exercise of reason might have procured them, and chosen rather to be short-lived queens than labour to obtain the sober pleasures that arise from equality. Exalted by their inferiority (this sounds like a contradiction), they constantly demand homage as women, though experience should teach them that the men who pride themselves upon paying this arbitrary insolent respect to the sex, with the most scrupulous exactness, are most inclined to tyrannize over, and despise the very weakness they cherish. Often do they repeat Mr Hume's[1] sentiments, when, comparing the French and Athenian character, he alludes to women – "But what is more singular in this whimsical nation, say I to the Athenians, is, that a frolic of yours during the saturnalia, when the slaves are served by their masters, is seriously continued by them through the whole year, and through the whole course of their lives, accompanied, too, with some circumstances, which still further augment the absurdity and ridicule. Your sport only elevates for a few days those whom fortune has thrown down, and whom she too, in sport, may really elevate for ever above you. But this nation gravely exalts those whom nature has subjected to them, and whose inferiority and infirmities are absolutely incurable. The women, though without virtue, are their masters and sovereigns."

[1] David Hume (1711–76), Scottish philosopher. Author of *A Treatise of Human Nature*, 1739–45.

Ah! why do women – I write with affectionate solicitude – condescend to receive a degree of attention and respect from strangers different from that reciprocation of civility which the dictates of humanity and the politeness of civilization authorize between man and man? And why do they not discover, when in the noon of beauty's power, that they are treated like queens only to be deluded by hollow respect, till they are led to resign, or not assume, their natural prerogatives? Confined, then, in cages like the feathered race, they have nothing to do but to plume themselves, and stalk with mock majesty from perch to perch. It is true they are provided with food and raiment, for which they neither toil nor spin; but health, liberty, and virtue are given in exchange. But where, amongst mankind, has been found sufficient strength of mind to enable a being to resign these adventitious prerogatives – one who, rising with the calm dignity of reason above opinion, dared to be proud of the privileges inherent in man? And it is vain to expect it whilst hereditary power chokes the affections, and nips reason in the bud.

The passions of men have thus placed women on thrones, and till mankind become more reasonable, it is to be feared that women will avail themselves of the power which they attain with the least exertion, and which is the most indisputable. They will smile – yes, they will smile, though told that:

In beauty's empire is no mean,
And woman, either slave or queen,
Is quickly scorned when not adored.

But the adoration comes first, and the scorn is not anticipated.

Louis XIV, in particular, spread factitious manners, and caught, in a specious way, the whole nation in his toils; for, establishing an artful chain of despotism, he made it the interest of the people at large individually to respect his station, and support his power. And women, whom he flattered by a puerile attention to the whole sex, obtained in his reign that prince-like distinction so fatal to reason and virtue.

A king is always a king, and a woman always a woman.[1] His authority and her sex ever stand between them and rational converse. With a lover, I grant, she should be so, and her sensibility will naturally lead her to endeavour to excite emotion, not to gratify her vanity, but her heart. This I do not allow to be coquetry; it is the artless impulse of nature. I only exclaim against the sexual desire of conquest when the heart is out of the question.

This desire is not confined to women. "I have endeavoured," says Lord

[1] And a wit always a wit, might be added, for the vain fooleries of wits and beauties to obtain attention, and make conquests, are much upon a par [M.W.].

Chesterfield,[1] "to gain the hearts of twenty women, whose persons I would not have given a fig for." The libertine who, in a gust of passion, takes advantage of unsuspecting tenderness, is a saint when compared with this cold-hearted rascal – for I like to use significant words. Yet only taught to please, women are always on the watch to please, and with true heroic ardour endeavour to gain hearts merely to resign or spurn them when the victory is decided and conspicuous.

I must descend to the minutiae of the subject.

I lament that women are systematically degraded by receiving the trivial attentions which men think it manly to pay to the sex, when in fact, they are insultingly supporting their own superiority. It is not condescension to bow to an inferior. So ludicrous, in fact, do these ceremonies appear to me that I scarcely am able to govern my muscles when I see a man start with eager and serious solicitude to lift a handkerchief or shut a door, when the *lady* could have done it herself, had she only moved a pace or two.

A wild wish has just flown from my heart to my head, and I will not stifle it, though it may excite a horse-laugh. I do earnestly wish to see the distinction of sex confounded in society, unless where love animates the behaviour. For this distinction is, I am firmly persuaded, the foundation of the weakness of character ascribed to woman; is the cause why the understanding is neglected, whilst accomplishments are acquired with sedulous care; and the same cause accounts for their preferring the graceful before the heroic virtues.

Mankind, including every description, wish to be loved and respected by *something*, and the common herd will always take the nearest road to the completion of their wishes. The respect paid to wealth and beauty is the most certain and unequivocal, and, of course, will always attract the vulgar eye of common minds. Abilities and virtues are absolutely necessary to raise men from the middle rank of life into notice, and the natural consequence is notorious – the middle rank contains most virtue and abilities. Men have thus, in one station at least, an opportunity of exerting themselves with dignity, and of rising by the exertions which really improve a rational creature; but the whole female sex are, till their character is formed, in the same condition as the rich, for they are born – I now speak of a state of civilization – with certain sexual privileges; and whilst they are gratuitously granted them, few will ever think of works of supererogation to obtain the esteem of a small number of superior people.

When do we hear of women who, starting out of obscurity, boldly claim respect on account of their great abilities or daring virtues? Where are they to be found? "To be observed, to be attended to, to be taken notice of with sympathy, complacency, and approbation, are all the advantages which

---

[1] Lord Chesterfield (1694–1773), English statesman and wit. Author of *Letters to his son*.

they seek." True! my male readers will probably exclaim; but let them, before they draw any conclusion, recollect that this was not written originally as descriptive of women, but of the rich. In Dr Smith's *Theory of Moral Sentiments*[1] I have found a general character of people of rank and fortune, that, in my opinion, might with the greatest propriety be applied to the female sex. I refer the sagacious reader to the whole comparison, but must be allowed to quote a passage to enforce an argument that I mean to insist on, as the one most conclusive against a sexual character. For if, excepting warriors, no great men of any denomination have ever appeared amongst the nobility, may it not be fairly inferred that their local situation swallowed up the man, and produced a character similar to that of women, who are *localized* – if I may be allowed the word – by the rank they are placed in by *courtesy*? Women, commonly called ladies, are not to be contradicted, in company, are not allowed to exert any manual strength; and from them the negative virtues only are expected, when any virtues are expected – patience, docility, good humour, and flexibility – virtues incompatible with any vigorous exertion of intellect. Besides, by living more with each other, and being seldom absolutely alone, they are more under the influence of sentiments than passions. Solitude and reflection are necessary to give to wishes the force of passions, and to enable the imagination to enlarge the object, and make it the most desirable. The same may be said of the rich; they do not sufficiently deal in general ideas, collected by impassioned thinking or calm investigation, to acquire that strength of character on which great resolves are built. But hear what an acute observer says of the great:

"Do the great seem insensible of the easy price at which they may acquire the public admiration; or do they seem to imagine that to them, as to other men, it must be the purchase either of sweat or of blood? By what important accomplishments is the young nobleman instructed to support the dignity of his rank, and to render himself worthy of that superiority over his fellow-citizens, to which the virtue of his ancestors had raised them? Is it by knowledge, by industry, by patience, by self-denial, or by virtue of any kind? As all his words, as all his motions are attended to, he learns an habitual regard to every circumstance of ordinary behaviour, and studies to perform all those small duties with the most exact propriety. As he is conscious how much he is observed, and how much mankind are disposed to favour all his inclinations, he acts, upon the most indifferent occasions, with that freedom and elevation which the thought of this naturally inspires. His air, his manner, his deportment, all mark that elegant and graceful sense of his own superiority, which those who are

---

[1] Adam Smith (1723–90), Scottish economist and philosopher. Author of *Wealth of Nations*, 1776, and *Theory of Moral Sentiments*, 1759.

born to inferior station can hardly ever arrive at. These are the arts by
which he proposes to make mankind more easily submit to his authority,
and to govern their inclinations according to his own pleasure; and in this
he is seldom disappointed. These arts, supported by rank and pre-
eminence, are, upon ordinary occasions, sufficient to govern the world.
Louis XIV, during the greater part of his reign, was regarded, not only in
France, but all over Europe, as the most perfect model of a great prince.
But what were the talents and virtues by which he acquired this great
reputation? Was it by the scrupulous and inflexible justice of all his
undertakings, by the immense dangers and difficulties with which they
were attended, or by the unwearied and unrelenting application with
which he pursued them? Was it by his extensive knowledge, by his
exquisite judgment, or by his heroic valour? It was by none of these
qualities. But he was, first of all, the most powerful prince in Europe, and
consequently held the highest rank among kings; and then, says his
historian, 'he surpassed all his courtiers in the gracefulness of his shape,
and the majestic beauty of his features. The sound of his voice, noble and
affecting, gained those hearts which his presence intimidated. He had a
step and a deportment which could suit only him and his rank, and which
would have been ridiculous in any other person. The embarrassment
which he occasioned to those who spoke to him, flattered that secret
satisfaction with which he felt his own superiority.' These frivolous
accomplishments, supported by his rank, and, no doubt too, by a degree
of other talents and virtues, which seems, however, not to have been much
above mediocrity, established this prince in the esteem of his own age, and
have drawn, even from posterity, a good deal of respect for his memory.
Compared with these, in his own times, and in his own presence, no other
virtue, it seems, appeared to have any merit. Knowledge, industry, valour,
and beneficence trembled, were abashed, and lost all dignity before
them."

Woman also thus "in herself complete", by possessing all these *frivolous*
accomplishments, so changes the nature of things:

> That what she wills to do or say
> Seems wisest, virtuousest, discreetest, best;
> All higher knowledge in *her presence* falls
> Degraded. Wisdom in discourse with her
> Loses discountenanced, and, like folly shows;
> Authority and reason on her wait.

And all this is built on her loveliness!

In the middle rank of life, to continue the comparison, men, in their
youth, are prepared for professions, and marriage is not considered as the
grand feature in their lives; whilst women, on the contrary, have no other

scheme to sharpen their faculties. It is not business, extensive plans, or any of the excursive flights of ambition, that engross their attention; no, their thoughts are not employed in rearing such noble structures. To rise in the world, and have the liberty of running from pleasure to pleasure, they must marry advantageously, and to this object their time is sacrificed, and their persons often legally prostituted. A man when he enters any profession has his eye steadily fixed on some future advantage (and the mind gains great strength by having all its efforts directed to one point), and, full of his business, pleasure is considered as mere relaxation; whilst women seek for pleasure as the main purpose of existence. In fact, from the education, which they receive from society, the love of pleasure may be said to govern them all; but does this prove that there is a sex in souls? It would be just as rational to declare that the courtiers in France, when a destructive system of despotism had formed their character, were not men, because liberty, virtue, and humanity, were sacrificed to pleasure and vanity. Fatal passions, which have ever domineered over the *whole* race!

The same love of pleasure, fostered by the whole tendency of their education, gives a trifling turn to the conduct of women in most circumstances; for instance, they are ever anxious about secondary things; and on the watch for adventures instead of being occupied by duties.

A man, when he undertakes a journey, has, in general, the end in view; a woman thinks more of the incidental occurrences, the strange things that may possibly occur on the road; the impression that she may make on her fellow-travellers; and, above all, she is anxiously intent on the care of the finery that she carries with her, which is more than ever a part of herself, when going to figure on a new scene; when, to use an apt French turn of expression, she is going to produce a sensation. Can dignity of mind exist with such trivial cares?

In short, women, in general, as well as the rich of both sexes, have acquired all the follies and vices of civilization, and missed the useful fruit. It is not necessary for me always to premise, that I speak of the condition of the whole sex, leaving exceptions out of the question. Their senses are inflamed, and their understandings neglected, consequently they become the prey of their senses, delicately termed sensibility, and are blown about by every momentary gust of feeling. Civilized women are, therefore, so weakened by false refinement, that, respecting morals, their condition is much below what it would be were they left in a state nearer to nature. Ever restless and anxious, their over-exercised sensibility not only renders them uncomfortable themselves, but troublesome, to use a soft phrase, to others. All their thoughts turn on things calculated to excite emotion and feeling, when they should reason, their conduct is unstable, and their opinions are wavering – not the wavering produced by deliberation or progressive views, but by contradictory emotions. By fits and starts, they are warm in many pursuits; yet this warmth, never concentrated into perseverance, soon exhausts itself; exhaled by its own heat, or meeting with some other fleeting passion, to which reason has never given any specific gravity, neutrality ensues. Miserable, indeed, must be that being whose cultivation of mind has only tended to inflame its passions! A distinction should be made between inflaming and strengthening them. The passions thus pampered, whilst the judgment is left unformed, what can be expected to ensue? Undoubtedly, a mixture of madness and folly!

This observation should not be confined to the *fair* sex; however, at present, I only mean to apply it to them.

Novels, music, poetry, and gallantry, all tend to make women the creatures of sensation, and their character is thus formed in the mould of folly during the time they are acquiring accomplishments, the only improvement they are excited, by their station in society, to acquire. This overstretched sensibility naturally relaxes the other powers of the mind, and prevents intellect from attaining that sovereignty which it ought to attain to render a rational creature useful to others, and content with its own station; for the exercise of the understanding, as life advances, is the only method pointed out by nature to calm the passions.

Satiety has a very different effect, and I have often been forcibly struck by an emphatical description of damnation; when the spirit is represented as continually hovering with abortive eagerness round the defiled body, unable to enjoy anything without the organs of sense. Yet, to their senses, are women made slaves, because it is by their sensibility that they obtain present power.

And will moralists pretend to assert that this is the condition in which one-half of the human race should be encouraged to remain with listless inactivity and stupid acquiescence? Kind instructors! what were we created for? To remain, it may be said, innocent; they mean in a state of childhood. We might as well never have been born, unless it were necessary that we should be created to enable man to acquire the noble privilege of reason, the power of discerning good from evil, whilst we lie down in the dust from whence we were taken, never to rise again.

It would be an endless task to trace the variety of meannesses, cares, and sorrows, into which women are plunged by the prevailing opinion, that they were created rather to feel than reason, and that all the power they obtain must be obtained by their charms and weakness:

Fine by defect, and amiably weak!

And, made by this amiable weakness entirely dependent, excepting what they gain by illicit sway, on man, not only for protection, but advice, is it surprising that, neglecting the duties that reason alone points out, and shrinking from trials calculated to strengthen their minds, they only exert themselves to give their defects a graceful covering, which may serve to heighten their charms in the eye of the voluptuary, though it sink them below the scale of moral excellence.

Fragile in every sense of the word, they are obliged to look up to man for every comfort. In the most trifling danger they cling to their support, with parasitical tenacity, piteously demanding succour; and their *natural* protector extends his arm, or lifts up his voice, to guard the lovely trembler – from what? Perhaps the frown of an old cow, or the jump of a mouse; a rat would be a serious danger. In the name of reason, and even common sense, what can save such beings from contempt; even though they be soft and fair.

These fears, when not affected, may produce some pretty attitudes; but they show a degree of imbecility which degrades a rational creature in a way women are not aware of – for love and esteem are very distinct things.

I am fully persuaded that we should hear of none of these infantine airs, if girls were allowed to take sufficient exercise, and not confined in close rooms till their muscles are relaxed, and their powers of digestion destroyed. To carry the remark still further, if fear in girls, instead of being cherished, perhaps, created, were treated in the same manner as cowardice in boys, we should quickly see women with more dignified aspects. It is true, they could not then with equal propriety be termed the sweet flowers that smile in the walk of man; but they would be more respectable members of society, and discharge the important duties of life by the light of their own reason. "Educate women like men," says Rousseau, "and the more they resemble our sex the less power they will have over us." This is the very point I aim at. I do not wish them to have power over men; but over themselves.

From REFORM ACT, 1832

The Industrial Revolution produced enormous force for electoral change in Britain, where an urban population expanding exponentially encountered a franchise historically weighted in favour of the rural landowners. (Some electoral boroughs were so "rotten" that the local squire effectively appointed or sold the encumbency.) The urbanites, rich and poor, were not only desirous of the vote but able to organize *en masse* to achieve it. It was in response to their widespread clamour that the Reform Act was passed – after the progressive Whig leader Earl Grey threatened to create a hundred Whig peers to get the measure through the Tory dominated House of Lords – and the franchise in the counties was extended to £10 copyholders and £50 short-leaseholders and tenants at will; in the boroughs £10 householders were granted the vote. Most rotten boroughs were eliminated.

The Act was received with national rejoicing, even though most of the workers who had campaigned for it were excluded from its benefit by the £10 qualification. They would go on to support the "Chartist" movement.

Nonetheless, the Reform Act was the decisive step towards universal suffrage in Britain. It increased the electorate by some 50 percent and ended the sale of Commons influence for money.

Whereas it is expedient to take effectual measures for correcting divers abuses that have long prevailed in the choice of members to serve in the commons house of parliament, to deprive many inconsiderable places of the right of returning members, to grant such privilege to large, populous, and wealthy towns, to increase the number of knights of the shire, to extend the elective franchise to many of His Majesty's subjects who have not heretobefore enjoyed the same, and to diminish the expense of elections: Be it therefore enacted by the king's most excellent Majesty, by and with the advice and consent of the lords spiritual and temporal, and commons, in this present parliament assembled, and by the authority of the same, that each of the boroughs enumerated in the Schedule marked A (56 in all) shall from and after the end of this present parliament cease to return any member or members to serve in parliament.

* * *

XVIII. That no person shall be entitled to vote in the election of a knight or knights of the shire to serve in any future parliament, or in the election of a member or members to serve in any future parliament for any city or town being a county of itself, in respect of any freehold lands or tenements whereof such person may be seised for his own life, or for the life of another, or for any lives whatsoever, except such person shall be in the actual and bona fide occupation of such lands or tenements, or except the same shall have come to such person by marriage, marriage settlement, devise, or promotion to any benefice or to any office, or except the same shall be of the clear yearly value of not less than £10 above all rents and charges payable out of or in respect of the same; any statute or usage to the contrary notwithstanding: provided always, that nothing in this act contained shall prevent any person now seised for his own life, or for the life of another, or for any lives whatsoever, of any freehold lands or tenements in respect of which he now has, or but for the passing of this act might acquire, the right of voting in such respective elections, from retaining or acquiring, so long as he shall be so seised of the same lands or tenements, such right of voting in respect thereof, if duly registered according to the respective provisions hereinafter contained.

XIX. That every male person of full age, and not subject to any legal incapacity, who shall be seised at law or in equity of any land or tenements of copyhold or any other tenure whatever except freehold, for his own life, or for the life of another, or for any lives whatsoever, or for any larger estate, of the clear yearly value of not less than £10 over and above all rents and charges payable out of or in respect of the same, shall be entitled to vote in the election of a knight or knights of the shire to serve in any future parliament for the county, or for the riding, parts, or division of the county, in which such lands or tenements shall be respectively situate.

XX. That every male person of full age, and not subject to any legal incapacity, who shall be entitled, either as lessee or assignee, to any lands or tenements, whether of freehold or of any other tenure whatever, for the unexpired residue, whatever it may be, of any term originally created for a period of not less than sixty years (whether determinable on a life or lives, or not), of the clear yearly value of not less than £10 over and above all rents and charges payable out of or in respect of the same, or for the unexpired residue, whatever it may be, of any term originally created for a period of not less than twenty years (whether determinable on a life or lives, or not), of the clear yearly value of not less than £50 over and above all rents and charges payable out of or in respect of the same, or who shall occupy as tenant any lands or tenements for which he shall be bona fide liable to a yearly rent of not less than £50, shall be entitled to vote in the election of a knight or knights of the shire to serve in any future parliament for the county, or for the riding, parts, or division of the county, in which such lands or tenements shall be respectively situate: provided always, that no person, being only a sublessee, or the assignee of any under-lease, shall have a right to vote in such election in respect of any such term of sixty years or twenty years as aforesaid, unless he shall be in the actual occupation of the premises.

XXI. That no public or parliamentary tax, nor any church rate, county rate, or parochial rate, shall be deemed to be any charge payable out of or in respect of any lands or tenements within the meaning of this act.

XXII. That in order to entitle any person to vote in any election of a knight of the shire or other member to serve in any future parliament, in respect of any messuages, lands, or tenements, whether freehold or otherwise, it shall not be necessary that the same shall be assessed to the land tax; any statute to the contrary notwithstanding.

*   *   *

XXVI. That notwithstanding anything hereinbefore contained no person shall be entitled to vote in the election of a knight or knights of the shire to serve in any future parliament unless he shall have been duly registered according to the provisions hereinafter contained; and that no person shall be so registered in any year in respect of his estate or interest in any lands or tenements, as a freeholder, copyholder, customary tenant, or tenant in ancient demesne, unless he shall have been in the actual possession thereof, or in the receipt of the rents and profits thereof for his own use for six calendar months at least next previous to the last day of July in such year, which said period of six calendar months shall be sufficient, any statute to the contrary notwithstanding; and that no person shall be so registered in any year, in respect of any lands or tenements held by him as such lessee or assignee, or as such occupier and tenant as aforesaid, unless he shall have been in the actual possession thereof, or in receipt of the rents and profits thereof for his own use, as the case may require, for twelve calendar months next previous to the last day of July in such year: provided always, that where any lands or tenements, which would otherwise entitle the owner, holder, or occupier thereof to vote in any such election, shall come to any person, at any time within such respective periods of six or twelve calendar months, by descent, succession, marriage, marriage settlement, devise, or promotion to any benefice in a church, or by promotion to any office, such person shall be entitled in respect thereof to have his name inserted as a voter in the election of a knight or knights of the shire in the lists then next to be made, by virtue of this act as hereinafter mentioned, and, upon his being duly registered according to the provisions hereinafter contained, to vote in such election.

XXVII. That in every city or borough which shall return a member or members to serve in any future parliament, every male person of full age, and not subject to any legal incapacity, who shall occupy, within such city or borough, or within any place sharing in the election for such city or borough, as owner or tenant, any house, warehouse, counting-house, shop, or other building, being, either separately, or jointly with any land within such city, borough, or place occupied therewith by him as owner, or therewith by him as tenant under the same landlord, of the clear yearly value of not less than £10, shall, if duly registered according to the provisions hereinafter contained, be entitled to vote in the election of a member or members to serve in any future parliament for such city or borough: provided always, that no such person shall be so registered in any year unless he shall have occupied such premises as aforesaid for twelve calendar months next previous to the last day of July in such year, nor unless such person, where such premises are situated in any parish or township in which there shall be a rate for the relief of the poor, shall have been rated in respect of such premises to all rates for the relief of the poor in such parish or township, made during the time of such his occupation so required as aforesaid, nor unless such person shall have paid, on or before the 20th of July in such year, all the poor's rates and assessed taxes which shall have become payable from him in respect of such premises previously to the 6th April then next preceding: provided also, that no such person shall be so registered in any year unless he shall have resided for six calendar months next previous to the last day of July in such year within the city or borough, or within the place sharing in the election for the city or borough, in respect of which city, borough, or place respectively he shall be entitled to vote, or within seven statute miles thereof or of any part thereof.

XXVIII. That the premises in respect of the occupation of which any person shall be entitled to be registered in any year, and to vote in the election for any city or borough as aforesaid, shall not be required to be the same premises, but may be different premises occupied in immediate succession by such person during the twelve calendar months next previous to the last day of July in such year, such person having paid on or before the 20th of July in such year, all the poor's rates and assessed taxes which shall previously to the 6th of April then next preceding have become payable from him in respect of all such premises so occupied by him in succession.

*   *   *

XXXVI. That no person shall be entitled to be registered in any year as a voter in the election of a member or members to serve in any future parliament for any city or borough who shall within twelve calendar months next previous to the last day of July in such year have received parochial relief or other alms, which by the law of parliament now disqualify from voting in the election of members to serve in parliament.

*   *   *

LXII. That at every contested election of a knight or knights to serve in any future parliament for any county, or for any riding, parts, or division of a county, the polling shall commence at nine o'clock in the forenoon of the next day but two after the day fixed for the election, unless such next day but two shall be Saturday or Sunday, and then on the Monday following, at the principal place of election, and also at the several places to be appointed as hereinafter directed for taking polls; and such polling shall continue for two days only, such two days being successive days; (that is to say) for seven hours on the first day of polling, and for eight hours on the second day of polling; and no poll shall be kept open later than four o'clock in the afternoon of the second day; any statute to the contrary notwithstanding.

LXIII. That the respective counties in England and Wales, and the respective ridings, parts, and divisions of counties, shall be divided into convenient districts for polling, and in each district shall be appointed a convenient place for taking the poll at all elections of a knight or knights of the shire to serve in any future parliament, and such districts and places for taking the poll shall be settled and appointed by the act to be passed in this present parliament for the purpose of setting and describing the divisions of the counties enumerated in the schedule marked (F.) to this act annexed; provided that no county, nor any riding, parts, or division of a county, shall have more than fifteen districts and respective places appointed for taking the poll for such county, riding, or division.

LXIV. That at every contested election for any county, riding, parts, or division of a county, the sheriff, under-sheriff, or sheriff's deputy shall, if required thereto by or on behalf of any candidate, on the day fixed for the election, and if not so required may if it shall appear to him expedient, cause to be erected a reasonable number of booths for taking the poll at the principal place of election, and also at each of the polling places so to be appointed as aforesaid, and shall cause to be affixed on the most conspicuous part of each of the said booths the names of the several parishes, townships, and places for which such booth is respectively allotted; and no person shall be admitted to vote at any such election in respect of any property situate in any parish, township or place, except at the booth so allotted for such parish, township or place, and if no booth shall be so allotted for the same, then at any of the booths for the same district; and in case any parish, township, or place shall happen not to be included in any of the districts to be appointed, the votes in respect of property situate in any parish, township, or places omitted shall be taken at the principal place of election for the county, or riding, parts, or division of the county, as the case may be.

       ★   ★   ★

LXXI. That from and after the end of this present parliament all booths erected for the convenience of taking polls shall be erected at the joint and equal expense of the several candidates, and the same shall be erected by contract with the candidates, if they shall think fit to make such contract, or if they shall not make such contract, then the same shall be erected by the sheriff or other returning officer at the expense of the several candidates as aforesaid, subject to such limitation as is hereinafter next mentioned; (that is to say) that the expense to be incurred for the booth or booths to be erected at the principal place of election or at any of the polling places so to be appointed as aforesaid, shall not exceed the sum of £40 in respect of any one such principal place of election or any one such polling place, and that the expense to be incurred for any booth or booths to be erected for any parish, district, or part of any city or borough shall not exceed the sum of £25 in respect of any one such parish district, or part; and that all deputies appointed by the sheriff or other returning officer shall be paid each two guineas by the day, and all clerks employed in taking the poll shall be paid each one guinea by the day, at the expense of the candidates at such election: provided always, that if any person shall be proposed without his consent, then the person so proposing him shall be liable to defray his share of the said expenses in like manner as if he had been a candidate; provided also, that the sheriff or other returning officer may, if he shall think fit, instead of erecting such booth or booths as aforesaid, procure or hire and use any houses or other buildings for the purpose of taking the poll therein, subject always to the same regulations, provisions, liabilities, and limitations of expense as are hereinbefore mentioned with regard to booths for taking the poll.

From DEMOCRACY IN AMERICA, 1835

Alexis de Tocqueville

A magistrate at Versailles, de Tocqueville (1805–59) was sent in 1831 to the USA to report on its penal system. He returned home to write the voluminous political treatise *De la Democratie en Amerique*. Although de Tocqueville found that democracy *lessened* liberty (because it needed greater centralized government), he allowed that democracy produced a more compassionate society.

We perceive that for several ages social conditions have tended to equality, and we discover that in the course of the same period the manners of society have been softened. Are these two things merely contemporaneous, or does any secret link exist between them, so that the one cannot go on without making the other advance? Several causes may concur to render the manners of a people less rude; but, of all these causes, the most powerful appears to me to be the equality of conditions. Equality of conditions and growing civility in manners are then, in my eyes, not only contemporaneous occurrences, but correlative facts . . .

When all the ranks of a community are nearly equal, as all men think and feel in nearly the same manner, each of them may judge in a moment of the sensations of all the others: he casts a rapid glance upon himself, and that is enough. There is no wretchedness into which he cannot readily enter, and a secret instinct reveals to him its extent. It signifies not that strangers or foes be the sufferers; imagination puts him in their place: something like a personal feeling is mingled with his pity, and makes himself suffer while the body of his fellow creature is in torture.

In democratic ages men rarely sacrifice themselves for one another; but they display general compassion for the members of the human race. They inflict no useless ills; and they are happy to relieve the griefs of others, when they can do so without much hurting themselves; they are not disinterested, but they are humane.

Although the Americans have in a manner reduced egotism to a social and philosophical theory, they are nevertheless extremely open to compassion . . .

When men feel a natural compassion for their mutual sufferings – when they are brought together by easy and frequent intercourse, and no sensitive feelings keep them asunder, it may readily be supposed that they will lend assistance to one another whenever it is needed. When an American asks for the cooperation of his fellow citizens it is seldom refused, and I have often seen it afforded spontaneously and with great good will. If an accident happens on the highway, everybody hastens to help the sufferer; if some great and sudden calamity befalls a family, the purses of a thousand strangers are at once willingly opened, and small but numerous donations pour in to relieve their distress.

It often happens among the most civilized nations of the globe, that a poor wretch is as friendless in the midst of a crowd as the savage in his wilds: this is hardly ever the case in the United States. The Americans, who are always cold and often coarse in their manners, seldom show insensibility; and if they do not proffer services eagerly, yet they do not refuse to render them.

All this is not in contradiction to what I have said before on the subject of individualism. The two things are so far from combating each other, that I can see how they agree. Equality of conditions, while it makes men feel their independence, shows them their own weakness: they are free, but exposed to a thousand accidents; and experience soon teaches them, that although they do not habitually require the assistance of others, a time almost always comes when they cannot do without it.

We constantly see in Europe that men of the same profession are ever ready to assist each other; they are all exposed to the same ills, and that is enough to teach them to seek mutual preservatives, however hard-hearted and selfish they may otherwise be. When one of them falls into danger, from which the others may save him by a slight transient sacrifice or a sudden effort, they do not fail to make the attempt. Not that they are deeply interested in his fate; for if, by chance, their exertions are unavailing, they immediately forget the object of them, and return to their own business; but a sort of tacit and almost involuntary agreement has been passed between them, by which each one owes to the others a temporary support which he may claim for himself in turn.

Extend to a people the remark here applied to a class, and you will understand my meaning. A similar covenant exists in fact between all the citizens of a democracy: they all feel themselves subject to the same weakness and the same dangers; and their interest, as well as their sympathy, makes it a rule with them to lend each other mutual assistance when required. The more equal social conditions become, the more do men display this reciprocal disposition to oblige each other. In democracies no great benefits are conferred, but good offices are constantly rendered: a man seldom displays self-devotion, but all men are ready to be of service to one another.

TO THE YOUNG MEN OF ITALY, 1848

Giuseppe Mazzini

Of the political legacy of the French Revolution, self-determination took the greatest grip on the West in the first half of the 19th century. Liberal nationalism stood for the rights of free men in a unified and independent country. It shaped the politics of Latin America, of Abraham Lincoln, as well as Europe.

In 1848 Europe exploded in a series of liberal nationalist revolts, including Italy where the "Young Italy" leader Giuseppe Mazzini (1805–72) made the address below in memory of two Italian patriots executed by Austrian occupation troops.

The revolt in Italy, like the remainder of the revolts in Europe, was ultimately unsuccessful. Nothing thwarted, Mazzini continued his fervoured agitation on behalf of *risorgimento* (the revival movement for Italian unification) until his death. His scattering of seeds was not in vain. Nine years later the Italians occupied Rome, the last enclave of foreign-held territory, and Italy was united for the first time since the days of the Roman Empire.

Speech in Milan, 1848

When I was commissioned by you, young men, to proffer in this temple a few words sacred to the memory of the brothers Bandiera and their fellow martyrs at Cosenza, I thought that some of those who heard me might exclaim with noble indignation: "Wherefore lament over the dead? The martyrs of liberty are only worthily honoured by winning the battle they have begun; Cosenza, the land where they fell, is enslaved; Venice, the city of their birth, is begirt by foreign foes. Let us emancipate them, and until that moment let no words pass our lips save words of war."

But another thought arose: "Why have we not conquered? Why is it that, while we are fighting for independence in the north of Italy, liberty is perishing in the south? Why is it that a war, which should have sprung to the Alps with the bound of a lion, has dragged itself along for four months, with the slow uncertain motion of the scorpion surrounded by a circle of fire? How has the rapid and powerful intuition of a people newly arisen to life been converted into the weary, helpless effort of the sick man turning from side to side? Ah! had we all arisen in the sanctity of the idea for which our martyrs died; had the holy standard of their faith preceded our youth to battle; had we reached that unity of life which was in them so powerful, and made of our every action a thought, and of our every thought an action; had we devoutly gathered up their last words in our hearts, and learned from them that liberty and independence are one; that God and the people, the fatherland and humanity, are the two inseparable terms of the device of every people striving to become a nation; that Italy can have no true life till she be one, holy in the equality and love of all her children, great in the worship of eternal truth, and consecrated to a lofty mission, a moral priesthood among the peoples of Europe – we should now have had, not war, but victory; Cosenza would not be compelled to venerate the memory of her martyrs in secret, nor Venice be restrained from honouring them with a monument; and we, gathered here together, might gladly invoke their sacred names, without uncertainty as to our future destiny, or a cloud of sadness on our brows, and say to those precursor souls: 'Rejoice! for your spirit is incarnate in your brethren, and they are worthy of you.'"

The idea which they worshipped, young men, does not as yet shine forth in its full purity and integrity upon your banner. The sublime programme which they, dying, bequeathed to the rising Italian generation, is yours; but mutilated, broken up into fragments by the false doctrines, which, elsewhere overthrown, have taken refuge amongst us. I look around, and I see the struggles of desperate populations, an alternation of generous rage and of unworthy repose; of shouts for freedom and of formulæ of servitude, throughout all parts of our peninsula; but the soul of the country, where is it? What unity is there in this unequal and manifold movement – where is the word that should dominate the hundred diverse and opposing counsels which mislead or seduce the multitude? I hear phrases usurping the national omnipotence – the Italy of the north – the league of the states – federative compacts between princes," – but Italy, where is it? Where is the common country, the country which the Bandiera hailed as thrice initiatrix of a new era of European civilization?

Intoxicated with our first victories, improvident for the future, we forgot the idea revealed by God to those who suffered; and God has punished our forgetfulness by deferring our triumph. The Italian movement, my countrymen, is, by decree of Providence, that of Europe. We arise to give a pledge of moral progress to the European world. But neither political fictions, nor dynastic aggrandizements, nor theories of expediency, can transform or renovate the life of the peoples. Humanity lives and moves through faith; great principles are the guiding stars that lead Europe towards the future. Let us turn to the graves of our martyrs, and ask inspiration of those who died for us all, and we shall find the secret of victory in the adoration of a faith. The angel of martyrdom and the angel of victory are brothers; but the one looks up to heaven, and the other looks down to earth; and it is when, from epoch to epoch, their glances meet between earth and heaven, that creation is embellished with a new life, and a people arises from the cradle or the tomb, evangelist or prophet.

I will sum up for you in a few words this faith of our martyrs; their external life is known to you all; it is now a matter of history and I need not recall it to you.

The faith of the brothers Bandiera, which was and is our own, was based upon a few simple uncontrovertible truths, which few, indeed, venture to declare false, but which are nevertheless forgotten or betrayed by most:–

God and the People.

God at the summit of the social edifice; the people, the universality of our brethren, at the base. God, the Father and Educator; the people, the progressive interpreter of his law.

No true society can exist without a common belief and a common aim. Religion declares the belief and the aim. Politics regulate society in the practical realization of that belief, and prepare the means of attaining that aim. Religion represents the principle, politics the application. There is but one sun in heaven for all the earth. There is one law for all those who people the earth. It is alike the law of the human being and of collective humanity. We are placed here below, not for the capricious exercise of our own individual faculties – our faculties and liberty are the means, not the end – not to work out our own happiness upon earth; happiness can only be reached elsewhere, and there God works for us; but to consecrate our existence to the discovery of a portion of the Divine law; to practise it as far as our individual circumstances and powers allow, and to diffuse the knowledge and love of it among our brethren.

We are here below to labour fraternally to build up the unity of the human family, so that the day may come when it shall represent a single sheepfold with a single shepherd – the spirit of God, the Law.

To aid our search after truth, God has given to us tradition and the voice of our own conscience. Wherever they are opposed, is error. To attain harmony and consistence between the conscience of the individual and the conscience of humanity, no sacrifice is too great. The family, the city, the fatherland, and humanity, are but different spheres in which to exercise our activity and our power of sacrifice towards this great aim. God watches from above the inevitable progress of humanity, and from time to time he raises up the great in genius, in love, in thought, or in action, as priests of His truth, and guides to the multitude on their way.

These principles – indicated in their letters, in their proclamations, and in their conversation – with a profound sense of the mission entrusted by God to the individual and to humanity, were to Attilio and Emilio Bandiera and their fellow martyrs the guide and comfort of a weary life; and, when men and circumstances had alike betrayed them, these principles sustained them in death, in religious serenity and calm certainty of the realization of their immortal hopes for the future of Italy. The immense energy of their souls arose from the intense love which informed their faith. And could they now arise from the grave and speak to you, they would, believe me, address you, though with a power very different from that which is given to me, in counsel not unlike this which I now offer to you.

Love! love is the flight of the soul towards God; towards the great, the sublime, and the beautiful, which are the shadow of God upon earth. Love your family, the partner of your life, those around you ready to share your joys and sorrows; love the dead who were dear to you and to whom you were dear. But let your love be the love taught you by Dante and by us – the love of souls that aspire together; do not grovel on the earth in search of a felicity which it is not the destiny of the creature to reach here below; do not yield to a delusion which inevitably would degrade you into egotism. To love is to give and take a promise for the future. God has given us love, that the weary soul may give and receive support upon the way of life. It is a flower springing up on the path of duty; but it cannot change its course. Purify, strengthen, and improve yourselves by loving. Act always – even at the price of increasing her earthly trials – so that the sister soul united to your own may never need, here or elsewhere, to blush through you or for you. The time will come when, from the height of a new life, embracing the whole past and comprehending its secret, you will smile together at the sorrows you have endured, the trials you have overcome.

Love your country. Your country is the land where your parents sleep, where is spoken that language in which the chosen of your heart, blushing, whispered the first word of love; it is the home that God has given you, that by striving to perfect yourselves therein, you may prepare to ascend to Him. It is your name, your glory, your sign among the people. Give to it your thoughts, your counsels, your blood. Raise it up, great and beautiful as it was foretold by our great men, and see that you leave it uncontaminated by any trace of falsehood or of servitude; unprofaned by dismemberment. Let it be one, as the thought of God. You are twenty-five millions of men, endowed with active, splendid faculties; possessing a tradition of glory the envy of the nations of Europe. An immense future is before you; you lift your eyes to the loveliest heaven, and around you smiles the loveliest land in Europe; you are encircled by the Alps and the sea, boundaries traced out by the finger of God for a people of giants – you are bound to be such, or nothing. Let not a man of that twenty-five millions remain excluded from the fraternal bond destined to join you together; let not a glance be raised to that heaven which is not the glance of a free man. Let Rome be the ark of your redemption, the temple of your nation. Has she not twice been the temple of the destinies of Europe? In Rome two extinct worlds, the Pagan and the Papal, are superposed like the double jewels of a diadem; draw from these a third world greater than the two. From Rome, the holy city, the city of love (Amour), the purest and wisest among you, elected by the vote and fortified by the inspiration of a whole people, shall dictate the pact that shall make us one, and represent us in the future alliance of the peoples. Until then you will either have no country or have her contaminated or profaned.

Love humanity. You can only ascertain your own mission from the aim set by God before humanity at large. God has given you your country as cradle, and humanity as mother; you cannot rightly love your brethren of the cradle if you love not the common mother. Beyond the Alps, beyond the sea, are other peoples now fighting or preparing to fight the holy fight of independence, of nationality, of liberty; other peoples striving by different routes to reach the same goal – improvement, association, and the foundation of an authority which shall put an end to moral anarchy and re-link earth to heaven; an authority which mankind may love and obey without remorse or shame. Unite with them; they will unite with you. Do not invoke their aid where your single arm will suffice to conquer; but say to them that the hour will shortly sound for a terrible struggle between right and blind force, and that in that hour you will ever be found with those who have raised the same banner as yourselves.

And love, young men, love and venerate the ideal. The ideal is the word of God. High above every country, high above humanity, is the country of the spirit, the city of the soul, in which all are brethren who believe in the inviolability of thought and in the dignity of our immortal soul; and the baptism of this fraternity is martyrdom. From that high sphere spring the principles which alone can redeem the peoples. Arise for the sake of these, and not from impatience of suffering or dread of evil. Anger, pride, ambition, and the desire of material prosperity are arms common alike to the peoples and their oppressors, and even should you conquer with these today, you would fall again tomorrow: but principles belong to the peoples alone, and their oppressors can find no arms to oppose them. Adore enthusiasm, the dreams of the virgin soul, and the visions of early youth, for they are a perfume of paradise which the soul retains in issuing from the hands of its Creator. Respect above all things your conscience; have upon your lips the truth implanted by God in your hearts, and, while labouring in harmony, even with those who differ from you, in all that tends to the emancipation of our soil, yet ever bear your own banner erect and boldly promulgate your own faith.

Such words, young men, would the martyrs of Cosenza have spoken, had they been living amongst you; and here, where it may be that, invoked by our love, their holy spirits hover near us, I call upon you to gather them up in your hearts and to make of them a treasure amid the storms that yet threaten you; storms which, with the name of our martyrs on your lips and their faith in your hearts, you will overcome.

God be with you, and bless Italy!

OPEN LETTER AGAINST SLAVERY, 1848

Frederick Douglass

Douglass (1817–95) was born into bondage in the American South. His *Narrative of the Life of Frederick Douglass* introduced many white people in the USA and Europe to the realities of slavery. He purchased his freedom (£150) following a successful lecture tour of Britain. The open letter below was published in the *North Star* newspaper on 8 September 1848. It was addressed to captain Thomas Auld, Douglass' former "master".

There were around 5 million slaves in America in 1848, almost all living in the South on cotton plantations.

Sir –

The long and intimate, though by no means friendly, relation which unhappily subsisted between you and myself, leads me to hope that you will easily account for the great liberty which I now take to address you in this open and public manner. The same fact may possibly remove any disagreeable surprise which you may experience on again finding your name coupled with mine, in any other way than in an advertisement, accurately describing my person, and offering a large sum for my arrest. In thus dragging you again before the public, I am aware that I shall subject myself to no inconsiderable amount of censure. I shall probably be charged with an unwarrantable, if not a wanton and reckless disregard of the rights and properties of private life. There are those north as well as south who entertain a much higher respect for rights which are merely conventional, than they do for rights which are personal and essential. Not a few there are in our country, who, while they have no scruples against robbing the labourer of the hard earned results of his patient industry, will be shocked by the extremely indelicate manner of bringing your name before the public. Believing this to be the case, and wishing to meet every reasonable or plausible objection to my conduct, I will frankly state the ground upon which I justify myself in this instance, as well as on former occasions when I have thought proper to mention your name in public. All will agree that a man guilty of theft, robbery, or murder, has forfeited the right to concealment and private life; that the community have a right to subject such persons to the most complete exposure. However much they may desire retirement, and aim to conceal themselves and their movements from the popular gaze, the public have a right to ferret them out, and bring their conduct before the proper tribunals of the country for investigation. Sir, you will undoubtedly make the proper application of these generally admitted principles, and will easily see the light in which you are regarded by me; I will not therefore manifest ill temper, by calling you hard names. I know you to be a man of some intelligence, and can readily determine the precise estimate which I entertain of your character. I may therefore indulge in language which may seem to others indirect and ambiguous, and yet be quite well understood by yourself.

I have selected this day on which to address you, because it is the anniversary of my emancipation; and knowing no better way, I am led to this as the best mode of celebrating that truly important event. Just ten years ago this beautiful September morning, yon bright sun beheld me a slave – a poor degraded chattel – trembling at the sound of your voice, lamenting that I was a man, and wishing myself a brute. The hopes which I had treasured up for weeks of a safe and successful escape from your grasp, were powerfully confronted at this last hour by dark clouds of doubt and fear, making my person shake and my bosom to heave with the heavy contest between hope and fear. I have no words to describe to you the deep agony of soul which I experienced on that never-to-be-forgotten morning – for I left by daylight. I was making a leap in the dark. The probabilities, so far as I could by reason determine them, were stoutly against the undertaking. The preliminaries and precautions I had adopted previously, all worked badly. I was like one going to war without weapons – ten chances of defeat to one of victory. One in whom I had confided, and one who had promised me assistance, appalled by fear at the trial hour, deserted me, thus leaving the responsibility of success or failure solely with myself. You, sir, can never know my feelings. As I look back to them, I can scarcely realize that I have passed through a scene so trying. Trying, however, as they were, and gloomy as was the prospect, thanks be to the Most High, who is ever the God of the oppressed, at the moment which was to determine my whole earthly career, His grace was sufficient; my mind was made up. I embraced the golden opportunity, took the morning tide at the flood, and a free man, young, active, and strong is the result.

I have often thought I should like to explain to you the grounds upon which I have justified myself in running away from you. I am almost ashamed to do so now, for by this time you may have discovered them yourself. I will, however, glance at them. When yet but a child about six years old, I imbibed the determination to run away. The very first mental effort that I now remember on my part, was an attempt to solve the mystery – why am I a slave? and with this question my youthful mind was troubled for many days, pressing upon me more heavily at times than others. When I saw the slave-driver whip a slave-woman, cut the blood out of her neck, and heard her piteous cries, I went away into the corner of the fence, wept and pondered over the mystery. I had, through some medium, I know not what, got some idea of God, the Creator of all mankind, the black and the white, and that he had made the blacks to serve the whites as slaves. How he could do this and be *good*, I could not tell. I was not satisfied with this theory, which made God responsible for slavery, for it pained me greatly, and I have wept over it long and often. At one time, your first wife, Mrs Lucretia, heard me singing and saw me shedding tears, and asked of me the matter, but I was afraid to tell her. I was puzzled with this question, till one night while sitting in the kitchen, I heard some of the old slaves talking of their parents having been stolen from Africa by white men, and were sold here as slaves. The whole mystery was solved at once. Very soon after this, my Aunt Jinny and Uncle Noah ran away, and the great noise made about it by your father-in-law, made me for the first time acquainted with the fact, that there were free states as well as slave states. From that time, I resolved that I would some day run away. The morality of the act I dispose of as follows: I am myself; you are yourself; we are two distinct persons, equal persons. What you are, I am. You are a man, and so am I. God created both, and made us separate beings. I am not by nature bond to you, or you to me. Nature does not make your existence depend upon me, or mine to depend upon yours. I cannot walk upon your legs, or you upon mine. I cannot breathe for you, or you for me; I must breathe for myself, and you for yourself. We are distinct persons, and are each equally provided with faculties necessary to our individual existence. In leaving you, I took nothing but what belonged to me, and in no way lessened your means for obtaining an honest living. Your faculties remained yours, and mine became useful to their rightful owner. I therefore see no wrong in any part of the transaction. It is true, I went off secretly; but that was more your fault than mine. Had I let you into the secret, you would have defeated the enterprise entirely; but for this, I should have been really glad to have made you acquainted with my intentions to leave.

You may perhaps want to know how I like my present condition. I am free to say, I greatly prefer it to that which I occupied in Maryland. I am, however, by no means prejudiced against the state as such. Its geography, climate, fertility, and products, are such as to make it a very desirable abode for any man; and but for the existence of slavery there, it is not impossible that I might again take up my abode in that state. It is not that I love Maryland less, but freedom more. You will be surprised to learn that people at the north labour under the strange delusion that if the slaves were emancipated at the south, they would flock to the north. So far from this being the case, in that event, you would see many old and familiar faces back again to the south. The fact is, there are few here who would not return to the south in the event of emancipation. We want to live in the land of our birth, and to lay our bones by the side of our fathers; and nothing short of an intense love of personal freedom keeps us from the south. For the sake of this most of us would live on a crust of bread and a cup of cold water.

Since I left you, I have had a rich experience. I have occupied stations which I never dreamed of when a slave. Three out of the ten years since I left you, I spent as a common labourer on the wharves of New Bedford, Massachusetts. It was there I earned my first free dollar. It was mine. I could spend it as I pleased. I could buy hams or herring with it, without asking any odds of anybody. That was a precious dollar to me. You remember when I used to make seven or eight, or even nine dollars a week in Baltimore, you would take every cent of it from me every Saturday night, saying that I belonged to you, and my earnings also. I never liked this conduct on your part – to say the best, I thought it a little mean. I would not have served you so. But let that pass. I was a little awkward about counting money in New England fashion when I first landed in New Bedford. I came near betraying myself several times. I caught myself saying phip, for fourpence; and at one time a man actually charged me with being a runaway, whereupon I was silly enough to become one by running away from him, for I was greatly afraid he might adopt measures to get me again into slavery, a condition I then dreaded more than death.

I soon learned, however, to count money, as well as to make it, and got on swimmingly. I married soon after leaving you; in fact, I was engaged to be married before I left you; and instead of finding my companion a burden, she was truly a helpmate. She went to live at service, and I to work on the wharf, and though we toiled hard the first winter, we never lived more happily. After remaining in New Bedford for three years, I met with William Lloyd Garrison, a person of whom you have *possibly* heard, as he is pretty generally known among slaveholders. He put it into my head that I might make myself serviceable to the cause of the slave, by devoting a portion of my time to telling my own sorrows, and those of other slaves, which had come under my observation. This was the commencement of a higher state of existence than any to which I had ever aspired. I was thrown into society the most pure, enlightened, and benevolent, that the country affords. Among these I have never forgotten you, but have invariably made you the topic of conversation – thus giving you all the notoriety I could do. I need not tell you that the opinion formed of you in these circles is far from being favourable. They have little respect for your honesty, and less for your religion.

But I was going on to relate to you something of my interesting experience. I had not long enjoyed the excellent society to which I have referred, before the light of its excellence exerted a beneficial influence on my mind and heart. Much of my early dislike of white persons was removed, and their manners, habits, and customs, so entirely unlike what I had been used to in the kitchen-quarters on the plantations of the south, fairly charmed me, and gave me a strong disrelish for the coarse and degrading customs of my former condition. I therefore made an effort so to improve my mind and deportment, as to be somewhat fitted to the station to which I seemed almost providentially called. The transition from degradation to respectability was indeed great, and to get from one to the other without carrying some marks of one's former condition, is truly a difficult matter. I would not have you think that I am now entirely clear of all plantation peculiarities, but my friends here, while they entertained the strongest dislike of them, regard me with that charity to which my past life somewhat entitles me, so that my condition in this respect is exceedingly pleasant. So far as my domestic affairs are concerned, I can boast of as comfortable a dwelling as your own. I have an industrious and neat companion, and four dear children – the oldest a girl of nine years, and three fine boys, the oldest eight, the next six, and the youngest four years old. The three oldest are now going regularly to school – two can read and write, and the other can spell, with tolerable correctness, words of two syllables. Dear fellows! they are all in comfortable beds, and are sound asleep, perfectly secure under my own roof. There are no slaveholders here to rend my heart by snatching them from my arms, or blast a mother's dearest hopes by tearing them from her bosom. These dear children are ours – not to work up into rice, sugar, and tobacco, but to watch over, regard, and protect, and to rear them to the paths of wisdom and virtue, and, as far as we can, to make them useful to the world and to themselves. Oh! sir, a slaveholder never appears to me so completely an agent of hell as when I think of and look upon my dear children. It is then that my feelings rise above my control. I meant to have said more with respect to my own prosperity and happiness, but thoughts and feelings which this recital has quickened, unfits me to proceed further in that direction. The grim horrors of slavery rise in all their ghastly terror before me; the wails of millions pierce my heart and chill my blood. I remember the chain, the gag, the bloody whip; the death-like gloom overshadowing the broken spirit of the fettered bondman; the appalling liability of his being torn away from wife and children, and sold like a beast in the market. Say not that this is a picture of fancy. You well know that I wear stripes on my back, inflicted by your direction; and that you, while we were brothers in the same church, caused this right hand, with which I am now penning this letter, to be closely tied to my left, and my person dragged at the pistol's mouth, fifteen miles, from the Bay side to Easton, to be sold like a beast in the market, for the alleged crime of intending to escape from your possession. All this, and more, you remember, and know to be perfectly true, not only of yourself, but of nearly all of the slaveholders around you.

At this moment, you are probably the guilty holder of at least three of my own dear sisters, and my only brother, in bondage. These you regard as your property. They are recorded on your ledger, or perhaps have been sold to human flesh-mongers, with a view to filling your own ever-hungry purse. Sir, I desire to know how and where these dear sisters are. Have you sold them? or are they still in your possession? What has become of them? are they living or dead? And my dear old grandmother, whom you turned out like an old horse to die in the woods – is she still alive? Write and let me know all about them. If my grandmother be still alive, she is of no service to you, for by this time she must be nearly eighty years old – too old to be cared for by one to whom she has ceased to be of service; send her to me at Rochester, or bring her to Philadelphia, and it shall be the crowning happiness of my life to take care of her in her old age. Oh! she was to me a mother and a father, so far as hard toil for my comfort could make her such. Send me my grandmother! that I may watch over and take care of her in her old age. And my sisters – let me know all about them. I would write to them, and learn all I want to know of them, without disturbing you in any way, but that, through your unrighteous conduct, they have been entirely deprived of the power to read and write. You have kept them in utter ignorance, and have therefore robbed them of the sweet enjoyments of writing or receiving letters from absent friends and relatives. Your wickedness and cruelty, committed in this respect on your fellow-creatures, are greater than all the stripes you have laid upon my back or theirs. It is an outrage upon the soul, a war upon the immortal spirit, and one for which you must give account at the bar of our common Father and Creator.

The responsibility which you have assumed in this regard is truly awful, and how you could stagger under it these many years is marvellous. Your mind must have become darkened, your heart hardened, your conscience seared and petrified, or you would have long since thrown off the accursed load, and sought relief at the hands of a sin-forgiving God. How, let me ask, would you look upon me, were I, some dark night, in company with a band of hardened villains, to enter the precincts of your elegant dwelling, and seize the person of your own lovely daughter, Amanda, and carry her off from your family, friends, and all the loved ones of her youth – make her my slave – compel her to work, and I take her wages – place her name on my ledger as property – disregard her personal rights – fetter the powers of her immortal soul by denying her the right and privilege of learning to read and write – feed her coarsely – clothe her scantily, and whip her on the naked back occasionally; more, and still more horrible, leave her unprotected – a degraded victim to the brutal lust of fiendish overseers, who would pollute, blight, and blast her fair soul – rob her of all dignity – destroy her virtue, and annihilate in her person all the graces that adorn the character of virtuous womanhood? I ask, how would you regard me, if such were my conduct? Oh! the vocabulary of the damned would not afford a word sufficiently infernal to express your idea of my God-provoking wickedness. Yet, sir, your treatment of my beloved sisters is in all essential points precisely like the case I have now supposed. Damning as would be such a deed on my part, it would be no more so than that which you have committed against me and my sisters.

I will now bring this letter to a close; you shall hear from me again unless you let me hear from you. I intend to make use of you as a weapon with which to assail the system of slavery – as a means of concentrating public attention on the system, and deepening the horror of trafficking in the souls and bodies of men. I shall make use of you as a means of exposing the character of the American church and clergy – and as a means of bringing this guilty nation, with yourself, to repentance. In doing this, I entertain no malice toward you personally. There is no roof under which you would be more safe than mine, and there is nothing in my house which you might need for your comfort, which I would not readily grant. Indeed, I should esteem it a privilege to set you an example as to how mankind ought to treat each other.

I am your fellow-man, but not your slave.
Frederick Douglass

From ON LIBERTY, 1859

John Stuart Mill

John Stuart Mill (1806–73) was the son of James Mill, the chief disciple of the Utilitarian Jeremy Bentham. Mill junior was educated (in an intellectually rigorous but emotionally negligible manner) by his father, and remained influenced by Utilitarianism – which advocated the greatest good for the greatest number – all his career as a philosopher. Unlike Bentham, John Stuart Mill was alive to the possibility of tyranny by the majority and the need to limit state power. He most fully explored these issues in *On Liberty*, published in 1859. Of particular import is Mill's proposition that the sole reason for "interfering with the liberty of action of any of their number is . . . to prevent harm to others. His own good, either physical or moral, is not a sufficient warrant". This is the gold standard definition and defence of the rights of the individual in Western society.

Mill's other works include *Utilitarianism*, 1863, *The Subjection of Women*, 1869, and the seminal work on logic, *System of Logic*, 1843.

The object of this Essay is to assert one very simple principle, as entitled to govern absolutely the dealings of society with the individual in the way of compulsion and control, whether the means used be physical force in the form of legal penalties, or the moral coercion of public opinion. That principle is, that the sole end for which mankind are warranted, individually or collectively, in interfering with the liberty of action of any of their number, is self-protection. That the only purpose for which power can be rightfully exercised over any member of a civilized community, against his will, is to prevent harm to others. His own good, either physical or moral, is not a sufficient warrant. He cannot rightfully be compelled to do or forbear because it will be better for him to do so, because it will make him happier because, in the opinions of others, to do so would be wise, or even right. These are good reasons for remonstrating with him, or reasoning with him or persuading him, or entreating him, but not for compelling him, or visiting him with any evil in case he do otherwise. To justify that, the conduct from which it is desired to deter him, must be calculated to produce evil to some one else. The only part of the conduct of any one, for which he is amenable to society, is that which concerns others. In the part which merely concerns himself, his independence is, of right, absolute. Over himself, over his own body and mind, the individual is sovereign.

It is perhaps, hardly necessary to say that this doctrine is meant to apply only to human beings in the maturity of their faculties. We are not speaking of children, or of young persons below the age which the law may fix as that of manhood or womanhood. Those who are still in a state to require being taken care of by others, must be protected against their own actions as well as against external injury. For the same reason, we may leave out of consideration those backward states of society in which the race itself may be considered as in its nonage. The early difficulties in the way of spontaneous progress are so great, that there is seldom any choice of means for overcoming them; and a ruler full of the spirit of improvement is warranted in the use of any expedients that will attain an end, perhaps otherwise unattainable. Despotism is a legitimate mode of government in dealing with barbarians, provided the end be their improvement, and the means justified by actually effecting that end. Liberty, as a principle, has no application to any state of things anterior to the time when mankind have become capable of being improved by free and equal discussion. Until then, there is nothing for them but implicit obedience to an Akbar or a Charlemagne, if they are so fortunate as to find one. But as soon as mankind have attained the capacity of being guided to their own improvement by conviction or persuasion (a period long since reached in all nations with whom we need here concern ourselves), compulsion, either in the direct form or in that of pains and penalties for non-compliance, is no longer admissible as a means to their own good, and justifiable only for the security of others.

It is proper to state that I forego any advantage which could be derived to my argument from the idea of abstract right, as a thing independent of utility. I regard utility as the ultimate appeal on all ethical questions; but it must be utility in the largest sense, grounded on the permanent interests of man as a progressive being. Those interests, I contend, authorize the subjection of individual spontaneity to external control, only in respect to those actions of each, which concern the interest of other people. If any one does an act hurtful to others, there is a *prima facie* case for punishing him, by law, or, where legal penalties are not safely applicable, by general disapprobation. There are also many positive acts for the benefit of others, which he may rightfully be compelled to perform; such as, to give evidence in a court of justice; to bear his fair share in the common defence, or in any other joint work necessary to the interest of the society of which he enjoys the protection; and to perform certain acts of individual beneficence, such as saving a fellow-creature's life, or interposing to protect the defenceless against ill-usage, things which whenever it is obviously a man's duty to do, he may rightfully be made responsible to society for not doing. A person may cause evil to others not only by his actions but by his inaction, and in either case he is justly accountable to them for the injury. The latter case, it is true, requires a much more cautious exercise of compulsion than the former. To make any one answerable for doing evil to others, is the rule; to make him answerable for not preventing evil, is, comparatively speaking, the exception. Yet there are many cases clear enough and grave enough to justify that exception. In all things which regard the external relations of the individual, he is *de jure* amenable to those whose interests are concerned, and if need be, to society as their protector. There are often good reasons for not holding him to the responsibility; but these reasons must arise from the special expediencies of the case: either because it is a kind of case in which he is on the whole likely to act better, when left to his own discretion, than when controlled in any way in which society have it in their power to control him; or because the attempt to exercise control would produce other evils, greater than those which it would prevent. When such reasons as these preclude the enforcement of responsibility, the conscience of the agent himself should step into the vacant judgment seat, and protect those interests of others which have no external protection; judging himself all the more rigidly, because the case does not admit of his being made accountable to the judgment of his fellow-creatures.

But there is a sphere of action in which society, as distinguished from the individual, has, if any, only an indirect interest; comprehending all that portion of a person's life and conduct which affects only himself, or if it also affects others, only with their free, voluntary, and undeceived consent and participation. When I say only himself, I mean directly, and in the first instance: for whatever affects himself, may affect others through himself; and the objection which may be grounded on this contingency, will receive consideration in the sequel. This, then, is the appropriate region of human liberty. It comprises, first, the inward domain of consciousness; demanding liberty or conscience, in the most comprehensive sense; liberty of thought and feeling; absolute freedom of opinion and sentiment on all subjects, practical or speculative, scientific, moral, or theological. The liberty of expressing and publishing opinions may seem to fall under a different principle, since it belongs to that part of the conduct of an individual which concerns other people; but, being almost of as much importance as the liberty of thought itself, and resting in great part on the same reasons, is practically inseparable from it. Secondly, the principle requires liberty of tastes and pursuits; of framing the plan of our life to suit our own character; of doing as we like, subject to such consequences as may follow: without impediment from our fellow-creatures, so long as what we do does not harm them, even though they should think our conduct foolish, perverse, or wrong. Thirdly, from this liberty of each individual, follows the liberty, within the same limits, of combination among individuals; freedom to unite, for any purpose not involving harm to others: the persons combining being supposed to be of full age, and not forced or deceived.

No society in which these liberties are not, on the whole, respected, is free, whatever may be its form of government; and none is completely free in which they do not exist absolute and unqualified. The only freedom which deserves the name, is that of pursuing our own good in our own way, so long as we do not attempt to deprive others of theirs, or impede their efforts to obtain it. Each is the proper guardian of his own health, whether bodily, or mental and spiritual. Mankind are greater gainers by suffering each other to live as seems good to themselves, than by compelling each to live as seems good to the rest . . .

★   ★   ★

What, then, is the rightful limit to the sovereignty of the individual over himself? Where does the authority of society begin? How much of human life should be assigned to individuality, and how much to society?

Each will receive its proper share, if each has that which more particularly concerns it. To individuality should belong the part of life in which it is chiefly the individual that is interested; to society, the part which chiefly interests society.

Though society is not founded on a contract, and though no good purpose is answered by inventing a contract in order to deduce social obligations from it, every one who receives the protection of society owes a return for the benefit, and the fact of living in society renders it indispensable that each should be bound to observe a certain line of conduct towards the rest. This conduct consists first, in not injuring the interests of one another; or rather certain interests, which, either by express legal provision or by tacit understanding, ought to be considered as rights; and secondly, in each person's bearing his share (to be fixed on some equitable principle) of the labours and sacrifices incurred for defending the society or its members from injury and molestation. These conditions society is justified in enforcing at all costs to those who endeavour to withhold fulfilment. Nor is this all that society may do. The acts of an individual may be hurtful to others, or wanting in due consideration for their welfare, without going the length of violating any of their constituted rights. The offender may then be justly punished by opinion, though not by law. As soon as any part of a person's conduct affects prejudicially the interests of others, society has jurisdiction over it, and the question whether the general welfare will or will not be promoted by interfering with it, becomes open to discussion. But there is no room for entertaining any such question when a person's conduct affects the interests of no persons besides himself; or needs not affect them unless they like (all the persons concerned being of full age, and the ordinary amount of understanding). In all such cases there should be perfect freedom, legal and social, to do the action and stand the consequences.

It would be a great misunderstanding of this doctrine to suppose that it is one of selfish indifference, which pretends that human beings have no business with each other's conduct in life, and that they should not concern themselves about the well-doing or well-being of one another, unless their own interest is involved. Instead of any diminution, there is need of a great increase of disinterested exertion to promote the good of others. But disinterested benevolence can find other instruments to persuade people to their good, than whips and scourges, either of the literal or the metaphorical sort. I am the last person to undervalue the self-regarding virtues; they are only second in importance, if even second, to the social. It is equally the business of education to cultivate both. But even education works by conviction and persuasion as well as by compulsion, and it is by the former only that, when the period of education is past, the self-regarding virtues should be inculcated. Human beings owe to each other help to distinguish the better from the worse, and encouragement to choose the former and avoid the latter. They should be for ever stimulating each other to increased exercise of their higher faculties; and increased direction of their feelings and aims towards wise instead of foolish, elevating instead of degrading, objects and contemplations. But neither one person, nor any number of persons, is warranted in saying to another human creature of ripe years, that he shall not do with his life for his own benefit what he chooses to do with it. He is the person most interested in his own well-being: the interest which any other person, except in cases of strong personal attachment, can have in it, is trifling, compared with that which he himself has; the interest which society has in him individually (except as to his conduct to others) is fractional, and altogether indirect: while, with respect to his own feelings and circumstances, the most ordinary man or woman has means of knowledge immeasurably surpassing those that can be possessed by any one else. The interference of society to overrule his judgment and purposes in what only regards himself, must be grounded on general presumptions; which may be altogether wrong, and even if right, are as likely as not to be misapplied to individual cases, by persons no better acquainted with the circumstances of such cases than those are who look at them merely from without. In this department, therefore, of human affairs, Individuality has its proper field of action. In the conduct of human beings towards one another, it is necessary that general rules should for the most part be observed, in order that people may know what they have to expect; but in each person's own concerns, his individual spontaneity is entitled to free exercise. Considerations to aid his judgment, exhortations to strengthen his will, may be offered to him, even obtruded on him, by others; but he himself is the final judge. All errors which he is likely to commit against advice and warning, are far outweighed by the evil of allowing others to constrain him to what they deem his good.

I do not mean that the feelings with which a person is regarded by others, ought not to be in any way affected by his self-regarding qualities or deficiencies. This is neither possible nor desirable. If he is eminent in any way of the qualities which conduce to his own good, he is, so far, a proper object of admiration. He is so much the nearer to the ideal perfection of human nature. If he is grossly deficient in those qualities, a sentiment the opposite of admiration will follow. There is a degree of folly, and a degree of what may be called (though the phrase is not unobjectionable) lowness or depravation of taste, which, though it cannot justify doing harm to the person who manifests it, renders him necessarily and properly a subject of distaste, or, in extreme cases, even of contempt: a person could not have the opposite qualities in due strength without entertaining these feelings. Though doing no wrong to any one, a person may so act as to compel us to judge him, and feel to him, as a fool, or as a being of an inferior order: and since this judgment and feeling are a fact which he would prefer to avoid, it is doing him a service to warn him of it beforehand, as of any other disagreeable consequence to which he exposes himself. It would be well, indeed, if this good office were much more freely rendered than the common notions of politeness at present permit, and if one person could honestly point out to another that he thinks him in fault, without being considered unmannerly or presuming. We have a right, also, in various ways, to act upon our unfavourable opinion of any one, not to the oppression of his individuality, but in the exercise of ours. We are not bound, for example, to seek his society; we have a right to avoid it (though not to parade the avoidance), for we have a right to choose the society most acceptable to us. We have a right, and it may be our duty, to caution others against him, if we think his example or conversation likely to have a pernicious effect on those with whom he associates. We may give others a preference over him in optional good offices, expect those which tend to his improvement. In these various modes a person may suffer very severe penalties at the hands of others, for faults which directly concern only himself; but he suffers these penalties only in so far as they are natural, and, as it were, the spontaneous consequences of the faults themselves, not because they are purposely inflicted on him for the sake of punishment. A person who shows rashness, obstinacy, self-conceit – who cannot live within moderate means – who cannot restrain himself from hurtful indulgences – who pursues animal pleasures at the expense of those of feeling and intellect – must expect to be lowered in the opinion of others, and to have a less share of their favourable sentiments; but of this he has no right to complain, unless he has merited their favour by special excellence in his social relations, and has thus established a title to their good offices, which is not affected by his demerits towards himself.

What I contend for is, that the inconveniences which are strictly inseparable from the unfavourable judgment of others, are the only ones to which a person should ever be subjected for that portion of his conduct and character which concerns his own good, but which does not affect the interests of others in their relations with him. Acts injurious to others require a totally different treatment. Encroachment on their rights; infliction on them of any loss or damage not justified by his own rights; falsehood or duplicity in dealing with them; unfair or ungenerous use of advantages over them; even selfish abstinence from defending them against injury – these are fit objects of moral reprobation, and, in grave cases, of moral retribution and punishment. And not only these acts, but the dispositions which lead to them, are properly immoral, and fit subjects of disapprobation which may rise to abhorrence. Cruelty of disposition; malice and ill-nature; that most antisocial and odious of all passions, envy; dissimulation and insincerity; irascibility on insufficient cause, and resentment disproportioned to the provocation; the love of domineering over others; the desire to engross more than one's share of advantages (the πλεονεξία of the Greeks; the pride which derives gratification from the abasement of others; the egotism which thinks self and its concerns more important than everything else, and decides all doubtful questions in its own favour – these are moral vices, and constitute a bad and odious moral character: unlike the self-regarding faults previously mentioned, which are not properly immoralities, and to whatever pitch they may be carried, do not constitute wickedness. They may be proofs of any amount of folly, or want of personal dignity and self-respect; but they are only a subject of moral reprobation when they involve a breach of duty to others, for whose sake the individual is bound to have care for himself. What are called duties to ourselves are not socially obligatory, unless circumstances render them at the same time duties to others. The term duty to oneself, when it means anything more than prudence, means self-respect or self-development; and for none of these is any one accountable to his fellow creatures, because for none of them is it for the good of mankind that he be held accountable to them.

The distinction between the loss of consideration which a person may rightly incur by defect of prudence or of personal dignity, and the reprobation which is due to him for an offence against the rights of others, is not a merely nominal distinction. It makes a vast difference both in our feelings and in our conduct towards him, whether he displeases us in things in which we think we have a right to control him, or in things in which we know that we have not. If he displeases us, we may express our distaste, and we may stand aloof from a person as well as from a thing that displeases us; but we shall not therefore feel called on to make his life uncomfortable. We shall reflect that he already bears, or will bear, the whole penalty of his error; if he spoils his life by mismanagement, we shall not, for that reason, desire to spoil it still further: instead of wishing to punish him, we shall rather endeavour to alleviate his punishment, by showing him how he may avoid or cure the evils his conduct tends to bring upon him. He may be to us an object of pity, perhaps of dislike, but not of anger or resentment; we shall not treat him like an enemy of society: the worst we shall think ourselves justified in doing is leaving him to himself, if we do not interfere benevolently by showing interest or concern for him. It is far otherwise if he has infringed the rules necessary for the protection of his fellow-creatures, individually or collectively. The evil consequences of his acts do not then fall on himself, but on others; and society, as the protector of all its members, must retaliate on him; must inflict pain on him for the express purpose of punishment, and must take care that it be sufficiently severe. In the one case, he is an offender at our bar, and we are called on not only to sit in judgment on him, but, in one shape or another, to execute our own sentence: in the other case, it is not our part to inflict any suffering on him, except what may incidentally follow from our using the same liberty in the regulation of our own affairs, which we allow to him in his.

The distinction here pointed out between the part of a person's life which concerns only himself, and that which concerns others, many persons will refuse to admit. How (it may be asked) can any part of the conduct of a member of society be a matter of indifference to the other members? No person is an entirely isolated being: it is impossible for a person to do anything seriously or permanently hurtful to himself, without mischief reaching at least to his near connections, and often far beyond them. If he injures his property, he does harm to those who directly or indirectly derived support from it, and usually diminishes, by a greater or less amount, the general resources of the community. If he deteriorates his bodily or mental faculties, he not only brings evil upon all who depended on him for any portion of their happiness, but disqualifies himself for rendering the services which he owes to his fellow-creatures generally; perhaps becomes a burthen on their affection or benevolence; and if such conduct were very frequent, hardly any offence that is committed would detract more from the general sum of good. Finally, if by his vices or follies a person does no direct harm to others, he is nevertheless (it may be said) injurious by his example; and ought to be compelled to control himself, for the sake of those whom the sight or knowledge of his conduct might corrupt or mislead.

And even (it will be added) if the consequences of misconduct could be confined to the vicious or thoughtless individual, ought society to abandon to their own guidance those who are manifestly unfit for it? If protection against themselves is confessedly due to children and persons under age, is not society equally bound to afford it to persons of mature years who are equally incapable of self-government? If gambling, or drunkenness, or incontinence, or idleness, or uncleanliness, are as injurious to happiness, and as great a hindrance to improvement, as many or most of the acts prohibited by law, why (it may be asked) should not law; so far as is consistent with practicability and social convenience, endeavour to repress these also? And as a supplement to the unavoidable imperfections of law, ought not opinion at least to organize a powerful police against these vices, and visit rigidly with social penalties those who are known to practise them? There is no question here (it may be said) about restricting individuality, or impeding the trial of new and original experiments in living. The only things it is sought to prevent are things which have been tried and condemned from the beginning of the world until now; things which experience has shown not to be useful or suitable to any person's individuality. There must be some length of time and amount of experience, after which a moral or prudential truth may be regarded as established, and it is merely desired to prevent generation after generation from falling over the same precipice which has been fatal to their predecessors.

I fully admit that the mischief which a person does to himself, may seriously affect, both through their sympathies and their interests, those nearly connected with him, and in a minor degree, society at large. When, by conduct of this sort, a person is led to violate a distinct and assignable obligation to any other person or persons, the case is taken out of the self-regarding class, and becomes amenable to moral disapprobation in the proper sense of the term. If, for example, a man, through intemperance or extravagance, becomes unable to pay his debts, or, having undertaken the moral responsibility of a family, becomes from the same cause incapable of supporting or educating them, he is deservedly reprobated, and might be justly punished; but it is for the breach of duty to his family or creditors, not for the extravagance. If the resources which ought to have been devoted to them, had been diverted from them for the most prudent investment, the moral culpability would have been the same. George Barnwell murdered his uncle to get money for his mistress, but if he had done it to set himself up in business, he would equally have been hanged. Again, in the frequent case of a man who causes grief to his family by addiction to bad habits, he deserves reproach for his unkindness or ingratitude; but so he may for cultivating habits not in themselves vicious, if they are painful to those with whom he passes his life, or who from personal ties are dependent on him for their comfort. Whoever fails in the consideration generally due to the interests and feelings of others, not being compelled by some more imperative duty, or justified by allowable self-preference, is a subject of moral disapprobation for that failure, but not for the cause of it, nor for the errors, merely personal to himself, which may have remotely led to it. In like manner, when a person disables himself, by conduct purely self-regarding, from the performance of some definite duty incumbent on him to the public, he is guilty of a social offence. No person ought to be punished simply for being drunk; but a soldier or a policeman should be punished for being drunk on duty. Whenever, in short, there is a definite damage, or a definite risk of damage, either to an individual or to the public, the case is taken out of the province of liberty, and placed in that of morality or law.

From ON THE ORIGIN OF SPECIES, 1859

Charles Darwin

"When on board HMS *Beagle*, as naturalist, I was much struck with certain facts in the distribution of the inhabitants of South America, and in the geological relations of the present to the past inhabitants of that continent. These facts seemed to me to throw might on the origin of species – that mystery of mysteries . . ." So wrote Charles Darwin in the introduction to *On the Origin of Species by Means of Natural Selection*, an epoch-shaking book which suggested that no species is immutable, but all have evolved down the millennia. In the struggle for existence success has lain with those creatures possessing advantageous mutations. Such "natural selection" was analogous, Darwin maintained, with the artificial selection of the horse or pigeon breeder.

On the Origin of Species thus directly challenged the prevailing creationist belief that all creatures were the handiwork of God. Evolutionism, however, after the initial horror, found general acceptance in the Western world, even when in *The Descent of Man*, 1871, Darwin proposed that humans had descended from primates.

Charles Robert Darwin (1809–82) was born in Shrewsbury, England. His maternal grandfather was Josiah Wedgwood, the founder of Wedgwood pottery; his paternal grandfather was Erasmus Darwin, a freethinking physician whose views of evolution anticipated his grandson's. For forty years Darwin lived at Downe in Kent where he wrote, in addition to *On the Origin* and *The Descent of Man*, numerous other books, mostly on botanical matters.

Darwin, it might be noted, did not kill God with science in *On the Origin of Species*. Although many modern biologists deny a Supreme Maker, many physicists maintain a divine Origin of the Universe.

Chapter III: Struggle for Existence

. . . I should premise that I use the term Struggle for Existence in a large and metaphorical sense, including dependence of one being on another, and including (which is more important) not only the life of the individual, but success in leaving progeny. Two canine animals in a time of dearth, may be truly said to struggle with each other which shall get food and live. But a plant on the edge of a desert is said to struggle for life against the drought, though more properly it should be said to be dependent on the moisture. A plant which annually produces a thousand seeds, of which on an average only one comes to maturity, may be more truly said to struggle with the plants of the same and other kinds which already clothe the ground. The mistletoe is dependent on the apple and a few other trees, but can only in a far-fetched sense be said to struggle with these trees, for if too many of these parasites grow on the same tree, it will languish and die. But several seedling mistletoes, growing close together on the same branch, may more truly be said to struggle with each other. As the mistletoe is disseminated by birds, its existence depends on birds; and it may meta-phorically be said to struggle with other fruit-bearing plants, in order to tempt birds to devour and thus disseminate its seeds rather than those of other plants. In these several senses, which pass into each other, I use for convenience' sake the general term of struggle for existence.

A struggle for existence inevitably follows from the high rate at which all organic beings tend to increase. Every being, which during its natural lifetime produces several eggs or seeds, must suffer destruction during some period of its life, and during some season or occasional year, otherwise, on the principle of geometrical increase, its numbers would quickly become so inordinately great that no country could support the product. Hence, as more individuals are produced than can possibly survive, there must in every case be a struggle for existence, either one individual with another of the same species, or with the individuals of distinct species, or with the physical conditions of life. It is the doctrine of Malthus applied with manifold force to the whole animal and vegetable kingdoms; for in this case there can be no artificial increase of food, and no prudential restraint from marriage. Although some species may be now increasing, more or less rapidly, in numbers, all cannot do so, for the world would not hold them.

There is no exception to the rule that every organic being naturally increases at so high a rate, that if not destroyed, the earth would soon be covered by the progeny of a single pair. Even slow-breeding man has doubled in twenty-five years, and at this rate, in a few thousand years, there would literally not be standing room for his progeny. Linnaeus has calculated that if an annual plant produced only two seeds – and there is no plant so unproductive as this – and their seedlings next year produced two, and so on, then in twenty years there would be a million plants. The elephant is reckoned to be the slowest breeder of all known animals, and I have taken some pains to estimate its probable minimum rate of natural increase: it will be under the mark to assume that it breeds when thirty years old, and goes on breeding till ninety years old, bringing forth three pair of young in this interval; if this be so, at the end of the fifth century there would be alive fifteen million elephants, descended from the first pair.

But we have better evidence on this subject than mere theoretical calculations, namely, the numerous recorded cases of the astonishingly rapid increase of various animals in a state of nature, when circumstances have been favourable to them during two or three following seasons. Still more striking is the evidence from our domestic animals of many kinds which have run wild in several parts of the world: if the statements of the rate of increase of slow-breeding cattle and horses in South America, and latterly in Australia, had not been well authenticated, they would have been quite incredible. So it is with plants: cases could be given of introduced plants which have become common throughout whole islands in a period of less than ten years. Several of the plants now most numerous over the wide plains of La Plata, clothing square leagues of surface almost to the exclusion of all other plants, have been introduced from Europe; and there are plants which now range in India, as I hear from Dr Falconer, from Cape Comorin to the Himalaya, which have been imported from America since its discovery. In such cases, and endless instances could be given, no one supposes that the fertility of these animals or plants has been suddenly and temporarily increased in any sensible degree. The obvious explanation is that the conditions of life have been very favourable, and that there has consequently been less destruction of the old and young, and that nearly all the young have been enabled to breed. In such cases the geometrical ratio of increase, the result of which never fails to be surprising, simply explains the extraordinarily rapid increase and wide diffusion of naturalized productions in their new homes.

In a state of nature almost every plant produces seed, and amongst animals there are very few which do not annually pair. Hence we may confidently assert, that all plants and animals are tending to increase at a geometrical ratio, that all would most rapidly stock every station in which they could any how exist, and that the geometrical tendency to increase must be checked by destruction at some period of life. Our familiarity with the larger domestic animals tends, I think, to mislead us: we see no great destruction falling on them, and we forget that thousands are annually slaughtered for food, and that in a state of nature an equal number would have somehow to be disposed of.

The only difference between organisms which annually produce eggs or seeds by the thousand, and those which produce extremely few, is, that the slow-breeders would require a few more years to people, under favourable conditions, a whole district, let it be ever so large. The condor lays a couple of eggs and the ostrich a score, and yet in the same country the condor may be the more numerous of the two: the Fulmar petrel lays but one egg, yet it is believed to be the most numerous bird in the world. One fly deposits hundreds of eggs, and another, like the *hippobosca*, a single one; but this difference does not determine how many individuals of the two species can be supported in a district. A large number of eggs is of some importance to those species, which depend on a rapidly fluctuating amount of food, for it allows them rapidly to increase in number. But the real importance of a large number of eggs or seeds is to make up for much destruction at some period of life; and this period in the great majority of cases is an early one. If an animal can in any way protect its own eggs or young, a small number may be produced, and yet the average stock be fully kept up; but if many eggs or young are destroyed, many must be produced, or the species will become extinct. It would suffice to keep up the full number of a tree, which lived on an average for a thousand years, if a single seed were produced once in a thousand years, supposing that this seed were never destroyed, and could be ensured to germinate in a fitting place. So that in all cases, the average number of any animal or plant depends only indirectly on the number of its eggs or seeds.

In looking at Nature, it is most necessary to keep the foregoing considerations always in mind – never to forget that every single organic being around us may be said to be striving to the utmost to increase in numbers; that each lives by a struggle at some period of its life; that heavy destruction inevitably falls either on the young or old, during each generation or at recurrent intervals. Lighten any check, mitigate the destruction ever so little, and the number of the species will almost instantaneously increase to any amount. The face of Nature may be compared to a yielding surface, with ten thousand sharp wedges packed close together and driven inwards by incessant blows, sometimes one wedge being struck, and then another with greater force . . .

. . . Many cases are on record showing how complex and unexpected are the checks and relations between organic beings, which have to struggle together in the same country. I will give only a single instance, which, though a simple one, has interested me. In Staffordshire, on the estate of a relation where I had ample means of investigation, there was a large and extremely barren heath, which had never been touched by the hand of man; but several hundred acres of exactly the same nature had been enclosed twenty-five years previously and planted with Scotch fir. The change in the native vegetation of the planted part of the heath was most remarkable, more than is generally seen in passing from one quite different soil to another: not only the proportional numbers of the heathplants were wholly changed, but twelve species of plants (not counting grasses and carices) flourished in the plantations, which could not be found on the heath. The effect on the insects must have been still greater, for six insectivorous birds were very common in the plantations, which were not to be seen on the heath; and the heath was frequented by two or three distinct insectivorous birds. Here we see how potent has been the effect of the introduction of a single tree, nothing whatever else having been done, with the exception that the land had been enclosed, so that cattle could not enter. But how important an element enclosure is, I plainly saw near Farnham, in Surrey. Here there are extensive heaths, with a few clumps of old Scotch firs on the distant hill-tops: within the last ten years large spaces have been enclosed, and self-sown firs are now springing up in multitudes, so close together that all cannot live. When I ascertained that these young trees had not been sown or planted, I was so much surprised at their numbers that I went to several points of view, whence I could examine hundreds of acres of the unenclosed heath, and literally I could not see a single Scotch fir except the old planted clumps. But on looking closely between the stems of the heath, I found a multitude of seedlings and little trees, which had been perpetually browsed down by the cattle. In one square yard, at a point some hundred yards distant from one of the old clumps, I counted thirty-two little trees; and one of them, judging from the rings of growth, had during twenty-six years tried to raise its head above the stems of the heath, and had failed. No wonder that, as soon as the land was enclosed, it became thickly clothed with vigorously growing young firs. Yet the heath was so extremely barren and so extensive that no one would ever have imagined that cattle would have so closely and effectually searched it for food.

Here we see that cattle absolutely determine the existence of the Scotch fir; but in several parts of the world insects determine the existence of cattle. Perhaps Paraguay offers the most curious instance of this; for here neither cattle nor horses nor dogs have ever run wild, though they swarm southward and northward in a feral state; and Azara and Rengger have shown that this is caused by the greater number in Paraguay of a certain fly, which lays eggs in the navels of these animals when first born. The increase of these flies, numerous as they are, must be habitually checked by some means, probably by birds. Hence, if certain insectivorous birds (whose numbers are probably regulated by hawks or beasts of prey) were to increase in Paraguay, the flies would decrease – then cattle and horses would become feral, and this would certainly greatly alter (as indeed I have observed in parts of South America) the vegetation: this again would largely affect the insects; and this, as we just have seen in Staffordshire, the insectivorous birds, and so onwards in ever-increasing circles of complexity. We began this series by insectivorous birds, and we have ended with them. Not that in nature the relations can ever be as simple as this. Battle within battle must ever be recurring with varying success; and yet in the long-run the forces are so nicely balanced, that the face of nature remains uniform for long periods of time, though assuredly the merest trifle would often give the victory to one organic being over another. Nevertheless so profound is our ignorance, and so high our presumption, that we marvel when we hear of the extinction of an organic being; and as we do not see the cause, we invoke cataclysms to desolate the world, or invent laws on the duration of the forms of life!

I am tempted to give one more instance showing how plants and animals, most remote in the scale of nature, are bound together by a web of complex relations. I shall hereafter have occasion to show that the exotic *Lobelia fulgens*, in this part of England, is never visited by insects, and, consequently, from its peculiar structure, never can set a seed. Many of our orchidaceous plants absolutely require the visits of moths to remove their pollen-masses and thus to fertilize them. I have, also, reason to believe that humble-bees are indispensable to the fertilization of the heartsease (*Viola tricolor*), for other bees do not visit this flower. From experiments which I have tried, I have found that the visits of bees, if not indispensable, are at least highly beneficial to the fertilization of our clovers; but humble-bees alone visit the common red clover (*Trifolium pratense*), as other bees cannot reach the nectar. Hence I have very little doubt, that if the whole genus of humble-bees became extinct or very rare in England, the heartsease and red clover would become very rare, or wholly disappear. The number of humble-bees in any district depends in a great degree on the number of field-mice, which destroy their combs and nests; and Mr H. Newman, who has long attended to the habits of humble-bees, believes that "more than two-thirds of them are thus destroyed all over England." Now the number of mice is largely dependent, as every one knows, on the number of cats; and Mr Newman says, "Near villages and small towns I have found the nests of humble-bees more numerous than elsewhere, which I attribute to the number of cats that destroy the mice." Hence it is quite credible that the presence of a feline animal in large numbers in a district might determine, through the intervention first of mice and then of bees, the frequency of certain flowers in that district!

In the case of every species, many different checks, acting at different periods of life, and during different seasons or years, probably come into play; some one check or some few being generally the most potent, but all concurring in determining the average number or even the existence of the species. In some cases it can be shown that widely-different checks act on the same species in different districts. When we look at the plants and bushes clothing an entangled bank, we are tempted to attribute their proportional numbers and kinds to what we call chance. But how false a view is this! Every one has heard that when an American forest is cut down, a very different vegetation springs up; but it has been observed that the trees now growing on the ancient Indian mounds, in the Southern United States, display the same beautiful diversity and proportion of kinds as in the surrounding virgin forests. What a struggle between the several kinds of trees must here have gone on during long centuries, each annually scattering its seeds by the thousand; what war between insect and insect – between insects, snails, and other animals with birds and beasts of prey – all striving to increase, and all feeding on each other or on the trees or their seeds and seedlings, or on the other plants which first clothed the ground and thus checked the growth of the trees! Throw up a handful of feathers, and all must fall to the ground according to definite laws; but how simple is this problem compared to the action and reaction of the innumerable plants and animals which have determined, in the course of centuries, the proportional numbers and kinds of trees now growing on the old Indian ruins!

Chapter IV: Natural Selection

. . . We shall best understand the probable course of natural selection by taking the case of a country undergoing some physical change, for instance, of climate. The proportional numbers of its inhabitants would almost immediately undergo a change, and some species might become extinct. We may conclude, from what we have seen of the intimate and complex manner in which the inhabitants of each country are bound together, that any change in the numerical proportions of some of the inhabitants, independently of the change of climate itself, would most seriously affect many of the others. If the country were open on its borders, new forms would certainly immigrate, and this also would seriously disturb the relations of some of the former inhabitants. Let it be remembered how powerful the influence of a single introduced tree or mammal has been shown to be. But in the case of an island, or of a country partly surrounded by barriers, into which new and better adapted forms could not freely enter, we should then have places in the economy of nature which would assuredly be better filled up, if some of the original inhabitants were in some manner modified; for, had the area been open to immigration, these same places would have been seized on by intruders. In such case, every slight modification, which in the course of ages chanced to arise, and which in any way favoured the individuals of any of the species, by better adapting them to their altered conditions, would tend to be preserved; and natural selection would thus have free scope for the work of improvement.

We have reason to believe, as stated in the first chapter, that a change in the conditions of life, by specially acting on the reproductive system, causes or increases variability; and in the foregoing case the conditions of life are supposed to have undergone a change, and this would manifestly be favourable to natural selection, by giving a better chance of profitable variations occurring; and unless profitable variations do occur, natural selection can do nothing. Not that, as I believe, any extreme amount of variability is necessary; as man can certainly produce great results by adding up in any given direction mere individual differences, so could Nature, but far more easily, from having incomparably longer time at her disposal. Nor do I believe that any great physical change, as of climate, or any unusual degree of isolation to check immigration, is actually necessary to produce new and unoccupied places for natural selection to fill up by modifying and improving some of the varying inhabitants. For as all the inhabitants of each country are struggling together with nicely balanced forces, extremely slight modifications in the structure or habits of one inhabitant would often give it an advantage over others; and still further modifications of the same kind would often still further increase the advantage. No country can be named in which all the native inhabitants are now so perfectly adapted to each other and to the physical conditions under which they live, that none of them could anyhow be improved, for in all countries, the natives have been so far conquered by naturalised productions, that they have allowed foreigners to take firm possession of the land. And as foreigners have thus everywhere beaten some of the natives, we may safely conclude that the natives might have been modified with advantage, so as to have better resisted such intruders.

As man can produce and certainly has produced a great result by his methodical and unconscious means of selection, what may not nature effect? Man can act only on external and visible characters: nature cares nothing for appearances, except in so far as they may be useful to any being. She can act on every internal organ, on every shade of constitutional difference, on the whole machinery of life. Man selects only for his own good; Nature only for that of the being which she tends. Every selected character is fully exercised by her; and the being is placed under well-suited conditions of life. Man keeps the natives of many climates in the same country; he seldom exercises each selected character in some peculiar and fitting manner; he feeds a long- and a short-beaked pigeon on the same food; he does not exercise a long-backed or long-legged quadruped in any peculiar manner; he exposes sheep with long and short wool to the same climate. He does not allow the most vigorous males to struggle for the females. He does not rigidly destroy all inferior animals, but protects during each varying season, as far as lies in his power, all his productions. He often begins his selection by some half-monstrous form; or at least by some modification prominent enough to catch his eye, or to be plainly useful to him. Under nature, the slightest difference of structure or constitution may well turn the nicely-balanced scale in the struggle for life, and so be preserved. How fleeting are the wishes and efforts of man!

How short his time! And consequently how poor will his products be, compared with those accumulated by nature during whole geological periods. Can we wonder, then, that nature's productions should be far "truer" in character than man's productions; that they should be infinitely better adapted to the most complex conditions of life, and should plainly bear the stamp of far higher workmanship?

It may be said that natural selection is daily and hourly scrutinizing, throughout the world, every variation, even the slightest; rejecting that which is bad, preserving, and adding up all that is good; silently and insensibly working, whenever and wherever opportunity offers, at the improvement of each organic being in relation to its organic and inorganic conditions of life. We see nothing of these slow changes in progress, until the hand of time has marked the long lapse of ages, and then so imperfect is our view into long past geological ages, that we only see that the forms of life are now different from what they formerly were.

Although natural selection can act only through and for the good of each being, yet characters and structures, which we are apt to consider as of very trifling importance, may thus be acted on. When we see leaf-eating insects green, and bark-feeders mottled-grey; the alpine ptarmigan white in winter, the red grouse the colour of heather, and the black grouse that of peaty earth, we must believe that these tints are of service to these birds and insects in preserving them from danger. Grouse, if not destroyed at some period of their lives, would increase in countless numbers; they are known to suffer largely from birds of prey; and hawks are guided by eyesight to their prey – so much so, that on parts of the Continent persons are warned not to keep white pigeons, as being the most liable to destruction. Hence I can see no reason to doubt that natural selection might be most effective in giving the proper colour to each kind of grouse, and in keeping that colour, when once acquired, true and constant. Nor ought we to think that the occasional destruction of an animal of any particular colour would produce little effect: we should remember how essential it is in a flock of white sheep to destroy every lamb with the faintest trace of black. In plants the down on the fruit and the colour of the flesh are considered by botanists as characters of the most trifling importance: yet we hear from an excellent horticulturist, Downing, that in the United States smooth-skinned fruits suffer far more from a beetle, a curculio, than those with down; that purple plums suffer far more from a certain disease than yellow plums; whereas another disease attacks yellow-fleshed peaches far more than those with other coloured flesh. If, with all the aids of art, these slight differences make a great difference in cultivating the several varieties, assuredly, in a state of nature, where the trees would have to struggle with other trees and with a host of enemies, such differences would effectually settle which variety, whether a smooth or downy, a yellow or purple fleshed fruit, should succeed.

In looking at many small points of difference between species, which, as far as our ignorance permits us to judge, seem to be quite unimportant, we must not forget that climate, food, etc., probably produce some slight and direct effect. It is, however, far more necessary to bear in mind that there are many unknown laws of correlation of growth, which, when one part of the organization is modified through variation, and the modifications are accumulated by natural selection for the good of the being, will cause other modifications, often of the most unexpected nature.

As we see that those variations, which under domestication appear at any particular period of life, tend to reappear in the offspring at the same period – for instance, in the seeds of the many varieties of our culinary and agricultural plants; in the caterpillar and cocoon stages of the varieties of the silkworm; in the eggs of poultry, and in the colour of the down of their chickens; in the horns of our sheep and cattle when nearly adult – so in a state of nature, natural selection will be enabled to act on and modify organic beings at any age, by the accumulation of profitable variations at that age, and by their inheritance at a corresponding age. If it profit a plant to have its seeds more and more widely disseminated by the wind, I can see no greater difficulty in this being effected through natural selection, than in the cotton-planter increasing and improving by selection the down in the pods on his cotton-trees. Natural selection may modify and adapt the larva of an insect to a score of contingencies, wholly different from those which concern the mature insect. These modifications will no doubt affect, through the laws of correlation, the structure of the adult; and probably in the case of those insects which live only for a few hours, and which never feed, a large part of their structure is merely the correlated result of successive changes in the structure of their larvae. So, conversely, modifications in the adult will probably often affect the structure of the larva; but in all cases natural selection will ensure that modifications consequent on other modifications at a different period of life, shall not be in the least degree injurious: for if they became so, they would cause the extinction of the species.

Natural selection will modify the structure of the young in relation to the parent, and of the parent in relation to the young. In social animals it will adapt the structure of each individual for the benefit of the community; if each in consequence profits by the selected change. What natural selection cannot do is to modify the structure of one species, without giving it any advantage, for the good of another species; and though statements to this effect may be found in works of natural history, I cannot find one case which will bear investigation. A structure used only once in an animal's whole life, if of high importance to it, might be modified to any extent by natural selection; for instance, the great jaws possessed by certain insects, and used exclusively for opening the cocoon – or the hard tip to the beak of nestling birds, used for breaking the egg. It has been asserted, that of the best short-beaked tumbler-pigeons more perish in the egg than are able to get out of it; so that fanciers assist in the act of hatching. Now, if nature had to make the beak of a full-grown pigeon very short for the bird's own advantage, the process of modification would be very slow, and there would be simultaneously the most rigorous selection of the young birds within the egg, which had the most powerful and hardest beaks, for all with weak beaks would inevitably perish: or, more delicate and more broken shells might be selected, the thickness of the shell being known to vary like every other structure.

Chapter VI: Difficulties on Theory

. . . He who believes that each being has been created as we now see it, must occasionally have felt surprise when he has met with an animal having habits and structure not at all in agreement. What can be plainer than that the webbed feet of ducks and geese are formed for swimming? Yet there are upland geese with webbed feet which rarely or never go near the water; and no one except Audubon has seen the frigate-bird, which has all its four toes webbed, alight on the surface of the sea. On the other hand, grebes and coots are eminently aquatic, although their toes are only bordered by membrane. What seems plainer than that the long toes of Grallatores are formed for walking over swamps and floating plants, yet the water-hen is nearly as aquatic as the coot; and the landrail nearly as terrestrial as the quail or partridge. In such cases, and many others could be given, habits have changed without a corresponding change of structure. The webbed feet of the upland goose may be said to have become rudimentary in function, though not in structure. In the frigate-bird, the deeply-scooped membrane between the toes shows that structure has begun to change.

He who believes in separate and innumerable acts of creation will say, that in these cases it has pleased the Creator to cause a being of one type to take the place of one of another type; but this seems to me only restating the fact in dignified language. He who believes in the struggle for existence and in the principle of natural selection, will acknowledge that every organic being is constantly endeavouring to increase in numbers; and that if any one being vary ever so little, either in habits or structure, and thus gain an advantage over some other inhabitant of the country, it will seize on the place of that inhabitant, however different it may be from its own place. Hence it will cause him no surprise that there should be geese and frigate-birds with webbed feet, either living on the dry land or most rarely alighting on the water; that there should be long-toed corncrakes living in meadows instead of in swamps; that there should be woodpeckers where not a tree grows; that there should be diving thrushes, and petrels with the habits of auks.

Chapter XI: Geographical Distribution

In considering the distribution of organic beings over the face of the globe, the first great fact which strikes us is, that neither the similarity nor the dissimilarity of the inhabitants of various regions can be accounted for by their climatal and other physical conditions. Of late, almost every author who has studied the subject has come to this conclusion. The case of America alone would almost suffice to prove its truth: for if we exclude the northern parts where the circumpolar land is almost continuous, all authors agree that one of the most fundamental divisions in geographical distribution is that between the New and Old Worlds; yet if we travel over the vast American continent, from the central parts of the United States to its extreme southern point, we meet with the most diversified conditions; the most humid districts, arid deserts, lofty mountains, grassy plains, forests, marshes, lakes, and great rivers, under almost every temperature. There is hardly a climate or condition in the Old World which cannot be paralleled in the New – at least as closely as the same species generally require; for it is a most rare case to find a group of organisms confined to any small spot, having conditions peculiar in only a slight degree; for instance, small areas in the Old World could be pointed out hotter than any in the New World, yet these are not inhabited by a peculiar fauna or flora. Notwithstanding this parallelism in the conditions of the Old and New Worlds, how widely different are their living productions!

In the southern hemisphere, if we compare large tracts of land in Australia, South Africa, and western South America, between latitudes 25° and 35°, we shall find parts extremely similar in all their conditions, yet it would not be possible to point out three faunas and floras more utterly dissimilar. Or again we may compare the productions of South America south of lat. 35° with those north of 25°, which consequently inhabit a considerably different climate, and they will be found incomparably more closely related to each other, than they are to the productions of Australia or Africa under nearly the same climate. Analogous facts could be given with respect to the inhabitants of the sea.

A second great fact which strikes us in our general review is, that barriers of any kind, or obstacles to free migration, are related in a close and important manner to the differences between the productions of various regions. We see this in the great difference of nearly all the terrestrial productions of the New and Old Worlds, excepting in the northern parts, where the land almost joins, and where, under a slightly different climate, there might have been free migration for the northern temperate forms, as there now is for the strictly arctic productions. We see the same fact in the great difference between the inhabitants of Australia, Africa, and South America under the same latitude: for these countries are almost as much isolated from each other as is possible. On each continent, also, we see the same fact; for on the opposite sides of lofty and continuous mountain-ranges, and of great deserts, and sometimes even of large rivers, we find different productions; though as mountain-chains, deserts, etc., are not as impassable, or likely to have endured so long as the oceans separating continents, the differences are very inferior in degree to those characteristic of distinct continents.

Turning to the sea, we find the same law. No two marine faunas are more distinct, with hardly a fish, shell, or crab in common, than those of the eastern and western shores of South and Central America; yet these great faunas are separated only by the narrow, but impassable, isthmus of Panama. Westward of the shores of America, a wide space of open ocean extends, with not an island as a halting-place for emigrants; here we have a barrier of another kind, and as soon as this is passed we meet in the eastern islands of the Pacific, with another and totally distinct fauna. So that here three marine faunas range far northward and southward, in parallel lines not far from each other, under corresponding climates; but from being separated from each other by impassable barriers, either of land or open sea, they are wholly distinct. On the other hand, proceeding still further westward from the eastern islands of the tropical parts of the Pacific, we encounter no impassable barriers, and we have innumerable islands as halting-places, until after travelling over a hemisphere we come to the shores of Africa; and over this vast space we meet with no well-defined and distinct marine faunas. Although hardly one shell, crab or fish is common to the above-named three approximate faunas of Eastern and Western America and the eastern Pacific islands, yet many fish range from the Pacific into the Indian Ocean; and many shells are common to the eastern islands of the Pacific and the eastern shores of Africa, on almost exactly opposite meridians of longitude.

A third great fact, partly included in the foregoing statements, is the affinity of the productions of the same continent or sea, though the species themselves are distinct at different points and stations. It is a law of the widest generality, and every continent offers innumerable instances. Nevertheless the naturalist in travelling, for instance, from north to south never fails to be struck by the manner in which successive groups of beings, specifically distinct, yet clearly related, replace each other. He hears from closely allied, yet distinct kinds of birds, notes nearly similar, and sees their nests similarly constructed, but not quite alike, with eggs coloured in nearly the same manner. The plains near the Straits of Magellan are inhabited by one species of *Rhea* (American ostrich), and northward the plains of La Plata by another species of the same genus; and not by a true ostrich or emeu, like those found in Africa and Australia under the same latitude. On these same plains of La Plata, we see the agouti and bizcacha, animals having nearly the same habits as our hares and rabbits and belonging to the same order of Rodents, but they plainly display an American type of structure. We ascend the lofty peaks of the Cordillera and we find an alpine species of bizcacha; we look to the waters, and we do not find the beaver or musk-rat, but the coypu and capybara, rodents of the American type. Innumerable other instances could be given. If we look to the islands off the American shore however much they may differ in geological structure, the inhabitants, though they may be all peculiar species, are essentially American. We may look back to past ages, as shown in the last chapter, and we find American types then prevalent on the American continent and in the American seas. We see in these facts some deep organic bond, prevailing throughout space and time, over the same areas of land and water, and independent of their physical conditions. The naturalist must feel little curiosity, who is not led to inquire what this bond is.

This bond, on my theory, is simply inheritance, that cause which alone, as far as we positively know, produces organisms quite like, or, as we see in the case of varieties nearly like each other. The dissimilarity of the inhabitants of different regions may be attributed to modification through natural selection and in a quite subordinate degree to the direct influence of different physical conditions. The degree of dissimilarity will depend on the migration of the more dominant forms of life from one region into another having been effected with more or less ease, at periods more or less remote; on the nature and number of the former immigrants; and on their action and reaction, in their mutual struggles for life; the relation of organism to organism being, as I have already often remarked, the most important of all relations. Thus the high importance of barriers comes into play by checking migration; as does time for the slow process of modification through natural selection. Widely-ranging species, abounding in individuals, which have already triumphed over many competitors in their own widely-extended homes will have the best chance of seizing on new places, when they spread into new countries. In their new homes they will be exposed to new conditions, and will frequently undergo further modification and improvement; and thus they will become still further victorious, and will produce groups of modified descendants. On this principle of inheritance with modification, we can understand how it is that sections of genera, whole genera, and even families are confined to the same areas, as is so commonly and notoriously the case.

I believe, as was remarked in the last chapter, in no law of necessary development. As the variability of each species is an independent property, and will be taken advantage of by natural selection only so far as it profits the individual in its complex struggle for life, so the degree of modification in different species will be no uniform quantity. If, for instance, a number of species which stand in direct competition with each other, migrate in a body into a new and afterwards isolated country, they will be little liable to modification; for neither migration nor isolation in themselves can do anything. These principles come into play only by bringing organisms into new relations with each other, and in a lesser degree with the surrounding physical conditions. As we have seen in the last chapter that some forms have retained nearly the same character from an enormously remote geological period, so certain species have migrated over vast spaces, and have not become greatly modified.

On these views, it is obvious, that the several species of the same genus, though inhabiting the most distant quarters of the world, must originally have proceeded from the same source, as they have descended from the same progenitor. In the case of those species, which have undergone during whole geological periods but little modification, there is not much difficulty in believing that they may have migrated from the same region; for during the vast geographical and climatal changes which will have supervened since ancient times, almost any amount of migration is possible. But in many other cases, in which we have reason to believe that the species of a genus have been produced within comparatively recent times, there is great difficulty on this head. It is also obvious that the individuals of the same species, though now inhabiting distant and isolated regions, must have proceeded from one spot, where their parents were first produced: for, as explained in the last chapter, it is incredible that individuals identically the same should ever have been produced through natural selection from parents specifically distinct.

We are thus brought to the question which has been largely discussed by naturalists, namely, whether species have been created at one or more points of the earth's surface. Undoubtedly there are very many cases of extreme difficulty, in understanding how the same species could possibly have migrated from some one point to the several distant and isolated points, where now found. Nevertheless the simplicity of the view that each species was first produced within a single region captivates the mind. He who rejects it, rejects the *vera causa* of ordinary generation with subsequent migration, and calls in the agency of a miracle. It is universally admitted, that in most cases the area inhabited by a species is continuous; and when a plant or animal inhabits two points so distant from each other, or with an interval of such a nature, that the space could not be easily passed over by migration, the fact is given as something remarkable and exceptional. The capacity of migrating across the sea is more distinctly limited in terrestrial mammals, than perhaps in any other organic beings; and, accordingly, we find no inexplicable cases of the same mammal inhabiting distant points of the world. No geologist will feel any difficulty in such cases as Great Britain having been formerly united to Europe, and consequently possessing the same quadrupeds. But if the same species can be produced at two separate points, why do we not find a single mammal common to Europe and Australia or South America? The conditions of life are nearly the same, so that a multitude of European animals and plants have become naturalized in America and Australia; and some of the aboriginal plants are identically the same at these distant points of the northern and southern hemispheres. The answer, as I believe, is, that mammals have not been able to migrate, whereas some plants, from their varied means of dispersal, have migrated across the vast and broken interspace. The great and striking influence which barriers of every kind have had on distribution, is intelligible only on the view that the great majority of species have been produced on one side alone, and have not been able to migrate to the other side. Some few families, many sub-families, very many genera, and a still greater number of sections of genera are confined to a single region; and it has been observed by several naturalists, that the most natural genera, or those genera in which the species are most closely related to each other, are generally local, or confined to one area. What a strange anomaly it would be, if, when coming one step lower in the series, to the individuals of the same species, a directly opposite rule prevailed; and species were not local, but had been produced in two or more distinct areas!

Hence it seems to me, as it has to many other naturalists, that the view of each species having been produced in one area alone, and having sub-sequently migrated from that area as far as its powers of migration and subsistence under past and present conditions permitted, is the most probable. Undoubtedly many cases occur, in which we cannot explain how the same species could have passed from one point to the other. But the geographical and climatal changes, which have certainly occurred within recent geological times, must have interrupted or rendered dis-continuous the formerly continuous range of many species. So that we are reduced to consider whether the exceptions to continuity of range are so numerous and of so grave a nature, that we ought to give up the belief, rendered probable by general considerations, that each species has been produced within one area, and has migrated thence as far as it could. It would be hopelessly tedious to discuss all the exceptional cases of the same species, now living at distant and separated points; nor do I for a moment pretend that any explanation could be offered of many such cases. But after some preliminary remarks, I will discuss a few of the most striking classes of facts; namely, the existence of the same species on the summits of distant mountain-ranges, and at distant points in the arctic and antarctic regions; and secondly (in the following chapter), the wide distribution of freshwater production; and thirdly, the occurrence of the same terrestrial species on islands and on the mainland, though separated by hundreds of miles of open sea. If the existence of the same species at distant and isolated points of the earth's surface can in many instances be explained on the view of each species having migrated from a single birthplace; then, considering our ignorance with respect to former climatal and geographical changes and various occasional means of transport, the belief that this has been the universal law, seems to me incomparably the safest.

In discussing this subject, we shall be enabled at the same time to consider a point equally important for us, namely, whether the several distinct species of a genus, which on my theory have all descended from a common progenitor, can have migrated (undergoing modification during some part of their migration) from the area inhabited by their progenitor. If it can be shown to be almost invariably the case, that a region, of which most of its inhabitants are closely related to, or belong to the same genera with the species of a second region, has probably received at some former period immigrants from this other region, my theory will be strengthened; for we can clearly understand, on the principle of modification, why the inhabitants of a region should be related to those of another region, whence it has been stocked. A volcanic island, for instance, upheaved and formed at the distance of a few hundreds of miles from a continent, would probably receive from it in the course of time a few colonists, and their descendants, though modified, would still be plainly related by inheritance to the inhabitants of the continent. Cases of this nature are common, and are, as we shall hereafter more fully see, inexplicable on the theory of independent creation. This view of the relation of species in one region to those in another does not differ much (by substituting the word variety for species) from that lately advanced in an ingenious paper by Mr Wallace, in which he concludes, that "every species has come into existence coincident both in space and time with a pre-existing closely allied species". And I now know from correspondence, that this coincidence he attributes to generation with modification.

The previous remarks on "single and multiple centres of creation" do not directly bear on another allied question – namely whether all the individuals of the same species have descended from a single pair, or single hermaphrodite, or whether, as some authors suppose, from many individuals simultaneously created. With those organic beings which never intercross (if such exist), the species, on my theory, must have descended from a succession of improved varieties, which will never have blended with other individuals or varieties, but will have supplanted each other; so that, at each successive stage of modification and improvement, all the individuals of each variety will have descended from a single parent. But in the majority of cases, namely, with all organisms which habitually unite for each birth, or which often intercross, I believe that during the slow process of modification the individuals of the species will have been kept nearly uniform by intercrossing; so that many individuals will have gone on simultaneously changing, and the whole amount of modification will not have been due, at each stage, to descent from a single parent. To illustrate what I mean: our English race-horses differ slightly from the horses of every other breed; but they do not owe their difference and superiority to descent from any single pair, but to continued care in selecting and training many individuals during many generations . . .

Chapter XIV: Recapitulation and Conclusion

. . . It may be asked how far I extend the doctrine of the modification of species. The question is difficult to answer, because the more distinct the forms are which we may consider, by so much the arguments fall away in force. But some arguments of the greatest weight extend very far. All the members of whole classes can be connected together by chains of affinities, and all can be classified on the same principle in groups subordinate to groups. Fossil remains sometimes tend to fill up very wide intervals between existing orders. Organs in a rudimentary condition plainly show that an early progenitor had the organ in a fully developed state; and this in some instances necessarily implies an enormous amount of modification in the descendants. Throughout whole classes various structures are formed on the same pattern, and at an embryonic age the species closely resemble each other. Therefore I cannot doubt that the theory of descent with modification embraces all the members of the same class. I believe that animals have descended from at most only four or five progenitors, and plants from an equal or lesser number.

Analogy would lead me one step further, namely, to the belief that all animals and plants have descended from some one prototype. But analogy may be a deceitful guide. Nevertheless all living things have much in common, in their chemical composition, their germinal vesicles, their cellular structure, and their laws of growth and reproduction. We see this even in so trifling a circumstance as that the same poison often similarly affects plants and animals; or that the poison secreted by the gall-fly produces monstrous growths on the wild rose or oak-tree. Therefore I should infer from analogy that probably all the organic beings which have ever lived on this earth have descended from some one primordial form, into which life was first breathed.

THE PROCLAMATION OF EMANCIPATION, 1863

Abraham Lincoln

Lincoln was born in 1809, of a poor Kentucky family. Under the guidance of his stepmother he acquired the rudiments of education, and in 1836 set up as a country lawyer in Springfield, Illinois. After election to the state legislature, he ran for the senate as a Republican (on a platform of no extension of slavery) in 1858, attracting national attention for his debates with Stephen A. Douglas. In May 1860, the Republican party nominated Lincoln as its presidential candidate. He won the presidency over a fatally divided Democratic party, only to see pro-slavery South Carolina lead a secession from the Union. Lincoln's unflagging conduct of the consequent civil war, his moral belief in the perpetuality of the Union and the freedom of the slaves established him as the saviour of his country and the emancipator of a race. He was assassinated by John Wilkes Booth on 14 April 1865, three days after the surrender of General Robert E. Lee at Appomattox Courthouse – the practical end of the civil war.

The text of *The Proclamation of Emancipation* is reproduced herewith.

The Proclamation of Emancipation.   1 January 1863
By the President of the United States of America:
A Proclamation.

Whereas, on the twenty-second day of September, in the year of our Lord one thousand eight hundred and sixty-two, a proclamation was issued by the President of the United States, containing among other things, the following, to wit:

"That on the first day of January, in the year of our Lord one thousand eight hundred and sixty-three, all persons held as slaves within any State or designated part of a State, the people whereof shall then be in rebellion against the United States, shall be then, thenceforward, and forever free; and the Executive Government of the United States, including the military and naval authority thereof, will recognize and maintain the freedom of such persons, and will do no act or acts to repress such persons, or any of them, in any efforts they may make for their actual freedom.

"That the Executive will, on the first day of January aforesaid, by proclamation, designate the States and parts of States, if any, in which the people thereof, respectively, shall then be in rebellion against the United States; and the fact that any State, or the people thereof, shall on that day be, in good faith, represented in the Congress of the United States by members chosen thereto at elections wherein a majority of the qualified voters of such State shall have participated, shall, in the absence of strong countervailing testimony, be deemed conclusive evidence that such State, and the people thereof, are not then in rebellion against the United States."

Now, therefore I, Abraham Lincoln, President of the United States, by virtue of the power in me vested as Commander-in-Chief, of the Army and Navy of the United States in time of actual armed rebellion against authority and government of the United States, and as a fit and necessary war measure for suppressing said rebellion, do, on this first day of January, in the year of our Lord one thousand eight hundred and sixty-three, and in accordance with my purpose, so to do publicly proclaimed for the full period of one hundred days, from the day first above mentioned, order and designate as the States and parts of States wherein the people thereof respectively, are this day in rebellion against the United States, the following, to wit:

Arkansas, Texas, Louisiana (except the Parishes of St Bernard, Plaquemines, Jefferson, St Johns, St Charles, St James, Ascension, Assumption, Terrebonne, Lafourche, St Mary, St Martin, and Orleans, including the City of New Orleans), Mississippi, Alabama, Florida, Georgia, South Carolina, North Carolina, and Virginia (except the forty-eight counties designated as West Virginia, and also the counties of Berkley, Accomac, Northampton, Elizabeth-City, York, Princess Ann, and Norfolk, including the cities of Norfolk and Portsmouth); and which excepted parts are, for the present, left precisely as if this proclamation were not issued.

And by virtue of the power, and for the purpose aforesaid, I do order and declare that all persons held as slaves within said designated States, and parts of States, are, and henceforward shall be free; and that the Executive Government of the United States, including the military and naval authorities thereof, will recognize and maintain the freedom of said persons.

And I hereby enjoin upon the people so declared to be free to abstain from all violence, unless in necessary self-defense; and I recommend to them that, in all cases when allowed, they labor faithfully for reasonable wages.

And I further declare and make known, that such persons of suitable condition will be received into the armed service of the United States to garrison forts, positions, stations, and other places, and to man vessels of all sorts in said service.

And upon this act, sincerely believed to be an act of justice, warranted by the Constitution, upon military necessity, I invoke the considerate judgment of mankind, and the gracious favor of Almighty God.

In witness whereof, I have hereunto set my hand and caused the seal of the United States to be affixed.

Done at the City of Washington, this first day of January, in the year of our Lord one thousand eight hundred and sixty-three, and of the Independence of the United States of America the eighty-seventh.

ABRAHAM LINCOLN.

By the President:
WILLIAM H. SEWARD, Secretary of State.

THE GETTYSBURG ADDRESS, 1863

Abraham Lincoln

Delivered by President Abraham Lincoln on 19 November, 1863, at the Union cemetery at Gettysburg, Philadelphia. It was the first time the world heard the words "government of the people, by the people, for the people."

Four score and seven years ago our fathers brought forth on this continent, a new nation, conceived in Liberty, and dedicated to the proposition that all men are created equal.

Now we are engaged in a great civil war, testing whether that nation, or any nation so conceived and so dedicated, can long endure. We are met on a great battle-field of that war. We have come to dedicate a portion of that field, as a final resting place for those who here gave their lives that the nation might live. It is altogether fitting and proper that we should do this.

But, in a larger sense, we cannot dedicate – we cannot consecrate – we cannot hallow – this ground. The brave men, living and dead, who struggled here, have consecrated it, far above our poor power to add or detract. The world will little note, nor long remember what we say here, but it can never forget what they did here. It is for us the living, rather, to be dedicated here to the unfinished work which they who fought here have thus far so nobly advanced. It is rather for us to be here dedicated to the great task remaining before us – that from these honoured dead we take increased devotion to that cause for which they gave the last full measure of devotion – that we here highly resolve that these dead shall not have died in vain – that this nation, under God, shall have a new birth of freedom – and that government of the people, by the people, for the people, shall not perish from the earth.

From A MANIFESTO, 1884

George Bernard Shaw

The *Manifesto* was written by Shaw (1856–1950) for the newly formed Fabian Society. Taking its name from Fabius Cunctator, the Roman general who had cautiously but successfully stopped Hannibal, the Society advocated "evolutionary" (ie non-revolutionary) socialism. Alongside the playwright Shaw, H.G. Wells was another early leading light of the organization, which made an indelible imprint on the British Labour Party.

The Fabians are associated for spreading the following opinions held by them and discussing their practical consequences.

That under existing circumstances wealth cannot be enjoyed without dishonour or foregone without misery.

That it is the duty of each member of the State to provide for his or her wants by his or her own Labour.

That a life interest in the Land and Capital of the nation is the birthright of every individual born within its confines and that access to this birthright should not depend upon the will of any private person other than the person seeking it.

That the most striking result of our present system of farming out the national Land and Capital to private persons has been the division of Society into hostile classes, with large appetites and no dinners at one extreme and large dinners and no appetites at the other.

That the practice of entrusting the Land of the nation to private persons in the hope that they will make the best of it has been discredited by the consistency with which they have made the worst of it; and that Nationalization of the Land in some form is a public duty.

That the pretensions of Capitalism to encourage Invention and to distribute its benefits in the fairest way attainable, have been discredited by the experience of the 19th century.

That, under the existing system of leaving the National Industry to organize itself Competition has the effect of rendering adulteration, dishonest dealing and inhumanity compulsory.

That since Competition amongst producers admittedly secures to the public the most satisfactory products, the State should compete with all its might in every department of production.

That such restraints upon free Competition as the penalties for infringing the Postal monopoly, and the withdrawal of workhouse and prison labor from the markets, should be abolished.

That no branch of Industry should be carried on at a profit by the central administration.

That the Public Revenue should be levied by a direct Tax; and that the central administration should have no legal power to hold back for the replenishment of the Public Treasury any portion of the proceeds of Industries administered by them.

That the State should compete with private individuals – especially with parents – in providing happy homes for children, so that every child may have a refuge from the tyranny or neglect of its natural custodians.

That Men no longer need special political privileges to protect them against Women and that the sexes should henceforth enjoy equal political rights.

That no individual should enjoy any Privilege in consideration of services rendered to the State by his or her parents or other relation.

That the State should secure a liberal education and an equal share in the National Industry to each of its units.

That the established Government has no more right to call itself the State than the smoke of London has to call itself the weather.

That we had rather face a Civil War than such another century of suffering as the present one has been.

From THE SOUL OF MAN UNDER SOCIALISM, 1891

Oscar Wilde

In which Wilde (1854–1900) posits the liberating possibilities of machines, a classic notion of mainstream European socialist thought from Karl Marx onwards.

Up to the present, man has been, to a certain extent, the slave of machinery, and there is something tragic in the fact that as soon as man had invented a machine to do his work he began to starve. This, however, is, of course, the result of our property system and our system of competition. One man owns a machine which does the work of five hundred men. Five hundred men are, in consequence, thrown out of employment, and, having no work to do, become hungry and take to thieving. The one man secures the produce of the machine and keeps it, and has five hundred times as much as he should have, and probably, which is of much more importance, a great deal more than he really wants. Were that machine the property of all, everybody would benefit by it. It would be an immense advantage to the community. All unintellectual labour, all monotonous, dull labour, all labour that deals with dreadful things, and involves unpleasant conditions, must be done by machinery. Machinery must work for us in coal mines, and do all sanitary services, and be the stoker of steamers, and clean the streets, and run messages on wet days, and do anything that is tedious or distressing. At present machinery competes against man. Under proper conditions machinery will serve man. There is no doubt at all that this is the future of machinery; and just as trees grow while the country gentleman is asleep, so while Humanity will be amusing itself, or enjoying cultivated leisure – which, and not labour, is the aim of man – or making beautiful things, or reading beautiful things, or simply contemplating the world with admiration and delight, machinery will be doing all the necessary and unpleasant work. The fact is, that civilization requires slaves. The Greeks were quite right there. Unless there are slaves to do the ugly, horrible, uninteresting work, culture and contemplation become almost impossible. Human slavery is wrong, insecure and demoralizing. On mechanical slavery, on the slavery of the machine, the future of the world depends. And when scientific men are no longer called upon to go down to a depressing East End and distribute bad cocoa and worse blankets to starving people, they will have delightful leisure in which to devise wonderful and marvellous things for their own joy and the joy of everyone else. There will be great storages of force for every city, and for every house if required, and this force man will convert into heat, light or motion, according to his needs. Is this Utopian? A map of the world that does include Utopia is not worth even glancing at, for it leaves out the one country at which Humanity is always landing. And when Humanity lands there, it looks out and, seeing a better country, sets sail. Progress is the realization of Utopias.

"J'ACCUSE", 1898

Emile Zola

Zola was the author of the Naturalist novels *L'Assomoir, La Terre* and *Germinal*. Champion of the French underdog, he espoused the cause of the French Army officer, Alfred Dreyfus, a Jew who had been unjustly court-martialled for passing national defence documents to a foreign government. Zola accordingly assailed the government in his celebrated open letter, "J'accuse", published in the liberal newspaper *L'Aurore*. For his impeachment of the military and its anti-semitic criminal conspiracy, Zola was found guilty, in a rigged case of libel, but avoided imprisonment by escaping to England for a year, to return a national hero. Dreyfus himself, when the clamour of anti-semitism had died down, was pardoned and later fought in the First World War. He was awarded the Legion of Honour.

To President Félix Faure of France (January 1898)

Mr President,

Permit me, I beg you, in return for the gracious favours you once accorded me, to be concerned with regard to your just glory and to tell you that your record, so fair and fortunate thus far, is now threatened with the most shameful, the most ineffaceable blot.

You escaped safe and sane from the basest calumnies; you conquered all hearts. You seem radiant in the glory of a patriotic celebration . . . and are preparing to preside over the solemn triumph of our Universal Exposition, which is to crown our great century of work, truth and liberty. But what a clod of mud is flung upon your name – I was about to say your reign – through this abominable Dreyfus affair. A court martial has but recently, by order, dared to acquit one Esterhazy – a supreme slap at all truth, all justice! And it is done; France has this brand upon her visage; history will relate that it was during your administration that such a social crime could be committed.

Since, they have dared, I too shall dare. I shall tell the truth because I
pledged myself to tell it if justice, regularly empowered, did not do so,
fully, unmitigatedly. My duty is to speak; I have no wish to be an
accomplice. My nights would be haunted by the spectre of the innocent
being, expiating under the most frightful torture, a crime he never
committed.

And it is to you, Mr President, that I shall out this truth, with the force of
my revolt as an honest man. To your honour, I am convinced that you are
ignorant of the crime. And to whom, then, shall I denounce the malignant
rabble of true culprits, if not to you, the highest magistrate in the
country? . . .

I accuse Colonel du Paty de Clam of having been the diabolical agent of
the judicial error, unconsciously, I prefer to believe, and of having
continued to defend his deadly work during the past three years through
the most absurd and revolting machinations.

I accuse General Mercier of having made himself an accomplice in one
of the greatest crimes of history, probably through weak-mindedness.

I accuse General Billot of having had in his hands the decisive proofs of
the innocence of Dreyfus and of having concealed them, and of having
rendered himself guilty of the crime of lèse humanity and lèse justice, out
of political motives and to save the face of the General Staff.

I accuse General Boisdeffre and General Gonse of being accomplices in
the same crime, the former no doubt through religious prejudice, the latter
out of *esprit de corps*.

I accuse General de Pellieux and Major Ravary of having made a
scoundrelly inquest, I mean an inquest of the most monstrous partiality,
the complete report of which composes for us an imperishable monument
of naïve effrontery.

I accuse the three handwriting experts, MM. Belhomme, Varinard and
Couard, of having made lying and fraudulent reports, unless a medical
examination will certify them to be deficient of sight and judgment.

I accuse the War Office of having led a vile campaign in the press,
particularly in *l'Éclair* and *l'Écho de Paris*, in order to misdirect public
opinion and cover up its sins.

I accuse, lastly, the first court martial of having violated all human right
in condemning a prisoner on testimony kept secret from him, and I accuse
the second court martial of having covered up this illegality by order,
committing in turn the judicial crime of acquitting a guilty man with full
knowledge of his guilt.

In making these accusations I am aware that I render myself liable to
articles 30 and 31 of Libel Laws of 29 July 1881, which punish acts of
defamation. I expose myself voluntarily.

As to the men I accuse, I do not know them, I have never seen them, I
feel neither resentment nor hatred against them. For me they are only

entities, emblems of social malfeasance. The action I take here is simply a revolutionary step designed to hasten the explosion of truth and justice.

I have one passion only, for light, in the name of humanity which has borne so much and has a right to happiness. My burning protest is only the cry of my soul. Let them dare, then, to carry me to the court of appeals, and let there be an inquest in the full light of the day!

I am waiting.

Mr President, I beg you to accept the assurances of my deepest respect.

Emile Zola

"NO SURRENDER": A SUFFRAGETTE ON HUNGER STRIKE, 1910

Lady Constance Lytton

Lytton was a prominent "suffragette", a campaigner for the extension of the franchise to women in Edwardian England. Like a number of other suffragettes imprisoned for acts of non-violent protest, Lytton undertook a hunger strike to draw further attention to the cause. The scene below is Walton Jail, Liverpool.

As a result of the long women's suffrage campaign, and in recognition of the part played by women in running many of Britain's services during the First World War (1914–18), all women over 30 were given the vote in 1918, and over 21 in 1928.

I was visited again by the Senior Medical Officer, who asked me how long I had been without food. I said I had eaten a buttered scone and a banana sent in by friends to the police station on Friday at about midnight. He said, "Oh, then, this is the fourth day; that is too long, I shall feed you, I must feed you at once," but he went out and nothing happened till about six o'clock in the evening, when he returned with, I think, five wardresses and the feeding apparatus. He urged me to take food voluntarily. I told him that was absolutely out of the question, that when our legislators ceased to resist enfranchising women then I should cease to resist taking food in prison. He did not examine my heart nor feel my pulse; he did not ask to do so, nor did I say anything which could possibly induce him to think I would refuse to be examined. I offered no resistance to being placed in position, but lay down voluntarily on the plank bed. Two of the wardresses took hold of my arms, one held my head and one my feet. One wardress helped to pour the food. The doctor leant on my knees as he stooped over my chest to get at my mouth. I shut my mouth and clenched my teeth. I had looked forward to this moment with so much anxiety lest my identity should be discovered beforehand, that I felt positively glad when the time had come. The sense of being overpowered by more force than I could possibly resist was complete, but I resisted nothing except with my mouth. The doctor offered me the choice of a wooden or steel gag; he explained elaborately, as he did on most subsequent occasions, that the steel gag would hurt and the wooden one not, and he urged me not to force him to use the steel gag. But I did not speak nor open my mouth, so that after playing about for a moment or two with the wooden one he finally had recourse to the steel. He seemed annoyed at my resistance and he broke into a temper as he plied my teeth with the steel implement. He found that on either side at the back I had false teeth mounted on a bridge which did not take out. The superintending wardress asked if I had any false teeth, if so, that they must be taken out; I made no answer and the process went on. He dug his instrument down on to the sham tooth, it pressed fearfully on the gum. He said if I resisted so much with my teeth, he would have to feed me through the nose. The pain of it was intense and at last I must have given way for he got the gag between my teeth, when he proceeded to turn it much more than necessary until my jaws were fastened wide apart, far more than they could go naturally. Then he put down my throat a tube which seemed to me much too wide and was something like four feet in length. The irritation of the tube was excessive. I choked the moment it touched my throat until it had got down. Then the food was poured in quickly; it made me sick a few seconds after it was down and the action of the sickness made my body and legs double up, but the wardresses instantly pressed back my head and the doctor leant on my knees. The horror of it was more than I can describe. I was sick over the doctor and wardresses, and it seemed a long time before they took the tube out. As the doctor left he gave me a slap on the cheek, not violently, but, as it were, to express his contemptuous disapproval, and he seemed to take for granted that my distress was assumed. At first it seemed such an utterly contemptible thing to have done that I could only laugh in my mind. Then suddenly I saw Jane Warton lying before me, and it seemed as if I were outside of her. She was the most despised, ignorant and helpless prisoner that I had seen. When she had served her time and was out of the prison, no one would believe anything she said, and the doctor when he had fed her by force and tortured her body, struck her on the cheek to show how he despised her! That was Jane Warton, and I had come to help her.

When the doctor had gone out of the cell, I lay quite helpless. The wardresses were kind and knelt round to comfort me, but there was nothing to be done, I could not move, and remained there in what, under different conditions, would have been an intolerable mess. I had been sick over my hair, which, though short, hung on either side of my face, all over the wall near my bed, and my clothes seemed saturated with it, but the wardresses told me they could not get me a change that night as it was too late, the office was shut. I lay quite motionless, it seemed paradise to be without the suffocating tube, without the liquid food going in and out of my body and without the gag between my teeth. Presently the wardresses all left me, they had orders to go, which were carried out with the usual promptness. Before long I heard the sounds of the forced feeding in the next cell to mine. It was almost more than I could bear, it was Elsie Howey, I was sure. When the ghastly process was over and all quiet, I tapped on the wall and called out at the top of my voice, which wasn't much just then, "No surrender," and there came the answer past any doubt in Elsie's voice, "No surrender."

REPRESENTATION OF THE PEOPLE ACT, 1918

Or, the end goal of a thousand years of libertarian struggle.

The Representation of the People Act (UK) was passed partly in gratitude to a generation which had fought and often died, in the trenches of the Western Front; partly it was passed because there was no other choice. The Liberal prime minister Lloyd George had promised returning First World War soldiers "a land fit for heroes to live in". In this land there could be nothing less than universal suffrage. All ranks of men, regardless of income or property, had fought in the war; all ranks of men required a say in the peace.

The franchise was also extended to women over 30.

The 1918 Act would be altered in subsequent decades to reduce the voting age (to 21 for women in 1928, to 18 for both men and women in 1969), but this was only refinement. The principle of universal suffrage was established.

A number of other democratic countries passed similar legislation at a similar time.

1. (1) A man shall be entitled to be registered as a parliamentary elector for a constituency (other than a university constituency) if he is of full age and not subject to any legal incapacity, and –
   (a) has the requisite residence qualification; or
   (b) has the requisite business premises qualification.
   (2) A man, in order to have the requisite residence qualification or business premises qualification for a constituency:
   (a) must on the last day of the qualifying period be residing in premises in the constituency, or occupying business premises in the constituency, as the case may be; and
   (b) must during the whole of the qualifying period have resided in premises, or occupied business premises, as the case may be, in the

constituency, or in another constituency within the same parliamentary borough or parliamentary county, or within a parliamentary borough or parliamentary county contiguous to that borough or county, or separated from that borough or county by water, not exceeding at the nearest point six miles in breadth, measured in the case of tidal water from low-water mark.

For the purposes of this subsection the administrative county of London shall be treated as a parliamentary borough.

(3) The expression "business premises" in this section means land or other premises of the yearly value of not less than ten pounds occupied for the purpose of the business, profession, or trade of the person to be registered . . .

4. (1) A woman shall be entitled to be registered as a parliamentary elector for a constituency (other than a university constituency) if she –

(a) has attained the age of thirty years; and

(b) is not subject to any legal incapacity; and

(c) is entitled to be registered as a local government elector in respect of the occupation in that constituency of land or premises (not being a dwelling-house) of a yearly value of not less than five pounds or of a dwelling-house, or is the wife of a husband entitled to be so registered.

(2) A woman shall be entitled to be registered as a parliamentary elector for a university constituency if she has attained the age of thirty years and either would be entitled to be so registered if she were a man, or has been admitted to and passed the final examination, and kept under the conditions required of women by the university the period of residence, necessary for a man to obtain a degree at any university forming, or forming part of, a university constituency which did not at the time the examination was passed admit women to degrees.

(3) A woman shall be entitled to be registered as a local government elector for any local government electoral area –

(a) where she would be entitled to be so registered if she were a man; and

(b) where she is the wife of a man who is entitled to be so registered in respect of premises in which they both reside, and she has attained the age of thirty years and is not subject to any legal incapacity.

For the purpose of this provision, a naval or military voter who is registered in respect of a residence qualification which he would have had but for his service, shall be deemed to be resident in accordance with the qualification.

SATYAGRAHA: CIVIL DISOBEDIENCE IN ACTION, INDIA, 1930

Webb Miller

Founded by Mohandas (a.k.a. Mahatma: "a great soul") Gandhi in 1920, the civil disobedience campaign sought by non-violent methods the over-throw of British rule in India. Gandhi himself was frequently arrested for this disobedience, only to continue his protests in gaol with "fasts unto death". In 1947 Britain granted Indian independence, somewhat as a result of Gandhi's long struggle and somewhat as result of its own post-war conscience (it had, after all fought the Second World War for "freedom" and against the "enslavement" of nations). Gandhi hailed the British decision as "the noblest act of the British nation". A year later, during communal strife between Muslims and Hindus, Gandhi was assassinated by a Hindu fanatic.

Venerated throughout Asia as a man of peace, Gandhi's philosophy and practice of non-violent civil disobedience deeply affected the many Western social protest movements of the 1950s and 1960s, but most notably the civil rights movement in the USA.

Below is a snapshot of *satyagraha*, non-violent civil disobedience, in action from 1930, the year of Gandhi's campaign against the Salt Tax. This latter accorded the government a monopoly of the resource. Webb Miller was a British journalist.

After plodding about six miles across country lugging a pack of sandwiches and two quart bottles of water under a sun which was already blazing hot, inquiring from every native I met, I reached the assembling place of the Gandhi followers. Several long, open, thatched sheds were surrounded by high cactus thickets. The sheds were literally swarming and buzzed like a beehive with some 2,500 Congress or Gandhi men dressed in the regulation uniform of rough homespun cotton *dhotis* and triangular Gandhi caps, somewhat like American overseas soldiers' hats. They chattered excitedly and when I arrived hundreds surrounded me, with evidences of hostility at first. After they learned my identity, I was warmly welcomed by young college-educated, English-speaking men and escorted to Mme Naidu. The famous Indian poetess, stocky, swarthy, strong-featured, bare-legged, dressed in rough, dark homespun robe and sandals, welcomed me. She explained that she was busy martialling her forces for the demonstration against the salt pans and would talk with me more at length later. She was educated in England and spoke English fluently.

Mme Naidu called for prayer before the march started and the entire assemblage knelt. She exhorted them, "Gandhi's body is in gaol but his soul is with you. India's prestige is in your hands. You must not use any violence under any circumstances. You will be beaten but you must not resist; you must not even raise a hand to ward off blows." Wild, shrill cheers terminated her speech.

Slowly and in silence the throng commenced the half-mile march to the salt deposits. A few carried ropes for lassoing the barbed-wire stockade around the salt pans. About a score who were assigned to act as stretcher-bearers wore crude, hand-painted red crosses pinned to their breasts; their stretchers consisted of blankets. Manilal Gandhi, second son of Gandhi, walked among the foremost of the marchers. As the throng drew near the salt pans they commenced chanting the revolutionary slogan, *Inquilab zindabad*, intoning the two words over and over.

The salt deposits were surrounded by ditches filled with water and guarded by 400 native Surat police in khaki shorts and brown turbans. Half-a-dozen British officials commanded them. The police carried *lathis* – five-foot clubs tipped with steel. Inside the stockade twenty-five native riflemen were drawn up.

In complete silence the Gandhi men drew up and halted 100 yards from the stockade. A picked column advanced from the crowd, waded the ditches, and approached the barbed-wire stockade, which the Surat police surrounded, holding their clubs at the ready. Police officials ordered the marchers to disperse under a recently imposed regulation which prohibited gatherings of more than five persons in any one place. The column silently ignored the warning and slowly walked forward. I stayed with the main body about 100 yards from the stockade.

Suddenly, at a word of command, scores of native police rushed upon the advancing marchers and rained blows on their heads with their steel-shod *lathis*. Not one of the marchers even raised an arm to fend off the blows. They went down like ten-pins. From where I stood I heard the sickening whacks of the clubs on unprotected skulls. The waiting crowd of watchers groaned and sucked in their breaths in sympathetic pain at every blow.

Those struck down fell sprawling, unconscious or writhing in pain with fractured skulls or broken shoulders. In two or three minutes the ground was quilted with bodies. Great patches of blood widened on their white clothes. The survivors without breaking ranks silently and doggedly marched on until struck down. When every one of the first column had been knocked down stretcher-bearers rushed up unmolested by the police and carried off the injured to a thatched hut which had been arranged as a temporary hospital.

Then another column formed while the leaders pleaded with them to retain their self-control. They marched slowly toward the police. Although every one knew that within a few minutes he would be beaten down, perhaps killed, I could detect no signs of wavering or fear. They marched steadily with heads up, without the encouragement of music or cheering or any possibility that they might escape serious injury or death. The police rushed out and methodically and mechanically beat down the second column. There was no fight, no struggle; the marchers simply walked forward until struck down. There were no outcries, only groans after they fell. There were not enough stretcher-bearers to carry off the wounded; I saw eighteen injured being carried off simultaneously, while forty-two still lay bleeding on the ground awaiting stretcher-bearers. The blankets used as stretchers were sodden with blood . . .

In the middle of the morning V.J. Patel arrived. He had been leading the Swaraj movement since Gandhi's arrest, and had just resigned as President of the Indian Legislative Assembly in protest against the British. Scores surrounded him, knelt, and kissed his feet. He was a venerable gentleman of about sixty with white flowing beard and moustache, dressed in the usual undyed, coarse homespun smock. Sitting on the ground under a mango tree, Patel said, "All hope of reconciling India with the British Empire is lost for ever. I can understand any government's taking people into custody and punishing them for breaches of the law, but I cannot understand how any government that calls itself civilized could deal as savagely and brutally with non-violent, unresisting men as the British have this morning."

By eleven the heat reached 116 degrees in the shade and the activities of the Gandhi volunteers subsided. I went back to the temporary hospital to examine the wounded. They lay in rows on the bare ground in the shade of an open, palm-thatched shed. I counted 320 injured, many still insensible with fractured skulls, others writhing in agony from kicks in the testicles and stomach. The Gandhi men had been able to gather only a few native doctors, who were doing the best they could with the inadequate facilities. Scores of the injured had received no treatment for hours and two had died. The demonstration was finished for the day on account of the heat.

I was the only foreign correspondent who had witnessed the amazing scene – a classic example of *satyagraha* or non-violent civil disobedience.

"THEIR FINEST HOUR":
SPEECH TO PARLIAMENT, 1940

Winston Churchill MP

The Second World War opened on 1 September 1939 when the panzers of Nazi Germany rolled into Poland. Although Hitler's previous territorial aggrandizements had met with complicity or paralysis by the Western democracies, Britain and France had explicitly guaranteed the integrity of Poland's borders. This time there was no, and could be no, appeasement. Thus Britain and France declared war on the Reich on Sunday 3rd September. Nine months of "phoney war" followed, before the German army launched a *Blitzkrieg* ("lightning war") invasion of the Low Countries and France in May 1940. The armies of these countries were humiliated by the *Wehrmacht*; by 20 May panzers had reached the English channel. Four weeks later France signed an armistice. Only Britain, which had managed to salvage part of its expeditionary force to France in "the miracle of Dunkirk", still stood against Nazi Germany.

But cometh the hour, cometh the man. The attack on France obliged the British Prime Minister, Neville Chamberlain, to quit office, dented as he was by his past policy of appeasement. A new coalition administration was formed under Winston Churchill. Born in 1874, a former soldier and war correspondent, Churchill had been something of a political maverick since first entering Parliament in 1900, switching from Conservative to Liberal to Conservative. He had, however, been the most consistent opponent of appeasement in the House of Commons during the 1930s. On assuming Prime Ministerial office (the beginning of his "walk with destiny") he offered the British people nothing but "blood, toil, tears and sweat" and pugnaciously led Britain's lone resistance to Germany and Italy, until her cause was joined in 1941 by the USSR and USA. Churchill inspired by deed and word; one of the great English orators, his speeches steeled an entire people to fight for liberty and also succoured the enslaved of Europe.

Following the successful conclusion in 1945 of the Second World War, Churchill led the Opposition in the House of Commons before returning as Prime Minister, 1951–55. He warned ceaselessly in this time against the tyranny of Stalinism behind the "Iron Curtain" (his phrase). Churchill died in 1965.

Below is the full text of Churchill's "Their Finest Hour" speech, delivered in the House of Commons on 18 June 1940 during the Fall of France and before the Nazis' air attack on the isles ("The Battle of Britain"). The speech begins with a magisterial state-of-the-war analysis before progressing to the famously stirring order to battle.

I spoke the other day of the colossal military disaster which occurred when the French High Command failed to withdraw the northern armies from Belgium at a moment when they knew that the French front was decisively broken at Sedan and on the Meuse.

This delay entailed the loss of fifteen or sixteen French divisions and threw out of action the whole of the British Expeditionary Force.

Our army were indeed rescued by the British Navy from Dunkirk, but only with the loss of all their cannon, vehicles and modern equipment. This loss inevitably took some weeks to repair, and in the first two of these weeks the Battle of France had been lost.

When we consider the heroic resistance made by the French Army against heavy odds in this battle, and the enormous loss inflicted upon the enemy and the evident exhaustion of the enemy, it might well be thought that these twenty-five divisions of the best troops – best trained and equipped – might have turned the scales. However, General Weygand had to fight without them.

Only three British divisions or their equivalent were able to stand in the line with their French comrades. They have suffered severely, but they have fought well. We sent every man we could to France, as fast as we could re-equip and transport their formations.

I am not reciting these facts for the purpose of recrimination. That I judge to be utterly futile and even harmful. We cannot afford it. I recite them in order to explain why it was we did not have, as we could have had, between twelve and fourteen British divisions fighting in the line in this battle instead of only three.

Now I put all this aside. I put it on the shelf from which the historians may select their documents in order to tell their story. We have to think of the future and not of the past. This also applies in a small way to our own affairs at home.

There are many who wish to hold an inquest upon the conduct of the government and of Parliament during the years which led up to this catastrophe. They wish to indict those who were responsible for the guidance of our affairs.

This also would be a foolish and pernicious process. There are too many in it. Let each man search his conscience and search his speeches, as I frequently search mine. Of this I am quite sure, that if we open a quarrel between the past and the present we shall find that we have lost the future.

Therefore I cannot accept the drawing of any distinctions between members of the present government which was formed in a moment of crisis in order to unite members of all parties and all sections of opinion. It has received the almost unanimous support of both Houses of Parliament and its members are going to stand together and, subject to the authority of the House of Commons, we are going to govern the country and fight the war.

It is absolutely necessary at a time like this that every Minister who tries each day to do his duty shall be respected and their subordinates must know that their chiefs are not threatened men who are here today and gone tomorrow.

Their directions must be punctually and effectively given. Without this concentrated power we cannot do what lies before us. I do not think it would be very advantageous for the House to prolong this debate this afternoon under the conditions of a public sitting. We are to have a secret session on Thursday that would be a better opportunity for many earnest expressions of opinion which may be desired for the House to discuss our vital matters without having everything read the next morning by our dangerous foe.

The military events which have happened in France during the last fortnight have not come to me with any sense of surprise; indeed, I indicated a fortnight ago as clearly as I could to the House, that the worst possibilities were open and I made it perfectly clear that whatever happened in France, it would make no difference to the resolve of Britain and the British Empire to fight on, if necessary for years, and if necessary alone.

During the last few days we have successfully brought off the great majority of troops which were on the lines of communication in France. A very large number, scores of thousands, and seven-eighths of all the troops we have sent to France since the beginning of the war. About 350,010 out of 400,000 men are safely back in this country. Others are still fighting with the French and fighting with considerable success.

We have also brought back a great mass of stores, rifles and munitions of all kinds which have accumulated in France during the last nine months. We have therefore in this island today a very large and powerful military force. This includes all our best trained and finest troops, including scores of thousands of those who have already measured their quality against the Germans and found themselves at no disadvantage.

We have under arms at the present time in this island over 1,250,000 men. Behind these we have the local defence volunteers, numbering

500,000, only a portion of whom, however, are armed with rifles or other firearms.

We have incorporated into our defence force a mass of weapons and we expect very large additions to these weapons in the near future. In preparation, we intend to call up, drill and train, further large numbers at once.

Those who are not called up or who are employed upon the vast business of munitions production in all its branches serve their country best by remaining at their ordinary work until they are required.

We also have the Dominion armies here. The Canadians had actually landed in France, but have now been safely withdrawn much disappointed and are here with all their artillery and equipment. These very high-class forces from the dominions will now take part in the defence of their mother country.

Lest the account which I have given of these large forces should raise the question why they did not take part in the great battle in France, I must make it clear that apart from the divisions training at home, only twelve divisions were equipped to fight on a scale which justified their being sent abroad. This was fully up to the number that the French had been led to expect would be available in France at the ninth month of the war. The rest of our forces at home will steadily increase.

Thus, the invasion of Great Britain at this time would require the transport across the seas of hostile armies on a very large scale and after they had been so transported, they would have to be continually maintained with all the immense mass of munitions and supplies which are required for continuous battle, as continuous battle it would be.

Now here is where we come to the navy. After all, we have a navy; some people seem to forget it. We must remind them. For more than thirty years I have been concerned in discussions about the possibility of an overseas invasion and I took the responsibility on behalf of the Admiralty at the beginning of the last war of allowing all the regular troops to be sent out of the country although our Territorials had only just been called up and were quite untried.

Therefore, these islands for several months were denuded of fighting forces, but the Admiralty had confidence in the defence by the navy, although at that time the Germans had a magnificent battle fleet in the proportion of 10 to 16 and even though they were capable of fighting a general engagement any day. Now they have only a couple of heavy ships worth speaking of.

We are also told that the Italian Navy is coming to gain sea superiority in these waters. If that is seriously intended, I can only say we shall be delighted to offer Mussolini free safeguarded passage through the Straits of Gibraltar in order that he may play the part which he aspires to do. There is general curiosity in the British Fleet to find out whether the

Italians are up to the level they were in the last war or whether they have fallen off.

Therefore, it seems to me that as far as sea-borne invasion on a great scale is concerned, we are far more capable of meeting it than we were at many periods in the last war and during the early months of this war before our troops were trained and while the British Expeditionary Force was abroad.

The navy was never intended to prevent the raids of bodies of five or ten thousand men flung across and thrown suddenly ashore at several points on the coast some dark night or foggy morning. The efficacy of sea power, especially under modern conditions, depends upon the invading force being of a large size and, if it is of a large size, the navy has something they can find and, as it were, bite on.

Now we must remember that even five divisions, even lightly equipped, would require 200 to 250 ships, and with modern air reconnaissance and photography it would not be easy to collect such an armada and marshal it across the seas with any powerful naval force to escort it with any possibility that it would not be intercepted long before it reached the coast and the men all drowned in the sea, or, at the worst, blown to pieces with their equipment when they were trying to land.

We have also a great system of mine fields, recently reinforced, through which we alone know the channel. If the enemy tries to sweep a channel through these mine fields it will be the task of the navy to destroy these mine-sweepers and any other force employed to protect them. There ought to be no difficulty about this, owing to our superiority at sea.

These are the well-tested and well-proved arguments on which we have relied for many years, but the question is whether there are any new methods by which they can be circumvented. Odd as it may seem, some attention has been given to this by the Admiralty whose prime duty and responsibility it is to destroy any large sea-borne expedition before it reaches or at the moment when it reaches these shores. It would not be useful to go into details and it might even suggest ideas to other people that they have not got and who would not be likely to give us any of their ideas in exchange.

All I would say is that untiring vigilance and mind-searching must be devoted to the subject, because, the enemy is crafty, cunning and full of novel treacheries and strategies.

The House may be assured that the utmost ingenuity is being displayed by competent officers, well trained in planning and thoroughly up to date, to measure and to counterwork the novel possibilities which many suggest are absurd but seem not utterly rash.

Some people will ask why it was that the British Navy was not able to prevent the movement of a large army from Germany into Norway across the Skagerrak. But conditions in the Channel and in the North Sea are in no way like those which prevail in the Skagerrak. In the Skagerrak, because of the distance, we could give no air support to our surface ships and consequently, lying as we did close to the enemy's main air power in Norwegian waters, we were compelled to use only our submarines.

We could not enforce a decisive blockade or interruption of the enemy's surface vessels. Our vessels took a heavy toll but could not prevent the invasion. But in the Channel and in the North Sea, on the other hand, our forces, aided by submarines, will operate with close and effective air assistance.

This brings me naturally to the great question of invasion from the air and the impending struggle between the British and German Air Forces.

It seems quite clear that no invasion on a scale beyond the capacity of our ground forces to crush speedily is likely to take place from the air until our air force has been definitely overpowered. In the meantime, there may be raids by parachute troops and attempted descents by air-borne soldiers. We ought to be able to give those gentry a warm reception, both in the air and if they reach the ground in any condition to continue their dispute. The great question is, can we break Hitler's air weapon?

Now, of course, it is a very great pity that we have not got an air force at least equal to that of the most powerful enemy within reach of our shores, but we have a very powerful air force, which has proved itself far superior in quality both in men and in many types of machines to what we have met so far in the numerous fierce air battles which have been fought.

In France, where we were at a considerable disadvantage and lost many machines on the ground in the airdromes, we were accustomed to inflict upon the enemy a loss of two to two-and-a-half to one. In the fighting over Dunkirk, which was a sort of No Man's Land, we undoubtedly gained a local mastery of the air and inflicted on the German Air Force losses on the scale of three or four to one.

Any one looking at the photographs of the re-embarkation, showing the masses of troops assembled on the beaches, affording an ideal target for hours at a time, must realize that this embarkation would not have been possible unless the enemy had resigned all hope of recovery of air superiority at that point.

In these islands the advantage to the defenders will be very great. We ought to improve upon that rate of three or four to one, which was realized at Dunkirk.

In addition, there are, of course, a great many injured machines and men who get down safely after an air fight. But all those who fall in an attack upon this island would land on friendly soil and live to fight another day, whereas all the injured enemy machines and their complements will be total losses, as far as the Germans are concerned.

During the great battle in France we gave very great and continuous aid to the French, both by fighters and bombers, but in spite of all pressure, we never allowed the entire metropolitan strength of our air force in fighters to be consumed. This decision was painful, but it was also right.

The battle was, however, lost by the unfortunate strategic opening and by the extraordinary unforeseen power of the armoured columns and by the very great preponderance of the German Army in numbers.

Our fighter air force might easily have been exhausted as a mere incident in that struggle and we should have found ourselves at the present time in a very unhappy plight. I am happy to inform the House that our fighter air strength is stronger at the present time relatively to the German, which has suffered terrible losses, than it has ever been. Consequently we believe ourselves to possess the capacity to continue the war in the air under better conditions than we have ever experienced before.

I look forward confidently to the exploits of our fighter pilots, who will have the glory of saving their native land and our island home from the most deadly of all attacks.

There remains the danger of the bombing attacks, which will certainly be made very soon upon us by the bomber forces of the enemy. It is quite true that these forces are superior in number to ours, but we have a very large bombing force also which we shall use to strike at the military targets in Germany without intermission.

I do not at all underrate the severity of the ordeal which lies before us, but I believe that our countrymen will show themselves capable of standing up to it and carrying on in spite of it at least as well as any other people in the world.

It will depend upon themselves, and every man and woman will have the chance of showing the finest qualities of their race and of rendering the highest service to their cause.

For all of us, whatever our sphere or station, it will be a help to remember the famous lines:

He nothing common did, or mean
Upon that memorable scene.

I have thought it right on this occasion to give the House and the country some indication of the solid, practical grounds upon which we are basing our invincible resolve to continue the war, and I can assure them that our professional advisers of the three services unitedly advise that we should do it, and that there are good and reasonable hopes of final victory.

We have fully informed all the self-governing dominions and we have received from all Prime Ministers messages couched in the most moving terms, in which they endorse our decision and declare themselves ready to share our fortunes and persevere to the end.

We may now ask ourselves in what way has our position worsened since the beginning of the war. It is worsened by the fact that the Germans have conquered a large part of the coast of the Allies in Western Europe, and many small countries have been overrun by them. This aggravates the possibility of air attack and adds to our naval preoccupation, but it in no way diminishes, but on the contrary definitely increases, the power of our long-distance blockade.

Should military resistance come to an end in France – which is not yet, though it will in any case be greatly diminished – the Germans can concentrate their forces both military and industrial upon us. But for the reason given to the House this will not be easy to apply.

If invasion becomes more imminent, we have been relieved from the task of maintaining a large army in France and we have a far larger and more efficient force here to meet it.

If Hitler can bring under despotic control the industries of the countries he has conquered, this will add greatly to his already vast armament output. On the other hand, this will not happen immediately and we are now assured of immense continued and increasing support in munitions of all kinds from the United States, and especially of airplanes and pilots from across the ocean. They will come from regions beyond the reach of enemy bombers.

I do not see how any of these factors can operate to our detriment, on balance, before the Winter comes, and the Winter will impose a strain upon the Nazi regime, with half Europe writhing and starving under its heel, which, for all their ruthlessness, will run them very hard.

We must not forget that from the moment we declared war on Sept. 3, it was always possible for Germany to turn all her air force on this country. There would also be other devices of invasion, and France could do little or nothing to prevent her. We have therefore lived under this danger during all these months.

In the meanwhile, however, we have enormously improved our methods of defence and we have learned what we had no right to assume at the beginning, of the individual superiority of our aircraft and pilots.

Therefore in casting up this dread balance sheet and contemplating our dangers with a disillusioned eye, I see great reasons for intense exertion and vigilance, but none whatever for panic or despair. During the first four months of the last war the Allies experienced nothing but disaster and disappointment, and yet at the end their morale was higher than that of the Germans, who had moved from one aggressive triumph to another.

During that war we repeatedly asked ourselves the question, "How are we going to win?" and no one was ever able to answer it with much precision, until at the end, quite suddenly and unexpectedly, our terrible foe collapsed before us and we were so glutted with victory that in our folly we cast it away.

We do not yet know what will happen in France or whether the French resistance will be prolonged both in France and in the French Empire overseas. The French Government will be throwing away great opportunities and casting away their future if they do not continue the war in accordance with their treaty obligations, from which we have not felt able to release them.

The House will have read the historic declaration in which, at the desire of many Frenchmen and of our own hearts, we have proclaimed our willingness to conclude at the darkest hour in French history a union of common citizenship in their struggle.

However matters may go in France or with the French Government, or another French Government, we in this island and in the British Empire will never lose our sense of comradeship with the French people.

If we are now called upon to endure what they have suffered, we shall emulate their courage, and if final victory rewards our toils they shall share the gain – aye, freedom shall be restored to all. We abate nothing of our just demands. Czechs, Poles, Norwegians, Dutch and Belgians, who have joined their causes with our own, all shall be restored.

What General Weygand called the Battle of France is over. The Battle of Britain is about to begin. On this battle depends the survival of Christian civilization.

Upon it depends our own British life and the long continuity of our institutions and our empire. The whole fury and might of the enemy must very soon be turned upon us. Hitler knows he will have to break us in this island or lose the war.

If we can stand up to him all Europe may be freed and the life of the world may move forward into broad sunlit uplands; but if we fail, the whole world, including the United States and all that we have known and cared for, will sink into the abyss of a new dark age made more sinister and perhaps more prolonged by the lights of a perverted science.

Let us therefore brace ourselves to our duty and so bear ourselves that if the British Commonwealth and Empire last for a thousand years, men will still say "This was their finest hour."

From FULL EMPLOYMENT IN A FREE SOCIETY, 1944

William Beveridge

Published by the British government at the height of World War II, *Full Employment in a Free Society* laid the basis for the "Welfare State". Its ideas and prescriptions influenced many western European countries.

1. The Report on Social Insurance and Allied Services which I presented to His Majesty's Government in November, 1942, takes Freedom from Want as its aim, and sets out a Plan for Social Security to achieve this aim. Want is defined as lack of income to obtain the means of healthy subsistence – adequate food, shelter, clothing and fuel. The Plan for Social Security is designed to secure, by a comprehensive scheme of social insurance, that every individual, on condition of working while he can and contributing from his earnings, shall have an income sufficient for the healthy subsistence of himself and his family, an income to keep him above Want, when for any reason he cannot work and earn. In addition to subsistence income during interruption of earnings, the Report proposes Children's Allowances to ensure that, however large the family, no child need ever to be in want, and medical treatment of all kinds for all persons when sick, without a charge on treatment, to ensure that no person need be sick because he has not the means to pay the doctor or the hospital.

44. Full employment cannot be won and held without a great extension of the responsibilities and powers of the State, exercised through organs of the central Government. No power less than that of the state can ensure adequate total outlay at all times, or can control, in the general interest, the location of industry and the use of land. To ask for full employment while objecting to these extensions of State activity is to will the end and refuse the means. It is like shouting for victory in total war while rejecting compulsory service and rationing . . . The underlying principle of the Report is to propose for the State only those things which the State alone can do or which it can do better than any local authority or than private

citizens . . . and to leave to those other agencies that which, if they will, they can do as well or better than the State. The policy for Full Employment is a policy to be carried through by democratic action, of public authorities, central and local, responsible ultimately to the voters, and of voluntary associations and private citizens consciously co-operating for a common purpose which they understand and approve.

THE CHARTER OF THE UNITED NATIONS, 1945

The UN was founded in 1945 as a forum for the nations of the world and the upholder of international peace. While its record of success in peace-keeping has been mixed, its welfare agencies, WHO and UNESCO, have significant achievements in health and education provision to their name.

We, the peoples of the United Nations

Determined to save succeeding generations from the scourge of war, which twice in our lifetime has brought untold sorrow to mankind, and

To reaffirm faith in fundamental human rights, in the dignity and worth of the human person, in the equal right of men and women and of nations large and small, and

To establish conditions under which justice and respect for the obligations arising from treaties and other sources of international law can be maintained, and

To promote social progress and better standards of life in larger freedom, and for these ends

To practise tolerance and live together in peace with one another as good neighbours and

To unite our strength to maintain international peace and security and

To ensure, by the acceptance of principles and the institution of methods, that armed force shall not be used, save in the common interest, and

To employ international machinery for the promotion of the economic and social advancement of all people, have resolved to combine our efforts to accomplish these aims.

Accordingly, our respective governments, through representatives assembled in the city of San Francisco, who have exhibited their full powers found to be in good and due form, have agreed to the present Charter of the United Nations and do hereby establish an international organization to be known as the United Nations.

Chapter I
Purposes

Article 1 – The purposes of the United Nations are:

1. To maintain international peace and security, and to that end: to take effective collective measures for the prevention and removal of threats to the peace and for the suppression of acts of aggression or other breaches of the peace, and to bring about by peaceful means, and in conformity with the principles of justice and international law, adjustment or settlement of international disputes or situations which might lead to a breach of the peace;

2. To develop friendly relations among nations based on respect for the principle of equal rights and self-determination of peoples, and to take other appropriate measures to strengthen universal peace;

3. To achieve international co-operation in solving international problems of an economic, social, cultural or humanitarian character, and in promoting and encouraging respect for human rights and for the fundamental freedoms for all without distinction as to race, sex, language or religion; and

4. To be a centre for harmonizing the actions of nations in the attainment of these common ends.

Chapter IV
The General Assembly Composition

Article 9 – The General Assembly shall consist of all the members of the United Nations.

Each member shall not have more than five representatives in the General Assembly.

Functions and Powers

Article 10 – The General Assembly may discuss any questions or any matters within the scope of the present Charter or relating to the powers and functions of any organs provided in the present Charter, and, except as provided in Article 12, may make recommendations to the members of the Nations or to the Security Council, or both, on any such questions or matters.

Chapter V The Security Council Composition

Article 23 – 1. The Security Council shall consist of eleven members of the United Nations. The United States of America, the United Kingdom of Great Britain and Northern Ireland, the Union of Soviet Socialist Republics, the Republic of China, and France, shall be permanent members of the Security Council. The General Assembly shall elect six other members of the United Nations to be non-permanent members of the Security Council, due regard being specially paid, in the first instance to the contribution of members of the United Nations to the maintenance of international peace and security and to the other purposes of the organization, and also to equitable geographical distribution.

Primary Responsibility

Article 24 – 1. In order to ensure prompt and effective action by the United Nations, its members confer on the Security Council primary responsibility for the maintenance of international peace and security and agree that in carrying out its duties under this responsibility the Security Council acts on their behalf.

Voting

Article 27 – 1. Each member of the Security Council shall have one vote:
   2. Decisions of the Security Council on procedural matters shall be made by an affirmative vote of seven members.
   3. Decisions of the Security Council on all other matters shall be made by an affirmative vote of seven members including the concurring votes of the permanent members; provided that, in decisions under Chapter VI and under Paragraph 3 of Article 52, a party to a dispute shall abstain from voting.

Procedure

Article 28 – 1. The Security Council shall be so organised as to be able to function continuously. Each member of the Security Council shall for this purpose be represented at all times at the seat of the organization.

Chapter VII
Action with Respect to Threats to the Peace, Breaches of the Peace and Acts of Aggression

Article 39 – The Security Council shall determine the existence of any threat to the peace, breach of the peace, or act of aggression and shall make recommendations, or decide what measures shall be taken in accordance with the provisions of Articles 41 and 42, to maintain or restore international peace and security.

Article 40 – In order to prevent an aggravation of the situation, the Security Council may, before making the recommendations or deciding upon the measures provided for in Article 39, call upon the parties concerned to comply with such provisional measures as it deems necessary or desirable. Such provisional measures shall be without prejudice to the rights, claims, or position of the parties concerned. The Security Council shall duly take account of failure to comply with such provisional measures.

Article 41 – The Security Council may decide what measures not involving the use of armed force are to be employed to give effect to its decisions, and it may call upon members of the United Nations to apply such measures. These may include complete or partial interruptions of economic relations and of rail, sea, air, postal, telegraphic radio, and other means of communication, and the severance of diplomatic relations.

Article 42 – Should the Security Council consider that measures provided for in Article 41 would be inadequate, or have proved to be inadequate, it may take such action by air, sea, or land forces as may be necessary to maintain or restore international peace and security. Such action may include demonstrations, blockade, and other operations by air, sea, or land forces of members of the United Nations.

Article 43 – 1. All members of the United Nations, in order to contribute to the maintenance of international peace and security, undertake to make available to the Security Council, on its call and in accordance with a special agreement or agreements, armed forces, assistance, and facilities, including rights of passage, necessary for the purpose of maintaining international peace and security.

2. Such agreement or agreements shall govern the numbers and types of forces, their degree of readiness and general locations, and nature of the facilities and assistance to be provided.

3. The agreement or agreements shall be negotiated as soon as possible on the initiative of the Security Council. They shall be concluded between the Security Council and member states or between the Security Council and groups of member states and shall be subject to ratification by the signatory states in accordance with their constitutional processes.

Article 44 – When the Security Council has decided to use force it shall, before calling upon a member not represented on it to provide armed forces in fulfilment of the obligations assumed under Article 43, invite that member, if the member so desires, to participate in the decisions of the Security Council concerning the employment of contingents of that member's forces.

Article 45 – In order to enable the United Nations to take urgent military measures, members shall hold immediately available air force contingents for combined international enforcement action. The strength and degree of readiness of these contingents and plans for their combined action shall be determined within the limits laid down in the special agreements referred to in Article 43, by the Security Council with the assistance of the Military Staff Committee.

Article 51 – Nothing in the present charter shall impair the inherent right of individual or collective self-defence, if an armed attack occurs against a member of the organization, until the Security Council has taken the measures necessary to maintain international peace and security. Measures taken by members in the exercise of this right of self-defence shall be immediately reported to the Security Council and shall not in any way affect the authority and responsibility of the Security Council under the present charter to take at any time such action as it may deem necessary in order to maintain or restore international peace and security.

Chapter VIII Regional Arrangements

Article 52 – 1. Nothing in the present charter precludes the existence of regional arrangements or agencies for dealing with such matters relating to the maintenance of international peace and security as are appropriate for regional action, provided that such arrangements or agencies and their activities are consistent with the purpose and principles of the organization.

2. The members of the United Nations entering into such arrangements or constituting such agencies shall make every effort to achieve peaceful settlement of local disputes through such regional arrangements or by such regional agencies before referring them to the Security Council.

UNIVERSAL DECLARATION OF HUMAN RIGHTS, 1948

The Universal Declaration was adopted by the General Assembly of the United Nations late on the night of 10 December 1948 without a single dissenting vote. Much of the immediate inspiration for the Universal Declaration came from the wartime US President, Franklin D. Roosevelt, who had termed the Second World War a battle of "four freedoms": for free speech and expression, for freedom to worship God in one's own way, freedom from want, freedom from fear. (Roosevelt's wife, Eleanor, chaired the UN commission which drafted the Universal Declaration.) Since 1948, the Universal Declaration has become the parent of most other rights documents in the world. Moreover, as an international common standard by which a sovereign country's rights and wrongs can be measured, the Universal Declaration has helped change that world: the freedom movements of Stalinist Eastern Europe and apartheid South Africa both used the Universal Declaration as leverage to topple the monolith.

Preamble

WHEREAS recognition of the inherent dignity and of the equal and inalienable rights of all members of the human family is the foundation of freedom, justice and peace in the world.

WHEREAS disregard and contempt for human rights have resulted in barbarous acts which have outraged the conscience of mankind, and the advent of a world in which human beings shall enjoy freedom of speech and belief and freedom from fear and want has been proclaimed as the highest aspiration of the common people.

WHEREAS it is essential, if man is not to be compelled to have recourse, as a last resort, to rebellion against tyranny and oppression, that human rights should be protected by the rule of law.

WHEREAS it is essential to promote the development of friendly relations between nations.

WHEREAS the peoples of the United Nations have in the Charter reaffirmed their faith in fundamental human rights, in the dignity and worth of the human person and in the equal rights of men and women and have determined to promote social progress and better standards of life in larger freedom.

WHEREAS Member States have pledged themselves to achieve, in co-operation with the United Nations, the promotion of universal respect for and observance of human rights and fundamental freedoms.

WHEREAS a common understanding of these rights and freedoms is of the greatest importance for the full realization of this pledge.

Now, Therefore, The General Assembly Proclaims

This universal declaration of human rights as a common standard of achievement for all peoples and all nations, to the end that every individual and every organ of society, keeping this Declaration constantly in mind, shall strive by teaching and education to promote respect for these rights and freedoms and by progressive measures, national and international, to secure their universal and effective recognition and observance, both among the peoples of Member States themselves and among the peoples of territories under their jurisdiction.

ARTICLE 1. All human beings are born free and equal in dignity and rights. They are endowed with reason and conscience and should act towards one another in a spirit of brotherhood.

ARTICLE 2. Everyone is entitled to all the rights and freedoms set forth in this Declaration, without distinction of any kind, such as race, colour, sex, language, religion, political or other opinion, national or social origin, property, birth or other status.

Furthermore, no distinction shall be made on the basis of the political, jurisdictional or international status of the country or territory to which a person belongs, whether it be independent, trust, non-self-governing or under any other limitation of sovereignty.

ARTICLE 3. Everyone has the right to life, liberty and security of person.

ARTICLE 4. No one shall be held in slavery or servitude; slavery and the slave trade shall be prohibited in all their forms.

ARTICLE 5. No one shall be subjected to torture or to cruel, inhuman or degrading treatment or punishment.

ARTICLE 6. Everyone has the right to recognition everywhere as a person before the law.

ARTICLE 7. All are equal before the law and are entitled without any discrimination to equal protection of the law. All are entitled to equal protection against any discrimination in violation of this Declaration and against any incitement to such discrimination.

ARTICLE 8. Everyone has the right to an effective remedy by the competent national tribunals for acts violating the fundamental rights granted him by the constitution or by law.

ARTICLE 9. No one shall be subjected to arbitrary arrest, detention or exile.

ARTICLE 10. Everyone is entitled in full equality to a fair and public hearing by an independent and impartial tribunal, in the determination of his rights and obligations and of any criminal charge against him.

ARTICLE 11. (1) Everyone charged with a penal offence has the right to be presumed innocent until proved guilty according to law in a public trial at which he has had all the guarantees necessary for his defence.

(2) No one shall be held guilty of any penal offence or of any act or omission which did not constitute a penal offence, under national or international law, at the time when it was committed. Nor shall a heavier penalty be imposed than the one that was applicable at the time the penal offence was committed.

ARTICLE 12. No one shall be subject to arbitrary interference with his privacy, family, home or correspondence, nor to attacks upon his honour and reputation. Everyone has the right to the protection of the law against such interference or attacks.

ARTICLE 13. (1) Everyone has the right to freedom of movement and residence within the borders of each state.

(2) Everyone has the right to leave any country, including his own, and to return to his country.

ARTICLE 14. (1) Everyone has the right to seek and to enjoy in other countries asylum from persecution.

(2) This right may not be invoked in the case of prosecutions genuinely arising from non-political crimes or from acts contrary to the purposes and principles of the United Nations.

ARTICLE 15. (1) Everyone has the right to a nationality.

(2) No one shall be arbitrarily deprived of his nationality nor denied the right to change his nationality.

ARTICLE 16. (1) Men and women of full age, without any limitation due to race, nationality or religion, have the right to marry and to found a family. They are entitled to equal rights as to marriage, during marriage, and at its dissolution.

(2) Marriage shall be entered into only with the free and full consent of the intending spouses.

(3) The family is the natural and fundamental group unit of society and is entitled to protection by society and the State.

ARTICLE 17. (1) Everyone has the right to own property alone as well as in association with others.

(2) No one shall be arbitrarily deprived of his property.

ARTICLE 18. Everyone has the right to freedom of thought, conscience and religion: this right includes freedom to change his religion or belief, and freedom, either alone or in community with others and in public or private, to manifest his religion or belief in teaching, practice, worship and observance.

ARTICLE 19. Everyone has the right to freedom of opinion and expression; this right includes freedom to hold opinions without interference and to seek, receive and impart information and ideas through any media and regardless of frontiers.

ARTICLE 20. (1) Everyone has the right to freedom of peaceful assembly and association.

(2) No one may be compelled to belong to an association.

ARTICLE 21. (1) Everyone has the right to take part in the government of his country, directly or through freely chosen representatives.

(2) Everyone has the right of equal access to public service in his country.

(3) The will of the people shall be the basis of the authority of government; this will shall be expressed in periodic and genuine elections which shall be by universal and equal suffrage and shall be held by secret vote or by equivalent free voting procedures.

ARTICLE 22. Everyone, as a member of society, has the right to social security and is entitled to realization, through national effort and international co-operation and in accordance with the organization and resources of each State, of the economic, social and cultural rights indispensable for his dignity and the free development of his personality.

ARTICLE 23. (1) Everyone has the right to work, to free choice of employment, to just and favourable conditions of work and to protection against unemployment.

(2) Everyone, without any discrimination, has the right to equal pay for equal work.

(3) Everyone who works has the right to just and favourable remuneration ensuring for himself and his family an existence worthy of human dignity, and supplemented, if necessary, by other means of social protection.

(4) Everyone has the right to form and to join trade unions for protection of his interests.

ARTICLE 24. Everyone has the right to rest and leisure, including reasonable limitation of working hours and periodic holidays with pay.

ARTICLE 25. (1) Everyone has the right to a standard of living adequate for the health and well-being of himself and his family, including food, clothing, housing and medical care and necessary social services, and the right to security in the event of unemployment, sickness, disability, widowhood, old age or other lack of livelihood in circumstances beyond his control.

(2) Motherhood and childhood are entitled to special care and assistance. All children, whether born in or out of wedlock, shall enjoy the same social protection.

ARTICLE 26. (1) Everyone has the right to education. Education shall be free, at least in the elementary and fundamental states. Elementary education shall be compulsory. Technical and professional education shall be made generally available and higher education shall be equally accessible to all on the basis of merit.

(2) Education shall be directed to the full development of the human personality and to the strengthening of respect for human rights and fundamental freedoms. It shall promote understanding, tolerance and friendship among all nations, racial or religious groups, and shall further the activities of the United Nations for the maintenance of peace.

(3) Parents shall have a prior right to choose the kind of education that shall be given to their children.

ARTICLE 27. (1) Everyone has the right freely to participate in the cultural life of the community, to enjoy the arts and to share in scientific advancement and its benefits.

(2) Everyone has the right to the protection of the moral and material interests resulting from any scientific, literary or artistic production of which he is the author.

ARTICLE 28. Everyone is entitled to a social and international order in which the rights and freedoms set forth in this Declaration can be fully realized.

ARTICLE 29. (1) Everyone has duties to the community in which alone the free and full development of his personality is possible.

(2) In the exercise of his rights and freedoms, everyone shall be subject only to such limitations as are determined by law solely for the purpose of securing due recognition and respect for the rights and freedoms of others and of meeting the just requirements of morality, public order and the general welfare in a democratic society.

(3) These rights and freedoms may in no case be exercised contrary to the purposes and principles of the United Nations.

ARTICLE 30. Nothing in this Declaration may be interpreted as implying for any State, group or person any right to engage in any activity or to perform any act aimed at the destruction of any of the rights and freedoms set forth herein.

THE NORTH ATLANTIC TREATY, 1949

Ratified on 4 April 1949, the Treaty sought to protect America and the Western democracies in the context of the new "Cold War" with Stalin's Soviet Union. On this textual foundation the North Atlantic Treaty Organization (NATO) was erected three years later.

The Parties to this Treaty reaffirm their faith in the purposes and principles of the Charter of the United Nations and their desire to live in peace with all peoples and all governments.

They are determined to safeguard the freedom, common heritage and civilization of their peoples, founded on the principles of democracy, individual liberty and the rule of law. They seek to promote stability and well-being in the North Atlantic area. They are resolved to unite their efforts for collective defence and for the preservation of peace and security. They therefore agree to this North Atlantic Treaty:

Article 1

The Parties undertake, as set forth in the *Charter of the United Nations*, to settle any international dispute in which they may be involved by peaceful means in such a manner that international peace and security and justice are not endangered, and to refrain in their international relations from the threat or use of force in any manner inconsistent with the purposes of the United Nations.

Article 2

The Parties will contribute toward the further development of peaceful and friendly international relations by strengthening their free institutions, by bringing about a better understanding of the principles upon which these institutions are founded, and by promoting conditions of stability and well-being. They will seek to eliminate conflict in their international economic policies and will encourage economic collaboration between any or all of them.

Article 3

In order more effectively to achieve the objectives of this Treaty, the Parties, separately and jointly, by means of continuous and effective self-help and mutual aid, will maintain and develop their individual and collective capacity to resist armed attack.

Article 4

The Parties will consult together whenever, in the opinion of any of them, the territorial integrity, political independence or security of any of the Parties is threatened.

Article 5

The Parties agree that an armed attack against one or more of them in Europe or North America shall be considered an attack against them all and consequently they agree that, if such an armed attack occurs, each of them, in exercise of the right of individual or collective self-defence recognized by Article 51 of the *Charter of the United Nations*, will assist the Party or Parties so attacked by taking forthwith, individually and in concert with the other Parties, such action as it deems necessary, including the use of armed force, to restore and maintain the security of the North Atlantic area.

Any such armed attack and all measures taken as a result thereof shall immediately be reported to the Security Council. Such measures shall be terminated when the Security Council has taken the measures necessary to restore and maintain international peace and security.

Article 6

For the purpose of Article 5, an armed attack on one or more of the Parties is deemed to include an armed attack:

- on the territory of any of the Parties in Europe or North America, on the Algerian Departments of France, on the territory of or on the Islands under the jurisdiction of any of the Parties in the North Atlantic area north of the Tropic of Cancer;

- on the forces, vessels, or aircraft of any of the Parties, when in or over these territories or any other area in Europe in which occupation forces of any of the Parties were stationed on the date when the Treaty entered into force or the Mediterranean Sea or the North Atlantic area north of the Tropic of Cancer.

Article 7

This Treaty does not affect, and shall not be interpreted as affecting in any way the rights and obligations under the Charter of the Parties which are members of the United Nations, or the primary responsibility of the Security Council for the maintenance of international peace and security.

Article 8

Each Party declares that none of the international engagements now in force between it and any other of the Parties or any third State is in conflict with the provisions of this Treaty, and undertakes not to enter into any international engagement in conflict with this Treaty.

Article 9

The Parties hereby establish a Council, on which each of them shall be represented, to consider matters concerning the implementation of this Treaty. The Council shall be so organized as to be able to meet promptly at any time. The Council shall set up such subsidiary bodies as may be necessary; in particular it shall establish immediately a defence committee which shall recommend measures for the implementation of Articles 3 and 5.

Article 10

The Parties may, by unanimous agreement, invite any other European State in a position to further the principles of this Treaty and to contribute to the security of the North Atlantic area to accede to this Treaty. Any State so invited may become a Party to the Treaty by depositing its instrument of accession with the Government of the United States of America. The Government of the United States of America will inform each of the Parties of the deposit of each such instrument of accession.

Article 11

This Treaty shall be ratified and its provisions carried out by the Parties in accordance with their respective constitutional processes. The instruments of ratification shall be deposited as soon as possible with the Government of the United States of America, which will notify all the other signatories of each deposit. The Treaty shall enter into force between the States which have ratified it as soon as the ratifications of the majority of the signatories, including the ratifications of Belgium, Canada, France, Luxembourg, the Netherlands, the United Kingdom and the United States, have been deposited and shall come into effect with respect to other States on the date of the deposit of their ratifications.

Article 12

After the Treaty has been in force for ten years, or at any time thereafter, the Parties shall, if any of them so requests, consult together for the purpose of reviewing the Treaty, having regard for the factors then affecting peace and security in the North Atlantic area, including the development of universal as well as regional arrangements under the Charter of the United Nations for the maintenance of international peace and security.

Article 13

After the Treaty has been in force for twenty years, any Party may cease to be a Party one year after its notice of denunciation has been given to the Government of the United States of America, which will inform the Governments of the other Parties of the deposit of each notice of denunciation.

Article 14

This Treaty, of which the English and French texts are equally authentic, shall be deposited in the archives of the Government of the United States of America. Duly certified copies will be transmitted by that Government to the Governments of other signatories.

"WE MUST ABOLISH THE CULT OF THE INDIVIDUAL": SPEECH TO THE 20th CONGRESS OF THE COMMUNIST PARTY OF THE SOVIET UNION, 1956

Nikita Khrushchev

In which Khrushchev (1894–1971), the General Secretary of the Communist Party of the Soviet Union, denounced the terror and self-cultism of Stalin.

Comrades! In the report of the Central Committee of the party at the twentieth congress, in a number of speeches by delegates to the Congress, as also formerly during the plenary CC/CPSU [Central Committee of the Communist Party of the Soviet Union] sessions, quite a lot has been said about the cult of the individual and about its harmful consequences.

After Stalin's death the Central Committee of the party began to implement a policy of explaining concisely and consistently that it is impermissible and foreign to the spirit of Marxism-Leninism to elevate one person, to transform him into a superman possessing supernatural characteristics akin to those of a god. Such a man supposedly knows everything, sees everything, thinks for everyone, can do anything, is infallible in his behaviour.

Such a belief about a man, and specifically about Stalin, was cultivated among us for many years.

At the present we are concerned with a question which has immense importance for the party now and for the future – [we are concerned] with how the cult of the person of Stalin has been gradually growing, the cult which became at a certain specific stage the source of a whole series of exceedingly serious and grave perversions of party principles, of party democracy, of revolutionary legality.

Because of the fact that not all as yet realize fully the practical consequences resulting from the cult of the individual, the great harm caused by the violation of the principle of collective direction of the party, and because of the accumulation of immense and limitless power in the hands of one person, the Central Committee of the party considers it absolutely necessary to make the material pertaining to this matter available to the twentieth congress of the Communist party of the Soviet Union.

In December, 1922, in a letter to the party congress Vladimir Ilyich wrote: "After taking over the position of Secretary General, Comrade Stalin accumulated in his hands immeasurable power and I am not certain whether he will be always able to use this power with the required care."

This letter, a political document of tremendous importance, known in the party history as Lenin's "testament," was distributed among the delegates to the twentieth party congress.

It was precisely during this period (1935–1937–1938) that the practice of mass repression through the Government apparatus was born, first against the enemies of Leninism – Trotskyites, Zinovievites, Bukharinites, long since politically defeated by the party, and subsequently also against many honest Communists, against those party cadres who had borne the heavy load of the Civil War, and the first and most difficult years of industrialization and collectivization, who actively fought against the Trotskyites and the rightists for the Leninist party line.

Stalin originated the concept "enemy of the people". This term automatically rendered it unnecessary that the ideological errors of a man or men engaged in a controversy be proven; this term made possible the use of the most cruel repression, violating all norms of revolutionary legality, against anyone who in any way disagreed with Stalin, against those who were only suspected of hostile intent, against those who had bad reputations in the main, and in actuality, the only proof of guilt used, against all norms of current legal science, was the "confession" of the accused himself; and, as subsequent probing proved, "confessions" were acquired through physical pressures against the accused.

It was determined that of the 139 members and candidates of the party's Central Committee who were elected at the seventeenth congress, ninety-eight persons, i.e., 70 percent, were arrested and shot (mostly in 1937–38).

The same fate met not only the Central Committee members but also the majority of the delegates to the seventeenth party congress. Of 1,966 delegates with either voting or advisory rights, 1,108 persons were arrested on charges of antirevolutionary crimes, i.e., decidedly more than a majority. This very fact shows how absurd, wild and contrary to common sense were the charges of counter-revolutionary crimes made, as we now see, against a majority of participants at the seventeenth party congress.

After the criminal murder of Sergei M. Kirov, mass repressions and brutal acts of violation of Socialist legality began. On the evening of

1 December 1934, on Stalin's initiative (without the approval of the Political Bureau, which was passed two days later, casually) the secretary of the Presidium of the Central Executive Committee, Abel S. Yenukidze, signed the following directive:

1. Investigative agencies are directed to speed up the cases of those accused of the preparation or execution of acts of terror.
2. Judicial organs are directed not to hold up the execution of death sentences pertaining to crimes of this category in order to consider the possibility of pardon, because the Presidium of the Central Executive Committee of the USSR does not consider as possible the receiving of petitions of this sort.
3. The organs of the Commissariat of Internal Affairs are directed to execute the death sentences against criminals of the above-mentioned category immediately after the passage of sentences.

This directive became the basis for mass acts of abuse against Socialist legality. During many of the fabricated court cases the accused were charged with "the preparation" of terroristic acts; this deprived them of any possibility that their cases might be re-examined, even when they stated before the court that their "confessions" were secured by force, and when, in a convincing manner, they disproved the accusations against them.

The majority of the Central Committee members and candidates elected at the seventeenth congress and arrested in 1937–8 were expelled from the party illegally through the brutal abuse of the party statute, because the question of their expulsion was never studied at the Central Committee Plenum.

Now when the cases of some of these so-called "spies" and "saboteurs" were examined it was found that all their cases were fabricated. Confessions of guilt of many arrested and charged with enemy activity were gained with the help of cruel and inhuman tortures.

Comrade Eikhe was arrested 29 April 1938, on the basis of slanderous materials, without the sanction of the prosecutor of the USSR, which was finally received fifteen months after the arrest.

Eikhe was forced under torture to sign ahead of time a protocol of his confession prepared by the investigative judges in which he and several other eminent party workers were accused of anti-Soviet activity.

On 1 October 1939, Eikhe sent his declaration to Stalin in which he categorically denied his guilt and asked for an examination of his case. In the declaration he wrote:

There is no more bitter misery than to sit in the jail of a government for which I have always fought.

On 4 February Eikhe was shot. It has been definitely established now that Eikhe's case was fabricated; he has been posthumously rehabilitated.

A large part of these cases are being reviewed now and a great part of them are being voided because they were baseless and falsified. Suffice it to say that from 1954 to the present time the Military Collegium of the Supreme Court has rehabilitated 7,679 persons, many of whom were rehabilitated posthumously.

The power accumulated in the hands of one person, Stalin, led to serious consequences during the great patriotic war.

A cable from our London Embassy dated 18 June 1941 stated:

> As of now Cripps is deeply convinced of the inevitability of armed conflict between Germany and the USSR which will begin not later than the middle of June. According to Cripps, the Germans have presently concentrated 147 divisions (including air force and service units) along the Soviet borders.

Despite these particularly grave warnings, the necessary steps were not taken to prepare the country properly for defence and to prevent it from being caught unawares.

When the Fascist armies had actually invaded Soviet territory and military operations began, Moscow issued the order that Stalin, despite evident facts, thought that the war had not yet started, that this was only a provocative action on the part of several undisciplined sections of the German army, and that our reaction might serve as a reason for the Germans to begin the war.

Stalin was very much interested in the assessment of Comrade Zhukov as a military leader. He asked me often for my opinion of Zhukov. I told him then, "I have known Zhukov for a long time; he is a good general and a good military leader."

After the war Stalin began to tell all kinds of nonsense about Zhukov, among others the following, "You praised Zhukov, but he does not deserve it. It is said that before each operation at the front Zhukov used to behave as follows: he used to take a handful of earth, smell it and say, 'We can begin the attack,' or the opposite, 'the planned operation cannot be carried out.'" I stated at that time, "Comrade Stalin, I do not know who invented this, but it is not true."

It is possible that Stalin himself invented these things for the purpose of minimizing the role and military talents of Marshal Zhukov.

All the more monstrous are the acts whose initiator was Stalin and which are rude violations of the basic Leninist principles of the nationality policy of the Soviet State. We refer to the mass deportations from their native places of whole nations, together with all Communists and Komsomols without any exception; this deportation action was not dictated by any military considerations.

The Ukrainians avoided meeting this fate only because there were too many of them and there was no place to which to deport them. Otherwise, he would have deported them also.

Let us also recall the "Affair of the Doctor Plotters". [Animation in the hall.] Actually there was no "affair" outside of the declaration of the woman doctor Timashuk, who was probably influenced or ordered by someone (after all, she was an unofficial collaborator of the organs of state security) to write Stalin a letter in which she declared that doctors were applying supposedly improper methods of medical treatment.

Such a letter was sufficient for Stalin to reach an immediate conclusion that there are doctor-plotters in the Soviet Union. He issued orders to arrest a group of eminent Soviet medical specialists. He personally issued advice on the conduct of the investigation and the method of interrogation of the arrested persons.

Stalin personally called the investigative judge, gave him instructions, advised him on which investigative methods should be used: these methods were simple – beat, beat and, once again, beat.

Comrades: The cult of the individual acquired such monstrous size chiefly because Stalin himself, using all conceivable methods, supported the glorification of his own person. This is supported by numerous facts. One of the most characteristic examples of Stalin's self-glorification and of his lack of even elementary modesty is the edition of his "Short Biography", which was published in 1948.

"Stalin is the worthy continuer of Lenin's work, or, as it is said in our party, Stalin is the Lenin of today." You see how well it is said; not by the nation but by Stalin himself.

Comrades: We must abolish the cult of the individual decisively, once and for all . . .

From "THE WIND OF CHANGE": SPEECH BEFORE THE SOUTH AFRICAN PARLIAMENT OF THE UNION, 1960

Harold Macmillan

The speech from which excerpts are printed below was delivered by the British Conservative prime minister in Cape Town, the legislative capital of South Africa on 3 February 1960. South Africa was then a racially segregated ("apartheid") society. In his speech, Macmillan noted the growth of African nationalism and stressed Britain's commitment to the granting of independence to its dependencies. He also indicated the British government's opposition to apartheid. Macmillan was heard in complete silence.

A year later, South Africa withdrew from the Commonwealth – the association of nations which had grown out of British settlement overseas – citing the organization's criticism of its racial policy as the cause.

Harold Macmillan was prime minister of Britain from 1957 until 1963.

. . . In the twentieth century, and especially since the end of the war, the processes which gave birth to the nation-states of Europe have been repeated all over the world. We have seen the awakening of national consciousness in peoples who have for centuries lived in dependence on some other power.

Fifteen years ago this movement spread through Asia . . .

Today, the same thing is happening in Africa. The most striking of all the impressions I have formed since I left London a month ago is of the strength of this African national consciousness. In different places it may take different forms, but it is happening everywhere. The wind of change is blowing through the continent.

Whether we like it or not, this growth of national consciousness is a political fact. We must all accept it as a fact. Our national policies must take account of it . . . [or] . . . we may imperil the precarious balance of east and west on which the peace of the world depends.

The world today is divided into three great groups. First, there are what we call the western Powers. You in South Africa and we in Britain belong to this group, together with our friends and allies in other parts of the Commonwealth, in the United States of America, and in Europe.

Secondly, there are the Communists – Russia and her satellites in Europe and China, whose population will rise by 1970 to the staggering total of eight hundred million. Thirdly, there are those parts of the world whose people are at present uncommitted either to Communism or to our western ideas. In this context we think first of Asia and of Africa.

As I see it, the great issue in this second half of the 20th century is whether the uncommitted peoples of Asia and Africa will swing to the east or to the west. Will they be drawn into the Communist camp? Or will the great experiments in self-government that are now being made in Asia and Africa, especially within the Commonwealth, prove so successful, and by their example so compelling, that the balance will come down in favour of freedom and order and justice?

The struggle is joined and it is a struggle for the minds of men. What is now on trial is much more than our military strength or our diplomatic and administrative skill. It is our way of life.

The uncommitted nations want to see before they choose. What can we show them to help them choose aright? Each of the independent members of the Commonwealth must answer that question for itself.

It is the basic principle for our modern Commonwealth that we respect each other's sovereignty in matters of internal policy. At the same time, we must recognize that, in this shrinking world in which we live today, the internal policies of one nation may have effects outside it. We may sometimes be tempted to say to each other, "Mind your own business." But in these days I would myself expand the old saying so that it runs, "Mind your own business, but mind how it affects my business too."

Let me be very frank with you, my friends. What Governments and Parliaments in the United Kingdom have done since the war in according independence to India, Pakistan, Ceylon, Malaya, and Ghana, and what they will do for Nigeria and the other countries now nearing independence – all this, though we take full and sole responsibility for it, we do in the belief that it is the only way to establish the future of the Commonwealth and of the free world on sound foundations.

All this, of course, is also of deep and close concern to you, for nothing we do in this small world can be done in a corner or remain hidden. What we do today in West, Central, and East Africa becomes known to everyone in the Union, whatever his language, colour, or tradition . . .

. . . it has been our aim, in countries for which we have borne responsibility, not only to raise the material standards of living but to create a society which respects the rights of individuals – a society in which men are given the opportunity to grow to their full stature, and that must in our view include the opportunity to have an increasing share in political power and responsibility; a society in which individual merit, and individual merit alone, is the criterion for man's advancement whether political or economic.

Finally, in countries inhabited by several different races, it has been our aim to find the means by which the community can become more of a community, and fellowship can be fostered between its various parts . . .

The attitude of the United Kingdom Government towards this problem was clearly expressed by the Foreign Secretary, Mr Selwyn Lloyd, speaking at the United Nations General Assembly on 17 September 1959. These are his words:–

> In those territories where different races or tribes live side by side, the task is to ensure that all the people may enjoy security and freedom and the chance to contribute as individuals to the progress and well being of these countries. We reject the idea of any inherent superiority of one race over another. Our policy therefore is nonracial. It offers a future in which Africans, Europeans, Asians, the peoples of the Pacific, and others with whom we are concerned, will all play their full part as citizens in the countries where they live and in which feelings of race will be submerged in loyalty to the new nations.

I have thought you would wish me to state plainly and with full candour the policy for which we in Britain stand . . .

I am well aware of the peculiar nature of the problems with which you are faced here in the Union of South Africa . . .

As a fellow member of the Commonwealth, it is our earnest desire to give South Africa our support and encouragement, but I hope you won't mind my saying frankly that there are some aspects of your policies which make it impossible for us to do this without being false to our own deep convictions about the political destinies of free men, to which in our own territories we are trying to give effect . . .

INAUGURAL ADDRESS, 1961

President John F. Kennedy

A former World War II naval hero, John F. Kennedy (1917–63) was the 35th president of the United States and the first Roman Catholic to hold that office. During his Democratic campaign for the presidency he developed the concept of the "New Frontier", the conquest of political and social injustice; as president, "JFK", helped by his Attorney General brother Robert Kennedy, championed the civil rights movement – including desegregation in schools and universities – and set in motion the legislation later renacted as Medicare. In foreign politics, after the fiasco of the CIA's Bay of Pigs invasion of Castro's Cuba and the imminence of nuclear war with the USSR over its placing of missiles on Cuba, Kennedy initiated a West–East thaw which fruited the Nuclear Test Ban Treaty. His other achievements in foreign policy included the creation of the Peace Corps and the Alliance for Progress with Latin America. On 22 November 1963, the youngest president in US history was assassinated while riding in a motor cavalcade in Dallas, Texas. His "New Frontier" vision outlasted him and continues to impact on American politics.

There follows the text of President Kennedy's Inaugural Address of 20 January 1961, his most vivid exposition of the beliefs and ideas behind the "New Frontier" approach.

Inaugural Address

Vice President Johnson, Mr Speaker, Mr Chief Justice, President Eisenhower, Vice President Nixon, President Truman, Reverend Clergy, fellow citizens:

We observe today not a victory of party but a celebration of freedom – symbolizing an end as well as a beginning – signifying renewal as well as change. For I have sworn before you and Almighty God the same solemn oath our forebears prescribed nearly a century and three-quarters ago.

The world is very different now. For man holds in his mortal hands the power to abolish all forms of human poverty and all forms of human life. And yet the same revolutionary beliefs for which our forebears fought are still at issue around the globe – the belief that the rights of man come not from the generosity of the state but from the hand of God.

We dare not forget today that we are the heirs of that first revolution. Let the word go forth from this time and place, to friend and foe alike, that the torch has been passed to a new generation of Americans – born in this century, tempered by war, disciplined by a hard and bitter peace, proud of our ancient heritage – and unwilling to witness or permit the slow undoing of those human rights to which this nation has always been committed, and to which we are committed today at home and around the world.

Let every nation know, whether it wishes us well or ill, that we shall pay any price, bear any burden, meet any hardship, support any friend, oppose any foe to assure the survival and the success of liberty.

This much we pledge – and more.

To those old allies whose cultural and spiritual origins we share, we pledge the loyalty of faithful friends. United, there is little we cannot do in a host of new cooperative ventures. Divided, there is little we can do – for we dare not meet a powerful challenge at odds and split asunder.

To those new states whom we welcome to the ranks of the free, we pledge our word that one form of colonial control shall not have passed away merely to be replaced by a far more iron tyranny. We shall not always expect to find them supporting our view. But we shall always hope to find them strongly supporting their own freedom – and to remember that, in the past, those who foolishly sought power by riding the back of the tiger ended up inside.

To those peoples in the huts and villages of half the globe struggling to break the bonds of mass misery, we pledge our best efforts to help them help themselves, for whatever period is required – not because the Communists may be doing it, not because we seek their votes, but because it is right. If a free society cannot help the many who are poor, it cannot save the few who are rich.

To our sister republics south of our border, we offer a special pledge – to convert our good words into good deeds – in a new alliance for progress – to assist free men and free governments in casting off the chains of poverty. But this peaceful revolution of hope cannot become the prey of hostile powers. Let all our neighbours know that we shall join with them to oppose aggression or subversion anywhere in the Americas. And let every other power know that this hemisphere intends to remain the master of its own house.

To that world assembly of sovereign states, the United Nations, our last best hope in an age where the instruments of war have far outpaced the instruments of peace, we renew our pledge of support – to prevent it from becoming merely a forum for invective – to strengthen its shield of the new and the weak – and to enlarge the area in which its writ may run.

Finally, to those nations who would make themselves our adversary, we offer not a pledge but a request: that both sides begin anew the quest for peace, before the dark powers of destruction unleashed by science engulf all humanity in planned or accidental self-destruction.

We dare not tempt them with weakness. For only when our arms are sufficient beyond doubt can we be certain beyond doubt that they will never be employed.

But neither can two great and powerful groups of nations take comfort from our present course – both sides overburdened by the cost of modern weapons, both rightly alarmed by the steady spread of the deadly atom, yet both racing to alter that uncertain balance of terror that stays the hand of mankind's final war.

So let us begin anew – remembering on both sides that civility is not a sign of weakness, and sincerity is always subject to proof. Let us never negotiate out of fear. But let us never fear to negotiate.

Let both sides explore what problems unite us instead of belabouring those problems which divide us.

Let both sides, for the first time, formulate serious and precise proposals for the inspection and control of arms – and bring the absolute power to destroy other nations under the absolute control of all nations.

Let both sides seek to invoke the wonders of science instead of its terrors. Together let us explore the stars, conquer the deserts, eradicate disease, tap the ocean depths and encourage the arts and commerce.

Let both sides unite to heed in all corners of the earth the command of Isaiah – to "undo the heavy burdens . . . [and] let the oppressed go free."

And if a beachhead of cooperation may push back the jungles of suspicion, let both sides join in creating a new endeavour – not a new balance of power, but a new world of law, where the strong are just and the weak secure and the peace preserved.

All this will not be finished in the first 100 days. Nor will it be finished in the first 1,000 days, nor in the life of this Administration, nor even perhaps in our lifetime on this planet. But let us begin.

In your hands, my fellow citizens, more than mine, will rest the final success or failure of our course. Since this country was founded, each generation of Americans has been summoned to give testimony to its national loyalty. The graves of young Americans who answered the call to service surround the globe.

Now the trumpet summons us again – not as a call to bear arms, though arms we need – not as a call to battle, though embattled we are – but a call to bear the burden of a long twilight struggle year in and year out, "rejoicing in hope, patient in tribulation" – a struggle against the common enemies of man: tyranny, poverty, disease and war itself.

Can we forge against these enemies a grand and global alliance, north and south, east and west, that can assure a more fruitful life for all mankind? Will you join in that historic effort?

In the long history of the world, only a few generations have been granted the role of defending freedom in its hour of maximum danger. I do not shrink from this responsibility – I welcome it. I do not believe that any of us would exchange places with any other people or any other generation. The energy, the faith, the devotion which we bring to this endeavour will light our country and all who serve it – and the glow from that fire can truly light the world.

And so, my fellow Americans: ask not what your country can do for you – ask what you can do for your country.

My fellow citizens of the world: ask not what America will do for you, but what together we can do for the freedom of man.

Finally, whether you are citizens of America or citizens of the world, ask of us here the same high standards of strength and sacrifice which we ask of you. With a good conscience our only sure reward, with history the final judge of our deeds, let us go forth to lead the land we love, asking His blessing and His help, but knowing that here on earth God's work must truly be our own.

"I HAVE A DREAM": SPEECH BEFORE THE CIVIL RIGHTS MARCH ON WASHINGTON, D.C, 1963

Martin Luther King, Jr

Delivered by Reverend King from the steps of the Lincoln Memorial on 28 August 1963 to an audience of around 250,00 civil rights marchers. The speech, with its "I have a dream" refrain, helped galvanize the American conscience; within two years, the Civil Rights Act and the Voting Rights Act effectively ended legal discrimination against Blacks in American society. King was awarded the Nobel Peace Prize. He was assassinated in 1968 by a white extremist, James Earl Ray.

I am happy to join with you today in what will go down in history as the greatest demonstration for freedom in the history of our nation.

Five score years ago, a great American, in whose symbolic shadow we stand, signed the Emancipation Proclamation. This momentous decree came as a great beacon light of hope to millions of Negro slaves who had been seared in the flames of withering injustice. It came as a joyous daybreak to end the long night of captivity.

But one hundred years later, we must face the tragic fact that the Negro is still not free. One hundred years later, the life of the Negro is still sadly crippled by the manacles of segregation and the chains of discrimination. One hundred years later, the Negro lives on a lonely island of poverty in the midst of a vast ocean of material prosperity. One hundred years later the Negro is still languishing in the corners of American society and finds himself an exile in his own land. So we have come here today to dramatize an appalling condition.

In a sense we have come to our nation's Capital to cash a check. When the architects of our republic wrote the magnificent words of the Constitution and the Declaration of Independence, they were signing a promissory note to which every American was to fall heir. This note was a promise that all men would be guaranteed the unalienable rights of life, liberty, and the pursuit of happiness.

It is obvious today that America has defaulted on this promissory note insofar as her citizens of colour are concerned. Instead of honouring this sacred obligation, America has given the Negro people a bad check; a check which has come back marked "insufficient funds". But we refuse to believe that the bank of justice is bankrupt. We refuse to believe that there are insufficient funds in the great vaults of opportunity of this nation. So we have come to cash this check – a check that will give us upon demand the riches of freedom and the security of justice. We have also come to this hallowed spot to remind America of the fierce urgency of *now*. This is no time to engage in the luxury of cooling off or to take the tranquilizing drug of gradualism. *Now* is the time to make real the promises of Democracy. *Now* is the time to rise from the dark and desolate valley of segregation to the sunlit path of racial justice. *Now* is the time to open the doors of opportunity to all of God's children. *Now* is the time to lift our nation from the quicksands of racial injustice to the solid rock of brotherhood.

It would be fatal for the nation to overlook the urgency of the moment and to underestimate the determination of the Negro. This sweltering summer of the Negro's legitimate discontent will not pass until there is an invigorating autumn of freedom and equality. 1963 is not an end, but a beginning. Those who hope that the Negro needed to blow off steam and will now be content will have a rude awakening if the Nation returns to business as usual. There will be neither rest nor tranquility in America until the Negro is granted his citizenship rights. The whirlwinds of revolt will continue to shake the foundations of our Nation until the bright day of justice emerges.

But there is something that I must say to my people who stand on the warm threshold which leads into the palace of justice. In the process of gaining our rightful place we must not be guilty of wrongful deeds. Let us not seek to satisfy our thirst for freedom by drinking from the cup of bitterness and hatred. We must forever conduct our struggle on the high plane of dignity and discipline. We must not allow our creative protest to degenerate into physical violence. Again and again we must rise to the majestic heights of meeting physical force with soul force. The marvellous new militancy which has engulfed the Negro community must not lead us to a distrust of all white people, for many of our white brothers, as evidenced by their presence here today, have come to realize that their destiny is tied up with our destiny and their freedom is inextricably bound to our freedom. We cannot walk alone.

And as we walk, we must make the pledge that we shall march ahead. We cannot turn back. There are those who are asking the devotees of civil rights, "When will you be satisfied?" We can never be satisfied as long as the Negro is the victim of the unspeakable horrors of police brutality. We can never be satisfied as long as our bodies, heavy with the fatigue of travel, cannot gain lodging in the motels of the highways and the hotels of the cities. We cannot be satisfied as long as the Negro's basic mobility is from a smaller ghetto to a larger one. We can never be satisfied as long as a Negro in Mississippi cannot vote and a Negro in New York believes he has nothing for which to vote. No, no, we are not satisfied, and we will not be satisfied until justice rolls down like waters and righteousness like a mighty stream.

I am not unmindful that some of you have come here out of great trials and tribulations. Some of you have come fresh from narrow jail cells. Some of you have come from areas where your quest for freedom left you battered by the storms of persecution and staggered by the winds of police brutality. You have been the veterans of creative suffering. Continue to work with the faith that unearned suffering is redemptive.

Go back to Mississippi, go back to Alabama, go back to South Carolina, go back to Georgia, go back to Louisiana, go back to the slums and ghettos of our modern cities, knowing that somehow this situation can and will be changed. Let us not wallow in the valley of despair.

I say to you today, my friends, that in spite of the difficulties and frustrations of the moment I still have a dream. It is a dream deeply rooted in the American dream.

I have a dream that one day this nation will rise up and live out the true meaning of its creed: "We hold these truths to be self-evident; that all men are created equal."

I have a dream that one day on the red hills of Georgia the sons of former slaves and the sons of former slaveowners will be able to sit down together at the table of brotherhood.

I have a dream that one day even the state of Mississippi, a desert state sweltering with the heat of injustice and oppression, will be transformed into an oasis of freedom and justice.

I have a dream that my four little children will one day live in a nation where they will not be judged by the colour of their skin but by the content of their character.

I have a dream today.

I have a dream that one day the state of Alabama, whose governor's lips are presently dripping with the words of interposition and nullification, will be transformed into a situation where little black boys and black girls will be able to join hand with little white boys and white girls and walk together as sisters and brothers.

I have a dream today.

I have a dream that one day every valley shall be exalted, every hill and mountain shall be made low, the rough places will be made plains, and the crooked places will be made straight, and the glory of the Lord shall be revealed, and all flesh shall see it together.

This is our hope. This is the faith with which I return to the South. With this faith we will be able to hew out of the mountain of despair a stone of hope. With this faith we will be able to transform the jangling discords of our nation into a beautiful symphony of brotherhood. With this faith we will be able to work together, to pray together, to struggle together, to go to jail together, to stand up for freedom together, knowing that we will be free one day.

This will be the day when all of God's children will be able to sing with new meaning "My country 'tis of thee, sweet land of liberty, of thee I sing. Land where my fathers died, land of the pilgrim's pride, from every mountainside, let freedom ring."

And if America is to be a great nation this must become true. So let freedom ring from the prodigious hilltops of New Hampshire. Let freedom ring from the mighty mountains of New York. Let freedom ring from the heightening Alleghenies of Pennsylvania!

Let freedom ring from the snowcapped Rockies of Colorado!

Let freedom ring from the curvaceous peaks of California!

But not only that; let freedom ring from Stone Mountain of Georgia!

Let freedom ring from Lookout Mountain of Tennessee!

Let freedom ring from every hill and mole hill of Mississippi. From every mountainside, let freedom ring.

When we let freedom ring, when we let it ring from every village and every hamlet, from every state and every city, we will be able to speed up that day when all of God's children, black men and white men, Jews and Gentiles, Protestants and Catholics, will be able to join hands and sing in the words of the old Negro spiritual, "Free at last! free at last! thank God almighty, we are free at last!"

From "I AM PREPARED TO DIE": SPEECH AT THE RIVONA TRIAL, 1964

Nelson Mandela

Nelson Rolihlahla Mandela (1918–) joined the African National Congress in 1944. For the next twenty years later, he played a leading part in the ANC's campaign against the white minority government of South Africa. Sentenced in 1964 to life imprisonment for political offences, Mandela became a symbol of anti-apartheid resistance. Internal and external pressure forced the South African president F.W. de Klerk to order Mandela's release in 1990. The gradual dismantlement of apartheid ensued, and in 1994 Mandela was elected president in South Africa's first full democratic elections.

Herewith is an excerpt from Mandela's defence speech at his 1964 trial.

Some of the things so far told to the court are true and some are untrue. I do not, however, deny that I planned sabotage. I did not plan it in a spirit of recklessness, nor because I have any love of violence. I planned it as a result of a calm and sober assessment of the political situation that had arisen after many years of tyranny, exploitation and oppression of my people by the whites.

I admit immediately that I was one of the persons who helped to form Umkonto We Sizwe ["Spear of the Nation", the military wing of the ANC], and that I played a prominent role in its affairs until I was arrested in August 1962. I, and the others who started the organization, did so for two reasons. First, we believed that as a result of government policy, violence by the African people had become inevitable, and that unless responsible leadership was given to canalize and control the feelings of our people there would be outbreaks of terrorism which would produce an intensity of bitterness and hostility between the various races of this country which is not produced even by war. Second, we felt that without violence there would be no way open to the African people to succeed in their struggle against the principle of white supremacy. All lawful modes of expressing opposition to this principle had been closed by legislation, and we were placed in a position in which we had either to accept a permanent state of inferiority, or to defy the government. We chose to defy the law. We first broke the law in a way which avoided any recourse to violence; when this form was legislated against, and then the government resorted to a show of force to crush the opposition to its policies, only then did we decide to answer violence with violence.

But the violence which we chose to adopt was not terrorism. We who formed Umkonto were all members of the African National Congress, and had behind us the ANC tradition of non-violence and negotiation as a means of solving political disputes. We believed that South Africa belonged to all the people who lived in it, and not to one group, be it black or white. We did not want an interracial war, and tried to avoid it to the last minute.

The African National Congress was formed in 1912 to defend the right of the African people which had been seriously curtailed by the South Africa Act, and which were then being threatened by the Native Land Act. For 37 years – that is until 1949 – it adhered strictly to a constitutional struggle. It put forward demands and resolutions; it sent delegations to the government in the belief that African grievances could be settled through peaceful discussion and that Africans could advance gradually to full political rights. But white governments remained unmoved, and the rights of Africans became less instead of becoming greater. In the words of my leader, Chief Luthuli, who became President of the ANC in 1952, and who was later awarded the Nobel Peace Prize:

> . . . who will deny that thirty years of my life have been spent knocking in vain, patiently, moderately and modestly at a closed and barred door? What have been the fruits of moderation? The past thirty years have seen the greatest number of laws restricting our rights and progress, until today we have reached a stage where we have almost no rights at all.

Even after 1949, the ANC remained determined to avoid violence. At this time, however, there was a change from the strictly constitutional means of protest which had been employed in the past. The change was embodied in a decision which was taken to protest against apartheid legislation by peaceful, but unlawful, demonstrations against certain laws. Pursuant to this policy the ANC launched the Defiance Campaign, in which I was placed in charge of volunteers. This campaign was based on the principles of passive resistance. More than 8,500 people defied apartheid laws and went to gaol. Yet there was not a single instance of violence in the course of this campaign on the part of any defier. I, and nineteen colleagues were convicted for the role which we played in organizing the campaign, but our sentences were suspended mainly because the Judge found that discipline and non-violence had been stressed throughout.

During the Defiance Campaign, the Public Safety Act and the Criminal Law Amendment Act were passed. These statutes provided harsher penalties for offences committed by way of protests against laws. Despite this, the protests continued and the ANC adhered to its policy of non-violence. In 1956, 156 leading members of the Congress Alliance, including myself, were arrested on a charge of High Treason and charges under the Suppression of Communism Act. The non-violent policy of the ANC was put in issue by the state, but when the court gave judgment some five years later it found that the ANC did not have a policy of violence. We were acquitted on all counts, which included a count that the ANC sought to set up a Communist State in place of the existing regime. The government has always sought to label all its opponents as communists.

In 1960, there was the shooting at Sharpeville, which resulted in the proclamations of a State of Emergency and the declaration of the ANC as an unlawful organization. My colleagues and I, after careful consideration, decided that we would not obey this decree. The African people were not part of the government and did not make the laws by which they were governed. We believed in the words of the Universal Declaration of Human Rights, that "the will of the people shall be the basis of authority of the government", and for us to accept the banning was equivalent to accepting the silencing of the Africans for all time. The ANC refused to dissolve, but instead went underground. We believed it was our duty to preserve this organization which had been built up with almost 50 years of unremitting toil. I have no doubt that no self-respecting white political organization would disband itself if declared illegal by a government in which it had no say.

In 1960 the government held a referendum which led to the establishment of the Republic. Africans, who constituted approximately 70 per cent of the population of South Africa, were not entitled to vote, and were not even consulted about the proposed constitutional change. All of us were apprehensive of our future under the proposed White Republic, and a resolution was taken to hold an All-In African Conference to call for a National Convention, and to organize mass demonstrations on the eve of the unwanted Republic, if the government failed to call the convention. The conference was attended by Africans of various political persuasions. I was the secretary of the conference and undertook to be responsible for organizing the national stay-at-home which was subsequently called to coincide with the declaration of the Republic. As all strikes by Africans are illegal, the person organizing such a strike must avoid arrest. I was chosen to be this person, and consequently I had to leave my home and family and my practice and go into hiding to avoid arrest.

The stay-at-home, in accordance with ANC policy, was to be a peaceful demonstration. Careful instructions were given to organizers and members to avoid any recourse to violence. The government's answer was to introduce new and harsher laws, to mobilize its armed forces, and to send Saracens, armed vehicles and soldiers into the townships in a massive show of force designed to intimidate the people. This was an indication that the government had decided to rule by force alone, and this decision was a milestone on the road to Umkonto.

It was only when all else had failed, when all channels of peaceful protest had been barred to us, that the decision was made to embark on violent forms of political struggle, and to form Umkonto We Sizwe. We did so not because we desired such a course, but solely because the government had left us with no other choice. In the Manifesto of Umkonto, published on 16 December 1961, which is Exhibit AD, we said: "The time comes in the life of any nation when there remain only two choices – submit or fight. That time has now come to South Africa. We shall not submit and we have no choice but to hit back by all means in our power in defence of our people, our future and our freedom." This was our feeling in June of 1961 when we decided to press for a change in the policy of the National Liberation Movement. I can only say that I felt morally obliged to do what I did.

LETTER TO THE SECRETARIAT OF THE SOVIET WRITERS' UNION, 1969

Aleksandr Solzhenitsyn

The novelist Solzhenitsyn (1918–) first encountered the displeasure of the Soviet Union's authorities when he criticized Stalin's conduct of World War II, a "crime" for which he served eight years in jail. After his release a complaint about censorship led to the banning of his novels *The Cancer Ward* and *The First Circle*. In 1969 he was expelled from the Soviet Writers' Union – to whom he sent the letter below in reply. In 1970 he was awarded the Nobel Prize for Literature. Eventually the Soviet government tired of him and deported him to West Germany. He later settled in the USA.

Shamelessly trampling underfoot your own statutes, you have expelled me in my absence, as at the sound of a fire-alarm, without even sending me a summons by telegram, without even giving me the four hours I needed to come from Ryazan and be present at the meeting. You have shown openly that the RESOLUTION preceded the "discussion". Was it less awkward for you to invent new charges in my absence? Were you afraid of being obliged to grant me ten minutes for my answer? I am compelled to substitute this letter for those ten minutes.

Blow the dust off the clock. Your watches are behind the times. Throw open the heavy curtains which are so dear to you – you do not even suspect that the day has already dawned outside. It is no longer that stifling, that sombre, irrevocable time when you expelled Akhmatova in the same servile manner. It is not even that timid, frosty period when you expelled Pasternak, whining abuse at him. Was this shame not enough for you? Do you want to make it greater? But the time is near when each of you will seek to erase his signature from today's resolution.

Blind leading the blind! You do not even notice that you are wandering in the opposite direction from the one you yourselves announced. At this time of crisis you are incapable of suggesting anything constructive, anything good for our society, which is gravely sick – only your hatred, your vigilance, your "hold on and don't let go".

Your clumsy articles fall apart; your vacant minds stir feebly – but you have no arguments. You have only your voting and your administration. And that is why neither Sholokhov nor any of you, of all the lot of you, dared reply to the famous letter of Lydia Chukovskaya, who is the pride of Russian publicistic writing. But the administrative pincers are ready for her: how could she allow people to read her book (*The Deserted House*) when it has not been published? Once the AUTHORITIES have made up their minds not to publish you – then stifle yourself, choke yourself, cease to exist, and don't give your stuff to anyone to read!

They are also threatening to expel Lev Kopelev, the frontline veteran, who has already served ten years in prison although he was completely innocent. Today he is guilty: he intercedes for the persecuted, he revealed the hallowed secrets of his conversation with an influential person, he disclosed an OFFICIAL SECRET. But why do you hold conversations like these which have to be concealed from the people? Were we not promised 50 years ago that never again would there be any secret diplomacy, secret talks, secret and incomprehensible appointments and transfers, that the masses would be informed of all matters and discuss them openly?

"The enemy will overhear" – that is your excuse. The eternal, omnipresent "enemies" are a convenient justification for your functions and your very existence. As if there were no enemies when you promised immediate openness. But what would you do without "enemies"? You could not live without "enemies"; hatred, a hatred no better than racial hatred, has become your sterile atmosphere. But in this way a sense of our single, common humanity is lost and its doom is accelerated. Should the antarctic ice melt tomorrow, we would all become a sea of drowning humanity, and into whose heads would you then be drilling your concepts of "class struggle"? Not to speak of the time when the few surviving bipeds will be wandering over radioactive earth, dying.

It is high time to remember that we belong first and foremost to humanity. And that man has distinguished himself from the animal world by THOUGHT and SPEECH. And these, naturally, should be FREE. If they are put in chains, we shall return to the state of animals.

OPENNESS, honest and complete OPENNESS – that is the first condition of health in all societies, including our own. And he who does not want this openness for our country cares nothing for his fatherland and thinks only of his own interest. He who does not wish this openness for his fatherland does not want to purify it of its diseases, but only to drive them inwards, there to fester.

SOURCES & ACKNOWLEDGMENTS

The editor has made every effort to locate all persons having any rights in the selections appearing in this anthology and to secure permission from the holders of such rights. Any queries regarding the use of material should be addressed to the editor c/o the publishers.

The editor acknowledges the following sources:

Part One: Age of Classical Civilization

Hammurabi, extracts from "The Code of Hammurabi" reprinted from *Documents from Old Testament Times*, ed. D. Winton Thomas, Thomas Nelson and Sons Ltd., 1958. Copyright © 1958 Thomas Nelson and Sons Ltd.

Anonymous, "The Teaching of Amenhope", reprinted from *Documents from Old Testament Times*, ed. D. Winton Thomas, Thomas Nelson and Sons Ltd., 1958. Copyright © 1958 Thomas Nelson and Sons Ltd.

Akhenaten, "The Hymn to Aten", reprinted from *Documents from Old Testament Times*, ed. D. Winton Thomas, Thomas Nelson and Sons Ltd., 1958. Copyright © 1958 Thomas Nelson and Sons Ltd.

"The Ten Commandments" reprinted from *The Holy Bible*, Authorized Version, Trinitarian Bible Society, London, n.d.

"The Twelve Tables", extracts reprinted from *The Library of Original Sources*, Vol III, Oliver J Thatcher, University Extension Research Co., 1901.

Thucydides, The Funeral Oration of Pericles', reprinted from *Arthur Mee's Book of Everlasting Things*, Hodder & Stoughton, n.d.

Plato, "Socrates on his Condemnation to Death", reprinted from *Socrates: The Apology and Crito etc*, trans Benjamin Jowett, Roberts Brothers, Boston (Mass) 1882.

Plato, extracts from "The Republic" reprinted from *The Portable Plato*, trans Benjamin Jowett, Viking, New York, 1948 (Ethics); *Great Dialogues of Plato*, trans WHD Rouse, ed Philip G. Rouse and Eric H. Warmington, New York, New American Library, 1961. Copyright © 1956, 1961 John Clive Graves Rouse (The Cave); *Portable Plato*, ibid, (Education for Leadership).

Aristotle, extracts from "The Politics" reprinted from *The Politics of Aristotle*, trans JEC Welldon, Book I, Macmillan & Co., London, 1883.

Aristotle, extracts from "Nicmachean Ethics" reprinted from *Politics: Aristotle*, trans H. Rackham, Heinemann, London, 1959. Copyright © 1959 H. Rackman.

"The Wisdom of Solomon" reprinted from *The Holy Bible*, Trinitarian Bible Society, London, n.d.

Lucretius, "De Rerum Natura", reprinted from *De Rerum Natura*, trans Thomas Busby, Bk IV, London, 1813.

Cicero, "First Oration Against Catiline", rprinted from *The World's Great Speeches*, ed. Lewis Copeland, Lawrence W. Lamm and Stephen J. McKenna, Dover Publications, Inc., Mineloa, New York, 1999.

Cicero, "On the State" reprinted from *De Republica, De Legibus*, trans CW Keyes, Harvard University Press, Mass., 1959. Copyright © 1959 Harvard University Press and CW Keyes.

St Luke, "The Birth of Christ", reprinted from *The Holy Bible*, Trinitarian Bible Society, London, n.d.

"The Sermon on the Mount", reprinted from *The Holy Bible*, Trinitarian Bible Society, London, n.d.

Aurelius, Marcus, "Meditations", extracts reprinted from *Marcus Aurelius: Meditations*, trans Maxwell Staniforth, Penguin Books, London, 1964. Copyright © 1964 Maxwell Staniforth.

Constantine and Licinius, "The Edict of Milan", reprinted from *Translations and Reprints from the Original Sources of European History*, Vol 4, ed. D.C. Munro, University of Pennsylvania Press, Philadelphia, 1897.

St Augustine, extracts from "The Confessions", reprinted from *Confessions of St Augustine*, trans C. Bigg, Methuen, London, 1919; "The City of God" reprinted from *The City of God*, trans J. Healey, Farran, Okeden & Welsh, London, 1890.

Part Two: The Age of Faith

"The Monastic Rule of St Benedict", extracts reprinted from *Readings in Ancient History*, Vol II, ed William Stearns Davis, Allyn & Bacon, New York, 1946.

Cappellanus, Andreas, "The Rules of Courtly Love", reprinted from *The Art of Courtly Love*, trans JJ Parry, Columbia University Press, New York, 1941. Copyright © 1941 Columbia University Press.

"Magna Carta", quoted in *Documents of Liberty*, ed Henry Marsh, David & Charles, Newton Abbot, 1971. Translation copyright © British Library.

Thomas of Celano, extracts from "The Life of St Francis" reprinted from *The Lives of S. Francis of Assisi by Brother Thomas of Celano*, trans AG Ferrers Howell, Methuen & Co., London, 1908.

St Thomas Aquinas, "The End of Man", reprinted from *Summa contra gentiles*, Book III, trans. English Dominican Fathers, Burns, Oates & Washbourne, London, 1928.

Edward I, "Writ to Summons of Parliament", reprinted from *Select Charters and Other Illistrations of English Constitutional History*, William Stubbs, Clarendon Press, Oxford, 1866.

Dante Alighieri, extracts from "The Divine Comedy" extracts reprinted from *Hell (L'Inferno)*, Penguin, Harmondsworth, 1949. Copyright © Dorothy L. Sayers 1949. Langland, Williams, "Piers Plowman's Port-est", extracted from *The Vision of Piers Plowman*, trans. H.W. Wells, Sheed & Ward, London, 1935.

Petrarca, Francesco, "Letter to Posterity", reprinted from *Petrarch, the First Modern Scholar and Man of Letters*, trans. JR Robinson and HW Rolfe, Putnam, New York, 1898.

Wyclif, John, extracts from "Wyclif's Doctrines" reprinted from *John Wyclif*, Herbert Workman, Oxford, 1926.

More, Sir Thomas, extracts from "Utopia" reprinted from *Utopia*, trans Raphe Robynson, Abraham Vele, London 1556, text modernized by PE Hallett, 1932.

Part Three: The Age of Freedom

Luther, Martin, "The Ninety-Five Theses", reprinted from *Translations and Reprints from the Original Sources of European History*, Vol 2, ed. JH Robinson, University of Pennsylvania, Philadelphia, 1894.

Luther, Martin, "Speech Before the Diet of Worms", reprinted *from The World's Great Speeches*, ed. Lewis Copeland, Lawrence W. Lamm and Stephen J. McKenna, Dover Publications, Inc., Mineloa, New York, 1999.

Foxe, John, "The Candle That Shall Never be Put out: The Martyrdom of Ridley and Latimer, reprinted from *Book of Martyrs*, James Whalley, Manchester, 1873.

"The Poor Law Act", reprinted from *Tudor Constitutional Documents* 1485–1603, JR Tanner, Cambridge University Press, Cambridge, 1922.

Bacon, Francis, extracts from "Novum Organum", extracts reprinted *The Works*, trans Basil Montague, Parry & Macmillan, Philadelphia, 1854.

Bradford, William, "The Mayflower Compact", reprinted from *Documents of American History*, ed Henry Steele Commager, Appleton, Century, Crofts, New York, 1949.

"The Petition of Right", reprinted from *The Constitutional Documents of the Puritan Revolution*, 1625–1660, SR Gardiner, Clarendon Press, Oxford, 1906.

Descartes, René, "The Discourse Upon Method", extracted from *The Philosophy of Descartes*, trans. Henry AP Torrey, New York, 1892.

Rushworth, John, "The Attempted Arrest of the Five Members", reprinted from *Historical Collections*, Boulter, London, 1682.

Winstanley, Gerrard, "A Declaration from the Poor Oppressed People of England", reprinted from *Gerrard Winstanley: Selected Writings*, ed Andrew Hopton, Aporia, 1989.

Milton, John, extracts from "Areopagitica" reprinted from *Areopagitica*, J. Deighton, London, 1791.

Bunyan, John, extracts from "The Pilgrims Progress", extracted from *The Pilgrim's Progress From This World to That Which is to Come*, Haughton & Co. London, 1880.

"Habeas Corpus Act", reprinted from *Select Documents of English Constitutional History*, ed GB Adams and HM Stephens, Macmillan, New York, 1901.

"The Bill of Rights" (Britain), reprinted from *Selection Documents of English Constitutional History*, ed GB Adams and HM Stephens, Macmillan, New York, 1901.

Locke, John, "The Second Treatise of Government", extracts reprinted from *Two Treatises of Government*, A. Millar, London, 1764.

Rousseau, Jean Jacques, extracts from "The Social Contract" reprinted from *The Social Contract and Discourses*, trans GDH Cole, Dent, London, 1973. Copyright revisions © 1973 JM Dent & Sons Ltd.

Rousseau, Jean Jacques, extracts from *Emile* quoted in *The Search for Personal Freedom*, vol II, Neal M. Cross et al, Wm. C. Brown Company Publishers, Dubuque, Iowa, 1976 (Book I); Emile, trans Barbara Foxley, JM Dent, London, 1999, revised by Grace Roosevelt, Institute for Learning Technologies, *http:projects.ilt,columbia.edu/pedagogies/Rousseau* n.d.

Voltaire, extracts from "The Philosophical Dictionary" reprinted from *The Philosophical Dictionary*, trans HI Woolf, Knopf, New York, 1924.

Beccaria, Cesare, "The Abolition of Torture", reprinted from *An Essay on Crimes and Punishments*, J. Almon, London, 1767.

"The Declaration of Independence", reprinted from *Documents of American History*. ed Henry Steele Commager, Appleton, Century, Crofts, New York, 1949.

Smith, Adam, extracts from *An Inquiry Into the Nature and Causes of the Wealth of Nations*, ed JET Rogers, Clarendon Press, Oxford, 1880.

Lessing, Gotthold Ephraim, "Religious Toleration", extracted from *Nathan The Wise*, trans William Jack, Glasgow, 1894.

"The Declaration of the Rights of Man and Citizen (France)", reprinted from *Constitutions and Other Select Documents Illustrative of the History of France*, FM Anderson, Minneapolis, 1908.

"The Bill of Rights", reprinted from *Documents of American History*, ed Henry Steele Commager, Appleton-Crofts, Inc., 1949. Copyright © 1949 Appleton-Century-Crofts, Inc.

Paine, Thomas, extracts from "Rights of Man" reprinted from *Rights of Man*, Wordsworth Editions Ltd., Ware, 1996.

Wollstonecraft, Mary, extract from "Vindication of the Rights of Woman" reprinted from *Vindication of the Rights of Woman*, Penguin Classics, Harmondsworth, 1983 "Reform Act" is reprinted from *Documents of Liberty*, ed Henry Marsh, David & Charles, Newton Abbot, 1971.

De Tocqueville, Alexis, extracts from "Democracy in America" quoted in *The Book of Virtues*, ed William J Bennett, Simon & Schuster, 1993.

Mazzini, Giuseppe, "To Young Men of Italy", reprinted from *The World's Great Speeches*, ed. Lewis Copeland, Lawrence W. Lamm & Stephen J. McKenna, Dover Publications, Inc., 1999.

Douglass, Frederick, "Open Letter Against Slavery", quoted in *Letters of a Nation*, ed Andrew Carroll, Kodansha America, Inc., 1997.

Mill, John Stuart, extract from "On Liberty" reprinted from *On Liberty*, JW Parker & Son, London, 1859.

Darwin, Charles, extracts from "On the Origin of Species" reprinted from *On the Origin of Species*, Wordsworth Editions Ltd 1998.

Lincoln Abraham, "The Proclamation of Emancipation" is reprinted from *Abraham Lincoln: Speeches and Letters*, ed Peter J. Parrish, J.M. Dent 1993.

Lincoln Abraham, "The Gettysburg Address" is reprinted from *Abraham Lincoln: Speeches and Letters*, ed Peter J. Parrish, J.M. Dent 1993.

Shaw, George Bernard, extract from "A manifesto" reprinted from *A Manifesto*, Fabian Tract No. 2, London, 1884.

Wilde, Oscar, extract from *The Soul of Man Under Socialism*, Arthur L Humphreys, London, 1912.

Zola, Emile, "J'accuse", quoted in *Treasury of the World's Greatest Letters*, ed. M. Lincoln Schuster, Simon & Schuster, 1948.

Lytton, Constance, "No Surrender" is an extract from *Prisons and Prisoners*, Virago, London, 1988.

Representation of the People Act, quoted in *Documents of Liberty*, ed Henry Marsh, David & Charles, 1971. Copyright © Her Majesty's Stationery Office.

Miller, Webb, "Satyagraha" is an extract from *I Found No Peace*, Victor Gollancz, London, 1938.

Churchill, Winston, "Their Finest Hour", quoted in *The World's Great Speeches*, ed. Lewis Copeland, Lawrence W. Lamm & Stephen J. McKenna, Dover Publications, Inc., 1999.

Beveridge, William, extract from *Full Employment in a Free Society*, George Allen & Unwin, London, 1944.

"Universal Declaration of Human Rights" quoted in *Documents & Descriptions*, ed RW Breach, Oxford University Press, Oxford, 1966.

"Universal Declaration of Human Rights", quoted in *A World Made New: Eleanor Roosevelt and the Universal Declaration of Human Rights*, Mary Ann Glendon, Random House, New York, 2001.

"The North Atlantic Treaty' reprinted from *NATO on-line library* website

Khrushchev, Nikita, "We Must Abolish the Cult of the Individual", reprinted from *The World's Great Speeches*, ed. Lewis Copeland, Lawrence W. Lamm & Stephen J. McKenna, Dover Publications, Inc., 1999.

Macmillan, Harold, extract from "The Wind of Change" speech reprinted from *Cardinal Documents in British History*, ed Robert Livingston Schulyer & Corinne Comstock Weston, D. Van Nostrand Company, Inc., 1961.

Kennedy, John F., "Inaugural Address", quoted in *The World's Great Speeches*, ed. Lewis Copeland, Lawrence W. Lamm & Stephen J. McKenna, Dover Publications, Inc., 1999. Copyright © 1963 Martin Luther King Jr., renewed 1991 Coretta Scott King.

Mandela, Nelson, "I am Prepared to Die", quoted in *The Chatto Book of Dissent*, ed Michael Rosen & David Widgery, Chatto, 1991.

Solzhenitsyn, Aleksandr, "Letter to the Secretariat of the Soviet Writers' Union", quoted in *The Chatto Book of Dissent*, ed Michael Rosen & David Widgery, Chatto, 1991.